SOCIOLOGY

First Canadian Edition

Sociology around the world

The countries that are identified on this map are cited in the book, either in the context of research studies or in relevant statistical data. Refer to the subject index for specific page references.

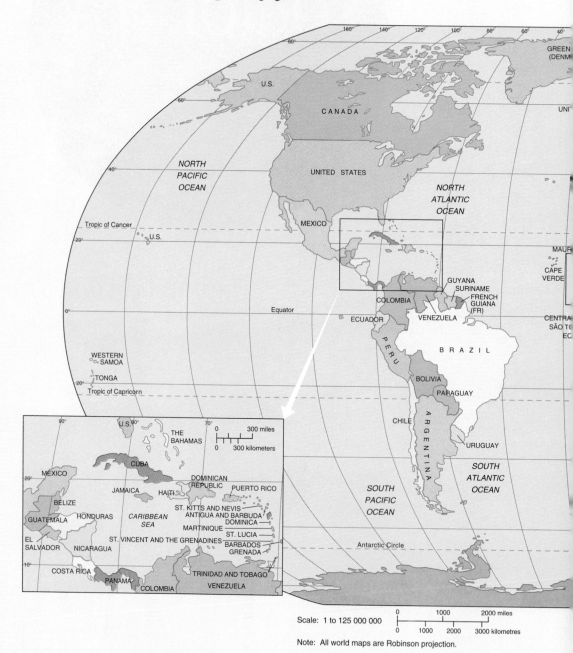

Scale: 1 to 125 000 000

Note: All world maps are Robinson projection.

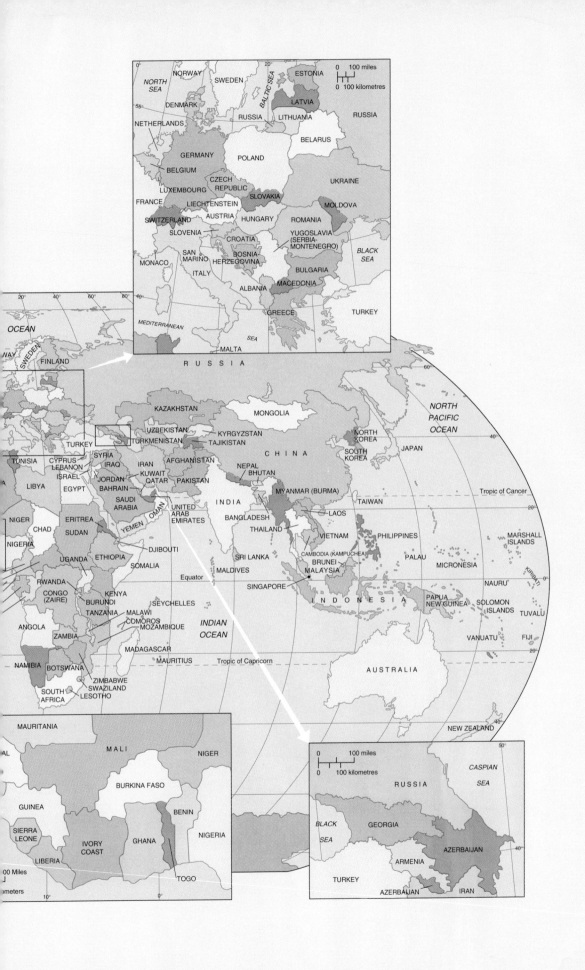

NORTH
SEA

NORWAY
SWEDEN
DENMARK
NETHERLANDS
GERMANY
BELGIUM
LUXEMBOURG
CZECH
REPUBLIC
FRANCE
LIECHTENSTEIN
SWITZERLAND
AUSTRIA
SLOVAKIA
SLOVENIA
CROATIA
SAN
MARINO
BOSNIA-
HERZEGOVINA
MONACO
ITALY
ALBANIA
MACEDONIA
GREECE
MEDITERRANEAN
SEA
MALTA

BALTIC SEA
ESTONIA
LATVIA
LITHUANIA
RUSSIA
RUSSIA
BELARUS
POLAND
UKRAINE
MOLDOVA
HUNGARY
ROMANIA
YUGOSLAVIA
(SERBIA-
MONTENEGRO)
BULGARIA
BLACK
SEA
TURKEY

0   100 miles
0   100 kilometres

OCEAN

SWEDEN
FINLAND

TURKEY

TUNISIA
CYPRUS
LEBANON
ISRAEL
LIBYA
EGYPT

NIGER
CHAD
NIGERIA
SUDAN
ERITREA
UGANDA
ETHIOPIA
RWANDA
CONGO
(ZAIRE)
BURUNDI
KENYA
TANZANIA
MALAWI
ANGOLA
COMOROS
MOZAMBIQUE
ZAMBIA
MADAGASCAR
NAMIBIA
BOTSWANA
ZIMBABWE
SWAZILAND
SOUTH
AFRICA
LESOTHO

SYRIA
IRAQ
IRAN
JORDAN
KUWAIT
QATAR
BAHRAIN
SAUDI
ARABIA
YEMEN
OMAN
UNITED
ARAB
EMIRATES
DJIBOUTI
SOMALIA
SEYCHELLES

AFGHANISTAN
PAKISTAN
NEPAL
BHUTAN
INDIA
BANGLADESH
MYANMAR (BURMA)
SRI LANKA
MALDIVES

Equator

INDIAN
OCEAN

Tropic of Capricorn
MAURITIUS

RUSSIA

KAZAKHSTAN
MONGOLIA
UZBEKISTAN
TURKMENISTAN
KYRGYZSTAN
TAJIKISTAN
CHINA
NORTH
KOREA
SOUTH
KOREA
JAPAN

TAIWAN
Tropic of Cancer
LAOS
THAILAND
VIETNAM
CAMBODIA (KAMPUCHEA)
BRUNEI
MALAYSIA
SINGAPORE
INDONESIA
PHILIPPINES
PALAU
MICRONESIA

NORTH
PACIFIC
OCEAN

MARSHALL
ISLANDS
KIRIBATI
NAURU
PAPUA
NEW GUINEA
SOLOMON
ISLANDS
TUVALU
VANUATU
FIJI

AUSTRALIA

NEW ZEALAND

MAURITANIA

MALI
NIGER
BURKINA FASO
GUINEA
BENIN
SIERRA
LEONE
IVORY
COAST
GHANA
NIGERIA
LIBERIA
TOGO

00 Miles
ometers

0   100 miles
0   100 kilometres

RUSSIA

CASPIAN
SEA

BLACK
SEA
GEORGIA
AZERBAIJAN
ARMENIA
TURKEY
AZERBAIJAN
IRAN

SOCIOLOGY

FIRST CANADIAN EDITION

Richard T. Schaefer
DePaul University

Edith Smith
University of Ottawa and
Carleton University

McGraw-Hill
Ryerson

Toronto   Montréal   Boston   Burr Ridge, IL   Dubuque, IA   Madison, WI   New York
San Francisco   St. Louis   Bangkok   Bogotá   Caracas   Kuala Lumpur   Lisbon   London
Madrid   Mexico City   Milan   New Delhi   Santiago   Seoul   Singapore   Sydney   Taipei

McGraw-Hill Ryerson

Sociology
First Canadian Edition

Copyright © 2005 by McGraw-Hill Ryerson Limited, a Subsidiary of The McGraw-Hill Companies. All rights reserved. Copyright © 2004, 2001, 1998, 1995, 1992, 1989, 1983, by The McGraw-Hill Companies. All rights reserved. No part of this publication may be reproduced or transmitted in any form or by any means, or stored in a data retrieval system, without the prior written permission of McGraw-Hill Ryerson Limited, or in the case of photocopying or other reprographic copying, a licence from The Canadian Copyright Licensing Agency (Access Copyright). For an Access Copyright licence, visit www.accesscopyright.ca or call toll free 1-800-893-5777.

Statistics Canada information is used with permission of the Minister of Industry, as Minister responsible for Statistics Canada. Information on the availability of the wide range of data from Statistics Canada can be obtained from Statistics Canada's Regional Offices, its World Wide Web site at http://www.statcan.ca, and its toll-free access number 1-800-263-1136.

ISBN: 0-07-094849-6

1 2 3 4 5 6 7 8 9 10 VH 0 9 8 7 6 5 4

Printed and bound in the United States of America

Care has been taken to trace ownership of copyright material contained in this text; however, the publisher will welcome any information that enables rectification of any reference or credit for subsequent editions.

Vice President, Editorial and Media Technology: Pat Ferrier
Senior Sponsoring Editor: James Buchanan
Senior Developmental Editor: Jennifer DiDomenico
Marketing Manager: Sharon Loeb
Supervising Editor: Jaime Duffy
Copy Editor: Laurel Sparrow
Production Coordinator: Madeleine Harrington
Composition: Bookman Typesetting Co. Inc./Chris Hudson
Cover Image: Ray Massey/Stone
Cover Design: Sharon Lucas
Printer: Von Hoffman Press

National Library of Canada Cataloguing in Publication Data

Schaefer, Richard T.
    Sociology/Richard T. Schaefer, Edith Smith; contributors: Richard Floyd,
    Bonnie Haaland.—1st Canadian ed.

Includes bibliographical references and indexes.
ISBN 0-07-094849-6

    1. Sociology.   I. Smith, Edith, 1951-   II. Floyd, Richard, 1946-   III. Haaland, Bonnie
IV. Title.

HM586.S318 2003   301   C2002-905550-4

Dedication

To my students, who sharpen my sociological imagination. R.T.S.

To Michael, my life partner, for being there and reminding me that the light at the end of the tunnel would grow brighter. And to my son, Christopher, for his questions and answers. E.S.

About the Authors

RICHARD T. SCHAEFER:
Professor, DePaul University; B.A. Northwestern University M.A., Ph.D. University of Chicago

Growing up in Chicago at a time when neighbourhoods were going through transitions in ethnic and racial composition, Richard T. Schaefer found himself increasingly intrigued by what was happening, how people were reacting, and how these changes were affecting neighbourhoods and people's jobs. His interest in social issues caused him to gravitate to sociology courses at Northwestern University, where he eventually received a B.A. in sociology.

"Originally as an undergraduate I thought I would go on to law school and become a lawyer. But after taking a few sociology courses, I found myself wanting to learn more about what sociologists studied, and fascinated by the kinds of questions they raised." This fascination led him to obtain his M.A. and Ph.D. in sociology from the University of Chicago. Dr. Schaefer's continuing interest in race relations led him to write his master's thesis on the membership of the Ku Klux Klan and his doctoral thesis on racial prejudice and race relations in Great Britain.

Dr. Schaefer went on to become a professor of sociology. He has taught introductory sociology for 30 years to students in colleges, adult education programs, nursing programs, and even a maximum-security prison. Dr. Schaefer's love of teaching is apparent in his interaction with his students. "I find myself constantly learning from the students who are in my classes and from reading what they write. Their insights into the material we read or current events that we discuss often become part of future course material and sometimes even find their way into my writing."

Dr. Schaefer is author of the fourth edition of *Sociology: A Brief Introduction* (McGraw-Hill, 2002). Dr. Schaefer is also the author of *Racial and Ethnic Groups,* now in its eighth edition, and *Race and Ethnicity in the United States,* second edition. His articles and book reviews have appeared in many journals, including: *American Journal of Sociology; Phylon: A Review of Race and Culture; Contemporary Sociology; Sociology and Social Research; Sociological Quarterly;* and *Teaching Sociology.* He served as president of the Midwest Sociological Society in 1994–1995.

Dr. Schaefer's advice to students is to "look at the material and make connections to your own life and experiences. Sociology will make you a more attentive observer of how people in groups interact and function. It will also make you more aware of people's different needs and interests—and perhaps more ready to work for the common good, while still recognizing people's individuality."

Taking Sociology to Work

EDITH SMITH:
Professor, University of Ottawa and Carleton University; B.Soc.Sc. University of Ottawa; M.A., Ph.D. Carleton University

Raised in a working-class family in Winnipeg, Manitoba, Edith Smith followed the path expected of her: graduating from high school, finding a job, and getting married. An interest in travel and experiencing the world meant that she migrated around the country, living in five different provinces and working in a variety of clerical positions. After becoming a mother Edith settled down in Ottawa, where she opened a small business and learned about writing and editing the words of others. Afraid that she had stopped thinking, she decided to return to university and complete her bachelor's degree, with the goal of applying her love of reading to a job involving books in a library. She discovered an enjoyment of sociology and with it a love of learning that would not let her stop with a Bachelor of Social Science.

As a single mother and an adult student in an environment filled with young people, Edith became fascinated with the experiences of other re-entry students and devoted her master's thesis to the subject. The following year she began her teaching career with sociology courses at a CEGEP in Hull, Quebec. From there she moved to the University of Ottawa, where she taught a variety of sociology courses—including introduction to family studies, gender relations, and education—while completing her doctoral degree at Carleton University, focusing on the sociology of adult education in Canada. Enjoying the diversity of campus environments and students, she now teaches part-time at both Carleton and the University of Ottawa.

Portions of Edith's master's thesis were published under the title "The Process As Empowerment: The Case of Female Re-entry Students," by Spirals Study No. 2. In addition, she has published articles in *The Canadian Journal for the Study of Adult Education*, and *Women's Education*. Edith has also presented research papers at both Canadian and international sociological conferences.

"From the very first day I stepped into a classroom, it felt like home. Having the opportunity to participate in this environment makes me feel very fortunate. My classroom philosophy is that everyone in the room is a student and a teacher, and this allows us all to learn from each other. Students have so much to teach me and after every course, I feel that I've gained more knowledge of my subject because of them. Together we develop our sociological imaginations, allowing us to look, more critically, through new windows on our social world."

Contents in Brief

Contents

 16 GOVERNMENT 434

 17 THE ECONOMY AND WORK 458

 18 HEALTH AND MEDICINE 482

21 COLLECTIVE BEHAVIOUR, SOCIAL MOVEMENTS, AND SOCIAL CHANGE 579

List of Boxes

Sociology in the Global Community

Research in Action

Global immigration patterns (Chapter 10)
The status of women around the world
(Chapter 11)
Issues of aging around the world (Chapter 12)
Transmission of cultural values (Chapter 15)
Homelessness worldwide (Chapter 19)
Population policy in China (Chapter 20)
The global disconnect in technology
(Chapter 20)

- **A focus on applying sociological thought.** The distinctive emphasis on social policy in the text shows students how to use sociology to examine such issues as reproductive technology, the AIDS crisis, and privacy and censorship. The Taking Sociology to Work boxes and Chapter 1 Appendix on careers provide examples of the various career paths open to Canadian students of sociology, and motivate students to engage with the material. Internet Connection exercises prompt students to apply the concepts they have learned while using a variety of resources on the World Wide Web.

The Plan for this Book

Sociology, First Canadian Edition, is divided into 21 chapters that study human behaviour from the perspective of sociologists. Part One ("The Sociological Perspective") sets the scene. The opening chapter ("Understanding Sociology") presents a brief history of the discipline and introduces the basic theories and perspectives employed in sociology. Chapter 2 ("Sociological Research") describes the major research methods.

The next five chapters (Part Two: "Organizing Social Life") focus on key sociological concepts. Chapter 3 ("Culture") illustrates how sociologists study the behaviour we have learned and share. Chapter 4 ("Socialization") reveals how humans are most distinctively social animals who learn the attitudes and behaviour viewed as appropriate in their particular cultures. We examine social interaction and social structure in Chapter 5 and the workings of groups and organizations in Chapter 6. Chapter 7 ("Deviance and Social Control") reviews how we conform to and deviate from established norms.

Part Three, "Social Inequality," considers the social hierarchies present in societies. Chapters 8 and 9 introduce us to the presence of social inequality in Canada (8) and worldwide (9). Chapter 10 ("Racial and Ethnic Inequality"), Chapter 11 ("Stratification by Gender"), and Chapter 12 ("Stratification by Age") analyze specific types of inequality.

Part Four examines the major social institutions of human society. Marriage, kinship, and divorce are some of the topics examined in Chapter 13 ("The Family and

Intimate Relationships"). Other social institutions that we consider are religion (Chapter 14), education (Chapter 15), government and politics (Chapter 16), the economy and work (Chapter 17), and health and medicine (Chapter 18)

The final chapters of the text, constituting Part Five ("Changing Society"), introduce major themes in our changing world. In Chapter 19 we examine the importance of communities and urbanization in our lives. Chapter 20 deals with population, technology and environmental issues. Finally, Chapter 21 presents a sociological analysis of collective behaviour, social movements, and the process of change.

Pedagogy to Hone the Sociological Imagination

The First Canadian Edition of *Sociology* offers a complete and integrated pedagogical system to help students to think sociologically.

Chapter Openers

Each chapter opens with graphic art that illustrates a key theme or concept of the chapter and a lively excerpt from writings of sociologists and others who explore sociological topics. For example, Chapter 3 begins with Horace Miner's classic take on Nacirema culture. Chapter 5 opens with a description of Zimbardo's mock prison study. John Ralston Saul's musings on the power of the modern media and marketing in *Voltaire's Bastards* introduce Chapter 6, and an excerpt from Thomas Homer-Dixon's *The Ingenuity Gap* sets the stage for Chapter 9's discussion of global stratification. Later, in Chapter 20, Po Brosnon profiles the inventor of Hotmail in an excerpt from *The Nudist on the Late Shift*.

Each excerpt is followed by a chapter overview that links it to key themes and describes the content of the chapter in narrative form.

Boxes

The First Canadian Edition of *Sociology* contains four types of themed boxes, three of which contain "Let's Discuss" questions to foster student involvement.

- **Research in Action** boxes present timely and relevant sociological findings on topics such as minority women and federal candidacy in Canada and impression management by students after exams.

- **Sociology in the Global Community** boxes provide a global perspective on topics such as disability as a master status, domestic violence, and population policy.

• **Eye on the Media** boxes illustrate how the media affect, and are affected by, social trends and events. Topics include the social construction of rock music as a social problem, coalition building in *Survivor*, and the Doukhobors and the Canadian media.

 • **Taking Sociology to Work** boxes profile Canadian individuals who majored in sociology and use its principles in their work. These people work in a variety of occupations and professions, and all share the conviction that their background in sociology has been valuable in their careers.

Social Policy Sections

The Social Policy sections that close Chapters 2 to 21 play a critical role in helping students to think like sociologists. They apply sociological principles and theories to important social and political issues debated by policymakers and the general public. These include multiculturalism (Chapter 3), reproductive technology (Chapter 13), religion in the schools (Chapter 14), and financing health care (Chapter 18). Each Social Policy section provides Canadian content while retaining a global perspective.

Illustrations

The photographs, cartoons, figures, and tables are closely linked to the themes of the chapters. The maps, titled "Mapping Life Nationwide" and "Mapping Life Worldwide," show the prevalence of a variety of social trends. A world map highlighting those countries used as examples in the text appears at the beginning of the book.

Cross-Reference Icons

When the text discussion refers to a concept introduced earlier in the book, an icon in the margin points the reader to the exact page, facilitating student comprehension and encouraging good study habits.

`p. 000`

Chapter Summaries

Each chapter includes a brief numbered summary to aid students in reviewing important concepts.

Critical Thinking Questions

After the summary, each chapter includes critical thinking questions that will help students analyze the social world in which they participate. Critical thinking is an essential element of the sociological imagination.

Additional Readings

An annotated list of books and journals concludes each chapter; these works have been selected as additional readings because of their sociological soundness and their accessibility for introductory students.

Internet Connection Exercises

An Internet exercise appears at the end of each chapter to take students online to analyze social issues relevant to chapter topics. Additional Internet Connection exercises are available at the Schaefer Online Learning Centre at **http://www.mcgrawhill.ca/college/schaefer**.

CBC Videos **CBC**

At the end of Chapters 1, 10, 11, 12, and 15, an icon leads students to the Online Learning Centre, where they can view CBC video segments related to chapter content. Each segment is accompanied by a series of discussion questions.

Enhancements Made for the First Canadian Edition

As described above, the First Canadian Edition of *Sociology* is fully adapted for a Canadian audience. All chapters and pedagogical features have been updated with Canadian data and examples and coverage of issues, concepts, and theories important to Canadian students and instructors, including a feminist sociological perspective on the chapter topic. Below is a chapter-by-chapter summary of just some of the content changes in this adaptation.

CHAPTER 1: Understanding Sociology

- Provides data on food banks in Edmonton
- Coverage of the Montreal Massacre and the *Firearms Act*
- New Table 1-1 provides Canadian data on specializations within sociology
- New section on modern developments in sociology in Canada
- Revised appendix focuses on sociology and careers in Canada

CHAPTER 2: Sociological Research

- New opening extract from *Generation on Hold* by J.E. Côté and A.L. Allahar, about contemporary youth and consumerism
- More material on the differences between quantitative and qualitative research methods is included
- Canadian studies on home-leaving serve as examples to illustrate the sociological research process

- New Research in Action box on framing survey questions for marginal populations
- Explanation of the CSAA Statement of Professional Ethics
- Figure 2-1: The Scientific Method has been reworked to reflect seven stages of the research process
- Provides a more complete breakdown of points in the "What is the Scientific Method?" section— much of this section has been rewritten with Canadian examples after each point
- New discussion on measuring nominal, ordinal, interval, and ratio variables
- New Taking Sociology to Work box—Angus Reid, Senior Fellow, Liu Centre for Studies of Global Issues, University of British Columbia
- Incorporation of Canadian data and policies into Social Policy section on studying human sexuality

CHAPTER 3: Culture

- Introduces multiculturalism and the cultural mosaic
- Expanded section on technology in section on "Development of Culture Around the World"
- New section on Canadian values in "Elements of Culture"
- New section on "Cultural Diversity in Canada"
- New Taking Sociology to Work box— Dr. Marylee Stephenson, CS/RESORS Consulting Ltd.
- New Social Policy section on multiculturalism

CHAPTER 4: Socialization

- New coverage of the gendered self and Marlene Mackie's theory of gender socialization
- New subsection on family and gender socialization
- Canadian data on gender bias in the classroom and bullying is included
- New subsection on peer group and gender socialization
- Canadian data on television viewing habits is included
- New coverage of the role of social class in gender socialization
- New Table 4-1 on the mass media's treatment of women
- Three new key terms added
- Coverage of daycare in Canada added to the Social Policy section

CHAPTER 5: Social Interaction and Social Structure

- New Taking Sociology to Work box on Cathy MacDonald, Dean, College Resources, Kwantlen University College
- New information on cyberspace communication's effect on the influence potential of status characteristics.
- Canadian data on Internet use
- New Research in Action box—"Teens at Work"
- Canadian examples—DAWN Canada and Campbell River Access Awareness Committee— added to the Sociology in the Global Community box
- New section on Durkheim's mechanical and organic solidarity in "Social Structure in Global Perspective"
- Extensive Canadianization of the Social Policy section
- Four new key terms: division of labour, mechanical solidarity, organic solidarity, and social cohesion

CHAPTER 6: Groups and Organizations

- New opening excerpt from John Ralston Saul's *Voltaire's Bastards: The Dictatorship of Reason in the West*
- New Eye on the Media box—"Surviving *Survivor*"
- Updated statistics and added Canadian statistics
- Section "Voluntary Organizations" rewritten from a Canadian perspective
- New Taking Sociology to Work box on János John Maté, Representative to the United Nations, Greenpeace International
- Social Policy box on sexual harassment fully updated with Canadian legislation, data, and policy initiatives

CHAPTER 7: Deviance and Social Control

- New chapter opening excerpt from *Victimless Crime? Prostitution, Drugs, Homosexuality, and Abortion* by Robert F. Meier and Gilbert Geis
- Reorganized chapter so that material on social control follows discussion of deviance
- New Research in Action box—"Street Kids"
- New Sociology in the Global Community box— "Singapore: A Nation of Campaigns"
- Canadian data on physical punishment of children is included
- Canadian data on prison sentencing is included
- New table—"Selected Cosmetic Procedures Performed by Members of the American Society

of Plastic and Reconstruction Surgeons in Canada and the U.S."
- New data on Internet addiction is included
- New coverage of spousal abuse and violence against women
- Canadian data on crime rates, with attention to regional differences, including new figure—"Crime Rates by Province and Territory, 2001"
- New Taking Sociology to Work box on Holly Johnson, Chief of Research, Canadian Centre for Justice Statistics, Statistics Canada
- Coverage of women's feeling of safety on Canadian campuses
- New Social Policy Section on illicit drug use in Canada

CHAPTER 8: Stratification and Social Mobility in Canada

- Added coverage of meritocracy
- New coverage of the concept of net worth and Canada's calculations of wealth
- Discussion of quintiles as Canadian example of social classes
- New tables and figures contain Canadian statistics
- Canadian examples of dealing with poverty are employed and differences in ideological and political approaches to "solving" the problem are addressed
- New Research in Action box on poverty in Canada is based on research by the Canadian Council on Social Development
- The Social Policy section has been rewritten from a Canadian perspective

CHAPTER 9: Social Inequality Worldwide

- New opening extract from Thomas Homer-Dixon's *The Ingenuity Gap*
- Coverage of Craig Kielburger, teenage founder of Free the Children
- New Canadian examples and links with the chapter opener in "Stratification in the World System"
- New discussion on Canadian identity and the Americanization of global culture
- Table 9-1 updated with 1999 statistics
- The case study on Mexico has been updated with new comparisons with Canada and current political and economic status information and statistics
- Figure 9-4 has been updated with 1999 Human Rights Index rankings
- The Social Policy section on universal human rights has been expanded and updated with

2000–2002 cases of human rights abuses, victories and debates including sections on women and sexual orientation

CHAPTER 10: Racial and Ethnic Inequality

- New opening excerpt from *Web of Hate: Inside Canada's Far Right Network*, by Warren Kinsella
- The chapter has been extensively rewritten to reflect Canada's policies of multiculturalism and to shift away from an American "race" perspective to a Canadian "ethnicity" perspective
- Focus on the social construction of racial and ethnic categories; discussion of "whiteness" as part of social construction of race
- Discussion of John Porter's concept of Canada as a "vertical mosaic"
- New Research in Action box—"Minority women and Federal Candidacy"
- Full discussion of implications of the *Canadian Citizenship Act* of 1967
- Coverage of the *Canadian Charter of Rights and Freedoms and the Multiculturalism Act* of 1988
- Canadian tables and figures with 1996 census data
- New section on "self-segregation" as a response by new Canadians
- Differentiation between pluralism and multiculturalism
- Discussion of racial groups in Canada covers First Nations people and Asian Canadians
- Discussion of ethnic groups in Canada focuses on French Canadians and Europeans
- New Eye on the Media box on Doukhobors and the Canadian media
- New Taking Sociology to Work box profiles Ivana Filice, educator, researcher, and consultant
- Social Policy Box on global immigration covers Canadian immigration policy initiatives

CHAPTER 11: Stratification by Gender

- New section on transgressing gender norms, including Table 11-1 on norm violations by women and by men as reported in experiment of sociology students
- "Women: The Oppressed Majority" rewritten from a current Canadian perspective
- Five of the tables and figures provide current Canadian statistics (the other three are more global in focus)
- Made substantial changes to the section on women in the workplace
- New section on the women's movement in Canada
- Extensive revisions to material on minority women and double jeopardy

- New Taking Sociology to Work box: Prudence Hannis, Community Activist with Quebec Native Women
- New Social Policy section—"Abortion and Sex Selection: The 'New Eugenics'"

CHAPTER 12: Stratification by Age

- Updated global perspectives based on UN Second World Assembly on Ageing held in Madrid in April 2002
- New tables and figures on world population aging
- Added current Canadian statistics from 2000 and 2001 on the aging population and its characteristics
- New section "The Aging of Canada" includes four new graphics (tables/figures/maps)
- Substantial revisions to the section on "Wealth and Income"
- Included Canadian organizations as examples of collective consciousness
- Social Policy section rewritten to reflect current world situation and to give Canada more visibility

CHAPTER 13: The Family and Intimate Relationships

- New figure—"Types of Family Households in Canada"
- New emphasis on diversity in Canadian families
- Increased emphasis on same-sex families
- Coverage of ethnicity and family (i.e., intermarriage, arranged marriages)
- New coverage of First Nations families
- Links between the intersection of race, class, gender, and sexual orientation with family are provided
- New figure—"Living Arrangements of Children in Canada"
- New Taking Sociology to Work box profiles Karla Jessen Williamson, Executive Director of the Arctic Institute of North America
- New coverage of single-parent families in Canada and globally
- New section on Family Violence in Canada with two new figures
- The Social Policy section has been substantially rewritten to address Canadian perspectives

CHAPTER 14: Religion

- New opening extract, "Grandfather was a Knowing Christian" by Noah Augustine, examines the conflict in religious identity among different generations of First Nations people

- Inclusion of First Nations among groups oppressed by major religions
- New section on denominations in Canada
- New table—"Religious Affiliation in Canada 1981–1999"
- New Taking Sociology to Work box profiles Pat Duffy Hutcheon, secular humanist
- Coverage of the Canadian Falun Gong member who was arrested and tortured in China
- The Social Policy section has been extensively revised to include Canadian policies on and examples of religious practices in schools in Saskatchewan, Quebec, and Ontario

CHAPTER 15: Education

- New opening extract from *Rituals of Failure* by Sandro Contenta
- Provides statistics on Canadian educational attainment and enrolment
- New figure—"Adults From OECD Countries Who Have Completed Post-Secondary Education"
- Coverage of Canada's use of residential schools for assimilation
- New Taking Sociology to Work box profiles Sarah Humphrey, behaviour technician and counsellor
- New coverage of education and family socioeconomic status in Canada
- New table—"Earnings by Gender and Educational Achievement"
- Research in Action box on violence in schools has been substantially revised
- New coverage of adult education and home schooling in Canada
- The Social Policy section has been rewritten from the perspective of Alberta's charter schools and Ontario's legislation on tax credits for independent school parents, and includes sections on Britain and New Zealand

CHAPTER 16: Government

- New opening excerpt from *Chips & Pop: Decoding the Nexus Generation* by Barnard, Cosgrave, and Welsh, examines the forces that are impacting on post-adolescents in contemporary Canadian society.
- Added the concept of "ideological power and authority"
- The Sociology in the Global Community box on terrorist violence has been substantially rewritten to reflect the events of September 11, 2001, and after
- Includes new material in Political Behaviour in Canada

- Added the concept of "majority government"
- New table on Voter Turnout in Federal Elections in Canada
- New Figure 16-1—"Federal Election Results from 1988–2000"
- New coverage of women in Canadian politics
- New Figure 16-2—"Gender & Vote Choice in Federal Elections, 1997 & 2000"
- The Research in Action box has been updated to include recent student protests in Canada
- New coverage of Canadian lobby and interest groups and multiculturalism as the Canadian version of the pluralist model of power
- New Social Policy box on gender equality

CHAPTER 17: The Economy and Work

- Added the concept of social democracy between coverage of capitalism and socialism
- Added the concept of oligopoly to the section on monopoly
- Coverage of Crown corporations as tolerated monopolies
- New figure on stress and work and how it affects job satisfaction, commitment and ultimately, absenteeism
- Coverage of changes in Canada's economy over the past century
- Coverage of the growth of the part-time labour force in Canada
- Two new figures showing labour force participation and wage gaps between men and designated groups under the *Employment Equity Act*
- New Social Policy section on employment equity

CHAPTER 18: Health and Medicine

- New chapter opening excerpt on smoking as an addiction by Peter Gzowski
- New coverage of the social meaning of illness under "Interactionist Perspectives"
- Labelling theory as applied to women's health throughout history
- Health Canada determinants of health are discussed in the section on social class and in Table 18-1, "Determinants of Health"
- New coverage of First Nations people and health
- New subsection under "Gender" discusses differences in life expectancy, and morbidity
- New subsection under "Age" discusses the recognition, in Canada, of growing incidence of brain diseases such as Alzheimer's and Parkinson's and what is being done about them

- New section, "Sexual Orientation," covers the lack of research on gays and lesbians and its impact on their health
- New section on health care in Canada
- Coverage of the role of government and the development and growth of the *Canada Health Act*
- Coverage of mental health in Canada
- Extensively revised Social Policy section covers Canada's role as world model of financed healthcare, public perceptions of healthcare problems, and responses to problems such as the Royal Commission on Health Care

CHAPTER 19: Communities and Urbanization

- New discussion of metropolitan influence zones (MIZs) and Census Metropolitan Areas (CMAs)
- New coverage of city/suburb migration patterns and gentrification in Canada
- Coverage of urbanization in Canada and the percentage of people living in four major urban centres
- The section on Issues Facing Cities has been rewritten to reflect Canadian reality
- New material on transportation in Canada and coverage of government emphasis on roads instead of public transit
- New coverage of the history of suburbs in Canada and their reflection of class, more than race, when compared to the U.S.
- Coverage of the development and decline of rural communities in Canada and the challenges now facing rural families and family farms
- The Social Policy box looks at homelessness from a Canadian perspective

CHAPTER 20: Population, the Environment, and Technology

- Added Technology section (from Chapter 22 in U.S. 7th edition)
- Added Canadian material on census and gathering of vital statistics
- New Figure 20-2 compares population pyramids of Kenya and Canada
- Reworked the three trends in internal migration to better fit the Canadian context: urbanization, "sunning of America," and the "doughnut" effect
- New Taking Sociology to Work box profiles Kelsie Lenor Wilson-Dorsett, Deputy Director, Department of Statistics, Government of Bahamas
- The environment section has been substantially revised to include Canadian examples

- New Research in Action box—"Protecting Canada's Species at Risk"
- Extensively revised Social Policy section reflects Canadian reality with regard to privacy and censorship in the global village

CHAPTER 21: Collective Behaviour, Social Movements, and Social Change

- Combined section on Social Change (from Chapter 22 in U.S. 7th edition) with Collective Behaviour and Social Movements
- Made social movements a major section instead of part of collective behaviour and used it as transition between collective behaviour leading to social movements leading to social change
- Added new examples from meetings of global leaders and current sports riots from the World Cup events
- Added section on Gender and Social Movements covering different roles within movements for males/females and the impact of female leadership within movements
- The Social Policy section has been substantially rewritten to reflect Canadian history, actions, and accomplishments of lesbian and gay rights movement

Support for Instructors

i-Learning Sales Specialist

Your *Integrated Learning Sales Specialist* is a McGraw-Hill Ryerson representative who has the experience, product knowledge, training, and support to help you assess and integrate any of the below-noted products, technology, and services into your course for optimum teaching and learning performance. Whether it's how to use our test bank software, helping your students improve their grades, or how to put your entire course on-line, your *i*-Learning Sales Specialist is there to help. Contact your local *i*-Learning Sales Specialist today to learn how to maximize all McGraw-Hill Ryerson resources!

iLearning Services Program

McGraw-Hill Ryerson offers a unique *i*Services package designed for Canadian faculty. Our mission is to equip providers of higher education with superior tools and resources required for excellence in teaching. For additional information visit **www.mcgrawhill. ca/highereducation/eservices/**.

The integrator

This pioneering instructional resource from McGraw-Hill Ryerson is your road map to all of the other elements of your text's support package. Keyed to the chapters and topics of *Sociology*, First Canadian Edition, the *i*ntegrator ties together all of the elements in your resource package, guiding you to where you'll find corresponding coverage in each of the related support package components—be it the Instructor's Manual, Test Bank, PowerPoint Slides, Online Learning Centre, or Student Study Guide.

Instructor's Resource Manual

This manual, adapted for Canada by author Edith Smith, provides instructors with additional lecture ideas, class discussion topics, essay questions, research topics, and CBC video cases.

Test Bank and Computerized Test Bank

The fully adapted test bank features short-answer questions, multiple-choice questions, and essay questions.

The test bank is also available electronically in a Brownstone format that allows instructors to select, edit, and/or write their own questions, print exams, and more.

Online Learning Centre

Visit the Schaefer Online Learning Centre at **www.mcgrawhill.ca/ college/schaefer** to download the *i*ntegrator, **Instructor's Resource Manual** and a complete set of **PowerPoint slides** to accompany the text. The site also features six **CBC video segments**.

PowerWeb

Add the Internet to your course. PowerWeb includes current articles, curriculum-based materials, weekly updates with assessment, informative and timely world news, refereed Web links, research tools, student study tools, interactive exercises, and much more. To learn more, visit **www.dushkin.com/powerweb**.

E-STAT

E-STAT is an educational resource designed by Statistics Canada and made available to Canadian educational institutions. Using 450 000 current CANSIM (Canadian Socio-economic Information Management System) Time Series and the most recent—as well as historical—census data, E-STAT lets you bring data to life in colourful graphs and maps. You can access such data as population, income, language, ethnic groups, federal debt, imports and exports, and more. Easy-to-use, thorough and dynamic, E-STAT is a stimulating teaching and learning resource that spurs students on to discover Canada, past and present.

Data Liberation Initiative

The Data Liberation Initiative (DLI) is a cost-effective method for improving data resources for Canadian post-secondary institutions. Prior to the start of the DLI program, Canadian universities and colleges had to purchase Statistics Canada data, file by file. With the advent of the DLI, participating post-secondary institutions pay an annual subscription fee that allows their faculty and students unlimited access to numerous Statistics Canada public-use microdata files, databases, and geographic files.

PageOut: The Course Web Site Development Centre

PageOut was designed for the professor just beginning to explore Web options. In less than an hour, even the novice computer user can create a course Web site with a template provided by McGraw-Hill (no programming knowledge required).

To find out more about PageOut, contact your *i*-Learning Sales Specialist.

Support for Students

Reel Society Interactive Movie CD-ROM

Exercise your sociological imagination and step into the world of Reel Society, an interactive movie that brings key sociological concepts to life. You become part of the story of several university students during three challenging days on campus. You take part by making decisions for them. You see the consequences of your choices. Through it all, a wide variety of issues and perspectives are shown for the purpose of relating sociological thought to real life. To learn more about Reel Society, visit **www.mhhe.com/reelsociety**.

Study to Go: A Mobile Learning Application for Palm and PocketPC

Do you use a handheld Personal Digital Assistant (PDA)? McGraw-Hill Ryerson's *Study to Go* application gives you the opportunity to study any time, anywhere. And it's free for students using *Sociology*! To download quizzes, key terms, and flashcards, visit the Online Learning Centre at **www.mcgrawhill.ca/college/schaefer**.

Study Guide

The fully adapted study guide includes a variety of resources for each chapter to help students review and succeed in the course.

Online Learning Centre

Visit the Schaefer Online Learning Centre at **www.mcgrawhill.ca/college/schaefer** to take multiple-choice chapter quizzes, view CBC video segments and answer related questions, search the book glossary, engage with additional Internet Connections for each chapter, and more.

ACKNOWLEDGMENTS

An endeavour of this magnitude cannot be completed without team effort. So I want to acknowledge the invaluable assistance of librarians (in particular Lorraine Albert at the University of Ottawa and Carolyn Gilmore at Dawson College), who were experts at leading me in the right direction. In addition, much-needed research assistance was given by Christine Constantin. I am indebted to Cindy Davey and Ivana Filice for sharing their knowledge, expertise, and encouragement. Don and Carolyn provided me with their editorial advice as well as a quiet place to work when urban life was too hectic. In fact, the unwavering support of family, friends, and colleagues was of more help than can be expressed.

I have received incredibly strong support and encouragement from a number of individuals at McGraw-Hill Ryerson: James Buchanan, sponsoring editor, and Jennifer DiDomenico, a developmental editor par excellence. Additional guidance and support were provided by Jaime Duffy, supervising editor, Laurel Sparrow, copy editor, Dianna Little, designer, and Madeleine Harrington, production coordinator.

Thanks to Richard Floyd and Bonnie Haaland of Kwantlen University College for their contributions to the text.

I would also like to express my thanks to those who submitted thoughtful and thorough reviews that helped to improve the textbook:

Robert Argue, Ryerson University

Morgan Holmes, Wilfrid Laurier University

Merle Jacobs, York University

Patricia Kachuk, University of British Columbia

Paul Lamy, University of Ottawa

Debra Langan, York University

Daniel MacInnes, St. Francis Xavier University

John Manzo, University of Calgary

Nicole Power, Memorial University of Newfoundland

Susan Prentice, University of Manitoba

Vince Sacco, Queen's University

Craig Seaton, Trinity Western University

William Shaffir, McMaster University

Murray Smith, Brock University

Ann Travers, Simon Fraser University

Kevin Wong, Brandon University

I also extend thanks to those reviewers who have contributed to previous editions of this text in the United States:

Jan AbuShakrah, Portland Community College, Patti Adler, University of Colorado, Cynthia D. Anderson, Iowa State University, Therese Baker, California State University, San Marcos, Chet Ballard, Valdosta State University, Judith Barker, Ithaca College, John W. Bedell, California State University, Fullerton, Kathleen Bennet DeMarrais, Northern Arizona University, Mary Bernstein, Arizona State University, H. B. (Keo) Cavalcanti, University of Richmond, Larry Clarke, Shoreline Community College, Linda Cook, Houston Community College, Ione Y. DeOllos, Ball State University, Jan Fiola, Moorhead State University, Michael Goslin, Tallahassee Community College, Lillian O. Holloman, Prince George's Community College, Mark Kassop, Bergen Community College, Janet Kroon, University of South Dakota, David R. Maines, Oakland University, Rebecca Matthews, University of Iowa, Peter Meiksins, Cleveland State University, Kenneth J. Mietus, Western Illinois University, Joel I. Nelson, University of Minnesota, Timothy J. Owens, Purdue University, Pete A. Padilla, Arizona State University, Earl Piercy, Trukee Meadows Community College, Diane Pike, Augsburg College, Ferris J. Ritchey, University of Alabama, Birmingham, Nathan Rousseau, Muskingum College, Jon Schlenker, University of Maine, Augusta, Kerry Strand, Hood College, John Tenuto, College of Lake County, Jacquelyn Troup, Cerritos College, Steven Vassar, Minnesota State University, Gina Walls, Parkland Community College, Elaine Wethington, Cornell University, Eric R. Wright, Indiana University-Purdue University, Indianapolis, Stephen Zehr, University of Southern Indiana.

I have been fortunate to have the opportunity to talk about sociology with students for many years. They have been incredibly helpful in the development of my own sociological imagination as well as in directing my research.

A Visual Preview of the First Canadian Edition

Sociology, First Canadian Edition, teaches students how to think critically about society and their own lives from a wide range of classical and contemporary sociological perspectives.

Timely "Sociology in the Global Community" Boxes

These boxes provide a global perspective on topics such as disability as a master status, slavery in the twenty-first century, and terrorist violence.

Stimulating "Research in Action" Boxes

These boxes present sociological findings on topics such as poverty in Canada, school-related violence, and gated communities.

Motivational "Taking Sociology to Work" Interviews

"Taking Sociology to Work" boxes profile Canadian individuals who majored in sociology and use its principles in their work.

Thought-Provoking "Eye on the Media" Boxes

These sections illustrate how the media affect—and are affected by—social trends and events. Topics featured in these boxes include constructing rock music as a social problem, the Doukhobors and the Canadian media, and political activism on the Internet.

Distinctive Social Policy Sections

These discussions, five of which are completely new to the First Canadian Edition, and all of which have been extensively adapted, provide a sociological perspective on contemporary social issues such as multiculturalism, immigration, and financing health care. These sections provide a global view of the issues and are organized around a consistent heading structure to make the material accessible.

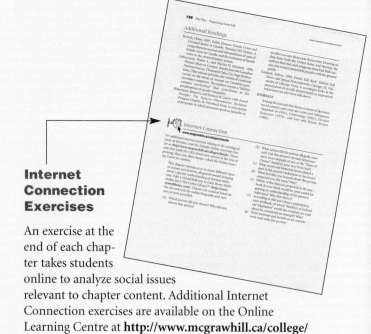

Helpful Cross-Reference System

Key concepts that have been introduced at an earlier point in the text are highlighted with an icon that includes a page number for review purposes.

Internet Connection Exercises

An exercise at the end of each chapter takes students online to analyze social issues relevant to chapter content. Additional Internet Connection exercises are available on the Online Learning Centre at **http://www.mcgrawhill.ca/college/schaefer.**

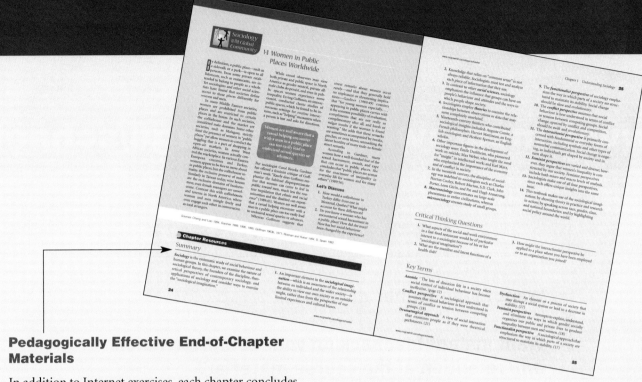

Pedagogically Effective End-of-Chapter Materials

In addition to Internet exercises, each chapter concludes with a point-by-point summary, glossary of key terms with page references, critical thinking questions, and suggested readings.

Practical Career Guide

"Careers in Sociology" appears as an appendix at the end of Chapter 1 and provides a glimpse of the opportunities available to those with degrees in sociology.

Online LearningCentre with POWERWEB

www.mcgrawhill.ca/college/schaefer

FOR THE STUDENT

- Want to get higher grades?

- Want instant feedback on your comprehension *and* retention of the course material?

- Want to know how ready you *really* are to take your next exam?

- Want the extra help at *your* convenience?

Of course you do!

Then check out your
Online Learning Centre!

- Online Quizzes
- Web Resources
- Web Research
  - CBC video clips

Sociology

First Canadian Edition

FOR THE INSTRUCTOR

- Want an easy way to test your students prior to an exam that *doesn't* create more work for you?

- Want to access your supplements *without* having to bring them all to class?

- Want to integrate current happenings into your lectures *without* all the searching and extra work?

- Want an *easy* way to get your course on-line?

- Want to *free up more time* in your day to get more done?

Of course you do!

Then check out your
Online Learning Centre!

- Downloadable Supplements
- PageOut
- Online Resources
- E-STAT
- CBC video clips

McGraw-Hill Ryerson

Higher Learning. Forward Thinking.™

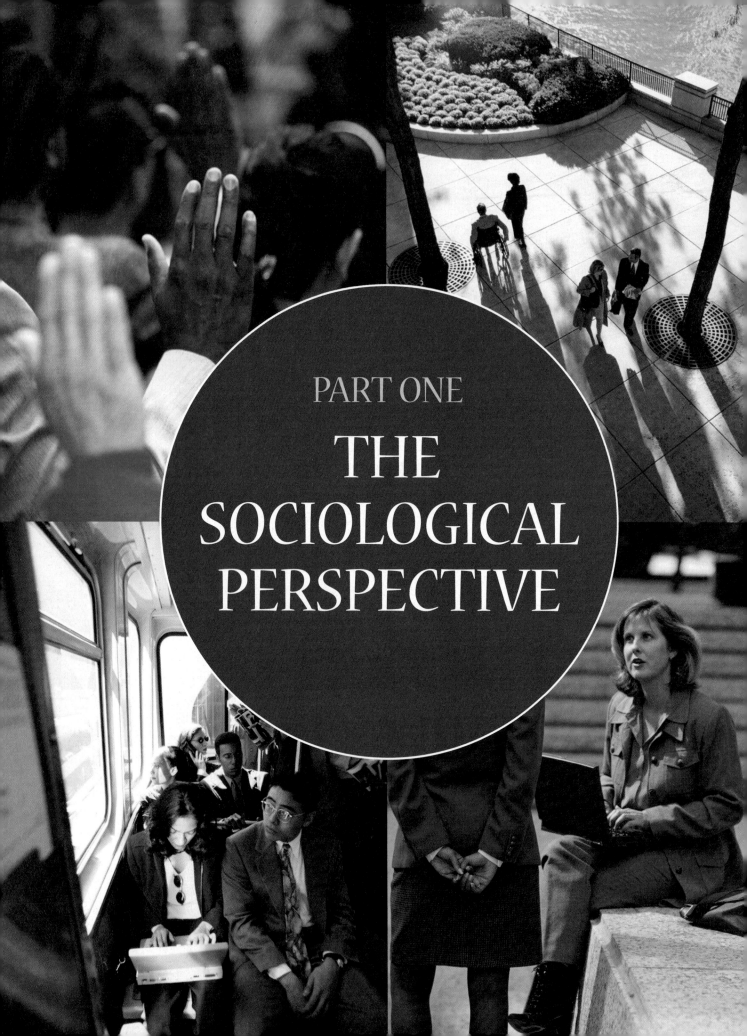

PART ONE
THE SOCIOLOGICAL PERSPECTIVE

Part One introduces the fundamental theories and research methods used by sociologists and other social scientists to understand social behaviour. Chapter 1: defines the sociological imagination; compares sociology with other social sciences; discusses the origins and founders of sociology; and presents the functionalist, conflict, feminist, and interactionist approaches that will be utilized throughout the book.

Chapter 2 outlines the basic principles and steps of the scientific method, examines the methods through which sociologists generate data for their research, and explores the ethical issues that sociologists face as they study human behaviour. These discussions of sociological theory and research provide the foundation for our study of the organization of social life (Part Two), social inequality (Part Three), social institutions (Part Four), and social change (Part Five).

UNDERSTANDING SOCIOLOGY

Sociology places us in the context of groups, cultures, and societies. People interact in all three of these settings in the Olympic games. This poster promotes the bid of Osaka, Japan, for the 2008 Summer Olympics.

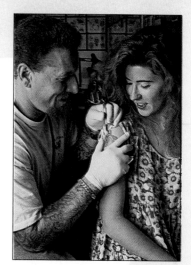

first walked into the Blue Mosque in the spring of 1996, when I came to accompany a friend getting her first tattoo. Before entering the clean, comfortable, and friendly shop, I had never thought about getting permanent body art myself. In fact, I had specifically promised my family that I would never become tattooed. After watching my friend go through the experience, I changed my mind and began wondering what forms of body modification I could sport myself. The shop's congenial atmosphere made it easy to return several times while choosing my own piercings and eventually my own tattoo. During my visits, I formed friendships with all the artists, and started dating and eventually married the shop's owner, Lefty. Our home became a stopping ground for tattooists traveling through town and a social center for the shop. . . .

My tattoo recreational life became a research interest after Lefty and I took a vacation to California. Renting a car and roaming the California coastline, we visited a score of tattoo shops, talked about the meaning of tattoos in society, and noted the many changes taking place in the tattoo industry. At the end of one of these conversations, Lefty mentioned that someone should do a study chronicling these changes. As a graduate student in Sociology looking for a dissertation topic, I quickly stepped up to the research task and Lefty willingly assumed the responsibility of key informant. . . .

As a tattooist's wife and a shop regular, I gained a unique view of this social world. Over the two-year participant observation study, I visited the shop between one hundred to two hundred times and was present during thousands of conversations between the tattoo artists at home and at social occasions. . . .

While at home and during social functions, I focused on the social world of professional tattooists while listening to daily conversations regarding their interactions with clients, their hopes, their frustrations, and their goals. The first time tattooees at the Blue Mosque were a unique set made up equally of men and women, ranging in age (18–60) more than heavily tattooed clients of the shop, and were more likely to be middle or upper middle class. My observations reflect the largely conventional, middle class experience of getting a first tattoo. (Irwin 1999a) ∎

What makes tattooing an appropriate subject for study in sociology? Uniting all sociological studies is their focus on *patterns* of human behaviour. Katherine Irwin's tattoo research, for example, tracked the dramatic change in what it meant to get a tattoo in the 1990s, as opposed to earlier periods, when tattooing was primarily associated with fringe groups like biker gangs, punk rockers, and skinheads. Tattoo clients of the 1990s, Irwin found, increasingly fit the image of avant-garde or hip individuals, seeking to make a statement about their identities but not to cut themselves off from mainstream society. By continuing to interact with that society, whether as students, or employees, or just members of conventional families, they were in fact making tattooing appear less unconventional. The tattoo has gradually become a badge of trendy social status, instead of a symbol of outcast status (Irwin 1998, 1999b, 2000).

Sociologists are not concerned with what one individual does or does not do, but with what people do as members of a group or interacting with one another, and what that means for the individuals and for society as a whole. Tattooing is, in fact, a subject that sociologists can study in any number of ways. They might examine its history (going back as far as 30 000 years) or its use in different groups, regions, and cultures. One study, for example, specifically looks at how the tattoos of prison gang members communicate their status, rank, and personal accomplishments. Another focuses on the emergence of Christian tattoo parlours, which offer images of Christ or banners that blaze "Born Again" (E. Gale 1999; Mascia-Lees and Sharpe 1992; Phelan and Hunt 1998).

As a field of study, then, sociology is extremely broad in scope. You will see throughout this book the range of topics sociologists investigate—from suicide to TV viewing habits, from Amish society to global economic patterns, from peer pressure to pickpocketing techniques. Sociology looks at how others influence our behaviour as well as how major social institutions like the government, religion, and the economy affect us.

This chapter will explore the nature of sociology as a field of inquiry and an exercise of the "sociological imagination." We'll look at the discipline as a science and consider its relationship to other social sciences. We will evaluate the contributions of three pioneering thinkers—Émile Durkheim, Max Weber, and Karl Marx—to the development of sociology. Next we will discuss a number of important theoretical perspectives used by sociologists. Finally, we will consider the ways sociology helps us to develop our sociological imagination. ■

What Is Sociology?

Sociology is the systematic study of social behaviour and human groups. It focuses primarily on the influence of social relationships on people's attitudes and behaviour and on how societies are established and change. This textbook deals with such varied topics as families, the workplace, street gangs, business firms, political parties, genetic engineering, schools, religions, and labour unions. It is concerned with love, poverty, conformity, discrimination, illness, technology, and community.

The Sociological Imagination

In attempting to understand social behaviour, sociologists rely on an unusual type of creative thinking. C. Wright Mills (1959) described such thinking as the *sociological imagination*—an awareness of the relationship between an individual and the wider society. This awareness allows all of us (not just sociologists) to comprehend the links between our immediate, personal social settings and the remote, impersonal social world that surrounds us and helps to shape us.

A key element in the sociological imagination is the ability to view one's own society as an outsider would, rather than only from the perspective of personal experiences and cultural biases. Consider something as simple as the practice of eating while walking. In Canada we think nothing of seeing people consuming coffee or chocolate bars as they walk along. Sociologists would see this as a pattern of acceptable behaviour because others regard it as acceptable. Yet sociologists need to go beyond one culture to place the practice in perspective. This "normal" behaviour is quite unacceptable elsewhere. For example, in Japan people do not eat while walking. Streetside sellers and vending machines dispense food everywhere, but the Japanese will stop to eat or drink whatever they buy before they continue on their way. In their eyes, to engage in another activity while eating shows disrespect for the food preparation, even if the food comes out of a vending machine.

Do you consider talking on a cell phone while driving "normal" behaviour? Some cultural practices are so new that their acceptability in a society is still being determined.

The sociological imagination allows us to go beyond personal experiences and observations to understand broader public issues. Unemployment, for example, is unquestionably a personal hardship for a man or woman without a job. However, C. Wright Mills pointed out that when unemployment is a social problem shared by millions of people, it is appropriate to question the way that a society is structured or organized. Similarly, Mills advocated using the sociological imagination to view divorce not simply as the personal problem of a particular man or woman, but rather as a societal problem, since it is the outcome of many marriages. And he was writing this in the 1950s, when the divorce rate was but a fraction of what it is today (I. Horowitz 1983).

Sociological imagination can bring new understanding to daily life around us. For example, growing numbers of Canadian families are turning to food banks to provide them with daily necessities. A 1999 report on hunger, homelessness, and food bank use published by Edmonton's Food Bank and the Edmonton Social Planning Council found that 54 percent of Edmonton families using food banks live on less than $1000 per month. The majority of these families (71 percent) reported that they turn to food banks because of ongoing money shortages. Female single parents with children under 12 were most likely to be clients of food banks (55 percent).

Many observers would uncritically applaud the distribution of tons of food to the needy. But let's look deeper. While supportive of and personally involved in such efforts, Miller and Schaefer (1993) have drawn on the sociological imagination to offer a more probing view of these activities. They note that powerful forces in United States society—such as the federal government, major food retailers, and other large corporations—have joined in charitable food distribution arrangements. Perhaps as a result, the focus of such relief programs is too restricted. The homeless are to be fed, not housed; the unemployed are to be given meals, not jobs. Relief efforts assist hungry individuals and families without challenging the existing social order (for example, by demanding a redistribution of wealth). Of course, without these limited successes in distributing food, starving people might assault patrons of restaurants, loot grocery stores, or literally die of starvation on the steps of city halls. Such critical thinking is typical of sociologists, as they draw on the sociological imagination to study a social issue—in this case, hunger in North America (Second Harvest 1997; Vladimiroff 1998).

Sociology and the Social Sciences

Is sociology a science? The term *science* refers to the body of knowledge obtained by methods based upon systematic observation. Just like other scientific disciplines, sociology engages in organized, systematic study of phenomena (in this case, human behaviour) in order to enhance understanding. All scientists, whether studying mushrooms or murderers, attempt to collect precise information through methods of study that are as objective as possible. They rely on careful recording of observations and accumulation of data.

Feeding the homeless seems entirely benevolent, but if we look deeper into this charitable action we might conclude that its focus is too narrow. The homeless also need shelter; the unemployed need jobs. Exercising the sociological imagination enables us to think critically as we examine social issues.

Of course, there is a great difference between sociology and physics and between psychology and astronomy. For this reason, the sciences are commonly divided into natural and social sciences. ***Natural science*** is the study of the physical features of nature and the ways in which they interact and change. Astronomy, biology, chemistry, geology, and physics are all natural sciences. ***Social science*** is the study of various aspects of human society. The social sciences include sociology, anthropology, economics, history, psychology, and political science.

These academic disciplines have a common focus on the social behaviour of people, yet each has a particular orientation. Anthropologists usually study past cultures and preindustrial societies that continue today, as well as the origins of men and women; this knowledge is used to examine contemporary societies, including even industrial societies. Economists explore the ways in which people produce and exchange goods and services, along with money and other resources. Historians are concerned with the peoples and events of the past and their significance for us today. Political scientists study international relations, the workings of government, and the exercise of power and authority. Psychologists investigate personality and individual behaviour. So what does sociology focus on? It emphasizes the influence that society has on people's attitudes and behaviour and the ways in which people shape society. Humans are social animals; therefore, sociologists scientifically examine our social relationships with people.

Let's consider how the different social sciences might approach the issue of gun control. This issue received increased public attention in Canada when Marc Lepine systematically shot and killed 14 female engineering students at École Polytechnique in Montreal on December 6, 1987. The event became known as the "Montreal Massacre" and was instrumental in the stricter gun control laws in Canada, in the form of registration requirements under the *Firearms Act*. Political scientists would look at the impact of political action groups, such as the National Firearm Association, on lawmakers. Historians would examine attitudes toward firearms and how guns were used over time in our country and elsewhere. Anthropologists would focus on the use of weapons in a variety of cultures as means of protection as well as symbols of power. Psychologists would look at individual cases and assess the impact guns have on their owners as well as on individual victims of gunfire. Economists would be interested in how firearm manufacture and sales affect communities. Sociologists would gather data to inform policymakers. For example, they would examine data from different regions to evaluate the effect of gun restrictions on the incidence of firearm accidents or violent crimes involving firearms. They would ask: What explanations can be offered for the gender, racial, age,

Table 1-1	**Specializations Within Sociology**

Aboriginal people/First Nations
Aging/social gerontology
Biotechnology
Community/urban and rural sociology
Comparative historical sociology
Criminal justice/corrections
Criminology
Cultural sociology
Demography
Development
Deviance/social control
Disability studies
Economic sociology
Education
Environmental sociology
Family studies
History of sociology/social thought
Labour process/labour studies
Leisure/sports/recreation
Media/mass communications
Medical sociology
Methodology
Migration and immigration
Nationalism
Occupations/professions
Organizational studies
Political sociology
Popular culture
Race/ethnicity/minority relations
Religion
Sex and gender
Social change
Social movements
Social policy
Social psychology
Socialization
Sociology of knowledge
Sociology of mental health
Sociology of work
Stratification/mobility
Theory

Source: Compiled by Edith Smith from data received from the Canadian Sociology and Anthropology Association, February 2002.

rural/urban, and geographic differences in gun ownership? How would these differences affect the formulation of government policy? Sociologists might also look at data that show how Canada compares to other nations (particularly the United States) in gun ownership and use.

Sociologists put their imagination to work in a variety of areas. Table 1-1 presents a list of the specializations within contemporary sociology. Throughout this text-book, the sociological imagination will be used to examine Canada (and other societies) from the viewpoint of respectful but questioning outsiders.

Sociology and Common Sense

Sociology focuses on the study of human behaviour. Yet we all have experience with human behaviour and at least some knowledge of it. All of us might well have theories about why people get tattoos, for example, or why people become homeless. Our theories and opinions typically come from "common sense"—that is, from our experiences and conversations, from what we read, from what we see on television, and so forth.

In our daily lives, we rely on common sense to get us through many unfamiliar situations. However, this common sense knowledge, while sometimes accurate, is not always reliable, because it rests on commonly held beliefs rather than on systematic analysis of facts. It was once considered "common sense" to accept that the earth was flat—a view rightly questioned by Pythagoras and Aristotle. Incorrect common sense notions are not just a part of the distant past; they remain with us today.

"Common sense" tells us that people panic when faced with natural disasters, such as floods, earthquakes,

Do disasters produce panic or an organized, structured response? Common sense might tell us the former, but, in fact, disasters bring out a great deal of structure and organization to deal with their aftermath. Prime Minister Jean Chrétien thanks rescue workers for their effort at the World Trade Center at Ground Zero, September 29, 2001.

or ice storms. However, these particular "common sense" notions—like the notion that the earth is flat—are untrue; they are not supported by sociological research. Disasters do not generally produce panic. In the aftermath of disasters and even explosions, greater social organization and structure emerges to deal with a community's problems. In Canada, for example, emergency response teams often coordinate public services and even certain services normally performed by the private sector, such as food distribution. Decision making becomes more centralized in times of disaster.

Like other social scientists, sociologists do not accept something as a fact because "everyone knows it." Instead, each piece of information must be tested and recorded, then analyzed in relationship to other data. Sociology relies on scientific studies in order to describe and understand a social environment. At times, the findings of sociologists may seem like common sense because they deal with facets of everyday life. The difference is that such findings have been *tested* by researchers. Common sense now tells us that the earth is round. But this particular common sense notion is based on centuries of scientific work upholding the breakthrough made by Pythagoras and Aristotle.

What Is Sociological Theory?

Why do people commit suicide? One traditional common sense answer is that people inherit the desire to kill themselves. Another view is that sunspots drive people to take their own lives. These explanations may not seem especially convincing to contemporary researchers, but they represent beliefs widely held as recently as 1900.

Sociologists are not particularly interested in why any one individual commits suicide; they are more concerned with the social forces that systematically cause some people to take their own lives. In order to undertake this research, sociologists develop a theory that offers a general explanation of suicidal behaviour.

We can think of theories as attempts to explain events, forces, materials, ideas, or behaviour in a comprehensive manner. Within sociology, a **theory** is a set of statements that seeks to explain problems, actions, or behaviour. An effective theory may have both explanatory and predictive power. That is, it can help us to develop a broad and integrated view of the relationships among seemingly isolated phenomena as well as to understand how one type of change in an environment leads to others.

Émile Durkheim (1951, original edition 1897) looked into suicide data in great detail and developed a highly original theory about the relationship between suicide and social factors. He was primarily concerned not with the personalities of individual suicide victims, but rather with suicide *rates* and how they varied from country to country. As a result, when he looked at the number of reported suicides in France, England, and Denmark in 1869, he also examined the populations of these nations to determine their rates of suicide. He found that whereas England had only 67 reported suicides per million inhabitants, France had 135 per million and Denmark had 277 per million. The question then became: "Why did Denmark have a comparatively high rate of reported suicides?"

Durkheim went much deeper into his investigation of suicide rates, and the result was his landmark work *Suicide,* published in 1897. Durkheim refused to accept unproven explanations regarding suicide automatically, including the beliefs that cosmic forces or inherited tendencies caused such deaths. Instead, he focused on such problems as the cohesiveness or lack of cohesiveness of religious, social, and occupational groups, in a particular place and time.

Durkheim's research suggested that suicide, while a solitary act, is related to group life. Protestants had much higher suicide rates than Catholics did; the unmarried had much higher rates than married people did; soldiers were more likely to take their lives than civilians were. In addition, it appeared that there were higher rates of suicide in times of peace than in times of war and revolution, and in times of economic instability and recession rather than in times of prosperity. Durkheim concluded that the suicide rates of a society reflected the extent to which people were or were not integrated into the group life of the society.

Émile Durkheim, like many other social scientists, developed a theory to explain how individual behaviour can be understood within a social context. He pointed out the influence of groups and societal forces on what had always been viewed as a highly personal act. Clearly, Durkheim offered a more *scientific* explanation for the causes of suicide than that of sunspots or inherited tendencies. His theory has predictive power, since it suggests that suicide rates will rise or fall in conjunction with certain social and economic changes.

Of course, a theory—even the best of theories—is not a final statement about human behaviour. Durkheim's theory of suicide is no exception; sociologists continue to examine factors that contribute to differences in suicide rates around the world and to a particular society's rate of suicide. For example, although the overall rate of suicide in New Zealand is only marginally higher than in the United States, the suicide rate among young people is 41 percent higher in New Zealand. Sociologists and psychiatrists from that country suggest that their remote, sparsely populated society maintains exaggerated standards of masculinity that are especially difficult for young

males. Gay adolescents who fail to conform to their peers' preference for sports are particularly vulnerable to suicide, as are Aboriginal youth on Canadian reserves (Shenon 1995; for a critique of Durkheim's work, see Douglas 1967).

The Development of Sociology

People have always been curious about sociological matters—such as how we get along, what we do, and whom we select as our leaders. Philosophers and religious authorities of ancient and medieval societies made countless observations about human behaviour. They did not test or verify these observations scientifically; nevertheless, these observations often became the foundation for moral codes. Several of the early social philosophers predicted that a systematic study of human behaviour would one day emerge. Beginning in the nineteenth century, European theorists made pioneering contributions to the development of a science of human behaviour. Each of them emerged out of a particular historical context that influenced their questions and their theories.

Early Thinkers: Comte, Martineau, and Spencer

The nineteenth century was an unsettling time in France. The French monarchy had been deposed earlier in the revolution of 1789, and Napoleon had subsequently suffered defeat in his effort to conquer Europe. Amidst this chaos, philosophers considered how society might be improved. Auguste Comte (1798–1857), credited with being the most influential of these philosophers of the early 1800s, believed that a theoretical science of society and a systematic investigation of behaviour were needed to improve society. He coined the term *sociology* to apply to the science of human behaviour.

Writing in the 1800s, Comte feared that the excesses of the French Revolution had permanently impaired France's stability. Yet he hoped that the study of social behaviour in a systematic way would eventually lead to more rational human interactions. In Comte's hierarchy of sciences, sociology was at the top. He called it the "queen" and its practitioners "scientist–priests." This French theorist did not simply give sociology its name; he also presented a rather ambitious challenge to the fledgling discipline.

Scholars were able to learn of Comte's works largely through translations by the English sociologist Harriet Martineau (1802–1876). But Martineau was a pathbreaker in her own right as a sociologist. She offered insightful observations of the customs and social practices of both her native Britain and the United States.

Harriet Martineau was an early pioneer of sociology who studied social behaviour both in her native England and in the United States.

Martineau's book *Society in America* (1962, original edition 1837) examines religion, politics, child rearing, and immigration in the young nation. Martineau gives special attention to social class distinctions and to such factors as gender and race.

Martineau's writings emphasized the impact that the economy, law, trade, and population could have on the social problems of contemporary society. She spoke out in favour of the rights of women, the emancipation of slaves, and religious tolerance. In Martineau's (1896) view, intellectuals and scholars should not simply offer observations of social conditions; they should act upon their convictions in a manner that will benefit society. In line with this view, Martineau conducted research on the nature of female employment and pointed to the need for further investigation of this important issue (Lengermann and Niebrugge-Brantley 1998). As we will see, feminist sociologists continue these ideas today.

Another important contributor to the discipline of sociology was Herbert Spencer (1820–1903). A relatively prosperous Victorian Englishman, Spencer (unlike Martineau) did not feel compelled to correct or improve society; instead, he merely hoped to understand it better. Drawing on Charles Darwin's study *On the Origin of Species,* Spencer applied the concept of evolution of the species to societies in order to explain how they change,

or evolve, over time. Similarly, he adapted Darwin's evolutionary view of the "survival of the fittest" by arguing that it is "natural" that some people are rich while others are poor.

Spencer's approach to societal change was extremely popular in his own lifetime. Unlike Comte and Martineau, Spencer suggested that societies are bound to change eventually; therefore, one need not be highly critical of present social arrangements or work actively for social change. This position appealed to many influential people in England and North America who had a vested interest in the status quo and were suspicious of social thinkers who endorsed change. One can see the influence of their historical context in the views of these early founders of sociological theories.

Émile Durkheim

Émile Durkheim made many pioneering contributions to sociology, including his important theoretical work on suicide. The son of a rabbi, Durkheim (1858–1917) was educated in both France and Germany. He established an impressive academic reputation and was appointed as one of the first professors of sociology in France. Above all, Durkheim will be remembered for his insistence that behaviour must be understood within a larger social context, not just in individualistic terms.

As one example of this emphasis, Durkheim (1947, original edition 1912) developed a fundamental thesis to help understand all forms of society through intensive study of the Arunta, an Australian tribe. He focused on the functions that religion performed for the Arunta and underscored the role that group life plays in defining that which we consider religious. Durkheim concluded that, like other forms of group behaviour, religion reinforces a group's solidarity.

Another of Durkheim's main interests was the consequences of work in modern societies. In his view, the growing division of labour found in industrial societies as workers became much more specialized in their tasks led to what he called *anomie*. **Anomie** refers to the loss of direction that a society feels when social control of individual behaviour has become ineffective. The state of anomie occurs when people have lost their sense of purpose or direction, often during a time of profound social change. In a period of anomie, people are so confused and unable to cope with the new social environment that they may resort to taking their own lives.

Like many other sociologists, Durkheim's interests were not limited to one aspect of social behaviour. Later in this book, we will consider his thinking on crime and punishment, religion, and the workplace. Few sociologists have had such a dramatic impact on so many different areas within the discipline.

Max Weber

Another important early theorist was Max Weber (pronounced "VAY-ber"). Born in Germany in 1864, Weber took his early academic training in legal and economic history, but he gradually developed an interest in sociology. Eventually, he became a professor at various German universities. Weber taught his students that they should employ **Verstehen**, the German word for "understanding" or "insight," in their intellectual work. He pointed out that we cannot analyze much of our social behaviour by the kinds of objective criteria we use to measure weight or temperature. To fully comprehend behaviour, we must learn the subjective meanings people attach to their actions—how they themselves view and explain their behaviour.

For example, suppose that a sociologist was studying the social ranking of students at a high school. Weber would expect the researcher to employ *Verstehen* to determine the significance of the high school's social hierarchy for its members. The researcher might examine the effects of athleticism or grades or social skills or physical appearance in the school. He or she would seek to learn how the students relate to others of higher or lower status. While investigating these questions, the researcher would take into account people's emotions, thoughts, beliefs, and attitudes (L. Coser 1977).

We also owe credit to Weber for a key conceptual tool: the ideal type. An **ideal type** is a construct, a made-up model that serves as a measuring rod against which actual cases can be evaluated. In his own works, Weber identified various characteristics of bureaucracy as an ideal type (discussed in detail in Chapter 6). In presenting this model of bureaucracy, Weber was not describing any particular business, nor was he using the term *ideal* in a way that suggested a positive evaluation. Instead, his purpose was to provide a useful standard for measuring how bureaucratic an actual organization is (Gerth and Mills 1958). Later in this textbook, we use the concept of ideal type to study the family, religion, authority, and economic systems and to analyze bureaucracy.

Although their professional careers coincided, Émile Durkheim and Max Weber never met and probably were unaware of each other's existence, let alone ideas. This was certainly not true of the work of Karl Marx. Durkheim's thinking about the impact of the division of labour in industrial societies was related to Marx's writings, while Weber's concern for a value-free, objective sociology was a direct response to Marx's deeply held convictions. Thus, it is not surprising that Karl Marx is viewed as a major figure in the development of sociology as well as several other social sciences (see Figure 1-1).

Karl Marx

Karl Marx (1818–1883) shared with Durkheim and Weber a dual interest in abstract philosophical issues and

FIGURE 1-1

Early Social Thinkers

Émile Durkheim
1858–1917

Max Weber
1864–1920

Karl Marx
1818–1883

	Émile Durkheim 1858–1917	Max Weber 1864–1920	Karl Marx 1818–1883
Academic training	Philosophy	Law, economics, history, philosophy	Philosophy, law
Key works	1893—*The Division of Labor in Society*	1904–1905—*The Protestant Ethic and the Spirit of Capitalism*	1848—*The Communist Manifesto*
	1897—*Suicide: A Study in Sociology*	1922—*Wirtschaft und Gesellschaft*	1867—*Das Kapital*
	1912—*Elementary Forms of Religious Life*		

the concrete reality of everyday life. Unlike the others, Marx was so critical of existing institutions that a conventional academic career was impossible, and although he was born and educated in Germany, he spent most of his life in exile, in Paris and London.

Marx's personal life was a difficult struggle. When a paper that he had written was suppressed, he fled his native land for France. In Paris, he met Friedrich Engels (1820–1895), with whom he formed a lifelong friendship. They lived at a time when European and North American economic life was increasingly being dominated by the factory rather than the farm.

In 1847, Marx and Engels attended secret meetings in London of an illegal coalition of labour unions, known as the Communist League. The following year, they prepared a platform called *The Communist Manifesto*, in which they argued that the masses of people who have no resources other than their labour (whom they referred to as the *proletariat*) should unite to fight for the overthrow of capitalist societies. In the words of Marx and Engels:

> The history of all hitherto existing society is the history of class struggles. . . . The proletarians have nothing to lose but their chains. They have a world to win. WORKING MEN OF ALL COUNTRIES UNITE! (Feuer 1959:7, 41).

After completing *The Communist Manifesto*, Marx returned to Germany, only to be expelled. He then moved to England, where he continued to write books and essays. Marx lived there in extreme poverty. He pawned most of his possessions, and several of his children died of malnutrition and disease. Marx clearly was an outsider in British society, a fact that may well have affected his view of Western cultures.

In Marx's analysis, society was fundamentally divided between classes that clash in pursuit of their own class interests. When he examined the industrial societies of his time, such as Germany, England, and the United States, he saw the factory as the centre of conflict between the exploiters (the owners of the means of production) and the exploited (the workers). Marx viewed these relationships in systematic terms; that is, he believed that an entire system of economic, social, and political relationships maintained the power and dominance of the owners over the workers. Consequently, Marx and Engels argued that the working class needed to overthrow the existing class system. Marx's influence on contemporary thinking has been dramatic. Marx's writings inspired those who were later to lead communist revolutions in Russia, China, Cuba, Vietnam, and elsewhere.

Even apart from the political revolutions that his work fostered, Marx's influence on contemporary thinking has been dramatic. Marx emphasized the *group* identifications and associations that influence an individual's place in society. This area of study is the major focus of contemporary sociology. Throughout this textbook, we will consider how membership in a particular gender classification, age group, racial group, or economic class affects a person's attitudes and behaviour. In an important sense, we can trace this way of understanding society back to the pioneering work of Karl Marx.

Modern Developments in North America

Sociology today builds on the firm foundation developed by Émile Durkheim, Max Weber, and Karl Marx. However, the discipline of sociology has certainly not remained stagnant over the last century. While Europeans have continued to make contributions to the discipline, sociologists from throughout the world have advanced sociological theory and research. Their new insights have helped them to better understand the workings of society.

In the United States

Charles Horton Cooley (1864–1929) was typical of the sociologists who came to prominence in the early 1900s. Cooley received his graduate training in economics but later became a sociology professor at the University of Michigan. Like other early sociologists, he had become interested in this "new" discipline while pursuing a related area of study.

Cooley shared the desire of Durkheim, Weber, and Marx to learn more about society. But to do so effectively, Cooley preferred to use the sociological perspective to look first at smaller units—intimate, face-to-face groups such as families, gangs, and friendship networks. He saw these groups as the seedbeds of society in the sense that they shape people's ideals, beliefs, values, and social nature. Cooley's work increased our understanding of groups of relatively small size.

In the early 1900s, many leading sociologists in the United States saw themselves as social reformers dedicated to studying and then improving a corrupt society systematically. They were genuinely concerned about the lives of immigrants in the nation's growing cities. Early female sociologists, in particular, often took active roles in poor urban areas as leaders of community centres known as *settlement houses*. For example, Jane Addams (1860–1935), an active member of the American Sociological Society, cofounded the famous Chicago settlement, Hull House.

Addams and other pioneering female sociologists commonly combined intellectual inquiry, social service work, and political activism—all with the goal of assisting the underprivileged and creating a more egalitarian society. Working with the black journalist and educator Ida B. Wells, Addams successfully prevented the implementation of a racial segregation policy in the Chicago public schools. Addams' efforts to establish a juvenile

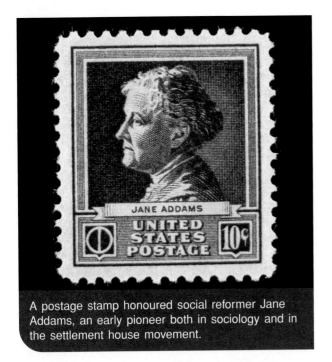

A postage stamp honoured social reformer Jane Addams, an early pioneer both in sociology and in the settlement house movement.

court system and a women's trade union also reflect the practical focus of her work (Addams 1910, 1930; Deegan 1991; Lengermann and Niebrugge-Brantley 1998).

By the middle of the twentieth century, however, the focus of the discipline had shifted. Sociologists for the most part restricted themselves to theorizing and gathering information; the aim of transforming society was left to social workers and others. This shift away from social reform was accompanied by a growing commitment to scientific methods of research and to value-free interpretation of data.

Another early sociologist, W.E.B. Du Bois (1868–1963), conducted research that he hoped would assist the struggle for a racially egalitarian society. Du Bois believed that knowledge was essential in combating prejudice and achieving tolerance and justice. Sociology, Du Bois contended, had to draw on scientific principles to study social problems such as those experienced by blacks in the United States. In addition, Du Bois made a major contribution to sociology through his in-depth studies of urban life—both white and black.

Du Bois had little patience for theorists such as Herbert Spencer who seemed content with the status quo. He advocated basic research on the lives of blacks that would separate opinion from fact, and he documented their relatively low status in Philadelphia and Atlanta. Du Bois believed that the granting of full political rights to blacks was essential to their social and economic progress in the United States. Many of his ideas challenging the status quo did not find a receptive audience within either the government or the academic world. As a result, Du Bois

became increasingly involved with organizations whose members questioned the established social order, and he helped found the National Association for the Advancement of Colored People, better known as the NAACP (Green and Driver 1978).

Sociologist Robert Merton (1968) made an important contribution to the discipline by successfully combining theory and research. For example, Merton produced a theory that is one of the most frequently cited explanations of deviant behaviour. He noted different ways in which people attempt to achieve success in life. In his view, some may not share the socially agreed-upon goal of accumulating material goods or the accepted means of achieving this goal. Merton bases his explanation of crime on individual behaviour—influenced by society's approved goals and means—yet it has wider applications. It helps to account for the high crime rates among the nation's poor, who may see no hope of advancing themselves through traditional roads to success. Chapter 7 discusses Merton's theory in greater detail.

In Canada

While sociologists were researching and teaching throughout the 1900s, the early courses took place within other disciplines such as history, political economy, or political science. Formal departments of sociology were established as early as 1922 (McGill University) and the 1950s (McMaster and Carleton Universities). However, the 1960s were a decade of primary importance in the history of the development of sociology in Canada. The University of Toronto set up its department in 1963. In the following year the first issue of the *Canadian Review of Sociology and Anthropology* was published, and the Canadian Sociology and Anthropology Association (CSAA) was established in 1965. Prior to that, sociologists and anthropologists were formally organized as a chapter of the Canadian Political Science Association. However, once the CSAA was formed, the growth in the field was phenomenal: from 61 sociologists working in Canadian universities in 1960 to 917 in the mid-1970s. By the 1980s, all universities offered courses in sociology. Today, a student can complete a sociology degree in 47 universities in Canada, and over half of them offer M.A. and/or Ph.D. programs.

The development of sociological thought in Canada reflects not only the history of the discipline in Europe but also the influence of academic theorists as well as activists in religious and social action movements. And unique to Canada, it also reflects the two solitudes of English and French Canada.

In Quebec, sociologists were oriented toward a social and political redefinition of changing Quebec society. For example, Leon Gérin's (1863–1951) empirical studies of rural and urban workers and their families stressed a concern for, and an awareness of, social problems and social change. While Gérin worked primarily outside of the university, his widely published work on family life in changing rural Quebec set the stage for academic sociology. Social scientists from within Laval University and the University of Montreal established a precedent of public involvement with the Catholic social action movement in their studies of social problems experienced as Quebec moved through the transition from rural to urban society. From the outset, francophone Canadian sociology revealed a tendency toward social and political engagement.

Early sociology in English Canada reflected a much more politically neutral nature. While appointments of sociologists to colleges across the country came from those with Methodist or Baptist backgrounds, the influence of American sociology led to the avoidance of the participatory model of Quebec sociologists. Instead, Anglo-Canadian sociologists were much more concerned with shaping the discipline into more reserved academic activity. S.D. Clark's (b1910) social historical work at the University of Toronto is a good example of the sensitivity to establishing a respectable discipline, distinct from history or political economy. Despite its links to American intellectuals such as Seymour M. Lipset, Clark recalls that, for the longest time, sociology in Canadian universities was seen as "a discipline concerned only with the gathering of useless facts" (Clark, 1979:396).

However, in 1965, with the publication of John Porter's *The Vertical Mosaic*, a uniquely Canadian sociology came of age. After graduating from the London School of Economics in 1949, Porter (1921–1979) took up teaching at Carleton University and began his landmark work exposing social inequality in Canada and theorizing ways to eradicate it. *The Vertical Mosaic* ensured international recognition for a distinctive Canadian sociology because of its scope and the importance of its theme, and its contributions continue to be seen in Canadian sociology.

We can see Porter's influence in *The Double Ghetto* by Pat and Hugh Armstrong (1978), which also reached a wide audience beyond the discipline that produced the study. The Armstrongs offered a detailed examination of women's work in the home and the paid labour market, concluding that work remains largely segregated by sex. With the publication of these two studies, "no public discussion of any import on the social issues with which they were concerned could disregard the documentation and acute analyses of the inequities in Canada . . . " (McFarlane, 1992:291) brought about by sociology in Canada.

Not only was Porter concerned with exposing social inequality, but his objective was also to influence policy toward a more open society through social and

John Porter's *The Vertical Mosaic* was a landmark in Canadian sociology.

educational reform. He believed that one of the roles of a social critic was to offer solutions to social problems. To some degree this objective was met by the very fact that sociologists are often asked to contribute to research for a variety of Royal Commissions whose recommendations become the basis for governmental policy. John Porter, more than any other theorist of his time, succeeded in generating a pride in and an attraction to the field, and thus he served to stimulate the development of Canadian sociology (Jones, 1992; Forcese & Richer, 1988; Hiller, 1982).

Contemporary sociology reflects the diverse contributions of earlier theorists. As sociologists approach such topics as divorce, drug addiction, and religious cults, they can draw on the theoretical insights of the discipline's pioneers. A careful reader can hear Comte, Martineau, Durkheim, Weber, Marx, Cooley, Porter, and many others speaking through the pages of current research. Sociology has also broadened beyond the intellectual confines of North America and Europe. Contributions to the discipline now come from sociologists studying and researching human behaviour in other parts of the world. In describing the work of today's sociologists, it is helpful to examine a number of influential theoretical approaches (also known as *perspectives*).

Major Theoretical Perspectives

Robert Merton emphasized that sociology should strive to bring together the "macro-level" and "micro-level" approaches to the study of society. *Macrosociology* concentrates on large-scale phenomena or entire civilizations. Thus, Émile Durkheim's cross-cultural study of suicide is an example of macro-level research. More recently, macrosociologists have examined international crime rates (see Chapter 7), the stereotype of Asians as a "model minority" (see Chapter 10), and the population patterns of Islamic countries (see Chapter 20). By contrast, *microsociology* stresses the study of: interactions in small groups. Examples of micro-level sociological research has included studies of: how divorced men and women disengage from significant social roles (see Chapter 5); how conformity can influence the expression of prejudiced attitudes (see Chapter 7); and how a teacher's expectations can affect a student's academic performance (see Chapter 15).

Sociologists view society in different ways. Some see the world basically as a stable and ongoing entity. They are impressed with the endurance of the family, organized religion, and other social institutions. Some sociologists see society as composed of many groups in conflict, competing for scarce resources. To other sociologists, the focus must be placed on the significance of factors such as gender, race, and class when examining inequalities that exist in both the public and private spheres of society. Yet to others, the most fascinating aspects of the social world are the everyday, routine interactions among individuals that we sometimes take for granted. These four views, the ones most widely used by sociologists, are the functionalist, conflict, feminist, and interactionist perspectives. They will provide an introductory look at the discipline.

Functionalist Perspective

Think of society as a living organism in which each part of the organism contributes to its survival. This view is the *functionalist perspective*, which emphasizes the way that parts of a society are structured to maintain its stability.

Talcott Parsons (1902–1979), a Harvard University sociologist, was a key figure in the development of functionalist theory. Parsons had been greatly influenced by the work of Émile Durkheim, Max Weber, and other European sociologists. For over four decades, Parsons dominated sociology in North America with his advocacy of functionalism. He saw any society as a vast network of connected parts, each of which helps to maintain the system as a whole. The functionalist approach holds that if an aspect of social life does not contribute to a society's stability or survival—if it does not serve some identifiably useful function or promote value consensus among members of a society—it will not be passed on from one generation to the next.

Let's examine prostitution as an example of the functionalist perspective. Why is it that a practice so widely condemned continues to display such persistence and vitality? Functionalists suggest that prostitution satisfies needs of patrons that may not be readily met through more socially acceptable forms of interaction such as courtship or marriage. The "buyer" receives sex without any responsibility for procreation or sentimental attachment; at the same time, the "seller" makes a living through this exchange.

Such an examination leads us to conclude that prostitution does perform certain functions that society seems to need. However, this is not to suggest that prostitution is a desirable or legitimate form of social behaviour. Functionalists do not make such judgments. Rather, advocates of the functionalist perspective hope to explain how an aspect of society that is so frequently attacked can nevertheless manage to survive (K. Davis 1937).

Manifest and Latent Functions

A university calendar typically states various functions of the institution. It may inform you, for example, that the university intends to "offer each student a broad education in classical and contemporary thought, in the humanities, in the sciences, and in the arts." However, it would be quite a surprise to find a calendar that declared, "This university was founded in 1895 to keep people between the ages of 18 and 22 out of the job market, thus reducing unemployment." No post-secondary institution would declare that this is its purpose. Yet societal institutions serve many functions, some of them quite subtle. The university, in fact, *does* delay people's entry into the job market.

Robert Merton (1968) made an important distinction between manifest and latent functions. *Manifest functions* of institutions are open, stated, conscious functions. They involve the intended, recognized consequences of an aspect of society, such as the university's role in certifying academic competence and excellence. By contrast, *latent functions* are unconscious or unintended functions and may reflect hidden purposes of an institution. One latent function of universities is to hold down unemployment. Another is to serve as a meeting ground for people seeking marital partners.

Dysfunctions

Functionalists acknowledge that not all parts of a society contribute to its stability all the time. A *dysfunction* refers to an element or a process of society that may actually disrupt a social system or lead to a decrease in stability.

We consider many dysfunctional behaviour patterns, such as homicide, as undesirable. Yet we should not automatically interpret dysfunctions as negative. The evaluation of a dysfunction depends on one's own values or, as the saying goes, on "where you sit." For example, the official view in prisons in the United States is that inmates'

Canadian soldiers fill a function by providing peace-keeping services in countries around the world. Two members of the Royal Canadian Regiment take a break while on patrol outside Coralici, Bosnia, in April 1999.

gangs should be eradicated because they are dysfunctional to smooth operations. Yet some guards have actually come to view the presence of prison gangs as functional for their jobs. The danger posed by gangs creates a "threat to security," requiring increased surveillance and more overtime work for guards (Hunt et al. 1993:400).

Conflict Perspective

In contrast to functionalists' emphasis on stability and consensus, conflict sociologists see the social world in continual struggle. The **conflict perspective** assumes that social behaviour is best understood in terms of conflict or tension between competing groups. Such conflict need not be violent; it can take the form of labour negotiations, gender relations, party politics, competition between religious groups for members, or disputes over the federal budget.

Throughout most of the 1900s, the functionalist perspective had the upper hand in sociology in North America. However, the conflict approach has become increasingly persuasive since the late 1960s. The rise of the feminist and gay rights movements, First Nations land claims, and confrontations at abortion clinics offered support for the conflict approach—the view that our social world is characterized by continual struggle between competing groups. Currently, the discipline of sociology accepts conflict theory as one valid way to gain insight into a society.

The Marxist View

As we saw earlier, Karl Marx viewed struggle between social classes as inevitable, given the exploitation of workers under capitalism. Expanding on Marx's work, sociologists and other social scientists have come to see conflict not merely as a class phenomenon but as a part of everyday life in all societies. Thus, in studying any culture, organization, or social group, sociologists want to know who benefits, who suffers, and who dominates at the expense of others. They are concerned with the conflicts between women and men, parents and children, and urban and rural areas, to name only a few. Conflict theorists are interested in how society's institutions—including the family, government, religion, education, and the media—may help to maintain the privileges of some groups and keep others in a subservient position. Their emphasis on social change and redistribution of resources makes conflict theorists more "radical" and "activist" than functionalists (Dahrendorf 1958). One important contribution of conflict theory is that it has encouraged sociologists to view society through the eyes of those segments of the population that rarely influence decision making. Early black sociologists such as Du Bois conducted research that they hoped would assist the struggle for a racially egalitarian society. And C. Wright Mills (1916–1962) was a renowned conflict theorist who believed that sociologists should become involved in social reform by exposing the power elite in whose hands the fate of our nations exist. Chapter 16 explores his theory in greater depth.

Feminist Perspectives

Feminist perspectives attempt to explain, understand, and eliminate the ways in which gender socially organizes our public and private lives to produce inequality between men and women. There are as many feminist perspectives as there are social and political philosophies; they run the gamut from liberal feminism to Marxist feminism to radical feminism, and from anarchist feminism to eco-feminism. There is no *one* feminist theory.

Feminist perspectives have been the major contributor to contemporary sociological theory, transforming the discipline by providing new frameworks within which gender inequality can be examined, analyzed, and changed. While the variety of feminist perspectives differ in terms of their views of the origins and solutions to gender inequality, they share a common starting point—the significance of gender in understanding social inequality. They begin from the standpoint of women and advocate solutions *for* women (Madoo-Lengermann and Niebrugge 1996).

Despite the differences, feminist theories agree on four common elements:

1. A desire to understand how gender is part of every aspect of social life

2. A belief that gender—along with class, race, and sexuality—is socially constructed, leading to inequality in the workplace, at home, in leisure activities, and in society at large

3. A belief that gender relations are not "natural"; rather, they are products of culture and history

4. An understanding of the necessity of advocacy for social change. (Jagger and Rothenberg 1984).

Feminist perspectives include both the macro and micro levels of analysis. For example, many feminist sociologists share the views of the conflict perspectives and analyze gender in the context of power relations, economic production, and state domination. For these sociologists, the inequality of women is embedded in the power structures of political systems (i.e., Maroney and Luxton 1987). How does this difference in power between males and females then trickle down into personal relations?

Other feminist sociologists, however, share the micro-level analysis of interactionist perspectives, examining our everyday social interaction from the standpoint of gendered patterns of behaviour. For example, there are particular patterns of interpersonal, face-to-face communication that occur more frequently in male–female interaction than between two members of the same sex (Tannen 1990, 1994). How do these patterns of micro-level behaviour help us to understand the larger macro

issues, such as economic inequality between men and women?

Dorothy Smith is a Canadian sociologist whose contributions to sociology in general, and to feminist sociology in particular, have become recognized worldwide. Smith argues for a sociology that is built on the everyday experiences of women, pointing out that in the past sociology has excluded these experiences. Her groundbreaking work, *The Everyday World as Problematic* (1987), has been influential in helping sociology students see the everyday world from the standpoint of women.

Margrit Eichler was among the first Canadian sociologists to recognize the ways in which sexism can influence research in social science (Nelson and Robinson 1999). Eichler examined sexist language, sexist concepts, an androcentric perspective, sexist methodology, and sexist interpretation of results (Eichler 1984). Her work has shown the way toward gender-neutral theorizing, conducting, and reporting of research.

Interactionist Perspective

Workers interacting on the job, encounters in public places like bus stops and parks, behaviour in small groups—these are all aspects of microsociology that catch the attention of interactionists. Whereas functionalist and conflict theorists both analyze large-scale societywide patterns of behaviour, the *interactionist perspective* generalizes about everyday forms of social interaction in order to understand society as a whole. In the 1990s, for example, the workings of juries became a subject of public scrutiny. High-profile trials ended in verdicts that left some people shaking their heads. Long before jury members were being interviewed on their front lawns following trials, interactionists tried to better understand behaviour in the small-group setting of a jury deliberation room, as shown in Box 1-1.

Interactionism is a sociological framework for viewing human beings as living in a world of meaningful objects. These "objects" may include material things, actions, other people, relationships, and even symbols.

While functionalist and conflict approaches were initiated in Europe, interactionism developed first in the United States. George Herbert Mead (1863–1931) is widely regarded as the founder of the interactionist perspective. Mead taught at the University of Chicago from 1893 until his death. His sociological analysis, like that of Charles Horton Cooley, often focused on human interactions within one-to-one situations and small groups. Mead was interested in observing the most minute forms of communication—smiles, frowns, nodding of one's head—and in understanding how such individual behaviour was influenced by the larger context of a group or society. Despite his innovative views, Mead only

In 1987, Canadian sociologist Dorothy E. Smith produced *The Everyday World as Problematic*, which has become a landmark in feminist sociology.

1-1 Decision Making in the Jury Box

Imagine you have been selected for a jury. How do you think you and the other jury members will arrive at a unanimous decision? How do opinions form? And how do they get changed? Your interaction with your fellow jurors is crucial in the decision-making process.

Few small groups have received as much attention in the 1990s as juries. Among the juries that have aroused great interest are the jury in the case of four Los Angeles police officers accused of beating Rodney King, the juries in the trials of Karla Homolka and Paul Bernardo, and the jury that acquitted O.J. Simpson of double homicide charges. Well before these highly publicized trials, social scientists were studying how juries reach their decisions.

Interactionists employ four types of research: interviews with jury members who attempt to reconstruct how they reached a verdict; observation of jurors as they sit through and react to events in the courtroom; videotapes and observation of actual jury deliberations (permitted by presiding judges in a few instances); and experiments that use volunteers to create mock juries. We'll consider here some findings about the influence of fellow jurors on decision making, the likelihood of finding defendants guilty, the effect that jury size has on outcomes, and recent changes in the jury experience.

In a 1957 motion picture, *Twelve Angry Men,* actor Henry Fonda played a juror who begins as the lone voice favouring acquittal of a criminal defendant, but in the end convinces the entire jury of the defendant's innocence. While the movie made for great drama, more recent research suggests that jurors generally do not change their minds after the first ballot. For example, a study of 225 cases indicated that if a majority of jurors votes to convict a defendant on the first ballot, there is only a 5 percent chance that the defendant will later be acquitted.

A jury's decision making may even occur before the first ballot. Despite judges' instructions to the contrary, many jurors form tentative verdict preferences early in a trial. Studies suggest that jurors with initial feelings of the defendants' being guilty or not guilty give disproportionate weight to supporting testimony that reinforces their initial verdict preferences, while discounting testimony that undermines their preferences.

> As with other small groups, participation in a jury can be an intense experience, especially in a long, combative criminal trial with a focus on violence and bloodshed.

Most research on jury decision making in criminal trials has focused on how juries decide if a defendant is guilty or not guilty. However, in a significant number of criminal cases, a defendant is tried on several counts, or there is a possibility of deciding that he or she is not guilty by reason of insanity. A number of studies have shown that jurors are more likely to convict a defendant on some charge if they are given several alternatives to an absolute verdict of not guilty.

Researchers have given special attention to comparisons of 6-person and 12-person juries. American state legislatures have shown an interest in reducing jury size to save money and expedite courtroom proceedings; social scientists have explored how this might affect a jury's decision making. In one study of criminal cases, the size of a jury had no impact on the likelihood of conviction when the defendant appeared not to be guilty. However, when the defendant's guilt seemed more obvious, 12-person juries were more reluctant to convict than 6-person juries.

Research on jury members needs to deal with changes in the experience of being a juror. For example, the rise in violent crime in the United States and improved methods of documenting the crime scene now mean that jurors are more likely to be exposed to images and descriptions of graphic violence and gore. Mental health professionals and social scientists have documented the trauma jurors sometimes suffer that can trigger classic symptoms of stress, such as depression, anxiety, weight loss, sleep loss, and disruptions in close social relationships. As with other small groups, participation in a jury can be an intense experience, especially in a long, combative criminal trial with a focus on violence and bloodshed.

Let's Discuss

1. Does it appear that jurors enter the deliberations with totally open minds? Why or why not?
2. What effect does smaller jury size have on decision making? What might be the reason for this?

Sources: Abramson 1994; Hare 1992; MacCoun 1989; Manzo 1996; Roan 1995; Sabini 1992.

occasionally wrote articles, and never a book. He was an extremely popular teacher, and most of his insights have come to us through edited volumes of lectures that his students published after his death.

The interactionist perspective is sometimes referred to as the *symbolic interactionist perspective,* because interactionists see symbols as an especially important part of human communication. Members of a society share the social meanings of symbols. In Canada, for example, a handshake symbolizes congeniality, while a middle-finger salute signifies disrespect. However, another culture might use different gestures to convey a feeling of congeniality or disrespect.

Consider the different ways in which various societies portray suicide without the use of words. People in Canada point a finger at the head (shooting); urban Japanese bring a fist against the stomach (stabbing); and the South Fore of Papua, New Guinea, clench a hand at the throat (hanging). These types of symbolic interaction are classified as forms of **nonverbal communication**, which can include many other gestures, facial expressions, and postures.

Since Mead's teachings have become well known, sociologists have expressed greater interest in the interactionist perspective. Many have moved away from what may have been an excessive preoccupation with the large-scale (macro) level of social behaviour and have redirected their attention toward behaviour that occurs in small groups (micro level).

Erving Goffman (1922–1982) popularized a particular type of interactionist method known as the **dramaturgical approach**. The dramaturgist compares everyday life to the setting of the theatre and stage. Just as actors project certain images, all of us seek to present particular features of our personalities while we hide other qualities. Thus, in a class, we may feel the need to project a serious image; at a party, we want to look relaxed and friendly.

The Sociological Approach

Which perspective should a sociologist use in studying human behaviour? Functionalist? Conflict? Interactionist? Feminist?

Sociology makes use of all four perspectives (see Table 1-2), since each offers unique insights into the same

Table 1-2 Comparing Major Theoretical Perspectives

	Functionalist	Conflict	Interactionist	Feminist
View of society	Stable, well integrated	Characterized by tension and struggle between groups	Active in influencing and affecting everyday social interaction	Characterized by gender and inequality; causes and solutions vary
Level of analysis emphasized	Macro	Macro	Micro analysis as a way of understanding the larger macro phenomena	Both macro and micro levels of analysis
Key concepts	Manifest functions Latent functions Dysfunction	Inequality Capitalism Stratification	Symbols Nonverbal communication Face-to-face	Standpoint of women Political action Gender inequality Oppression
View of the individual	People are socialized to perform societal functions	People are shaped by power, coercion, and authority	People manipulate symbols and create their social worlds through interaction	Differs according to social class, race, ethnicity, age, sexual orientation, and physical ability
View of the social order	Maintained through cooperation and consensus	Maintained through force and coercion	Maintained by shared understanding of everyday behaviour	Maintained through standpoints that do not include those of women
View of social change	Predictable, reinforcing	Change takes place all the time and may have positive consequences	Reflected in people's social positions and their communications with others	Essential in order to bring about equality
Example	Public punishments reinforce the social order	Laws reinforce the positions of those in power	People respect laws or disobey them based on their own past experience	Spousal violence, date rape, and economic inequality need to be eliminated
Proponents	Émile Durkheim Talcott Parsons Robert Merton	Karl Marx W.E.B. DuBois C. Wright Mills	George Herbert Mead Charles Horton Cooley Erving Goffman	Dorothy Smith Margrit Eichler

issue. Think about how Katherine Irwin went about studying the tattoo culture in the United States today (described in the chapter opening). She focused on the tattoo's use as a symbol of hip social status (functionalist perspective), and she examined the tensions between a parent and a child who decides to get tattooed, and the disapproval an employer might show toward a tattooed employee (conflict perspective). Research into the actual process of getting tattooed, including the negotiations between the tattoo artist and the tattooee, made use of the interactionist perspective. Box 1-2 shows how television might look from the functionalist, conflict, interactionist, and feminist points of view.

No one approach to a particular issue is "correct." This textbook assumes that we can gain the broadest understanding of our society by drawing on all four perspectives in the study of human behaviour and institutions. These perspectives overlap as their interests coincide but can diverge according to the dictates of each approach and of the issue being studied. A sociologist's theoretical orientation influences his or her approach to a research problem in important ways.

Developing the Sociological Imagination

In this book, we will be illustrating the sociological imagination in several different ways: by showing theory in practice and research in action; by speaking across race, gender, class, and national boundaries; and by highlighting social policy throughout the world.

Theory in Practice

We will illustrate how the four sociological perspectives—functionalist, conflict, interactionist, and feminist—are helpful in understanding today's issues. Sociologists do not necessarily declare "here I am using functionalism," but their research and approaches do tend to draw on one or more theoretical frameworks, as will become clear in the pages to follow.

Research in Action

Sociologists actively investigate a variety of issues and social behaviour. We have already seen that such research might involve the meaning of tattoos, television programs, and decision making in the jury box. Often the research has direct applications to improving people's lives, as in the case of increasing the participation of blacks in Canada and the United States in diabetes test-

ing. Throughout the rest of the textbook, the research performed by sociologists and other social scientists will shed light on group behaviour of all types.

Speaking Across Race, Gender, Class, and National Boundaries

Sociologists include both men and women, people from a variety of socioeconomic backgrounds (some privileged and many not), and individuals from a wealth of ethnic, national, and religious origins. In their work, sociologists seek to draw conclusions that speak to all people—not just the affluent or powerful. This is not always easy. Insights into how a corporation can increase its profits tend to attract more attention and financial support than do, say, the merits of a needle exchange program for low-income, urban residents. Yet sociology today, more than ever, seeks to better understand the experiences of *all* people. In Box 1-3, we take a look at how a woman's role in public places is defined differently from that of a man in different parts of the world.

Social Policy Throughout the World

One important way we can use the sociological imagination is to enhance our understanding of current social issues throughout the world. Beginning with Chapter 2, which focuses on research, each chapter will conclude with a discussion of a contemporary social policy issue. In some cases, we will examine a specific issue facing national governments. For example, government funding of child-care centres will be discussed in Chapter 4, Socialization, sexual harassment in Chapter 6, Groups and Organizations, and the search for shelters in Chapter 19, Communities and Urbanization. These social policy sections will demonstrate how fundamental sociological concepts can enhance our critical thinking skills and help us to better understand current public policy debates taking place around the world.

Sociologists expect the next quarter-century to be perhaps the most exciting and critical period in the history of the discipline. This is because of a growing recognition—both in Canada and around the world—that current social problems *must* be addressed before their magnitude overwhelms human societies. We can expect sociologists to play an increasingly important role in the government sector by researching and developing public policy alternatives. It seems only natural for this textbook to focus on the connection between the work of sociologists and the difficult questions confronting the policy-makers and people of Canada.

1-2 Looking at Television from Four Perspectives

Television to most of us is that box sitting on the shelf or table that diverts us, occasionally entertains us, and sometimes puts us to sleep. But sociologists would look much deeper at the medium. Here is what they would find using the four sociological perspectives.

FUNCTIONALIST VIEW

In examining any aspect of society, including television, functionalists emphasize the contribution it makes to overall social stability. Functionalists regard television as a powerful force in communicating the common values of our society and in promoting an overall feeling of unity and social solidarity:

- Television vividly presents important national and international news. On a local level, television communicates vital information on everything from storm warnings and school closings to locations of emergency shelters.
- Television in Canada reflects the diversity of its people. For example, there are stations broadcasting not only in English or French, but also in languages of the First Nations people or immigrants from Asia, etc.
- Television programs transmit valuable learning skills (*Sesame Street*) and factual information (the CBC National News).
- Television "brings together" members of a community or even a nation by broadcasting important events and ceremonies (press conferences, parades, and state funerals) and through coverage of disasters such as the September 11, 2001 terrorist attacks on the United States.
- Television contributes to economic stability and prosperity by promoting and advertising services and (through shopping channels) serving as a direct marketplace for products.

CONFLICT VIEW

Conflict theorists argue that the social order is based on coercion and exploitation. They emphasize that television reflects and even exacerbates many of the divisions of our society and world, including those based on gender, race, ethnicity, and social class:

- Television is a form of big business in which profits are more important than the quality of the product (programming).
- Television's decision makers are overwhelmingly white, male, and prosperous; by contrast, television programs tend to ignore the lives and ambitions of subordinate groups, among them working-class people, visible minorities, First Nations people, gays and lesbians, people with disabilities, and older people.

> On a local level, television communicates vital information on everything from storm warnings and school closings to locations of emergency shelters.

- Television distorts the political process, as candidates with the most money (often backed by powerful lobbying groups) buy exposure to voters and saturate the air with attack commercials.
- By exporting *Survivor, Baywatch,* and other programs around the world, U.S. television undermines the distinctive traditions and art forms of other societies and encourages their cultural and economic dependence on the United States.

INTERACTIONIST VIEW

In studying the social order, interactionists are especially interested in shared understandings of everyday behaviour. Consequently, interactionists examine television on the micro level by focusing on how day-to-day social behaviour is shaped by television:

- Television literally serves as a babysitter or a "playmate" for many children for long periods of their lives.
- Friendship networks can emerge from shared viewing habits or from recollections of a cherished series from the past. Family members and friends often gather for parties centred on the broadcasting of popular events such as the Stanley Cup game, the Academy Awards, or even series like *Survivor.*
- Television allows Canadians to understand their differences and their distinctiveness. Shows such as "This Hour Has 22 Minutes" not only satirize political and cultural events in this country, but segments on the program allow us to laugh as a group when others, such as Americans, are satirized for being uninformed about issues north of their border.
- The frequent appearance of violence in news and entertainment programming creates feelings of fear and may actually make interpersonal relations more aggressive.
- The power of television encourages political leaders and even entertainment figures to manipulate symbols carefully (through public appearances) and attempt to convey self-serving definitions of social reality.

FEMINIST VIEWS

Data gathered from various feminist studies have demonstrated that gender is constructed by social factors, thus television plays an important role not only in reflecting society's ideas about gender, but also in constructing its own images:

- Television reinforces gender inequality through its portrayal of women as subordinate and powerless, and men as dominant and powerful.
- Television objectifies women through its portrayal of women as objects to be admired for their physical appearance and sexual attractiveness.
- Television creates the false impression that all women are the same—young, white, middle-class, slim, and heterosexual.

Despite their differences, functionalists, conflict theorists, interactionists, and feminists would agree that there is much more to television than simply "entertainment." They would also agree that television and other popular forms of culture are worthy subjects for serious study by sociologists.

Let's Discuss

1. What functions does television serve? What might be some "dysfunctions"?
2. If you were a television network executive, which perspective would influence your choice of programs? Why?

1-3 Women in Public Places Worldwide

By definition, a public place—such as a sidewalk or a park—is open to all persons. Even some private establishments, such as restaurants, are intended to belong to people as a whole. Yet sociologists and other social scientists have found that societies define access to these places differently for women and men.

In many Middle Eastern societies, women are prohibited from public places and are restricted to certain places in the house. In such societies, the coffeehouse and the market are considered male domains. Some other societies, such as Malagasy, strictly limit the presence of women in "public places" yet allow women to conduct the haggling that is a part of shopping in open-air markets. In some West African societies, women actually control the marketplace. In various Eastern European countries and Turkey, women appear to be free to move about in public places, but the coffeehouse remains the exclusive preserve of males. Similarly in Taiwan today, wine houses are the exclusive domains of businessmen; even female managers are unwelcome. Contrast this with coffeehouses and taverns in North America, where women and men mingle freely and even engage each other in conversation as total strangers.

While casual observers may view both private and public space in North America as gender-neutral, private all-male clubs do persist, and even in public spaces women experience some inequality. Erving Goffman, an interactionist, conducted classic studies of public spaces, which he found to be innocuous settings for routine interactions, such as "helping" encounters when a person is lost and asks for directions.

> Women are well aware that a casual helping encounter with a man in a public place can too easily lead to undesired sexual queries or advances.

But sociologist Carol Brooks Gardner has offered a feminist critique of Goffman's work: "Rarely does Goffman emphasize the habitual disproportionate fear that women can come to feel in public toward men, much less the routine trepidation that ethnic and racial minorities and the disabled can experience" (1989:45). Women are well aware that a casual helping encounter with a man in a public place can too easily lead to undesired sexual queries or advances.

Whereas Goffman suggests that street remarks about women occur rarely—and that they generally hold no unpleasant or threatening implications—Gardner (1989:49) counters that "for young women especially, . . . appearing in public places carries with it the constant possibility of evaluation, compliments that are not really so complimentary after all, and harsh or vulgar insults if the woman is found wanting." She adds that these remarks are sometimes accompanied by tweaks, pinches, or even blows, unmasking the latent hostility of many male-to-female street remarks.

According to Gardner, many women have a well-founded fear of the sexual harassment, assault, and rape that can occur in public places. She concludes that "public places are arenas for the enactment of inequality in everyday life for women and for many others" (1989:56).

Let's Discuss

1. How would a coffeehouse in Turkey differ from one in Montreal, Quebec? What might account for these differences?
2. Do you know a woman who has encountered sexual harassment in a public place? How did she react? How has her social behaviour been changed by the experience?

Sources: Cheng and Liao 1994; Gardner 1989, 1990, 1995; Goffman 1963b, 1971; Rosman and Rubel 1994; D. Spain 1992.

● Chapter Resources

Summary

Sociology is the systematic study of social behaviour and human groups. In this chapter, we examine the nature of sociological theory, the founders of the discipline, theoretical perspectives of contemporary sociology, and applications of sociology and consider ways to exercise the "sociological imagination."

1. An important element in the **sociological imagination**—which is an awareness of the relationship between an individual and the wider society—is the ability to view our own society as an outsider might, rather than from the perspective of our limited experiences and cultural biases.

2. Knowledge that relies on "common sense" is not always reliable. Sociologists must test and analyze each piece of information that they use.

3. In contrast to other *social sciences,* sociology emphasizes the influence that groups can have on people's behaviour and attitudes and the ways in which people shape society.

4. Sociologists employ *theories* to examine the relationships between observations or data that may seem completely unrelated.

5. Nineteenth-century thinkers who contributed sociological insights included: Auguste Comte, a French philosopher; Harriet Martineau, an English sociologist; and Herbert Spencer, an English scholar.

6. Other important figures in the development of sociology were: Émile Durkheim, who pioneered work on suicide; Max Weber, who taught the need for "insight" in intellectual work; and Karl Marx, who emphasized the importance of the economy and of conflict in society.

7. In the twentieth century, the discipline of sociology was indebted to sociologists such as Charles Horton Cooley, Robert Merton, S.D. Clark, John Porter, Leon Gérin, and Pat and Hugh Armstrong.

8. *Macrosociology* concentrates on large-scale phenomena or entire civilizations, whereas *microsociology* stresses study of small groups.

9. The *functionalist perspective* of sociology emphasizes the way in which parts of a society are structured to maintain its stability. Social change should be slow and evolutionary.

10. The *conflict perspective* assumes that social behaviour is best understood in terms of conflict or tension between competing groups. Social change, spurred by conflict and competition, should be swift and revolutionary.

11. The *interactionist perspective* is primarily concerned with fundamental or everyday forms of interaction, including symbols and other types of nonverbal communication. Social change is ongoing, as individuals get shaped by society and in turn shape it.

12. *Feminist perspectives* are varied and diverse; however, they argue that women's inequality is constructed by our society. Feminist perspectives include both micro and macro levels of analysis.

13. Sociologists make use of all four perspectives, since each offers unique insights into the same issue.

14. This textbook makes use of the sociological imagination: by showing theory in practice and research in action; by speaking across race, gender, class, and national boundaries; and by highlighting social policy around the world.

Critical Thinking Questions

1. What aspects of the social and work environment in a fast-food restaurant would be of particular interest to a sociologist because of his or her "sociological imagination"?

2. What are the manifest and latent functions of a health club?

3. How might the interactionist perspective be applied to a place where you have been employed or to an organization you joined?

Key Terms

Anomie   The loss of direction felt in a society when social control of individual behaviour has become ineffective. (page 12)

Conflict perspective   A sociological approach that assumes that social behaviour is best understood in terms of conflict or tension between competing groups. (18)

Dramaturgical approach   A view of social interaction that examines people as if they were theatrical performers. (21)

Dysfunction   An element or a process of society that may disrupt a social system or lead to a decrease in stability. (17)

Feminist perspectives   Attempts to explain, understand, and eliminate the ways in which gender socially organizes our public and private lives to produce inequality between men and women. (18)

Functionalist perspective   A sociological approach that emphasizes the way in which parts of a society are structured to maintain its stability. (17)

Ideal type   A construct or model that serves as a measuring rod against which actual cases can be evaluated. (13)

Interactionist perspective   A sociological approach that generalizes about fundamental or everyday forms of social interaction. (19)

Latent functions   Unconscious or unintended functions; hidden purposes. (17)

Macrosociology   Sociological investigation that concentrates on large-scale phenomena or entire civilizations. (16)

Manifest functions   Open, stated, and conscious functions. (17)

Microsociology   Sociological investigation that stresses the study of interactions in small groups and often uses laboratory experimental studies. (17)

Natural science   The study of the physical features of nature and the ways in which they interact and change. (9)

Nonverbal communication   The sending of messages through the use of posture, facial expressions, and gestures. (21)

Science   The body of knowledge obtained by methods based upon systematic observation. (8)

Social science   The study of various aspects of human society. (9)

Sociological imagination   An awareness of the relationship between an individual and the wider society. (7)

Sociology   The systematic study of social behaviour and human groups. (7)

Theory   In sociology, a set of statements that seeks to explain problems, actions, or behaviour. (10)

Verstehen   The German word for "understanding" or "insight"; used to stress the need for sociologists to take into account people's emotions, thoughts, beliefs, and attitudes. (13)

Additional Readings

Bailey, Gordon, and Noga Gayle. 1993. *Sociology: An Introduction From the Classics to Contemporary Feminists*. Toronto: Oxford University Press. An anthology of essential readings that explores the development of sociological thought from the writings of Durkheim, Weber, and Marx to the more contemporary theorizing by feminist sociologists such as Dorothy Smith.

Glassner, Barry. 1999. *The Culture of Fear*. New York: Basic Books. Glassner looks at how people's fears of crime, drug use, and other social problems are growing, even though the social reality often does not match the public perceptions.

Levin, Jack. 1999. *Sociological Snapshots 3: Seeing Social Structure and Change in Everyday Life*. Thousand Oaks, CA: Pine Forge Press. The sociological imagination is employed to look at everything from elevator culture and television soap operas to religious cults and the death penalty.

McDonald, Lynn. 1994. *Women Founders of the Social Sciences*. Ottawa: Carlton University Press. The author examines the important but often overlooked contributions of such pioneers as Mary Wollstonecraft, Harriet Martineau, Beatrice Webb, Jane Addams, and many more.

Internet Connection

www.mcgrawhill.ca/college/schaefer

For additional Internet exercises relating to sociological theory and sociological fields of inquiry, visit the Schaefer Online Learning Centre at **http://www.mcgrawhill.ca/college/schaefer**. *Please note that while the URLs listed were current at the time of printing, these sites often change—check the Online Learning Centre for updates.*

Sociologists use four main theoretical perspectives when analyzing the social world, including events both historical and current. Log onto Yahoo! (**http://www.yahoo.com** or **http://www.yahoo.ca**) and choose one of the breaking stories from the "In the News" section. Follow the links given, reading articles and viewing pictures from online newspapers and networks on your chosen story. Next, apply functionalist, conflict, interactionist, and feminist perspectives to the story (Table 1-2 in your textbook will be especially helpful).

(a) How would Karl Marx and conflict thinkers view such an event? Is there tension and struggle between groups? Which groups?

(b) How would Émile Durkheim and functionalist thinkers examine the story? Can you apply concepts such as manifest functions, latent functions, and dysfunctions?

(c) What would be the perspective of George Herbert Mead and other interactionists? What symbols are being used to describe the story by the media? Can you apply dramaturgy to the events? Are players in the story trying to project a certain image using symbols?

(d) How might one feminist theorist interpret this event? How could you apply the role of gender in this analysis?

(e) Which perspective did you find to be the most interesting? Is one perspective better suited than the others to analyze the story? Why or why not?

CBC Video

Visit the Schaefer Online Learning Centre at **http://www.mcgrawhill.ca/college/schaefer** to view the CBC video segment "A Community in Despair: The Case of Port Hardy" and answer related questions.

Appendix CAREERS IN SOCIOLOGY

An undergraduate degree in sociology doesn't just serve as excellent preparation for future graduate work in sociology. It also provides a strong liberal arts background for entry-level positions in business, social services, foundations, community organizations, not-for-profit groups, law enforcement, and governmental jobs. Many fields—among them marketing, public relations, and broadcasting—now require investigative skills and an understanding of diverse groups found in today's multi-ethnic and multinational environment. Moreover, a sociology degree requires accomplishment in oral and written communication, interpersonal skills, problem solving, and critical thinking—all job-related skills that may give sociology graduates an advantage over those who pursue more technical degrees (Benner and Hitchcock 1986; Billson and Huber 1993).

Consequently, while few occupations specifically require an undergraduate degree in sociology, such academic training can be an important asset in entering a wide range of occupations. Just to bring this home, a number of chapters highlight a real-life professional who describes how the study of sociology has helped in his or her career. Look for the "Taking Sociology to Work" boxes.

The accompanying figure summarizes sources of employment for those with B.A. degrees in sociology. It shows that the areas of social work, counselling, social service work, clergy, probation, and administrative service management offer career opportunities for sociology graduates. Undergraduates who know where their career interests lie are well advised to enrol in sociology courses and specialties best suited for those interests. For example, students hoping to become health planners would take a class in medical sociology; students seeking employment as social science research assistants would focus on courses in statistics and methods. Internships, such as placements at city planning agencies and survey research organizations, afford another way for sociology students to prepare for careers. Studies show that students who choose an internship placement have less trouble finding jobs, obtain better jobs, and enjoy greater job satisfaction than students without internship placements (Salem and Grabarek 1986).

Many post-secondary students view social work as the field most closely associated with sociology. Traditionally, social workers received their undergraduate training in sociology and allied fields such as psychology and

Occupations for 1995 Sociology Graduates in Canada, 1997	
	Percent of bachelor's degree graduates
Psychologists, social workers, counsellors, clergy and probation officers	12.8
Library, correspondence and related information clerks	9.8
Administrative service managers	9.1
Paralegal, social services workers and occupations in education and religion	7.5
Security guards and related occupations	5.1
Self-employed	1.4

Note: Percentages do not add up to 100 because these statistics include only bachelor's degree graduates who entered the labour force, and those not pursuing their education on a full-time basis six to nine months after graduation.

Source: Human Resources Development Canada 2000.

counselling. After some practical experience, social workers would generally seek a master's degree in social work (M.S.W.) to be considered for supervisory or administrative positions. Today, however, some students choose (where it is available) to pursue an undergraduate degree in social work (B.S.W.). This degree prepares graduates for direct service positions such as caseworker or group worker.

Many students continue their sociological training beyond the bachelor's degree. More than 25 universities in Canada have graduate programs in sociology that offer Ph.D. and/or master's degrees. These programs differ greatly in their areas of specialization, course requirements, costs, and research and teaching opportunities available to graduate students (Association of Universities and Colleges of Canada 2001).

Higher education is an important source of employment for sociologists with graduate degrees. About

SOCIOLOGY GRADUATE?

OH YEAH, THAT HAS FUTURE CEO WRITTEN ALL OVER IT.

Many people believe a sociology degree doesn't prepare you for the job market (let alone the CEO's office). The truth is more than 90% of liberal arts students start their careers within six months of graduation. But university isn't job training. It's broader. It's mind training. So a sociology grad can jump into the high-tech field of telecommunications. And, in some cases, end up running the company. Just like Carol Stephenson, President and CEO of Lucent Technologies Canada.

UNIVERSITY OF TORONTO
Faculty of Arts and Science

STEPHENSON
CAROL
897137063

UNIVERSITY OF TORONTO. GREAT MINDS FOR A GREAT FUTURE.

The skills acquired through studying sociology can be applied to a number of positions in government, business, and community organizations. University of Toronto sociology graduate Carol Stephenson became the CEO of Lucent Technologies Canada.

80 percent of recent Ph.D. recipients in sociology sought employment in post-secondary institutions. These sociologists teach not only majors committed to the discipline but also students hoping to become doctors, nurses, lawyers, police officers, and so forth.

For sociology graduates interested in academic careers, the road to a Ph.D. degree (or doctorate) can be long and difficult. This degree symbolizes competence in original research; each candidate must prepare a book-length study known as a *dissertation*. Typically, a doctoral student in sociology will engage in four to seven years of intensive work, including the time required to complete the dissertation. Yet even this effort is no guarantee of a job as a sociology professor.

The good news is that over the next 10 years, the demand for instructors is expected to increase because of

boom generation, as well as the anticipated slow but steady growth in the post-secondary student population in Canada. Nonetheless, anyone who launches an academic career must be prepared for considerable uncertainty and competition in the post-secondary job market.

Of course, not all people working as sociologists teach or hold doctoral degrees. Take government, for example. Statistics Canada relies on people with sociological training to interpret data for other government departments and the general public. Virtually every department depends on survey research—a field in which sociology students can specialize—in order to assess everything from community needs to the morale of the department's own workers. In addition, people with sociological training can put their academic knowledge to effective use in corrections, health sciences, community development, and recreational services. Some people working in government or private industry have a master's degree (M.A.) in sociology; others have a bachelor's degree (B.A.).

A 1996 survey of 11 sociology departments in Canada showed that approximately 20 percent of Ph.D. graduates use their sociological skills outside the academic world, either in government or the private sector (Davies and Denton 1996). A renewed interest in applied sociology has led to the hiring of an increasing number of sociologists with graduate degrees by businesses, industry, hospitals, and nonprofit organizations. Indeed, studies show that many sociology graduates are making career changes from social service areas to business and commerce. As an undergraduate major, sociology is excellent preparation for employment in many parts of the business world (Billson 1994).

Whether you take a few courses in sociology or actually complete a degree, you will benefit from the critical thinking skills developed in this discipline. Sociologists emphasize the value of being able to analyze, interpret, and function within a variety of working situations; this is an asset in virtually any career. Moreover, given the rapid technological change evident in the last decade and the expanding global economy, all of us will need to adapt to substantial social change, even in our own careers. Sociology provides a rich conceptual framework that can serve as a foundation for flexible career development and can assist us in taking advantage of new employment

SOCIOLOGICAL RESEARCH

What Is the Scientific Method? 33

Major Research Designs 40

Ethics of Research 44

Technology and Sociological Research 48

Social Policy and Sociological Research: Studying Human Sexuality 49

Boxes

Appendix I: Understanding Tables and Graphs 52

Appendix II: Writing a Library Research Report 53

Canada's first census was carried out in 1666, when the population of the French colony was counted at just over 3000. In 1871, the initial national count was performed in accordance with an act of parliament. Beginning in 1918, the Dominion Bureau of Statistics, later Statistics Canada, took on the task of counting the Canadian people every five years. Since then, on the '1' years (1921, 1931, etc.) a major survey has been performed, and on the '6' years (1926, 1936, etc.) a smaller-scale count has been done.

The dissent we are now witnessing is a manifestation of the frustration and alienation felt by a disenfranchised and economically manipulated group. The rioting in major Western cities, the growing necessity for armed guards in violence-prone high schools where students carry weapons, the formation of violent gangs, even in small towns, high levels of un- and underemployment, epidemic levels of suicide, and mindless consumerism are all part of the same problem that leaves many young people aimlessly groping to come of age in the 1990s. . .

[T]he changing circumstances confronting young people as they grow up and try to come of age in advanced industrial societies . . . include the long wait adolescents must face between the time when they become physically mature and when they are considered to be socially mature, or "adult." The delay is characterized by economic and social marginality; sequestration into age-segregated groups, and extended financial and emotional dependence on parents. The young are also subject to manipulation and control by a variety of groups formed by adults who are out to protect their own interests.

. . . we propose that as we moved into the most recent phase of industrial capitalism, which began in the 1950s, the coming-of-age process has become even longer, primarily because the labor of adolescents and youth is no longer needed, except in service industries. Consequently, young people have lost a "franchise." Now they participate less in the labor force, and when they do, it is in a more subservient manner. Accordingly, fewer young people have the full rights and privileges of citizenship, and they must wait longer before they are fully recognized as adults. In addition to not being able to make a meaningful contribution to the economy, young people have been forced to remain in school longer, where they are under the watchful eye of massive educational bureaucracies.

. . . young people have been targeted as consumers rather than as producers by the service, leisure, information, and high-technology sectors of the advanced industrial economy. In other words, young people have increasingly been targeted as consumers of "leisure industries" (e.g., media and music) and "identity industries" (e.g., fashion and education).

. . . these leisure and identity industries have merged to create a culture in which coming of age involves allying oneself with one of these forces—for example, adopting one of the images manufactured by the leisure industries, or predicating an identity on the credentials conferred by the educational system.

. . . young people today face a situation where conflict, chaos, and confusion underlie a superficial harmony. Developing a viable adult identity has become an increasingly tenuous process for those coming of age because many of the identities they are sold by adult profiteers are illusory and fleeting. *(Côté and Allahar 1994: xiv–xvii)* ■

This excerpt comes from the book *Generation on Hold*, by Côté and Allahar. It is an attempt to examine adolescence from a variety of multidisciplinary and sociological perspectives. Even though the authors looked at adolescence from different angles, their studies have one thing in common: all of the research cited in the book was done using the scientific method outlined in this chapter.

For instance, in *Teen Trends: A Nation in Motion*, Reginald Bibby and Donald Posterski use qualitative instruments to capture the attitudes of Canadian students about violence in high schools, concluding that the phenomenon is considered to be very serious (Côté et al. 1994:141). The authors of this research gathered their data directly from the youth population using surveys.

By contrast, Lucie Norbert, in her study of underemployment among university graduates in Canada, used existing data files to conclude that 43 percent of the graduates whose employment outcomes were tracked reported being in a job that did not require a degree (Côté et al. 1994:126). This kind of archival research is a cost-effective way to produce a profile of a demographic group selected from the larger population.

For his study of the socioeconomic environment and life course of First Nations youth in Canada, David Ross (Côté et al. 1994:77) used a combination of first person interviews and archival records to conclude that these young people are marginalized to an even greater extent than are mainstream youth. Ross' examination of education outcomes shows that over three-quarters of reserve First Nations persons have not finished high school. Interviews reveal that the situation is even worse for those living in the far North, where a lack of access to services and facilities leads many to crime as a way of escaping the deprivation that is so prevalent.

Sociologists and other social scientists face new and complex challenges every time they venture to confirm a hypothesis through original research. While methods are well defined under the "scientific" paradigm, the *choice* of method often involves applying a little creativity.

Effective sociological research can be quite thought-provoking. It may suggest many new questions about social interactions that require further study, such as why we make assumptions about people's intentions based merely on their gender or age or race. In some cases, rather than raising additional questions, a study will simply confirm previous beliefs and findings.

This chapter will examine the research process used in conducting sociological studies. We will first look at the steps that make up the scientific method in doing research. Then we will take a look at various techniques commonly used in sociological research, such as experiments, surveys, observations, and use of secondary sources. We will pay particular attention to the ethical challenges sociologists face in studying human behaviour and to the debate raised by Max Weber's call for "value neutrality" in social science research. We will also examine the role that technology plays in research today. The social policy section considers the difficulties in researching human sexuality.

Whatever the area of sociological inquiry and whatever the perspective of the sociologist—whether functionalist, conflict, interactionist, feminist, or any other—there is one crucial requirement: imaginative, responsible research that meets the highest scientific and ethical standards. ∎

What Is the Scientific Method?

Like all of us, sociologists are interested in the central questions of our time. Is the family falling apart? Is there too much crime in Canada? Are we lagging behind in our ability to feed the world population? Such issues concern most people, whether or not they have academic training. However, unlike the typical citizen, the sociologist has a commitment to the use of the scientific method in studying society. The *scientific method* is a systematic, organized series of steps that ensures maximum objectivity and consistency in researching a problem.

The scientific method can be applied to either quantitative or qualitative research. **Quantitative research** (think "quantity") looks at data that can easily be measured and expressed in numbers. For example, it answers survey questions such as, "At what age did you leave home?" or "How many times per week do you go to the mall?" **Qualitative research** (think "quality") looks at data that is observed, described, and interpreted but is difficult to express in numbers. For example, it involves observations about consumer behaviour, or conversational interviews, or transcripts from a focus group.

Many of us will never actually conduct scientific research. Why, then, is it important that we understand the scientific method? Because it plays a major role in the workings of our society.

We are constantly being bombarded with "facts" or "data." Almost daily, advertisers cite supposedly scientific studies to prove that their products are superior. Such

FIGURE 2-1

The Scientific Method

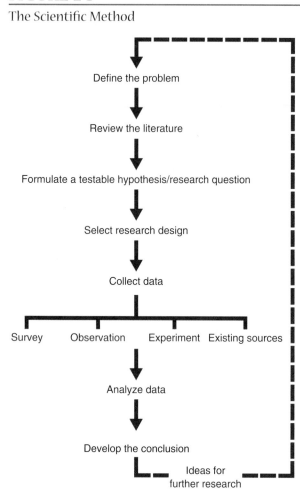

Define the problem

↓

Review the literature

↓

Formulate a testable hypothesis/research question

↓

Select research design

↓

Collect data

Survey   Observation   Experiment   Existing sources

↓

Analyze data

↓

Develop the conclusion

Ideas for further research

The scientific method allows sociologists, objectively and logically, to evaluate the facts collected. This can lead to further ideas for sociological research.

claims may be accurate or exaggerated. We can make better evaluations of the information—and will not be fooled so easily—if we are familiar with the standards of scientific research. These standards are quite stringent and demand adherence that is as strict as possible.

The scientific method requires precise preparation in developing useful research. Otherwise, the research data collected may not prove useful. Sociologists and other researchers follow seven basic steps in the scientific method: (1) defining the problem, (2) reviewing the literature, (3) formulating the hypothesis, (4) selecting the research design, (5) collecting the data, (6) analyzing the data, and (7) developing the conclusion (see Figure 2-1). We'll use an actual example to illustrate the workings of the scientific method.

1. Defining the Problem

During the latter part of the 1990s, the stereotypical image of young people desperate to escape the parental home faded somewhat from the popular imagination. During this time, there was plenty of anecdotal evidence pointing to the trend for youth to remain at home several years longer than their parents' generation had done. Despite the pervasiveness of this anecdotal evidence, we need proper research employing the scientific method to confirm the existence of and to pinpoint the causes associated with such social change. In other words, we need to know "the facts." This is where social scientists have a role to play.

Two studies were undertaken to address this challenge. The first, by Zhao, Rajulton, and Ravanera (1995), looked at the influence of family structure, gender, and culture on the timing of children's home-leaving. The second, by Gee, Mitchell, and Wister (1995), examined the increase in co-residence between young adults and

As the Zhao (1995) study shows, Canadian youth leave home for a variety of reasons. Many, like these Montreal students, move out as part of the transition from high school to university.

their parents. This study sought to confirm that this increase is a result of the fact that adult children stay under the parental roof longer than similar age cohorts did traditionally, and that they are more likely to return home after leaving.

The first step in any research project is to state, as clearly as possible, what you hope to investigate—that is, *define the problem*. In the examples cited above, the researchers were interested in two facets of the same issue. The Zhao study focused exclusively on the variables that influenced home-leaving, while the Gee research looked at this event in terms of its influence on a secondary life-choice—returning to the parental home.

Early on, any social science researcher must develop an operational definition of each concept being studied. An **operational definition** is an explanation of an abstract concept that is specific enough to allow the research team to measure the concept. While many concepts may not appear to be abstract—"happiness," or "threat," for example—they cannot be measured without using some sort of marker or indicator. If you wanted to determine someone's level of happiness, you would have to select a marker, such as smiling or laughter, to gauge its presence.

In the Gee study, the researchers wanted to examine the effects of the "child's main activity" on the probability of returning to the parental home. Activity, as a concept, is abstract, and requires an operational definition in order for the findings to have any value. For the purposes of the study, "activity" was defined as "going to school" or "going to work."

In the Zhao study, "stability in the home" was identified as one of the key variables influencing children's leaving of their parental home. Since "stability" is abstract in the sense that it cannot be measured in and of itself, the researchers were required to find a concrete indicator. They did this by using marital status of the parents, adopting categories such as "Married," "Common Law," and "Single Parent," as defined by Statistics Canada in the 1990 General Social Survey.

2. Reviewing the Literature

Once you have determined your research topic and defined the problem, you need to ask yourself what is already known about the topic. That is where step 2, reviewing the literature, comes in. By conducting a *review of the literature*—the relevant scholarly studies and information—researchers get to know what others have already done on the topic. This helps the researcher refine the problem under study, clarify possible techniques to be used in collecting data, eliminate or reduce avoidable mistakes, and decide on the contribution the research will make to the research problem/topic.

The phenomenon of young adult children remaining longer in or returning to the parental home—coined "the cluttered nest" (Zhao 1995:122)—is a relatively new one, but there is no lack of relevant research. Prior to the 1960s, the age at which children left the home had fallen continuously since the beginning of the twentieth century. The dramatic shift in this trend has made the study of intergenerational living a burgeoning area of research.

Both the Zhao and the Gee studies required a review of this existing research. They would have read the studies that have been done throughout North America (Boyd and Pryor 1989; Boyd and Norris 1994; Glick and Lin 1986; Grigsby and McGowan 1986) and in Europe (Aquilino 1990). Zhao et al. relied on research done in a number of areas to inform their study: Cherlin (1992) is cited for examining the effect of cohabitation on individualism, and Kiernan (1992) offered the authors insight into the relationship between step-parents and a child's decision to leave home.

3. Formulating the Hypothesis or Research Question

After reviewing earlier research and drawing on the contributions of sociological theorists, researchers now need to formulate the specific focus of their project. This is done either by setting a *research question*, in the case of a qualitative study, or by *creating a hypothesis*, in the case of a quantitative study. Finding the answer to the research question is the goal of the qualitative study. Whereas qualitative research begins with a question, quantitative research begins with an answer, the hypothesis. A **hypothesis** is a speculative statement about the relationship between two or more factors known as *variables*. Income, religion, occupation, and gender can all serve as variables in a study. We can define a **variable** as a measurable trait or characteristic that is subject to change under different conditions.

Researchers who formulate a hypothesis generally must suggest how one aspect of human behaviour influences or affects another. The variable hypothesized to cause or influence another is called the **independent variable**. The second variable is termed the **dependent variable** because its action "depends" on the influence of the independent variable.

Zhao hypothesized that the timing of children's home-leaving (the dependent variable) would be influenced by the number of children in the family, whether the parents were the child's natural or step-parents, and by the ethnic affiliation of the household (all independent variables). Specifically, it was suggested that children with more than two siblings would leave home earlier than others, that stepfamilies result in earlier home-leaving, and that children whose parents are immigrants,

FIGURE 2-2

Causal Logic

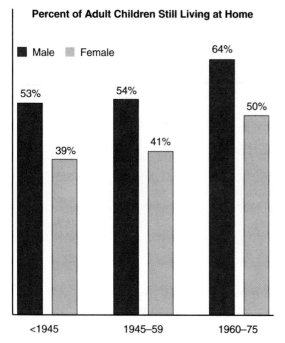

Percent of Adult Children Still Living at Home

■ Male   ▨ Female

In *causal logic* an independent variable (often designated by the symbol *x*) influences a dependent variable (generally designated as *y*); thus, *x* leads to *y*. For example, in the graph above, gender is the independent variable (*x*) and "probability of still living at home" is the dependent variable (*y*). Notice that the first two pairs of variables are taken from studies already described in this textbook.

Source: Gee et al. 1995.

especially non-European, are likely to take up separate residence at a younger age.

The Gee study focused on the phenomenon of young adult children returning to live in the parental home. The researchers developed a number of hypotheses, including that higher parental socioeconomic status (independent variable) would influence the likelihood of children returning home, and that the child's marital status (independent variable) would affect the child's decision whether or not to return to the parental home (dependent variable). Gee determined that homes where the parents' socioeconomic status was higher were less often "cluttered nests." Also, as intuition would suggest, children who have spouses of their own are not as inclined to return home.

Identifying independent and dependent variables—in this case, what causes home-leaving—is a critical step in clarifying cause-and-effect relationships in society. As shown in Figure 2-2, *causal logic*, or *causality*, involves the relationship between a condition or variable and a particular consequence, with one event leading to the

other. To claim a causal relationship between two variables, three criteria must be met (Lazarsfeld 1959):

1. The independent variable must be present before the dependent variable
2. There must be empirical evidence of a cause-and-effect link between the variables
3. The cause-and-effect link cannot be explained by a third factor.

Consider, for example, the September 11, 2001, attacks on the Pentagon and the World Trade Center. To support their claim that Osama bin Laden (the independent variable) caused the disasters (the dependent variable), the Americans had to meet Lazarfeld's criteria: that bin Laden had contact with the terrorists prior to September 11; that bin Laden had motivation and means for such an act; and that the contact between the Al Qaeda leader and the terrorists could not be reasonably attributed to another factor.

A ***control variable*** is a factor held constant to test the relative impact of the independent variable. For example, if researchers wanted to know how adults feel about restrictions on smoking in public places, they would probably attempt to use a respondent's smoking behaviour as a control variable. That is, how do smokers versus nonsmokers feel about smoking in public places? Consequently, the researchers would compile separate statistics on how smokers and nonsmokers feel about antismoking regulations.

A ***correlation*** exists when a change in one variable coincides with a change in the other. Correlations are an indication that causality *may* be present; they do not necessarily indicate causation. Sociologists seek to identify the *causal* link between variables; this causal link is generally advanced by researchers in their hypotheses.

4. Selecting the Research Design

Now that you are prepared with a specific research question or hypothesis, you have to select a research design that will ensure who (the sample) and what (the variables) will give you answers to your question. Social scientists begin this step by carefully selecting a sample of the population or group of people that they wish to study.

Selecting the Sample

A ***representative sample*** is a selection from a larger population that is statistically typical of that population. There are many kinds of samples, but the one social scientists most frequently use is the random sample. In a ***random sample***, every member of an entire population being studied has the same chance of being selected. Thus, if researchers want to examine the opinions of people listed in a city directory (a book that, unlike the

Whether it is the census or any other type of research, sampling methods have a direct impact on the accuracy of the results.

telephone directory, lists all households), they might call every 10th or 50th or 100th name listed. This would constitute a random sample. The advantage of using specialized sampling techniques is that sociologists do not need to question everyone in a population.

Sampling is a complex aspect of research design. In Box 2-1, we consider the approach some researchers took when trying to create an appropriate sample of people in the world's most populous nation—China. We'll also see how they made use of data from the sample.

Measuring the Variables

Four types of measures are used in sociology: nominal, ordinal, interval, and ratio. A *nominal* measure is one that only identifies membership in a category. For instance, a young person is either of driving age or not.

An *ordinal* measure is one that allows for the various states of the variable to be ranked but not necessarily compared. For instance, classifying Driver A as having driven longer than Driver B indicates that A has more experience than B, but not how much. It could be one month or 20 years.

An *interval* measure is used when there are predictable intervals between the various states of the variable, allowing them to be compared. In a study of young drivers, this could be the number of months they have been driving, enabling the researcher to say that A has been at the wheel six months longer than B.

Just a slight change in the sample, from "young drivers" to "adolescents," would transform the interval measurement into a *ratio* measure—one that allows for precise comparisons, and in which there is a zero value. For instance, if two drivers have 15 and 5 years behind the wheel, respectively, then the first driver has three times

the experience of the second. Also, some adolescents will not have their driver's licence yet, and so will have no driving experience.

5. Collecting the Data

Once you have defined the problem, reviewed the literature, formulated your hypothesis or research question, and selected a research design, the next step is to collect the data. You begin by deciding which data-gathering technique(s) to use. There are four general methods: survey research, experiments, observation, and using secondary sources. The first two methods or techniques are used primarily in quantitative research, while the latter two are more often used in qualitative research. While they will be discussed in more detail later in the chapter, the following brief explanations provide an introduction to the basic idea behind each technique.

Survey research is the gathering of data by directly questioning members of the population being studied. Survey is the most commonly used method in social research, primarily because it enables the collection of large amounts of data while minimizing cost. While most surveys are designed to collect quantitative information, open-ended questions that ask for an opinion, and in-depth interviews, can be used to examine qualitative issues.

Experiment, the measurement of cause and effect in a controlled environment, is seldom used in sociology because of the difficulties in reproducing realistic social conditions in a laboratory.

Observation is the recording of events and impressions in a real-life social situation. Observation can be used in either quantitative or qualitative studies. For

Sociology in the Global Community   2-1 "Sent-Down" in China

Imagine arriving at school and learning that the entire college was being closed and that, in fact, the government was closing *all* universities. Furthermore, since there was no school for you to attend, you were now being taken to the countryside to work on farms so the country could increase agricultural production.

This is basically what happened to students in China from 1967 to 1978, a period historians refer to as the Cultural Revolution, when China was trying to rid itself of outside influences. During this time, 17 million young urban people—about a third of the youth entering the labour force—were the victims of the government's "send-down" policy. They were forced to live and work in rural areas rather than attend school or work at government jobs they may have held.

Sociologists Xueguang Zhou and Liren Hou of Duke University were interested in what impact these state policies had on the people's lives. To

learn more, the researchers decided to interview those who were "sent-down" as well as comparable people who were not sent to rural areas. They did their representative sampling in several stages: first selecting cities from different geographical areas, then systematically selecting blocks within those cities, and finally randomly selecting and interviewing adults within the blocks.

> 17 million young urban people were the victims of the government's "send-down" policy.

They accumulated a sample of 2793 people, of whom 855 had been sent-down.

Zhou and Hou found that those who stayed in rural areas more than six years were likely to marry later, have fewer children, and hold poorer jobs than those who spent less time or those who stayed in urban areas. While these

differences may be expected, some findings were surprising. For example, those who were sent-down for only a few years were more likely to graduate from college than those young people who were never sent-down. The researchers argue that many of the youths who left "early" from rural areas were well-connected politically and therefore probably came from more prosperous backgrounds. Also, these young people may have resolved to overcome quickly the adverse effects of the state policy.

Let's Discuss

1. How did the researchers make sure their sample was representative? Do you think selecting names from a phone book would produce the same results? How would you go about selecting a sample population?
2. Describe the independent and dependent variables in this study. (Refer to page 35 if you need to.)

Source: Zhou and Hou 1999.

---

instance, researchers looking into youth consumerism might record the number of bags each adolescent is carrying while leaving a mall. This would be a quantitative study. Or, the research team might record their impressions of youths' satisfaction in a store: Do they look happy as they leave? This would be qualitative.

Using secondary sources involves the use of already existing data that was collected by others. This can include archives, government documents (i.e., census data), and content analysis of written, aural, or visual material. This method of data collection looks at existing data and/or studies with an eye to reinterpreting them qualitatively from a fresh angle, or viewing them in a larger context with other studies of the same research problem.

In recent years, social research has increasingly used a combination of survey and observation to gather more comprehensive data. Focus groups are a good example of this method. In these settings, group facilitators guide the

discussion with specific questions to which they record the answers. At the same time, they make notes about the qualitative aspects of the process, like body language and tone of voice.

6. Analyzing the Data

Once data has been gathered (collected), it needs to be interpreted. Sociologists use many complex interpretive tools in assessing the meaning of their data. Only a few of the most basic measures are presented below.

One way to determine the significance of data is to calculate proportions. The fact that 400 survey respondents left their parents' home at the age of 14 does not tell us very much. The raw numbers must be analyzed for meaning. If we know that the sample size is 500, though, the "400" might tell us something significant about the population being studied—80 percent left home at an early age. If the sample is 50 000, however, we know that

400 is too small a proportion (0.8 percent of the total) to be meaningful.

Finding the *measure of central tendency* is another way to determine the significance of data. There are three of these measures—mean, median, and mode. The *mean* is the average. In our example, this would be the average age at which the respondents left their parental home. The *median* is the number at which 50 percent of respondents fall below and 50 percent above. In the Zhao study, analysis showed that the median age at which men left home in 1945 was 21.25. This indicates that half of all men moved out of their parental home by the time they were this age. The *mode* is the most frequent answer to a question. More men left the parental home at this age than any other.

When the research question is as straightforward as "At what age did you leave home?", answers inevitably come out as numbers: "I left home at 18." This is *quantitative data*—data that is numerical and self-explanatory; "18" needs no interpretation. Often, however, questions elicit responses that are not so clear-cut. This is referred to as *qualitative data*, which requires interpretation. A young woman who says she left home because her parents were too strict simply gives us an opinion. There is no right or wrong answer, and the one she has provided can only inform the research if we understand what "strict" means. The answer needs to be interpreted within the context of the study.

Ensuring Validity and Reliability

The scientific method requires that research results be both valid and reliable. **Validity** refers to the degree to which a measure or scale truly reflects the phenomenon under study. For Zhao, a valid measure of the reasons why young adults leave home depended on gathering accurate data. One of the considerations for this study was settling on a specific definition of "leaving home." The researchers had to decide if a temporary absence such as living away for school or a summer job represented departure. To deal with this problem, the Zhao team was careful to look only at those children who had left home permanently.

Reliability refers to consistency of results. In a research project, reliability is achieved if a particular measure repeatedly provides substantially similar findings. For example, to be reliable, the question, "Why did you return home?" would have to produce the same findings for the Gee research team each time it was asked of a different sample group for the same population.

7. Developing the Conclusion

Scientific studies, including those conducted by sociologists, do not aim to answer all the questions that can be raised about a particular subject. Therefore, the conclusion of a research study represents both an end and a beginning. It terminates a specific phase of the investigation, but it should also generate ideas for future study. Both Zhao and Gee recognize a need for ongoing research in their areas.

Supporting Hypotheses

Sociological studies do not always generate data that support the original hypothesis. In many instances, a hypothesis is refuted, and researchers must reformulate their conclusions. Unexpected results may also lead sociologists to re-examine their methodology and make changes in the research design.

Using the existing literature, Zhao was able to identify several independent variables influencing the age of home-leaving for young adults. For instance, the Zhao team hypothesized that children living in homes where the parental relationship was cohabitational, rather than formalized through marriage, would leave home earlier. The same outcome was predicted for single-parent families—that children would strike out on their own at a younger age. The team also hypothesized that the presence of a stepfamily would encourage early exit from the parental nest. As to the effects of ethnicity, Zhao et al. were looking for confirmation that the parents' cultural affiliation is a critical causal factor in home-leaving. It was hypothesized that children coming from homes where the cultural norms emphasized strong familial relations, such as those in Asia and Eastern Europe, would live with their parents for a longer period.

However, while Zhao's hypotheses were supported, it is important to recognize that evidence refuting one or more of these would have been just as valuable. For instance, if the research team had discovered that stability in the parental home had no effect on leaving, this would be an important finding.

In Summary: The Scientific Method

Let us briefly summarize the process of the scientific method through a review of the example. Both Zhao and Gee *defined the problem*, identifying the issue to be focused on—either home-leaving or return to the parental home. They *reviewed the literature*, examining what other researchers had already done in the area of interest, which helped them *formulate hypotheses* or research questions about the connection between various environmental factors and children leaving the parental home. They *selected a research design* and a *sample*, identifying their population and how they would choose it, and then they *selected a research method*, a format or technique for data collection. Finally, they *collected and analyzed the data*, using statistics to extract the meaning from the raw numbers.

Major Research Designs

An important aspect of sociological research is deciding how to collect the data needed to answer the research question or test the hypothesis. Selection of the research technique is a critical step for sociologists and requires creativity and ingenuity. Because the choice of technique or methodology is so important, we need to understand this aspect of the scientific process fully. For this reason, the following section expands on the brief definitions of the various types of data collection methods provided earlier.

p. 37

Surveys

Almost all of us have responded to surveys of one kind or another. We may have been asked what kind of detergent we use, which political candidate we intend to vote for, or what our favourite television program is. A *survey* is a study, generally in the form of an interview or questionnaire, that provides sociologists with information concerning how people think and act. Among Canada's best-known surveys of opinion are the Ipsos–Reid and Decima polls. As anyone who watches the news during political campaigns knows, polls have become a staple of political life.

When you think of surveys, you may recall seeing many "person on the street" interviews on local television news shows. While such interviews can be highly entertaining, they are not necessarily an accurate indication of public opinion. First, they reflect the opinions of only those people who happen to be at a certain location. Such a sample can be biased in favour of commuters, middle-class shoppers, or factory workers, depending on which street or area the newspeople select. Second, television interviews tend to attract outgoing people who are willing to appear on the air, while they frighten away others who may feel intimidated by a camera. As we've seen, a survey must be based on precise, representative sampling if it is genuinely to reflect a broad range of the population.

In preparing to conduct a survey, sociologists must not only develop representative samples; they must exercise great care in the wording of questions. An effective survey question must be simple and clear enough for people to understand it. It must also be specific enough so that there are no problems in interpreting the results. Even questions that are less structured ("What do you think of programming on educational television?") must be carefully phrased to solicit the type of information desired. Box 2-2 illustrates some of the challenges researchers face in phrasing survey questions for marginal populations. Surveys can be indispensable sources of information, but only if the sampling is done properly and the questions are worded accurately.

There are two main forms of surveys: the *interview* and the *questionnaire*. An **interview** involves face-to-face or telephone questioning of a respondent to obtain desired information. A **questionnaire**, on the other hand, is a research instrument employed to obtain desired information from a respondent and can be administered either in person or through the mail.

Each of these has its own advantages. An interviewer can obtain a high response rate because people find it more difficult to turn down a personal request for an interview than to throw away a written questionnaire. In addition, a skilful interviewer can go beyond written questions and "probe" for a subject's underlying feelings and reasons, making interviews a valuable technique for gathering qualitative research data. On the other hand, questionnaires have the advantage of being cheaper, especially when large samples are used, as in quantitative research. As you can see, surveys are used in both qualitative and quantitative research, depending on the specific survey method chosen in the research design stage.

Studies have shown that characteristics of the interviewer have an impact on survey data. To get around this problem, Canadian sociologists Richard Floyd and Stephen Dooley (Floyd and Dooley 1998) developed the Target Inclusion Model (TIM). Researchers using the TIM recruit members of the target population as part of the research team, both during the development of the survey and in the field as interviewers. Being interviewed by their peers puts street youth, for example, at ease during the data-gathering process.

Experiments

When sociologists want to study a possible cause-and-effect relationship, they may conduct experiments. An experiment is an artificially created situation that allows the researcher to manipulate variables.

In the classic method of conducting an experiment, two groups of people are selected and matched for similar characteristics such as age or education. The researchers then assign the subjects to one of two groups—the experimental or the control group. The **experimental group** is exposed to an independent variable; the **control group** is not. Thus, if scientists were testing a new type of antibiotic drug, they would administer that drug to an experimental group but not to a control group.

Sociologists don't often rely on this classic form of experiment because it generally involves manipulating human behaviour in an inappropriate manner, especially

Research in Action

2-2 Framing Survey Questions for Marginal Populations

The most difficult populations to study are those that exist at the margins of society. Groups as disparate as senior citizens and street youth share a common social status: they operate outside the mainstream.

Both groups, as you might expect, are suspicious of the world around them. Seniors fear exploitation and being physically or financially harmed. Research has shown that many street youth come from dysfunctional backgrounds, so for them the fear is of those in positions of authority. This creates challenges for the researcher, particularly in the area of communication.

For instance, when creating a questionnaire for seniors, one of the basic rules is not to ask direct questions about financial status. Nothing will put a senior respondent on his or her guard more quickly than to ask, "How much money do you have in the bank?" But what do you do in these circumstances if it is critical to your study to determine socioeconomic status?

One strategy is to ask questions that will indirectly give you the information you need. In this instance, you might be able to ask the respondents what make and model of car they own, or whether they own their own home. Questions like these will provide a solid indication of their financial situation.

> One strategy is to ask questions that will indirectly give you the information you need.

In approaching the street youth population, the research team is not only faced with skepticism, but also with a language barrier created by the jargon of the street. If you were to ask a street youth whether his or her mother was living, the question might be misconstrued, either deliberately or unintentionally. Young people who live on the street frequently adopt street parents to replace those they have left behind, an understandable practice when you consider that the majority of them come from abusive home environments. Here the question would have to include the phrase "birth mother" to be clear.

In building questions for a survey, the researcher must take into account the characteristics of the population to be studied. Not all questions mean the same thing to all people.

Let's Discuss

1. Think of a marginal population other than street youth or seniors. How do these people qualify as "marginal"?
2. What difficulty might you encounter in creating questions to ask this group?
3. Compose a question that overcomes this difficulty.

in a laboratory setting. However, there are sociologists whose area of research falls into the social psychological domain, and they may use experiments as a means of research. Canadian sociologist Martha Foschi has conducted a series of experiments over the past 30 years, focusing on diffuse status characteristics—those characteristics that provide status across situations (e.g., age, gender, ethnicity, etc.)—and expectation states (the expectations, created by status characteristics, that someone brings to a social interaction).

In one such experiment, subjects are paired with someone of the opposite sex, and their willingness to accept influence from that other person is measured. In this experiment, the subjects perform a task that they are told will test their visual perception by having them gauge the amount of white on a slide containing black and white blocks. The subjects perform this task once, and are given information about their performance. Then, they are asked to do a second set of evaluations using the same sensory skill, only this time they are given access to

second opinions. After making their initial determination of whether the slide has more black or white, they are shown the other individual's choice, and asked if they want to change their selection.

The experiment looks at how often subjects change their mind when the other person is a woman compared to how often they change it when the other person is a man. The findings indicate that people are more willing to be influenced by someone who is male than someone who is female. Over the course of many years, Dr. Foschi's experiments have provided valuable information about the interplay of status characteristics and influence.

In some experiments, as in observation research, the presence of a social scientist or other observer may affect the behaviour of people being studied. The recognition of this phenomenon grew out of an experiment conducted during the 1920s and 1930s at the Hawthorne plant of the Western Electric Company. A group of researchers set out to determine how to improve the productivity of workers at the plant. The investigators manipulated such

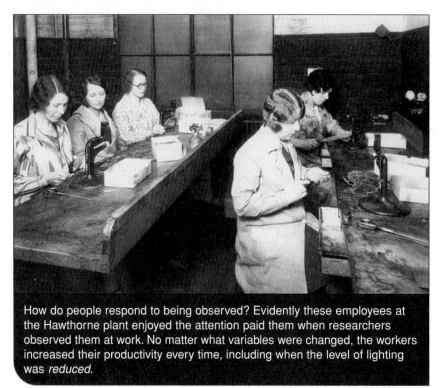

How do people respond to being observed? Evidently these employees at the Hawthorne plant enjoyed the attention paid them when researchers observed them at work. No matter what variables were changed, the workers increased their productivity every time, including when the level of lighting was *reduced.*

variables as the lighting and working hours to see what impact changes in them had on productivity. To their surprise, they found that *every* step they took seemed to increase productivity. Even measures that seemed likely to have the opposite effect, such as reducing the amount of lighting in the plant, led to higher productivity.

Why did the plant's employees work harder even under less favourable conditions? Their behaviour apparently was influenced by the greater attention being paid to them in the course of the research and by the novelty of being subjects in an experiment. Since that time, sociologists have used the term **Hawthorne effect** to refer to subjects of research who deviate from their typical behaviour because they realize that they are under observation (S. Jones 1992; Lang 1992; Pelton 1994).

Observation

Investigators who collect information through direct participation and/or observation of a group, tribe, or community under study are engaged in observation. This method allows sociologists to examine certain behaviours and communities that could not be investigated through other research techniques.

As we mentioned earlier, observation research is the most common form of *qualitative research,* relying on what is seen in field or naturalistic settings more than on statistical data. Generally, such studies focus on small groups or communities rather than large groups or whole

nations. An increasingly popular form of qualitative research in sociology today is ethnography. **Ethnography** refers to efforts to describe an entire social setting through extended, systematic observation. William Whyte's study, described below, involved understanding behaviour of not just the people on one street corner, but all facets of life in an urban neighbourhood. Anthropologists rely heavily on ethnography. Much as an anthropologist seeks to understand the people of some Polynesian island, the sociologist as an ethnographer seeks to understand and present to us an entire way of life in some setting.

Quantitative research collects and reports data primarily in numerical form. Most of the survey research discussed so far in this textbook has been this type of research. While quantitative research can make use of larger samples than qualitative research, it can't look at a topic in the same depth. Neither type of research is necessarily better; indeed we are usually best informed when we rely on studies using a variety of research designs that look at both qualitative and quantitative aspects of the same subject.

In some cases, the sociologist actually "joins" a group for a period of time to get an accurate sense of how it operates. This is called *participant observation.* In the tattoo study described in Chapter 1, the researcher was a participant observer.

During the late 1930s, in the classic example of participant-observation research we referred to a moment ago, William F. Whyte moved into a low-income Italian neighbourhood in Boston. For nearly four years, he was a member of the social circle of "corner boys" that he describes in *Street Corner Society.* Whyte revealed his identity to these men and joined in their conversations, bowling, and other leisure-time activities. His goal was to gain greater insight into the community that these men had established. As Whyte (1981:303) listened to Doc, the leader of the group, he "learned the answers to questions I would not even have had the sense to ask if I had been getting my information solely on an interviewing basis." Whyte's work was especially valuable, since, at the time, the academic world had little direct knowledge of the poor and tended to rely for information on the records of social service agencies, hospitals, and courts (Adler and Johnson 1992).

The initial challenge that Whyte faced—and that every participant observer encounters—was to gain acceptance into an unfamiliar group. It is no simple matter for a university-trained sociologist to win the trust of a religious cult, a youth gang, a poor rural community, or a First Nations group. It requires a great deal of patience and an accepting, nonthreatening type of person.

Observation research poses other complex challenges for the investigator. Sociologists must be able to fully understand what they are observing. In a sense, then, researchers such as William F. Whyte must learn to see the world as the group sees it in order to fully comprehend the events taking place around them.

This raises a delicate issue. If the research is to be successful, the observer cannot allow the close associations or even friendships that inevitably develop to influence the subjects' behaviour or the conclusions of the study. Anson Shupe and David Bromley (1980), two sociologists who have used participant observation, have likened this challenge to that of "walking a tightrope." Even while working hard to gain acceptance from the group being studied, the participant observer *must* maintain some degree of detachment.

Managers may rely on observation research to improve working conditions or productivity. For example, when Norway's shipping industry was faced with severe cutbacks, a team of researchers worked aboard a merchant ship as part of an effort to improve the social organization and efficiency of Norway's fleet. Similarly, when faced with growing competition in the photocopying industry, Xerox Corporation employed a research team to propose cost-cutting measures to managers and union leaders. In each case, the methodology of participant observation proved useful in solving practical problems (W. Whyte 1989).

Use of Secondary Sources

Sociologists do not necessarily have to collect new data in order to conduct research and test hypotheses. The term *secondary analysis* refers to a variety of research techniques that make use of already existing sources, or publicly accessible information and data. In the case study of the effect of family type on children leaving home, the researchers made use of existing data. In conducting secondary source analysis, researchers often utilize data in ways unintended by the initial collectors of information. For example, census data are compiled for specific uses by the government but are valuable for marketing specialists in locating everything from bicycle stores to nursing homes.

Sociologists consider secondary analysis to be *nonreactive*, since it does not influence people's behaviour. As an example, Émile Durkheim's statistical analysis of suicide neither increased nor decreased human self-destruction. Subjects of an experiment or observation research are often aware that they are being watched—an awareness that can influence their behaviour—but this is not the case with secondary analysis. Researchers, then, can avoid the Hawthorne effect by using secondary analysis.

There is one inherent problem, however: the researcher who relies on data collected by someone else may not find exactly what is needed. Social scientists studying family violence can use statistics from police and social service agencies on *reported* cases of spouse abuse and child abuse. Yet such government bodies have no precise data on *all* cases of abuse.

Many social scientists find it useful to study cultural, economic, and political documents, including sources such as newspapers, periodicals, television shows, scripts, diaries, songs, folklore, and legal papers (see Table 2-1 for more examples). In examining these sources, researchers employ a technique known as *content analysis*, which is the systematic coding and objective recording of data from written, aural, or visual materials.

Using content analysis, Erving Goffman conducted a pioneering

This African city in the Ivory Coast provides a rich setting for observation research. An ethnographer would take note of the interaction of Western and African cultures in the everyday life.

Table 2-1	Existing Sources Used in Sociological Research

Most frequently used sources

Statistics Canada

Crime statistics

Birth, death, marriage, and divorce statistics

Other sources

Newspapers and periodicals

Personal journals, diaries, e-mail, and letters

Records and archival material of religious organizations, corporations, and other organizations

Transcripts of radio programs

Videotapes of motion pictures and television programs

Websites

Song lyrics

Scientific records (such as patent applications)

Speeches of public figures (such as politicians)

Votes cast in elections or by elected officials on specific legislative proposals

Attendance records for public events

Videotapes of social protests and rallies

Literature, including folklore

Content analysis of recent films finds this unstated message: smoking is cool. In this still from *Fight Club*, Brad Pitt is shown enjoying his cigarette. If the movie industry is made aware of the extent of smoking in films and the message that it sends to young viewers, perhaps it will try to alter the message.

exploration of how advertisements in 1979 portrayed women as inferior to men. Women typically were shown being subordinate to or dependent on others or being instructed by men. They used caressing and touching gestures more than men. Even when presented in leadership-type roles, women were likely to be shown in seductive poses or gazing out into space. Similarly, researchers today are analyzing films to look at the increase in smoking in motion pictures, despite increased public health concerns. This type of content analysis can have clear social policy implications if it draws the attention of the motion picture industry to the message it may be delivering (especially to young people) that smoking is acceptable, even desirable. For example, a 1999 content analysis found that tobacco use appeared in 89 percent of the 200 most popular movie rentals in the United States (Goffman 1979; Kang 1997; and Roberts et al. 1999).

These examples underscore the value of using existing sources in studying contemporary material. Researchers have learned, in addition, that such analysis can be essential in helping us to understand social behaviour from the distant past. For example, sociologist Karen Barkey (1991) examined village court records from the seventeenth century Ottoman Empire (centred in modern-day Turkey) to assess the extent of peasant rebellions against the empire and, more specifically, its tax policies. Barkey could hardly have relied on surveys, observations, or experiments to study the Ottoman Empire; like other scholars studying earlier civilizations, she turned to secondary analysis.

Ethics of Research

A biochemist cannot inject a serum into a human being unless the serum has been thoroughly tested and the subject agrees to the shot. To do otherwise would be both unethical and illegal. Sociologists must also abide by certain specific standards in conducting research—a *code of ethics*. The professional society of the discipline, the Canadian Sociology and Anthropology Association (CSAA), published a code of ethics in 1994. Below is a short excerpt from the CSAA's *Statement of Professional Ethics*. The complete statement is available online at **http://alcor.concordia.ca/~csaa1/eng/englcode.htm**.

Organizing and initiating research

1. Codes of professional ethics arise from the need to protect vulnerable or subordinate populations from harm incurred, knowingly or unknowingly, by the intervention of researchers into their lives and cultures. Sociologists and anthropologists have a responsibility to respect the rights, and be concerned with the welfare, of all the vulnerable and subordinate populations affected by their work. . .

Protecting people in the research environment

9. Researchers must respect the rights of citizens to privacy, confidentiality and anonymity, and not to be studied. Researchers should make every effort to determine whether those providing information wish to remain anonymous or to receive recognition and then respect their wishes. . .

Informed consent

12. Researchers must not expose respondents to risk of personal harm. Informed consent must be obtained when the risks of research are greater than the risks of everyday life. . .

Covert research and deception

17. Subjects should not be deceived if there is any reasonably anticipated risk to the subjects or if the harm cannot be offset or the extent of the harm be reasonably predicted.

On the surface, these and the rest of the basic principles of the CSAA's *Statement of Professional Ethics* probably seem clear-cut. How could they lead to any disagreement or controversy? However, many delicate ethical questions cannot be resolved simply by reading the *Statement*. For example, should a sociologist engaged in participant-observation research *always* protect the confidentiality of subjects? What if the subjects are members of a religious cult allegedly engaged in unethical and possibly illegal activities? What if the sociologist is interviewing political activists and is questioned by police about his or her research?

Most sociological research uses *people* as sources of information—as respondents to survey questions, subjects of observation, or participants in experiments. In all cases, sociologists need to be certain that they are not invading the privacy of their subjects. Generally, this is handled by assuring those involved of anonymity and by guaranteeing that personal information disclosed will remain confidential. However, a study by William Zellner raised important questions about the extent to which sociologists can threaten people's right to privacy.

Accident or Suicide?

An ethical issue—with the right to know posed against the right to privacy—became apparent in research on automobile accidents in which fatalities occur. Sociologist William Zellner (1978) wanted to learn if fatal car crashes are sometimes suicides that have been disguised as accidents in order to protect family and friends (and perhaps to collect otherwise unredeemable insurance benefits). These acts of "autocide" are by nature covert.

In his efforts to assess the frequency of such suicides, Zellner sought to interview the friends, co-workers, and family members of the deceased. He hoped to obtain information that would allow him to ascertain whether the deaths were accidental or purposeful. Zellner told the people approached for interviews that his goal was to contribute to a reduction of future accidents by learning

Are some people who die in single-occupant car crashes actually suicides? One sociological study of possible "autocides" concluded that at least 12 percent of such accident victims have in fact committed suicide. But the study also raised some ethical questions concerning the right to know and the right to privacy.

about the emotional characteristics of accident victims. He made no mention of his suspicions of autocide, out of fear that potential respondents would refuse to meet with him.

Zellner eventually concluded that at least 12 percent of all fatal single-occupant crashes are suicides. This information could be valuable for society, particularly since some of the probable suicides actually killed or critically injured innocent bystanders in the process of taking their own lives. Yet the ethical questions still must be faced. Was Zellner's research unethical because he misrepresented the motives of his study and failed to obtain his subjects' informed consent? Or was his deception justified by the social value of his findings?

The answers to these questions are not immediately apparent. Zellner appeared to have admirable motives and took great care in protecting confidentiality. He did not reveal names of suspected suicides to insurance companies, though Zellner did recommend that the insurance industry drop double indemnity (payment of twice the person's life insurance benefits in the event of accidental death) in the future.

Zellner's study raised an additional ethical issue: the possibility of harm to those who were interviewed. Subjects were asked if the deceased had "talked about suicide" and if they had spoken of how "bad or useless" they were. Could these questions have led people to guess the true intentions of the researcher? Perhaps, but according to Zellner, none of the informants voiced such suspicions. More seriously, might the study have caused the bereaved to *suspect* suicide—when before the survey they had accepted the deaths as accidental? Again, there is no evidence to suggest this, but we cannot be sure.

Given our uncertainty about this last question, was the research justified? Was Zellner taking too big a risk in asking the friends and families if the deceased victims had spoken of suicide before their deaths? Does the right to know outweigh the right to privacy in this type of situation? And who has the right to make such a judgment? In practice, as in Zellner's study, it is the *researcher,* not the subjects of inquiry, who makes the critical ethical decisions. Therefore, sociologists and other investigators bear the responsibility for establishing clear and sensitive boundaries for ethical scientific investigation.

Preserving Confidentiality

Like journalists, sociologists occasionally find themselves subject to questions from law enforcement authorities or to legal threats because of knowledge they have gained in conducting research and maintaining confidentiality. This situation raises profound ethical questions.

In 1994, Russel Ogden was a graduate student at Simon Fraser University (SFU). In his research, Ogden conducted interviews with people involved in assisted suicide or euthanasia among persons with AIDS. A newspaper report about the study came to the attention of the Vancouver coroner, who was already holding an inquest into the death of an "unknown female." Ogden's thesis reported that two research participants had knowledge about her death. The coroner subpoenaed Ogden to identify his sources, but he cited a promise of "absolute confidentiality" and refused to name them. This promise had been authorized by SFU's Research Ethics Board.

The coroner initially found Ogden to be in contempt of court but later accepted a common law argument that the communications between Ogden and his participants were privileged. In doing so, the coroner released Ogden from "any stain or suggestion of contempt." Ogden's battle in coroner's court was fought without the support of his university. He sued SFU, unsuccessfully, to recover his legal costs. However, the judge condemned SFU for failing to protect academic freedom and urged the university to remedy the situation. SFU's president responded with a written apology to Ogden, compensation for legal costs and lost wages, and a guarantee that the university would assist "any researchers who find themselves in the position of having to challenge a subpoena" (Lowman and Palys 2000).

This case points to the delicate balance researchers and sponsoring institutions must maintain between the value of research, the confidentiality of the subjects, and the threat of litigation. Of these three, the confidentiality of those who agree to participate in research requires priority if the integrity of neutral, incisive social science study is to be maintained.

Neutrality and Politics in Research

The ethical considerations of sociologists lie not only in the methods they use but also in the way they interpret results. Max Weber (1949, original edition 1904) recognized that personal values would influence the questions that sociologists select for research. In his view, that was perfectly acceptable, but under no conditions could a researcher allow his or her personal feelings to influence the *interpretation* of data. In Weber's phrase, sociologists must practise **value neutrality** in their research.

As part of this neutrality, investigators have an ethical obligation to accept research findings even when the data run counter to their own personal views, to theoretically based explanations, or to widely accepted beliefs. For example, Émile Durkheim challenged popular conceptions when he reported that social (rather than supernatural) forces were an important factor in suicide.

p. 11

Some sociologists believe that it is impossible for scholars to prevent their personal values from influencing their work. If that is true, then Weber's insistence on value-free sociology may lead the public to accept sociological conclusions without exploring the biases of the researchers. Furthermore, drawing on the conflict perspective, Alvin Gouldner (1970), among others, has suggested that sociologists may use objectivity as a sacred justification for remaining uncritical of existing institutions and centres of power. These arguments are attacks not so much on Weber himself as on how his goals have been incorrectly interpreted. As we have seen, Weber was quite clear that sociologists may bring values to their subject matter. In his view, however, they must not confuse their own values with the social reality under study (Bendix 1968).

Let's consider what might happen when researchers bring their own biases to the investigation. A person investigating the impact of intercollegiate sports on alumni contributions, for example, may focus only on the highly visible, revenue-generating sports of football and basketball and neglect the so-called "minor sports" such as tennis or soccer that are more likely to involve women athletes. Despite the early work of Dorothy Smith and others, sociologists still need to be reminded that the discipline often fails to consider adequately *all* people's social behaviour.

One of the frequent criticisms levelled against all of the social sciences, but at sociology in particular because of its cultural focus, is that the concepts and theories are not broadly representative. The charge of **Eurocentrism** refers to the fact that the sociological knowledge base has essentially been built to reflect the European standards of its authors.

Sociology has also been accused of **androcentrism**, a tendency to represent the world from a male perspective. Recently, feminist sociologist Shulamit Reinharz (1992) has argued that sociological research should not only be inclusive but should also be open to bringing about social change and drawing on relevant research by nonsociologists. Reinharz maintains that research should always analyze whether women's unequal social status has affected the study in any way.

To avoid Eurocentrism in the study of children leaving home, which we have been using as an example throughout this chapter, one might broaden it to include a cross-cultural perspective. It is possible that, due to tradition, young people growing up in first-generation, immigrant homes in Canada may leave home much later than others in their age cohort. The issue of value neutrality does not mean you can't have opinions, but it does mean you must work to overcome any biases, however unintentional, that you may bring to the research.

Even the most experienced researchers, however, face situations in which their professional resolve is put to the test. In the study of street youth mentioned earlier in this chapter, the field research team encountered tragedy, literally, on every street corner.

One case involved a girl whom the team met on their first night of doing interviews. The 14-year-old had arrived in the large Canadian city only hours earlier, and was already high. Concerned about her vulnerability in this situation, researchers questioned their police liaison officer about possible interventions. The experienced officer told them that there was nothing he could legally do, despite his belief that the girl was now caught in a subculture that would inevitably result in her rapid deterioration. Confirming the researchers' worst fears, the officer was brutal in his assessment of the girl's prospects, suggesting that she would probably be quickly caught up in the drug and sex trade.

The patrolman's insight was borne out in the subsequent months of the study. Encountering the girl time and again, the research team watched as she went from being a typical (though stoned) teenager on that first night, to a hardened, streetwise, and battered shell of her former self when the data-gathering ended just three months later.

These homeless youth in a Toronto tent city represent one of the most difficult populations for researchers to access. The lack of a permanent address hinders most sampling procedures.

The dilemma for the researchers was to fight their instincts to be "good Samaritans" and help the girl. The debriefings after that first night and many subsequent nights included discussions of options, which ranged from having one of the researchers take her home, to finding her a job, to pressuring the government to step in, to going to the media with the story. The consensus was that *something* had to be done. Yet in the end, nothing was. The team concluded, to their professional credit, that if neutrality was to be maintained they could not attempt to assist the girl.

There are two good reasons for their decision. First, and perhaps most important, there is always the potential that intervention by outsiders would put the girl's well-being at risk by marginalizing her within her own social network. Street youth are very distrustful of those who do not belong to their group. Second, if word of the team's intervention had spread among the street youth population, there may have been negative consequences for the validity of the project sample.

Technology and Sociological Research

Advances in technology have affected all aspects of life, and sociological research is no exception. The increased speed and capacity of computers have enabled sociologists to handle much larger sets of data. In the recent past, only people with large grants or major institutional support could easily work with census data. Now anyone with a desktop computer and modem can access information to learn more about social behaviour. Moreover, data from foreign countries concerning crime statistics and health care are just as available as information from our own country.

Researchers usually rely on computers to deal with quantitative data—that is, numerical measures—but electronic technology is also assisting us with qualitative data, such as information obtained in observation research. Numerous software programs such as *Ethnograph* and *NUD*IST* allow the researcher not only to record his or her observations, like a word-processing program, but also to identify common behavioural patterns or similar concerns expressed in interviews. For example, after observing students in a university cafeteria over several weeks and putting your observations into the computer, you could then group all your observations related to certain variables, such as "sorority" or "study group."

The Internet affords an excellent opportunity to communicate with fellow researchers as well as to locate useful information on social issues posted on websites. It would be impossible to calculate all the sociological

postings on Internet mailing lists or World Wide Web sites. Of course, you need to apply the same critical scrutiny to Internet material that you would use on any printed resource.

While the development of the Internet has become invaluable for research purposes, that is not to say that it is not misused. Having easy access to research and papers from around the world has led to an increase in using material without giving credit to its source, or even outright plagiarism. In 2002, headlines were made when a group of Canadian high school students was found to have downloaded material from the Internet and used words without indicating the quoted sections or providing references. The same situation arose in a class on ethics in engineering at Carleton University, resulting in charges of academic fraud to these students. Just as you need to be critical of the quality of Internet material, you must also treat it as you would any other reference material from the library.

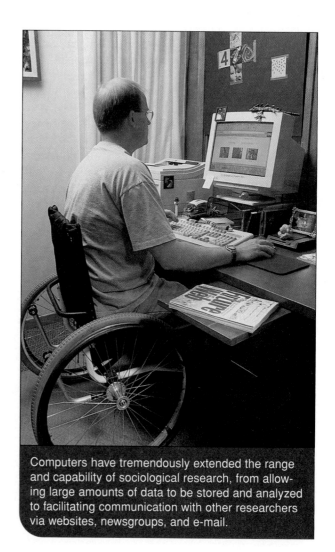

Computers have tremendously extended the range and capability of sociological research, from allowing large amounts of data to be stored and analyzed to facilitating communication with other researchers via websites, newsgroups, and e-mail.

ANGUS REID:
Liu Centre for Studies of Global Issues

Angus Reid is a Senior Fellow at the Liu Centre for the Study of Global Issues at the University of British Columbia. The name "Angus Reid," however, is most often associated with public opinion and market research. After completing his Ph.D. in sociology at Carleton University and teaching at the University of Manitoba, in 1979 he founded Angus Reid Group Inc. In 2000, his Vancouver-based company merged with the French company, Ipsos Group, and became one of North America's largest market research companies with regional offices in cities such as New York, Toronto, San Francisco, Ottawa, Montreal, Calgary, Winnipeg, and St. Louis.

The company conducts research for governments, media organizations, corporations, and public affairs organizations. Some of the company's research includes a global poll on the Palestinian–Israeli conflict, a study of the time European and American youth spend online, a poll of music file-sharing on the Internet, and Canadians' views on capital punishment. Reid stated that the company "provides clients with a broad sociological context, not just data" (Canadian Press Newswire 2000).

As of 2002, Reid began applying his experience in public opinion research around the world in his new position at a university centre dedicated to global issues.

How useful is the Internet for conducting survey research? That's unclear as yet. It is relatively easy to send out or post on an electronic bulletin board a questionnaire and solicit responses. It is an inexpensive way to reach large numbers of potential respondents and get a quick return of responses. However, there are some obvious dilemmas. How do you protect a respondent's anonymity? Second, how do you define the potential audience? Even if you know to whom you sent the questionnaire, the respondents may forward it on to others.

While web-based surveys are still in their early stages, the initial results are promising. For example, InterSurvey has created a pool of Internet respondents, initially selected by telephone to be a diverse and representative sample. Using similar methods to locate 50 000 adult respondents in 33 nations, the National Geographic Society conducted an online survey that focused on migration and regional culture. Social scientists are closely monitoring these new approaches to gauge how they might revolutionize one type of research design (W. Bainbridge 1999; R. Morin 2000).

SOCIAL POLICY AND SOCIOLOGICAL RESEARCH

Studying Human Sexuality

The Issue

Historically, the subject of human sexuality has been viewed as a private issue in Canadian society. It was a topic to be discussed awkwardly by parents and their children, or in hushed tones among friends. But as Canadian culture in particular and the social standards of Western societies in general have undergone a transformation in recent decades, the formerly taboo topic has become public fare. Sex education is a regular part of high-school education, with topics such as birth control being discussed in the classroom. In the media, television has established new, and previously unimaginable boundaries. *Sex and the City* has weekly plot lines focusing on the sexual attitudes and exploits of its young female characters. *Queer as Folk* is a successful television show that explores sexuality in gay and lesbian relations.

You can find similar plots in dozens of TV shows today. Human sexuality is a topic of drama and comedy as well as life. Certainly, it is an important aspect of human behaviour. As we will see, however, it is a difficult topic to research because of all the preconceptions, myths, and beliefs we bring to the topic of sexuality.

Yet, in this age of devastating sexually transmitted diseases, there is no better time to increase our scientific understanding of human sexuality.

The Setting

We have few reliable national data on patterns of sexual behaviour. Until recently, the only comprehensive study of sexual behaviour was the famous two-volume Kinsey Report prepared in the 1940s (Kinsey et al. 1948, 1953). While the Kinsey Report is still widely quoted, the volunteers interviewed for the report were not representative of the adult population. Since then, social scientific studies of sexual behaviour have typically been rather limited in scope but still useful.

In part, we have few reliable data on patterns of sexual behaviour because it is difficult for researchers to obtain accurate information about this sensitive subject. Moreover, until AIDS emerged in the 1980s, there was little scientific demand for data on sexual behaviour, except in specific areas such as contraception. Finally, even though the AIDS crisis has reached dramatic proportions (as will be discussed in the social policy section of Chapter 5), government funding for studies of sexual behaviour is controversial. Ironically, perhaps, given Canadians' history of dwelling in the shadow of their more flamboyant neighbours to the south, the government in Ottawa has never been as reluctant as Washington about funding research on sexual issues. A good example of such government-funded research is found in the General Social Survey data in Figure 2-3.

Sociological Insights

The controversy surrounding research on human sexual behaviour raises the issue of value neutrality. And this becomes especially delicate when one considers the relationship of sociology to the government. The government has become the major source of funding for sociological research. Yet Max Weber urged that sociology remain an autonomous discipline and not become unduly influenced by any one segment of society. According to his ideal of value neutrality, sociologists must remain free to reveal information whether it is embarrassing to government or, for that matter, is supportive of government institutions. Thus, researchers investigating a prison riot must be ready to examine objectively not only the behaviour of inmates but also the conduct of prison officials before and during the outbreak.

Conflict theorists and feminists, among others, are critical of some research that claims to be objective. In

Research into sexual behaviour in Canada is complicated by the sensitivity of the subject.

turn, their research is occasionally criticized for not sufficiently addressing Weber's concern for value neutrality. In any case, maintaining objectivity may be difficult if sociologists fear that findings critical of government or business institutions will jeopardize their chances of obtaining support for new research projects.

The issue of bias associated with research funding approached by the Canadian Sociology and Anthropology Association (in its *Statement of Professional Ethics*) is different from the way it is handled by the American Sociological Association. American researchers are required to reveal funding sources. The American code of ethics, however, does not address whether a sociologist who accepts funding from a particular agency may also accept its perspective on what needs to be studied.

The Canadian code focuses more on the implications of funding affiliations. The Canadian Sociology and Anthropology Association's *Statement of Professional Ethics* says:

> Researchers must guard against the uncritical promotion
> of research, which in design, execution, or results,

FIGURE 2-3

Women Whose First Conjugal Union Was Common-Law Were Nearly Twice as Likely to Separate

	Age in 1995			
Proportion of women separating if	60–69	50–59	40–49	30–39
	Born in			
	1926–1935	1936–1945	1946–1955	1956–1965
Married first	25	30	36	33
Common-law first (including those separated after marrying their partner)	—	77	60	63

— Sample too small to produce reliable estimate.
Source: Statistics Canada 2000e.

furthers the power of states, corporations, churches, or other institutions, over the lives and cultures of research subjects. . . .

and

Researchers should be sensitive to the possible exploitation of individuals and groups. . . .

The Canadian code warns that it is inappropriate for studies to be designed to fit marketing plans or the agenda of some government agency. The implications for research on human sexuality are significant.

Lewis Coser (1956:27) has argued that as sociologists in the United States have increasingly turned from basic sociological research to applied research for government agencies and the private sector, "they have relinquished to a large extent the freedom to choose their own problems, substituting the problems of their clients for those which might have interested them on purely theoretical grounds." Viewed in this light, the importance of government and corporate funding for sociological studies raises troubling questions for those who cherish Weber's ideal of value neutrality in research. As we'll see in the next section, applied sociological research on human sexuality has run into barriers.

Policy Initiatives

Research on sexual behaviours and/or attitudes toward sex have always been met with some skepticism by funding agencies. Governments, perhaps concerned about political fallout, have resisted proposals that address issues in this area. This has been particularly true in the United States. While Canada's reputation as a more conservative society would seem to suggest that the

government in Ottawa would be less willing than that in Washington to sponsor studies of sexuality, the reverse appears to be the case.

The federal government, through its socioeconomic research arm, Statistics Canada, has funded a number of studies of Canadians' sexual activities, including a recent examination of these behaviours in young people and an ongoing series of reports on the age at which Canadians first experience intercourse.

This openness can be taken as an indication of the ability of funding agencies in Canada to remain objective when determining the value of a research proposal. This neutrality provides scientists, particularly social scientists such as sociologists, with the ability to examine trends and phenomena in Canadian society without being constrained by a political agenda.

It is quite a different story in the United States, where researchers have been forced to rely on private, corporate funding for projects such as the one undertaken by sociologists Laumann, Gagnon, Michaels, and Michael, described below. Whether such an alliance could be formed in Canada without contravening the CSAA's standards, which warn against research resulting in the increased power of corporations, is open to debate.

In 1991, the United States Senate voted 66–34 to forbid funding any survey on adult sexual practices. Despite the vote, sociologists Edward Laumann, John Gagnon, Stuart Michaels, and Robert Michael developed the National Health and Social Life Survey (NHSLS) to better understand the sexual practices of adults in the United States. The researchers raised U.S.$1.6 million of *private* funding to make their study possible.

The researchers made great efforts to ensure privacy during the NHSLS interviews, as well as confidentiality of responses and security in maintaining data files. Perhaps because of this careful effort, the interviewers did not typically experience problems even though they were asking people about their sexual behaviour. All interviews were conducted in person, although there was also a confidential form that included questions about such sensitive subjects as family income and masturbation. The researchers used several techniques to test the accuracy of subjects' responses, such as asking redundant questions at different times in different ways during the 90-minute interview. These careful procedures helped establish the validity of the NHSLS findings.

Let's Discuss

1. Why is human sexuality a difficult subject to research? Would you feel comfortable answering questions about your own sex life?
2. How does value neutrality become an important issue in research sponsored by the government?
3. If you were to conduct a survey in your community of people who engage in premarital sex, how would you set it up?

Appendix I

UNDERSTANDING TABLES AND GRAPHS

Tables allow social scientists to summarize data and make it easier for them to develop conclusions. A cross-tabulation is a type of table that illustrates the relationship between two or more characteristics.

During 1999, the Angus Reid Group conducted a survey of Canadians aged 18 and over. Each respondent was asked: "Do you think homosexual couples who wish to marry should or should not qualify for legal recognition of the marriage?" There is no way that, without some type of summary, analysts in the Angus Reid Group could examine the hundreds of individual responses and reach firm conclusions. However, through the use of the cross-tabulation presented in the accompanying table, we can quickly see that older people, and those from the Prairie provinces and Alberta are less likely to favour legal recognition of same-sex marriages.

Graphs, like tables, can be quite useful for sociologists. Illustration A (on page 53) shows a type of pictorial graph that often appears in newspapers and magazines. It documents that in 1996 the United States had more than 12 times the number of personal computers per 1000 people than did Mexico and nearly twice as many as Canada. However, this graph relies on a visual misrepresentation. Through use of two dimensions—length and width—the graph inflates the presence of personal computers in the United States. Although the U.S. "computer" should appear 12 times as large as the Mexican computer, it actually appears much larger. Thus, Illustration A misleads readers about the comparison among the three nations. Illustration B, a bar graph, makes a more accurate comparison.

Attitudes on Legalization of Same-Sex Marriage

Group	Opposed	In favour
Adults in Quebec	36%	61%
Adults in British Columbia	43%	54%
Adults in Ontario	44%	53%
Adults in Atlantic Canada	49%	48%
Adults in Saskatchewan and Manitoba	53%	42%
Adults in Alberta	56%	43%
Ages 18 to 34	32%	66%
Ages 35 to 54	40%	57%
Ages over 54	64%	32%
Females	41%	56%
Males	47%	50%

Source: Ontario Consultants on Religious Tolerance 2001.

PERSONAL COMPUTERS IN CANADA, MEXICO, AND THE UNITED STATES

Illustration A (*misleading*)

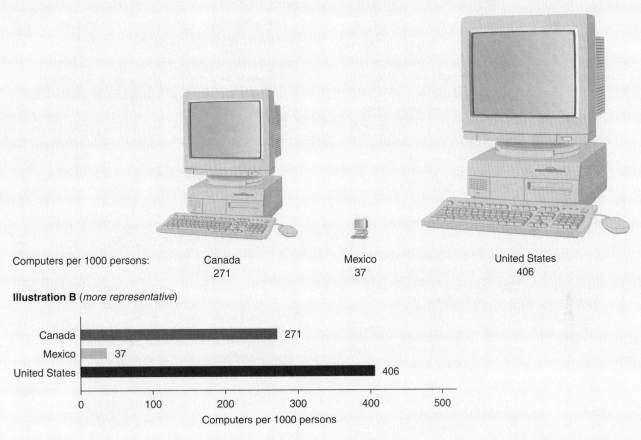

Computers per 1000 persons:

| Canada | Mexico | United States |
| 271 | 37 | 406 |

Illustration B (*more representative*)

Canada 271
Mexico 37
United States 406

0   100   200   300   400   500

Computers per 1000 persons

Source: For data, World Bank 2000:226–227.

Appendix II

WRITING A LIBRARY RESEARCH REPORT

Let's say that you have decided to write a report on cohabitation (unmarried couples living together). How do you go about doing the necessary library research? Students must follow procedures similar to those used by sociologists in conducting original research. First, you must define the problem that you wish to study—perhaps in this case, how much cohabitation occurs and what its impact is on marital happiness later. The next step is to review the literature, which generally requires library research.

The following steps will be helpful in finding information:

1. Check this textbook and other textbooks that you own. Don't forget to begin with the materials closest at hand. At the end of each chapter of this textbook is a listing of books, journals, and electronic sources of information (including CD-ROMs and sites on the Internet and web).

2. Use the library catalog. Most academic libraries now use computerized systems that access not only the library's collection but also books and magazines from other libraries available through interlibrary loans. These systems allow you to search for books by author or title. You can use title searches to locate books by subject as well. For example, if you search the title base for the keyword "cohabitation," you will learn where books with that word somewhere in the title are located in the library's book stacks. Near these books will be other works on cohabitation that may not happen to have that word in the title. You may also want to search other related keywords, such as "unmarried couples."

3. Investigate using computerized periodical indexes if available in your library. *Sociological Abstracts* online covers most sociological writing since 1974. A recent search found more than 420 articles having to do with cohabitation. Some dealt with laws about cohabitation while others focused on trends in other countries. Expanded Academic Index covers general-interest periodicals (*Time, Ms., National Review, Atlantic Monthly,* and so forth) for the most recent four years; it also indexes the *New York Times* for the last six months. These electronic systems may be connected to a printer, allowing you to produce your own printout complete with bibliographic information and sometimes even abstracts of articles.

4. Consult the *Encyclopedia of the Social Sciences,* which concentrates on material of interest to social scientists. Each article includes references for further information.

5. Examine government documents. The Canadian government, provinces and cities, and the United Nations publish information on virtually every subject of interest to social science researchers. Publications of Statistics Canada, for example, include tables showing the number of unmarried couples living together and some social characteristics of these households. Many university libraries have access to a wide range of government reports. Consult the librarian for assistance in locating such materials.

6. Use newspapers. Major newspapers publish indexes annually or even weekly that are useful in locating information about specific events or issues.

7. Ask people, organizations, and agencies concerned with the topic for information and assistance. Be as specific as possible in making requests. You might receive very different information on the issue of cohabitation from talking with marriage counsellors and with clergy from different religions.

8. If you run into difficulties, consult the instructor, teaching assistant, or librarian.

Once you have completed all research, the task of writing the report can begin. Here are a few tips:

- Be sure the topic you have chosen is not too broad. You must be able to cover it adequately in a reasonable amount of time and a reasonable number of pages.
- Develop an outline for your report. You should have an introduction and a conclusion that relate to each other—and the discussion should proceed logically throughout the paper. Use headings within the paper if they will improve clarity and organization.
- Do not leave all the writing until the last minute. It is best to write a rough draft, let it sit for a few days, and then take a fresh look before beginning revisions.
- If possible, read your paper *aloud.* Doing so may be helpful in locating sections or phrases that don't make sense.

Remember that you *must* cite all information you have obtained from other sources. If you use an author's exact words, it is essential that they be placed in quotation marks. Even if you reworked someone else's ideas, you must indicate the source of these ideas.

Some professors may require that students use footnotes in research reports. Others will allow students to employ the form of referencing used in this textbook, which follows the format of the Canadian Sociology and Anthropology Association. If you see "(Merton 1968:27)" listed after a statement or paragraph, it means that the material has been adapted from page 27 of a work published by Merton in 1968 and listed in the reference section at the back of this textbook.

● Chapter Resources

Summary

Sociologists are committed to the use of the scientific method in their research efforts. In this chapter, we examine the basic principles of the scientific method and study various techniques used by sociologists in conducting research.

1. There are seven basic steps in the *scientific method*: defining the problem, reviewing the literature, formulating the hypothesis, selecting the research design, collecting data and analyzing it, and then developing the conclusion.

2. Whenever researchers wish to study abstract concepts, such as intelligence or prejudice, they must develop workable *operational definitions*.

3. A *hypothesis* usually states a possible relationship between two or more variables.

4. By using sampling techniques, sociologists avoid having to test everyone in a population.
5. According to the scientific method, research results must possess both *validity* and *reliability*.
6. The two principal forms of *survey* research are the *interview* and the *questionnaire*.
7. When sociologists wish to study a cause-and-effect relationship, they may conduct an *experiment*.
8. *Observation* allows sociologists to study certain behaviours and communities that cannot be investigated through other research methods.
9. Sociologists also make use of existing sources in *secondary analysis* and *content analysis*.
10. The Canadian Sociology and Anthropology Association (CSAA) *Statement of Professional*

Ethics calls for objectivity and integrity in research, respect for the subject's privacy, and confidentiality.
11. Max Weber urged sociologists to practise *value neutrality* in their research by ensuring that their personal feelings do not influence the interpretation of data.
12. Technology today plays an important role in sociological research, whether it be a computer database or information from the Internet.
13. The increased involvement of corporations in funding university-based research has made it more difficult to maintain objectivity.

Critical Thinking Questions

1. Suppose that your sociology instructor has asked you to do a study of homelessness. Which research technique (survey, observation, experiment, existing sources) would you find most useful? How would you use that technique to complete your assignment?

2. How can a sociologist genuinely maintain value neutrality while studying a group that he or she finds repugnant (for example, a white supremacist organization, a satanic cult, or a group of prison inmates convicted of rape)?
3. Why is it important for sociologists to have a code of ethics?

Key Terms

Androcentrism   A world view that favours the male perspective. (47)
Causal logic   The relationship between a condition or variable and a particular consequence, with one event leading to the other. (36)
Code of ethics   The standards of acceptable behaviour developed by and for members of a profession. (44)
Content analysis   The systematic coding and objective recording of data, from written, aural, or visual materials. (43)
Control group   Subjects in an experiment who are not introduced to the independent variable by the researcher. (40)
Control variable   A factor held constant to test the relative impact of an independent variable. (36)
Correlation   A relationship between two variables whereby a change in one coincides with a change in the other. (36)
Dependent variable   The variable in a causal relationship that is subject to the influence of another variable. (35)

Ethnography   The study of an entire social setting through extended systematic observation. (42)
Eurocentrism   A world view that assumes European values are the desired standard. (47)
Experiment   The measurement of cause and effect in a controlled environment. (37)
Experimental group   Subjects in an experiment who are exposed to an independent variable introduced by a researcher. (40)
Hawthorne effect   The unintended influence that observers or experiments can have on their subjects. (42)
Hypothesis   A speculative statement about the relationship between two or more variables. (35)
Independent variable   The variable in a causal relationship that, when altered, causes or influences a change in a second variable. (35)
Interview   A face-to-face or telephone questioning of a respondent to obtain desired information. (40)
Observation   Recording of events and impressions in a real-life social situation. (37)

Operational definition An explanation of an abstract concept that is specific enough to allow a researcher to measure the concept. (35)

Qualitative research Research that relies on what is seen in field or naturalistic settings more than on statistical data. (33)

Quantitative research Research that collects, measures, and reports data primarily in numerical form. (33)

Questionnaire A research instrument employed to obtain desired information from a respondent. (40)

Random sample A sample for which every member of the entire population has the same chance of being selected. (36)

Reliability The extent to which a measure provides consistent results. (39)

Representative sample A selection from a larger population that is statistically typical of that population. (36)

Scientific method A systematic, organized series of steps that ensures maximum objectivity and consistency in researching a problem. (33)

Secondary analysis A variety of research techniques that make use of publicly accessible information and data. (43)

Survey A study, generally in the form of interviews or questionnaires, that provides sociologists and other researchers with information concerning how people think and act. (40)

Survey research The gathering of data by directly questioning members of the population being studied. (37)

Using secondary sources A method of data collection that involves the use of already existing data collected by others, qualitatively reinterpreting data or viewing it in a larger context. (38)

Validity The degree to which a scale or measure truly reflects the phenomenon under study. (39)

Value neutrality Objectivity of sociologists in the interpretation of data. (46)

Variable A measurable trait or characteristic that is subject to change under different conditions. (35)

Additional Readings

Canadian Sociology and Anthropology Association. *Canadian Review of Sociology and Anthropology.* Montreal: CSAA. Since its inception in 1964, the *Review* has provided peer-reviewed articles and critiques on topics of sociology and anthropology. This journal provides an excellent scholarly source for research about social issues in Canada.

Denzin, Norman K., and Yvonna S. Lincoln, eds. 2000. *Handbook of Qualitative Research.* 2nd ed. Thousand Oaks, CA: Sage. The 40 articles in this anthology cover newer techniques used in conducting observation and biographical research, as well as ethical issues facing researchers.

Ericksen, Julia A. 1999. *Kiss and Tell: Surveying Sex in the Twentieth Century.* Cambridge, MA: Harvard University Press. Evaluates the methodology of the hundreds of surveys of human sexuality conducted by sociologists and other social scientists.

Kirby, Sandra L., and Kate McKenna. 1989. *Experience Research Social Change: Methods from the Margins.* Toronto: Garamond Press. This book is intended as a how-to guide, and shows that people can be treated as 'subjects' rather than 'objects' through every stage of the research process.

JOURNALS

Among the journals that focus on methods of sociological and other social scientific research are the following: *Irb: A Review of Human Subjects Research* (founded in 1979), *Journal of Contemporary Ethnography* (1971), *Qualitative Research* (1977), *Sociological Methods and Research* (1972), *Sociological Methodology* (1954), and *Sociological Inquiry* (1930).

Many sociological journals are now available on the Internet, but one specific journal on research is available only online. You can locate *Sociological Research Online* at **http://www.socresonline.org.uk/socresonline/**.

Internet Connection

www.mcgrawhill.ca/college/schaefer

For additional Internet exercises relating to content analysis and codes of ethics, visit the Schaefer Online Learning Centre at **http://www.mcgrawhill.ca/college/schaefer**. *Please note that while the URLs listed were current at the time of printing, these sites often change—check the Online Learning Centre for updates.*

A variety of websites offer compilations of Canadian research sources available on the Internet. One of the best can be found at **http://www.canadiansocialresearch.net**. This site provides access to hundreds of data sources including those from both government and non-government organizations, as well as the corporate world. By looking for answers to the following questions on any particular site you find linked there, you can gain a working familiarity with the site's potential. All of the following information can be found through the site's links.

(a) Find the official site for your home province. Which ministry is responsible for post-secondary education?

(b) What programs assist disabled persons in Manitoba to achieve independent living?

(c) Find an electronic meeting place designed specifically to meet the needs of needs of Aboriginal youth. How is this site being used? What issues are being raised by the contributors?

(d) The Canadian Council on Social Development claims that the 2001 federal budget fell short of achieving its goal to "help Canadians through difficult times." What argument is presented to support that claim?

(e) See if your community has an official website. Does it have information about social programs?

(f) What is the mandate of the International Council of Canadian Studies?

PART TWO

ORGANIZING SOCIAL LIFE

ociologist Peter Berger (1963:18–19) once observed that the "sociologist is a person intensively, endlessly, shamelessly interested" in the doings of people. In Part Two, we begin our study of the organization of social life within human communities and societies.

Chapter 3 examines the basic element of any society: its culture. It considers the development of culture, cultural universals, and variations among cultures. Chapter 4 presents the lifelong socialization process through which we acquire culture and are introduced to social structure. Chapter 5 examines social interaction and the major aspects of social structure: statuses, roles, groups, and institutions. Chapter 6 focuses on the impact of groups and organizations on social behaviour. Chapter 7 examines attempts to enforce acceptance of social norms, as well as behaviour that violates norms.

CULTURE

One of many comic book stalls that line the streets near a railroad station in Bombay, India. At first glance, the comic books may look different from those in North America, but closer inspection reveals some common themes—adventure, romance, beauty, and crime.

Nacirema culture is characterized by a highly developed market economy which has evolved in a rich natural habitat. While much of the people's time is devoted to economic pursuits, a large part of the fruits of these labors and a considerable portion of the day are spent in ritual activity. The focus of this activity is the human body, the appearance and health of which loom as a dominant concern in the ethos of the people. While such concern is certainly not unusual, its ceremonial aspects and associated philosophy are unique.

The fundamental belief underlying the whole system appears to be that the human body is ugly and that its natural tendency is to debility and disease. Incarcerated in such a body, man's only hope is to avert these characteristics through the use of the powerful influences of ritual and ceremony. Every household has one or more shrines devoted to this purpose. The more powerful individuals in this society have several shrines in their houses, and, in fact, the opulence of a house is often referred to in terms of the number of such ritual centers it possesses. . . .

While each family has at least one such shrine, the rituals associated with it are not family ceremonies but are private and secret. The rites are normally only discussed with children, and then only during the period when they are being initiated into these mysteries. I was able, however, to establish sufficient rapport with the natives to examine these shrines and to have the rituals described to me.

The focal point of the shrine is a box or chest which is built into the wall. In this chest are kept the many charms and magical potions without which no native believes he could live. These preparations are secured from a variety of specialized practitioners. The most powerful of these are the medicine men, whose assistance must be rewarded with substantial gifts. However, the medicine men do not provide the curative potions for their clients, but decide what the ingredients should be and then write them down in an ancient and secret language. This writing is understood only by the medicine men and by the herbalists who, for another gift, provide the required charm. *(Miner 1956)* ■

nthropologist Horace Miner cast his observant eyes on the intriguing behaviour of the Nacirema. If we look a bit closer, however, some aspects of this culture may seem familiar, for what Miner is describing is actually the culture of the United States ("Nacirema" is "American" spelled backward). The "shrine" is the bathroom, and we are correctly informed that in this culture a measure of wealth is often how many bathrooms are in one's house. The bathroom rituals make use of charms and magical potions (beauty products and prescription drugs) obtained from specialized practitioners (such as hairstylists), herbalists (pharmacists), and medicine men (physicians). Using our sociological imagination we could update the Nacirema "shrine" by describing blow-dryers, mint-flavoured dental floss, Water Piks, and hair gel.

We begin to appreciate how to understand behaviour when we step back and examine it thoughtfully, objectively—whether it is "Nacirema" culture or another one. Take the case of Fiji, an island in the Pacific. A recent study showed that for the first time eating disorders were showing up among the young people there. This was a society where, traditionally, "you've gained weight" was a compliment and "your legs are skinny" was a major insult. Having a robust, nicely rounded body was the expectation for both men and women. What happened to change this cultural ideal? With the introduction of cable television in 1995, many Fiji islanders, especially girls, have come to want to look like the thin-waisted stars of American television shows like *Ally McBeal* and *Friends*, rather than their own full-bodied mothers and aunts. By understanding life in Fiji, we can also come to understand our own society much better (Becker 1995; Becker and Burwell 1999).

The study of culture is basic to sociology. In this chapter we will examine the meaning of culture and society as well as the development of culture from its roots in the prehistoric human experience to the technological advances of today. The major aspects of culture—including language, norms, sanctions, and

values—will be defined and explored. We will see how cultures develop a dominant ideology, and how functionalist and conflict theorists view culture. The discussion will focus both on general cultural practices found in all societies and on the wide variations that can distinguish one society from another. The social policy section will look at the conflicts in cultural values that underlie current debates about multiculturalism. ■

The children in this Indonesian village are drawn to the house with the television. What effect do you think watching *Friends* would have on them? Using our sociological imagination to look at the influence of television on other cultures can help us to understand TV's impact on our own culture.

Culture and Society

Culture is the totality of learned, socially transmitted customs, knowledge, material objects, and behaviour. It includes the ideas, values, customs, and artifacts (for example, CDs, comic books, and birth control devices) of groups of people. Patriotic attachment to the game of hockey in Canada is an aspect of culture, as is national addiction to the tango in Argentina.

Sometimes people refer to a particular person as "very cultured" or to a city as having "lots of culture." That use of the term *culture* is different from our use in this textbook. In sociological terms, *culture* does not refer solely to the fine arts and refined intellectual taste. It consists of all objects and ideas within a society, including ice cream cones, rock music, and slang words. Sociologists consider both a portrait by Rembrandt and a portrait by a billboard painter to be aspects of a culture. A tribe that cultivates soil by hand has just as much of a culture as a people that relies on computer-operated machinery. Each people has a distinctive culture with its own characteristic ways of gathering and preparing food, constructing homes, structuring the family, and promoting standards of right and wrong.

Sharing a similar culture helps to define the group or society to which we belong. A fairly large number of people are said to constitute a **society** when they live in the same territory, are relatively independent of people outside their area, and participate in a common culture. Mexico City is more populous than many nations of the world, yet sociologists do not consider it a society in its own right. Rather, it is seen as part of—and dependent on—the larger society of Mexico.

A society is the largest form of human group. It consists of people who share a common heritage and culture. Members of the society learn this culture and transmit it from one generation to the next. They even preserve their distinctive culture through literature, art, video recordings, and other means of expression. If it were not for the social transmission of culture, each generation would have to reinvent television, not to mention the wheel.

Having a common culture also simplifies many day-to-day interactions. For example, when you buy an airline ticket, you know you don't have to bring along hundreds of dollars in cash. You can pay with a credit card. When you are part of a society, there are many small (as well as more important) cultural patterns that you take for granted. You assume that theatres will provide seats for the audience, that physicians will not disclose confidential information, and that parents will be careful when crossing the street with young children. All these assumptions reflect the basic values, beliefs, and customs of the culture of Canada.

Language is a critical element of culture that sets humans apart from other species. Members of a society generally share a common language, which facilitates day-to-day exchanges with others. When you ask a hardware store clerk for a flashlight, you don't need to draw a picture of the instrument. You share the same cultural term for a small, battery-operated, portable light. However, if you were in England and needed this item, you would have to ask for an "electric torch." Of course, even within the same society, a term can have a number of different meanings. In Canada, *grass* signifies both a plant eaten by grazing animals and an intoxicating drug.

Development of Culture Around the World

We've come a long way from our prehistoric heritage. As we begin a new millennium, we can transmit an entire book around the world via the Internet, we can clone cells, and we can prolong lives through organ transplants. The human species has produced such achievements as the ragtime compositions of Scott Joplin, the poetry of Emily Dickinson, the paintings of Vincent Van Gogh, the novels of Jane Austen, and the films of Akira Kurosawa. We can peer into the outermost reaches of the universe, and we can analyze our innermost feelings. In all these ways, we are remarkably different from other species of the animal kingdom.

The process of expanding culture has been underway for thousands of years. The first archaeological evidence of humanlike primates places our ancestors back many millions of years. About 700 000 years ago, people built hearths to harness fire. Archaeologists have uncovered tools that date back about 100 000 years. From 35 000 years ago we have evidence of paintings, jewellery, and statues. By that time, marriages, births, and deaths had already developed elaborate ceremonies (Harris 1997; Haviland 1999).

Tracing the development of culture is not easy. Archaeologists cannot "dig up" weddings, laws, or governments, but they are able to locate items that point to the emergence of cultural traditions. Our early ancestors were primates that had characteristics of human beings. These curious and communicative creatures made important advances in the use of tools. Recent studies of chimpanzees in the wild have revealed that they frequently use sticks and other natural objects in ways learned from other members of the group. However, unlike chimpanzees, our ancestors gradually made tools from increasingly durable materials. As a result, the items could be reused and refined into more effective implements.

Cultural Universals

Despite their differences, all societies have developed certain common practices and beliefs, known as **cultural universals**. Many cultural universals are, in fact, adaptations to meet essential human needs, such as people's need for food, shelter, and clothing. Anthropologist George Murdock (1945:124) compiled a list of cultural universals. Some of these include athletic sports, cooking, funeral ceremonies, medicine, and sexual restrictions.

The cultural practices listed by Murdock may be universal, but the manner in which they are expressed varies from culture to culture. For example, one society may let its members choose their own marriage partners. Another may encourage marriages arranged by the parents.

Sports are a cultural universal, but the variety of expression is endless. Shown here: traditional Japanese archery, and camel racing in Saudi Arabia.

Not only does the expression of cultural universals vary from one society to another, but it also may change dramatically over time within a society. Thus, the most popular styles of dancing in North America today are sure to be different from the styles dominant in the 1950s or the 1970s. Each generation, and each year for that matter, most human cultures change and expand through the processes of innovation and diffusion.

Innovation

The process of introducing an idea or object that is new to a culture is known as *innovation*. Innovation interests sociologists because of the social consequences that introducing something new can have in any society. There are two forms of innovation: discovery and invention. A *discovery* involves making known or sharing the existence of an aspect of reality. The finding of the DNA molecule and the identification of a new moon of Saturn are both acts of discovery. A significant factor in the process of discovery is the sharing of new-found knowledge with others. By contrast, an *invention* results when existing cultural items are combined into a form that did not exist before. The bow and arrow, the automobile, and the television are all examples of inventions, as are Protestantism and democracy.

Diffusion and Technology

You don't have to sample gourmet food to eat "foreign" foods. Breakfast cereal originally comes from Germany, candy from the Netherlands, and chewing gum from Mexico. The United States has also "exported" foods to other lands. Residents of many nations enjoy pizza, which was popularized in the United States. However, in Japan they add squid, in Australia it is eaten with pineapple, and in England people like kernels of corn with the cheese.

Just as a culture does not always discover or invent its foods, it may also adopt ideas, technology, and customs from other cultures. Sociologists use the term *diffusion* to refer to the process by which a cultural item is spread from group to group or society to society. Diffusion can occur through a variety of means, among them exploration, military conquest, missionary work, the influence of the mass media, tourism, and the Internet.

Early in human history, culture changed rather slowly through discovery. Then, as the number of discoveries in a culture increased, inventions became possible. The more inventions there were, the more rapidly additional inventions could be created. In addition, as diverse cultures came into contact with one another, they could each take advantage of the other's innovations. Thus, when people in Canada read a newspaper, we look at characters invented by the ancient Semites, printed by a process invented in Germany, on a material invented in China (Linton 1936).

Today the world seems a very small place when we consider the cultural diffusion that has occurred. People in diverse countries have contact with each other more than ever before, partly due to technological advances. Some even suggest that globalization has produced a global cultural link because of the movement of goods, information, and people around the world (Featherstone 1990). The global economy allows for the flow of goods through international trade that is greater than ever. Marshall McLuhan's concept of a "global village" in the 1960s was just the tip of the iceberg when compared to the flow of information through our current global satellite-based communication. People are moving around the globe, whether for travel purposes, to study abroad, or to relocate for business purposes. These changes in behaviour and knowledge have a large impact on cultural diffusion as new ideas, products, and ways of living are crossing borders and oceans daily. However, the flow of goods, information, and people has not been even—those with greater economic and political power also have greater influence over cultural diffusion.

Nations tend to feel a loss of identity when they accept culture from outside. Countries throughout the world decry American exports, from films to language to Bart Simpson. Movies produced in the United States account for 65 percent of the global box office. Magazines as diverse as *Cosmopolitan* and *Reader's Digest* sell two issues abroad for every one they sell in the United States. *The X-Files* airs in 60 countries. These examples of canned culture all facilitate the diffusion of cultural practices (Farhi and Rosenfeld 1998).

Many societies try to protect themselves from the invasion of too much culture from other countries, especially the economically dominant United States. The Canadian government, for example, requires that 35 percent of a station's daytime radio programming be Canadian songs or artists (see Figure 3-1). In Brazil, a toy manufacturer has eclipsed Barbie's popularity by designing a doll named Susi that looks more like Brazilian girls. Susi has a slightly smaller chest, much wider thighs, and darker skin than Barbie. Her wardrobe includes the skimpy bikinis favoured on Brazilian beaches as well as a soccer shirt honouring the Brazilian team. According to the toy company's marketing director, "we wanted Susi to be more Latin, more voluptuous. We Latins appreciate those attributes." Brazilians seem to agree: Before Christmas in 1999, five Susi dolls were sold for every two Barbies (DePalma 1999; Downie 2000).

Technology in its many forms has now increased the speed by which aspects of culture are shared and has broadened the distribution of cultural elements. Sociologist Gerhard Lenski has defined **technology** as "information about how to use the material resources of the environment to satisfy human needs and desires" (Nolan and Lenski 1999:41). Today's technological developments no longer have to await publication in journals with limited circulation. Press conferences, often simultaneously carried on the Internet, now trumpet new developments.

Technology not only accelerates the diffusion of scientific innovations but also transmits culture. Later, in Chapter 20, we will discuss the concern in many parts of the world that the English language and North American culture dominate the Internet and World Wide Web. Control, or at least dominance, of technology influences the direction of diffusion of culture. Websites abound with the most superficial aspects of Canadian and American culture but little information about the pressing issues faced by citizens of other nations. People all over the world find it easier to visit electronic chat rooms about daytime television soaps like *All My Children* than to learn about their own government's policies on daycare or infant nutrition programs.

Sociologist William F. Ogburn (1922) made a useful distinction between the elements of material and nonmaterial culture. **Material culture** refers to the tangible physical or technological aspects of our daily lives, including food items, houses, factories, and raw

---

FIGURE 3-1

What Is Canadian?

Canadians try to ward off American influence by controlling what is played on the radio. The government requires that 35 percent of a station's programming in the daytime be Canadian. But what is Canadian? A complicated set of rules gives points based on whether the artist, the composer, the lyricist, or the production is Canadian. A song that earns two points meets the government requirements. Canadian Céline Dion singing "My Heart Will Go On" would not be classified as Canadian.

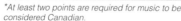

Céline Dion		Lenny Kravitz
Canadian	**Nationality**	Not Canadian
"My Heart Will Go On"	**Song**	"American Woman"
Not Canadian	**Lyricist**	Canadian
Not Canadian	**Composer**	Canadian
1 point*		2 points*

*At least two points are required for music to be considered Canadian.

Source: DePalma 1999.

materials. ***Nonmaterial culture*** refers to ways of using material objects and to customs, beliefs, philosophies, governments, and patterns of communication. Generally, the nonmaterial culture is more resistant to change than the material culture. Consequently, Ogburn introduced the term ***culture lag*** to refer to the period of maladjustment when the nonmaterial culture is still adapting to new material conditions. For example, the ethics of using the Internet, particularly privacy and censorship issues, have not yet caught up with the explosion in Internet use and technology. Technology has a globalizing effect as diverse cultures become interconnected through the material and nonmaterial elements of its use. Technological applications such as the Internet provide a shared element of material culture, while the behaviours employed and attitudes acquired while participating in an online chat room contribute to shared nonmaterial culture.

Diffusion can involve a single word like "cyber" or an entirely new orientation toward living, which may be transmitted through advances in electronic communication. Sociologist George Ritzer (1995b) coined the term "McDonaldization of society" to describe how the principles of fast-food restaurants developed in the United States have come to dominate more and more sectors of societies throughout the world. For example, hair salons and medical clinics now take walk-in appointments. In Hong Kong, sex selection clinics offer a menu of items—from fertility enhancement to methods of increasing the likelihood of producing a child of the desired sex. Religious groups—from evangelical preachers on local stations or websites to priests at the Vatican Television Center—use marketing techniques similar to those that sell "happy meals."

McDonaldization is associated with the melding of cultures, so that we see more and more similarities in cultural expression. In Japan, for example, African entrepreneurs have found a thriving market for hip-hop fashions popularized by teens in the United States. In Austria, the McDonald's organization itself has drawn on the Austrians' love of coffee, cake, and conversation to create the McCafe as part of its fast-food chain. Many observers believe that McDonaldization and the use of technology to spread elements of culture through diffusion both serve to dilute the distinctive aspects of a society's culture (Alfino et al. 1998; T. Clark 1994; Ritzer 1995b; Rocks

1999). (Cultural diffusion via the media is discussed in more detail in Chapter 4.)

Elements of Culture

Each culture considers its own distinctive ways of handling basic societal tasks as "natural." But, in fact, methods of education, marital ceremonies, religious doctrines, and other aspects of culture are learned and transmitted through human interactions within specific societies. Parents in India are accustomed to arranging marriages for their children, whereas most parents in Canada leave marital decisions up to their offspring. Lifelong residents of Naples consider it natural to speak Italian, whereas lifelong residents of Buenos Aires feel the same way about Spanish. We'll now take a look at the major aspects of culture that shape the way the members of a society live—language, norms, sanctions, and values.

Language

The English language makes extensive use of words dealing with war. We speak of "conquering" space, "fighting" the "battle" of the bulge, "waging a war" on drugs, making a "killing" on the stock market, and "bombing" an examination; something monumental or great is "the bomb." An observer from an entirely different and warless culture could gauge the importance that war and the military have had on our lives simply by recognizing the prominence that militaristic terms have in our language.

It's back to the classroom for these business executives. Conducting business overseas in today's global economy requires language skills.

In the old West, words such as *gelding, stallion, mare, piebald,* and *sorrel* were all used to describe one animal—the horse. Even if we knew little of this period of history, we could conclude from the list of terms that horses were quite important in this culture. The Slave First Nations people, who live in the Northwest Territories, have 14 terms to describe ice, including eight for different kinds of "solid ice" and others for "seamed ice," "cracked ice," and "floating ice." Clearly, language reflects the priorities of a culture (Basso 1972; Haviland 1999).

Language is, in fact, the foundation of every culture. **Language** is an abstract system of word meanings and symbols for all aspects of culture. It includes speech, written characters, numerals, symbols, and gestures and expressions of nonverbal communication. Figure 3-2 shows where the major languages of the world are spoken.

Language is not an exclusively human attribute. Although they are incapable of human speech, primates such as chimpanzees have been able to use symbols to communicate. However, even at their most advanced level, animals operate with essentially a fixed set of signs with fixed meanings. By contrast, humans can manipulate symbols in order to express abstract concepts and rules and to transmit culture to the next generation.

Unlike some other elements of culture, language permeates all parts of society. Certain cultural skills, such as cooking or carpentry, can be learned without the use of language through the process of imitation. However, is it possible to transmit complex legal and religious systems to the next generation simply by observing how they are performed? You could put on a black robe and sit behind a bench as a judge does, but would you ever be able to understand legal reasoning without language? People invariably depend on language for the use and transmission of the rest of a culture.

While language is a cultural universal, striking differences in the use of language are evident around the world. This is the case even when two countries use the same spoken language. For example, an English-speaking person from Canada who is visiting London may be puzzled the first time an English friend says "I'll ring you up." The friend means "I'll call you on the telephone." Similarly, the meanings of nonverbal gestures vary from one culture to another. Whereas residents of North America attach positive meanings to the commonly used "thumbs up" gesture, this gesture has only vulgar connotations in Greece (Ekman et al. 1984).

Sapir–Whorf Hypothesis

Language does more than simply describe reality; it also serves to *shape* the reality of a culture. For example, most people in the southern parts of Canada cannot easily make the verbal distinctions about ice that are possible in the Slave First Nations culture. As a result, they are less likely to notice such differences.

The **Sapir–Whorf hypothesis**, named for two linguists, describes the role of language in interpreting our world. According to Sapir and Whorf, since people can conceptualize the world only through language, language *precedes* thought. Thus, the word symbols and grammar of a language organize the world for us. The Sapir–Whorf hypothesis also holds that language is not a "given." Rather, it is culturally determined and leads to different interpretations of reality by focusing our attention on certain phenomena.

In a literal sense, language may colour how we see the world. Berlin and Kay (1991) have noted that humans possess the physical ability to make millions of colour distinctions, yet languages differ in the number of colours that are recognized. The English language distinguishes between yellow and orange, but some other languages do not. In the Dugum Dani language of New Guinea's West Highlands, there are only two basic colour terms—*modla* for "white" and *mili* for "black." By contrast, there are 11 basic terms in English. Russian and Hungarian, though, have 12 colour terms. Russians have terms for light blue and dark blue, while Hungarians have terms for two different shades of red.

If language precedes thought as the Sapir–Whorf hypothesis describes, does it then create our reality? Many sociologists find that the hypothesis overemphasizes the relationships between language, thought, and behaviour. They agree that our values and beliefs are expressed through words, and language can influence our behaviour and understanding of reality, but it does not *determine* it.

For example, gender-related language can reflect—although in itself it will not determine—the traditional acceptance of men and women in certain occupations. Each time we use a term such as *mailman, policeman,* or *fireman,* we are implying (especially to young children) that these occupations can be filled only by males. Yet many women work as *letter carriers, police officers,* and *firefighters*—a fact that is being increasingly recognized and legitimized through the use of such nonsexist language (Henley et al. 1985; Eichler 1988).

Language can also transmit stereotypes related to race. Look up the meanings of the adjective *black* in dictionaries published in the United States. You will find *dismal, gloomy* or *forbidding, destitute of moral light or goodness, atrocious, evil, threatening, clouded with anger.* By contrast, dictionaries list *pure* and *innocent* among the meanings of the adjective *white.* Through such patterns of language, our culture reinforces positive associations with the term (and skin colour) *white* and negative associations with *black.* Is it surprising, then, that a list preventing people from working in a profession is called

FIGURE 3-2

Languages of the World

Mapping Life WORLDWIDE

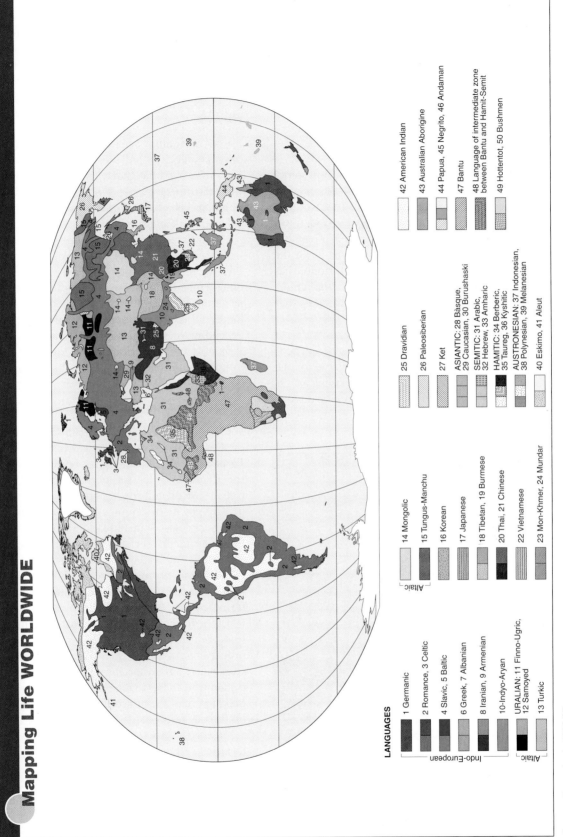

Source: Espenshade 1990:25.

a *blacklist,* while a lie that we think of as somewhat acceptable is called a *white lie?*

Language can shape how we see, taste, smell, feel, and hear. It also influences the way we think about the people, ideas, and objects around us. Language communicates a culture's most important norms, values, and sanctions to people. That's why the introduction of a new language into a society is such a sensitive issue in many parts of the world.

Nonverbal Communication

You know the appropriate distance to stand from someone when you talk informally. You know the circumstances under which it is appropriate to touch others, with a pat on the back or by taking someone's hand. If you are in the midst of a friendly meeting and one member suddenly sits back, folds his arms, and turns down the corners of his mouth, you know at once that trouble has arrived. These are all examples of *nonverbal communication,* the use of gestures, facial expressions, and other visual images to communicate.

We are not born with these expressions. We learn them, just as we learn other forms of language, from people who share our same culture. This is as true for the basic expressions of smiling, laughter, and crying as it is for more complex emotions such as shame or distress (Fridlund et al. 1987).

Nonverbal communication can take many forms. The Canadian flag at half mast in Niagara after September 11, 2001, symbolized respect and grief for those who lost their lives in the terrorist attacks.

Like other forms of language, nonverbal communication is not the same in all cultures. For example, sociological research at the micro level documents that people from various cultures differ in the degree to which they touch others during the course of normal social interaction.

Norms

"Wash your hands before dinner." "Thou shalt not kill." "Respect your elders." All societies have ways of encouraging and enforcing what they view as appropriate behaviour while discouraging and punishing what they consider to be improper behaviour. *Norms* are established standards of behaviour maintained by a society.

In order for a norm to become significant, it must be widely shared and understood. For example, in movie theatres in Canada, we typically expect that people will be quiet while the film is shown. Because of this norm, an usher can tell a member of the audience to stop talking so loudly. Of course, the application of this norm can vary, depending on the particular film and type of audience. People attending a serious artistic film will be more likely to insist on the norm of silence than those attending a slapstick comedy or horror movie.

Types of Norms

Sociologists distinguish between norms in two ways. First, norms are classified as either formal or informal. *Formal norms* generally have been written down and specify strict rules for punishment of violators. In Canada, we often formalize norms into laws, which must be very precise in defining proper and improper behaviour. Sociologist Donald Black (1995) has termed *law* to be "governmental social control," establishing laws as formal norms enforced by the state. Laws are just one example of formal norms. The requirements for a university major and the rules of a card game are also considered formal norms.

By contrast, *informal norms* are generally understood but they are not precisely recorded. Standards of proper dress are a common example of informal norms. Our society has no specific punishment or sanction for a person who comes to school, say, wearing a monkey suit. Making fun of the nonconforming student is usually the most likely response.

Norms are also classified by their relative importance to society. When classified in this way, they are known as *mores* and *folkways.*

Mores (pronounced "mor-ays") are norms deemed highly necessary to the welfare of a society, often because they embody the most cherished principles of a people. Each society demands obedience to its mores; violation

MARYLEE STEPHENSON:
Founder and President, CS/RESORS Consulting

Marylee Stephenson holds ultimate responsibility for the organization, management, and quality of all work undertaken in her socioeconomic research company, CS/RESORS Consulting. Stephenson manages the company, collaborating with senior associates in Ottawa, Montreal, and Vancouver, as well as those associates who are brought onto the team for projects in other parts of Canada.

Stephenson brings a strong academic background to her research work. Her education includes an M.A. in sociology from the University of Essex in Britain, and a Ph.D. from the University of British Columbia. She has five years' experience as Senior Research Officer and then Director of Research with the Canadian Advisory Council on the Status of Women. It was the latter experience that developed her skills in managing projects that are national in scope. From a methodological standpoint, she is particularly well versed in the use of qualitative methodologies.

Among the areas in which Stephenson specializes are justice issues, especially as they relate to vulnerable or minority groups, women's issues, employment issues, and tourism and recreation. She has written several books, including the only visitor's guide to all of the national parks of Canada, and a guidebook to the Galapagos Islands. The combination of academic, governmental, and private sector experience gives Stephenson a very broad background in social policy issues. She has a clear understanding of the research and policy culture within which these three levels operate.

Interestingly, Stephenson has recently developed a distinctive application of her combined analytical and presentation skills—as a very busy stand-up comic. She delivers comedy and commentary at conferences and workshops, and in clubs and cafes across Canada (see **www.sociocomic.com**).

---

can lead to severe penalties. Thus, Canada has strong mores against murder and child abuse, which have been institutionalized into formal norms.

Folkways are norms governing everyday behaviour. Folkways play an important role in shaping the daily behaviour of members of a culture. Consider, for example, something as simple as footwear. In Japan it is a folkway for youngsters to wear flip-flop sandals while learning to walk. A study of Japanese adults has found that, even barefoot, they walk as if wearing flip-flops—braking their thigh muscles and leaning forward as they step. This folkway may even explain why Japan produces so few competitive runners (Stedman 1998).

Society is less likely to formalize folkways than mores, and their violation raises comparatively little concern. For example, walking up a "down" escalator in a department store challenges our standards of appropriate behaviour, but it will not result in a fine or a jail sentence.

In many societies around the world, folkways exist to reinforce patterns of male dominance. Various folkways reveal men's hierarchical position above women within the traditional Buddhist areas of Southeast Asia. In the sleeping cars of trains, women do not sleep in upper berths above men. Hospitals that house men on the first floor do not place women patients on the second floor. Even on clotheslines, folkways dictate male dominance:

women's attire is hung lower than that of men (Bulle 1987).

Acceptance of Norms

People do not follow norms, whether mores or folkways, in all situations. In some cases, they can evade a norm because they know it is weakly enforced. It is illegal for young Canadian teenagers to drink alcoholic beverages, yet drinking by minors is common throughout the nation.

In some instances, behaviour that appears to violate society's norms may actually represent adherence to the norms of a particular group. Teenage drinkers conform to the standards of a peer group. Conformity to group norms also governed the behaviour of the members of a religious cult associated with the Branch Davidians. In 1993, after a deadly gun battle with United States federal officials, nearly 100 members of the cult defied government orders to abandon their compound near Waco, Texas. After a 51-day standoff, the United States Department of Justice ordered an assault on the compound and 86 cult members died.

Norms are violated in some instances because one norm conflicts with another. For example, suppose that you live in an apartment building and one night hear the screams of the woman next door, who is being beaten by her husband. If you decide to intervene by ringing their doorbell or calling the police, you are violating the norm of "minding your own business" while, at the same time, following the norm of assisting a victim of violence.

Even when norms do not conflict, there are always exceptions to any norm. The same action, under different circumstances, can cause one to be viewed either as a hero or as a villain. Secretly taping telephone conversations is normally considered illegal and abhorrent. However, it can be done with a court order to obtain valid evidence for a criminal trial. We would heap praise on a government agent who uses such methods to convict an organized crime figure. In our culture, we tolerate killing another human being if it is in self-defence, and we actually reward killing in times of war.

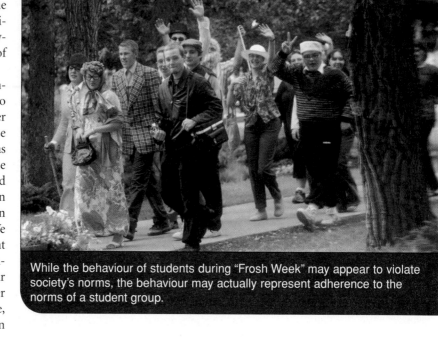

While the behaviour of students during "Frosh Week" may appear to violate society's norms, the behaviour may actually represent adherence to the norms of a student group.

Acceptance of norms is subject to change as the political, economic, and social conditions of a culture are transformed. For example, under traditional norms in Canada, a woman was expected to marry, raise children, and remain at home if her husband could support the family without her assistance. However, these norms have been changing in recent decades, in part as a result of the contemporary feminist movement (see Chapter 11). As support for traditional norms weakens, people feel free to violate them more frequently and openly and are less likely to be punished for doing so.

Sanctions

Suppose that a football coach sends a 13th player onto the field. Or imagine a business school graduate showing up in shorts for a job interview at a large bank. Or consider a driver who neglects to put any money into a parking meter. These people have violated widely shared and understood norms. So what happens? In each of these situations, the person will receive sanctions if his or her behaviour is detected.

Sanctions are penalties and rewards for conduct concerning a social norm. Note that the concept of *reward* is included in this definition. Conformity to a norm can lead to positive sanctions such as a pay raise, a medal, a word of gratitude, or a pat on the back. Negative sanctions include fines, threats, imprisonment, and stares of contempt.

Table 3-1 summarizes the relationship between norms and sanctions. As you can see, the sanctions that

are associated with formal norms (those written down and codified) tend to be formalized as well. If a football coach sends too many players onto the field, the team will be penalized 15 yards. The driver who fails to put money in the parking meter will be given a ticket and expected to pay a fine. But sanctions for violations of informal norms can vary. The business school graduate who comes to the bank interview in shorts will probably lose any chance of getting the job; on the other hand, he or she might be so brilliant the bank officials will overlook the unconventional attire.

Table 3-1	**Norms and Sanctions**	
Norms	***Sanctions***	
	Positive	**Negative**
Formal	Salary bonus	Demotion
	Testimonial dinner	Firing from a job
	Medal	Jail sentence
	Diploma	Expulsion
Informal	Smile	Frown
	Compliment	Humiliation
	Cheers	Belittling

Applying sanctions entails first *detecting* violations of norms or obedience to norms. A person cannot be penalized or rewarded unless someone with the power to provide sanctions is aware of the person's actions. Therefore, if none of the officials in the football game realizes that there is an extra player on the field, there will be no penalty. If the police do not check the parking meter, there will be no fine or ticket. Furthermore, there can be *improper* application of sanctions in certain situations. The referee may make an error in counting the number of football players and levy an undeserved penalty on one team for "too many players on the field."

The entire fabric of norms and sanctions in a culture reflects that culture's values and priorities. The most cherished values will be most heavily sanctioned; matters regarded as less critical, on the other hand, will carry light and informal sanctions.

Values

We each have our own personal set of standards—which may include such things as caring or fitness or success in business—but we also share a general set of objectives as members of a society. Cultural *values* are these collective conceptions of what is considered good, desirable, and proper—or bad, undesirable, and improper—in a culture. They indicate what people in a given culture prefer as well as what they find important and morally right (or wrong). Values may be specific, such as honouring one's parents and owning a home, or they may be more general, such as health, love, and democracy. Of course, the members of a society do not uniformly share its values. Angry political debates and billboards promoting conflicting causes tell us that much. In Box 3-1 we explore how rock music reflects people's values. Those whose values conflict with the music tend to regard the music as a social problem.

Values influence people's behaviour and serve as criteria for evaluating the actions of others. There is often a direct relationship among the values, norms, and sanctions of a culture. For example, if a culture highly values the institution of marriage, it may have norms (and strict sanctions) that prohibit the act of adultery. If a culture views private property as a basic value, it will probably have stiff laws against theft and vandalism.

In a study by the federal government, Citizens' Forum on Canada's Future, conducted between November 1990 and July 1991, 400 000 Canadians were asked which values they thought of as "Canadian" values (1991: 35–45).

The values that emerged included:

1. *Equality and fairness in a democratic society.*
2. *Consultation and dialogue.* Canadians believe that, as citizens, we value our ability to resolve problems and differences peacefully, through discussion, debate, and negotiation.

3. *Accommodation and tolerance.* Accommodation of the differences in Canadian society—ethnic, linguistic, and regional—is considered to be a value of Canadian culture.
4. *Support for diversity.* Canadians value diversity and support it as a part of what makes us Canadian.
5. *Compassion and generosity.* Caring about others, particularly those who are less fortunate, and our willingness to act to make our society more humane, are values Canadians espouse.
6. *Respect for Canada's national beauty.* Preserving Canada's natural environment for future generations is a highly prized value of its citizens.
7. *Commitment to freedom, peace, and nonviolent change.* Canadians want to see their country as a leader in peacemaking and resolution of international conflicts.

People's values may differ according to factors such as their age, gender, region, ethnic background, and language. For example, in a major study by Bibby and Posterski, Canadian teens were found to value what many Canadians have valued for some time. These values include relationships, freedom, success, and comfortable living (1992:18). However, the means through which to achieve these goals were valued differently by the teens compared to the adult group. The values of hard work, honesty, politeness, and forgiveness are considered increasingly less important to Canadian teens.

Figure 3-3 shows the decline in the importance of these values between 1984 and 1992 for Canadian teens,

FIGURE 3-3

Valued Means of Teenagers and Adults

Percent Viewing as "Very Important"

	Youth		Adults	
	1984	1992	1985	1990
Cleanliness	79	72	75	69
Honesty	85	70	96	89
Humour	—	69	—	—
Forgiveness	66	59	75	55
Intelligence	63	56	61	58
Politeness	64	53	70	62
Working hard	69	49	67	58
Creativity	—	45	—	38
Imagination	42	—	41	41
Generosity	—	40	—	52

Source: Bibby and Posterski 1992:19.

3-1 Knockin' Rock—Making Music a Social Problem

In 1990 rock band Judas Priest was sued by the parents of two boys who carried out a suicide pact. The parents claimed that the lyrics of Priest's song "Beyond the Realms of Death" encouraged the boys to opt out of life. That case was dismissed, but it symbolizes the antagonism that rock music has aroused in society, creating a cultural divide between generations.

In fact, rock music has come under attack for decades as the source of all sorts of evils—sexual promiscuity, teen pregnancy, drug use, satanism, suicide, abuse of women, and communism, to name just a few. Critics, who generally come from the religious and political right, point to the obscene lyrics of heavy metal, the anger of rap songs, the decadent lifestyles of rock artists, and the explicit movements and gestures of the performers as causes of deviant behaviour in the youth generation.

The criticisms have had an impact. The United States Senate held hearings about obscene music, and record companies instigated voluntary labelling to alert buyers to explicit lyrics. Cities and towns have cancelled public performances of controversial rock musicians (Marilyn Manson was even paid U.S.$40 000 *not* to play in South Carolina). In the 1950s Ed Sullivan instructed his TV camera crew to show Elvis Presley only from the waist up while he was performing. Anxious parents today attempt to monitor the music their kids buy and the music videos they watch. In a word, rock music has been made into a social problem.

But is rock truly a social problem in that it causes undesirable behaviour?

Sociologist Deena Weinstein thinks not. In her research she found "no sociologically credible evidence that rock caused sexual promiscuity, rape, drug abuse, satanism, and suicide. Indeed, there is clear evidence that it is not the cause of such behaviours" (1999). That is not to say that rock music has no part to play in these problems. According to Weinstein, rock music functions as a symbolic rebellion. It reflects the values of those who cherish the music, and these may be values that other groups in society want to inhibit.

> **Rock music has come under attack for decades as the source of all sorts of evils—sexual promiscuity, teen pregnancy, drug use, satanism, suicide, abuse of women, and communism, to name just a few.**

Rock music legitimizes the "disapproved" behaviours by giving them a symbolic form and making them public. Weinstein acknowledges, however, that symbols can have "complex and varied relations to behaviour."

Weinstein shows how the symbolic function of rock has changed over succeeding generations, matching the concerns and values of each youth generation. In the 1950s early "rock'n'roll" expressed the rebellion of teenagers against a society conforming to respectable middle-class codes. In the 1960s rock provided an outlet for

feelings of political rebellion and a desire for consciousness expansion. The 1970s and 1980s gave rise to a number of distinct styles catering to special audiences. For example, the defiance of rap music and the satanic appeals of heavy metal symbolized the alienation of marginalized youth.

In every decade, rock's detractors have tended to be the older generation—generally white, middle class, politically conservative, and religious. They are intent on preserving the cultural values they hold dear and passing these on intact and unchanged to the generations to follow. Bewildered by rapid social changes and a youth culture resisting adult authority, the older generation makes rock into a convenient scapegoat for all its own fears and failures. The result is that people are more concerned with "killing the messenger" than paying attention to the message embedded in rock's symbolic rebellion. But, as Weinstein (1999) points out, "what could be more gratifying for a young symbolic rebel than to be thought of by the adult world as really important, as really dangerous?"

Let's Discuss

1. Does rock music today reflect your values? Why or why not? What kind of effect (if any) does the music have on the behaviour of those you know?
2. How would a conflict theorist and a functionalist look at the interplay of rock music and its supporters and detractors?

Sources: Weinstein 1999, 2000.

as well as comparing the level of importance attributed to these values by adults.

Canadians were often thought of as the most deferential people in the Western world, but that seems to have changed. In his book, *The Decline of Deference* (1996), Neil Nevitte used findings from the World Values Survey

to describe how Canadians have changed in the past few decades. We have lost faith in our major institutions such as organized religion, marriage, the monarchy, political parties, Canada Pension Plan, banks, and even Canada Post. Canadians are refusing to defer to traditional leaders and authorities, and are now looking elsewhere for information as we learn to make our own individual decisions. Nevitte uses the example of Canadians saying "no" to things like the *Charlottetown Accord*, the separatist leadership in Quebec, and to longstanding political parties such as the Progressive Conservatives in federal elections. The antiglobalization movement is an excellent example of people saying "no" to political and economic leaders' proposals for a global economy. Increasingly, instead of deferring to them, Canadians are finding ways to take decision-making powers away from our leaders, as we become more knowledgeable and informed about the ways and values of other cultures around the globe.

Culture and the Dominant Ideology

Both functionalist and conflict theorists agree that culture and society are in harmony with each other, but for different reasons. Functionalists maintain that stability requires a consensus and the support of society's members; consequently, there are strong central values and common norms. This view of culture became popular in sociology beginning in the 1950s. It was borrowed from British anthropologists who saw cultural traits as all working toward stabilizing a culture. From a functionalist perspective, a cultural trait or practice will persist if it

p. 17 → performs functions that society seems to need or contributes to overall social stability and consensus. This view helps explain why widely condemned social practices such as prostitution continue to survive.

Conflict theorists agree that a common culture may exist, but they argue that it serves to maintain the privileges of certain groups. Moreover, while protecting their own self-interests, powerful groups may keep others in a subservient position. The term ***dominant ideology*** describes the set of cultural beliefs and practices that helps to maintain powerful social, economic, and political interests. This concept was first used by Hungarian Marxist Georg Lukacs (1923) and Italian Marxist Antonio Gramsci (1929). In Karl Marx's view, a capitalist society has a dominant ideology that serves the interests of the ruling class. Box 3-2 illustrates that there is a dominant ideology about poverty that derives its strength from the more powerful segments of society.

From a conflict perspective, the dominant ideology has major social significance. Not only do a society's most powerful groups and institutions control wealth and property; even more important, they control the means of producing beliefs about reality through religion, education, and the media. For example, if all of a society's most important institutions tell women that they should be subservient to men, this dominant ideology will help to control women and keep them in a subordinate position (Abercrombie et al. 1980, 1990; R. Robertson 1988).

Neither the functionalist nor the conflict perspective can alone explain all aspects of a culture. For example, we can trace the custom of tossing rice at a bride and groom back to the wish to have children and to the view of rice as a symbol of fertility, rather than to the powerlessness of the proletariat. Nevertheless, certain cultural practices in our society and others clearly benefit some to the detriment of many. These practices may indeed promote social stability and consensus—but at whose expense?

Cultural Diversity

Each culture has a unique character. The Inuit people of this country have little in common with farmers in Southeast Asia. Cultures adapt to meet specific sets of circumstances, such as climate, level of technology, population, and geography. This adaptation to different conditions shows up in differences in all elements of culture, including norms, sanctions, values, and language. Thus, despite the presence of cultural universals such as courtship and religion, there is still great diversity among the world's many cultures. Moreover, even within a single nation, certain segments of the populace develop cultural patterns that differ from the patterns of the dominant society.

Aspects of Cultural Diversity

Subcultures

Residents of a retirement community, workers on an offshore oil rig, rodeo cowboys, street gangs, goth music fans—all are examples of what sociologists refer to as *subcultures*. A **subculture** is a segment of society that shares a distinctive pattern of mores, folkways, and values that differs from the pattern of the larger society. In a sense, a subculture can be thought of as a culture existing within a larger, dominant culture. The existence of many subcultures is characteristic of complex and diverse societies such as Canada.

You can get an idea of the impact of subcultures within Canada by considering the variety of seasonal traditions in December. The religious and commercial celebration of the Christmas holiday is an event well entrenched in the dominant culture of our society. However, the Jewish subculture observes Hanukkah, Muslims observe Ramadan (which falls at different times during the year, but at present is occurring during the winter months), and some people join in rituals celebrating the winter solstice.

Members of a subculture participate in the dominant culture, while at the same time engaging in unique and distinctive forms of behaviour. Frequently, a subculture will develop an ***argot***, or specialized language, that

Why do we think people are poor? *Individualistic* explanations emphasize personal responsibility: Poor people lack the proper work ethic, lack ability, or are unsuited to the workplace because of problems like drinking or drug abuse. *Structural* explanations, on the other hand, lay the blame for poverty on such external factors as inferior educational opportunities, prejudice, and low wages in some industries. Research documents that people in Canada and the United States generally go along with the individualistic explanation. The dominant ideology in Canada and the United States holds that people are poor largely because of their own shortcomings.

In a world survey assessing the causes of poverty, Canadians were asked "Why are there people in this country who live in need?" (Institute for Social Research 1994). Canadians responded, with equal frequency, that personal laziness and societal injustice caused poverty (31.8 percent for each reason). Countries such as Sweden, where individualistic

beliefs are not as strong as in North America, responded that societal injustice far outweighed personal laziness as being the cause of poverty.

How pervasive is this individualistic view? Do the poor and rich alike subscribe to it? In seeking answers, sociologists have conducted studies of how various groups of people view poverty.

> ... the dominant ideology holds that people are poor largely because of their own shortcomings.

The research has shown that people with lower incomes are more likely than the wealthy to see the larger socioeconomic system as the cause of poverty. In part this structural view, focusing on the larger job market, relieves them of some personal responsibility for their plight, but it also reflects the social reality to which they are close. On the other hand, the wealthy tend to embrace the dominant

individualistic view because continuation of the socioeconomic status quo is in their best interest. They also prefer to regard their own success as the result of their own accomplishments, with little or no help from external factors.

Is the dominant ideology on poverty widespread? Yes, but it appears that the individualist ideology is dominant in Canadian society not because of a lack of alternatives, but because those who see things differently lack the political influence and status needed to get the ear of the mainstream culture.

Let's Discuss

1. Does support for the dominant ideology about poverty divide along income lines among racial and ethnic minorities? Why or why not?
2. Does your university administration have a "dominant ideology"? How is it manifested? Are there any groups that challenge it? On what basis?

Sources: Bobo 1991; Institute for Social Research 1994.

distinguishes it from the wider society. For example, if you were to join a band of pickpockets you would need to learn what the dip, dish, and tailpipe are expected to do (see Figure 3-4).

An argot allows "insiders," the members of the subculture, to understand words with special meanings. It also establishes patterns of communication that "outsiders" can't understand. Sociologists associated with the interactionist perspective emphasize that language and symbols offer a powerful way for a subculture to feel cohesive and maintain its identity.

Subcultures develop in a number of ways. Often a subculture emerges because a segment of society faces problems or even privileges unique to its position. Subcultures may be based on common age (teenagers or old people), region (Newfoundlanders), ethnic heritage (Indo-Canadians), occupation (firefighters), or beliefs (environmentalists). Certain subcultures, such as

FIGURE 3-4

The Argot of Pickpockets

Source: Gearty 1996.

Cultures vary because they need to adapt to the special conditions of their environment. Peruvians who live in the high Andes near the equator must adapt to a climate that can range from hot to cold within a single day. These women in Cuzco wear layers of clothing and cover their heads both for warmth and for protection from the high-altitude sun.

more cars, larger and larger homes, and an endless array of material goods. Instead, they expressed a desire to live in a culture based on more humanistic values, such as sharing, love, and coexistence with the environment.

When a subculture conspicuously and deliberately *opposes* certain aspects of the larger culture, it is known as a **counterculture**. Countercultures typically thrive among the young, who have the least investment in the existing culture, yet the most to gain from changes to it. For example, antiglobalization protesters are often young people who want to live in a world that is not dominated by a few corporate leaders with power to control the global economy. They promote change on a global level. In most cases, a 20-year-old can adjust to new cultural standards more easily than someone who has spent 60 years following the patterns of the dominant culture (Zellner 1995).

An example of a counterculture in Canadian history is the *Front du libération du Québec* (FLQ). In 1970, the FLQ opposed the social, economic, political, and

computer "hackers," develop because of a shared interest or hobby. In still other subcultures, such as that of prison inmates, members have been excluded from conventional society and are forced to develop alternative ways of living.

Functionalist and conflict theorists agree that variation exists within a culture. Functionalists view subcultures as variations of particular social environments and as evidence that differences can exist within a common culture. However, conflict theorists suggest that variation often reflects the inequality of social arrangements within a society. A conflict perspective would view the challenge to dominant social norms by Quebec separatists, the feminist movement, and disabled groups as a reflection of inequity based on ethnicity, gender, and disability status. Conflict theorists also argue that subcultures sometimes emerge when the dominant society unsuccessfully tries to suppress a practice, such as the use of illegal drugs.

Countercultures

By the end of the 1960s, an extensive subculture had emerged in North America, composed of young people turned off by a society they believed was too materialistic and technological. This group primarily included political radicals and "hippies" who had "dropped out" of mainstream social institutions. These young men and women rejected the pressure to accumulate more and

"IT'S ENDLESS. WE JOIN A COUNTER-CULTURE; IT BECOMES THE CULTURE. WE JOIN ANOTHER COUNTER-CULTURE; IT BECOMES THE CULTURE..."

Cultures change. Aspects we once regarded as unacceptable—such as men wearing earrings and people wearing jeans in the workplace—and associated with fringe groups are now widely accepted. Countercultural practices are sometimes absorbed by the mainstream culture.

educational institutions of the dominant culture of Quebec. Its activities included the murder of a prominent Quebec politician and the kidnapping of a British Trade Commissioner posted in Quebec. The FLQ produced a manifesto containing all of its demands, which was broadcast through public media.

Culture Shock

Anyone who feels disoriented, uncertain, out of place, or even fearful when immersed in an unfamiliar culture may be experiencing **culture shock**. For example, a resident of Canada who visits certain areas in China and wants a local dinner may be stunned to learn that the specialty is scorpion. Similarly, someone from a strict Islamic culture may be shocked upon first seeing the comparatively provocative dress styles and open displays of affection that are common in North American and various European cultures. Culture shock can also occur within the larger confines of one's own culture. For example, a 14-year-old boy from a small town in northern Saskatchewan might feel the effects of culture shock while visiting Toronto for the first time. The speed of the traffic, the level of the street noise and the intensity and variation of external stimuli may cause him to feel disoriented and uncomfortable with his surroundings.

All of us, to some extent, take for granted the cultural practices of our society. As a result, it can be surprising and even disturbing to realize that other cultures do not follow our "way of life." The fact is that customs that seem strange to us are considered normal and proper in other cultures, which may see *our* mores and folkways as odd.

Cultural Diversity in Canada

If a tourist were to travel across Canada for the first time, he or she would most certainly be struck by this country's diversity—diversity of region, ethnicity, race, and language. Cultural diversity, as the traveller would observe, is greatest in Canada's metropolitan areas, where the greatest number of cultural minorities and particularly visible minorities reside. On the basis of his or her observations of cultural diversity, the traveller might conclude that Canada is a "multicultural" society. But what does multiculturalism really mean? Does it simply describe (numerically) the variety of cultures represented in Canada?

Multiculturalism is not only a description of the reality of Canada's cultural makeup—"what is" (Fleras and Kunz 2001)—but, in Canada, it is an explicit policy set out by the government. **Multiculturalism** is a policy that promotes cultural and racial diversity and full and equal participation of individuals and communities of all origins as a fundamental characteristic of Canadian identity. The federal Multiculturalism Program of 1997 has three main goals (Communications Canada 2001):

1. *Identity*—fostering a society where people of all backgrounds feel a sense of attachment and belonging to Canada
2. *Civic participation*—developing citizens who are actively involved in their communities and country
3. *Social justice*—building a country that ensures fair and equitable treatment of people of all origins.

Multiculturalism can also take the form of an ideology—a set of beliefs, goals, ideals, and attitudes about what multiculturalism *should be*. The ideal of multiculturalism in Canada has two desirable outcomes: the survival of ethnic groups and their cultures, and tolerance of this

Women in certain areas of Thailand traditionally elongated their necks by wearing layers of coils. The custom began dying out until the Thai people discovered that tourists would pay money to be "shocked" by the practice. These girls are members of the "Long Neck" tribe.

diversity as reflected by an absence of prejudice towards ethnic minorities (Weinfeld, 1994). In embracing multiculturalism as an ideology, Canadians often compare their society's way of expressing cultural diversity to the way it is expressed in the United States (Fleras and Kunz 2001). The analogy of the "mosaic" is commonly used to describe Canada's cultural diversity, where various tiles represent distinct cultural groups that collectively form the whole. In the United States, the "melting pot" analogy represents the model of assimilation, in which Americans become more like one another, rather than distinct from one another.

Support for the "mosaic" version of Canada has been declining and shifting toward the "melting pot." Across region, age, and education levels, in 1985, 56 percent of Canadians said they preferred the "mosaic" and 28 percent the "melting pot." In 1995, only 44 percent preferred the mosaic, while 40 percent preferred the melting pot (Bibby 1995).

While Canadians' attitudes about what is meant by multiculturalism may be changing, they are overwhelmingly in support of it, according to a nationwide poll conducted by Environics. Just three months after the events of September 11, 2001, Canadians' support for an open, tolerant approach to multiculturalism was "rock solid." Canadians in all provinces believe that the multiculturalism policy introduced in 1971 makes this country a distinct and more tolerant nation. In response to a question of whether the policy should be preserved and enhanced by government, 82 percent said "yes" (Cobb 2002). Multiculturalism is, however, not without its critics. Some argue that it is a divisive rather than unifying force in Canada, while others claim that it is only "window dressing," diverting attention from the real problems of ethnic and racial prejudice and discrimination (Nelson and Fleras 1998).

The American Influence

One of the original purposes of multiculturalism was to establish a national uniqueness that would make Canadians distinct from Americans (Bibby 1990). In 1972, Prime Minister Pierre Trudeau stated that, if we implement this policy, "We become less like others; we become less susceptible to cultural, social, or political envelopment by others" (Bibby 1990:49). Despite the significant Americanization of Canadian life, the view that Americans have "too much power in our nation's affairs" has not increased since the 1970s (Bibby 1995).

Even though Canadians generally hold the view that Americans do not have "too much power" in our society, Canadians frequently consider Americans to be their favourite authors, TV personalities, and screen stars (Bibby 1995). Given Canadians' reliance on American culture (particularly outside Quebec) our "heroes" may

be those that are defined by America (Bibby 1995). In 1995, when Canadians were asked to name the greatest living Canadian, 73 percent said "no one came to mind" (Bibby 1995:47). Furthermore, when asked what characteristics describe Americans and Canadians, Canadians felt that the traits of confidence, patriotism, and risk-taking had greater applicability to Americans, while generosity was a trait more applicable to Canadians. As Figure 3-5 illustrates, Canadian teenagers view the description "world's best at what they do" as applicable to Americans almost 50 percent more often than they view it applying to Canadians (Bibby 1995). If Canadian broadcasting and publishing regulations promoting Canadian cultural content were not in place, one might wonder how much more "Americanized" our cultural preferences might be. In 1995, 64 percent of Canadians believed that "CBC television continues to play a unique role in enhancing Canadian culture" (Bibby 1995:1210).

Attitudes Toward Cultural Diversity

Ethnocentrism

Many everyday statements reflect our attitude that our culture is best. We use terms such as *underdeveloped, backward,* and *primitive* to refer to other societies. What "we" believe is a religion; what "they" believe is superstition and mythology (Spradley and McCurdy 1980).

It is tempting to evaluate the practices of other cultures on the basis of our own perspectives. Sociologist William Graham Sumner (1906) coined the term **ethnocentrism** to refer to the tendency to assume that one's culture and way of life constitute the norm or are superior to all others. The ethnocentric person sees his or her own group as the centre or defining point of culture

FIGURE 3-5

Applicability of Traits to Canadians and Americans
Traits describe "very well" or "fairly well"

	Adults		Teenagers	
	Canadians	Americans	Canadians	Americans
Confident	61%	87%	66%	91%
Patriotic	58	92	47	89
Generous	84	53	**	**
Risk-takers	33	82	43	84
World's best	56	48	40	62

Source: Bibby 1995:49.

and views all other cultures as deviations from what is "normal."

Those Westerners who are contemptuous of India's Hindu religion and culture because of its view of cattle as sacred are engaged in ethnocentrism. As another manifestation of ethnocentrism, people in one culture may dismiss as unthinkable the mate-selection or child-rearing practices of another culture. We might, in fact, be tempted to view the Nacirema culture from an ethnocentric point of view—until we learn it is a culture similar to our own that Miner describes (see the chapter opening).

Conflict theorists point out that ethnocentric value judgments serve to devalue diversity and to deny equal opportunities. The treatment of First Nations children in Christian-based residential schools during the middle of the last century is an example of ethnocentrism that conflict theorists might point to in Canadian history. Church authorities were so convinced of the cultural superiority of their own beliefs that they set out to deny First Nations children the expression of their own cultural beliefs and practices.

Functionalists note that ethnocentrism serves to maintain a sense of solidarity by promoting group pride. Canadians' view of our country as peaceful, safe, and relatively free from violence may create a feeling of national solidarity when comparing ourselves to our American neighbours.

Cultural Relativism

While ethnocentrism evaluates foreign cultures using the familiar culture of the observer as a standard of correct behaviour, **cultural relativism** views people's behaviour from the perspective of their own culture. It places a priority on understanding other cultures, rather than dismissing them as "strange" or "exotic." Unlike ethnocentrism, cultural relativism employs the kind of

value neutrality in scientific study that Max Weber saw as so important (see Chapter 2). p. 46

Cultural relativism stresses that different social contexts give rise to different norms and values. Thus, we must examine practices such as polygamy, bullfighting, and monarchy within the particular contexts of the cultures in which they are found. While cultural relativism does not suggest that we must unquestionably *accept* every cultural variation, it does require a serious and unbiased effort to evaluate norms, values, and customs in light of their distinctive culture.

There is an interesting extension of cultural relativism, referred to as *xenocentrism*. **Xenocentrism** is the belief that the products, styles, or ideas of one's society are *inferior* to those that originate elsewhere (W. Wilson et al. 1976). In a sense, it is a reverse ethnocentrism. For example, people in Canada often assume that French wine or Japanese electronic devices are superior to our own. Are they? Or are people unduly charmed by the lure of goods from exotic places? Such fascination with overseas products can be damaging to competitors in Canada. Some U.S. companies have responded by creating products that *sound* European, such as Häagen-Dazs ice cream (made in Teaneck, New Jersey). Conflict theorists are most likely to consider the economic impact of xenocentrism in the developing world. Consumers in developing nations frequently turn their backs on locally produced goods and instead purchase items imported from Europe or North America.

How one views one's culture—whether from an ethnocentric point of view or through the lens of cultural relativism—has important consequences in the area of social policy. An important issue today is the extent to which a nation should accommodate diverse cultures by implementing multiculturalism policies. We'll take a closer look at this issue in the next section.

SOCIAL POLICY AND CULTURE

Multiculturalism

The Issue

In 1971, multiculturalism became official government policy in Canada. It was a policy established to promote tolerance for cultural minorities or, in the words of then Prime Minister Pierre Elliot Trudeau, to "explore the delights of many cultures." Although the Canadian policy on multiculturalism provides an alternative to the American melting pot approach to cultural diversity, it has

generated a good deal of conflict and faced a great deal of opposition (Nelson and Fleras 1995).

Much of the conflict surrounding multiculturalism stems from the variety of meanings or definitions Canadians have for the concept. The term *multiculturalism* can be used to refer to: (a) the fact (what is, i.e., the existing composition of Canadian society); (b) an ideology (what should be); (c) a policy (what is proposed); (d) a process (what really happens); (e) a critical discussion (what is being challenged); and (f) a social movement (collective resistance) (Fleras and Elliott 1999). In general, multiculturalism can be defined as a process through which Canadians come to be engaged in their society as different from one another, yet equal to one another (Fleras and Kunz 2001).

The Setting

Citizenship and Immigration Canada reports that Canada accepts more immigrants, in proportion to the size of its population, than any other country in the world. One in every six residents of this country was born outside Canada. The five top sources for immigration since 1998 have been countries in Asia (Citizenship and Immigration 2001). According to the 2001 Census, 38 percent of Canadians declared their ethnicity to be that of "multiple origins"; that is, they declared two or more ethnic origins. Overall, multicultural minorities tend to live in Canada's large urban centres, making Vancouver, Montreal, and Toronto the most culturally diverse regions of the country. Approximately three-quarters of all immigrants who arrived in Canada in the 1990s settled in one of these three centres (Fleras and Kunz 2001, Statistics Canada 2003a).

Sociological Insights

From the standpoint of the two major sociological macro-level perspectives—conflict theory and functionalist theory—the implementation of multiculturalism as a social policy has two distinct interpretations. Conflict sociologists view multiculturalism as an attempt to "empower minorities to pursue the dual goals of ethnicity and equality" (Nelson and Fleras 1998:259). It is seen as an attempt to nurture, preserve, and protect different cultural traditions in the midst of domination by one cultural group. Multiculturalism policies also aim to make diversity, and the inevitable struggles that result, an accepted and welcome element of the cultural fabric of Canadian life, thus shifting attention away from the lack of cultural diversity of those in positions of power.

Functionalist sociologists view culture as something that all Canadians share. It is the common values that unite and integrate us, resulting in a shared sense of identity. Therefore, according to functionalist thinkers, the more we diversify Canadian culture, the less we share in common; the more we hyphenate our identities (e.g., Indo-Canadian, Chinese-Canadian, Italian-Canadian, etc.), the less "Canadian" we actually become. Promoting acceptance of diversity of many subcultures leads to a lack of consensus about what the core values of a Canadian should be.

Policies on multiculturalism attempt to preserve, protect, and nurture different cultural traditions in the midst of domination by one cultural group.

However, both functionalist and conflict theorists have criticized multiculturalism for a number of reasons. Sociologists Fleras and Elliott (1999) argue that criticisms regarding multiculturalism can be classified into four categories:

- Those that claim that multiculturalism is "divisive" and serves to weaken Canadian society
- Those that see multicultural programs and policies as "regressive," as a tool to pacify the needs and legitimate claims of the minority cultural groups
- Those that consider the efforts of multiculturalism to be "ornamental" or superficial, with much form and little substance
- Those that consider multiculturalism as an "impractical" policy in a capitalist society such as Canada, where the principles of individualism, private property, profit, and consumerism prevail (Fleras and Elliott 1999).

Policy Initiatives

Official multiculturalism in Canada currently comes under the portfolio of Citizenship and Canadian Identity, which is in turn under the Ministry of Canadian Heritage. According to Fleras and Kunz (2001), policies on multiculturalism have evolved from those in the 1970s, which celebrated Canadians' differences (e.g., cultural sensitivity training programs). The 1980s attempted to "manage" diversity through policies on employment equity and race relations, while the 1990s brought policy objectives of inclusion and integration of cultural minorities. The current policies on multiculturalism encourage the full participation of all cultural groups, based on the goals of social justice. As Fleras and Kunz (2001:16) state, "Emphasis is on what we have in common as rights-bearing and equality-seeking individuals rather than on what separates or divides us." Special activities such as Black History Month and the "Racism: Stop It!" campaign, which focus on the promotion of social justice, have been created by the federal government's multicultural programs.

Fleras and Elliott (1999) state that multiculturalism is not what divides Canada, but is rather what unites us, separating us and making us distinct from Americans. As noted earlier, the 2002 Environics poll found that 82 percent of Canadians supported this notion. Multiculturalism policies focus on eliminating institutional barriers for minority groups and, therefore, attempt to break down the "vertical mosaic."

Let's Discuss

1. How might someone with an ethnocentric point of view look at multiculturalism?
2. Describe how functionalist theorists would explain recent developments in multicultural programs in Canada.
3. Did you attend a school where multicultural programs were in place? What was your perception of such a program?

● Chapter Resources

Summary

Culture is the totality of learned, socially transmitted customs, knowledge, material objects, and behaviour. This chapter examines the basic elements that make up a culture, social practices common to all cultures, and variations that distinguish one culture from another.

1. Sharing a similar culture helps to define the group or society to which we belong.
2. Anthropologist George Murdock has compiled a list of **cultural universals**, general practices found in every culture, including courtship, family, games, language, medicine, religion, and sexual restrictions.
3. Human culture is constantly expanding through **innovation**, including both **discovery** and **invention**.
4. **Diffusion**—the spread of cultural items from one place to another—also changes cultures. But societies resist ideas that seem too foreign as well as those that are perceived as threatening to their own values and beliefs.
5. **Language**, an important element of culture, includes speech, written characters, numerals, symbols, and gestures and other forms of

nonverbal communication. Language both describes culture and shapes it for us.
6. Sociologists distinguish between **norms** in two ways. They are classified as either **formal** or **informal** norms and as **mores** or **folkways**.
7. The more cherished **values** of a culture will receive the heaviest sanctions; matters that are regarded as less critical, on the other hand, will carry light and informal sanctions.
8. The **dominant ideology** of a culture describes the set of cultural beliefs and practices that help to maintain powerful social, economic, and political interests.
9. In a sense, a **subculture** can be thought of as a culture existing within a larger, dominant culture. **Countercultures** are subcultures that deliberately oppose aspects of the larger culture.
10. People who measure other cultures by the standard of their own engage in **ethnocentrism**. Using **cultural relativism** allows us to view people from the perspective of their own culture.
11. **Multiculturalism** is a process through which citizens come to be engaged in their society as different from one another, yet equal to one another.

Critical Thinking Questions

1. Select three cultural universals from George Murdock's list (see p. 64) and analyze them from a functionalist perspective. Why are these practices found in every culture? What functions do they serve?
2. Drawing on the theories and concepts presented in the chapter, apply sociological analysis to one subculture with which you are familiar. Describe the norms, values, argot, and sanctions evident in that subculture.
3. In what ways is the dominant ideology of Canada evident in the nation's literature, music, movies, theatre, television programs, and sporting events?

Key Terms

Argot   Specialized language used by members of a group or subculture. (76)

Counterculture   A subculture that deliberately opposes certain aspects of the larger culture. (77)

Cultural relativism   The viewing of people's behaviour from the perspective of their own culture. (80)

Cultural universals   General practices found in every culture. (64)

Culture   The totality of learned, socially transmitted customs, knowledge, material objects, and behaviour. (63)

Culture lag   Ogburn's term for a period of maladjustment during which the nonmaterial culture is still adapting to new material conditions. (67)

Culture shock   The feeling of surprise and disorientation that is experienced when people witness cultural practices different from their own. (78)

Diffusion   The process by which a cultural item is spread from group to group or society to society. (65)

Discovery   The process of making known or sharing the existence of an aspect of reality. (65)

Dominant ideology   A set of cultural beliefs and practices that helps to maintain powerful social, economic, and political interests. (75)

Ethnocentrism   The tendency to assume that one's own culture and way of life represent the norm or are superior to all others. (79)

Folkways   Norms governing everyday social behaviour whose violation raises comparatively little concern. (71)

Formal norms   Norms that generally have been written down and that specify strict rules for punishment of violators. (70)

Informal norms   Norms that generally are understood but are not precisely recorded. (70)

Innovation   The process of introducing new elements into a culture through either discovery or invention. (65)

Invention   The combination of existing cultural items into a form that did not previously exist. (65)

Language   An abstract system of word meanings and symbols for all aspects of culture. It also includes gestures and other nonverbal communication. (68)

Law   Governmental social control. (70)

Material culture   The tangible physical or technological aspects of our daily lives. (66)

Mores   Norms deemed highly necessary to the welfare of a society. (70)

Multiculturalism   A policy that promotes cultural and racial diversity and full and equal participation of individuals and communities of all origins as a fundamental characteristic of Canadian identity. (78)

Nonmaterial culture   Cultural adjustments to material conditions, such as customs, beliefs, patterns of communication, and ways of using material objects. (67)

Norms   Established standards of behaviour maintained by a society. (70)

Sanctions   Penalties and rewards for conduct concerning a social norm. (72)

Sapir–Whorf hypothesis   A hypothesis concerning the role of language in shaping cultures. It holds that language is culturally determined and serves to influence our mode of thought. (68)

Society   A fairly large number of people who live in the same territory, are relatively independent of people outside it, and participate in a common culture. (64)

Subculture   A segment of society that shares a distinctive pattern of mores, folkways, and values that differs from the pattern of the larger society. (76)

Technology   Information about how to use the material resources of the environment to satisfy human needs and desires. (66)

Values   Collective conceptions of what is considered good, desirable, and proper—or bad, undesirable, and improper—in a culture. (73)

Xenocentrism   The belief that the products, styles, or ideas of one's society are inferior to those that originate elsewhere. (80)

Additional Readings

Bibby, Reginald. 1995. *The Bibby Report: Social Trends Canadian Style.* Toronto: Stoddart. Based on national surveys of 1975, 1980, 1985, 1990, and 1995, this book examines Canadians' values on such issues as multiculturalism, Americanization, bilingualism, and spirituality.

Fleras, Augie, and Jean Lock Kunz. 2001. *Media and Minorities: Representing Diversity in Multicultural Canada.* Toronto: Thomson Educational Publishing. Fleras and Kunz analyze and assess the representation of minority groups in the mass media against a backdrop of Canada's commitment to multiculturalism.

Kraybill, Donald B., and Steven M. Nott. 1995. *Amish Enterprises: From Plows to Profits.* Baltimore: Johns Hopkins University Press. An examination of how the Amish have adapted to capitalism in the United States while maintaining their distinctive values and subculture.

Weinstein, Deena. 2000. *Heavy Metal: The Music and Its Culture.* Cambridge, MA: Da Capo. A sociologist examines the subculture associated with "heavy metal" music and efforts to curtail this subculture.

Zellner, William M. 1995. *Countercultures: A Sociological Analysis.* New York: St. Martin's. An overview of six countercultures found in the United States: the Unification Church, the Church of Scientology, satanists, skinheads, survivalists, and the Ku Klux Klan.

JOURNALS

Among the journals that focus on issues of culture and diversity are *Cross-Cultural Research* (founded in 1994), *Culture* (1981), *Culture and Tradition* (1976), *Ethnology* (1962), *Multiculturalism* (1977), *MultiCultural Social* Change (1979), and *Theory, Culture, and Society* (1982).

Internet Connection

www.mcgrawhill.ca/college/schaefer

*For additional Internet exercises relating to culture and nonverbal communication, visit the Schaefer Online Learning Centre at **http://www.mcgrawhill.ca/college/schaefer**. Please note that while the URLs listed were current at the time of printing, these sites often change—check the Online Learning Centre for updates.*

Your textbook offers a contrast of subcultures and countercultures. In general, both groups are segments of society that share distinctive features, such as argots, beliefs, and particular dress codes. However, a counterculture conspicuously and deliberately opposes certain aspects of the larger culture in a way that a subculture does not. To see this difference in action, compare the Amish described through the links found at **http://dir.yahoo.com/Society_and_Culture/ Religion_and_Spirituality/Faiths_and_Practices/ Christianity/Denominations_and_Sects/Amish** to street gangs described through the links found at **http://dir.yahoo.com/Society_and_Culture/ Cultures_and_Groups/Gangs**. For each of the two groups, explore the following:

(a) Identify the argot of the group. Describe some specific examples of special forms of verbal, written, and gestural communication. How are those gestures and words used to communicate? What kinds of messages are sent through the argot? In what ways can a subculture or counterculture make use of an argot to build solidarity among its members, while at the same time keeping outsiders at a distance?

(b) What special clothing or dress codes are used? What symbols and messages do members communicate through clothing? What purpose does specialized dress serve for the group?

(c) What are some of the special practices or beliefs of the group? Do these beliefs or practices put the group at odds with the larger culture? How so?

(d) What purpose or meaning can being a member of the group have for those who belong?

(e) Draw some comparisons and contrasts between the two groups. What do the Amish and street gangs have in common? In what ways are they different? Why would the Amish be labelled a subculture, but street gangs a counterculture? Do you agree with these labels? Why or why not?

Schools can sometimes be stressful arenas of socialization. This poster informs schoolchildren in Japan that they can call a hotline and receive advice concerning stress, bullying by classmates, and corporal punishment from their teachers.

I n sixth grade, the popular girls' clique split into two subgroups, whose leaders were Tiffany and Emily. The girls from the two groups liked each other, but the leaders did not. Tiffany was jealous of the attention Emily got from her followers and from the popular boys, wanting centre stage all to herself. Emily resented Tiffany's intrusions and manipulations. They polarized their groups against each other.

By spring, Tiffany could no longer control her hatred. She persuaded one of the less popular boys to steal Emily's backpack, empty it, and take it into the rest room and smear it with excrement. Emily discovered her backpack missing, searched for it, and alerted her teacher. The backpack was finally found in the boys' rest room (where it could not be traced back to Tiffany), clogging up a toilet, soaking in urine and feces. Although the school administrators interviewed numerous people to try to uncover the truth, they were never able to solve the crime.

Tiffany used Emily's anguish to ridicule her, portray her as weak, and turn the bulk of the popular people (boys and girls) against her. The following year Emily's parents sent her to boarding school.

* * *

One day Larry, Brad, and Trevor were at Rick's house. Larry had just turned twelve and had a lot of birthday money in his wallet. Brad noticed Larry's wallet lying on Rick's bed and climbed on top of it. He motioned Trevor to join him. From his perch, Brad asked Larry where his wallet was, and when Larry could not find it, Brad accused Rick of stealing it. Despite Rick's fervent denials, Brad eventually convinced Larry of Rick's guilt, whipping him into a frenzy of anger and outrage. Larry tore Rick's room apart looking for his wallet. Brad slyly showed Trevor the wallet he was sitting on, inviting him to join him in conspiratorial silence.

Brad's accusations, Larry's fear for his money and anger at Rick, and Rick's pathetic denials escalated to the point where Larry began threatening to break Rick's things if he did not turn over the wallet. Helplessly, Rick professed innocence and ignorance. Larry broke Rick's lamp. Then he smashed the telephone in Rick's room (a birthday gift) to the floor, shattering it. He stomped on video games. Rick wailed and cried. Larry ran out of the room, moving to the kitchen to find more things to destroy, his anger out of control. Rick followed him, screaming, terrified. As Larry was about to throw down a blender, Rick's mother came home and stopped him. Assessing the situation, she sent the three boys home. Searching the house, she found the wallet on the bed and called Larry's mother.

The next day in school, Brad and Trevor bragged exultantly to everybody about their caper. Rick was out of the group. *(Adler and Adler 1998:2–3)* ∎

atricia and Peter Adler's intensive research into preadolescent culture began with their own children, when they were five and nine. As participant observers, the parents jumped into the lives of their children, their children's friends, and children of their own friends as well as other children in their community over a period of eight years. They uncovered a dynamic peer culture—one in which the preadolescents' interactions help influence behaviour and determine such things as status, popularity, and friendships. In their book *Peer Power,* the Adlers show that children are active agents in creating their social world and getting socialized into it; they are not just the passive objects of socialization by parents, teachers, and other authority figures in their lives. These researchers found that while each child has his or her own special issues and experiences, the peer culture influences behaviour and helps form lifelong behavioural patterns.

What makes us behave the way we do? How do we know what behaviour is expected of us or acceptable during different stages in our lives? How do we learn to become social beings?

Sociologists, in general, are interested in the patterns of behaviour and attitudes that emerge *throughout* the life course, from infancy to old age. These patterns are part of the process of **socialization,** whereby people learn the attitudes, values, and behaviours appropriate for members of a particular culture. Socialization occurs through human interactions at every stage throughout our lives. We learn a great deal from those people most important in our lives—immediate family members, best friends, and teachers. But we also learn from people we see on the street, on television, on the Internet, and in films and magazines. From a microsociological perspective, socialization helps us to discover how to behave "properly" and what to expect from others if we follow (or challenge) society's norms and values. From a macrosociological perspective, socialization provides for the transmission of a culture from one generation to the next and thereby for the long-term continuance of a society.

Socialization affects the overall cultural practices of a society, and it also shapes our self-images. For example, in North America, a person who is viewed as "too heavy" or "too short" does not conform to the ideal cultural standard of physical attractiveness. This kind of unfavourable evaluation can significantly influence the person's self-esteem. In this sense, socialization experiences can help shape our personalities. In everyday speech, the term **personality** is used to refer to a person's typical patterns of attitudes, needs, characteristics, and behaviour.

This chapter will examine the role of socialization in human development. It begins by analyzing the nature versus nurture debate, or the interaction of heredity and environmental factors. We pay particular attention to how people develop perceptions, feelings, and beliefs about themselves. The chapter will also explore the lifelong nature of the socialization process, as well as important agents of socialization, among them the family, schools, peers, and the media. Finally, the social policy section will focus on the socialization experience of group child care for young children. ■

The Role of Socialization

What makes us who we are? Is it the genes we are born with? Or the environment in which we grow up? Researchers have traditionally clashed over the relative importance of biological inheritance and environmental factors in human development—a conflict called the *nature versus nurture* (or *heredity versus environment*) debate. Today, most social scientists have moved beyond this debate, acknowledging instead the *interaction* of these variables in shaping human development. However, we can better appreciate how heredity and environmental factors interact and influence the socialization process if we first examine situations in which one factor operates almost entirely without the other (Homans 1979).

Environment: The Impact of Isolation

In the 1994 movie *Nell,* Jodie Foster played a young woman hidden since birth by her mother in a backwoods cabin. Raised without normal human contact, Nell crouches like an animal, screams wildly, and speaks or sings in a language all her own. This movie was drawn from the actual account of an emaciated 16-year-old boy who mysteriously appeared in 1828 in the town square of Nuremberg, Germany (Lipson 1994).

The Case of Isabelle

Some viewers may have found the story of Nell difficult to believe, but the painful childhood of Isabelle was all too real. For the first six years of her life, Isabelle lived in almost total seclusion in a darkened room. She had little contact with other people, with the exception of her mother, who could neither speak nor hear. Isabelle's mother's parents had been so deeply ashamed of Isabelle's illegitimate birth that they kept her hidden away from the world. Authorities finally discovered the child in 1938, when Isabelle's mother escaped from her parents' home, taking her daughter with her.

When she was discovered at age six, Isabelle could not speak. She could merely make various croaking sounds. Her only communications with her mother were simple gestures. Isabelle had been largely deprived of the typical interactions and socialization experiences of childhood. Since she had actually seen few people, she initially showed a strong fear of strangers and reacted almost like a wild animal when confronted with an unfamiliar person. As she became accustomed to seeing certain individuals, her reaction changed to one of extreme apathy. At first, it was believed that Isabelle was deaf, but she soon began to react to nearby sounds. On tests of maturity, she scored at the level of an infant rather than a six-year-old.

Specialists developed a systematic training program to help Isabelle adapt to human relationships and socialization. After a few days of training, she made her first attempt to verbalize. Although she started slowly, Isabelle quickly passed through six years of development. In a little over two months, she was speaking in complete sentences. Nine months later, she could identify both words and sentences. Before Isabelle reached the age of nine, she was ready to attend school with other children. By her 14th year, she was in sixth grade, doing well in school, and emotionally well-adjusted.

Yet, without an opportunity to experience socialization in her first six years, Isabelle had been hardly human in the social sense when she was first discovered. Her inability to communicate at the time of her discovery—despite her physical and cognitive potential to learn—and her remarkable progress over the next few years underscore the impact of socialization on human development (K. Davis 1940, 1947).

Isabelle's experience is important for researchers because it is one of few cases of children reared in total isolation. Unfortunately, however, there are many cases of children raised in extremely neglectful social circumstances. Recently, attention has focused on infants and young children in orphanages in the formerly communist countries of Eastern Europe. For example, in Romanian orphanages, babies lie in their cribs for 18 or 20 hours a day, curled against their feeding bottles and receiving little adult care. Such minimal attention continues for the first five years of their lives. Many of them are fearful of human contact and prone to unpredictable antisocial behaviour. This situation came to light as families in North America and Europe began adopting thousands of these children. The adjustment problems for about 20 percent of them were often so dramatic that the adopting families suffered guilty fears of being ill-fit adoptive parents. Many of them have asked for assistance in dealing with the children. Slowly, efforts are being made to introduce the deprived youngsters to feelings of attachment that they never had experienced before (V. Groza et al. 1999; M. Talbot 1998).

Increasingly, researchers are emphasizing the importance of early socialization experiences for children who grow up in more normal environments. We now know that it is not enough to care for an infant's physical needs; parents must also concern themselves with children's social development. If, for example, children are discouraged from having friends, they will miss out on social interactions with peers that are critical for emotional growth.

Primate Studies

Studies of animals raised in isolation also support the importance of socialization in development. Harry Harlow (1971), a researcher at the primate laboratory of the University of Wisconsin, conducted tests with

These children in a Romanian orphanage enjoy little adult contact and spend much of their time confined to cribs. This neglect can result in adjustment problems later in life.

rhesus monkeys that had been raised away from their mothers and away from contact with other monkeys. As was the case with Isabelle, the rhesus monkeys raised in isolation were fearful and easily frightened. They did not mate, and the females who were artificially inseminated became abusive mothers. Apparently, isolation had had a damaging effect on the monkeys.

A creative aspect of Harlow's experimentation was his use of "artificial mothers." In one such experiment, Harlow presented monkeys raised in isolation with two substitute mothers—one cloth-covered replica and one covered with wire that had the ability to offer milk. Monkey after monkey went to the wire mother for the life-giving milk, yet spent much more time clinging to the more motherlike cloth model. In this study, the monkeys valued the artificial mothers that provided a comforting physical sensation (conveyed by the terry cloth) more highly than those that provided food. It appears that the infant monkeys developed greater social attachments from their need for warmth, comfort, and intimacy than from their need for milk.

While the isolation studies discussed above may seem to suggest that inheritance can be dismissed as a factor in the social development of humans and animals, studies of twins provide insight into a fascinating interplay between hereditary and environmental factors.

The Influence of Heredity

Oskar Stohr and Jack Yufe are identical twins who were separated soon after their birth and raised on different continents in very different cultural settings. Oskar was reared as a strict Catholic by his maternal grandmother in the Sudetenland of Czechoslovakia. As a member of the Hitler Youth movement in Nazi Germany, he learned to hate Jews. By contrast, his brother Jack was reared in Trinidad by the twins' Jewish father. Jack joined an Israeli kibbutz (a collective settlement) at age 17 and later served in the Israeli army. But when they were reunited in middle age, some startling similarities emerged:

> Both were wearing wire-rimmed glasses and mustaches, both sported two pocket shirts with epaulets. They share idiosyncrasies galore: they like spicy foods and sweet liqueurs, are absent-minded, have a habit of falling asleep in front of the television, think it's funny to sneeze in a crowd of strangers, flush the toilet before using it, store rubber bands on their wrists, read magazines from back to front, dip buttered toast in their coffee (Holden 1980).

The twins also were found to differ in many important respects: Jack is a workaholic; Oskar enjoys leisure-time activities. Whereas Oskar is a traditionalist who is domineering toward women, Jack is a political liberal who is much more accepting of feminism. Finally, Jack is

extremely proud of being Jewish, while Oskar never mentions his Jewish heritage (Holden 1987).

Oskar and Jack are prime examples of the interplay of heredity and environment. For a number of years, researchers at the Minnesota Center for Twin and Adoption Research have been studying pairs of identical twins reared apart to determine what similarities, if any, they show in personality traits, behaviour, and intelligence. Thus far, the preliminary results from the available twin studies indicate that both genetic factors and socialization experiences are influential in human development. Certain characteristics, such as temperaments, voice patterns, and nervous habits, appear to be strikingly similar even in twins reared apart, suggesting that these qualities may be linked to hereditary causes. However, identical twins reared apart differ far more in their attitudes, values, types of mates chosen, and even drinking habits; these qualities, it would seem, are influenced by environmental patterns. In examining clusters of personality traits among such twins, the Minnesota studies have found marked similarities in their tendency toward leadership or dominance, but significant differences in their need for intimacy, comfort, and assistance.

Researchers have also been impressed with the similar scores on intelligence tests of twins reared apart in *roughly similar* social settings. Most of the identical twins register scores even closer than those that would be expected if the same person took a test twice. At the same time, however, identical twins brought up in *dramatically different* social environments score quite differently on intelligence tests—a finding that supports the impact of socialization on human development (McGue and Bouchard 1998).

We need to be cautious when reviewing the studies of twin pairs and other relevant research. Widely broadcast findings have often been based on extremely small samples and preliminary analysis. For example, one study (not involving twin pairs) was frequently cited as confirming genetic links with behaviour. Yet the researchers had to retract their conclusions after they increased the sample from 81 to 91 cases and reclassified two of the original 81 cases. After these changes, the initial findings were no longer valid. Critics add that the studies on twin pairs have not provided satisfactory information concerning the extent to which these separated identical twins may have had contact with each other, even though they were "raised apart." Such interactions—especially if they were extensive—could call into question the validity of the twin studies (Kelsoe et al. 1989).

Psychologist Leon Kamin fears that overgeneralizing from the Minnesota twin results—and granting too much importance to the impact of heredity—may lead to blaming the poor and downtrodden for their unfortunate condition. As this debate continues, we can certainly anticipate numerous efforts to replicate the research and clarify the interplay between hereditary and environmental factors in human development (Horgan 1993; Leo 1987; Plomin 1989; Wallis 1987).

Sociobiology

Do the *social* traits that human groups display have biological origins? As part of the continuing debate on the relative influences of heredity and the environment, there has been renewed interest in sociobiology in recent years. *Sociobiology* is the systematic study of the biological bases of social behaviour. Sociobiologists basically apply naturalist Charles Darwin's principles of natural selection to the study of social behaviour. They assume that particular forms of behaviour become genetically linked to a species if they contribute to its fitness to survive (van den Berghe 1978). In its extreme form, sociobiology suggests that *all* behaviour is the result of genetic or biological factors and that social interactions play no role in shaping people's conduct.

Sociobiology does not seek to describe individual behaviour on the level of "Why is Fred more aggressive than Jim?" Rather, sociobiologists focus on how human nature is affected by the genetic composition of a *group* of people who share certain characteristics (such as men or women, or members of isolated tribal bands). Many sociologists are highly critical of sociobiologists' tendency to explain, or seemingly justify, human behaviour on the basis of nature, rather than its cultural and social basis.

Conflict theorists (like functionalists and interactionists) believe that people's behaviour rather than their genetic structure defines social reality. Conflict theorists fear that the sociobiological approach could be used as an argument against efforts to assist disadvantaged people, such as schoolchildren who are not competing successfully (M. Harris 1997).

Edward O. Wilson, a zoologist at Harvard University, has argued that there should be parallel studies of human behaviour with a focus on both genetic and social causes. Certainly most social scientists would agree that there is a biological basis for social behaviour. But there is less support for the most extreme positions taken by certain advocates of sociobiology (S. Begley 1998; Gove 1987; Wilson 1975, 1978; see also Guterman 2000; Segerstråle 2000).

The Self and Socialization

We all have various perceptions, feelings, and beliefs about who we are and what we are like. How do we come to develop these? Do they change as we age?

We were not born with these understandings. Building on the work of George Herbert Mead (1964b),

sociologists recognize that we create our own designation: the self. The *self* is a distinct identity that sets us apart from others. It is not a static phenomenon but continues to develop and change throughout our lives.

Sociologists and psychologists alike have expressed interest in how the individual develops and modifies the sense of self as a result of social interaction. The work of sociologists Charles Horton Cooley and George Herbert Mead, pioneers of the interactionist approach, has been especially useful in furthering our understanding of these important issues (Gecas 1982).

p. 19

Sociological Approaches to the Self

Cooley: Looking-Glass Self

In the early 1900s, Charles Horton Cooley advanced the belief that we learn who we are by interacting with others. Our view of ourselves, then, comes not only from direct contemplation of our personal qualities but also from our impressions of how others perceive us. Cooley used the phrase **looking-glass self** to emphasize that the self is the product of our social interactions with other people.

The process of developing a self-identity or self-concept has three phases. First, we imagine how we present ourselves to others—to relatives, friends, even strangers on the street. Then we imagine how others evaluate us (attractive, intelligent, shy, or strange). Finally, we develop some sort of feeling about ourselves, such as respect or shame, as a result of these impressions (Cooley 1902; Howard 1989).

A subtle but critical aspect of Cooley's looking-glass self is that the self results from an individual's "imagination" of how others view him or her. As a result, we can develop self-identities based on *incorrect* perceptions of how others see us. A student may react strongly to a teacher's criticism and decide (wrongly) that the instructor views the student as stupid. This misperception can easily be converted into a negative self-identity through the following process: (1) the teacher criticized me, (2) the teacher must think that I'm stupid, (3) I *am* stupid. Therefore, the student's concept of self leads to behaviour based on this self-identity and mirrors the looking-glass self. Yet self-identities are also subject to change. If the student receives an "A" at the end of the course, he or she will probably no longer feel stupid.

Mead: Stages of the Self

George Herbert Mead continued Cooley's exploration of interactionist theory. Mead (1934, 1964a) developed a useful model of the process by which the self emerges, defined by three distinct stages: the preparatory stage, the play stage, and the game stage.

During the *preparatory stage,* children merely imitate the people around them, especially family members with whom they continually interact. Thus, a small child will bang on a piece of wood while a parent is engaged in carpentry work or will try to throw a ball if an older sibling is doing so nearby.

As they grow older, children become more adept at using symbols to communicate with others. *Symbols* are the gestures, objects, and language that form the basis of human communication. By interacting with relatives and friends, as well as by watching cartoons on television and looking at picture books, children in the preparatory stage begin to understand the use of symbols. Like spoken languages, symbols vary from culture to culture and even between subcultures. Raising one's eyebrows may mean astonishment in North America, but in Peru it means "money" or "pay me," while in the Pacific island nation of Tonga it means "yes" or "I agree" (R. Axtell 1990).

Mead was among the first to analyze the relationship of symbols to socialization. As children develop skill in communicating through symbols, they gradually become more aware of social relationships. As a result, during the

"Say cheese!" Children imitate the people around them, especially family members they continually interact with, during the *preparatory stage* described by George Herbert Mead.

play stage, the child becomes able to pretend to be other people. Just as an actor "becomes" a character, a child becomes a doctor, parent, superhero, or ship's captain.

Mead, in fact, noted that an important aspect of the play stage is role playing. **Role taking** is the process of mentally assuming the perspective of another, thereby enabling one to respond from that imagined viewpoint. For example, through this process, a young child will gradually learn when it is best to ask a parent for favours. If the parent usually comes home from work in a bad mood, the child will wait until after dinner when the parent is more relaxed and approachable.

In Mead's third stage, the *game stage,* the child of about eight or nine years old no longer just plays roles but begins to consider several actual tasks and relationships simultaneously. At this point in development, children grasp not only their own social positions, but also those of others around them—just as in a football game the players must understand their own and everyone else's positions. Consider a girl or boy who is part of a scout troop out on a weekend hike in the mountains. The child must understand what he or she is expected to do, but also must recognize the responsibilities of other scouts as well as the leaders. This is the final stage of development under Mead's model; the child can now respond to numerous members of the social environment.

Mead uses the term **generalized others** to refer to the attitudes, viewpoints, and expectations of society as a whole that a child takes into account. Simply put, this concept suggests that when an individual acts, he or she takes into account an entire group of people. For example, a child will not act courteously merely to please a particular parent. Rather, the child comes to understand that courtesy is a widespread social value endorsed by parents, teachers, and religious leaders.

At the game stage, children can take a more sophisticated view of people and the social environment. They now understand what specific occupations and social positions are and no longer equate Mr. Sahota only with the role of "librarian" or Ms. La Haigue only with "principal." It has become clear to the child that Mr. Sahota can be a librarian, a parent, and a marathon runner at the same time and that Ms. La Haigue is one of many principals in our society. Thus, the child has reached a new level of sophistication in his or her observations of individuals and institutions.

Mead: Theory of the Self

Mead is best known for his theory of the self. According to Mead (1964b), the self begins as a privileged, central position in a person's world. Young children picture themselves as the focus of everything around them and find it difficult to consider the perspectives of others. For example, when shown a mountain scene and asked to

A young gymnast is receiving guidance from her coach. Individuals such as coaches, teachers, friends, and parents often play a major role in shaping a person's self.

describe what an observer on the opposite side of the mountain sees (such as a lake or hikers), young children describe only objects visible from their own vantage point. This childhood tendency to place ourselves at the centre of events never entirely disappears. Many people with a fear of flying automatically assume that if any plane goes down, it will be the one they are on. And who reads the horoscope section in the paper without looking at their own horoscope first? And why else do we buy lottery tickets if we do not imagine ourselves winning?

As people mature, the self changes and begins to reflect greater concern about the reactions of others. Parents, friends, co-workers, coaches, and teachers are often among those who play a major role in shaping a person's self. Mead used the term *significant others* to refer to those individuals who are most important in the development of the self. Many young people, for example, find themselves drawn to the same kind of work their parents engage in (Schlenker 1985).

Goffman: Presentation of the Self

How do we manage our "self"? How do we display to others who we are? Erving Goffman, a sociologist associated with the interactionist perspective, suggested that many of our daily activities involve attempts to convey impressions of who we are.

Early in life, the individual learns to slant his or her presentation of the self in order to create distinctive appearances and satisfy particular audiences. Goffman (1959) refers to this altering of the presentation of the self as *impression management*. Box 4-1 provides an everyday example of this concept by describing how students engage in impression management after getting their examination grades.

In examining such everyday social interactions, Goffman makes so many explicit parallels to the theatre that his view has been termed the *dramaturgical approach*. According to this perspective, people resemble performers in action. For example, a clerk may try to appear busier than he or she actually is if a supervisor happens to be watching. A customer in a singles' bar may try to look as if he or she is waiting for a particular person to arrive.

Goffman (1959) has also drawn attention to another aspect of the self—*face-work*. How often do you initiate some kind of face-saving behaviour when you feel embarrassed or rejected? In response to a rejection at the singles' bar, a person may engage in face-work by saying, "There really isn't an interesting person in this entire crowd." We feel the need to maintain a proper image of the self if we are to continue social interaction.

Goffman's approach is generally regarded as an insightful perspective on everyday life, but it is not without its critics. Writing from a conflict perspective, sociologist Alvin Gouldner (1970) sees Goffman's work as implicitly reaffirming the status quo, including social class inequalities. Using Gouldner's critique, one might ask if women and minorities are expected to deceive both themselves and others while paying homage to those with power. In considering impression management and other concepts developed by Goffman, sociologists must remember that by describing social reality, one is not necessarily endorsing its harsh impact on many individuals and groups (S. Williams 1986).

Mackie: The Gendered Self

Marlene Mackie has examined the process by which one has gender added to the self-identity. She defines *gender socialization* as the "processes through which individuals learn to become feminine and masculine according to the expectations current in their society" (Mackie 1991:75). She writes of the important role of *learning* in the acquisition of femininity and masculinity and how this interacts with biology.

4-1 Impression Management by Students after Exams

When you get an exam back, you probably react differently with fellow classmates, depending on the grades that you and they earned. This is all part of impression management, as sociologists Daniel Albas and Cheryl Albas (1988) demonstrated. They explored the strategies that post-secondary students use to create desired appearances after receiving their grades on exams. Albas and Albas divide these encounters into three categories: those between students who have all received high grades (Ace–Ace encounters), those between students who have received high grades and those who have received low or even failing grades (Ace–Bomber encounters), and those between students who have all received low grades (Bomber–Bomber encounters).

Ace–Ace encounters occur in a rather open atmosphere because there is comfort in sharing a high mark with another high achiever. It is even acceptable to violate the norm of modesty and brag when among other Aces since, as one student admitted, "It's much easier to admit a high mark to someone who has done better than you, or at least as well."

Ace–Bomber encounters are often sensitive. Bombers generally attempt to avoid such exchanges because "you . . . emerge looking like the dumb one" or "feel like you are lazy or unreliable." When forced into interactions with Aces, Bombers work to appear gracious and congratulatory. For their part, Aces offer sympathy and support for the dissatisfied Bombers and even rationalize their own "lucky" high scores.

> **When forced into interactions with Aces, Bombers work to appear gracious and congratulatory.**

To help Bombers save face, Aces may emphasize the difficulty and unfairness of the examination.

Bomber–Bomber encounters tend to be closed, reflecting the group effort to wall off the feared disdain of others. Yet, within the safety of these encounters, Bombers openly share their disappointment and engage in expressions of mutual self-pity that they themselves call "pity parties." They devise face-saving excuses for their poor performances, such as "I wasn't feeling well all week" or "I had four exams and two papers due that week." If the grade distribution in a class included particularly low scores, Bombers may blame the professor, who will be attacked as a sadist, a slave driver, or simply an incompetent.

As is evident from these descriptions, students' impression management strategies conform to society's informal norms regarding modesty and consideration for less successful peers. In classroom settings, as in the workplace and in other types of human interactions, efforts at impression management are most intense when status differentials are more pronounced, as in encounters between the high-scoring Aces and the low-scoring Bombers.

Let's Discuss

1. What social norms govern the students' impression management strategies?
2. How do you react with those who have received higher or lower grades than you? Do you engage in impression management? How would you like others to react to your grade?

Source: Albas and Albas 1988.

Mackie theorizes about four concepts central to gender socialization: sex; gender assignment; gender identity; and gender expression. The first, *sex*, refers to the biological fact of being born with either XX or XY chromosomes and particular genitalia. Eventually, hormones (estrogen or testosterone) are secreted in different degrees and at maturity, distinct reproductive equipment is present in females and males. The second concept, *gender assignment*, is dependent on the sex of the child. The doctor or midwife inspects the external genitalia and assigns a gender label of either "it's a boy" or "it's a girl" to the newborn. This label or classification sorts the child into one of two categories of human beings. This initial gender assignment causes the child eventually to develop a gender identity and to learn appropriate expressions of gender. The *gender identity*, or "personal conviction" of being female or male, ordinarily emerges early in life and remains unchanged. It becomes taken-for-granted in spite of the fact that the gender identity organizes the rest of a person's beliefs about self and about others. Eventually, the child who was assigned a "girl/boy" label, based on female or male sex organs, begins to identify the self as a girl/boy. And experience teaches us quite quickly about *gender expression*, about how to express femininity or masculinity. Spencer Cahill stated that one behaves in ways that culture interprets "as indicative of a normal sexual nature" (1980:130). And as we master this gender expression, we collectively reinforce the "naturalness," normality, and legitimacy of our society's expectations of sex/ gender (West and Zimmerman 2000:141).

Goffman's and Mackie's work represents a logical progression of the sociological efforts begun by Cooley and Mead on how personality is acquired through socialization and how we manage the presentation of our self to others. Cooley stressed the process by which we come to create a self; Mead focused on how the self develops as we learn to interact with others; Goffman emphasized the ways in which we consciously create images of ourselves for others. Mackie takes it one step further by showing how gender plays a role in each of these processes: creating a self, interacting with others, and consciously presenting an image of our gendered self for others.

Psychological Approaches to the Self

Psychologists have shared the interest of Cooley, Mead, and other sociologists in the development of the self. Early work in psychology, such as that of Sigmund Freud (1856–1939), stressed the role of inborn drives—among them the drive for sexual gratification—in channelling human behaviour. More recently, psychologists such as Jean Piaget have emphasized the stages through which human beings progress as the self develops.

Like Charles Horton Cooley and George Herbert Mead, Freud believed that the self is a social product and that aspects of one's personality are influenced by other people (especially one's parents). However, unlike Cooley and Mead, he suggested that the self has components that are always fighting with each other. According to Freud, our natural impulsive instincts are in constant conflict with societal constraints. Part of us seeks limitless pleasure, while another part seeks out rational behaviour. By interacting with others, we learn the expectations of society and then select behaviour most appropriate to our own culture. (Of course, as Freud was well aware, we sometimes distort reality and behave irrationally.)

Research on newborn babies by the Swiss child psychologist Jean Piaget (1896–1980) has underscored the importance of social interactions in developing a sense of self. Piaget found that newborns have no self in the sense of a looking-glass image. Ironically, though, they are quite self-centred; they demand that all attention be directed toward them. Newborns have not yet separated themselves from the universe of which they are a part. For these babies, the phrase "you and me" has no meaning; they understand only "me." However, as they mature, children are gradually socialized into social relationships even within their rather self-centred world.

In his well-known *cognitive theory of development*, Piaget (1954) identifies four stages in the development of children's thought processes. In the first, or *sensorimotor*, stage, young children use their senses to make discoveries. For example, through touching they discover that their hands are actually a part of themselves. During the second, or *preoperational*, stage, children begin to use words and symbols to distinguish objects and ideas. The milestone in the third, or *concrete operational*, stage is that children engage in more logical thinking. They learn that even when a formless lump of clay is shaped into a snake, it is still the same clay. Finally, in the fourth, or *formal operational*, stage, adolescents are capable of sophisticated abstract thought and can deal with ideas and values in a logical manner.

Piaget has suggested that moral development becomes an important part of socialization as children develop the ability to think more abstractly. When children learn the rules of a game such as checkers or jacks, they are learning to obey societal norms. Those under eight years old display a rather basic level of morality: rules are rules, and there is no concept of "extenuating circumstances." However, as they mature, children become capable of greater autonomy and begin to experience moral dilemmas as to what constitutes proper behaviour.

According to Jean Piaget, social interaction is the key to development. As they grow older, children give increasing attention to how other people think and why they act in particular ways. In order to develop a distinct personality, each of us needs opportunities to interact with others. As we saw earlier, Isabelle was deprived of the chance for normal social interactions, and the consequences were severe (Kitchener 1991).

Socialization and the Life Course

The Life Course

Adolescents among the Kota people of the Congo in Africa paint themselves blue, Mexican American girls go on a daylong religious retreat before dancing the night away, Egyptian mothers step over their newborn infants seven times, and North American students may throw hats in the air. These are all ways of celebrating *rites of passage*, a means of dramatizing and validating changes in a person's status through rituals. The Kota rite marks the passage to adulthood. The colour blue, viewed as the colour of death, symbolizes the death of childhood. Hispanic girls in the United States celebrate reaching womanhood with a *quinceañera* ceremony at age 15. In Miami, Florida, the popularity of the *quinceañera* supports a network of party planners, caterers, dress designers, and the Miss Quinceañera Latina pageant. For

Body painting is a ritual marking the passage to puberty among young people in Liberia in Northern Africa.

Sociologists and other social scientists have moved away from identifying specific life stages that we are all expected to pass through at some point. Indeed, people today are much less likely to follow an "orderly" progression of life events (leaving school, then obtaining their first job, then getting married) than they were in the past. For example, an increasing number of women in Canada are beginning or returning to post-secondary education after marrying and having children. With such changes in mind, researchers are increasingly reluctant to offer sweeping generalizations about stages in the life course.

We encounter some of the most difficult socialization challenges (and rites of passage) in the later years of life. Assessing one's accomplishments, coping with declining physical abilities, experiencing retirement, and facing the inevitability of death may lead to painful adjustments. Old age is further complicated by the negative way that many societies view and treat senior citizens. The common stereotypes of senior citizens as helpless and dependent may well weaken an older person's self-image. However, as we will explore more fully in Chapter 12, many older people continue to lead active, productive, fulfilled lives—whether within the paid labour force or as retirees.

Anticipatory Socialization and Resocialization

The development of a social self is literally a lifelong transformation that begins in the crib and continues as one prepares for death. Two types of socialization occur at many points throughout the life course: anticipatory socialization and resocialization.

Anticipatory socialization refers to the processes of socialization in which a person "rehearses" for future positions, occupations, and social relationships. A culture can function more efficiently and smoothly if members become acquainted with the norms, values, and behaviour associated with a social position before actually assuming that status. Preparation for many aspects of adult life begins with anticipatory socialization during childhood and adolescence and continues throughout our lives as we prepare for new responsibilities.

You can see the process of anticipatory socialization take place when high school students start to consider which post-secondary institutions they may attend. Traditionally, this meant looking at publications received in the mail or making campus visits. However, with new technology, more and more students are using the Internet to begin their educational experience. Institutions are investing more time and money in developing attractive websites where students can take "virtual" campus walks and hear audio clips of everything from the campus cheer to a sample zoology lecture.

thousands of years, Egyptian mothers have welcomed their newborns to the world in the Soboa ceremony by stepping over the seven-day-old infant seven times. North American students may celebrate their graduation from university by hurling their hats skyward (D. Cohen 1991; Garza 1993; McLane 1995; Quadagno 1999).

These specific ceremonies mark stages of development in the life course. They indicate that the socialization process continues throughout all stages of the human life cycle. Sociologists and other social scientists use the life-course approach in recognition that biological changes mould but do not dictate human behaviour from birth until death.

Within the cultural diversity of Canada, each individual has a "personal biography" that is influenced by events both in the family and in the larger society. While the completion of religious confirmations, school graduations, marriage, and parenthood can all be regarded as rites of passage in our society, people do not necessarily experience them at the same time. The timing of these events depends on such factors as one's gender, economic background, where one lives (region and urban or rural area), and even when one was born.

Occasionally, assuming new social and occupational positions requires us to unlearn a previous orientation. **Resocialization** refers to the process of discarding former behaviour patterns and accepting new ones as part of a transition in one's life. Often resocialization occurs when there is an explicit effort to transform an individual, as happens in therapy groups, prisons, religious conversion settings, and political indoctrination camps. The process of resocialization typically involves considerable stress for the individual, much more so than socialization in general or even anticipatory socialization (Gecas 1992).

Resocialization is particularly effective when it occurs within a total institution. Erving Goffman (1961) coined the term **total institutions** to refer to institutions—such as prisons, the military, mental hospitals, and convents—that regulate all aspects of a person's life under a single authority. Because the total institution is generally cut off from the rest of society, it provides for all the needs of its members. Quite literally, the crew of a merchant vessel at sea becomes part of a total institution. So elaborate are its requirements, and so all-encompassing are its activities, a total institution often represents a miniature society.

Goffman (1961) has identified four common traits of total institutions:

- All aspects of life are conducted in the same place and are under the control of a single authority
- Any activities within the institution are conducted in the company of others in the same circumstances—for example, novices in a convent or army recruits
- The authorities devise rules and schedule activities without consulting the participants
- All aspects of life within a total institution are designed to fulfill the purpose of the organization. Thus, all activities in a monastery might be centred on prayer and communion with God (Davies 1989; P. Rose et al. 1979).

People often lose their individuality within total institutions. For example, a person entering prison may experience the humiliation of a **degradation ceremony** as he or she is stripped of clothing, jewellery, and other personal possessions. Even the person's self is taken away to some extent; the prison inmate loses a name and becomes known to authorities as a number. From this point on, scheduled daily routines allow for little or no personal initiative. The individual becomes secondary and rather invisible in the overbearing social environment (Garfinkel 1956).

Back in 1934, the world was gripped by the birth of quintuplets to Oliva and Elzire Dionne in Northern Ontario. In the midst of the Depression, people wanted to hear and see all they could about these five girls, born generations before fertility drugs made multiple births

How would you like to be "on view" for thousands of tourists? That was the fate of the Dionne quintuplets during the 1930s near the village of Corbeil in Ontario. The five little girls were removed from their parents and kept under sharp watch in a nine-room compound called "Quintland"—a form of a *total institution.*

more common. What seemed like a heartwarming story, however, turned out to be a tragic case of Goffman's total institutionalization. The government of Ontario soon took the quintuplets from their home and set them up in a facility complete with an observation gallery overlooking their playground. Each month, 10 000 tourists paid an entry fee to view the five little "Cinderellas." When the girls left the nine-room compound, it was always to raise money for some worthwhile cause or to merchandise some product. Within their compound, even their parents and their older siblings had to make appointments to see them. A child psychiatrist responsible for their child rearing ordered that they never be spanked—or hugged (to prevent the chance of infection).

After nine years, the quintuplets were reunited with their family. But the legacy of total institutionalization persisted. Sharp divisions and jealousies had developed between the five girls and other siblings. The parents were caught up in charges of doing too much or too little for all their children. In 1997 the three surviving quintuplets made public a poignant letter to the parents of recently born septuplets in Iowa:

> We three would like you to know we feel a natural affinity and tenderness for your children. We hope your children receive more respect than we did. Their fate should be no different from that of other children. Multiple births should not be confused with entertainment, nor should they be an opportunity to sell products. . . .
>
> Our lives have been ruined by the exploitation we suffered at the hands of the government of Ontario, our place of birth. We were displayed as a curiosity three times a day for millions of tourists. . . .
>
> We sincerely hope a lesson will be learned from examining how our lives were forever altered by our childhood experiences. If this letter changes the course of events for these newborns, then perhaps our lives will have served a higher purpose (Dionne et al. 1997:39).

It is to be hoped that the Iowa septuplets won't find themselves in the position of the Dionne women in 1998, waging a lawsuit against the government for the way they were raised in an institutional environment.

Agents of Socialization

As we have seen, the continuing and lifelong socialization process involves many different social forces that influence our lives and alter our self-images. *Agents of socialization* are those groups and people who influence our self-images, attitudes, and behaviours.

The family is the most important agent of socialization in Canada, especially for children. We'll also give particular attention in this chapter to five other agents of socialization: the school, the peer group, the mass media, the workplace, and the state. The role of religion in socializing young people into society's norms and values will be explored in Chapter 14.

Family

Children in Amish communities are raised in a highly structured and disciplined manner. But they are not immune to the temptations posed by their peers in the non-Amish world—"rebellious" acts such as dancing, drinking, and riding in cars. Still, Amish families don't get too concerned; they know the strong influence they ultimately exert over their offspring (see Box 4-2). The same is true for the family in general. It is tempting to say that the "peer group" or even the "media" really raise kids these days, especially when the spotlight falls on young people involved in shooting sprees and hate

crimes. Almost all available research, however, shows that the role of the family in socializing a child cannot be underestimated (W. Williams 1998; for a different view see J. Harris 1998).

The lifelong process of learning begins shortly after birth. Since newborns can hear, see, smell, taste, and feel heat, cold, and pain, they are constantly orienting themselves to the surrounding world. Human beings, especially family members, constitute an important part of their social environment. People minister to the baby's needs by feeding, cleansing, carrying, and comforting the baby.

The caretakers of a newborn are not concerned with teaching social skills per se. Nevertheless, babies are hardly asocial. An infant enters an organized society, becomes part of a generation, and typically joins a family. Depending on how they are treated, infants can develop strong social attachments and dependency on others.

Most infants go through a relatively formal period of socialization generally called *habit training*. Caregivers impose schedules for eating and sleeping, for terminating breast- or bottle-feeding, and for introducing new foods. In these and other ways, infants can be viewed as objects of socialization. Yet they also function as socializers. Even as the behaviour of a baby is being modified by interactions with people and the environment, the baby is causing others to change their behaviour patterns. He or she converts adults into mothers and fathers, who, in turn, assist the baby in progressing into childhood (Rheingold 1969).

As both Charles Horton Cooley and George Herbert Mead noted, the development of the self is a critical aspect of the early years of one's life. However, how children develop this sense of self can vary from one society to another. For example, parents in Canada would never think of sending six-year-olds to school unsupervised. But this is the norm in Japan, where parents push their children to commute to school on their own from an early age. In cities like Tokyo, first-graders must learn to negotiate buses, subways, and long walks. To ensure their safety, parents carefully lay out rules: never talk to strangers; check with a station attendant if you get off at the wrong stop; if you miss your stop stay on to the end of the line, then call; take stairs, not escalators; don't fall asleep. Some parents equip the children with cell phones or pagers. One parent acknowledges that she worries, "but after they are 6, children are supposed to start being independent from the mother. If you're still taking your child to school after the first month, everyone looks at you funny" (Tolbert 2000:17).

In Canada, social development includes exposure to cultural assumptions regarding gender, class, and race. Fleras and Kunz (2001) argue that the news media tend to undermine the contributions of minorities in Canadian society, emphasizing "their status as athletes, entertainers, or criminals, while occasional fawning reference

Key Terms

Agents of socialization Those groups and people who influence our self-images, attitudes, and behaviours. (99)

Anticipatory socialization Processes of socialization in which a person "rehearses" for future positions, occupations, and social relationships. (97)

Cognitive theory of development Jean Piaget's theory explaining how children's thought progresses through four stages. (96)

Degradation ceremony An aspect of the socialization process within total institutions, in which people are subjected to humiliating rituals. (98)

Dramaturgical approach A view of social interaction that examines people as if they were theatrical performers. (94)

Face-work The efforts of people to maintain the proper image and avoid embarrassment in public. (94)

Gender roles Expectations regarding the proper behaviour, attitudes, and activities of males and females. (101)

Gender socialization The processes through which individuals learn to become feminine and masculine according to the expectations current in their society. (94)

Generalized others The attitudes, viewpoints, and expectations of society as a whole that a child takes into account in his or her behaviour. (93)

Impression management The altering of the presentation of the self in order to create distinctive appearances and satisfy particular audiences. (94)

Looking-glass self A concept that emphasizes the self as the product of our social interactions with others. (92)

Peer group The group of people with whom we associate who are approximately our own age or who have a similar social status. (102)

Personality In everyday speech, a person's typical patterns of attitudes, needs, characteristics, and behaviour. (89)

Resocialization The process of discarding former behaviour patterns and accepting new ones as part of a transition in one's life. (98)

Rites of passage Rituals marking the symbolic transition from one social position to another. (96)

Role taking The process of mentally assuming the perspective of another, thereby enabling one to respond from that imagined viewpoint. (93)

Self A distinct identity that sets us apart from others. (92)

Significant others Those individuals who are most important in the development of the self, such as parents, friends, and teachers. (94)

Socialization The process whereby people learn the attitudes, values, and behaviours appropriate for members of a particular culture. (89)

Sociobiology The systematic study of biological bases of social behaviour. (92)

Symbols The gestures, objects, and language that form the basis of human communication. (93)

Total institutions Institutions that regulate all aspects of a person's life under a single authority, such as prisons, the military, mental hospitals, and convents. (98)

Additional Readings

Adler, Patricia A. and Peter Adler. 1998. *Peer Power: Preadolescent Culture and Identity.* New Brunswick, NJ: Rutgers University Press. Based on eight years of observation research, sociologists discuss the role of peer groups and family as they relate to popularity, social isolation, bullying, and boy–girl relationships.

Goffman, Erving. 1959. *The Presentation of Self in Everyday Life.* New York: Doubleday. Goffman demonstrates his interactionist theory that the self is managed in everyday situations in much the same way that a theatrical performer carries out a stage role.

Graydon, Shari. 2001. "The Portrayal of Women in Media: The Good, the Bad and the Beautiful." pp. 179–195 in McKie, Craig and Benjamin D. Singer (eds). *Communications in Canadian Society.* Toronto: Thomson. Graydon outlines the mass media's role (with special attention to advertising) in constructing images and ideals of women in our society.

Pollack, William. 1998. *Real Boys: Rescuing Our Sons from the Myths of Boyhood.* New York: Henry Holt. A clinical psychologist looks at the disenchantment experienced by so many boys because their true emotions are kept hidden.

Sadker, Myra and David Sadker. 1994. *Failing at Fairness: How America's Schools Cheat Girls*. New York: Scribner. A gender-based examination of the treatment of girls in the United States' school system.

JOURNALS

Among the journals that deal with socialization issues are *Adolescence* (founded in 1966), *Journal of Adolescence* (1978), *Journal of Personality and Social Psychology* (1965), *Media, Culture and Society* (1979), and *Young Children* (1945).

 Internet Connection

www.mcgrawhill.ca/college/schaefer

For additional Internet exercises relating to daycare around the world and MediaWatch, a Canadian nonprofit feminist organization working to eliminate sexism in the mass media, visit the Schaefer Online Learning Centre at **http://www.mcgrawhill.ca/college/schaefer**. *Please note that while the URLs listed were current at the time of printing, these sites often change—check the Online Learning Centre for updates.*

Erving Goffman's exploration of total institutions offers a sociological perspective of daily life inside prisons, the military, mental hospitals, and convents. Review the list of four common traits shared by all total institutions on page 98 of your text. Then, log onto the Cybrary of the Holocaust (**http://remember.org**). Spend time learning about the Holocaust in general, and life in concentration camps in particular, utilizing the video, photographs, stories, and research links on the site.

(a) What story or image had the greatest impact on you? Why? What new facts did you learn through your online visit?

(b) Reflecting on Goffman's ideas, identify how Nazi-run concentration camps qualify as total institutions. What occurred during the degradation ceremony to which prisoners were exposed upon entering the camps?

(c) What/who was the authority in the camps under which all aspects of life were conducted?

(d) In what specific ways were the activities of prisoners monitored by others?

(e) What was the daily routine of prisoners? What control, if any, did they have over their own lives?

(f) What were the main purposes of these camps, and how were prisoners forced to fulfill those purposes?

(g) Has looking at the Holocaust through a sociological lens changed the way you view this time in history? How so?

If this picture offends you, we apologize. If it doesn't, perhaps we should explain. Because, although this picture looks innocent enough, to the Asian market, it symbolizes death. But then, not every one should be expected to know that.

That's where we come in. Over the last 7 years Intertrend has been guiding clients to the Asian market with some very impressive results. Clients like California Bank & Trust, Disneyland, GTE, JCPenney, Nestle, Northwest Airlines, Sempra Energy, The Southern California Gas Company and Western Union have all profited from our knowledge of this country's fastest growing and most affluent cultural market. And their success has made us one of the largest Asian advertising agencies in the country.

We can help you as well. Give us a call or E-mail us at jych@intertrend.com. We can share some more of our trade secrets. We can also show you how we've helped our clients succeed in the Asian market. And that's something that needs no apology.

InterTrend Communications
19191 South Vermont Ave., Suite 400
Torrance, CA 90502
310.324.6313   fax 310.324.6848

OOOOPS.

In our social interaction with other cultures it is important to know what social rules apply. In Japan, for example, it is impolite to leave your chopsticks sticking up in the rice bowl—a symbol of death for the Japanese and an insult to their ancestors. This poster was created by an advertising agency that promises to steer its North American clients clear of such gaffes in the Asian market.

The quiet of a summer Sunday morning in Palo Alto, California was shattered by a screeching squad car siren as police swept through the city picking up college students in a surprise mass arrest. Each suspect was charged with a felony, warned of his constitutional rights, spread-eagled against the car, searched, handcuffed and carted off in the back seat of the squad car to the police station for booking.

After being fingerprinted and having identification forms prepared for his "jacket" (central information file), each prisoner was left isolated in a detention cell to wonder what he had done to get himself into this mess. After a while, he was blindfolded and transported to the "Stanford County Prison." Here he began the induction process of becoming a prisoner—stripped naked, skin searched, deloused, and issued a uniform, bedding, soap and towel. By late afternoon when nine such arrests had been completed, these youthful "first offenders" sat in dazed silence on the cots in their barren cells.

These men were part of a very unusual kind of prison, an experimental or mock prison, created by social psychologists for the purpose of intensively studying the effects of imprisonment upon volunteer research subjects. When we planned our two-week long simulation of prison life, we were primarily concerned about understanding the process by which people adapt to the novel and alien environment in which those called "prisoners" lose their liberty, civil rights, independence and privacy, while those called "guards" gain social power by accepting the responsibility for controlling and managing the lives of their dependent charges. . . .

Our final sample of participants (10 prisoners and 11 guards) were selected from over 75 volunteers recruited through ads in the city and campus newspapers. . . . Half were randomly assigned to role-play being guards, the others to be prisoners. Thus, there were no measurable differences between the guards and the prisoners at the start of this experiment. . . .

At the end of only six days we had to close down our mock prison because what we saw was frightening. It was no longer apparent to most of the subjects (or to us) where reality ended and their roles began. The majority had indeed become prisoners or guards, no longer able to clearly differentiate between role playing and self. There were dramatic changes in virtually every aspect of their behavior, thinking and feeling. In less than a week the experience of imprisonment undid (temporarily) a lifetime of learning; human values were suspended, self-concepts were challenged and the ugliest, most base, pathological side of human nature surfaced. We were horrified because we saw some boys (guards) treat others as if they were despicable animals, taking pleasure in cruelty, while other boys (prisoners) became servile, dehumanized robots who thought only of escape, of their own individual survival and of their mounting hatred for the guards. *(Zimbardo et al. 1974:61, 62, 63; Zimbardo 1972:4)* ■

The Zimbardo study effectively demonstrates the way in which social interaction can be and is determined by the social institutions within which it takes place. While the student guards quickly assumed the abusive characteristics associated with their roles within the prison environment, they would have been unlikely to behave the same way if, for instance, they had been asked to watch over (guard) children in a schoolyard. Institutional-specific expectations informed their actions. Sociologists use the term ***social interaction*** to refer to the ways in which people respond to one another, whether face to face or over the telephone or computer. In the mock prison, social interactions between guards and prisoners were highly impersonal. The guards addressed the prisoners by number rather than name, and wore reflector sunglasses that made eye contact with them impossible.

As in many real-life prisons, the simulated prison at Stanford University had a social structure in which guards held virtually total control over prisoners. The term ***social structure*** refers to the way in which a society is organized into predictable relationships. The social structure of Zimbardo's mock prison influenced the interactions between the guards and prisoners.

Zimbardo (1992:576) notes that it was a real prison "in the minds of the jailers and their captives." His simulated prison experiment, first conducted more than 25 years ago, has subsequently been repeated (with similar findings) in many countries.

The concepts of social interaction and social structure, which are closely linked to each other, are central to sociological study. Sociologists observe patterns of behaviour closely to understand and accurately describe the social interactions of a community or society and the social structure in which they take place.

This chapter begins by considering how social interaction shapes the way we view the world around us. The chapter will focus on the five basic elements of social structure: statuses, social roles, groups, social networks and technology, and social institutions. Groups are important because much of our social interaction occurs in them. Social institutions such as the family, religion, and government are a fundamental aspect of social structure. We will contrast the functionalist, conflict, feminist, and interactionist approaches to the study of social institutions. We will also examine the typologies developed by Ferdinand Tönnies, Émile Durkheim and Gerhard Lenski for comparing modern societies with simpler forms of social structure. The social policy section will consider the AIDS crisis and its implications for social institutions throughout the world. ■

Social Interaction and Reality

According to sociologist Herbert Blumer (1969:79), the distinctive characteristic of social interaction among people is that "human beings interpret or 'define' each other's actions instead of merely reacting to each other's actions." In other words, our response to someone's behaviour is based on the *meaning* we attach to his or her actions. Reality is shaped by our perceptions, evaluations, and definitions.

These meanings typically reflect the norms and values of the dominant culture and our socialization experiences within that culture. As interactionists emphasize, the meanings that we attach to people's behaviour are shaped by our interactions with them and with the larger society. Consequently, social reality is literally constructed from our social interactions (Berger and Luckmann 1966).

Defining and Reconstructing Reality

How do we define our social reality? As an example, let us consider something as simple as how we regard tattoos

(refer back to Chapter 1). Even as recently as a few years ago, many of us in Canada considered tattoos as something "weird" or "kooky." We associated them with fringe countercultural groups, such as punk rockers, bike gangs, and skinheads. A tattoo elicited an automatic negative response among many people. Now, however, so many people, including society's trendsetters, are tattooed and the ritual of getting a tattoo has become so legitimized, the mainstream culture regards tattoos differently. At this point, as a result of increased social interactions with those people, tattoos look perfectly at home to us in a number of settings.

The ability to define social reality reflects a group's power within a society. Indeed, one of the most crucial aspects of the relationship between dominant and subordinate groups is the ability of the dominant or majority group to define a society's values. Sociologist William I. Thomas (1923), an early critic of theories of racial and gender differences, saw that the "definition of the situation" could mould the thinking and personality of the individual. Writing from an interactionist perspective, Thomas observed that people respond not only to the objective features of a person or situation but also to the meaning that the person or situation has for them. For example, in Philip Zimbardo's mock prison experiment, student "guards" and "prisoners" accepted the definition of the situation (including the traditional roles and behaviour associated with being a guard or prisoner) and acted accordingly.

As we have seen throughout the last 40 years, groups that have been historically marginalized in Canadian society—such as French Canadians, women, visible minorities, senior citizens, gays and lesbians, and people with physical or mental disabilities—have fought to redefine their place in society. An important aspect of the process of social change involves reconstructing social reality. Members of subordinate groups challenge traditional definitions and begin to perceive and experience reality in a new way.

Feminists have struggled to highlight the importance of the construction of reality in limiting women's participation in society. At the macro level, male-dominated institutions have established a reality that legitimizes and perpetuates the power imbalance between men and women.

The world champion boxer Muhammad Ali insisted on his own political views (including refusing to serve in the Vietnam War), his own religion (Black Muslim), and his own name (Muhammad Ali). Not only did Ali change the world of sports, but he also had a hand in altering the world of race relations in the U.S. (Remnick 1998).

Viewed from a sociological perspective, Ali was redefining social reality by looking much more critically at the racist thinking and terminology that restricted him.

Negotiated Order

As we have seen, people can reconstruct social reality through a process of internal change as they take a different view of everyday behaviour. Yet people also reshape reality by negotiating changes in patterns of social interaction. The term **negotiation** refers to the attempt to reach agreement with others concerning some objective. Negotiation does not involve coercion; it goes by many names, including *bargaining, compromising, trading off, mediating, exchanging, "wheeling and dealing,"* and *collusion*. It is through negotiation as a form of social interaction that society creates its social structure (Strauss 1977; see also G. Fine 1984).

Negotiation occurs in many ways. As interactionists point out, some social situations, such as buying groceries, involve no mediation, while other situations require significant amounts of negotiation. For example, we may negotiate with others regarding time ("When should we arrive?"), space ("Can we have a meeting at your house?"), or even assignment of places while waiting for concert tickets. In traditional societies, impending marriage often leads to negotiations between the families of the future husband and wife. For example, anthropologist Ray Abrahams (1968) has described how the Labwor people of Africa arrange for an amount of property to go from the groom's to the bride's family at the time of marriage. In the view of the Labwor, such bargaining over an exchange of cows and sheep culminates not only in a marriage but, more importantly, in the linking of two clans or families.

While such family-to-family bargaining is common in traditional cultures, negotiation can take much more elaborate forms in modern industrial societies. Consider the tax laws of Canada. From a sociological perspective, such laws are formal norms (reflected in federal and provincial codes). The entire tax

Boxing champion Muhammad Ali has helped to redefine stereotypes throughout his career. As an athlete, he contributed to the creation of a new social reality for American blacks; now, as a person with Parkinson's Disease, he is establishing a public presence for those with degenerative conditions.

CATHY MACDONALD:
Dean, College Resources,
Kwantlen University College

As a dean of a diverse set of services—from library stacks to daycare—at the largest university college in Canada, Cathy MacDonald faces logistical challenges that require a clear understanding of systems, the most important of which are those involving the coordination of human activities. MacDonald, whose undergraduate major was sociology, was drawn to her academic specialty by a keen interest in group dynamics and social organization.

As an administrator responsible for library and communication resources, she believes her foundation in sociology has played an important role throughout her working life. "My professional work, first as a librarian and later as an administrator, has always involved dealing with people. The theoretical course background received in university has been a key factor in my career success," MacDonald says.

The implication is clear: sociology offers a broad-based foundation in people and human systems management skills that can be a valuable asset in a variety of career settings.

code undergoes revision through negotiated outcomes involving many competing interests, including big business, foreign nations, and political action committees (see Chapter 16). On an individual level, taxpayers, if audited, will mediate with agents of the Canada Customs and Revenue Agency. Changes in the taxpayers' individual situations will occur through such negotiations. The tax structure of Canada can hardly be viewed as fixed; rather, it reflects the sum of negotiations for change at any time (Maines 1977, 1982; J. Thomas 1984).

Negotiations underlie much of our social behaviour. Most elements of social structure are not static and are therefore subject to change through bargaining and exchanging. For this reason, sociologists use the term *negotiated order* to underscore the fact that the social order is continually being constructed and altered through negotiation. **Negotiated order** refers to a social structure that derives its existence from the social interactions through which people define and redefine its character. At a micro level, feminist theory views these negotiations as skewed by a socialization process that teaches one gender that the other is superior. Under circumstances where women are taught to be deferential to men, any negotiated order will inevitably favour those with power—in this case, men.

We can add negotiation to our list of cultural universals because all societies provide guidelines or norms within which negotiations take place. The recurring role of negotiation in social interaction and social structure will be apparent as we examine statuses, social roles, groups, social networks and technology, and social institutions (Strauss 1977).

p. 64

Elements of Social Structure

We can examine predictable social relationships in terms of five elements: statuses, social roles, groups, social networks and technology, and social institutions. These elements make up social structure just as a foundation, walls, and ceilings make up a building's structure. The elements of social structure are developed through the lifelong process of socialization, described in Chapter 4.

Statuses

We normally think of a person's "status" as having to do with influence, wealth, and fame. However, sociologists use **status** to refer to any of the full range of socially defined positions within a large group or society—from the lowest to the highest position. Within our society, a person can occupy the status of prime minister of Canada, fruit picker, son or daughter, violinist, teenager, resident of Halifax, dental technician, or neighbour. Clearly, a person holds more than one status simultaneously.

Ascribed and Achieved Status

Sociologists view some statuses as *ascribed,* while they categorize others as *achieved* (see Figure 5-1). An **ascribed status** is "assigned" to a person by society without regard for the person's unique talents or characteristics. Generally, this assignment takes place at birth; thus, a person's racial background, gender, and age are all considered ascribed statuses. These characteristics are biological in origin but are significant mainly because of the

FIGURE 5-1

Social Statuses

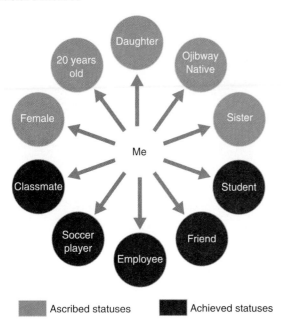

Ascribed statuses   Achieved statuses

The person in this figure—"me"—occupies many positions in society, each of which involves distinct statuses. How would you define your statuses?

social meanings they have in our culture. Conflict theorists are especially interested in ascribed statuses, since these statuses often confer privileges or reflect a person's membership in a subordinate group. The social meanings of race and ethnicity, gender, and age will be analyzed more fully in Chapters 10, 11, and 12.

In most cases, there is little that people can do to change an ascribed status. But we can attempt to change the traditional constraints associated with such statuses. As an example, the Canadian Association of Retired Persons (CARP)—an activist political group founded in 1984 to work for the rights of older people—has tried to modify society's negative and confining stereotypes of senior citizens (see Chapter 12). As a result of their work and that of other groups supporting older citizens, the ascribed status of "senior citizen" is no longer as difficult for millions of older people.

An ascribed status does not necessarily have the same social meaning in every society. In a cross-cultural study, sociologist Gary Huang (1988) confirmed the long-held view that respect for senior citizens is an important cultural norm in China. In many cases, the prefix "old" is used respectfully: calling someone "old teacher" or "old person" is like calling a judge in North America "your honour." Huang points out that positive age-seniority distinctions in language are absent in North America;

consequently, we view the term *old man* as more of an insult than a celebration of seniority and wisdom.

Unlike ascribed statuses, an ***achieved status*** comes to us largely through our own efforts. Both "bank president" and "prison guard" are achieved statuses, as are "lawyer," "student," "advertising executive," and "skateboarder." You must do something to acquire an achieved status—go to school, learn a skill, establish a friendship, or invent a new product. As we see in the next section, our achieved status is heavily influenced by our ascribed status. Being male, for example, will decrease the likelihood that a person would consider being a child care worker.

One of the interesting effects of increased cyberspace communication has been to limit the influence potential of status characteristics. It is impossible to tell someone's race or even age over the Internet, and therefore, the stereotypes that might alter one person's treatment of another in real life are simply not present. Although they are perhaps more evident, even achieved status characteristics may be difficult to discern in this medium. While disguising one's level of education may ultimately prove impossible, it is easy for the unemployed labourer to claim to be a self-made construction millionaire.

Master Status

Each person holds many different statuses; some may indicate higher social positions, and some, lower positions. How is one's overall social position viewed by others in light of these conflicting statuses? According to sociologist Everett Hughes (1945), societies deal with such inconsistencies by agreeing that certain statuses are more important than others. A ***master status*** is a status that dominates other statuses and thereby determines a person's general position within society. For example, Arthur Ashe, who died of AIDS in 1993, had a remarkable career as a tennis star; but at the end of his life, his status as a well-known personality with AIDS may have outweighed his statuses as a retired athlete, an author, and a political activist. As we will see in Box 5-1, throughout the world many people with disabilities find that their status as "disabled" is given undue weight and overshadows their actual ability to perform successfully in meaningful employment.

Society places such importance on external characteristics that they often come to dominate our lives. Indeed, such ascribed statuses often influence achieved status. Ron Nicolaye's life has been influenced by a number of these characteristics: he is an Aboriginal Canadian from the northeast coast of Vancouver Island and he is in a wheelchair. Within the traditional society where Ron grew up, either of these characteristics could have qualified to create a master status that limited his potential. However, this has not come to be. A great advocate of the environment and a keen participant in outdoor activities,

5-1 Disability as a Master Status

The Campbell River Access Committee had a difficult time convincing Vancouver Island officials that there was a need for wheelchair access to wilderness sites. However, after a demonstration of their abilities to traverse rough ground, climb into and out of canoes, and deal with the tasks of setting up a camp, outdoor enthusiasts in wheelchairs were afforded the access for which they had asked. Stereotypes about the disabled are gradually falling away as a result of such feats. But the status of disabled still carries a stigma, as it has for ages.

Throughout history and around the world, people with disabilities have often been subjected to cruel and inhuman treatment. For example, in the early twentieth century, the disabled were frequently viewed as subhuman creatures who were a menace to society. In fact, many state legislatures in the United States passed compulsory sterilization laws aimed at "handicapped people." In Japan more than 16 000 women with disabilities were involuntarily sterilized with government approval from 1945 to 1995. Sweden recently apologized for the same action taken against 62 000 of its citizens in the 1970s.

Such blatantly hostile treatment of people with disabilities generally gave way to a *medical model,* which views the disabled as chronic patients. Increasingly, however, people concerned with the rights of the disabled have criticized this model as well. In their view, it is the unnecessary and _discriminatory barriers present in the environment—both physical and attitudinal—that stand in the way of people with disabilities more than any biological limitations do. Applying a *civil rights model,* activists emphasize that those with disabilities face widespread prejudice, discrimination, and segregation. For example, most voting places are inaccessible to wheelchair users and fail to provide ballots that can be used by those unable to read print.

Drawing on the earlier work of Erving Goffman, contemporary sociologists have suggested that society has attached a stigma to many forms of disability and that this stigma leads to prejudicial treatment. Indeed, people with disabilities frequently observe that the nondisabled see them only as blind, wheelchair users, and so forth, rather than as complex human beings with individual strengths and weaknesses, whose blindness or use of a wheelchair is merely one aspect of their lives.

> In Japan more than 16 000 women with disabilities were involuntarily sterilized with government approval from 1945 to 1995.

A review of studies of people with disabilities disclosed that most academic research on the subject does not differentiate gender—thereby perpetuating the view that a disability overrides other personal characteristics. Consequently, disability serves as a master status.

Without question, people with disabilities occupy a subordinate position in the United States and Canada. By 1970, a strong political movement for disability rights had emerged across both countries. Since then, women and men involved in this movement have been working to challenge negative views of disabled people and to modify the social structure by reshaping laws, institutions, and environments so that people with disabilities can be fully integrated into mainstream society.

DisAbled Women's Network (DAWN) Canada is an example of an organization that recognizes that women and men with disabilities experience different needs. DAWN was established in 1985 and currently works to ensure that disabled women get the services and supports needed, that they have access to opportunities that nondisabled people take for granted, and that they have freedom of choice in all aspects of their lives. Issues DAWN has addressed include poverty, employment equity, violence, sexuality, health, isolation, and new reproductive technologies (NRTs).

The effort to overcome the master status is global in nature. The African nation of Botswana has plans to assist its disabled, most of whom live in rural areas and are in need of special services relating to mobility and economic development. Kenya, however, fails to outlaw discrimination against people with disabilities, even though its constitution outlaws discrimination on the basis of other characteristics, including sex, tribe, race, place of origin, creed, or religion. In many countries, disability rights activists are targeting issues essential to overcoming master status and to being a full citizen, such as employment, housing, and access to public buildings.

Let's Discuss

1. Does your campus present barriers to disabled students? If so, what kind of barriers—physical, attitudinal, or both? Describe some of them.
2. Why do you think nondisabled people see disability as the most important characteristic of a disabled person? What can be done to help people see beyond the wheelchair and the seeing-eye dog?

Sources: Albrecht et al. 2000; Goffman 1963a; Gove 1980; D. Murphy 1997; Newsday 1997; Ponczek 1998; Shapiro 1993; Willet and Deegan 2000.

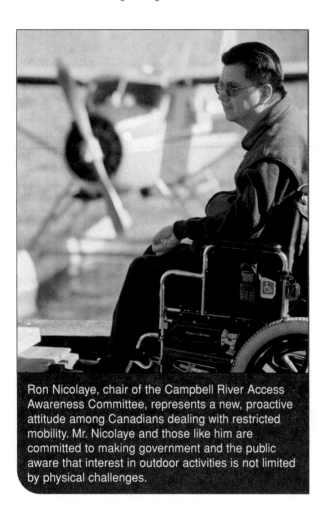

Ron Nicolaye, chair of the Campbell River Access Awareness Committee, represents a new, proactive attitude among Canadians dealing with restricted mobility. Mr. Nicolaye and those like him are committed to making government and the public aware that interest in outdoor activities is not limited by physical challenges.

Ron has devoted his energies to identifying and procuring opportunities for the disabled. He is chair of the Campbell River Access Awareness Committee, a local advocacy group that advises the mayor and city council of its community.

Social Roles

What Are Social Roles?

Throughout our lives, we are acquiring what sociologists call *social roles*. A **social role** is a set of expectations for people who occupy a given social position or status. Thus, in Canada, we expect that taxi drivers will know how to get around a city, that secretaries will be reliable in handling phone messages, and that police officers will take action if they see a citizen being threatened. With each distinctive social status—whether ascribed or achieved—come particular role expectations. However, actual performance varies from individual to individual. One secretary may assume extensive administrative responsibilities, while another may focus on clerical duties. Similarly, in Philip Zimbardo's mock prison experiment, some students were brutal and sadistic as guards, but others were not.

Roles are a significant component of social structure. Viewed from a functionalist perspective, roles contribute to a society's stability by enabling members to anticipate the behaviour of others and to pattern their own actions accordingly. Yet social roles can also be dysfunctional by restricting people's interactions and relationships. If we view a person *only* as a "computer geek" or a "teacher," it will be difficult to relate to this person as a friend or neighbour.

Role Conflict

Imagine the delicate situation of a woman who has worked for a decade as a police constable and has recently been promoted to sergeant. How is this woman expected to relate to her longtime friends and co-workers? Should she still go out to lunch with them, as she has done almost daily for years? Is it her responsibility to recommend the firing of an old friend who cannot keep up with the demands of the job?

Role conflict occurs when incompatible expectations arise from two or more social positions held by the same person. Fulfillment of the roles associated with one status may directly violate the roles linked to a second status. In the example above, the newly promoted sergeant will experience a serious conflict between certain social and occupational roles.

Role conflicts call for important ethical choices. In the example just given, the new sergeant has to make a difficult decision about how much allegiance she owes her friend whose work is unsatisfactory. Our culture tells us that success is more important than friendship. If friends are holding us back, we should leave them and pursue our ambitions. Yet, at the same time, we are told that abandoning our friends is contemptible. The sergeant must decide whether she will risk her promotion out of concern for her friend.

Another type of role conflict occurs when individuals move into occupations that are not common among people with their ascribed status. Male preschool teachers and female police officers experience this type of role conflict. In the latter case, female officers must strive to reconcile their workplace role in law enforcement with the societal view of women, which does not embrace many skills needed in police work. Research has shown that role conflict is often associated more with the pressures put on people when they try to break free of traditional gender assignments, than with the role itself. Women who occupy roles that are gender-typed as masculine report having higher rates of role conflict than those engaged in traditional feminine roles (and vice versa for men) (Basow 1992). Feminist theorists have argued that the elimination of institutionalized role expectations is critical to the full

Imagine you are a journalist walking down this alley as you witness the mugging going on here. What do you do? Try to stop the crime? Or take a picture for your magazine? This was the role conflict that Sarah Leen, a professional photographer, experienced when she stopped to change a lens and take a picture of this scene. At the same time, Leen felt fear for her own safety. People in certain professions—among them, journalism—commonly experience role conflict during disasters, crimes, and other distressing situations.

In the opening example, social psychologist Philip Zimbardo unexpectedly experienced role strain. He initially saw himself merely as a university professor directing an imaginative experiment in which students played the roles of either guard or inmate. However, he soon found that as a professor, he is also expected to look after the welfare of the students or at least not to endanger them.

Parks Canada employees also experience role strain. For generations their primary role has been to help visitors enjoy the beauty that the park system offers. However, increasingly, the social problems of the larger society, ranging from traffic jams to crime, have intruded, as more and more people seek to "escape" the routine workday world. Employees now find themselves torn between encouraging tourists to explore certain activities and curtailing activities that might interfere with the enjoyment of others, or even worse, actually harm the park. Park employees in parts of Africa face similar role strain. Photo safaris generate huge revenues for countries such as Kenya, but national wildlife refuges also are a target for people who traffic in illegal animal skins or ivory. Park employees have to carry out two very different tasks at the same time—to be welcoming ambassadors to visitors and a government enforcer of park regulations.

integration of women into modern Canadian society (C. Fletcher 1995; S. Martin 1994).

Role Strain

Role conflict describes the situation of a person dealing with the challenge of occupying two social positions simultaneously. However, even a single position can cause problems. Sociologists use the term ***role strain*** to describe difficulties that result from the differing demands and expectations associated with the same social position.

The role strain experienced by Canadian women has been a focus of feminist theory for the past few decades. Initially the emphasis was on the "Superwoman Syndrome," which described women who felt compelled to be "experts" in their work both in the paid labour force and in the home. Current research tends to focus more on the differences in role strain between married women and men. It appears to be a greater concern for women because of their unequal position in society in general: married women report that inequity brings with it more work overload, more responsibility for parental and caring work, less power than their spouse, and lack of emotional support in their role strain (Basow 1992).

Role Exit

Often, when we think of assuming a social role, we focus on the preparation and anticipatory socialization that a person undergoes for that role. Even though leaving a role can be just as demanding, only recently have social scientists given more attention to the adjustments involved in *leaving* social roles.

Sociologist Helen Rose Fuchs Ebaugh (1988) developed the term ***role exit*** to describe the process of disengagement from a role that is central to one's self-identity and re-establishment of an identity in a new role. Drawing on interviews with 185 people—among them ex-convicts, divorced men and women, recovering alcoholics, ex-nuns, former doctors, retirees, and transsexuals—Ebaugh (herself a former nun) studied the process of voluntarily exiting from significant social roles.

Ebaugh has offered a four-stage model of role exit. The first stage begins with *doubt*—as the person experiences frustration, burnout, or simply unhappiness with an accustomed status and the tasks associated with this social position. The second stage involves a *search for alternatives.* A person unhappy with his or her career may take a leave of absence; an unhappily married couple may begin what the partners see as a temporary separation.

The third stage of role exit is the *action stage* or *departure.* Ebaugh found that the vast majority of her respondents could identify a clear turning point that made them feel it was essential to take final action and leave their job, end their marriage, or engage in another type of role exit. However, 20 percent of respondents saw their role exit as a gradual, evolutionary process that had no single turning point. The last stage of role exit involves the *creation of a new identity.*

Many of you participated in a role exit when you made the transition from high school to university. At the same time, you may have declared your independence by exiting from the role of "living with your parents." By moving out and setting up one's own residence, one establishes a different status for oneself in society. Sociologist Ira Silver (1996) has made a study of the central role that material objects play in this type of transition. The objects that students choose to leave at home (like stuffed animals and dolls) are associated with their prior identities. They may remain deeply attached to these objects but do not want them to be seen as part of their new independent identities. The objects they bring with them symbolize how they now see themselves and how they wish to be perceived. CDs, clothes, and wall posters, for example, all are calculated to say, "This is me." This is an example of Cooley's looking-glass self and Goffman's theory of impression management discussed in Chapter 4.

pp. 92–94 ◀

Groups

In sociological terms, a ***group*** is any number of people with similar norms, values, and expectations who interact meaningfully with one another on a regular basis. The members of a women's hockey team, of a hospital's business office, or of a garage band constitute a group. However, the entire staff of a large hospital would not be considered a group, since the staff members rarely interact with one another at one time. Perhaps the only point at which they all come together is an annual party.

Every society is composed of many groups in which daily social interaction takes place. We seek out groups to establish friendships, to accomplish certain goals, and to fulfill social roles that we have acquired. We'll explore the various types of groups in which people interact in detail in Chapter 6, where sociological investigations of group behaviour will also be examined.

Groups play a vital part in a society's social structure. Much of our social interaction takes place within groups and is influenced by their norms and sanctions. Being a teenager or a retired person takes on special meanings when you interact within groups designed for people with that particular status. The expectations associated with many social roles, including those accompanying the statuses of brother, sister, and student, become more clearly defined in the context of a group.

New technology has broadened the definition of groups to include those who interact electronically—a significant number of Canadians. Internet use took its biggest jump ever in 2000 when 53 percent of Canadians aged 15 and over used the Internet at home, work, school, or other location, according to the General Social Survey. Use is greatest in those aged 15–24, where 92 percent used it at least once in the previous year and 45 percent use it daily, mostly from home. Canadians from Alberta and British Columbia were the most likely to use the Internet (61 percent) while those from Quebec were the least likely (44 percent), primarily due to language barriers. The majority of Internet users use it for e-mail

The pictures in this student's dorm room in India may signify his attempt to create a new identity, the final stage in role exit.

(84 percent) or for getting information on goods and services (75 percent), although one-quarter of Canadians go to the Internet for banking and shopping purposes (Statistics Canada 2000a, 2000b; Rotermann 2001).

For the human participant, online exchanges offer a new opportunity to alter one's image—what Goffman (1959) refers to as impression management. How might you present yourself to an online discussion group?

Social Networks and Technology

Groups do not merely serve to define other elements of the social structure, such as roles and statuses; they also are an intermediate link between the individual and the larger society. We are all members of a number of different groups and through our acquaintances make connections with people in different social circles. These connections are known as a **social network**—that is, a series of social relationships that link a person directly to others and therefore indirectly to still more people. Social networks may constrain people by limiting the range of their interactions, yet these networks may also empower people by making available vast resources (N. Lin 1999).

Involvement in social networks—commonly known as *networking*—is especially valuable in finding employment. For example, while looking for a job one year after finishing school, Albert Einstein was successful only when a classmate's father put him in touch with his future employer. These kinds of contacts, even if they are weak and distant, can be crucial in establishing social networks and facilitating transmission of information.

With advances in technology, we can now maintain social networks electronically. We don't need face-to-face contacts for knowledge sharing anymore. It is not uncommon for those looking for employment or for a means of identifying someone with common interests to first turn to the Internet. First impressions now begin on the web. A survey of university students found that 79 percent consider the quality of an employer's website important in deciding whether or not to apply for a job there (Jobtrak.com 2000b).

Sociologist Manuel Castells (1996, 1997, 1998) views the emerging electronic social networks as fundamental to new organizations and the growth of existing businesses and associations. One emerging

electronic network, in particular, is changing the way people interact. "Texting" began first in Asia in 2000 and has now taken off in North America and Europe. It refers to wireless e-mails exchanged over cell phones in the small screens featured in newer models. Initially, texting was popular among young users, who sent shorthand messages such as "WRU" (where are you?) and "CU2NYT" (see you tonight). But now the business world has seen the advantages of transmitting updated business or financial e-mails via cell phones or handheld personal computer organizers. Sociologists, however, caution that such devices create a workday that never ends and that increasingly people are busy checking their digital devices rather than holding conversations with those around them (W. Arnold 2000; K. Hafner 2000).

A study released in 2000 documented a rise in the amount of time people are spending online in their homes. The increase suggests that face-to-face interactions may well be declining, since there are only so many hours in anyone's day. Indeed, a third of the respondents said they spent more than five hours a week online while at home. Of those heavy users, 8 percent reported attending fewer social events as a result of their surfing, and 13 percent said they were spending less time with family and friends. Of course, the Internet can also promote social contacts, especially among those who have few opportunities, such as the disabled and the geographically

Even though you may not be totally sure to whom you are "talking" online, the Internet has added a massive new dimension to social interaction.

There has been a longstanding tradition in Canadian society that young people participate in the labour force from an early age. For generations, that tradition has included newspaper routes and babysitting as youngsters, moving on to part-time work on weekends and summers in the teenage years. However, the place of Canadian youth in the negotiated order of the economy has changed in recent years as teens have become entrenched as regular and significant participants in the workforce. Researchers Andrew Jackson and Sylvain Schetagne reported on this shift in their 2001 paper "Still Struggling: An Update on Teenagers at Work."

Other research reports, such as that of Boyce mentioned in the previous chapter, suggest that teens are working more today than ever before, but Jackson and Schetagne's results reveal that during the first three-quarters of the 1990s, the participation rate fell from 51.6 percent in 1989 to 37.1 percent in 1997. This overall number includes a reduction in both part-time employment during the school year (from 43.6 percent to 30.2 percent) and summer employment (from 65.5 percent to 44.2 percent). They did find, however, that the numbers increased after 1997, to 41.1 percent in 1999. Boyce's study referred to 46 percent of teens working in 2000. However, Jackson and Schetagne found there are more teenaged workers, now, than there were a decade ago, but this is primarily

> **There are in fact more teenage workers now than there were a decade ago, but this is primarily because there are more teenagers now than there were a decade ago.**

because there are more teenagers now than there were a decade ago. So while the number working has increased, the percent of teens working in the first half of the 1990s had declined.

Another contradiction is found in "Still Struggling." The authors found that participation has increased at all age levels for teens, and that 17- to 19-year-olds work significantly more than those who are 15–16 (60.3 percent versus 33.3 percent). Once again, the numbers are deceiving because they indicate the number of teens who have worked ". . . *at least one week a year.*"

One important finding to emerge involves the gendered distribution of work. Over the decade of the 1990s, the longstanding employment gap between girls and boys was virtually eliminated. By 1999, girls made up a larger proportion of students who held jobs during the school year (36.3 percent versus 32.3 percent), and girls were less than 1 percent behind boys when it came to summer employment (49.8 percent versus 49.3 percent).

Let's Discuss

1. Did you have a summer job while in high school? Have you found it easier or more difficult to get a job in recent years?

2. How have you and your friends been affected by the diminished opportunities for youth? How long has it taken you to find a part-time or summer job?

Source: Jackson and Schetagne 2001.

isolated. Significantly, the number of retired people who frequent chat rooms created for older users has increased sharply. Participants at websites such as ThirdAge report that they have formed new online friendships to replace old ones formed at the workplace (Galant 2000; Nie and Erbring 2000). In Chapter 20, we will examine further the ways in which computer technology has assisted the formation of larger and even international social networks.

In the workplace, networking pays off more for men than for women because of the traditional presence of men in leadership positions. A 1997 survey of executives found that 63 percent of men use networking to find new jobs compared to 41 percent of women; 31 percent of the women use classified advertisements to find jobs, compared to only 13 percent of the men (Carey and McLean 1997). Still, women at all levels of the paid labour force are beginning to make effective use of social networks. A study of women who were leaving the welfare rolls in the U.S. to enter the paid workforce found that networking was an effective tool in their search for employment. Informal networking also helped them to locate child care and better housing—both of which are key to successful employment (Carey and McLean 1997; Henly 1999).

In a recent study of informal networks among middle-aged managers at four Fortune 500 firms, Herminia Ibarra (1995) of the Harvard Business School noted the impact of race on networking. Whereas white managers often participate in all-white social networks, black managers are more likely to be part of racially integrated networks—in part because there are comparatively fewer blacks with whom to network. Race and gender clearly play a role in face-to-face networking, but electronic networking allows one to assume different or, at least, ambiguous social identities (Moskos 1991; S. Turkle 1995; L. Williams 1994).

Social Institutions

The mass media, the government, the economy, the family, and the health care system are all examples of social institutions found in our society. *Social institutions* are organized patterns of beliefs and behaviour with the goal of meeting society's basic needs, such as replacing personnel (the family) and preserving order (the government).

By studying social institutions, sociologists gain insight into the structure of a society. For example, the institution of religion adapts to the segment of society that it serves. Church work has a very different meaning for ministers who serve a skid row area, a remote northern community, or a suburban middle-class community. Religious leaders assigned to a skid row mission will focus on tending to the ill and providing food and shelter. By contrast, clergy in affluent suburbs will be occupied with counselling those considering marriage and divorce, arranging youth activities, and overseeing cultural events.

Functionalist View

One way to understand social institutions is to see how they fulfill essential functions. Anthropologist David F. Aberle and his colleagues (1950) and sociologists Raymond Mack and Calvin Bradford (1979) have identified five major tasks, or functional prerequisites, that a society or relatively permanent group must accomplish if it is to survive (see Table 5-1):

1. *Replacing personnel.* Any group or society must replace personnel when they die, leave, or become incapacitated. This is accomplished through such means as immigration, annexation of neighbouring groups of people, acquisition of slaves, or normal sexual reproduction of members. The Shakers, a religious sect that immigrated to the United States in 1774, are a conspicuous example of a group that has *failed* to replace personnel. Their religious beliefs commit the Shakers to celibacy; to survive, the group must recruit new members. At first, the Shakers proved quite successful in attracting members and reached a peak of about 6000 members during the 1840s. However, as of 1999, the only Shaker community left was a farm in Maine with seven members (Swanson 1999).

2. *Teaching new recruits.* No group can survive if many of its members reject the established behaviour and responsibilities of the group. Thus, finding or producing new members is not sufficient. The group must encourage recruits to learn and

Table 5-1	**Functions and Institutions**
Functional prerequisite	**Social institutions**
Replacing personnel	Family Government (immigration)
Teaching new recruits	Family (basic skills) Economy (occupations) Education (schools) Religion (sacred teachings)
Producing and distributing goods and services	Family (food preparation) Economy Government Health Care Canada program
Preserving order	Family (child rearing, regulation of sexuality) Government Religion (morals)
Providing and maintaining a sense of purpose	Government (social democracy) Religion

accept its values and customs. This learning can take place formally within schools (where learning is a manifest function) or informally through interaction and negotiation in peer groups (where instruction is a latent function).

3. *Producing and distributing goods and services.* Any relatively permanent group or society must provide and distribute desired goods and services for its members. Each society establishes a set of rules for the allocation of financial and other resources. The group must satisfy the needs of most members at least to some extent, or it will risk the possibility of discontent and, ultimately, disorder.

4. *Preserving order.* Every group or society must have a means for maintaining order if it is to survive. This means having institutions and standards that organize the members of the group and their activities in a way that supports the existing structure. The native people of Newfoundland and Labrador, Canada's newest province, for example, survived the initial European contact, but were

ultimately destroyed by people who believed them to be less than human. The last member of the Beothuk nation, a woman who spent her final years in servitude to the white community, died in 1829. During the preceding 200 years, Beothuk numbers had been decimated as a result of indifferent treatment and exploitation at the hands of newcomers. Victims of abuse, and exposed to previously unknown diseases such as smallpox and measles, the Beothuk eventually succumbed. They were unable to preserve their order and protect themselves from attack because of their marginalized position.

Sister Marie, who belongs to the last surviving Shaker community in the United States, checks the supplies in a refrigerator at the group's home in Maine. The Shakers have found no effective way to replace their personnel —an essential task if a group is to become a permanent part of society.

5. *Providing and maintaining a sense of purpose.* People must feel motivated to continue as members of a society in order to fulfill the previous four requirements. The behaviour of U.S. prisoners of war (POWs) while in confinement during the war in Vietnam is a testament to the importance of maintaining a sense of purpose. While in prison camps, some of these men mentally made elaborate plans for marriage, family, children, reunions, and new careers. A few even built houses in their minds—right down to the last doorknob or water faucet. By holding on to a sense of purpose—their intense desire to return to their homeland and live normal lives—the POWs refused to allow the agony of confinement to destroy their mental health.

Many aspects of a society can assist people in developing and maintaining a sense of purpose. For some people, religious values or personal moral codes are most crucial; for others, national or tribal identities are especially meaningful. Whatever these differences, in any society there remains one common and critical reality. If an individual does not have a sense of purpose, he or she has little reason to contribute to a society's survival.

This list of functional prerequisites does not specify how a society and its corresponding social institutions will perform each task. For example, the U.S. protects itself from external attack by amassing a frightening arsenal of weaponry, while Canada makes determined efforts

to remain neutral in world politics and to promote co-operative relationships with its neighbours. No matter what its particular strategy, any society or relatively permanent group must attempt to satisfy all these functional prerequisites for survival. If it fails on even one condition, as the Beothuks did, the society runs the risk of extinction.

Conflict View

Conflict theorists do not concur with the functionalist approach to social institutions. While both perspectives agree that institutions are organized to meet basic social needs, conflict theorists object to the implication that the outcome is necessarily efficient and desirable.

From a conflict perspective, the present organization of social institutions is no accident. Major institutions, such as education, help to maintain the privileges of the most powerful individuals and groups within a society, while contributing to the powerlessness of others. As one example, public schools in Canada are financed largely through property taxes. This allows more-affluent areas to provide their children with better-equipped schools and better-paid teachers than low-income areas can afford. As a result, children from prosperous communities are better prepared to compete academically than children from impoverished communities. The structure of our country's educational system permits and even promotes such unequal treatment of schoolchildren.

Conflict theorists argue that social institutions such as education have an inherently conservative nature.

Without question, it has been difficult to implement educational reforms that promote equal opportunity—whether in the area of education, ESL, or mainstreaming of students with disabilities. From a functionalist perspective, social change can be dysfunctional, since it often leads to instability. However, from a conflict view, why should we preserve the existing social structure if it is unfair and discriminatory?

Social institutions also operate in gendered and racist environments, as conflict theorists, as well as feminists and interactionists, have pointed out. In schools, offices, and governmental institutions, assumptions are made about what people can do that reflect the sexism and racism of the larger society. For instance, many people assume that women cannot make tough decisions—even those in the top echelons of corporate management. Others assume that all black students at elite universities represent affirmative action admissions. Inequality based on gender, economic status, race, and ethnicity thrives in such an environment—to which we might add discrimination based on age, physical disability, and sexual orientation. The truth of this assertion can be seen in routine decisions to advertise jobs and provide or withhold fringe benefits like child care and parental leave.

Feminist Views

As was pointed out in Chapter 1, feminist theories, rather than presenting a single perspective, analyze the social world at a number of different levels. But whether the focus is on the family, the business world, or the political arena, feminist theorists share the view that institutional discrimination is at the core of women's exclusion from a broader level of participation in Canadian society as a whole.

In the family, women have traditionally been socialized to submissive roles within the household, deferring to the culturally established authority of fathers and husbands. This results in the "Superwoman" role strain discussed earlier. While Canadian women have made inroads into the paid labour force, the addition of this new set of responsibilities has not led to a similar reduction in their traditional domestic duties. The result is that women continue to do most of the cleaning, cooking, and child care in Canadian homes, despite the expectation that they also make a full financial contribution to the two-income household. According to Pat and Hugh Armstrong in a recent paper on women and work (2000:2), "Care work is women's work. Paid and unpaid, located at home, in voluntary organizations or in the labour force, the overwhelming majority of care is provided by women."

To describe the interlocking models of oppression that are built into most institutions, feminist sociologist Patricia Hill Collins (1991) coined the phrase *matrix of domination*. This is an implicit interconnectedness among the various institutions in society that results in the standards of one spilling over to influence the standards of others. For example, the paternalistic patterns of authority found in one institution can be expected to have parallels in others—male dominance in the family supports male dominance in business, politics, education, and so on.

One of the unique features of feminist theorists is their concern with the proactive potential of theorizing. Their analysis of the role of institutions in perpetuating female marginalization is not merely an academic exercise, but rather a knowledge directed towards urging policymakers to intervene in restructuring decision-making processes so that those in less-advantaged groups will not remain mired at the bottom of Canadian society's power hierarchy.

Interactionist View

Social institutions affect our everyday behaviour, whether we are driving down the street or waiting in a long

Interactionist theory analyzes exchanges that occur during social contact. These rafters must communicate quickly and clearly to ensure that their trip through treacherous water is a safe one.

shopping line. Sociologist Mitchell Duneier (1994a, 1994b) studied the social behaviour of the word processors, all women, who work in the service centre of a large Chicago law firm. Duneier was interested in the informal social norms that emerge in this work environment and the rich social network that these female employees have created.

The Network Center, as it is called, is merely a single, windowless room in a large office building where the firm occupies seven floors. This centre is staffed by two shifts of word processors, who work either from 4:00 P.M. to midnight or midnight to 8:00 A.M. Each word processor works in a cubicle with just enough room for her keyboard, terminal, printer, and telephone. Work assignments for the word processors are placed in a central basket and then completed according to precise procedures.

At first glance, we might think that these women labour with little social contact, apart from limited work breaks and occasional conversations with their supervisor. However, drawing on the interactionist perspective, Duneier learned that despite working in a large office, these women find private moments to talk (often in the halls or outside the washroom) and share a critical view of the law firm's attorneys and day-shift secretaries. Indeed, the word processors routinely suggest that their assignments represent work that the "lazy" secretaries should have completed during the normal workday. Duneier (1994b) tells of one word processor who resented the lawyers' superior attitude and pointedly refused to recognize or speak with any attorney who would not address her by name.

Interactionist theorists emphasize that our social behaviour is conditioned by the roles and statuses that we accept, the groups to which we belong, and the institutions within which we function. For example, the social roles associated with being a judge occur within the larger context of the criminal justice system. The status of "judge" stands in relation to other statuses, such as attorney, plaintiff, defendant, and witness, as well as to the social institution of government. While the symbolic aspects of courts and jails are awesome, the judicial system derives its continued significance from the roles people carry out in social interactions (Berger and Luckmann 1966).

Social Structure in Global Perspective

Modern societies are complex, especially when compared with earlier social arrangements. Sociologists Ferdinand Tönnies, Émile Durkheim, and Gerhard Lenski have offered important typologies for contrasting modern societies with simpler forms of social structure.

For Tönnies, the emergence of industrial society represented a loss of community. He saw the transformation as a dehumanizing one, forcing people to interact as machines rather than as neighbours. While Durkheim examined similar societies as Tönnies, he was more fascinated with what bonds are created to hold together a society that is going through change. He looked to the division of labour as a source of cohesion. Lenski, on the other hand, viewed the process of technological advancement as evolutionary. From his perspective, humans could only benefit from the efficiencies of the machine age.

Tönnies's *Gemeinschaft* and *Gesellschaft*

Ferdinand Tönnies (1855–1936) was appalled by the rise of an industrial city in his native Germany during the late 1800s. In his view, this city marked a dramatic change from the ideal type of a close-knit community, which Tönnies (1988, original edition 1887) termed *Gemeinschaft*, to that of an impersonal mass society known as *Gesellschaft*.

The *Gemeinschaft* (pronounced guh-MINE-shoft) community is typical of rural life. It is a small community in which people have similar backgrounds and life experiences. Virtually everyone knows one another, and social interactions are intimate and familiar, almost as one might find among kinfolk. There is a commitment to the larger social group and a sense of togetherness among community members. People relate to others in a personal way, not just as "clerk" or "manager." With this more personal interaction comes less privacy: we know more about everyone.

Social control in the *Gemeinschaft* community is maintained through informal means such as moral persuasion, gossip, and even gestures. These techniques work effectively because people are genuinely concerned about how others feel toward them. Social change is relatively limited in the *Gemeinschaft;* the lives of members of one generation may be quite similar to those of their grandparents.

By contrast, the *Gesellschaft* (pronounced guh-ZELL-shoft) is an ideal type characteristic of modern urban life. Most people are strangers and feel little in common with other community residents. Relationships are governed by social roles that grow out of immediate tasks, such as purchasing a product or arranging a business meeting. Self-interests dominate, and there is generally little consensus concerning values or commitment to the group. As a result, social control must rely on more formal techniques, such as laws and legally defined punishments. Social change is an important aspect of life in the *Gesellschaft;* it can be strikingly evident even within a single generation.

Do you think many of the people at this party know each other? Strangers who congregate together can be part of a *Gesellschaft*.

Table 5-2 summarizes the differences between the *Gemeinschaft* and the *Gesellschaft* as described by Tönnies. Sociologists have used these terms to compare social structures stressing close relationships with those that emphasize less personal ties. It is easy to view *Gemeinschaft* with nostalgia as a far better way of life than the "rat race" of contemporary existence. However, the more intimate relationships of the *Gemeinschaft* come with a price. The prejudice and discrimination found within *Gemeinschaft* can be quite confining; more emphasis is placed on such ascribed statuses as family background than on people's unique talents and achievements. In addition, *Gemeinschaft* tends to be distrustful of the individual who seeks to be creative or just to be different.

Durkheim's Mechanical and Organic Solidarity

Émile Durkheim (1858–1917) was interested in what keeps a group/society together, especially as it is experiencing change. His answer to this question involved

social cohesion or the degree to which members of a group feel united by shared values and beliefs. He found that the cohesion was related to the *division of labour* or the ways in which jobs were divided up among the members. Using an evolutionary approach, Durkheim examined the change in societies and developed a typology that placed them in categories of either *mechanical solidarity* or *organic solidarity*.

The expression *mechanical solidarity* was used to describe the social cohesion of simple, preindustrial society, where the division of labour was minimal and people shared very similar lifestyles, performed the same tasks, and had common beliefs. It was their similarity that held them together. Since everyone was engaged in the same lifestyle (primarily agricultural), little specialization of labour was necessary. Imagine a society in which everyone grew their own wheat, milled their own flour, and turned it into bread for their own tables.

However, as societies moved toward industrialization and increased in size, the division of labour became much more specialized. *Organic solidarity* refers to the social cohesion of industrial society, where people are dependent on one another because of the different and specialized tasks each performs. The term "organic" makes reference to the organs of the body, where each organ is dependent on the others to function properly. Durkheim spoke of the interdependence of these societies—people needed each other for the completion of tasks. Rather than growing their own wheat and turning it into bread, these jobs became divided up: someone was responsible for the planting and harvesting of the wheat, someone else was the miller, transporting the flour to the bakery involved yet another job, as did the baking and selling of the bread until it appeared on the table. The diversity of tasks is indicative of a complex division of labour and this was also reflected in the different beliefs

"I'd like to think of you as a person, David, but it's my job to think of you as personnel."

With organic solidarity, people are likely to relate to one another in terms of their roles rather than their individual backgrounds.

Table 5-2 Comparison of *Gemeinschaft* and *Gesellschaft*

Gemeinschaft	*Gesellschaft*
Rural life typifies this form.	Urban life typifies this form.
People share a feeling of community that results from their similar backgrounds and life experiences.	People perceive little sense of commonality. Their differences in background appear more striking than their similarities.
Social interactions, including negotiations, are intimate and familiar.	Social interactions, including negotiations, are more likely to be task-specific.
There is a spirit of cooperation and unity of will.	Self-interests dominate.
Tasks and personal relationships cannot be separated.	The task being performed is paramount; relationships are subordinate.
There is little emphasis on individual privacy.	Privacy is valued.
Informal social control predominates.	Formal social control is evident.
There is less tolerance of deviance.	There is greater tolerance of deviance.
Emphasis is on ascribed statuses.	There is more emphasis on achieved statuses.
Social change is relatively limited.	Social change is very evident—even within a generation.

and variety of lifestyles found in these societies. It was their difference rather than their similarity that brought about their cohesion based on their need for one another—their interdependence.

Lenski's Sociocultural Evolution Approach

Sociologist Gerhard Lenski takes a very different view of society and social structure. Rather than distinguishing between two opposite types of societies, as Tönnies had, Lenski sees human societies as undergoing change according to a dominant pattern, known as *sociocultural evolution*. This term refers to the "process of change and development in human societies that results from cumulative growth in their stores of cultural information" (Lenski et al. 1995:75). In the sections that follow, we will examine the consequences of sociocultural evolution for the social structure of a society.

In Lenski's view, a society's level of technology is critical to the way it is organized. He defines *technology* as "information about the ways in which the material resources of the environment may be used to satisfy human needs and desires" (Nolan and Lenski 1999:414). The available technology does not completely define the form that a particular society and its social structure take.

Nevertheless, a low level of technology may limit the degree to which it can depend on such things as irrigation or complex machinery.

Preindustrial Societies

How does a preindustrial society organize its economy? If we know that, it is possible to categorize the society. The first type of preindustrial society to emerge in human history was the ***hunting-and-gathering society***, in which people simply rely on whatever foods and fibres are readily available. Technology in such societies is minimal. People are organized in groups and are constantly on the move in search of food. There is little division of labour into specialized tasks.

Hunting-and-gathering societies are composed of small, widely dispersed groups. Each group consists almost entirely of people related to one another. As a result, kinship ties are the source of authority and influence, and the social institution of the family takes on a particularly important role. Tönnies would certainly view such societies as examples of *Gemeinschaft*. Durkheim applied to them the term *mechanical solidarity*.

Since resources are scarce, there is relatively little inequality in terms of material goods. Social differentiation within the hunting-and-gathering society is based on such ascribed statuses as gender, age, and family background. The last hunting-and-gathering societies were located in the southern tip of South America and in the Kalahari Desert of Southwest Africa; they had virtually disappeared by the close of the twentieth century (Nolan and Lenski 1999).

Horticultural societies, in which people plant seeds and crops rather than subsist merely on available foods, emerged about 10 000 to 12 000 years ago. Members of horticultural societies are much less nomadic than hunters and gatherers. They place greater emphasis on the production of tools and household objects. Yet technology within horticultural societies remains rather limited. People cultivate crops with the aid of digging sticks or hoes (J. Wilford 1997).

The last stage of preindustrial development is the *agrarian society*, which emerged about 5000 years ago. As in horticultural societies, members of agrarian societies are primarily engaged in the production of food. However, the introduction of new technological innovations such as the plow allows farmers to increase their crop yield dramatically. They can cultivate the same fields over generations, thereby allowing the emergence of still larger settlements.

The social structure of the agrarian society continues to rely on the physical power of humans and animals (as opposed to mechanical power). Nevertheless, the social structure has more carefully defined roles than in horticultural societies. Individuals focus on specialized tasks, such as repair of fishing nets or work as a blacksmith. As human settlements become more established and stable, social institutions become more elaborate and property rights take on greater importance. The comparative permanence and greater surpluses of agrarian society make it more feasible to create artifacts such as statues, public monuments, and art objects and to pass them on from one generation to the next.

Industrial Societies

Although the Industrial Revolution did not topple monarchs, it produced changes every bit as significant as those resulting from political revolutions. The Industrial Revolution, which began largely in England during the period 1760 to 1830, was a scientific revolution focused on the application of nonanimal (mechanical) sources of power to labour tasks. It involved changes in the social organization of the workplace, as people left the homestead and began working in central locations such as factories.

As the Industrial Revolution proceeded, a new form of social structure emerged. An *industrial society* is a society that depends on mechanization to produce its goods and services. Industrial societies relied on new inventions that facilitated agricultural and industrial production and on new sources of energy such as steam. Many societies underwent an irrevocable shift from an agrarian-oriented economy to an industrial base. No longer did an individual or a family typically make an entire product. Instead, specialization of tasks and manufacturing of goods became increasingly common. Workers, generally men but also women and even children, left the home to labour in central factories.

The process of industrialization had distinctive social consequences. Families and communities could not continue to function as self-sufficient units. Individuals, villages, and regions began to exchange goods and services and become interdependent. As people came to rely on the labour of members of other communities, the family lost its unique position as the source of power and authority. The need for specialized knowledge led to more formalized education, and education emerged as a social institution distinct from the family. This is an example of the complexity in a division of labour to which Durkheim was referring in his concept of *organic solidarity*.

Postindustrial and Postmodern Societies

When the sociocultural evolutionary approach first appeared in the 1960s, it paid relatively little attention to how maturing industrialized societies may change with the emergence of even more advanced forms of technology. More recently, in evaluating the increasingly rapid pace of technological and social change, Gerhard Lenski and his collaborators have observed,

> The only things that might conceivably slow the rate of technological innovation in the next several decades are nuclear war, collapse of the world economy, or an environmental catastrophe. Fortunately, none of these appears likely in that time frame. (Lenski et al. 1995:441)

Lenski and other sociologists have studied the significant changes in the occupational structure of industrial societies as they shift from manufacturing to service economies. Social scientists call these technologically advanced nations *postindustrial societies*. Sociologist Daniel Bell (1999) defines *postindustrial society* as a society whose economic system is engaged primarily in the processing and control of information. The main output of a postindustrial society is services rather than manufactured goods. Large numbers of people become involved in occupations devoted to the teaching, generation, or dissemination of ideas.

Taking a functionalist perspective, Bell views this transition from industrial to postindustrial society as a positive development. He sees a general decline in organized working-class groups and a rise in interest groups concerned with such national issues as health, education, and the environment. Bell's outlook is functionalist because he portrays postindustrial society as basically consensual. Organizations and interest groups will engage in an open and competitive process of decision making. The level of conflict between diverse groups will diminish, and there will be much greater social stability.

Conflict theorists take issue with Bell's analysis of postindustrial society. For example, Michael Harrington (1980), who alerted the nation to the problems of the poor in his book *The Other America*, was critical of the significance that Bell attached to the growing class of white-collar workers. Harrington conceded that scientists, engineers, and economists are involved in important political and economic decisions, but he disagreed with Bell's claim that they have a free hand in decision making, independent of the interests of the rich. Harrington followed in the tradition of Marx by arguing that conflict between social classes will continue in postindustrial society.

More recently, sociologists have gone beyond discussing postindustrial societies to the ideal type of *postmodern society*. A **postmodern society** is a technologically sophisticated society that is preoccupied with consumer goods and media images (Brannigan 1992). Such societies consume goods and information on a mass scale. Postmodern theorists take a global perspective and note the ways that aspects of culture cross national boundaries (Lyotard 1993). For example, residents of Manitoba may listen to reggae music from Jamaica, eat sushi and other types of Japanese food, and wear clogs from Sweden.

Postmodern theorists point to this diversity in their rejection of the notion that the social world can be explained by a single paradigm. The intermingling of cultures and ideologies that characterizes the modern, electronically connected planet has led to a relativist approach. Postmodernists reject science as a panacea, arguing that no single explanation can accurately explain the causes and consequences of postmodern global society.

The emphasis of postmodern theorists is on describing new, emerging cultural forms and patterns of social interaction. Within sociology, the postmodern view offers support for integrating the insights of various theoretical perspectives—functionalism, conflict theory, and interactionism—while also incorporating feminist theories and other contemporary approaches. Indeed, feminist

sociologists argue optimistically that, with its indifference to hierarchies and distinctions, postmodernism will discard traditional values of male dominance in favour of gender equality. Yet others contend that despite new technology, postindustrial and postmodern societies can be expected to experience the problems of inequality that have plagued industrial societies (Ritzer 1995a; Sale 1996; Smart 1990; B. Turner 1990; van Vucht Tijssen 1990).

Ferdinand Tönnies, Émile Durkheim, and Gerhard Lenski present three visions of society's social structure. While different, each approach is useful, and this textbook will draw on them all. The sociocultural evolutionary approach emphasizes a historical perspective. It does not picture different types of social structures coexisting within the same society. Consequently, according to this approach, one would not expect a single society to include hunters and gatherers along with a postmodern culture. By contrast, sociologists frequently observe that a *Gemeinschaft* and a *Gesellschaft* can be found in the same society. For example, a rural Ontario community less than 100 kilometres from Toronto is linked to the metropolitan area by the technology of the modern information age.

The work of Tönnies, Durkheim, and Lenski reminds us that a major focus of sociology has been to identify changes in social structure and the consequences for human behaviour. At the macro level, we see society shifting to more advanced forms of technology. The social structure becomes increasingly complex, and new social institutions assume functions previously performed by the family. On the micro level, these changes affect the nature of social interactions between people. Each individual takes on multiple social roles, and people come to rely more on social networks rather than solely on kinship ties. As the social structure becomes more complex, people's relationships tend to become more impersonal, transient, and fragmented.

In the social policy section that follows, we will examine the impact of the AIDS crisis on social structure and social interaction.

SOCIAL POLICY AND SOCIAL STRUCTURE

The AIDS Crisis

The Issue

In his novel *The Plague,* Albert Camus (1948:34) wrote, "There have been as many plagues as wars in history, yet always plagues and wars take people equally by surprise." Regarded by many as the distinctive plague of the

modern era, AIDS certainly caught major social institutions—particularly the government, the health care system, and the economy—by surprise when it was initially noticed by medical practitioners in the 1970s. It has since spread around the world. While there are encouraging new therapies, there is currently no way to eradicate AIDS by medical means. Therefore, it is essential to protect people by reducing the transmission of the fatal virus. But how is this to be done? And whose responsibility is it? What roles do social institutions have?

The Setting

AIDS is the acronym for *acquired immune deficiency syndrome*. Rather than being a distinct disease, AIDS is actually a predisposition to disease caused by a virus, the human immunodeficiency virus (HIV). This virus gradually destroys the body's immune system, leaving the carrier vulnerable to infections, such as pneumonia, that those with healthy immune systems can generally resist. Transmission of the virus from one person to another appears to require either intimate sexual contact or exchange of blood or bodily fluids (whether from contaminated hypodermic needles or syringes, transfusions of infected blood, or transmission from an infected mother to her child before or during birth). Health practitioners pay particular attention to methods of transmitting HIV because there is no cure or vaccine for AIDS at this time.

The first cases of HIV–AIDS in Canada were reported in 1980. While the overall numbers are staying fairly stable, the number of new cases has declined in only injecting drug users (IDU), while others, such as the category of men who have sex with men (MSM) have begun to increase again in recent years. At the end of 1999, 49 800 people in Canada were living with HIV–AIDS. From 1996 to 1999, there was a 30 percent rise in incident HIV infections among MSM and a 27 percent drop among IDU. The suggestion is that health officials are working with drug users to provide free needles and more easy disposal of used ones, while the MSM category's rise is thought to be due to a renewed confidence in medications, which leads to a reduction in safe sex practices in the homosexual community. The incidence rate for women went up by 48 percent and for the Aboriginal population the increase was 91 percent (Health Canada May 2001).

Worldwide, AIDS is on the increase, with an estimated 34.2 million people infected and 2.8 million dying annually (see Figure 5-2). AIDS is not evenly distributed, and those areas least equipped to deal with it—the developing nations of Africa and South Asia—face the greatest challenge (Kaiser Family Foundation 2000; UNAIDS 2000).

FIGURE 5-2

The Geography of HIV

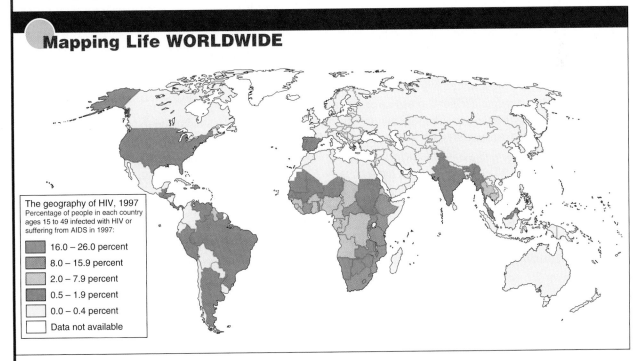

Mapping Life WORLDWIDE

The geography of HIV, 1997
Percentage of people in each country ages 15 to 49 infected with HIV or suffering from AIDS in 1997:

- 16.0 – 26.0 percent
- 8.0 – 15.9 percent
- 2.0 – 7.9 percent
- 0.5 – 1.9 percent
- 0.0 – 0.4 percent
- Data not available

Source: United Nations data reproduced by L. Altman 1998:A1.

Sociological Insights

Dramatic crises like the AIDS epidemic are likely to bring about certain transformations in a society's social structure. From a functionalist perspective, if established social institutions cannot meet a crucial need, new social networks are likely to emerge to fill that function. In the case of AIDS, self-help groups—especially in the gay communities of major cities—have organized to care for the sick, educate the healthy, and lobby for more responsive public policies. Health Canada has undergone realignment, moving its Bureau of AIDS–HIV to the newly created Centre for Infectious Disease Prevention and Control. Every major community across Canada has seen the development of self-help organizations such as Positive Women's Network, YouthCo (helping young people with AIDS), and Healing Our Spirit (created to meet the special challenges faced by Aboriginals).

The label of "person with AIDS" or "HIV-positive" often functions as a master status. Indeed, people with AIDS or infected with the virus face a powerful dual stigma. Not only are they associated with a lethal and contagious disease, but they have a disease that disproportionately afflicts already stigmatized groups, such as gay males and intravenous drug users. This linkage with stigmatized groups delayed recognition of the severity of the AIDS epidemic; the media took little interest in the disease until it seemed to be spreading beyond the gay community. Viewed from a conflict perspective, policymakers were slow to respond to the AIDS crisis because those in high-risk groups—gay men and IV drug users—were comparatively powerless. However, studies have shown that people with the virus and with AIDS who receive appropriate medical treatment are living longer than before. This may put additional pressure on policymakers to address the issues raised by the spread of AIDS (Epstein 1997; Shilts 1987).

On the micro level of social interaction, observers widely forecast that AIDS would lead to a more conservative sexual climate—among both homosexuals and heterosexuals—in which people would be much more cautious about involvement with new partners. Yet it appears that many sexually active people have not heeded precautions about "safe sex." Data from studies conducted in the 1990s indicated that there is growing complacency about AIDS, even among those most vulnerable (*AIDS Alert* 1999).

Another interactionist concern is the tremendous impact that taking the appropriate medication has on one's daily routine. Tens of thousands of AIDS patients are having to reorder their lives around their medical regimens. Even patients without the symptoms of HIV find the concentrated effort that is needed to fight the disease—taking 95 doses of 16 different medications every 24 hours—extremely taxing. Think for a moment about the effect such a regimen would have on your own life, from eating and sleeping to work, study, child care, and recreation (see Figure 5-3).

Policy Initiatives

Given the absence of a medical cure or vaccine, policy initiatives emphasize the need for more information about how AIDS is contracted and spread. In an address before the American Sociological Association, Canadian sociologist Barry Adam (1992) argued that sociologists can make an important contribution to AIDS-related research. He outlined four directions for such sociological research:

- How is information about AIDS produced and distributed? Is the distribution of information about how to have "safer sex" being limited or even censored?
- How does an AIDS "folklore"—false information about remedies and cures—emerge and become integrated into a community? Why do certain communities and individuals resist or ignore scientific information about the dangers of AIDS?
- How are medical and social services made available to people with AIDS? Why are these services often denied to the poorest patients?
- How is *homophobia* (fear of and prejudice against homosexuality) related to fears concerning AIDS? In what ways does homophobia correlate with other forms of bias?

Adam's questions underscore the impact of the AIDS crisis on social interaction and social structure. Addressing these questions will allow policymakers to better assess such initiatives as sex education programs in schools, needle exchange programs, and policies regarding AIDS testing.

AIDS has struck all societies, but not all nations can respond in the same manner. In some nations, cultural practices may prevent people from dealing with the AIDS epidemic realistically. They are less likely to take the necessary preventive measures, including more open discussion of sexuality, homosexuality, and drug use. Prevention has shown signs of working among target groups, such as drug users, pregnant women, and gay men and lesbians, but these initiatives are few and far

FIGURE 5-3

Daily Dosing for AIDS

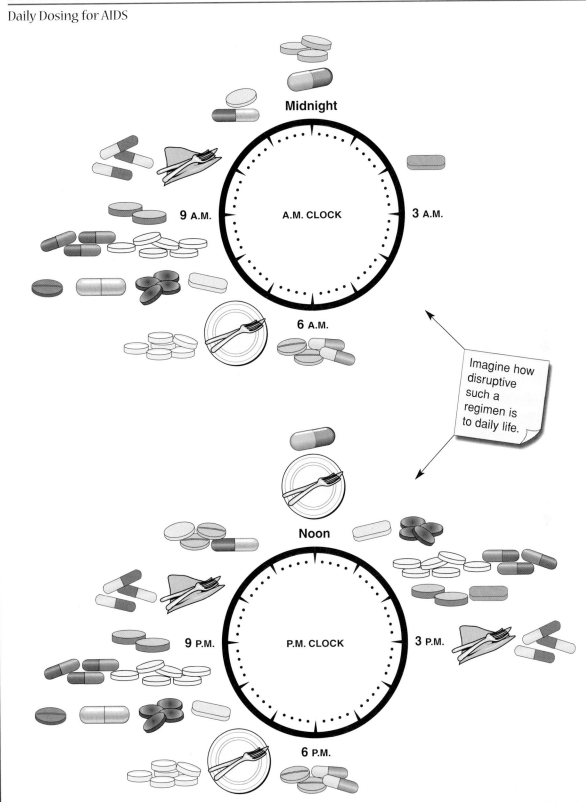

Note: Regimen may vary due to individual reactions to medications taken together. Shapes and colours of the 16 different prescription drugs are symbolic rather than realistic.

Source: Schaefer in consultation with Roxane Laboratories 2000.

between in developing nations. The prescribed treatment for a pregnant woman to reduce mother-to-baby transmission of AIDS costs about U.S.$1000—many times the average annual income in Africa, which accounts for 90 percent of the world's AIDS deaths. Even more costly is the medication for adult patients with HIV, which can cost over U.S.$71 000 per year (Pear 1997a; Sawyer 2000; Specter 1998b; Sternberg 1999).

The issues that divide rich and poor nations also manifest themselves within industrial nations. Canadians with HIV–AIDS have had to struggle to gain access to treatment. The social stigma originally associated with these conditions, and the fragmented decision-making process created by provincial jurisdiction, were just two of the obstacles to be overcome. A recent study by the Canadian AIDS Society concluded that the degree of success of advocacy groups has varied by region. Respondents rated the quality of treatment and care provided by the provincial and territorial governments, and assigned an overall grade of 'B–' to

programs in Canada. Quebec and Labrador came away with the highest rating with 46 percent of the respondents classifying programs there as "excellent" or "good." Access to drugs also varies by region, with per-patient costs ranging from $8000 to $12 000 across the country.

Let's Discuss

1. Has information on how to avoid getting AIDS been made available to you? Do you personally know of a case in which such information was withheld from someone or censored? If so, why and by whom?

2. Have you come across AIDS "folklore" (misinformation) on your campus or in your neighbourhood? If so, how widespread do you think it is?

3. If you were a sociologist who wanted to understand why some people knowingly ignore the dangers of AIDS, how would you go about studying the problem?

● Chapter Resources

Summary

Social interaction refers to the ways in which people respond to one another. *Social structure* refers to the way in which a society is organized into predictable relationships. This chapter examines the basic elements of social structure—statuses, social roles, groups, social networks and technology, and social institutions.

1. We shape our social reality based on what we learn through our social interactions. Social change comes from redefining or reconstructing social reality. Sometimes change is *negotiated*.

2. An *ascribed status* is generally assigned to a person at birth, whereas an *achieved status* is attained largely through one's own effort.

3. In Canada, ascribed statuses, such as race and gender, can function as *master statuses* that have an important impact on one's potential to achieve a desired professional and social status.

4. With each distinctive status—whether ascribed or achieved—comes particular *social roles*, the set of expectations for people who occupy that status. *Role strain* refers to a situation when the demands made in a single role put too much stress on the

individual trying to fulfill them. *Role conflict* occurs when meeting the requirements of one role contravenes the requirements of another.

5. Much of our patterned behaviour takes place within *groups* and is influenced by the norms and sanctions established by groups. Groups serve as links to *social networks* and their vast resources.

6. The mass media, the government, the economy, the family, and the health care system are all examples of *social institutions*.

7. One way to understand social institutions is to see how they fulfill essential functions, such as replacing personnel, training new recruits, and preserving order.

8. The conflict perspective argues that social institutions help to maintain the privileges of the powerful while contributing to the powerlessness of others.

9. Interactionist theorists emphasize that our social behaviour is conditioned by the roles and statuses that we accept, the groups to which we belong, and the institutions within which we function.

10. Feminist perspectives draw our attention to the fact that social structure can make stratification seem normal. For example, assumptions about women's child care responsibilities contribute to significant reductions in women's earnings over a lifetime, creating and reinforcing economic dependency and vulnerability. The challenge for Canadian society is to recognize that the historical power imbalance between men and women is sustained by social structures, and without systemic solutions, it cannot be displaced.

11. Ferdinand Tönnies distinguished the close-knit community of **Gemeinschaft** from the impersonal mass society known as **Gesellschaft**.

12. Émile Durkheim was curious about the cohesive elements of society. He saw the changes that occurred in simple societies with **mechanical solidarity** as the division of labour became more specialized. He believed that they evolved into complex societies with **organic solidarity** as members became interdependent.

13. Gerhard Lenski views human societies as changing historically along one dominant pattern, which he calls **sociocultural evolution.**

14. The AIDS crisis affects every social institution, including the family, the schools, the health care system, the economy, and the government.

Critical Thinking Questions

1. People in certain professions seem particularly susceptible to role conflict. For example, journalists commonly experience role conflict during disasters, crimes, and other distressing situations. Should they offer assistance to the needy or cover breaking news as reporters? Select two other professions and discuss the types of role conflict they might experience.

2. The functionalist, conflict, feminist, and interactionist perspectives can all be used in analyzing social institutions. What are the strengths or weaknesses in each perspective's analysis of social institutions?

3. In what ways does HIV serve to underscore issues of race, class, and gender in Canada today?

Key Terms

Achieved status   A social position attained by a person largely through his or her own efforts. (118)

Agrarian society   The most technologically advanced form of preindustrial society. Members are primarily engaged in the production of food but increase their crop yield through such innovations as the plow. (131)

Ascribed status   A social position "assigned" to a person by society without regard for the person's unique talents or characteristics. (117)

Division of labour   The ways in which jobs are divided up among the members of a group or society. (129)

Gemeinschaft   Close-knit communities, often found in rural areas, in which strong personal bonds unite members. (128)

Gesellschaft   Communities, often urban, that are large and impersonal, with little commitment to the group or consensus on values. (128)

Group   Any number of people with similar norms, values, and expectations who interact meaningfully with one another. (122)

Homophobia   Fear of and prejudice against homosexuality. (134)

Horticultural societies   Preindustrial societies in which people plant seeds and crops rather than subsist merely on available foods. (131)

Hunting-and-gathering society   A preindustrial society in which people rely on whatever foods and fibres are readily available in order to live. (130)

Industrial society   A society that depends on mechanization to produce its goods and services. (131)

Master status   A status that dominates other statuses and thereby determines a person's general position within society. (118)

Mechanical solidarity   The social cohesion of simple, preindustrial society, where the division of labour was minimal and people shared very similar lifestyles, performed the same tasks, and had common beliefs. (129)

Negotiated order   A social structure that derives its existence from the social interactions through which people define and redefine its character. (117)

Negotiation The attempt to reach agreement with others concerning some objective. (116)

Organic solidarity The social cohesion of industrial society, where people are dependent on one another because of the different and specialized tasks each performs. (129)

Postindustrial society A society whose economic system is primarily engaged in the processing and control of information. (131)

Postmodern society A technologically sophisticated society that is preoccupied with consumer goods and media images. (132)

Role conflict Difficulties that occur when incompatible expectations arise from two or more social positions held by the same person. (120)

Role exit The process of disengagement from a role that is central to one's self-identity and re-establishment of an identity in a new role. (121)

Role strain Difficulties that result from the differing demands and expectations associated with the same social position. (121)

Social cohesion The degree to which members of a group feel united by shared values and beliefs. (129)

Social institutions Organized patterns of beliefs and behaviour with the goal of meeting society's basic needs. (125)

Social interaction The ways in which people respond to one another. (115)

Social network A series of social relationships that link a person directly to others and therefore indirectly to still more people. (123)

Social role A set of expectations for people who occupy a given social position or status. (120)

Social structure The way in which a society is organized into predictable relationships. (115)

Sociocultural evolution The process of change and development in human societies that results from cumulative growth in their stores of cultural information. (130)

Status A term used by sociologists to refer to any of the full range of socially defined positions within a large group or society. (117)

Technology Information about the ways in which the material resources of the environment may be used to satisfy human needs and desire. (130)

Additional Readings

Epstein, Steven. 1996. *Impure Science: AIDS, Activism, and the Politics of Knowledge.* Berkeley, CA: University of California Press. A sociologist examines AIDS research from the perspective of how it has been influenced by social and political forces.

Ignatieff, Michael. 2000. *The Rights Revolution.* CBC Massey Lectures Series. Toronto: House of Anansi Press. Ignatieff looks at Canada as a liberal society heading into the twenty-first century, and argues that the proliferation of individual and special interest group rights that has occurred in recent decades does not pose a threat to the stability of our society.

Kephart, William M., and William M. Zellner. 1998. *Extraordinary Groups: An Examination of Unconventional Life-Styles.* 6th ed. New York: St. Martin's. Among the groups described in this very readable book are the Amish, the Oneida community, the Mormons, Hasidic Jews, Jehovah's Witnesses, and the Romani (commonly known as Gypsies).

Putnam, Robert D. 2000. *Bowling Alone: The Collapse and Revival of American Community.* New York: Simon and Schuster. A public policy scholar considers whether what he calls "social capital"—community activity and group participation—has declined in the last few decades.

Internet Connection

For additional Internet exercises relating to the Zimbardo prison experiment and Gemeinschaft *and* Gesellschaft, *visit the Schaefer Online Learning Centre at **http://www.mcgrawhill.ca/college/schaefer**. Please note that while the URLs listed were current at the time of printing, these sites often change—check the Online Learning Centre for updates.*

Visit the website **http://www.prisonexp.org**. This website deals with Philip Zimbardo's ill-fated 1971 experiment dealing with human relations in an artificial prison setting. Explore the site and see if you can find answers to these questions:

(a) Why do you think there is still a fascination with this study even 30 years after it apparently failed?

(b) What insights about this experiment has Zimbardo had over time?

(c) Can you explain how the environment the researchers created developed social networks?

(d) Can you think of a parallel situation from your own life experience, in which social circumstances influenced you to become a member of a group very quickly? What were the consequences of that involvement?

(e) Would you participate in a similar experiment today? Why or why not?

GROUPS AND ORGANIZATIONS

Groups come in all sizes and cover a broad array of interests. The group shown here is the Flying Seven, the first women's aviator club in Canada. From left to right: Miss Jean Pike, Miss Tosca Trasolini, Mrs. E. Flaherty, Mrs. F. Gilbert, President Elainne Roberge, Miss Margaret Fane, and Miss Rolie Moore.

For decades there has been an all-out war between two soft drinks of almost identical taste—Coca-Cola and Pepsi-Cola. Hundreds of millions have been sunk into financing this war. More important, billions have been spent by the public on one or the other of the products. Both drinks lay claim to the same properties— youth, freedom, physical exploits, having fun and getting girls or, conversely, getting boys. In many parts of the Third World, they also possess the properties necessary to help political freedom defeat dictatorship. Coke, in particular, has become a minor idol which promises freedom, money and escape to bigtime individualism in the West.

Clearly we are not talking about soft drinks. We are dealing here with what people want to believe about themselves. After all, you can scarcely claim to possess freedom of spirit and existential individualism on the grounds that you consume the same soft drink as three billion other people. This is conformism, not nonconformism.

The same could be said about the millions of McDonald's hamburgers eaten daily around the world. Clearly, this modern success story has nothing to do with selling the best hamburger. One look at the thin, grayish patties is enough to eliminate that possibility. One taste confirms that the meat is almost indistinguishable from the soft, innocuous bun and gooey ketchup. Sweetness seems to run each of these elements together. This is not a good hamburger. For that matter, McDonald's isn't even about people choosing the hamburger they like best. The corporation's approach has never seemed to involve winning the public through the mechanism of choice. Mac McDonald himself made it clear that he was removing freedom of choice: "if you gave people a choice there would be chaos."

And yet at some level, conscious or unconscious, people are convinced that by going to McDonald's they are demonstrating a sort of individualism—an individualism which turns its back on the middle-class social convention by going out and eating a Big Mac. They don't have to dress up or eat decent, let alone good food or, indeed, eat off plates or clear the table or wash dishes or deal with some snooty waiter or make conversation or sit up straight or sit still. They don't even have to sit down. Eating a McDonald's and drinking a Coke is an act of nonconformity and tens of millions of people are doing exactly that every day. *(Ralston Saul 1993)* ■

n this excerpt from *Voltaire's Bastards: The Dictatorship of Reason in the West*, John Ralston Saul refers to the power of modern media and marketing to influence our perceptions of which groups we belong to. McDonald's and other major transnational corporations spend billions of dollars a year to make sure that the groups we see as desirable, and subsequently join, are defined for us. Consumers have been convinced that the drive-through lane is the route to independence and self-expression, even though it is simply a path from one group in society—the "old" generation, with its tradition of family dinners around the dining table—to another—the "new" generation of movers and shakers who don't have time for such things.

In his book, *The McDonaldization of Society*, sociologist George Ritzer contemplates the enormous influence of this corporation on modern-day culture and social life. Ritzer defines **McDonaldization** as "the process by which the principles of the fast food restaurant are coming to dominate more and more sectors of American society as well as the rest of the world" (Ritzer 2000:1). In other words, corporate marketing is now able to set standards that become part of the culture in Canada and many other societies.

Despite the runaway success of McDonald's and its imitators, and the widely applauded economic benefits attributed to them, Saul sees such organizations as having effects on people's lives that may be far from constructive. On top of the propagandizing that leads a gullible public into joining client-base groups unwittingly, there is the waste and environmental degradation created by billions of disposable containers and the dehumanized work routines of fast-food crews. We must ask the question: Would people choose to become members of a group devoted to eating tasteless hamburgers were it not for the influence of mass marketing?

This chapter considers the impact of groups, group membership, and organizations on social interaction. It will begin by noting the distinctions between various types of groups, with particular attention given to the dynamics of small groups. We will examine how and why formal organizations came into existence and describe Max Weber's model of the modern bureaucracy. We'll also look at technology's impact on the organization of the workplace. The social policy section will focus on the issue of sexual harassment, which has become a major concern of both governmental and private-sector organizations. ■

Understanding Groups

In everyday speech, people use the term *group* to describe any collection of individuals, whether three strangers sharing an elevator or hundreds attending a rock concert.

p. 122 ◄ However, in sociological terms a **group** is any number of people with similar norms, values, and expectations who interact with one another meaningfully on a regular basis. People that gather together regularly to have their morning coffee at the local McDonald's, the Canadian Olympic Team, and the Ontario Minor Hockey Association are all considered examples of groups. The important point is that members of a group share some sense of belonging. This characteristic distinguishes groups from mere *aggregates* of people, such as passengers who happen to be together on an airplane flight, or from *categories* who share a common feature (such as being retired) but otherwise do not act together.

Consider the case of an *a cappella* singing group. It has agreed-upon values and social norms. All members want to improve their singing skills and schedule lots of performances. In addition, like many groups, the singing ensemble has both a formal and an informal structure. The members meet regularly to rehearse; they choose leaders to run the rehearsals and manage their affairs. At the same time, some group members may take on unofficial leadership roles by coaching new members in singing techniques and performing skills.

The study of groups has become an important part of sociological investigation because they play such a key role in the expression and transmission of culture. As we interact with others, we pass on our ways of thinking and acting—from language and values to ways of dressing and leisure activities.

Types of Groups

Sociologists have made a number of useful distinctions between types of groups—primary and secondary groups, in-groups and out-groups, and reference groups.

Primary and Secondary Groups

Charles Horton Cooley (1902:2357) coined the term **primary group** to refer to a small group characterized by intimate, face-to-face association and cooperation. The members of a family constitute a primary group. Members of a work crew can also be part of a primary group. Perhaps ironically, given Saul's introduction to McDonald's at the beginning of this chapter, one of the goals of the company's training program is to create a team atmosphere in the workplace so employees feel a sense of connection similar to that in the family.

Primary groups play a pivotal role both in the socialization process (see Chapter 4) and in the development of roles and statuses (see Chapter 5). When we find ourselves identifying closely with a group, it is probably a primary group. However, people in Canada participate in many groups that are not characterized by close bonds of friendship, such as large university classes and fan clubs. The term **secondary group** refers to a formal, impersonal group in which there is little social intimacy or mutual understanding (see Table 6-1). As in the McDonald's example above, the distinction between primary and secondary groups is not always clear-cut.

Secondary groups often emerge in the workplace among those who share special understandings about their occupation. Almost all of us have come into contact with people who deliver food, but, using observation research, two sociologists have given us new understanding of the secondary group ties that emerge in this occupation (see Box 6-1).

In-Groups and Out-Groups

A group can hold special meaning for members because of its relationship to other groups. People in one group sometimes feel antagonistic toward or threatened by another group, especially if the group is perceived as being different culturally or racially. Sociologists identify these "we" and "they" feelings by using two terms first employed by William Graham Sumner (1906:1213): *in-group* and *out-group*.

An **in-group** can be defined as any group or category to which people feel they belong. Simply put, it comprises everyone who is regarded as "we" or "us." The in-group may be as narrow as one's family or as broad as an entire society. The very existence of an in-group implies that there is an out-group viewed as "they" or "them." More formally, an **out-group** is a group or category to which people feel they do not belong.

One typical consequence of in-group membership is a feeling of distinctiveness and superiority among members, who see themselves as better than people in the out-group. A double standard held by members of the in-group can enhance this sense of superiority. Proper behaviour for the in-group is simultaneously viewed as unacceptable behaviour for the out-group. Sociologist Robert Merton (1968:480–88) describes this process as the conversion of "in-group virtues" into "out-group vices." This differential standard is apparent in worldwide discussions of terrorism. When a group or a nation takes aggressive actions, it usually justifies them as necessary,

Table 6-1	Comparison of Primary and Secondary Groups	
Primary group	**Secondary group**
Generally small	Usually large
Relatively long period of interaction	Short duration, temporary
Intimate, face-to-face association	Little social intimacy or mutual understanding
Some emotional depth in relationships	Relationships generally superficial
Cooperative, friendly	More formal and impersonal

"So long, Bill. This is my club. You can't come in."

An exclusive social club is an in-group whose members consider themselves superior to others.

6-1 Pizza Delivery Employees as a Secondary Group

We all tend to take pizza delivery for granted. We may not even take note of the person who brings the pizza to our door. But sociologists Patrick Kinkade and Michael Katovich did. Using an interactionist perspective they explored the social relationships that developed among urban pizza delivery drivers as they socialized during work while waiting for orders and after work in bars. In fact, one of the researchers spent 18 months as a pizza delivery person at three locales in Ft. Worth, Texas. What they found was that pizza deliverers form a tight network based on the ordinary transactions and the occasional dangerous interactions of their profession.

Within their culture, the pizza delivery drivers take risks and receive minimal rewards. While attacks on them are usually publicized, they are not documented statistically. But the drivers themselves are well aware of the possible dangers and talk to one another a great deal about them. During the observation period, two drivers were robbed and eight others were "tailed," resulting in four automobile accidents.

The researchers found that the world of this secondary group is "hypermasculine," with racist and sexist overtones. The drivers uniformly characterized the dangers to their safety as coming from members of racial and ethnic communities, even when there was no evidence of this. The drivers also regularly boasted of their sexual prowess and told and retold accounts of sexual favours they received from customers.

> Within their culture, the pizza delivery drivers take risks and receive minimal rewards.

Among the 106 drivers studied by the researchers, five types emerged:

- *The comedian.* This individual uses humour to neutralize or trivialize the anxiety felt over runs into neighbourhoods perceived as high-risk.
- *The adventurer.* The adventurer claims to invite problems and actually looks forward to testing himself in dangerous situations.
- *The denier.* This individual attempts to neutralize anxiety by suggesting that a problem does not exist or is exaggerated.
- *The fatalist.* This person recognizes and admits the risk of danger but simply accepts it without making any effort to neutralize it.
- *The pro.* The pro generally has had a long history in the delivery business, having worked for several pizza services and, commonly, having been an assistant manager, if not a manager, at one of the other stores.

In general, the researchers found through observation and interview that urban pizza deliverers derive more satisfaction from their secondary group membership than from monetary rewards. Group membership and identity, therefore, are very important. The study shows how people, especially in urban environments, make use of secondary groups to "carve out a niche" in the larger social world. They accept their identity as a delivery person and assume a particular type that they feel comfortable with.

Let's Discuss

1. Have you ever belonged to a work-related secondary group? If so, was your membership in the group a rewarding experience?
2. Think about a secondary group to which you belong. Can you identify any common role types? If so, describe them.

Source: Kinkade and Katovich 1997.

even as civilians are hurt and killed. Opponents are quick to label such actions with the emotion-laden term of "terrorist" and see condemnation from the world community. Yet these same people may themselves retaliate with actions that hurt civilians, which the first group will then condemn.

Since the September 11, 2001, attacks on the United States, this differential standard has been apparent in the rhetoric of the American government and the supporters of the terrorists' actions. On the one hand, many Americans see nothing wrong with bombing villages and killing civilians as a cost of eliminating terrorism. On the other hand, supporters of the terrorists see nothing wrong with flying an airplane into a skyscraper to make a statement about their beliefs. Supporters of both sides—members of their in-groups—have no trouble applauding the actions of those with whom they identify, and condemning the actions of the other group.

Conflict between in-groups and out-groups can turn violent on a personal as well as a political level. In 1999,

JÁNOS JOHN MATÉ:
Representative to the United Nations,
Greenpeace International

János John Maté graduated from Simon Fraser University in 1972 with a master's degree in sociology. Since that time, his understanding of the social world has served him in a variety of careers ranging from producing gala concerts to counselling couples to reporting on human rights for the National Film Board of Canada. But from the time he joined Greenpeace in 1989, his passion has been environmental issues. Maté began as director of the organization's Canada Nuclear Disarmament Campaign before coordinating the first antinuclear delegation to Israel. In 1995, he sailed to Moruroa from Tahiti to protest nuclear testing in the South Pacific. In the early 1990s, Maté began to focus his attentions on the depletion of the ozone layer, becoming Director of Greenpeace Canada's campaign to raise public awareness of the thinning of the planet's atmosphere. He has moved on to similar duties with Greenpeace International, coordinating the promotion and adoption of Greenfreeze, an environmentally friendly alternative to the ozone-destroying chemical used in refrigerators and car air conditioners for decades. Today, Maté is the organization's representative to the United Nations' Meeting of Parties to the Montreal Protocol, a group dedicated to stopping and reversing damage to the ozone in the earth's atmosphere. Throughout his career, Maté has benefited from the insight into the structures and processes of social life provided to him by his sociological background.

two disaffected students at Columbine High School in Littleton, Colorado, launched an attack on the school that left 15 students and teachers dead, including themselves. One week later, a 16-year-old former student walked into W.R. Myers High School in the small town of Taber, Alberta, and shot two students, killing one and seriously wounding the other. In both of these cases and others similar to them, the individuals involved claimed to have been victims of harassment for being different. Not being able to fit into one of their school's cliques may have prompted them to strike out against more popular classmates, with dire consequences.

Reference Groups

Both in-groups and primary groups can dramatically influence the way an individual thinks and behaves. Sociologists use the term **reference group** when speaking of any group that individuals use as a standard for evaluating themselves and their own behaviour. For example, a high school student who aspires to join a social circle will begin dressing like these peers, listening to the same music, and hanging out at the same stores and clubs.

Reference groups have two basic purposes. They serve a normative function by setting and enforcing standards. The high school student who wants the approval of the in-group will have to follow the

In William Golding's novel *Lord of the Flies*, a group of boys from an English prep school is marooned on a tropical island after their plane crashes, killing all the adults on board. Written as a fable about human nature, the novel describes the breakdown of social order among the boys, who divide into in- and out-groups and begin warring on one another. This frame from Peter Brook's film version dramatizes one of their savage confrontations.

group's dictates at least to some extent. Reference groups also perform a comparison function by serving as a standard against which people can measure themselves and others (Merton and Kitt 1950). For example, a snowboarder who can "tweak a Canadian Bacon" or "slam a Crippler" may be reluctant to include someone whose best half-pipe manoeuvre is a straight 180 as part of her in-group.

In many cases, people model their behaviour after groups to which they do not yet belong but to which they aspire to belong in the future. For example, a university student majoring in finance may 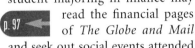 read the financial pages of *The Globe and Mail* and seek out social events attended by successful businesspeople. The student is engaging in the process of anticipatory socialization by using the Bay Street corporate elite as a reference group to which he or she aspires.

Often, two or more reference groups influence us at the same time. Our family members, peers, and co-workers all shape different aspects of our self-evaluation. In addition, certain reference group attachments change during the life cycle. This is dramatically demonstrated as young people go through adolescence, often finding that their group of friends from Grade 9 no longer appeals to them in Grade 10. We shift reference groups as we take on different statuses during our lives.

Studying Small Groups

Studying small groups is an important aspect of sociological research. The term ***small group*** is used to refer to a group small enough for all members to interact simultaneously, that is, to talk with one another or at least be well acquainted. Certain primary groups, such as families, may also be classified as small groups. However, many small groups are secondary in nature, and may be formed spontaneously. On the morning of September 11, 2001, for example, in the skies over rural Pennsylvania, a group of strangers created a small group when they joined together to prevent terrorists from crashing a fourth plane into a preselected target.

We may think of small groups as being informal and unpatterned; yet, interactionist researchers have revealed that there are distinct and predictable processes at work in the functioning of small groups. Airlines and hospitals

Groups come in all sizes. This group of puppeteers, a secondary group, has 120 members.

have developed sophisticated training programs in recent years to deal with the communication challenges found in cockpits and operating rooms. Studies had shown that the skewed distribution of power within flight crews, for example, led to situations in which the pilot—the authority figure in the group—failed to communicate with or be receptive to communication from the rest of his small group. The result was predictable dysfunction at times when the need for clear communication was the greatest (Sexton and Helmreich 2000; Waitzkin and Stoeckle 1976).

Size of a Group

At what point does a collection of people become too large to be called a small group? That is not clear. If there are more than 20 members, it is difficult for individuals to interact regularly in a direct and intimate manner. But even within a range of 2 to 20 people, group size can substantially alter the quality of social relationships. For example, as the number of group participants increases, the most active communicators become even more active relative to others. Therefore, a person who dominates a group of 3 or 4 members will be relatively more dominant in a 15-person group.

Group size also has noticeable social implications for members who do not assume leadership roles. In a larger group, each member has less time to speak, more points of view to absorb, and a more elaborate structure in which to function. At the same time, an individual has greater freedom to ignore certain members or viewpoints than he or she would in a smaller group. Clearly, it is harder to disregard someone in a 4-person workforce than in an office with 30 employees, or someone in a string quartet than in a high school band with 50 members.

German sociologist Georg Simmel (1858–1918) is credited as the first sociologist to emphasize the importance of interaction processes within groups. Reflecting on group size, Simmel (1950, original edition 1917) suggested that smaller groups have distinctive qualities and patterns of interaction that inevitably disappear as they expand in size. Larger groups, in Simmel's view, develop particular forms of interaction that are unnecessary in small groups.

The simplest of all social groups or relationships is the *dyad*, or two-member group. A romantic couple constitutes a dyad, as does a business partnership or a singing duo. In a dyad, one is able to achieve a special level of intimacy that cannot be duplicated in larger groups. However, as Simmel (1950) noted, a dyad, unlike any other group, can be destroyed by the loss of a single member. Therefore, the threat of termination hangs over a dyadic relationship perhaps more than over any other type.

Obviously, the introduction of one additional person to a dyad dramatically transforms the character of the small group. The dyad now becomes a three-member group, or *triad*. The new member has at least three basic ways of interacting with and influencing the dynamics of the group. The new person may play a *unifying* role within a triad. When a married couple has its first child, the baby may serve to bind the group closer together. A newcomer may also play a *mediating* role within a three-person group. If two roommates in an apartment are perpetually sniping at each other, the third roommate may attempt to remain on good terms with both and arrange compromise solutions to problems. Finally, a member of a triad can choose to employ a *divide-and-rule* strategy. This is the case, for example, with a coach who hopes to gain greater control over two assistants by making them rivals (Nixon 1979).

Coalitions

As groups grow to the size of triads or larger, we can expect coalitions to develop. A *coalition* is a temporary or permanent alliance geared toward a common goal. Coalitions can be broad-based or narrow, and can take on many different objectives. Sociologist William Julius Wilson (1999b) has described community-based organizations that include whites and visible minorities, working-class and affluent, who have banded together to work for improved sidewalks, better drainage systems, and comprehensive street paving. Out of this type of coalition building, Wilson hopes, will emerge better interracial understanding.

Some coalitions are intentionally short-lived. When Toronto announced its intention to submit a bid for the 2008 Summer Olympics, local community groups expressed their concerns by banding together to create a group called "Bread not Circuses" (BnC). This coalition of over 30 disparate community organizations, including the Toronto Disaster Relief Committee, a group fighting for the homeless, and the St. Lawrence Neighbourhood Association, a group defending the rights of condominium and house owners, combined their resources to oppose the bid. Their efforts may have been a factor when, on July 13, 2001, the Games were awarded to Beijing. The popular TV show *Survivor* demonstrated the power of the coalition, however short-term it might be (see Box 6-2).

The effects of group size and coalition on group dynamics are but two of the many aspects of the small group that sociologists have studied. Another area, conformity and deviance, is examined in Chapter 7. While it is clear that small-group encounters have a considerable influence on our lives, we are also deeply affected by much larger groupings of people, as we'll see in the next section.

Understanding Organizations

Formal Organizations and Bureaucracies

As contemporary societies have shifted to more advanced forms of technology and their social structures have become more complex, our lives have become increasingly dominated by large secondary groups referred to as *formal organizations* and designed for a specific purpose. A *formal organization* is a special-purpose group designed and structured for maximum efficiency. The Nova Scotia Symphony, the McDonald's fast-food industry, Canadian Association of Snowboard Instructors, and the school you attend are all examples of formal organizations. Organizations vary in their size, specificity of goals, and degree of efficiency, but they all are structured in such a way as to facilitate the management of large-scale operations. They also have a bureaucratic form of organization (described in the next section of the chapter).

In our society, formal organizations fulfill an enormous variety of personal and societal needs and shape the lives of every one of us. In fact, formal organizations have become such a dominant force that we must create organizations to supervise other organizations, such as the Ontario Securities Commission to regulate the brokerage companies. It sounds much more exciting to say that we live in the "computer age" than in the "age of formal organization"; however, the latter is probably a more accurate description of our times (Azumi and Hage 1972; Etzioni 1964).

6-2 Surviving *Survivor*—A Sociological View

Richard, Kelly, Rudy, and Susan all want to get ahead of other members of their group. So they agree to form a coalition aimed at keeping the other members from advancing or from receiving precious resources. Sometimes the coalition breaks down, but in the end its members prevail. Along the way they give out disinformation, deny their collusion, and even appear to be friendly to those they scheme against.

Sound like office politics? It well could be, but you probably recognize the four coalition members as the final four castaways in the first *Survivor*, the hit TV show in the summer of 2000.

> **The *Survivor* castaways knew that after the 39 days of filming, they would have nothing to do with one another beyond publicity appearances.**

This four-person coalition, calling itself the "Tagi Alliance," turned on fellow members of the Tagi tribe, voting them off the island one by one at tribal councils, and eventually banded against the remaining contestants in the merged tribe the last six weeks of the 12-episode contest. Coalitions like theirs occur in all organizations from schools to corporate boardrooms.

But what would sociologists have to say about the *Survivor* coalition? They would be quick to point out that this coalition does not truly represent everyday coalition-building. Coalitions can be temporary, but usually the members have to weigh the long-term social consequences of what they do against others. The *Survivor* castaways knew that after the 39 days of filming, they would have nothing to do with one another beyond publicity appearances. While the stakes were high (U.S.$1 million to the final survivor) and emotions were high, there were virtually no long-term social implications. For example, Susan expressed her strong dislike of Kelly in an emotional speech at the final tribal council, but what did it matter? They were not co-workers or classmates or family members.

Many observers have billed this type of show as "reality TV" and use the term to describe such offshoots as *Big Brother* and *Chains of Love*. Sociologists, however, would note that there is nothing real about taking 16 middle-class (or better) individuals and placing them on the island of Pulau Tiga to compete for a million-dollar windfall. That island is a part of Malaysia, a nation representative of much of the world's people who would welcome just one of the *Survivor* castaways' pre-island paycheques. Malaysians have a per capita annual income that is just a

The "Tagi Alliance": Kelly, Rudy, Susan, and Richard (left to right).

fraction of that of Canadians. Now that is reality!

Let's Discuss

1. Put yourself in the place of one of the TV show's castaways. Would you have joined a coalition? What would have been the advantages and disadvantages of such an action?
2. Did you watch the 2000 *Survivor* show? If so, why do you think the ringleader of the coalition won the contest? Would you have voted for him against Kelly to be the winner? Why or why not?
3. What constitutes reality in programs designated as "reality TV"?

Source: For GNP data, Haub and Cornelius 2000.

Ascribed statuses such as gender, race, and ethnicity influence how we see ourselves within formal organizations. For example, a study of women lawyers in the largest law firms in the United States found significant differences in these women's self-images. In firms in which fewer than 15 percent of partners were women, the female lawyers were likely to believe that "feminine" traits were strongly devalued and that masculinity was equated with success. As one female attorney put it, "Let's face it:

this is a man's environment, and it's sort of Jock City, especially at my firm." Women in firms where female lawyers were well represented in positions of power (where more than 15 percent of partners were women) had a stronger desire for and higher expectations of promotion (Ely 1995:619).

A number of feminists have written about women's experience with being a "token"—sole, or almost sole—representative of their sex in a particular business or job category. Rosabeth Moss Kanter speaks of the visibility that comes with tokenism and the perception of power that ordinarily accompanies it. However, for women in token positions, visibility is more of a source of vulnerability than power. There is a tendency for others to interpret their actions as either typical out-group behaviour or unusual behaviour *for that group* (Kanter 1977). Generalities are made of their mistakes ("Her presentation was weak—I knew a woman couldn't handle this"), and there is a tendency to discount successes ("For a woman, her strategy was tough. Someone must have helped her with it.") (Lips 1991:166). The impact of race, ethnicity, and gender on people's experiences and career prospects will be examined more fully in Chapters 10 and 11.

Characteristics of a Bureaucracy

A *bureaucracy* is a component of formal organization in which rules and hierarchical ranking are used to achieve efficiency. Rows of desks staffed by seemingly faceless people, endless lines and forms, impossibly complex language, and frustrating encounters with red tape—all these unpleasant images have combined to make *bureaucracy* a dirty word and an easy target in political campaigns. As a result, few people want to identify their occupation as "bureaucrat" despite the fact that all of us perform various bureaucratic tasks. Elements of bureaucracy enter into almost every occupation in a postindustrial society such as Canada.

Complaints about bureaucracy are not limited to developed countries. In 1993, the bureaucratic nature of the United Nations' humanitarian efforts in Somalia came under attack. The five international agencies designated to run relief efforts in Somalia had more than 12 000 employees, of whom only 116 were serving in the impoverished, war-torn African nation. Moreover, like many bureaucracies, the relief apparatus was slow in dealing with a drastic problem. In the words of a former United Nations worker in Somalia, "The average UN person takes 15 days to reply to a fax. . . . 3000 people can die in 15 days" (Longworth 1993:9).

Max Weber (1947, original edition 1922), first directed researchers to the significance of bureaucratic structure. In an important sociological advance, Weber emphasized the basic similarity of structure and process found in the otherwise dissimilar enterprises of religion, government, education, and business. Weber saw bureaucracy as a form of organization quite different from the family-run business. For analytical purposes, he developed an *ideal type* of bureaucracy that would reflect the most characteristic aspects of all human organizations. By *ideal type* Weber meant a construct or model that could serve as a point of reference against which specific cases could be evaluated. In actuality, perfect bureaucracies do not exist; no real-world organization corresponds exactly to Weber's ideal type.

Weber proposed that whether the purpose is to run a church, a corporation, or an army, the ideal bureaucracy displays five basic characteristics. A discussion of those characteristics, as well as the *dysfunctions* (or potential negative consequences) of a bureaucracy, follows. (Table 6-2 summarizes the discussion.)

Table 6-2 Characteristics of a Bureaucracy

Characteristic	Positive consequence	Negative consequence	
		For the individual	For the organization
Division of labour	Produces efficiency in large-scale corporation	Produces trained incapacity	Produces a narrow perspective
Hierarchy of authority	Clarifies who is in command	Deprives employees of a voice in decision making	Permits concealment of mistakes
Written rules and regulations	Let workers know what is expected of them	Stifle initiative and imagination	Lead to goal displacement
Impersonality	Reduces bias	Contributes to feelings of alienation	Discourages loyalty to company
Employment based on technical qualifications	Discourages favouritism and reduces petty rivalries	Discourages ambition to improve oneself elsewhere	Allows Peter Principle to operate

1. Division of Labour.   Specialized experts are employed in each position to perform specific tasks. In a university's bureaucracy, the admissions officer does not do the job of registrar; the educational advisors don't see to the maintenance of buildings. Durkheim's concept of *organic solidarity* can be seen here. The group is held together by interdependence where the performance of each of these individual workers is dependent to some degree on the performance of the others, within the division of labour. By working at a specific task, people are more likely to become highly skilled and carry out a job with maximum efficiency. This emphasis on specialization is so basic a part of our lives that we may not realize that it is a fairly recent development in Western culture. The fragmentation of tasks at a McDonald's franchise is a perfect example of this specialization.

p. 129

Unfortunately, the fragmentation of work into smaller and smaller tasks can divide workers and remove any connection they might feel to the overall objective of the bureaucracy. In *The Communist Manifesto* (written in 1848), Karl Marx and Friedrich Engels charged that the capitalist system reduces workers to a mere "appendage of the machine" (Feuer 1959). Such a work arrangement, they wrote, produces extreme *alienation*—a condition of estrangement or dissociation from the surrounding society. For example, at McDonald's, the people who make the french fries cannot take credit for someone's dining experience because they contributed but a small part of the overall meal. (Alienation will be discussed in greater detail in Chapter 17.) According to both Marx and conflict theorists, restricting workers to very small tasks also weakens their job security, since new employees can be easily trained to replace them.

Although division of labour has certainly enhanced the performance of many complex bureaucracies, in some cases it can lead to *trained incapacity*; that is, workers become so specialized that they develop blind spots and fail to notice obvious problems. Even worse, they may not *care* about what is happening in the next department. For example, when a baggage conveyor at Pearson International Airport in Toronto failed during the 2001 Christmas season, all of the other systems at Air Canada continued to function as usual. The result: several thousand travellers waited for hours to claim their bags. This is evidence that huge bureaucracies have caused workers in Canada and other developed nations to become less productive on the job.

The explosion of the United States space shuttle *Challenger* in 1986, in which seven astronauts died, is one of the most dramatic examples of the negative consequences of a bureaucratic division of labour. While the *Challenger* disaster is remembered primarily as a technical failure, its roots lay in the social organization of the National Aeronautics and Space Administration (NASA), whose officials decided to proceed with the launch despite a potentially serious problem. According to sociologist Diane Vaughan (1996, 1999), the defect that caused the

The 1986 *Challenger* disaster was not just a technical failure, but an example of the negative consequences of the bureaucratic division of labour.

accident was discovered as early as 1977; in 1985 it was labelled a "launch constraint" (reason not to launch). On the day the *Challenger* was scheduled to take off, engineers from a company that manufactured a critical part recommended that NASA cancel the launch, but the 34 people who participated in the final prelaunch teleconference ignored their warning. Ultimately, no one was held responsible for the catastrophe. At its worst, a narrow division of labour can allow everyone to avoid responsibility for a critical decision.

2. Hierarchy of Authority. Bureaucracies follow the principle of hierarchy; that is, each position is under the supervision of a higher authority. A president heads a university bureaucracy; he or she selects members of the administration, who in turn hire their own staff. In parliament, it is the prime minister who has the authority to name cabinet ministers, and to hire senior bureaucrats in the federal system. In the Roman Catholic church, the pope is the supreme authority; under him are cardinals, bishops, and so forth. In some social hierarchies, the ultimate authority may be obscure. In the Canadian confederation, for example, the prime minister is seen as holding the highest-ranking position in the country (within a democracy, however, it is the voters who have the final word). Even at McDonald's, there is a shift supervisor, crew chief, trainers, and managers, all of whom have authority that is defined within the company's employee handbook.

3. Written Rules and Regulations. What if the financial awards officer gave you a scholarship for having such a friendly smile? It would certainly be a pleasant surprise, but it would also be "against the rules."

Rules and regulations, as our frustrating interactions with phone companies and financial services have demonstrated, are an important characteristic of bureaucracies. Ideally, through such procedures, a bureaucracy ensures uniform performance of every task. This prohibits you from receiving a scholarship for a nice smile, but it also guarantees that no one else will, either.

On the other hand, the written rules and regulations of bureaucracies generally offer employees clear standards as to what is considered an adequate (or exceptional) performance. In addition, procedures provide a valuable sense of continuity in a bureaucracy. Individual workers will come and go, but the structure and past records give the organization a life of its own that outlasts the services of any one bureaucrat.

Of course, rules and regulations can overshadow the larger goals of an organization and become dysfunctional. If blindly applied, they will no longer serve as a means to achieving an objective but instead will become important (and perhaps too important) in their own

right. This would certainly be the case if a hospital emergency room physician failed to treat a seriously injured person because of having no valid proof that the person was a member of a provincial medical plan. Robert Merton (1968) has used the term *goal displacement* to refer to overzealous conformity to official regulations.

4. Impersonality. Max Weber wrote that in a bureaucracy, work is carried out *sine ira et studio,* "without hatred or passion." Bureaucratic norms dictate that officials perform their duties without the personal consideration of people as individuals. This is intended to guarantee equal treatment for all people; however, it also contributes to the often cold and uncaring feeling associated with modern organizations. We typically think of big government and big business when we think of impersonal bureaucracies. But today even small companies have telephone systems greeting callers with an electronic menu. E-mail addresses are sought under the guise of efficiency, but they also make it less likely that a response will be direct and personal. While McDonald's may try to achieve a sense of in-group membership within a shift team, how to deal with customers is prescribed. Ensuring equal treatment of all customers means there is little or no room for personal initiative.

5. Employment Based on Technical Qualifications. Within a bureaucracy, hiring is based on technical qualifications rather than on favouritism, and performance is measured against specific standards. At a McDonald's franchise, written personnel policies dictate who gets promoted. However, in all provinces with a labour-standards branch of government, people often have a right to appeal if they believe that particular rules have been violated. Such procedures protect bureaucrats against arbitrary dismissal, provide a measure of security, and encourage loyalty to the organization.

In this sense, the "impersonal" bureaucracy can be an improvement over nonbureaucratic organizations. University faculty members, for example, are ideally hired and promoted according to their professional qualifications, including degrees earned and research published, and not because of favours they do for the dean. Once they are granted tenure, their jobs are protected against the whims of individuals in positions of authority.

Although any bureaucracy ideally will value technical and professional competence, personnel decisions do not always follow this ideal pattern. Dysfunctions within bureaucracy have become well publicized, particularly because of the work of Laurence J. Peter. According to the *Peter Principle*, every employee within a hierarchy tends to rise to his or her level of incompetence (Peter and Hull 1969). The Principle states that workers are promoted every time they do their job well, and it is only after they move into a position in which they are incompetent that they will stop advancing up the hierarchy. This hypothesis, which has not been directly or systematically tested, reflects a possible dysfunctional outcome of structuring advancement on the basis of merit. Talented people receive promotion after promotion until, sadly, they finally achieve positions that they cannot handle with their usual competence (Blau and Meyer 1987).

The five characteristics of bureaucracy, developed by Max Weber more than 75 years ago, describe an ideal type rather than offer a precise definition of an actual bureaucracy. Not every formal organization will possess all of Weber's characteristics. In fact, there can be wide variation among actual bureaucratic organizations. In Box 6-3, we consider how some bureaucracies actually function in different cultural settings, including Weber's native country of Germany.

Bureaucratization as a Process

Sociologists have used the term ***bureaucratization*** to refer to the process by which a group, organization, or social movement becomes increasingly bureaucratic. Normally, we think of bureaucratization in terms of large organizations. In a typical citizen's nightmare, one may have to speak to 10 or 12 individuals in a corporation or government agency to find out which official has jurisdiction over a particular problem. Callers can get transferred from one department to another until they finally

hang up in disgust. One of the ironies of this situation is that the inefficiency of this process may serve the goals of the organization by discouraging some callers, such as those wishing to lodge complaints, who might otherwise put a strain on resources.

Bureaucratization also takes place within small-group settings. American sociologist Jennifer Bickman Mendez (1998) studied domestic houseworkers employed in central California by a nationwide franchise. She found that housekeeping tasks were minutely defined, to the point that employees had to follow 22 written steps for cleaning a bathroom. Complaints and special requests went not to the workers, but to an office-based manager. The impersonality and efficiency of this bureaucratic system is yet another example of the McDonaldization of the workplace.

Oligarchy: Rule by a Few

Conflict theorists have examined the bureaucratizing influence on social movements. German sociologist Robert Michels (1915) studied socialist parties and labour unions in Europe before the First World War, and found that such organizations were becoming increasingly bureaucratic. The emerging leaders of these organizations—even some of the most radical—had a vested interest in clinging to power. If they lost their leadership posts, they would have to return to full-time work as manual labourers.

Through his research, Michels originated the idea of the ***iron law of oligarchy***, which describes how even a democratic organization will develop into a bureaucracy ruled by a few (the oligarchy). Almost everyone who has ever had to do group work as part of a class project has, at one time or another, watched as a few individuals took over the group and ran it as their own. Why do these oligarchies emerge? People who achieve leadership roles usually have the skills, knowledge, or charismatic appeal (as Weber noted) to direct, if not control, others. Michels argues that the rank and file of a movement or organization look to leaders for direction and thereby reinforce the process of rule by a few. In addition, members of an oligarchy are strongly motivated to maintain their leadership roles, privileges, and power.

Michels's insights continue to be relevant today. Contemporary labour unions in Canada and

These members of the Toronto Symphony Orchestra must be technically proficient and professionally trained, or they will never make beautiful music together. Technical qualification is one of the characteristics of a well-structured bureaucracy.

6-3 The Varying Cultures of Formal Organizations

The Canadian negotiator in a business deal with a German company is running late for an appointment in Berlin. He rushes into his German counterpart's office, drops his briefcase on the woman's desk while apologizing, "I'm terribly sorry for keeping you waiting, Elsa," and proceeds to regale Elsa with an amusing story about his taxi ride to the office. Unwittingly, he has violated four rules of polite behaviour in German organizations: punctuality, personal space, privacy, and proper greetings. In German formal organizations, meetings take place on time, business is not mixed with pleasure or joking, greetings are formal, and the casual use of first names is frowned upon.

Now picture a formal business meeting that takes place in a corporation in France. A Japanese negotiating team enters the conference room, but is dismayed to find a round table. The Japanese do not use round tables in business settings. They prefer to sit facing the opposite side and have a prescribed seating order, with the power position in the middle, flanked by interpreters, key advisers, note takers, and finally the most junior personnel at the ends. The French negotiators get down to business and make direct offers, for which they expect quick answers from the Japanese team. But the protocol in Japanese organizations is to nurture business relationships first and conduct indirect negotiations until the real decision making can take place later in private.

> **The Japanese do not use round tables in business settings.**

What these examples show is that national cultures influence formal organizations. They reflect the ways we all have been socialized. Geert Hofstede, an international management scholar based in the Netherlands, calls these ingrained patterns of thinking, feeling, and acting *mental programs* (or "software of the mind"). If business is to be successful, the participants have to have some understanding of the customs, values, and procedures of other cultures. In the examples above, this holds true equally for the Germans *and* the Canadians, for the French *and* the Japanese.

Hofstede explored some of the cross-cultural differences in formal organizations by means of a study of IBM employees in 50 different countries. Since the respondents to his survey were matched in almost every respect *except for nationality*, he felt the national differences in their answers would show up clearly. He found four dimensions in which the countries differed:

1. *Power distance.* This refers to the degree to which a culture thinks it is appropriate to distribute power unequally and to accept the decisions of power holders. At one extreme on this dimension are the Arab countries, Guatemala, Malaysia, and the Philippines, each of which tolerates hierarchy and inequality and believes the actions of authorities should not be challenged. At the opposite end of this scale are Austria, Denmark, Israel, and New Zealand. The North American business model—both in Canada and the United States—leans toward the hierarchical model.

Sources: Frazee 1997; Hofstede 1997; Lustig and Koester 1999.

elsewhere bear little resemblance to those originally organized after spontaneous activity by exploited workers. Conflict theorists have pointed to the longevity of union leaders, who are not always responsive to the needs and demands of membership and seem more concerned with maintaining their own positions and power. Feminist theorists have pointed to the bureaucratization process as a tool used by a patriarchal society to sustain male dominance.

At least one study, however, raises questions about Michels's views. Based on her research on "pro-choice" organizations, which endorse a woman's right to make choices in reproductive issues, sociologist Suzanne Staggenborg (1988) disputes the assertion that formal organizations with professional leaders inevitably become conservative and oligarchical. Indeed, she notes that many formal organizations in the pro-choice movement appear to be more democratic than informal groups; the routinized procedures that they follow make it more difficult for leaders to grab excessive power. Feminist groups within the Canadian women's movement have also experimented with different decision-making formats. While consensus was one of the original models for women's groups, many found it untenable because of the inability to resolve conflicts. Saskatoon Women's Liberation chose to retain the original feminist concern that every member's voice be heard, by applying a form of participatory democracy with a goal ". . . that everyone

2. *Uncertainty avoidance.* Cultures differ in how much they can tolerate uncertainty and adapt to change. Those that feel threatened by uncertainty will establish more structure; examples include Greece, Portugal, and Uruguay. At the other extreme are countries that minimize rules and rituals, accept dissent, and take risks in trying new things: Denmark, Ireland, Jamaica, and Singapore can be found among these nations. Canadian society is one that encourages open debate and critical thinking of both ideas and systems.

3. *Individualism/collectivism.* This dimension refers to how cultures vary in encouraging people to be unique and independent versus conforming and interdependent. In other words, what is the balance between allegiance to the self and to the group? Canadian culture, in part because of its commitment to multiculturalism, tends to be neutral in its expectations between these two styles. Other cultures, however, have more directive guidelines. Guatemala, Indonesia, Pakistan, and West Africa all take a collectivist orientation: absolute loyalty to the group and an emphasis on belonging. On the other hand, Australia, Belgium, the Netherlands, and the United States are highly individualistic societies, valuing the autonomy of the individual.

4. *Masculinity/femininity.* To what extent do cultures prefer achievement, assertiveness, and acquisition of wealth (masculinity) to nurturance, social support, and quality of life (femininity)? Countries high in the masculinity index include Austria, Italy, Japan, and Mexico. High-scoring feminine cultures include Chile, Portugal, Sweden, and Thailand. While Canada tends to follow the American consumer-based model, there is a greater emphasis on nonmaterial quality of life factors here.

Hofstede's data come with some baggage attached. His respondents were for the most part males working in one large multinational corporation. Their point of view may be unique to their gender and level of education. Moreover, he collected his data in 1974; since then economic and political changes are sure to have affected cultural patterns. Still, his work is valuable for showing the cultural differences within the range of his respondents and for alerting all of us, and especially those in the business community, of the need to understand the cultural settings of formal organizations.

Let's Discuss

1. With which of the four business negotiating styles (Canadian, German, Japanese, French) would you feel most comfortable in a business setting? Do your classmates' answers differ based on their nationality or cultural background?

2. Analyze your campus culture. How much power distance is there between students, professors, and administrators? How much individualism is tolerated on your campus? How much pressure is there to conform?

---

should participate in the group and that everyone is equally responsible for and to the group" (Adamson et al. 1988:244) (see also E. Scott 1993).

While the "iron law" may sometimes help us to understand the concentration of formal authority within organizations, sociologists recognize that there are a number of checks on leadership. Groups often compete for power within a formal organization. For example, in an automotive corporation, divisions manufacturing heavy machinery and passenger cars compete against each other for limited research and development funds. Moreover, informal channels of communication and control can undercut the power of top officials of an organization.

Bureaucracy and Organizational Culture

How does bureaucratization affect the average individual who works in an organization? The early theorists of formal organizations tended to neglect this question. Max Weber, for example, focused on management personnel within bureaucracies, but he had little to say about workers in industry or clerks in government agencies.

According to the ***classical theory*** of formal organizations, also known as the ***scientific management approach***, workers are motivated almost entirely by economic rewards. This theory stresses that productivity is limited only by the physical constraints of workers. Therefore, workers are treated as a resource, much like the machines that began to replace them in the twentieth century. Management attempts to achieve maximum work efficiency through scientific planning, established performance standards, and careful supervision of workers and production. Planning under the scientific management approach involves efficiency studies but not studies of workers' attitudes or feelings of job satisfaction. Minimum-wage policies adopted by franchises like McDonald's appear to reject the idea that workers are motivated only by wages as opposed to job satisfaction. However, their adoption of scientific management processes serves to ensure that the system will provide a predictable outcome regardless of employee motivation.

It was not until workers certified union membership (a process that had failed at several other McDonald's franchises in Canada)—and forced management to recognize that they were not objects—that theorists of formal organizations began to revise the classical approach. Along with management and administrators, social scientists became aware that informal groups of workers have an important impact on organizations (Perrow 1986). An alternative way of considering bureaucratic dynamics, the **human relations approach**, emphasizes the role of people, communication, and participation within a bureaucracy. This type of analysis reflects the interest of interactionist theorists in small-group behaviour. Unlike planning under the scientific management approach, planning based on the human relations perspective focuses on workers' feelings, frustrations, and emotional need for job satisfaction. McDonald's, to its credit, does provide opportunities for employee feedback via suggestion boxes and meetings. In Box 6-3, we saw how understanding human relations in the corporate structure can enhance doing business abroad.

The gradual move away from a sole focus on physical aspects of getting the job done—and toward the concerns and needs of workers—led advocates of the human relations approach to stress the less formal aspects of bureaucratic structure. Informal structures and social networks within organizations develop partly as a result of people's ability to create more direct forms of communication than under the formal structure. Charles Page (1946) has used the term *bureaucracy's other face* to refer to the unofficial activities and interactions that are such a basic part of daily organizational life.

A series of classic studies illustrates the value of the human relations approach. The Hawthorne studies p. 42 alerted sociologists to the fact that research subjects may alter their behaviour to match the experimenter's expectations. The major focus of the Hawthorne studies, however, was the role of social factors in workers' productivity. One aspect of the research investigated the switchboard-bank wiring room, where 14 men were making parts of switches for telephone equipment.

The researchers discovered that these men were producing far below their physical capabilities. This was especially surprising because they would earn more money if they produced more parts.

Why was there such an unexpected restriction of output? The men feared that if they produced switch parts at a faster rate, their pay rate might be reduced or some might lose their jobs. As a result, this group of workers established its own (unofficial) norm for a proper day's work. The workers created informal rules and sanctions to enforce their norm. Yet management was unaware of such practices and actually believed that the men were working as hard as they could (Roethlisberger and Dickson 1939; for a different perspective, see S. Vallas 1999).

Recent research has underscored the impact of informal structures within organizations. Sociologist James Tucker (1993) studied everyday forms of resistance by temporary employees working in short-term positions. Tucker points out that informal social networks can offer advice to a temporary employee on how to pursue a grievance. For example, a female receptionist working for an automobile dealer was being sexually harassed both physically and verbally by a male supervisor. Other female employees, who were aware of the supervisor's behaviour, suggested that she complain to the manager of the dealership. Although the manager said there was little that he could do, he apparently spoke with the supervisor and the harassment stopped. We will examine sexual harassment within organizations in the social policy section.

Technology's Impact on the Workplace

In 1968, Stanley Kubrick's motion picture *2001: A Space Odyssey* dazzled audiences with its futuristic depiction of travel to Jupiter. With 2001 behind us, it is clear that we have not lived up to this target of outer space exploration. However, what about the portrayal of computers? In *2001* a mellow-voiced computer named HAL is very efficient and helpful to the crew, only to try to take over the entire operation and destroy the crew in the process. While computers may now successfully compete against chess champions, they are as far short of achieving the artificial intelligence of HAL as earthlings are of accomplishing manned travel to Jupiter.

Still, the computer today is a commanding presence in our lives, and in the workplace in particular. It is not just that the computer makes tedious, routine tasks easier, such as checking spelling in a term paper. It has affected the workplace in far more dramatic ways (Liker et al. 1999).

Automation

Jeremy Rifkin (1996)—the president of the Foundation on Economic Trends—noted that computer-generated

Telecommuters are linked to their supervisors and colleagues through computer terminals, phones, and fax machines.

Thus, telecommuting may move society further along the continuum from *Gemeinschaft* to *Gesellschaft*. On a more positive note, telecommuting may be the first social change that pulls fathers and mothers back into the home rather than pushing them out. The trend, if it continues, should also increase autonomy and job satisfaction for many employees (Nie 1999).

Electronic Communication

Electronic communication in the workplace has generated some heat lately. On the one hand, e-mailing is a convenient way to push messages around, especially with the CC (carbon copy) button. It's democratic too—lower-status employees are more likely to participate in e-mail discussion than in face-to-face communications, which gives organizations the benefit of the experiences and views of more of their workforce. But e-mailing is almost too easy to use. According to Statistics Canada, 96.6 percent of public organizations and 52.2 percent of private businesses in Canada use e-mail (Statistics Canada 1999g). Students can get a sense of the massive volume of correspondence that moves through this medium by looking at their own in-boxes. Not only are there messages from friends and business contacts, but there is a steady flow of unsolicited material. At Computer Associates, a software company, managers were receiving 300 e-mails a day each and people were e-mailing colleagues in the next cubicle. To deal with the electronic chaos, the company's CEO took the unusual step of banning all e-mails from 9:30 to 12 and 1:30 to 4. Other companies have limited the number of CCs that can be sent and banned systemwide messages (Gwynne and Dickerson 1997; Sproull and Kiesler 1991). Some post-secondary institutions in Canada have faced similar problems, and have responded by banning systemwide messages.

There are other problems with e-mail. It doesn't convey body language, which in face-to-face communication can soften insensitive phrasing and make unpleasant messages (such as a reprimand) easier to take. It also leaves a permanent record, and that can be a problem if messages are written thoughtlessly. Finally, as will be discussed in detail in Chapter 20, companies can monitor e-mail as a means of "watching" their employees. Dartmouth College professor Paul Argenti advises those who use e-mail, "Think before you write. The most important thing to know is what not to write" (Gwynne and Dickerson 1997:90).

automation has completely transformed the nature of manufacturing. Every year, the proportion of the Canadian workforce engaged in physical tasks, such as those found in manufacturing, shrinks. By 2020, less than 2 percent of the global workforce will be performing factory work. Moreover, automation is reshaping the service sector of the economy in a similar way, leading to substantial reductions in employees ("downsizing") and the increasing use of temporary or contingent workers (see Chapter 17).

Telecommuting

Increasingly, the workforce is turning into *telecommuters* in many industrial countries. *Telecommuters* are employees of business firms or government agencies who work full-time or part-time at home rather than in an outside office and who are linked to their supervisors and colleagues through computer terminals, phones, and fax machines (see Chapter 17). A 1998 study by Ottawa-based Ekos Research suggested that 1.5 million Canadians would be telecommuting by 2001. The study also found that the idea of working from home was either "Appealing" or "Very Appealing" to 55 percent of the population, and that one-third of respondents would forgo a 5 to 10 percent raise to be able to telecommute (Ekos Research 1998).

What are the social implications of this shift toward the virtual office? From an interactionist perspective, the workplace is a major source of friendships; restricting face-to-face social opportunities could destroy the trust that is created by face-to-face "handshake agreements."

Voluntary Associations

"Caring Canadians, Involved Canadians: Highlights from the 2000 National Survey on Giving, Volunteering and Participating" (NSGVP) reports on a study conducted on Canadians' participation in philanthropy in the year preceding the United Nations' International Year of Volunteers (IYV) (Hall et al. 2001). The study found that 6.5 million Canadians (27 percent of the population aged 15 and older) were involved in voluntary associations in 2000. *Voluntary associations* are organizations established on the basis of common interest, whose members volunteer or even pay to participate. Girl Guides, Kiwanis, Canadian Cancer Society, Minor Hockey Association, Canadian National Institute for the Blind, and the Canadian Legion are all examples of organizations considered voluntary associations. One of the largest voluntary associations, The Canadian Automobile Association, has over 4 million members, while one of the smallest, the Canadian Association of Gift Planners (organizer of the 'Leave a Legacy' program), has 21 members in Canada.

The categories of *formal organization* and *voluntary association* are not mutually exclusive. Large voluntary associations such as the Lions Club and the Chamber of Commerce have structures similar to those of profit-making corporations, including bureaucracies with clear lines of command. At the same time, certain formal organizations, such as CUSO and the Movement for Canadian Literacy, have philanthropic and educational goals usually found in voluntary associations. Interestingly, the Liberal Party of Canada and the Canadian Auto Workers union are considered examples of voluntary associations. While membership in a political party or union can be a condition of employment and therefore not genuinely voluntary, political parties and labour unions are usually included in discussions of voluntary associations.

Participation in voluntary associations is not unique to Canada. In a cross-cultural study, three Canadian sociologists examined membership in voluntary associations in 15 countries. Religious memberships were found to be prominent in Canada, the United States, the Netherlands, Ireland, and Northern Ireland. By contrast, union participation was highest in Great Britain, Norway, and Sweden. While people's country of residence may influence the types of voluntary associations they join, membership in such organizations is clearly a common social pattern (Curtis et al. 1992). NSGVP found that "Canadians donate money and volunteer time to support the arts, local sports clubs, medical research, food banks, shelters, international relief efforts, and their own places of worship, among many other causes" (Hall et al. 2001:9).

Membership in voluntary associations is not random. The most consistent predictor of participation is socioeconomic status—that is, a person's income, education, and occupation. People of higher socioeconomic status are more likely to belong to and participate actively in such organizations. Partly, this reflects the cost of group memberships, which may exclude people with limited income from joining (Sills 1968:365–66; J. Williams et al. 1973).

According to the 2000 NSGVP, while Canada's volunteers come from all walks of life, "there are some characteristics that distinguish those who volunteer from those who do not" (Hall et al. 2001:33). The rate of volunteering is higher for youth (aged 15–24) and for those in their mid-adult years (aged 35–54). Women are slightly more likely than men to participate, and volunteers are likely to be married. Level of education also comes into play, with people having more education showing a greater tendency to volunteer. And employed people, especially those with part-time employment, are more likely to volunteer than those who were unemployed or not in the labour force.

However, as shown in Table 6-3, the characteristics of those who spend the *most time* in volunteer activities are different. While older Canadians (aged 65 and over) are

CARP is a voluntary association of people aged 50 and older, both retired and working, that advocates for the needs of older Canadians. Members are kept informed throught its magazine, "Fifty Plus".

Table 6-3	Percentage Volunteering and Average Hours Volunteered During the Year, Canadians Aged 15 and Older, 2000		
Characteristic		**Percent**	**Average hours**
Age			
15–24		29	130
25–34		24	131
35–44		30	153
45–54		30	158
55–64		28	181
65 and older		18	269
Sex			
Male		25	170
Female		28	155
Marital status			
Married or common-law		28	165
Single, never married		26	136
Separated, divorced		25	181
Widowed		17	253
Education			
Less than high school		19	154
High school diploma		23	150
Some post-secondary		33	173
Post-secondary certificate or diploma		28	165
University degree		39	166
Labour force status			
Employed		28	147
Full-time		27	145
Part-time		33	155
Unemployed		25	175
Not in the labour force		24	193
Household income			
Less than $20 000		17	207
$20 000–$39 999		21	179
$40 000–$59 999		26	162
$60 000–$79 999		31	156
$80 000–$99 999		35	127
$100 000 or more		39	150

Source: Adapted from Hall et al. 2001:34.

least likely to volunteer, this age group performs the most hours of volunteering. And men, those who are widowed or separated/divorced, those who are unemployed or not in the labour force, and those with household incomes of less than $20 000 contribute the most hours of volunteer work. Although participation varies across the population of Canada, most people (59 percent) restrict their volunteering to one organization in a year, while 15 percent volunteered for three or more organizations (Hall et al. 2001:33–40).

Sociologists have applied a functionalist analysis to the study of voluntary associations. David Sills (1968:373–376) has identified several key functions that these groups serve within our society. First, they mediate between individuals and government. Professional associations such as the Canadian Medical Association mediate between their members and government in such matters as licensing and legislation. Second, voluntary associations give people training in organizational skills that is invaluable for future officeholders—and for better performance within most jobs. Of Canadians who volunteered in 2000, 62 percent reported that they believed this would help them in the job market. Third, organizations such as the National Anti-Poverty Association, the National Action Committee on the Status of Women (NAC), and the Canadian Association of Retired Persons (CARP) help to bring traditionally disadvantaged and underrepresented groups into the political mainstream. Finally, voluntary associations assist in governing. During the influx of South Asian refugees in the late 1970s and early 1980s, religious and charitable groups became deeply involved in helping the federal government resettle refugees.

The importance of voluntary associations—and especially of their unpaid workers (or volunteers)—is increasingly being recognized. Traditionally, unpaid work has been devalued in Canada, even though the skill levels, experience, and training demands are often comparable with those of wage labour. Viewed from a conflict perspective, the critical difference has been that a substantial amount of volunteer work is performed by women. Feminists and conflict theorists agree that, like the unpaid child care and household labour of homemakers, the effort of volunteers has been too often ignored by scholars—and awarded too little respect by the larger society—because volunteering is viewed as "women's work." Failure to recognize women's volunteerism thereby obscures a critical contribution women make to a society's social structure (Daniels 1987, 1988).

Organizational Change

Just as individuals and relationships change, so too do organizations, both formal and voluntary. The most obvious changes often involve personnel: a new prime minister of Canada is elected, an executive is fired, a star athlete retires. However, sociologists are most interested in how the organization itself changes.

These changes often relate to other social institutions, particularly the government. Its regulatory statutes, licensing procedures, tax laws, and contracting for goods and services directly influence the structure of formal organizations. Government policies relating to affirmative action (see Chapter 17) or disability rights (see Chapter 5) influence the internal decisions of organizations and may even require the hiring of new personnel.

In addition, an organization's goals may change over time along with its leaders and structure. A church starts a basketball league; an oil company purchases a movie studio; a tobacco firm begins to manufacture ballpoint pens. Such actions take place when an organization decides that its traditional goals are no longer adequate. It must then modify its previous objectives or cease to exist.

Goal Multiplication

If an organization concludes that its goals must change, it will typically establish additional goals or expand upon its traditional objectives. For example, in the 1970s many universities began continuing education programs to meet the needs of potential students holding full-time jobs and wishing to take classes at night. In 1980, the Elderhostel movement opened campuses in North America to older people who could live and learn along with much younger students.

Goal multiplication takes place when an organization expands its purposes. Generally, this is the result of changing social or economic conditions that threaten the organization's survival. The YMCA has practised such goal multiplication. Reflecting its name, the Young Men's Christian Association had a strong evangelistic focus during its beginnings in Canada in the 1850s. Bible study and tent revival meetings were provided by the early YMCAs. However, by the early 1900s, the YMCA had begun to diversify its appeal. It attempted to interest members by offering gymnasium facilities and residence quarters. Gradually, women, Lutherans, Roman Catholics, Jews, and the "unchurched" were accepted and even recruited as members.

The most recent phase of goal multiplication at the YMCA began after the Second World War. In larger urban areas, the organization became involved in providing employment training and juvenile delinquency programs. As a result, the YMCA received substantial funding from the federal government and corporate sponsors. This was a dramatic change for an organization whose income had previously come solely from membership fees and charitable contributions.

The YMCA's impressive range of activities currently includes social service programs for the disabled, daycare centres, fitness classes for office workers, residence dormitories for students and single adults, "learning for living" classes for adults, and senior citizens' facilities (Schmidt 1990).

These transitions in the YMCA were not always smooth. At times, major contributors and board members withdrew support because of opposition to organizational changes; they preferred the YMCA to remain as it had been. However, the YMCA has survived and grown by expanding its goals from evangelism to general community service (Etzioni 1964:13; Zald 1970).

Goal Succession

Unlike goal multiplication, *goal succession* occurs when a group or organization has either realized or been denied its goal. It must then identify an entirely new objective that can justify its existence. Cases of goal succession are rare because most organizations never fully achieve their goals. If they do, as in the case of a committee supporting

The Young Men's Christian Association (YMCA) has experienced goal multiplication in recent decades. Its range of activities currently includes social service programs for people with disabilities, daycare centres, fitness classes for office workers, residence dormitories for students and single adults, and senior citizens' facilities.

a victorious candidate for public office, they usually dissolve.

Sociologist Peter Blau (1964: 241–246), who coined the term *succession of goals*, noted that organizations do not necessarily behave in a rigid manner when their goals are achieved or become irrelevant. Rather, they may shift toward new objectives. A case in point is the Foundation for Infantile Paralysis, popularly known for its annual March of Dimes campaign. For some time, the foundation's major goals were to support medical research on polio and to provide assistance for victims of the disease. However, in 1955 the Salk vaccine was found to be an effective protection against paralytic polio. This left the foundation, so to speak, "unemployed." A vast network of committed staff members and volunteers was suddenly left without a clear rationale for existence. The group might have disbanded at this point, but instead it selected a new goal—combating arthritis and birth defects—and took on a new name (Etzioni 1964; Sills 1957).

Goal succession can also occur when programs seem to succeed through failure. For example, government agencies that are responsible for enforcing drug laws continue to exist because they fail to put drug pushers out of business. Likewise, prisons fail to rehabilitate inmates, thereby guaranteeing the steady return of many clients.

SOCIAL POLICY AND ORGANIZATIONS

Sexual Harassment

The Issue

In 1999, Canadian space researcher Judith Lapierre took part in a Russian simulation that involved living in a replica of a Mir space station for 110 days. The 32-year-old former nurse shared the cramped quarters with three men—an Austrian, a Japanese, and a Russian—as well as another four-man Russian crew. When she emerged from the isolation study, Lapierre accused one of the Russians of sexual harassment. According to Lapierre, the colleague had attempted to kiss her forcibly on New Year's Day. The cosmonaut's behaviour was condemned by the Russian space agency, and he subsequently apologized.

In 1994, 29 female employees from the Mitsubishi Corporation's auto plant at Normal, Illinois, filed a private lawsuit, accusing the company of fostering a climate of sexual harassment. Three years later, the company settled the lawsuit with 27 of the women for U.S.$9.5 million, and then with 350 other women for another U.S.$34 million.

The Canadian Labour Code was amended in 1984 to include *sexual harassment*. In that legislation, the federal government set labour standards that made employers responsible for responding to complaints about sexual harassment. Then, in 1987, the Supreme Court of Canada ruled on a case involving a federal employee and the Treasury Board, which expanded that responsibility. The Court held that employers should also be expected to establish and maintain a workplace that is free from sexual harassment.

In the Canada Labour Code, ***sexual harassment*** is defined as:

> Any conduct, comment, gesture or contact of a sexual nature (a) that is likely to cause offense or humiliation to any employee; or (b) that might, on reasonable grounds, be perceived by that employee as placing a condition of a sexual nature on employment or on any opportunity for training or promotion (Section 247.1).

The Setting

Sexual harassment is not new, but it has received increased attention in many parts of the world as growing numbers of women enter the paid labour force and growing numbers of people in positions of influence pay attention to victims' stories. Feminist analysis has gone a long way toward raising consciousness of the potential for victimization in a paternalistic setting. In a recent 10-year period, the proportion of women participating in the labour force has grown by at least 12 percent in Ireland, the Netherlands, South Korea, the United States, and Canada. A comparison of labour force participation rates between Canadian men and women aged 25–44 years shows that 90 percent of men and 80 percent of women worked for pay in 2000. Almost half of Canada's labour force (47 percent) was female.

Women of all ages and racial and ethnic groups—and men as well—have been the victims of sexual harassment. Such harassment may occur as a single encounter or as a repeated pattern of behaviour. Surveys

Sexual harassment can be as subtle as an unwanted hand on the shoulder. Repeated actions of this kind can lead to a "hostile environment."

typically show that 20 to 50 percent of women feel victimized by sexual harassment. Even higher proportions can be found if nonverbal forms of harassment, such as the posting of pornography in the workplace, are included (S. Welsh 1999:170–171).

Sociological Insights

In Canada, actions in the workplace are deemed to be sexual harassment when they can reasonably be perceived as such, and result in restricting someone's access to or participation in employment. Whether it occurs in the government, in the corporate world, or in universities, sexual harassment generally takes place in organizations in which the hierarchy of authority finds white males at the top and women's work is valued less than men's. One survey in the private sector in the United States found that black women were three times more likely than white women to experience sexual harassment. From a conflict perspective, it is not surprising that women—and especially women of colour—are most likely to become victims of sexual harassment. These groups are typically an organization's most vulnerable employees in terms of job security (J. Jones 1988).

Many bureaucracies have traditionally given little attention to the pervasive sexual harassment in their midst; the emotional costs of this discrimination suffered largely by female employees have not been a major concern. However, more regulations prohibiting sexual harassment have been issued as managers and executives confront the costs of sexual harassment *for the*

organization, and today, many formal organizations are developing zero tolerance for sexual harassment. Nine out of 10 companies now have rules and regulations dealing with the issue. However, many of these are weak and constitute only a single paragraph in the company handbook (Cloud 1998).

Policy Initiatives

As indicated earlier, sexual harassment has been defined by the Canadian Labour Code. Beyond requiring employers to be vigilant in dealing with incidents of sexual harassment, the Code also makes it mandatory for organizations, whether they be corporate or not-for-profit, to be proactive in creating and distributing a formal statement of policy that outlines their guidelines for defining and responding to sexual harassment. Although we have been focusing on sexual harassment in the workplace, there are similar issues on university campuses. See Table 6-4, a quiz designed to raise students' awareness of sexual harassment.

The policy for dealing with sexual harassment in Canada is still evolving as courts at all levels hear cases and reach conclusions that are not necessarily consistent. The confusion will continue, but the old patriarchal system in which male bosses behaved as they pleased with female subordinates is ending. Organizations are developing their own formal regulations in anticipation of the problems they may face, in an effort to create a climate that is nonhostile for all workers. And most large formal organizations have initiated sensitivity and diversity training, to increase employees' awareness of situations that might lead to complaints of harassment or intolerance. To be effective, such training must be ongoing and an integral part of an organization's behavioural norms. Occasional antibigotry lectures and one-shot sessions on the theme of "Let's avoid harassment" are unlikely to accomplish the desired results (Fernandez 1999).

The battle against sexual harassment is being fought not only in Canada but around the world. In 1991, the European Economic Community established a code of conduct that holds employers ultimately responsible for combating sexual harassment. In 1992, France joined many European countries in banning such behaviour. That same year, in an important victory for Japan's

| Table 6-4   **When Does a Joke or Flirtation Become Sexual Harassment?** |

True or false?	**Answers**
1. Anyone who is offended by a dirty joke has a poor sense of humour.	1. False. Some jokes offend because the point of the joke is to make someone feel worthless or humiliated. If someone feels less valuable than others when they hear a joke, then it's no joking matter.
2. It's okay to tell somebody you think they look really nice.	2. True. Compliments about a person such as "You look really cool" are usually appreciated. Sexual comments about the body are less likely to be received as compliments.
3. Staring at somebody's body shows that you really like them.	3. False. Although eye contact usually happens without making anyone uncomfortable, it can cross the line. A quick glance or a smile is usually considered flirting; constant staring at your body's sexual places is not.
4. It's not a big deal for students and teachers to flirt with one another.	4. False. Flirting happens between peers—it is not appropriate between people in authority and somebody over whom they have control.
5. Patting somebody on the bottom is a way of flirting with them.	5. False. Flirting is not patting, grabbing, pinching or groping.
6. If nobody complains when you wear a T-shirt with a sexual message, it means you haven't offended anybody.	6. False. Just because nobody complains doesn't mean it's okay. There are lots of reasons why people don't tell about sexual harassment. They may not want to attract attention or be called a "prude" or a "rat."
7. It shouldn't bother you to be teased about your body and appearance.	7. False. Although teasing and good-natured joking are part of life, constant teasing is hurtful. Boys, girls, women, and men are all affected by harassment.
8. A teacher who continually makes students uneasy should be told to stop.	8. True. If students worry that a teacher will purposefully say things that embarrass them, it is not just a form of teasing. What the teacher is doing should be reported to parents or school authorities and the teacher should be told to stop.

Source: Public Legal and Education Services of New Brunswick 2001.

feminist movement, a district court ruled that a small publishing company and one of its male employees had violated the rights of a female employee because of crude remarks that led her to quit her job. The complainant had charged that her male supervisor had spread rumours about her, telling others that she was promiscuous. When she attempted to get him to stop making such comments, she was advised to quit her job. In the view of the complainant's lawyer, "Sexual harassment is a big problem in Japan, and we hope this will send a signal to men that they have to be more careful" (Kanagae 1993; Perlez 1996; Pollack 1996; Weisman 1992:A3).

Let's Discuss

1. Have you ever been sexually harassed, either at work or at school? If so, did you complain about it? What was the outcome?

2. In the instances of sexual harassment you are personally familiar with, was there a difference in power between the victim and the person being harassed? If so, was the difference in power based on gender, age, status, or race?

3. Use the quiz in Table 6-4 to explore the attitudes of your classmates. What did you find? Based on these findings, do you think there is a need for a sexual harassment awareness program at your school?

● Chapter Resources

Summary

Social interaction among human beings is necessary to the transmission of culture and the survival of every society. This chapter examines the social behaviour of groups and formal organizations.

1. When we find ourselves identifying closely with a group, it is probably a *primary group*. A *secondary group* is more formal and impersonal.
2. People tend to see the world in terms of *in-groups* and *out-groups,* a perception often fostered by the very groups to which they belong.
3. *Reference groups* set and enforce standards of conduct and perform a comparison function for people's evaluations of themselves and others.
4. Interactionist researchers have revealed that there are distinct and predictable processes at work in the functioning of *small groups*. The simplest group is a *dyad,* composed of two members. *Triads* and larger groups increase ways of interacting and allow for *coalitions* to form.
5. As societies have become more complex, large *formal organizations* have become more powerful and pervasive.

6. Max Weber argued that, in its ideal form, every *bureaucracy* will share these five basic characteristics: division of labour, hierarchical authority, written rules and regulations, impersonality, and employment based on technical qualifications.
7. Bureaucracy can be understood as a process and as a matter of degree; thus, an organization is more or less bureaucratic than other organizations.
8. When leaders of an organization build up their power, it can lead to oligarchy (rule by a few).
9. The informal structure of an organization can undermine and redefine official bureaucratic policies.
10. Technology has transformed the workplace through automation, telecommuting, and electronic communication.
11. People belong to *voluntary associations* for a variety of purposes—for example, to share in joint activities or to get help with personal problems.
12. *Sexual harassment* has been reported not only in government workplaces and in private-sector organizations but also in schools.

Critical Thinking Questions

1. Think about how behaviour is shaped by reference groups. Drawing on your own experience, what different reference groups at different periods have shaped your outlook and your goals? In what ways have they done so?
2. Within a formal organization, are you likely to find primary groups, secondary groups, in-groups, out-groups, and reference groups? What functions do these groups serve for the formal organization? What dysfunctions might occur as a result of their presence?

3. Max Weber identified five basic characteristics of bureaucracy. Select an actual organization with which you are familiar (for example, your university, a business at which you work, a religious institution or civic association to which you belong) and apply Weber's analysis to that organization. To what degree does it correspond to Weber's ideal type of bureaucracy?

Key Terms

Alienation   A condition of estrangement or dissociation from the surrounding society. (151)

Bureaucracy   A component of formal organization in which rules and hierarchical ranking are used to achieve efficiency. (150)

Bureaucratization   The process by which a group, organization, or social movement becomes increasingly bureaucratic. (153)

Classical theory   An approach to the study of formal organizations that views workers as being motivated almost entirely by economic rewards. (155)

Coalition   A temporary or permanent alliance geared toward a common goal. (148)

Dyad   A two-member group. (148)

Dysfunction   An element or a process of society that may disrupt a social system or lead to a decrease in stability. (150)

Formal organization   A special-purpose group designed and structured for maximum efficiency. (148)

Goal displacement   Overzealous conformity to official regulations within a bureaucracy. (152)

Goal multiplication   The process by which an organization expands its purpose. (160)

Goal succession   The process through which an organization identifies an entirely new objective because its traditional goals have been either realized or denied. (160)

Group   Any number of people with similar norms, values, and expectations who interact meaningfully with one another on a regular basis. (143)

Human relations approach   An approach to the study of formal organizations that emphasizes the role of people, communication, and participation within a bureaucracy and tends to focus on the informal structure of the organization. (156)

Ideal type   A construct or model that serves as a point of reference against which specific cases can be evaluated. (150)

In-group   Any group or category to which people feel they belong. (144)

Iron law of oligarchy   A principle of organizational life under which even democratic organizations will become bureaucracies ruled by a few individuals. (153)

McDonaldization   The process by which the principles of the fast-food restaurant have come to dominate certain sectors of society, both in Canada and throughout the world. (143)

Out-group   A group or category to which people feel they do not belong. (144)

Peter Principle   A principle of organizational life according to which each individual within a hierarchy tends to rise to his or her level of incompetence. (152)

Primary group   A small group characterized by intimate, face-to-face association and cooperation. (143)

Reference group   Any group that individuals use as a standard in evaluating themselves and their own behaviour. (146)

Scientific management approach   Another name for the *classical theory* of formal organizations. (155)

Secondary group   A formal, impersonal group in which there is little social intimacy or mutual understanding. (144)

Sexual harassment   Any conduct, comment, gesture or contact of a sexual nature that is likely to cause offense or humiliation to any employee or that might, on reasonable grounds, be perceived by that employee as placing a condition of a sexual nature on employment or on any opportunity for training or promotion. (161)

Small group   A group small enough for all members to interact simultaneously, that is, to talk with one another or at least be acquainted. (147)

Telecommuters   Employees of business firms or government agencies who work full-time or part-time at home rather than in an outside office and who are linked to their supervisors and colleagues through computer terminals, phone lines, and fax machines. (157)

Trained incapacity   The tendency of workers in a bureaucracy to become so specialized that they develop blind spots and fail to notice obvious problems. (151)

Triad   A three-member group. (148)

Voluntary associations   Organizations established on the basis of common interest, whose members volunteer or even pay to participate. (158)

Additional Readings

Adamson, Nancy, Linda Briskin, and Margaret McPhail. 1988. *Feminist Organizing For Change: The Contemporary Women's Movement in Canada*. Toronto: Oxford University Press. Using a historical and theoretical approach, the authors develop an understanding of 'feminist practice,' which leads to an exploration of both feminist organizing and organizations.

Alfino, Mark, John S. Caputo, and Robin Wynyard. 1998. *McDonaldization Revisited: Critical Essays on Consumer Culture*. Westport, CT: Praeger. A multidisciplinary look at George Ritzer's approach to Max Weber's theory of rationalization and how it has been applied first to McDonald's restaurants and now to institutions worldwide.

Fagenson, Ellen A. 1993. *Women in Management: Trends, Issues, and Challenges in Managerial Diversity*. Newbury Park, CA: Sage. This anthology focuses on the continued underrepresentation of women in managerial positions within formal organizations.

Nishiguchi, Toshihiro. 1994. *Strategic Industrial Sourcing: The Japanese Advantage*. New York: Oxford University Press. Drawing on eight years of research and more than 1000 interviews, Nishiguchi offers insight into how very large industrial corporations have developed in Japan and have come to dominate that nation's economy.

Vaughan, Diane. 1996. *The Challenger Launch Decision: Risky Technology, Culture, and Deviance at NASA*. Chicago: University of Chicago Press. A detailed look at the work culture of the National Aeronautics and Space Administration (NASA) and its suppliers— and the impact of that work culture on the fatal launch of the United States space shuttle *Challenger* in 1986.

JOURNALS

Among the journals that focus on the study of groups and organizations are *Administration and Society* (founded in 1969), *Organizational Studies* (1980), *Small Group Research* (formerly *Small Group Behavior*, 1970), *Social Psychology Review* (1948), and *Work and Occupations* (1974).

 Internet Connection

www.mcgrawhill.ca/college/schaefer

For additional Internet exercises relating to Max Weber's examination of bureaucracies and technology's impact on the workplace, visit the Schaefer Online Learning Centre at **http://www.mcgrawhill.ca/college/schaefer**. *Please note that while the URLs listed were current at the time of printing, these sites often change—check the Online Learning Centre for updates.*

The construction of fair, clear, and workable social policy regarding sexual harassment has become a challenge for modern organizations and institutions. Review your textbook's discussion of sexual harassment at the end of this chapter. Then, direct your web browser to a search engine such as alltheweb (**http://www.alltheweb.com**) or Lycos (**http://www.lycos.com**). Search for your university's homepage and find the sexual harassment policy. If this policy is not online, try the name of another school in your area. After reflecting on your textbook's discussion and on the website, answer the following:

(a) How does the university define sexual harassment? How does it compare to the definition offered in your book?

(b) Who is included in this definition? Do you feel that any groups or persons have been left out of the definition who should be included?

(c) What examples are given of sexual harassment?

(d) What are the consequences for those who engage in such behaviour?

(e) If you were to draft the next version of this policy, what changes would you make? Why?

DEVIANCE AND
SOCIAL CONTROL

Cigarette smoking has become stigmatized in Canada. This newspaper advertisement, sponsored by Health Canada, reverses the typical advertising strategy of equating smoking with sexiness.

PART THREE

SOCIAL INEQUALITY

All men—and women—may have been created equal but they don't live in perfect equality. Part Three focuses on the structure and processes of social inequality. Chapter 8 examines the important sociological concepts of stratification and social mobility, as well as inequality based on social class, with special emphasis on Canada. In Chapter 9, we consider stratification and social mobility abroad and give particular attention to the unequal relationship between the world's industrialized and developing nations. Chapter 10 deals with issues of prejudice and discrimination against racial and ethnic groups. Chapter 11 discusses inequality based on gender and the position of women as an oppressed majority. Chapter 12 analyzes the aging process from a sociological perspective and examines inequality based on age.

hotjobs.com™ presents WorkWorld™

Internet & High-Tech Career Expo

Real Jobs.   **Real Companies.**   **Real Easy.**

Before entering:

1

Select Location ⬍

2 Choose:
○ Exhibitor
◉ Opportunity Seeker

▶ ENTER

As the twenty-first century begins, high-tech jobs symbolize unlimited opportunity. But these opportunities do not exist for millions of less skilled people. Even the ability to do job searches online, as reflected in this website for Hotjobs.com, is very limited for these people.

I n the early 1990s, the McDonald's Corporation launched a television ad campaign featuring a young black man named Calvin, who was portrayed sitting atop a Brooklyn stoop in his Golden Arches uniform while his friends down the sidewalk passed by, giving him a hard time about holding down a "McJob." After brushing off their teasing with good humour, Calvin is approached furtively by one young black man who asks, *sotto voce,* whether Calvin might help him get a job too. He allows that he could use some earnings and that despite the ragging he has just given Calvin, he thinks the uniform is really pretty cool—or at least that having a job is pretty cool. . . .

Americans have always been committed to the moral maxim that work defines the person. We carry around in our heads a rough tally that tells us what kinds of jobs are worthy of respect and what kinds are to be disdained, a pyramid organized by the income a job carries, the sort of credentials it takes to secure a particular position, the qualities of an occupation's incumbents—and we use this system of stratification (ruthlessly at times) to boost the status of some and humiliate others. . . .

Kimberly, a 20-year-old African American woman, began working at Burger Barn when she was 16 and discovered firsthand how her "friends" would turn on her for taking a low-wage job. Fortunately, she found a good friend at work who steadied her with a piece of advice:

> Say it's a job. You are making money. Right? Don't care what nobody say. You know? If they don't like it, too bad. They sitting on the corner doing what they are doing. You got to work making money. You know? Don't bother with what anybody has to say about it.

Kim's friend and adviser, a Burger Barn veteran who had long since come to terms with the insults of his peers, called upon a general status hierarchy that places the working above the nonworking as a bulwark against the slights. The advice Kim gleaned from her friend and her manager made a big difference in helping her to see that she deserves her dignity.

> Kids come in here . . . they don't have enough money. I'll be like, "You don't have enough money; you can't get [the food you ordered]." One night this little boy came in here and cursed me out. He [said], "That's why you are working at [Burger Barn]. You can't get a better job. . . ." I was upset and everything. I started crying. [My manager] was like, "Kim, don't bother with him. I'm saying, *you got a job.* You know. It is a *job.*" (Newman 1999:86, 102). ∎

ontrary to popular belief, the majority of poor people in North America do work. They just don't earn enough to lift themselves out of poverty. And they are very often overlooked by social scientists and policymakers, who tend to focus on the jobless poor in addressing issues of poverty. Katherine Newman, an anthropologist and professor of urban studies at Harvard University, aimed to counteract this neglect and misapprehension with her poignant look at the everyday life of the working poor, *No Shame in My Game.* The working poor are, in fact, a significant segment of the labour force.

Newman and her researchers followed the lives of 200 workers in large fast-food restaurants in New York City's Harlem over the course of a year and a half. They also tracked what happened to 100 unsuccessful job-seekers in the community. Their research techniques included interviews, visits to homes and schools, observation through on-site work at the restaurants, and personal diaries kept by the subjects of the study. The study threw light on the plight of the working poor—the struggle to get a job and to keep it, the stigma of taking low-level jobs, the long hours for low pay, the conflicting demands of family and school—and put a human face on this largely "invisible" population. In the course of doing so, Newman revealed layers of hierarchy even within the lower social class. This study's results apply to the Canadian context as well.

Ever since people first began to speculate about the nature of human society, their attention has been drawn to the differences between individuals and groups within any society. The term *social inequality* describes a condition in which members of a society have different amounts of wealth, prestige, or power. Some degree of social inequality characterizes every society.

When a system of social inequality is based on a hierarchy of groups, sociologists refer to it as *stratification:* a structured ranking of entire groups of people that perpetuates an unequal distribution of economic rewards and power in a society. These unequal rewards are evident not only in the distribution of wealth and income, but even in the distressing mortality rates of impoverished communities. Stratification involves the ways in which society's systems perpetuate social inequalities, thereby producing groups of people arranged in rank order from low to high.

In Canada, socioeconomic inequities are considered to be a product of individual qualities and effort. *Meritocracy* refers to a system where individuals earn their place in society—they are where they are because of merit. There is some debate about whether capitalist countries such as Canada and the United States are true meritocracies. Evidence suggests that there are significant advantages to being born into a wealthy Canadian family.

Stratification is a crucial subject of sociological investigation because of its pervasive influence on human interactions and institutions. It inevitably results in social inequality because certain groups of people stand higher in social rankings, control scarce resources, wield power, and receive special treatment. As we will see in this chapter, the consequences of stratification are evident in the unequal distribution of wealth and income within industrial societies. The term *income* refers to salaries, wages, and monies brought in by investments. By contrast, **wealth** is an inclusive term encompassing all of a person's material assets, including land, stocks, and other types of property. *Net worth* is the amount by which the value of someone's assets exceeds his or her debts. In Canada, it is used interchangeably with *wealth*.

This chapter focuses on the unequal distribution of socially valued rewards within human societies. First, we will examine three general systems of stratification. We will pay particular attention to Karl Marx's theories of class and to Max Weber's analysis of the components of stratification. The feminist perspective gives us a glimpse into stratification based on gender and the role of patriarchy in maintaining inequality. In addition, we will consider and compare functionalist and conflict theorists' explanations for the existence of stratification.

The second part of the chapter will explain how sociologists measure social class. We will examine the consequences of stratification in terms of wealth and income, health, educational opportunities, and other life chances. In the third part of the chapter, the movement of individuals up and down the social hierarchies of Canada will be examined. Finally, in the social policy section, we will address the issue of welfare reform in North America and Europe. ■

Understanding Stratification

Systems of Stratification

Look at the three general systems of stratification examined here—slavery, castes, and social classes—as ideal types useful for purposes of analysis. An *ideal type*, as defined by Weber, refers to the pure, abstract form of a social concept, not necessarily one that exists in the real world. It serves as a model of essential components against which to compare reality. Any stratification system may include elements of more than one type.

To understand these systems better, it may be helpful to review the distinction between *achieved status* and *ascribed status,* described in Chapter 5. *Ascribed status* is a social position "assigned" to a person without regard for that person's unique characteristics or talents. By contrast, *achieved status* is a social position attained by a person largely through his or her own effort. The two are closely linked. Canada's most affluent families generally inherit wealth and status, while many members of racial and ethnic minorities inherit disadvantaged status. Age and gender, as well, are ascribed statuses that influence a person's wealth and social position.

Slavery

The most extreme form of legalized social inequality for individuals or groups is *slavery.* What distinguishes this oppressive system of stratification is that enslaved individuals are *owned* by other people. They treat these human beings as property, just as if they were household pets or appliances.

Slavery, an ascribed status, has varied in the way it has been practised. In ancient Greece, slaves were mainly captives of war and piracy. Although succeeding generations could inherit slave status, it was not necessarily permanent. A person's status might change depending on which city-state happened to triumph in a military conflict. In effect, all citizens had the potential of becoming slaves or of being granted freedom, depending on the circumstances of history.

Even the Upper Canada 1793 *Act Against Slavery* failed to liberate Canadian blacks who were already owned by white masters. According to the Act, the freedom afforded to slaves was done in a way that caused the least inconvenience to the owners. For example, the status of those who were slaves at the time that the Act was passed retained their status—they were still the property of their masters. In other words, they were still slaves. Children born to slaves after the Act was passed would only become free once they reached the age of 25. On the more positive side, the Act prohibited new slaves from being brought into the province. In addition, slaves who reached the province on their own initiative after 1793 were to be considered free people. As Box 8-1 shows, millions of people around the world continue to live as slaves.

Castes

Castes are hereditary systems of rank, usually religiously dictated, that tend to be fixed and immobile. The caste system is generally associated with Hinduism in India and other countries. In India there are four major castes, called *varnas.* A fifth category of outcastes—the Harijan, previously referred to as *untouchables*—is considered to be so lowly and unclean as to have no place within this system of stratification. There are also many minor castes. Caste membership is an ascribed status (at birth, children automatically assume the same position as their parents). Each caste is quite sharply defined, and members are expected to marry within that caste.

Caste membership generally determines one's occupation or role as a religious functionary. An example of a lower caste in India is the *Dons,* whose main work is the undesirable job of cremating bodies. The caste system promotes a remarkable degree of differentiation. Thus,

Jacob Lawrence's painting, *Harriet Tubman* Series No. 9, graphically illustrates the torment of slavery as once practised in the United States. Slavery is the most extreme form of legalized social inequality.

8-1 Slavery in the Twenty-First Century

More than 100 million people around the world were still enslaved at the end of the twentieth century, according to estimates by Britain's Anti-Slavery International, the world's oldest human rights organization. And yet the 1948 Universal Declaration of Human Rights, which is supposedly binding on all members of the United Nations, holds that "No one shall be held in slavery or servitude; slavery and the slave trade shall be prohibited in all their forms" (Masland 1992:30, 32).

The United States considers any person a slave who is unable to withdraw his or her labour voluntarily from an employer. In many parts of the world, however, bonded labourers are imprisoned in virtual lifetime employment as they struggle to repay small debts. Indeed, the Bonded Labor Liberation Front has found workers paying off debts that are eight *centuries* old. Many nannies are brought into Canada on special work visas that require them to live with their employers for two years—imagine the labour abuses and bondage issues that could result from this kind of "slavery"!

The Swiss-based human rights group Christian Solidarity International has focused worldwide attention on the plight of slaves in the West African nation of Sudan. The organiza-tion solicits funds and uses them to buy slaves their freedom—at about $50 a slave. Several thousand members of the Dinka tribe have now regained their freedom that way. Some people believe that this program only encourages the Sudanese to enter the slave trade in order to receive payments, but the entire situation dramatically shows that slavery in the world did not end in the 1800s.

> More than 100 million people around the world were still enslaved at the end of the century.

While contemporary slavery may be most obvious in Third World countries, it also afflicts the industrialized nations of the West. Throughout Europe, guest workers and maids are employed by masters who hold their passports, subject them to degrading working conditions, and threaten them with deportation if they protest. Similar tactics are used essentially to imprison young women from Eastern Europe who have been brought (through deceptive promises) to work in the sex industries of Belgium, France, Germany, Greece, the Netherlands, and Switzerland.

Within North America, illegal immigrants are forced to labour for years under terrible conditions to pay off debts or out of fear of being turned over to immigration authorities. In New York City, dozens of deaf Mexican immigrants were forced to peddle trinkets in the subways and streets. In Florida and South Carolina, young women were lured from overseas with offers of landscaping jobs only to find themselves prostitutes in agricultural migrant camps. In Los Angeles, Thai immigrants were forced to work in a sweatshop an average of 84 hours a week at the meagre wage of $1.60 per hour, supposedly to pay off debts as high as $30 000 to the smugglers who brought them into California. This series of events finally led in 1998 to the creation of a federal task force to investigate and prosecute modern-day slavery in the United States.

Let's Discuss

1. Why are many bonded labourers around the world in the position of slaves?
2. If you were in the position of an illegal immigrant working for what amounts to slave labour, what would you do? Should those who seek the help of the authorities be deported?

Sources: Bales 1999; I. Fisher 1999; McDonnell and Becker 1996; Navarro 1998; *New York Times* 1997; Scheer 1998; C. Tyler 1991.

---

the single caste of chauffeurs has been split into two separate subcastes: drivers of luxury cars have a higher status than drivers of economy cars.

In recent decades, industrialization, urbanization, and increased participation in the global community have led to changes in India's rigid caste system. Many villagers have moved to urban areas where their low-caste status is unknown. Schools, hospitals, factories, and public transportation facilitate contacts between different castes that were previously avoided at all costs. In addition, the government has tried to reform the caste system. India's constitution, adopted in 1950, includes a provision abolishing discrimination against the Harijan, who had traditionally been excluded from temples, schools, and most forms of employment. Yet the caste system prevails, and its impact is now evident in electoral politics, as various political parties compete for the support of frustrated outcaste voters who constitute one-third of India's electorate. For the first time India has someone from a Harijan background serving in the symbolic but high-status position of president. Meanwhile, however, dozens of low-caste people continue to be killed for overstepping their lowly status in life (C. Dugger 1999; U. Schmetzer 1999).

Social Classes

A *class system* is a social ranking based primarily on economic position in which achieved characteristics can influence social mobility. In contrast to slavery and caste systems, the boundaries between classes are imprecisely defined, and one can move from one stratum, or level, of society to another. Yet class systems maintain stable stratification hierarchies and patterns of class divisions, and they too are marked by unequal distribution of wealth and power.

Income inequality is a basic characteristic of a class system. In 2000, the median family income in Canada rose by 2 percent to $51 000 (Statistics Canada 2002b). This represents the middle figure where half the incomes are higher and half are lower. In the previous year, the average (mean) income of a Canadian family was $68 347. The discrepancy between these two numbers is due to the fact that some Canadians made significantly more than the median, thus pulling up the overall average. The average income for families with two earners was $78 815, while families with a single earner brought in an average of $58 085 (Statistics Canada 2001b).

In Figure 8-1 we see the salaries made by CEOs (chief executive officers) in Canada and around the world. The existence of social classes in this country is emphasized by the fact that these administrators made 10 times the median income of the average Canadian worker. When we make the comparison with the income of someone earning the country's highest minimum wage, the gap is staggering.

Sociologist Daniel Rossides (1997) has conceptualized the class system of capitalist societies using a five-class model: the upper class, the upper-middle class, the lower-middle class, the working class, and the lower class. While the lines separating social classes in his model are not so sharp as the divisions between castes, he shows that members of the five classes differ significantly in ways other than income level.

FIGURE 8-1

Around the World: What's a CEO Worth?

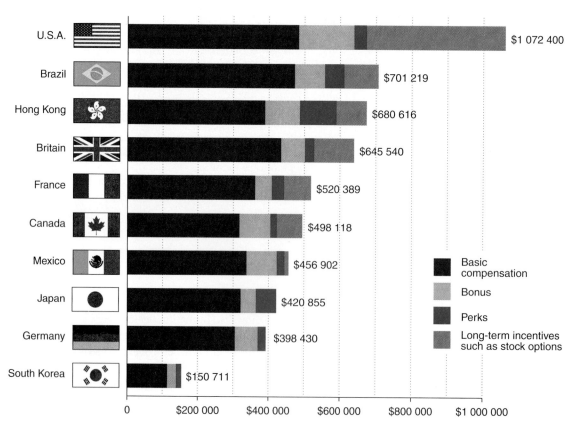

Note: The average annual pay package of the chief executive officer (CEO) of an industrial company with annual revenues of $250 million to $500 million in 10 countries. Figures are from April 1998 and are not weighted to compensate for different costs of living or levels of taxation.

Source: Towers Perrin in A. Bryant 1999:Section 4, p. 1.

In Canada, the study of social class is generally done through the comparison of *income quintiles*. Earners are separated into five groups (quintiles), each representing 20 percent of the population. While there is no official recognition of these categories as classes, they can be seen in comparison with Rossides' five-class model. There is little doubt of the implications associated with them, particularly as they apply to the upper and lower groups. In 1998, for instance, the 20 percent of Canadians at the bottom of the income scale took home just 7.1 percent of all the income earned in the country. By comparison, the top 20 percent of earners claimed 38.8 percent of the total. In real dollars, those at the top took home, on average, almost six times more than those at the bottom (Sauve 2000).

An important part of any claim of stratification has to do with establishing the institutionalized nature of the social inequalities. While income is certainly a marker of inequality in a meritocracy such as Canada, the argument can be made that everyone has equal access to opportunities and that differences in income and wealth reflect an individual's effort and talents, and inequities therefore are justified. Canadians seem to have accepted, to some degree, that disparity in income is a predictable and acceptable cost associated with our free market economy.

However, the differences found in market income are mirrored in another area where that argument is less convincing. This area is government transfers, the money that the federal government or the provinces give back to Canadian taxpayers. During the same year when top Canadian earners were enjoying six times the income of those at the other end of the income scale, they were also receiving monies from governments at the same disproportionate rate. The numbers indicate that the top group was given 39 percent of all government transfers, while the bottom quintile received just over 6 percent of the pie (StatsCan, Survey of Consumer Finances; Sauve 2000). While not conclusive evidence of a stratified society, these numbers do suggest that the unequal distribution of income is not entirely linked to achievement, in Canada's class system.

Social class is one of the independent or explanatory variables most frequently used by social scientists to shed light on social issues. In later chapters, we will analyze the relationships between social class and divorce patterns (Chapter 13), religious behaviour (Chapter 14), and formal schooling (Chapter 15), as well as other relationships in which social class is a variable.

Perspectives on Stratification

Sociologists have engaged in heated debates and reached varying conclusions about stratification and social inequality. No theorist stressed the significance of class for society—and for social change—more strongly than Karl Marx. Marx viewed class differentiation as the crucial determinant of social, economic, and political inequality. By contrast, Max Weber questioned Marx's emphasis on the overriding importance of the economic sector and argued that stratification should be viewed as having many dimensions.

Karl Marx's View of Class Differentiation

Sociologist Leonard Beeghley (1978:1) aptly noted that "Karl Marx was both a revolutionary and a social scientist." Marx was concerned with stratification in all types of human societies, beginning with primitive agricultural tribes and continuing into feudalism. But his main focus was on the effects of economic inequality on all aspects of nineteenth-century Europe. The plight of the working class made him feel that it was imperative to strive for changes in the class structure of society.

In Marx's view, social relations during any period of history depend on who controls the primary mode of economic production, such as land or factories. Differential access to scarce resources shapes the relationship between groups. Thus, under the feudal estate system, most production was agricultural, and the land was owned by the nobility. Peasants had little choice but to work according to terms dictated by those who owned the land.

Using this type of analysis, Marx examined social relations within **capitalism**—an economic system in which the means of production are largely in private hands and the main incentive for economic activity is the accumulation of profits (Rosenberg 1991). Marx focused on two classes—the bourgeoisie and the proletariat. The **bourgeoisie**, or capitalist class, owns the means of production, such as factories and machinery, while the **proletariat** is the working class. In capitalist societies, the members of the bourgeoisie maximize profit in competition with other firms. In the process, they exploit workers, who must exchange their labour for subsistence wages. In Marx's view, members of each class share a distinctive culture. He was most interested in the culture of the proletariat, but he also examined the ideology of the bourgeoisie, through which it justifies its dominance over workers.

According to Marx, exploitation of the proletariat will inevitably lead to the destruction of the capitalist system because the workers will revolt. But, first, the working class must develop **class consciousness**—a subjective awareness of common vested interests and the need for collective political action to bring about social change. Workers must often overcome what Marx termed **false consciousness**, or an attitude held by members of a class that does not accurately reflect its objective position. A worker with false consciousness may adopt an individualistic viewpoint toward capitalist exploitation ("*I* am being exploited by *my* boss"). By contrast, the class-conscious worker realizes that *all* workers are being exploited by the bourgeoisie and have a common stake in revolution (Vanneman and Cannon 1987).

For Karl Marx, class consciousness is part of a collective process whereby the proletariat comes to identify the bourgeoisie as the source of its oppression. Ultimately, the proletariat will overthrow the rule of the bourgeoisie and the government (which Marx saw as representing the interests of capitalists) and will eliminate private ownership of the means of production. In his rather utopian view, classes and oppression will cease to exist in the postrevolutionary workers' state.

How accurate were Marx's predictions? He failed to anticipate the emergence of labour unions, whose power in collective bargaining weakens the stranglehold that capitalists maintain over workers. Moreover, as contemporary conflict theorists note, he did not foresee the extent to which political liberties and relative prosperity could contribute to "false consciousness." He could not have foreseen some of the complications that exist now, such as labourers who are also shareholders, as is the case in many high-tech companies where employees are given stocks and stock options in addition to a salary. They are therefore both worker and part-owner, which means they do not fit the strict definition of either proletariat or capitalist bourgeoisie. And many people have come to view themselves as individuals striving for improvement in "free" societies with substantial mobility rather than as downtrodden members of social classes facing a collective fate. Still, the Marxist approach to the study of class is useful in stressing the importance of stratification as a determinant of social behaviour and the fundamental separation in many societies between two distinct groups, the rich and the poor.

Max Weber's View of Stratification

Unlike Karl Marx, Max Weber insisted that no single characteristic (such as class) totally defines a person's position within the stratification system. Instead, writing in 1916, he identified three analytically distinct components of stratification: class, status, and power (Gerth and Mills 1958).

Weber used the term *class* to refer to people who have a similar level of wealth and income. For example, some Canadian workers try to support their families through jobs that pay the minimum wage (such as the working poor described in the chapter opener). According to Weber's definition, these wage earners constitute a class because they have the same economic position and fate. While Weber agreed with Marx on the importance of the economic dimension of stratification, he argued that

the actions of individuals and groups could not be understood *solely* in economic terms.

Weber used the term *status group* to refer to people who rank the same in prestige or lifestyle. An individual gains status through membership in a desirable group, such as the medical profession. But status is not the same as economic class standing. In our culture, a successful plumber may be in a higher income class than a professor. Yet the plumber is widely regarded as a member of the blue-collar working status group, while the professor holds high status.

For Weber, the third major component of stratification reflects a political dimension. *Power* is the ability to exercise one's will over others. In Canada, power stems from membership in particularly influential groups, such as corporate boards of directors, government bodies, and advocacy groups. Conflict theorists generally agree that two major sources of power—big business and government—are closely interrelated (see Chapters 16 and 17).

In Weber's view, then, each of us has not one rank in society but three. Our position in a stratification system reflects some combination of class, status, and power. Each factor influences the other two, and in fact the rankings on these three dimensions often tend to coincide. This phenomenon is called *status consistency* and refers to the fact that when someone has a high ranking in one area, they tend to be similarly placed in the others.

Pierre Trudeau, one of Canada's most beloved prime ministers, came from a background in Montreal's elite community. Trudeau was the son of a wealthy French-Canadian businessman, a position in life that afforded him the best of opportunities, including an education at the esteemed London School of Economics.

Of course, status can be inconsistent. Wayne Gretzky has enviable status in income, prestige, and occupation. However, Canada's most famous athlete has little educational status. John Diefenbaker, Canada's prime minister from 1957 through 1963, came from modest roots. Diefenbaker lived most of his early life in the rural communities of Saskatchewan and the Northwest Territories, and earned his law degree in his home province after serving his country in the First World War.

At the same time, these dimensions of stratification may operate somewhat independently in determining a person's position. A widely published poet may achieve high status while earning a relatively modest income. Successful professional athletes have little power but enjoy a relatively high position in terms of class and status. To understand the workings of a culture more fully, sociologists must carefully evaluate the ways in which it distributes its most valued rewards, including wealth and income, status, and power (Duberman 1976; Gerth and Mills 1958).

How would it feel to be a member of the Supreme Court of Canada? Do you think that all Canadians have equal access to this building?

Is Stratification Universal?

Must some members of society receive greater rewards than others? Do people need to feel socially and economically superior to others? Can social life be organized without structured inequality? These questions have been debated for centuries, especially among political activists. Utopian socialists, religious minorities, and members of recent countercultures have all attempted to establish communities that, to some extent or other, would abolish inequality in social relationships.

Social science research has found that inequality exists in all societies—even the simplest. For example, when anthropologist Gunnar Landtman (1968, original edition 1938) studied the Kiwai Papuans of New Guinea, he initially noticed little differentiation among them. Every man in the village did the same work and lived in similar housing. However, on closer inspection, Landtman observed that certain Papuans—the men who were warriors, harpooners, and sorcerers—were described as "a little more high" than others. By contrast, villagers who were female, unemployed, or unmarried were considered "down a little bit" and were barred from owning land.

Stratification is universal in that all societies maintain some form of differentiation among members. Depending on its values, a society may assign people to distinctive ranks based on their religious knowledge, skill in hunting, beauty, trading expertise, or ability to provide health care. But why has such inequality developed in human societies? And how much differentiation among people, if any, is actually essential?

Functionalist, conflict, and feminist sociologists offer contrasting explanations for the existence and necessity of social stratification. Functionalists maintain that a differential system of rewards and punishments is necessary for the efficient operation of society. Conflict theorists argue that competition for scarce resources results in significant political, economic, and social inequality. Feminist sociologists analyze the historical position of disadvantage for women, determined by institutional and cultural influences. Ours is a gender stratified society, they say.

Functionalist View

Would people go to school for many years to become physicians if they could make as much money and gain as much respect working as street cleaners? Functionalists say no, which is partly why they believe that a stratified society is universal.

In the view of Kingsley Davis and Wilbert Moore (1945), society must distribute its members among a variety of social positions. It must not only make sure that these positions are filled but also see that they are staffed by people with the appropriate talents and abilities. Rewards, including money and prestige, are based on the importance of a position and the relative scarcity of qualified personnel. Yet this assessment often devalues work performed by certain segments of society, such as women's work as homemakers or occupations traditionally filled by women or low-status work in fast-food outlets.

Davis and Moore argue that stratification is universal and that social inequality is necessary so that people will be motivated to fill functionally important positions. But, critics say, unequal rewards are not the only means of encouraging people to fill critical positions and occupations. Personal pleasure, intrinsic satisfaction, and value orientations also motivate people to enter particular careers. Functionalists agree but note that society must use some type of reward to motivate people to enter unpleasant or dangerous jobs, as well as jobs that require a long training period. This response does not justify stratification systems in which status is largely inherited, such as slave or caste societies. Similarly, it is difficult to explain the high salaries our society offers to professional athletes or entertainers on the basis of how critical these jobs are to the survival of society (R. Collins 1975; Kerbo 1996; Tumin 1953, 1985).

Even if stratification is inevitable, the functionalist explanation for differential rewards does not explain the wide disparity between the rich and the poor. Critics of the functionalist approach point out that the richest 10 percent of households account for 20 percent of the nation's income in Sweden, 25 percent in France, and 24 percent in Canada. In their view, the level of income inequality found in contemporary industrial societies cannot be defended—even though these societies have a legitimate need to fill certain key occupations (World Bank 2000:238–239).

Conflict View

p. 13

The writings of feminist scholars have done much to advance conflict theory in recent years, but the writings of Karl Marx are at the heart of conflict theory, as we saw in Chapter 1. Marx viewed history as a continuous struggle between the oppressors and the oppressed that would ultimately culminate in an egalitarian, classless society. In terms of stratification, he argued that the dominant class under capitalism—the bourgeoisie—manipulated the economic and political systems in order to maintain control over the exploited proletariat. Marx did not believe that stratification was inevitable, but he did see inequality and oppression as inherent in capitalism (E. Wright et al. 1982).

Like Marx, contemporary conflict theorists believe that human beings are prone to conflict over such scarce resources as wealth, status, and power. However, where Marx focused primarily on class conflict, more recent theorists have extended this analysis to include conflicts based on gender, race, age, and other dimensions. British sociologist Ralf Dahrendorf is one of the most influential contributors to the conflict approach.

Dahrendorf (1959) modified Marx's analysis of capitalist society to apply to *modern* capitalist societies. For Dahrendorf, social classes are groups of people who share common interests resulting from their authority relationships. In identifying the most powerful groups in society, he includes not only the bourgeoisie—the owners of the means of production—but also the managers of industry, legislators, the judiciary, heads of the government bureaucracy, and others. In that respect, Dahrendorf has merged Marx's emphasis on class conflict with Weber's recognition that power is an important element of stratification (Cuff et al. 1990).

Conflict theorists, including Dahrendorf, contend that the powerful of today, like the bourgeoisie of Marx's time, want society to run smoothly so that they can enjoy their privileged positions. Because the status quo suits those with wealth, status, and power, they have a clear interest in preventing, minimizing, or controlling societal conflict.

One way for the powerful to maintain the status quo is to define and disseminate the society's dominant ideology. In Chapter 3, we noted that the term *dominant ideology* describes a set of cultural beliefs and practices that helps to maintain powerful social, economic, and political interests. For Karl Marx, the dominant ideology in a capitalist society serves the interests of the ruling class. From a conflict perspective, the social significance of the dominant ideology is that a society's most powerful groups and institutions not only control wealth and property, but, even more important, they control the means of producing beliefs about reality primarily through religion, education, and the media (Abercrombie et al. 1980, 1990; Robertson 1988).

p. 75

The powerful, such as leaders of government, also use limited social reforms to buy off the oppressed and reduce the danger of challenges to their dominance. For example, minimum wage laws and unemployment compensation unquestionably give some valuable assistance to needy men and women. Yet these reforms also serve to pacify those who might otherwise rebel. Of course, in the view of conflict theorists, such manoeuvres can never entirely eliminate conflict, since workers will continue to demand equality, and the powerful will not give up their control of society.

Conflict theorists see stratification as a major source of societal tension and conflict. They do not agree with Davis and Moore that stratification is functional for a society or that it serves as a source of stability. Rather, conflict sociologists argue that stratification will inevitably lead to instability and to social change (R. Collins 1975; L. Coser 1977).

Lenski's Viewpoint

Let's return to the question posed earlier—"Is stratification universal?"—and consider the sociological response. Some form of differentiation is found in every culture, from the most primitive to the most advanced industrial societies of our time. Sociologist Gerhard Lenski, in his sociocultural evolution approach (refer back to Chapter 5), described how economic systems change as their level of technology becomes more complex, beginning with hunting and gathering and culminating eventually with industrial society. In subsistence-based, hunting-and-gathering societies, people focus on survival. While inequality and differentiation are evident, a stratification system based on social class does not emerge because there is no real wealth to be claimed.

p. 130

As a society advances in technology, it becomes capable of producing a considerable surplus of goods. The emergence of surplus resources greatly expands the possibilities for inequality in status, influence, and power and allows a well-defined rigid social class system to develop. In order to minimize strikes, slowdowns, and industrial sabotage, the elites may share a portion of the economic surplus with the lower classes, but not enough to reduce their power and privilege.

As Lenski argued, the allocation of surplus goods and services controlled by those with wealth, status, and power reinforces the social inequality that accompanies stratification systems. While this reward system may once have served the overall purposes of society, as functionalists contend, the same cannot be said for the large disparities separating the haves from the have-nots in current societies. In contemporary industrial society, the degree of social and economic inequality far exceeds the need to provide for goods and services (Lenski 1966; Nolan and Lenski 1999).

Feminist Views

A number of feminist perspectives incorporate the ideas of both Marx and Weber, but they add further critical analyses of the impact of patriarchal structures when examining stratification. As feminist theories analyze the status of women in society, they show that Canadian women have historically been disadvantaged. Regardless of the indicator used—class, status, or power—women endure an inferior position within our social structure.

When we look at income levels as the indicator of class, the figures reveal that even after more than 30 years of proactive feminism, the wage gap between the earnings of females and males continues to exist. Almost three-quarters of the female wage earners in Canada are concentrated in a few female-dominated sectors where earnings continue to be low. In addition, the persistence of a traditional distribution of household responsibilities has a detrimental effect on workforce participation. According to Katherine Marshall, Canadian women are expected to carry the major load of daily housework, even in homes with two full-time earners. In 28 percent of these households, women are responsible for the unpaid chores of the home (Marshall 1999:26).

The status of women in Canada is a reflection of their struggle to gain equality in the workplace. Ghettoization in low paying, female-dominated sectors, and the continuing expectation that women will shoulder most of the unpaid work in the home, has served to limit women's ability to advance in careers and other status-enhancing paths. The underrepresentation of women in positions of power does not help. While some Canadian women do hold political and corporate positions of power, their numbers do not come close to matching the 51 percent of the total population that women represent. These issues will be discussed further in relation to family (Chapter 13), government (Chapter 16) and the world of work (Chapter 17).

The concern for feminists is the degree to which the current situation is due to structural influences. In other words, given that women are as inherently capable as men, their second-class status in our society must be explained by external, or structural, factors. If the social position of women is determined by institutional and cultural influences, then the argument can be made that Canada is a stratified society—stratified by gender. And if, as the statistics show, women of colour are at an even lower position in the Canadian hierarchy, then this is further evidence of stratification along yet another dimension—race. This will be further explored in Chapters 10 and 11.

Stratification by Social Class

Measuring Social Class

We're continually assessing how wealthy people are by looking at the cars they drive, the houses in which they live, the clothes they wear, and so on. Yet it is not as easy to locate an individual within our social hierarchies as it would be in slavery or caste systems of stratification. To determine someone's class position, sociologists generally rely on the objective method.

The **objective method** of measuring social class views class largely as a statistical category. Researchers assign individuals to social classes on the basis of criteria such as occupation, education, income, and residence. The key to the objective method is that the *researcher,* rather than the person being classified, identifies an individual's class position.

The first step in using this method is to decide what indicators or causal factors will be measured objectively, whether wealth, income, education, occupation, or a combination of these. The prestige ranking of occupations has proven to be a useful indicator of a person's class position. For one thing, it is much easier to determine accurately than income or wealth. The term **prestige** refers to the respect and admiration that an occupation holds in a society. "My daughter, the physicist" connotes something very different from "my daughter, the waitress." Prestige is independent of the particular individual who occupies a job, a characteristic that distinguishes it from esteem. **Esteem** refers to the reputation that a specific person has earned within an occupation. Therefore, one can say that the position of prime minister has high prestige, even though it has been occupied by people with varying degrees of esteem. A hairdresser may have the esteem of his clients, but he lacks the prestige of a corporation president.

Table 8-1 ranks the prestige of a number of well-known occupations. In a series of surveys in the United States, sociologists assigned prestige rankings to about 500 occupations, ranging from physician to newspaper vendor. The highest possible prestige score was 100, and

Table 8-1 Prestige Rankings of Occupations

Occupation	Score	Occupation	Score
Physician	86	Secretary	46
Lawyer	75	Insurance agent	45
Dentist	74	Bank teller	43
Professor	74	Nurse's aide	42
Architect	73	Farmer	40
Clergy	69	Correctional officer	40
Pharmacist	68	Receptionist	39
Registered nurse	66	Barber	36
High school teacher	66	Child care worker	35
Accountant	65	Hotel clerk	32
Airline pilot	60	Bus driver	32
Police officer and detective	60	Truck driver	30
Preschool teacher	55	Retail clerk (shoes)	28
Librarian	54	Garbage collector	28
Firefighter	53	Waiter and waitress	28
Social worker	52	Bartender	25
Electrician	51	Farm worker	23
Funeral director	49	Janitor	22
Mail carrier	47	Newspaper vendor	19

Sources: J. Davis and Smith 1998:1,242–1,246; Nakao and Treas 1990, 1994; NORC 1994.

the lowest was 0. Physician, lawyer, dentist, and professor were the most highly regarded occupations. Sociologists have used such data to assign prestige rankings to virtually all jobs and have found a stability in rankings from 1925 to 1991. Similar studies in other countries have also developed useful prestige rankings of occupations (Hodge and Rossi 1964; Lin and Xie 1988; Treiman 1977).

Studies of social class tend to neglect the occupations and incomes of *women* as determinants of social rank. In an exhaustive study of 589 occupations, sociologists Mary Powers and Joan Holmberg (1978) examined the impact of women's participation in the paid labour force on occupational status. Since women tend to dominate the relatively low-paying occupations, such as bookkeepers and secretaries, their participation in the workforce leads

to a general upgrading of the status of most male-dominated occupations. More recent research conducted in both North America and Europe has assessed the occupations of husbands *and* wives in determining the class positions of families. (Sørensen 1994). With more than half of all married women now working outside the home (see Chapter 11), this approach seems long overdue, but it also raises some questions. For example, how is class or status to be judged in dual-career families—by the occupation regarded as having greater prestige, the average, or some other combination of the two occupations?

Sociologists—and, in particular, feminist sociologists in Great Britain—are drawing on new approaches in assessing women's social class standing. One approach is to focus on the individual (rather than the family or household) as the basis of categorizing a woman's class position. Thus, a woman would be classified based on her own occupational status rather than that of her spouse (O'Donnell 1992).

Another feminist effort to measure the contribution of women to the economy reflects a more clearly political agenda. International Women Count Network, a global grassroots feminist organization, has sought to give a monetary value to women's unpaid work. Besides providing symbolic recognition of women's role in labour, this value would also be used to calculate pension programs and benefits that are based on wages received. In 1995 the United Nations placed a U.S.$11 trillion price tag on unpaid labour by women, largely in child care, housework, and agriculture. Whatever the figure today, the continued undercounting of many workers' contribution to a family and to an entire economy makes virtually all measures of stratification in need of reform (United Nations Development Programme 1995; Wages for Housework Campaign 1999).

Another complication in measuring social class is that advances in statistical methods and computer technology have multiplied the factors used to define class under the objective method. No longer are sociologists limited to annual income and education in evaluating a person's class position. Today, studies are published that use as criteria the value of homes, sources of income, assets, years in present occupations, neighbourhoods, and considerations regarding dual careers. Adding these variables will not necessarily paint a different picture of class differentiation, but it does allow sociologists to measure class in a more complex and multidimensional way.

Whatever the technique used to measure class, the sociologist is interested in real and often dramatic differences in power, privilege, and opportunity in a society. The study of stratification is a study of inequality. Nowhere is this more evident than in the distribution of wealth and income.

Consequences of Social Class

Wealth and Income

By all measures, income in Canada is distributed unevenly. Nobel prizewinning economist Paul Samuelson has described the situation in the following words: "If we made an income pyramid out of a child's blocks, with each layer portraying $500 of income, the peak would be far higher than Mount Everest, but most people would be within a few feet of the ground" (Samuelson and Nordhaus 1998:344). Recent data support Samuelson's analogy. As Figure 8-2 shows, in 1998 the top fifth (or 20 percent of the nation) accounted for 39 percent of total after-tax income. By contrast, the bottom fifth accounted for only 7 percent of after-tax income.

Wealth in Canada is much more unevenly distributed than income. As Figure 8-2 shows, in 1999 the richest fifth of the population held almost 64 percent of the nation's wealth. The discrepancy in wealth and income has been an enduring part of the Canadian class structure. Back in the seventeenth century, Natives and the Habitants lived in spartan circumstances while the owners of the Hudson's Bay Company lived lives of luxury. With the arrival of the Industrial Revolution and the labour movement early in the twentieth century, Southern Ontario and Quebec saw some of the historical inequities being addressed. However, in recent years the evidence suggests that the trend has been reversed.

The middle class, historically considered the bellwether of Canada's opportunities for social mobility, suffered significant job losses in the 1990s. This can be attributed to structural changes in the workplace. Particularly hard hit were middle management and skilled blue-collar workers. Both of these sectors have felt the impact of technological change that either made their work redundant or reduced its complexity substantially. Those at the middle of the corporate structure watched as their organizational and information management functions were taken over by more affordable and

FIGURE 8-2

Comparison of Distribution of Income and Wealth in Canada

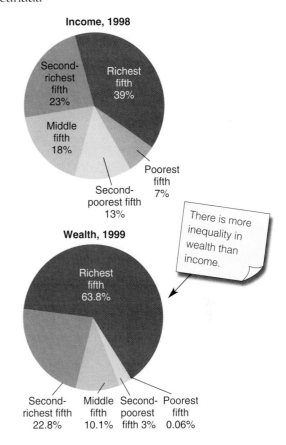

Note: Data on wealth do not add to 100 percent due to rounding.

Sources: Calculations of income data (after-tax family income) based on Sauve 2000. Calculations of data on wealth based on Statistics Canada 2001a.

accessible desktop computers. The blue-collar workers in processing and assembly facilities suffered a similar fate at the robotic arms of computer-controlled devices.

A 1993 study completed by Clarence Lochhead and Vivian Shalla for the Council on Social Development concluded: ". . . the labour market today is producing greater inequality among families with children than it did a decade ago, with especially severe income losses among lower-middle income earners and the poor" (Lochhead et al. 1996). In the decade 1984–1993, workers in the middle and lower income groups saw their wages fall in real terms. By contrast, those at the top of the ladder saw their incomes increase. In families with children under the age of 18, for example, the households ranked in the second quintile experienced a drop of $2985. During the same time, those in the top quintile enjoyed an increase of $5059. Lochhead and Shalla conclude that the increasing income inequality in Canada's

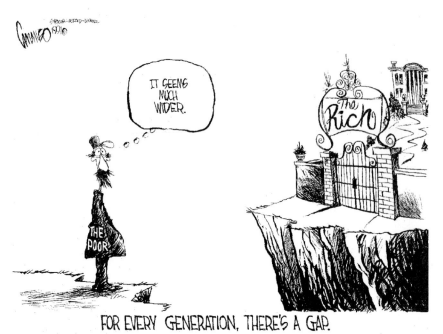

FOR EVERY GENERATION, THERE'S A GAP.

wage distribution is producing a 'two-tiered society,' suggesting that Canada is headed down a road where those two tiers will comprise the very rich on one level and the very poor on the other.

Poverty

While determining wealth in Canada is fairly straightforward, determining poverty is more complicated. Unlike most of the developed world, Canada does not have an official poverty line. Instead, Statistics Canada, the federal government's data gathering and analysis arm, uses four different markers. These range from comparisons of income to comparisons of expenditures. For example, the *low income measure* (LIM) compares a household's income against the median of an equivalent family. Any unit whose income is less than half that median is defined as poor.

The more common marker, the **low income cut-off** (**LICO**), is generally what people mean by a poverty line in Canada. It uses the amount a household spends on the basics—food, shelter, and clothing—to make the same determination. Statistics Canada classifies a family as being poor if it spends 64 percent or more of after-tax income on the basics (Sauve 2000). The National Council of Welfare's Fact Sheet on poverty lines for 2000 states that a family of four, living in a city of 500 000 or more, is considered poor if its income is less than $34 572. This represents a $10 000 difference from the LIM. Not having a set measure of the social condition of poverty presents policymakers and public program administrators with clear challenges.

In January 2001, Statistics Canada began using a new measure of poverty, one designed to reflect more than the

relationship between income and distribution. The **market basket measure** (**MBM**) will take into consideration more than subsistence needs, by calculating the amounts needed by various households to live a life comparable to the standards of its community. In other words, someone living in a town where 90 percent of the residents have Internet access would have the cost of that access included on his or her essential needs list.

Studying Poverty   Like the Canadian government, sociologists and other social scientists find their efforts to better understand poverty complicated by the difficulty of defining it. This problem is evident even in government programs that conceive of poverty in either absolute or relative terms. **Absolute poverty** in developed countries refers to a minimum level of subsistence below which no family should be expected to live. This standard theoretically remains unchanged from year to year. Policies concerning minimum wages, housing standards, or hot lunch programs for children in schools in low-income neighbourhoods imply a need to bring citizens up to some predetermined level of existence. Canada's provincial governments, which have set the minimum wage paid to workers within their borders since 1996, have all, with the exception of Ontario, increased the minimum wage since then (see Table 8-2 for the minimum wage rates across Canada). Some of the increases have been meagre, like Alberta's 25-cent raise over five years. Others have been greater but still modest, like the 85-cent increase legislated in Manitoba.

By contrast, **relative poverty** is a floating standard of deprivation by which people at the bottom of a society, whatever their lifestyles, are judged to be disadvantaged *in comparison with the rest of the community in which they live*. Policies and programs in the **social safety net**, those initiatives designed to alleviate the harshest conditions associated with being at the bottom of the income scale, are the domain of the provinces. Most current social programs view poverty in relative terms. Therefore, even if the poor of the 1990s are better off in absolute terms than the poor of the 1930s or 1960s, they are still seen as deserving special assistance from government.

There has been an ongoing debate in Canada over the usefulness of any official measure of poverty. Critics from the right argue that the almost complete absence of absolute poverty means that low-income Canadians are

Table 8-2 Minimum Wages for Experienced Adult Workers, by Province, as of December 2002

Province/territory	Wage
Alberta	$5.90
British Columbia	$8.00
Manitoba	$6.50
New Brunswick	$6.00
Newfoundland and Labrador	$6.00
Northwest Territories	$6.50
Nova Scotia	$6.00
Nunavut	$6.50
Ontario	$6.85
Prince Edward Island	$6.00
Quebec	$7.00
Saskatchewan	$6.65
Yukon Territory	$7.20

Source: HRDC 2002.

on seasonal workers in particular. The provincial jurisdiction over welfare has meant that there is no consistency in either access or standards across the country. With hardline conservative governments in Ontario and Alberta, standards covering accessibility to welfare have changed dramatically. The result is that the number of people in those provinces who are able to qualify for assistance has shrunk. In Ontario, the Progressive Conservative government of Mike Harris experimented with the idea of "workfare," a program that would require able welfare recipients to work for their cheques. The Social Policy section later in this chapter examines legislation associated with addressing poverty. It is quite clear that poverty, particularly when it is not absolute, is a subjective determination. With this in mind, we will consider just who it is that makes up the poor in Canada.

Who Are the Poor?   Not only does the category of the poor defy any simple definition, it counters common stereotypes about "poor people." For example, many people in Canada believe that the vast majority of the poor are able to work but will not. Yet many poor adults *do* work outside the home. In fact, income statistics show that over 60 percent of Canadian households that could be classified as poor have at least one individual who works full-time, year-round. This figure suggests that the stereotype of the "lazy poor" is more one of convenience than of fact.

A sizable number of the poor live in urban centres, but a majority live outside those neighbourhoods we might consider low-income. Poverty is no stranger in rural areas, ranging from Maritime fishing villages to hard-hit farming regions of Saskatchewan to First Nations communities. Yet, there is considerable variation in income by regions in Canada. The latest available statistics on incomes by province are from the 2001 Census, which shows that the provinces with the highest median family income are Ontario ($61 024), Alberta ($60 142), and British Columbia ($54 840). Median family income is lower in the Maritime provinces, with Newfoundland being the lowest (at $41 214) (Statistics Canada 2003f).

Canada's First Nations people are also at risk of poverty. Partly this is the case because they lag behind the rest of the population in terms of education, labour force participation, and income. Another aspect of their poverty has to do with systemic discrimination on the part of society's institutions, which will be explored in greater detail in Chapter 10. On average, Canada's Aboriginal people fare poorly in economic matters. However, Gerber (1990:42–43) states that, while the image of First Nations in poverty does apply to the aggregate, one can also find Aboriginal people "distributed across the range of class sites."

not starving to death on the streets, and that their lot is more one of inconvenience than desperation. These proponents of meritocracy and individual responsibility take the functionalist position that poverty serves as a motivator. They also suggest that current measures of poverty are reflective of a socialist agenda, and classify far too many Canadians as poor. On the other side of the debate are the liberal thinkers, who take the position that poverty in a society as wealthy as Canada's is unconscionable. These proponents of social programs to prevent or at least reduce the incidence of poverty see the existing poverty lines as being too punitive in that they fail to acknowledge the plight of many Canadians who struggle with minimum wage and/or sporadic employment in an attempt to provide the basics of life for their families.

Over the past decade, changes to some of the cornerstones of Canada's safety net have pleased the former group and infuriated the latter. At the federal level, more stringent standards in determining who is eligible to receive employment insurance had a dramatic impact

Included among the groups most affected by poverty in Canada are senior citizens, particularly women, and children, particularly those living in single-parent families with their mothers. One surprising addition to this list comes from the revelation in recent years that some families of men and women who are part of the lower ranks of the Canadian armed forces have been forced to use food banks to supplement their wages. Table 8-3 provides additional statistical information regarding these low-income people in Canada. (The situation of the most destitute poor in Canada and worldwide, the homeless, will be examined in the social policy section of Chapter 18.) Box 8-2 gives further information on poverty in our country.

Currently women make up more than half the poor in this country. As seen in Figure 8-3, women have higher poverty rates for every age group except those 45 to 54 years of age. The greatest percentage (and the largest sex differences) of poverty can be seen in the senior population of Canada (National Council of Welfare 2000). What makes women's poverty more alarming than men's is that a woman living below the poverty line is more than three times as likely as a man to have children who are wholly or substantially dependent on her. During the last 20 years, female-headed families have become an increasing proportion of Canada's low-income population. In addition, the aging population has seen a rise in the numbers—but not the rate—of female senior citizens living in poverty. Even able-bodied, single women are overrepresented among the poor. In 1998, this type of woman was 25 percent more likely to be poor than was a man of similar characteristics (Statistics Canada 1998d). The single greatest predictor of poverty among women in Canada is whether they are living without a spouse. Almost half (49 percent) of women over 65 and 41 percent of women under 65 who are unattached live in poverty in Canada. This alarming trend, known as the *feminization of poverty*, is evident not just in Canada but around the world.

Conflict theorists and other observers trace the higher rates of poverty among women to three distinct factors: the difficulty in finding affordable child care, sexual harassment, and sex discrimination in the labour market (see Chapter 11) (Dalaker and Proctor 2000:vi).

p. 217

p. 305

Take another look at Table 8-3, which shows that 37 percent of all single-parent families fall into the lowest income group. It is important to note, however, that within this number there is a significant overrepresentation of female-headed families. The same pattern is evident outside of Canada. In 1999, 11.8 percent of all people in the United States lived in poverty, compared to 27.8 percent of households headed by single mothers. This trend is also noticeable throughout Europe, in developing countries, and even in three widely differing nations whose legislation on behalf of women is the most advanced in the world: Israel, Sweden, and Russia. Similar to the situation in Canada, in these countries, national health care programs, housing subsidies, and other forms of government assistance cushion the impact of poverty somewhat, yet the feminization of poverty still advances (Abowitz 1986; Stanley 1995; Statistics Sweden 1999).

Sociologist William Julius Wilson (1980, 1987, 1989, 1996) and other social scientists have used the term **underclass** to describe the long-term poor who lack training and skills. While estimates vary depending on the definition, this group tends to consist disproportionately of women, visible minorities, and senior citizens in Canadian society.

Conflict theorists, among others, have expressed alarm at the portion of the population living on this lower rung of the stratification hierarchy and at society's reluctance to address the lack of economic opportunities for these people. Often, portraits of the underclass seem to

Table 8-3 **Low Income Rates in Canada**

Group	1990	1991	1992	1993	1994	1995	1996	1997	1998	1999
Individuals	28.2	30.8	30.5	30.9	30.4	30.5	32.6	31.9	30.1	29.9
Single parents	42.7	45.3	41.1	41.3	42.2	42.4	45.2	42.1	36.7	36.9
Couples w/ child	6.8	7.8	7.2	8.8	8.4	9.8	9.7	9.2	7.4	7.3
Couples w/o child	5.6	6.5	5.5	6.6	6.2	6.7	7.2	6.4	5.5	6.1
Senior citizens	2.5	2.6	2.6	4.0	2.5	2.1	2.9	3.7	3.5	2.2

Source: Adapted from Statistics Canada 1999c.

The Canadian Council on Social Development (CCSD) is a non-profit organization dedicated to "advancing economic and social security to all Canadians." The Council sees social issue research as a key to understanding the rationale and the potential impact of government and corporate policies. The organization has undertaken a broad range of data gathering and analysis that enable it to serve as a source of information and a respected advocate for Canadians.

Each year, the Council publishes a compendium of its findings on Canada's lower socioeconomic class in *The Canadian Fact Book on Poverty*. In the 2000 edition, it concluded that millions of Canadians lived in poverty, not because there were insufficient resources to provide adequate food, shelter, and clothing to all, but rather because of the skewed distribution of wealth in this country. Of particular concern was the number of Canadian children living in economically dysfunctional circumstances. The following are some of the conclusions from *The Canadian Fact Book on Poverty, 2000*:

- Children from homes with less than $20 000 annual income are 1.3 times more likely to live in substandard housing than are middle-class children.
- Poor children are 2.4 times more likely than children from wealthy homes to live in neighbourhoods with disproportionately high levels of crime.

> Of particular concern was the number of Canadian children living in economically dysfunctional circumstances.

- Poor children are more likely to be aggressive.
- Poor children are more likely to be hyperactive.
- Poor children are more likely to suffer from serious health problems such as speech or hearing impairment.
- Poor children are more likely to become involved in delinquent behaviours.

- Poor children are less likely to participate in skill-building activities.

But the Council also found that children were not the only ones whose lives were negatively impacted by poverty. Adults living in households where the earnings were less than $30 000 had the following characteristics:

- Poor adults were more likely to be in poor-to-fair health.
- Poor adults were twice as likely to have serious health problems as those with high-incomes.
- Poor adults were more likely to suffer from chronic conditions such as asthma, high blood pressure, and ulcers.
- Poor adults had higher scores on the mental health distress index.
- Poor adults had a much lower sense of self-esteem.

Let's Discuss

1. What can be done to lessen the impact of poverty on Canadian children?
2. Who has the responsibility of ensuring that a nation's children do not live in poverty?

Source: Canadian Council on Social Development 2000.

"blame the victims" for their own plight while ignoring other factors that push people into poverty.

Poverty, of course, is not a new phenomenon. Yet the concept of the underclass describes a chilling development: individuals and families, whether employed or unemployed, who are beyond the reach of any safety net provided by existing social programs. Moreover, membership in the underclass is not an intermittent condition but a long-term attribute. The underclass is understandably alienated from the larger society and engages sporadically in illegal behaviour. These illegal acts do little to encourage society to address the long-term problems of the underclass.

Analysis of the poor reveals that they are not a static social class. The overall composition of the poor changes continually, with some individuals and families moving above the poverty level after a year or two while others slip below it. Still, there are thousands of people who remain in poverty for many years at a time.

Explaining Poverty Why is it that pervasive poverty continues within nations of vast wealth such as Canada and the United States? Sociologist Herbert Gans (1995) has applied functionalist analysis to the existence of poverty and argues that various segments of society actually *benefit* from the existence of the poor. Gans has identified a number of social, economic, and political functions that the poor perform for society, among them the following:

FIGURE 8-3

Poverty Rates for Persons by Age Group and Sex, 1998

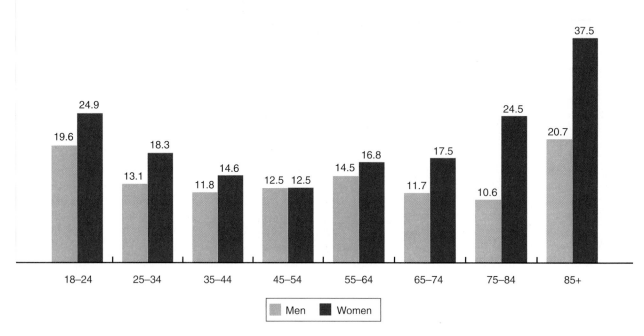

Source: National Council of Welfare 2000.

- The presence of poor people means that society's dirty work—physically dirty or dangerous, dead-end and underpaid, undignified, and menial jobs—will be performed at low cost.
- Poverty creates jobs for occupations and professions that "service" the poor. It creates both legal employment (public health experts, welfare caseworkers) and illegal jobs (drug dealers, numbers "runners").
- The identification and punishment of the poor as deviants upholds the legitimacy of conventional social norms and "mainstream values" regarding hard work, thrift, and honesty (see Chapter 7).

Poverty hits women particularly hard throughout the world, a situation known as the "feminization of poverty." Shown here are women and children in India.

p. 176

Functionalists point out that some people, such as the officials (standing) who deal with the homeless, actually benefit from the existence of poverty. Many occupations "service" the poor.

- Within a relatively hierarchical society, the existence of poor people guarantees the higher status of the more affluent. As psychologist William Ryan (1976) has noted, affluent people may justify inequality (and gain a measure of satisfaction) by "blaming the victims" of poverty for their disadvantaged condition.

- Because of the lack of political power, the poor often absorb the costs of social change. Under the policy of deinstitutionalization, mental patients released from long-term hospitals have been "dumped" primarily into low-income communities and neighbourhoods. Similarly, halfway houses for rehabilitated drug abusers are often rejected by more affluent communities and end up in poorer neighbourhoods.

In Gans's view, then, poverty and the poor actually satisfy positive functions for many nonpoor groups in Canada.

Stratification and Life Chances

Max Weber saw class as closely related to people's *life chances*—that is, their opportunities to provide themselves with material goods, positive living conditions, and favourable life experiences (Gerth and Mills 1958). Life chances are reflected in such measures as housing, education, and health. Occupying a higher position in a society improves your life chances and brings greater access to social rewards. By contrast, people in the lower social classes are forced to devote a larger proportion of their limited resources to the necessities of life.

The affluent and powerful not only have more material possessions than others; they also benefit in many nonmaterial ways. This fact was brought home to us by the hit motion picture *Titanic,* which showed that one's "life" chances had literal consequences in determining who would survive the ship's sinking in 1912 (see Box 8-3). We can also see the effects of life chances in education. Canadian children from high-income families with low high school achievement are more likely to attend university than are children from less affluent families with the highest levels of achievement. This gap in educational opportunities has remained consistent for decades.

In Canada, there are clear financial consequences associated with level of education. A report by the Council of Education Ministers Canada (CEMC), indicated a clear association between the probability of being unemployed and educational attainment. For example, someone with less than a high school diploma is three times more likely than someone with a university degree to be unemployed as a young adult, for longer periods (CEMC 1995).

While Canadians have access to universal health care through the federally mandated system, wealthy Canadians have always been able to travel to the U.S. or elsewhere to gain faster, and in come cases, more advanced, treatment. Reduction in federal transfer payments to the provinces over the course of the 1990s, combined with cost-cutting budgets like those of Ontario, Alberta, and Saskatchewan, has created what some analysts call ". . . a creeping privatization of the health care system" (NAPO 1998). Constrained public spending led to a 20 percent increase in the share of health care dollars coming directly from Canadians' pockets to the providers during the first half of the 1990s. This shift to services not covered by the government puts those Canadians with limited resources at a clear disadvantage.

In addition, class is increasingly being viewed as an important predictor of health. Children from impoverished backgrounds suffer more frequently from serious health problems such as sensory and/or cognitive dysfunctions (Canadian Council on Social Development 2000). These conditions transfer to adults, and become exacerbated by a disproportionate incidence of chronic problems such as asthma, high blood pressure, and alcoholism.

8-3 Social Class in the Movie *Titanic* and on the *SS Titanic*

The movie *Titanic* has been phenomenally successful. Millions of people in Canada, the United States, Japan, Germany, China, and elsewhere in the world have paid to see the film. By 2000, box office sales had surpassed U.S.$1.8 billion internationally, making it the most successful motion picture ever. While the special effects depicting the ship's breakup on an iceberg were spectacular, film audiences were mainly drawn to the story of how aristocratic 17-year-old Rose, facing a loveless marriage to a society figure, became attracted to working-class Jack.

They were not travelling together on that ill-fated maiden voyage of the *Titanic*. Rose was ensconced in first-class luxury while Jack was travelling in third class, or steerage, thanks to a ticket he won in a poker game. Still, for purposes of the plot, they managed to meet on board. Jack had to borrow a suit and act "properly" in order to pass the class line and gain entrance to the stuffy first-class dining room. But Rose had no trouble leaving her rich friends for a bawdy evening among those in the lower decks.

> The first attempt to alert steerage passengers to the need to head to the boat deck came at least 45 minutes after the other passengers were alerted.

The story of Rose and Jack was attractive because it was so romantic. After all, it typified a social class fantasy of the rich and poor falling in love and then struggling to survive. The theme of love between social class misfits is not new to motion pictures—consider Eliza Doolittle and Professor Henry Higgins in *My Fair Lady* and Vivian Ward and Edward Lewis in *Pretty Woman*. However, the fictional tale of Rose and Jack is particularly ironic because it uses as a backdrop a real tragedy that reinforces the fact that social inequality outweighs any iceberg.

When the *Titanic* sank in 1912, 1502 passengers and crew members perished and only 705 survived. The luxury liner was supposed to be "unsinkable," but there were still contingency plans for leading passengers to lifeboats in case of emergency. There was one glitch: These procedures were established only for first- and second-class passengers. Approximately 62 percent of the first-class passengers came away alive; even one-third of the first-class male passengers survived, despite a rule of "women and children first." In third class, only 25 percent of the passengers survived. Did the crew and the White Star Line purposely make the 381 steerage passengers expendable? There is no reason to think that, but, like all poorer people on land, they were given less thought and sometimes no thought at all. The first attempt to alert steerage passengers to the need to head to the boat deck came at least 45 minutes after the other passengers were alerted. Clogged passageways made it difficult for steerage passengers to find the lifeboats without being carefully guided. The real-life counterparts of Jack had little chance to survive the calamity. Stratification does make a difference for a person's life chances.

Let's Discuss

1. If you were a passenger on the *Titanic*, how would you be able to distinguish the upper and lower classes? What features on board kept the classes separate?
2. Why did so many more first-class passengers survive the ship's sinking than did lower-class passengers?

Sources: Butler 1998; Riding 1998; K. Crouse 1999.

This combination of decreased access to health care and identification of medical conditions that correlate highly with low incomes is, on its own, reason for concern. But if this trend is considered in light of the changes that have taken place in the distribution of income over the last few decades, the implications are dramatic. Between 1989 and 1998, the poorest quintile of Canadians saw its share of the national income drop by 5.2 percent. During the same time period, the top group of earners saw its share rise by 6.6 percent (Sauve 2000). Each of these changes represents the movement of billions of dollars from the pockets of the have-nots in Canada to the bank accounts of the haves.

If health care is becoming increasingly privatized and the distribution of income is becoming increasingly skewed, as the data suggest, then the conclusion to be drawn is that few Canadians will be able to access the health care they will need in the future.

Like disease, crime can be particularly devastating when it attacks the poor. People in low-income families are more likely to be assaulted, raped, or robbed than are the most affluent people. Furthermore, if accused of a crime, a person with low income and status is likely to be represented by an overworked public defender. Whether innocent or guilty, such a person may sit in jail for months, unable to raise bail (Perkins and Klaus 1996).

Even the administration of lotteries underscores differences in life chances. A lottery participant is six times more likely to be struck by lightning than to win the jackpot, yet provincial lotteries like Lotto 6/49 aim at low-income residents in their lottery promotions. Video lottery terminals are more heavily concentrated in poor neighbourhoods than in wealthy communities. Lottery advertisements are most frequent at the beginning of each month, when welfare and cheques for other forms of government assistance tend to arrive. Based on studies of lottery purchases, lottery executives view the poor as more likely than the affluent to spend a high portion of their earnings for the very unlikely chance of winning the jackpot (Novak and Schmid 1999).

Some people have hoped that the Internet revolution would help level the playing field by making information and markets uniformly available. Unfortunately, however, not everyone is able to get onto the "infohighway," and so yet another aspect of social inequality has emerged—the *digital divide*. The poor, minorities, and those who live in rural communities and inner cities are least likely to have access to a computer (National Telecommunications Information Administration 1999).

Even in the workplace, those at the bottom of the socioeconomic ladder are disadvantaged. While only 41 percent of workers with a high-school education worked at a computer, 85 percent of those with a university degree did so. Only 36 percent of individuals with an annual income of less than $20 000 used a computer at work, compared with 80 percent of those with an income of $60 000 or more (Perspectives June 2001). At home, the disparity was even more marked. In a 1998 survey conducted by Angus Reid, 62.2 percent of those with incomes in the highest quintile had computers at home. Only 15.4 percent of those falling in the lowest income group made the same claim.

Wealth, status, and power may not ensure happiness, but they certainly provide additional ways of coping with one's problems and disappointments. For this reason, the opportunity for advancement is of special significance to those who are on the bottom of society looking up. These people want the rewards and privileges that are granted to high-ranking members of a culture.

Social Mobility

Alexander Mackenzie began his working life as a stonemason yet managed to move up the career ladder to become Canada's second prime minister. Calvin Woodrow Ruck was a porter on the Canadian National Railway for years, before becoming a social worker and then being appointed to the Senate of Canada. The rise of a child from a poor background to some position of great prestige, power, or financial reward is an example of social mobility. The term *social mobility* refers to movement of individuals or groups from one position in a society's stratification system to another. But how significant— how frequent, how dramatic—is mobility in a class society such as Canada?

Open Versus Closed Class Systems

Sociologists use the terms *open class system* and *closed class system* to indicate the amount of social mobility in a society. An **open system** implies that the position of each individual is influenced by the person's *achieved* status. An open class system encourages competition among members of society. Canada and other developed nations are moving toward this ideal type by attempting to reduce barriers faced by women, racial and ethnic minorities, and people born to lower social classes.

At the other extreme of social mobility is the **closed system**, which allows little or no possibility of moving up. The slavery and caste systems of stratification are examples of closed systems. In such societies, social placement is based on *ascribed* statuses, such as race or family background, which cannot be changed.

Types of Social Mobility

An airline pilot who becomes a police officer moves from one social position to another of the same rank. Each occupation has the same prestige ranking: 60 on a scale ranging from a low of 0 to a high of 100 (see Table 8-1 on page 212). Sociologists call this kind of movement *horizontal mobility*. However, if the pilot were to become a lawyer (prestige ranking of 75), he or she would experience *vertical mobility*, the movement from one social position to another of a different rank. Vertical mobility can also involve moving *downward* in a society's stratification system, as would be the case if the airline pilot becomes a bank teller (ranking of 43). Pitirim Sorokin (1959, original edition 1927) was the first sociologist to distinguish between horizontal and vertical mobility.

Most sociological analysis, however, focuses on vertical rather than horizontal mobility.

One way of examining vertical social mobility is to contrast intergenerational and intragenerational mobility. *Intergenerational mobility* involves changes in the social position of children relative to their parents. Thus, a plumber whose father was a physician provides an example of downward intergenerational mobility. A film star whose parents were both factory workers illustrates upward intergenerational mobility.

Intragenerational mobility involves changes in social position within a person's adult life. A woman who enters the paid labour force as a teacher's aide and eventually becomes superintendent of the school district experiences upward intragenerational mobility. A professional athlete who fails to find work in the media after retirement will probably suffer downward intragenerational mobility.

Social Mobility in Canada

The belief in upward mobility is an important aspect of our society. Does this mean that Canada is indeed a land of opportunity for all? Not unless such ascriptive characteristics as race, gender, and family background have ceased to be significant in determining one's future prospects.

The Impact of Occupational Structure

Two sociological studies conducted a decade apart offer insight into the degree of mobility in the occupational structure of the United States (Blau and Duncan 1967; Featherman and Hauser 1978). Taken together, these investigations lead to several noteworthy conclusions. First, occupational mobility (both intergenerational and intragenerational) has been common among males. Approximately 60 to 70 percent of sons are employed in higher-ranked occupations than their fathers.

Second, the mobility that does take place tends to be in small increments. Thus, the child of a labourer may become a craftsperson, but the odds against reaching the top socioeconomic levels are extremely high unless one begins from a relatively privileged position.

Third, as the later study by Featherman and Hauser (1978) documents, occupational mobility among African Americans remains sharply limited by racial discrimination. Featherman and Hauser offer evidence of a modest decline in the significance of race; yet, we must regard their conclusions with some caution, since they did not consider households with no adult male present or individuals who were not counted in the labour force.

There is evidence of a similar phenomenon in Canada, where even the opportunity to participate in the labour force, at any level, has been compromised during the last decade. Between 1989 and 1997 for instance, the working age population in Canada grew by 10.2 percent while the number of available jobs grew at little more than half that rate (5.5 percent) (CCSD 2000). This increased competition for employment was particularly hard on young people who found themselves victims of the "right-sizing" corporate agenda of the 1990s. This generation is faced with a depleted labour market, reduced by layoffs and narrowed by a just-in-time mentality. The twenty-somethings of today have been cautioned that they are to be the first in over 100 years not expected to surpass the standard of living enjoyed by their parents. In other words, their chances of enjoying either inter- or intragenerational socioeconomic mobility are in question.

The Impact of Education

Another conclusion of both studies is that education plays a critical role in social mobility. The impact of formal schooling on adult status is even greater than that of family background, although the likelihood of a child acquiring a university degree increases with the family's socioeconomic status.

However, education's impact on mobility has diminished somewhat in the last decade. An undergraduate degree—a B.A. or a B.Sc.—serves less as a guarantee of upward mobility than it did in the past simply because more and more entrants into the job market now hold such a degree. Moreover, intergenerational mobility is declining, since there is no longer such a stark difference between generations. In earlier decades many high school-educated parents successfully sent their children to university, but today's university students are increasingly likely to have at least one parent with a degree (Hout 1988).

Research suggests that for the poor, social mobility is becoming more and more difficult to achieve. Studies by sociologist Greg Duncan (1994; Duncan and Yeung 1995) and by economist Ann Huff Stevens (1994) report that in the late 1980s, the opportunity to advance out of poverty in the United States narrowed significantly for poor people in general and especially for young women and African American children.

The Impact of Gender

Studies of mobility, even more than those of class, have traditionally ignored the significance of gender, but some research findings are now available that explore the relationship between gender and mobility.

Women's employment opportunities are much more limited than men's (as Chapter 11 will show). Moreover, according to recent research, women whose skills far exceed the jobs offered them are more likely than men to withdraw entirely from the paid labour force. This withdrawal violates an assumption common to traditional

Preet Heer is part of a young generation of visible minority women who have overcome traditional stratification of Canadian society. Ms. Heer is a graduate student at the School of Community and Regional Planning at the University of British Columbia.

salary ranges and limited prospects for advancement in many of these positions mean there is not much possibility of upward mobility. Moreover, self-employment as shopkeepers, entrepreneurs, independent professionals, and the like—an important road to upward mobility for men—is difficult for women, who find it hard to secure the necessary financing. Although sons commonly follow in the footsteps of their fathers, women are unlikely to move into their fathers' positions. Consequently, gender remains an important factor in shaping social mobility within Canada. Women are especially likely to be trapped in poverty and unable to rise out of their low-income status regardless of the society in which they live (P. Smith 1994).

In recent decades, many male workers in North America and elsewhere have experienced downward mobility, including unemployment. (As we will see in Chapter 17, this has resulted in part from corporate "downsizing," "restructuring," and more recently, "right-sizing" as well as plant closings.) For the first time since the Second World War, university-educated men in their late 40s and 50s—who may have assumed they were in their prime earning years—are experiencing a significant decline in wages. Some have lost high-level jobs at major corporations and have shifted (after periods of unemployment) to lower-paying positions at small companies or to self-employment.

The social policy section that follows takes into consideration the very limited prospects of mobility experienced by those on welfare. Can they find jobs that allow them to leave the welfare system, or are they doomed to remain trapped in poverty year after year? We'll see how governments at home and abroad have dealt with this difficult issue.

mobility studies: that most people will aspire to upward mobility and seek to make the most of their opportunities.

A decade-long study revealed that the increased full-time participation of women in the Canadian labour force was largely responsible for growth in the category of employees who earned more than $37 000. The gender-based wage gap narrowed modestly over the decade 1984 to 1994, but remained substantial. By 1995, women earned, on average, 65 cents for every dollar earned by men—up from 52 cents in 1980. Statistics Canada's recent release of income data from 2001 reveals that the gap has widened slightly—women are down to 64 cents for every male dollar (Statistics Canada 2003e). For full-time workers only, the wage gap narrowed from 64 cents to 70 cents earned by women for every dollar earned by men. Women earned an average of $35 258 while men received $49 250 (Statistics Canada 2003e).

In contrast to men, women have a rather large range of clerical occupations open to them. But the modest

SOCIAL POLICY AND STRATIFICATION

Rethinking Welfare in North America and Europe

The Issue

- After five years on Ontario's welfare roll, a single mother of two is a success story. The 28-year-old has landed a job at a storage company and moved up to a $9 an hour customer service position. But at the same time, a worker in a nearby hotel, earning just $6.85 an hour, worries about being edged back into unemployment by the stiff competition for low-wage jobs.
- A single mother in Paris, France, waited for four months to obtain a place in government-subsidized daycare for her daughter. Now she can seek a full-time job, but she is concerned about government threats to curtail such services to keep taxes down (Simons 1997).
- A woman in Massachusetts tacks up a handwritten advertisement in the public housing project in which she lives to say that she is available to clean yards and braid hair for a few extra dollars. The sign lists a friend's phone number; she doesn't have a phone of her own (Vobejda and Havenmann 1997).

These are the faces of people living on the edge—often women with children seeking to make a go of it amidst changing social policies. Governments in all parts of the world are searching for the right solution to welfare: How much subsidy should they provide? How much responsibility should fall on the shoulders of the poor?

The Setting

By the 1990s, there was intense debate in Canada and other Western democracies over the issue of welfare. Welfare programs were costly, and there was widespread concern (however unfounded) that welfare payments discouraged recipients from seeking jobs. Those at both ends of the political and ideological spectrum vowed to "end welfare as we know it" (Pear 1996:20).

Conservative governments, like those in Ontario and Alberta, set up the goal of making people who relied on the public purse accountable. *Workfare*—a program that requires able-bodied welfare recipients to work for their money—was seen as a way of discouraging abuses of the system and providing some degree of dignity to those

who had to rely on welfare. At the other end of the spectrum, social democrats like the New Democratic Party government in British Columbia, looked for ways to improve the living conditions and increase rates for those on welfare by revamping existing programs.

Countries vary widely in their commitment to social service programs. Because the Canadian system places some social assistance programs under federal direction (i.e., employment insurance), and others under provincial programs (i.e., welfare), the exact amount spent by the country on these initiatives is difficult to determine. However, most industrialized nations devote a higher proportion of their expenditures to housing, social security, welfare, and unemployment compensation than the 54 percent devoted by the United States. For example, in 1997, 71 percent of Switzerland's central government spending went to these social service areas, and in Ireland it was 60 percent. A study by sociologist Greg Duncan (1994) of welfare programs in the United States and seven European nations found that a higher proportion of the poor escape poverty in Europe than in the United States. Apparently, the greater benefits facilitate upward mobility (World Bank 2000:256–257).

Sociological Insights

Many sociologists tend to view the debate over welfare throughout industrialized nations from a conflict perspective: the haves in positions of policymaking listen to the interests of other haves, while the cries of the have-nots are drowned out. Critics of so-called welfare reform believe that Canada's economic problems are unfairly being blamed on welfare spending and the poor. From a conflict perspective, this backlash against welfare recipients reflects deep fears and hostility toward the nation's visible minorities.

Those critical of the backlash note that "welfare scapegoating" conveniently ignores the lucrative federal handouts that go to *affluent* individuals and families. For example, while federal employment insurance benefits were being cut by 40 percent during the 1990s, millions of dollars were spent to finance trips by Team Canada, a trade delegation including the prime minister and executives from some of the country's most profitable companies. The group travelled the globe drumming up business opportunities for those enterprises.

In the U.S., the National Association of Home Builders, an ardent defender of the mortgage-interest deduction, estimates that it costs the American government U.S.$60 billion a year in lost taxes. This deduction generally benefits affluent taxpayers who own their own homes. According to one study, more than 44 percent of the benefits from this tax break go to the 5 percent of tax-payers with the highest incomes, who together save themselves $22 billion annually (Goodgame 1993; Johnston 1996).

Those who take a conflict perspective also urge policymakers and the general public to look

Moving off welfare often requires job training. The "workfare" program illustrated here is preparing workers for construction jobs.

closely at *corporate welfare*—the tax breaks, direct payments, and grants that the government makes to corporations—rather than to focus on the comparatively small allowances being given to mothers on welfare and their children. These messages have received mixed response. Overall, in Canada, despite the increase in poverty during the decade of the 1990s, the number of people on welfare has dropped. Between 1994 and 1995 for example, the drop was almost 1 percent, or close to 30 000 recipients. The number in Alberta dropped by 18.3 percent, but in British Columbia rose by 5.9 percent, reflecting the priorities of the governments in those provinces (HRDC 1997).

Policy Initiatives

The direction of social policy in Canada over the past decade has been toward a leaner, more restrictive access to government subsidies for the poor. At the federal level, changes to qualifications for employment insurance resulted in a reduction of $6 billion in spending in this area between 1990 and 1996. This is despite an announced cumulative surplus of $20 billion in the fund by 1998. In the provincially controlled area of social assistance, a number of provinces that have historically offered the highest benefits, including Ontario and Prince Edward Island, have cut benefits most dramatically (NAPO 1998). A 1999 survey showed that the biggest needs of welfare-to-work employees were child care and

transportation—services rarely provided by employers. At the same time that suggestions mount to provide such services for former welfare recipients, the working poor complain that "we get nothing" (Fuller and Kagan 2000; Welfare to Work Partnership 1999).

European countries have witnessed many of the same citizen demands as found in North America: Keep our taxes low, even if it means reducing services to the poor. However, nations in Eastern and Central Europe have faced a special challenge since the end of communism. The governments in those nations had traditionally provided an impressive array of social services, but they differed from capitalist systems in several important respects. First, the communist system was premised on full employment, so there was no need to provide unemployment insurance; social services focused on the old and the disabled. Second, subsidies, such as for housing and even utilities, played an important role. With new competition from the West and tight budgets, some of these countries (as well as Sweden, despite its long history of social welfare programs) are beginning to realize that a system of universal coverage is no longer affordable and must be replaced by more targeted programs. Some of these countries' residents have sought refuge in Western Europe, putting new demands on social service systems there just as people are calling for a moratorium on higher taxes (World Bank 1997:55–57; Kuptsch and Mazie 1999).

Both in North American and in Europe, people are beginning to turn to private means of supporting themselves. For instance, they are investing money for their later years rather than depending on government social security programs. But that solution only works if you have a job and can save money. Increasing proportions of people are seeing the gap between themselves and the affluent growing with fewer government programs aimed to assist them. Solutions are frequently left to the private sector, while government policy initiatives at the national level all but disappear.

Let's Discuss

1. How has the level of spending for social services in Canada changed over the 1990s? What accounts for the differences?
2. Do you think welfare recipients should be required to work? What kind of support should they be given?
3. Have welfare reform programs introduced by different provincial governments been successful? Why or why not?

Chapter Resources

Summary

Stratification is the structured ranking of entire groups of people that perpetuates unequal economic rewards and power in a society. In this chapter, we examine three general systems of stratification, the explanations offered by functionalist, feminist, and conflict theorists for the existence of social inequality, the relationship between stratification and social mobility, and stratification within the world system.

1. Some degree of *social inequality* characterizes all cultures.
2. Systems of *stratification* include *slavery, castes,* and social *class.*
3. Karl Marx saw that differences in access to the means of production created social, economic, and political inequality and distinct classes of owners and labourers.
4. Max Weber identified three analytically distinct components of stratification: *class, status,* and *power.*
5. Functionalists argue that stratification is necessary so that people will be motivated to fill society's important positions; conflict theorists see stratification as a major source of societal tension and conflict.
6. As feminist theories examine the status of women in a society, they show that regardless of the

indicator used—class, status, or power—women endure an inferior position within our social structure.

7. One consequence of social class in Canada is that both *wealth* and *income* are distributed unevenly.
8. The category of the "poor" defies any simple definition and counters common stereotypes about "poor people." The long-term poor who lack training and skills form an *underclass.*
9. Functionalists find that the poor satisfy positive functions for many of the nonpoor in Canada.
10. One's *life chances*—opportunities for obtaining material goods, positive living conditions, and favourable life experiences—are related to one's social class. Occupying a higher social position improves a person's life chances.
11. *Social mobility* is more likely to be found in an *open system* that emphasizes achieved status than in a *closed system* that focuses on ascribed characteristics. Race, gender, and family background are important factors in mobility.
12. Many governments are struggling with how much of their tax revenue to spend on welfare programs. There is a growing sentiment in Canada in favour of putting welfare recipients to work.

Critical Thinking Questions

1. Groups like the Canadian Council on Social Development exist to monitor the social health of the country. Do you think they serve a worthwhile purpose? How would you compare the value of the research done by the CCSD to that of the business-sponsored Fraser Institute? Does Canada benefit from having advocates for both ends of the ideological spectrum?

2. Sociological study of stratification generally is conducted at the macro level and draws most heavily on the functionalist and conflict perspectives. How might sociologists use the *interactionist* perspective to examine social class inequalities within a university community?

3. Imagine that you have an opportunity to spend a year in a developing country studying inequality in that nation. How would you draw on the research designs of sociology (surveys, observation, experiments, existing sources) to better understand and document stratification in this developing country?

Key Terms

Absolute poverty A standard of poverty based on a minimum level of subsistence below which families should not be expected to live. (214)

Achieved status A social position attained by a person largely through his or her own efforts. (204)

Ascribed status A social position "assigned" to a person by society without regard for the person's unique talents or characteristics. (204)

Bourgeoisie Karl Marx's term for the capitalist class, comprising the owners of the means of production. (207)

Capitalism An economic system in which the means of production are largely in private hands and the main incentive for economic activity is the accumulation of profits. (207)

Castes Hereditary systems of rank, usually religiously dictated, that tend to be fixed and immobile. (204)

Class A group of people who have a similar level of wealth and income. (208)

Class consciousness In Karl Marx's view, a subjective awareness held by members of a class regarding their common vested interests and need for collective political action to bring about social change. (207)

Class system A social ranking based primarily on economic position in which achieved characteristics can influence social mobility. (206)

Closed system A social system in which there is little or no possibility of individual mobility. (221)

Dominant ideology A set of cultural beliefs and practices that helps to maintain powerful social, economic, and political interests. (210)

Esteem The reputation that a particular individual has earned within an occupation. (211)

False consciousness A term used by Karl Marx to describe an attitude held by members of a class that does not accurately reflect their objective position. (207)

Horizontal mobility The movement of an individual from one social position to another of the same rank. (221)

Ideal type As defined by Weber, refers to the pure, abstract form of a social concept, not necessarily one that exists in the real world. (204)

Income Salaries and wages. (203)

Intergenerational mobility Changes in the social position of children relative to their parents. (222)

Intragenerational mobility Changes in a person's social position within his or her adult life. (222)

Life chances People's opportunities to provide themselves with material goods, positive living conditions, and favourable life experiences. (219)

Low Income Cut-Off (LICO) Until January 2001, the Canadian equivalent of a poverty line. If the amount a household spends on the basics—food, shelter, and clothing—exceeds a certain proportion of income (the actual figure fluctuates with economic conditions, but generally falls just under 60 percent), then that household is classified as poor. (214)

Market Basket Measure (MBM) A measure that takes into consideration more than subsistence needs, by calculating the amounts needed by various households to live a life comparable to community standards. (214)

Meritocracy A system where individuals earn their place in society. (203)

Net worth The amount by which the value of someone's assets exceeds his or her debts. In Canada, it is used interchangeably with wealth. (203)

Objective method A technique for measuring social class that assigns individuals to classes on the basis of such criteria as occupation, education, income, and place of residence. (211)

Open system A social system in which the position of each individual is influenced by his or her achieved status. (221)

Power The ability to exercise one's will over others. (208)

Prestige The respect and admiration that an occupation holds in a society. (211)

Proletariat Karl Marx's term for the working class in a capitalist society. (207)

Relative poverty A floating standard of deprivation by which people at the bottom of a society, whatever their lifestyles, are judged to be disadvantaged in comparison with the nation as a whole. (214)

Slavery A system of enforced servitude in which people are legally owned by others and in which enslaved status is transferred from parents to children. (204)

Social inequality A condition in which members of a society have different amounts of wealth, prestige, or power. (203)

Social mobility Movement of individuals or groups from one position in a society's stratification system to another. (221)

Social safety net A system of social programs, such as welfare, employment insurance, Canada Pension Plan, etc., designed to alleviate the harshest conditions associated with being at the bottom of the income chain. (214)

Status consistency The notion that someone with high status in one area—income, for instance—is likely to be similarly ranked in other areas. (208)

Status group People who have the same prestige or lifestyle, independent of their class positions. (208)

Stratification A structured ranking of entire groups of people that perpetuates an unequal and stable distribution of economic rewards and power in a society. (203)

Underclass Long-term poor people who lack training and skills. (216)

Vertical mobility The movement of a person from one social position to another of a different rank. (221)

Wealth An inclusive term encompassing all of a person's material assets, including land and other types of property. (203)

Additional Readings

BOOKS

Bluestone, Barry, and Bennett Harrison. 1999. *Growing Prosperity: The Battle for Growth with Equity in the 21st Century.* Boston: Harrison Century Foundation/Houghton Mifflin. A critical look at the impact of the red-hot United States economy on the entire population.

Bonacich, Edna, and Richard Appelbaum. 2000. *Behind the Label: Inequality in the Los Angeles Apparel Industry.* Berkeley: University of California Press. Examines the new wave of sweatshops that has made Los Angeles the largest centre of clothing production in the United States.

McQuaig, Linda. 1998. *The Cult of Impotence: Selling the Myth of Powerlessnness in the Global Economy.* Toronto: Penguin Books. A challenge to the perception that globalization is inevitable, and that average citizens of the world have little or no power to stop or influence the process.

The World Bank. *World Development Report.* New York: Oxford University Press. Published annually by the International Bank for Reconstruction and Development (the United Nations agency more commonly referred to as the World Bank), this volume provides a vast array of social and economic indicators regarding world development.

JOURNALS

Among the journals that focus on issues of stratification, social class, and social mobility are *American Journal of Economics and Sociology* (founded in 1941), *Humanity and Society* (1977), and *Journal of Poverty* (1997). See also *The Daily*, a series published by Statistics Canada (available at **www.statcan.ca/Daily**).

Internet Connection

For additional Internet exercises relating to stratification in Canada, visit the Schaefer Online Learning Centre at **http://www.mcgrawhill.ca/college/schaefer**. *Please note that while the URLs listed were current at the time of printing, these sites often change—check the Online Learning Centre for updates.*

Marginalization and inequality are a central focus of this chapter. The Canadian Council on Social Development is an organization devoted to researching social issues in this country. Explore its webpages at **http://www.gdsourcing.com/works/CCSD.htm** to find the answers to the following questions:

(a) What are the factors limiting access to computers?
(b) Identify several consequences of childhood poverty.
(c) How does disability affect employment access?
(d) Do a comparison of urban and rural poverty in Canada.
(e) What is the Personal Security Index?
(f) What social trends are changing public education in Canada?

SOCIAL INEQUALITY WORLDWIDE

This poster advertising "Asian Week" at McDonald's in Germany attests to the global reach of multinational corporations today. But while the world is shrinking through aspects of globalization like this, there is still a huge gap between rich and poor nations and between rich and poor citizens within nations.

ncome per person, averaged globally, currently rises by about 0.8 percent per year, but in more than 100 countries in the last 15 years income has actually dropped. Some 1.3 billion people—about 30 percent of the population of the developing world—remain in absolute poverty, living on less than a dollar a day. And the gulf between the poorest and the wealthiest people on the planet is widening very fast. In 1960, the income of the richest 20 percent of the world's population was 30 times that of the poorest 20 percent; in 1998, it was 82 times greater. The combined wealth of the world's richest 225 people (a total of $1 trillion) exceeds the annual income of the poorest 47 percent of the planet's population, about 2.5 billion people. Indeed, the assets of the world's three richest individuals or families—Microsoft's Bill Gates, the Walton family of Wal-Mart stores, and the renowned investor Warren Buffett—are now greater than the combined GDPs of the 48 poorest countries. Meanwhile, as the rich get richer in the developed countries, average household consumption in Africa has plummeted 20 percent over the last 25 years. In India, an estimated 60 percent of all newborns are in such poor condition from malnutrition, low birth weight, and other causes that they would be immediately placed in intensive care were they born in California. Never in human history have we seen such differentials between rich and poor.

. . . [A]bout half the people on the planet—some three billion, all told—rely on agriculture for their main income, and of that perhaps one billion of these agriculturalists are mainly subsistence farmers, which means they survive by eating what they grow. Over 40 percent of people on the planet—about 2.4 billion—use fuelwood, charcoal, straw, or cow dung as their main source of energy; 50 to 60 percent rely on these biomass fuels for at least some of their primary energy needs. Over 1.2 billion people lack access to clean drinking water; many are forced to walk kilometres to get what water they can find. And about a billion people depend directly on fishing for a large proportion of their animal protein.

These people live mainly in Asia, Africa, and Latin America. They depend on local natural resources for their day-to-day survival, and they have little access to the vast technical ingenuity so abundant in the rich countries of North America, Europe, and East Asia. Deforestation, polluted water, depleted fisheries and eroded cropland harshly affect their lives in countless immediate and intimate ways, and natural resources will remain critically important to their well-being for decades to come. Yet many of us manage to ignore the contradiction these people present to our rosy world-view, because we rarely see them or go to the places where they live. *(Homer-Dixon 2000:32–36)* ■

Thomas Homer-Dixon is Director of the Peace and Conflict Studies, an undergraduate program at the University of Toronto. In his award winning book, *The Ingenuity Gap*, Homer-Dixon writes about the critical gap between our need for ideas to solve problems in a world that seems too complex and too fast-paced to manage, and our actual supply of those ideas. He states that poor countries are particularly vulnerable to ingenuity gaps, but rich countries are also caught dangerously between a requirement for ingenuity and an increasingly uncertain supply.

Students protesting sweatshop labour in developing countries mock Nike with its own slogan: "Just do it."

One focus in the book is on technical disparities that implicitly segregate some parts of the planet from others. Specifically, Homer-Dixon points to the primitive mechanisms upon which most of the world's population depends as evidence of the failure of modern systems to distribute the benefits of technological evolution equally. However, even in those areas where the economics of the developed world have begun to make inroads, benefits to the local people are minimal.

In their 1998 book, *Nike Culture*, sociologists Robert Goldman and Stephen Papson examined the global stratification that Nike, and other companies like it, help to perpetuate. People can pay hundreds of dollars for a pair of celebrity-endorsed sports shoes, yet the workers who manufacture the product are rewarded with pennies. Critics of Nike's practices have claimed that in 1996, the 45 Indonesian workers who participated in making a pair of Air Pegasus shoes shared a total of U.S.$1.60. Other stories of Vietnamese and Chinese women who are subject to health and safety hazards, pitifully underpaid, and physically harassed by shop floor managers have also helped to fuel concern about human rights violations.

Craig Kielburger, a teenager from Ontario, has been fighting the global battle against child labour since he was 12 years old. In 1995, Craig flew to Asia, where he visited factories and saw, firsthand, the frightening conditions under which children younger than he laboured, producing goods for multinational corporations. When he returned home, Craig helped found Free the Children, an international movement against child labour. Meetings with leaders like Nelson Mandela, Mother Theresa, and the Pope have given Craig a profile that has captured the attention of corporations. In 1998, Nike announced that it would no longer buy products from suppliers who hired workers under the age of 16.

However, Nike is not their only target. Many apparel manufacturers contract out their production to take advantage of cheap labour and overhead costs. Other initiatives have also appeared to protest the exploitation of children in the Third World. A campus-based, student movement—ranging from sit-ins and "knit-ins" to demonstrations and building occupation—has been aimed at ridding campus stores of all products made in sweatshops, both at home and abroad. Pressed by their students, many colleges and universities have agreed to adopt antisweatshop codes governing the products they make and stock on campus. And Nike and Reebok, partly in response to student protests, have raised the wages of some 100 000 workers in their Indonesian factories (to about 20 cents an hour—still far below what is needed to raise a family) (Appelbaum and Dreier 1999).

The global corporate and technological culture focuses our attention on worldwide stratification, as seen in the enormous gap between those enjoying wealth and those destitute from poverty.

This chapter will focus on stratification around the world, beginning with an examination of who controls the world marketplace. The impact of colonialism and neocolonialism on social inequality will be studied, as will world systems analysis, the immense power of multinational corporations, and the consequences of modernization. After this macro-level examination of the disparity between rich and poor countries, we will focus on stratification *within* the nations of the world through discussions of the distribution of wealth and income, comparative perspectives on prestige, and comparative social mobility. To better understand inequality in another country, we will present a case study of stratification in Mexico. Finally, in the social policy section, we will address the issue of international human rights and the violations of human rights evident around the world. ■

Stratification in the World System

Kwabena Afari is a pineapple exporter in Ghana. But for years his customers had to show a great deal of ingenuity to get in touch with him. First a call had to be placed to Accra, the capital city. Someone there would call the post office in Afari's hometown. Then the post office would send a messenger to his home. Afari has recently solved his problem by getting a cellular phone, but his longtime dilemma symbolizes the problems of the roughly 600 million people who live in sub-Saharan Africa and are being left behind by the trade and foreign investment transforming the global economy. One African entrepreneur notes, "It's not that we have been left behind. It's that we haven't even started" (Buckley 1997:8).

It is true that technology, the information highway, and innovations in telecommunications have all made the world a smaller and more unified place. Yet while the world marketplace is gradually shrinking in space and tastes, the profits of business are not being equally shared. There remains a substantial disparity between the world's have and have-not nations. For example, in 1995, the average value of goods and services produced per citizen (per capita gross national product) in Canada, the United States, Japan, Switzerland, and Norway was more than $25 000. By contrast, the figure was under $200 in six poorer countries. The 140 developing nations accounted for 78 percent of the world's population but possessed only about 16 percent of all wealth (Haub and Cornelius 1999). As Homer-Dixon points out in the chapter opener, the gap between those nations at the top and those at the bottom continues to increase dramatically. In 1960 the countries at the top had incomes 30 times those at the other end of the ranking. By 1995, that figure had risen to 82 times (United Nations 1998). These contrasts are illustrated in Figure 9-1. Three forces discussed below are particularly responsible for the domination of the world marketplace by a few nations: the legacy of colonialism, the advent of multinational corporations, and modernization.

Colonialism, Neocolonialism, and World Systems Analysis

Colonialism is the maintenance of political, social, economic, and cultural domination over a people by a foreign power for an extended period of time (W. Bell 1981b). In simple terms, it is rule by outsiders. The long reign of the British Empire over much of North America, parts of Africa, and India is an example of colonial domination. The same can be said of French rule over Algeria, Tunisia, and other parts of North Africa. Relations between the colonial nation and colonized people are similar to those between the dominant capitalist class and the proletariat as described by Karl Marx.

By the 1980s, this form of colonialism had largely disappeared. Most of the world's nations that were colonies before the First World War had achieved political independence and established their own governments. However, for many of these countries, the transition to genuine self-rule was not yet complete. Colonial domination had established patterns of economic exploitation that continued even after nationhood was achieved—in part because former colonies were unable to develop their own industry and technology. Their dependence on more industrialized nations, including their former colonial masters, for managerial and technical expertise, investment capital, and manufactured goods kept former colonies in a subservient position. Such continuing dependence and foreign domination constitute ***neocolonialism***. While Canada has been able to escape such dependence on Britain, its former colonial master, we have come under the influence of another global power.

A major issue that continues to be a concern for Canadians revolves around the question of defining ourselves as an independent entity. The uncertainty focuses on the possibility of a distinct Canadian identity while existing tenuously in the shadow of the United States. One of former prime minister Pierre Trudeau's famous remarks was that living next door to the Americans was like "sleeping with an elephant." This perception is

FIGURE 9-1

Gross National Product per Capita, 2000

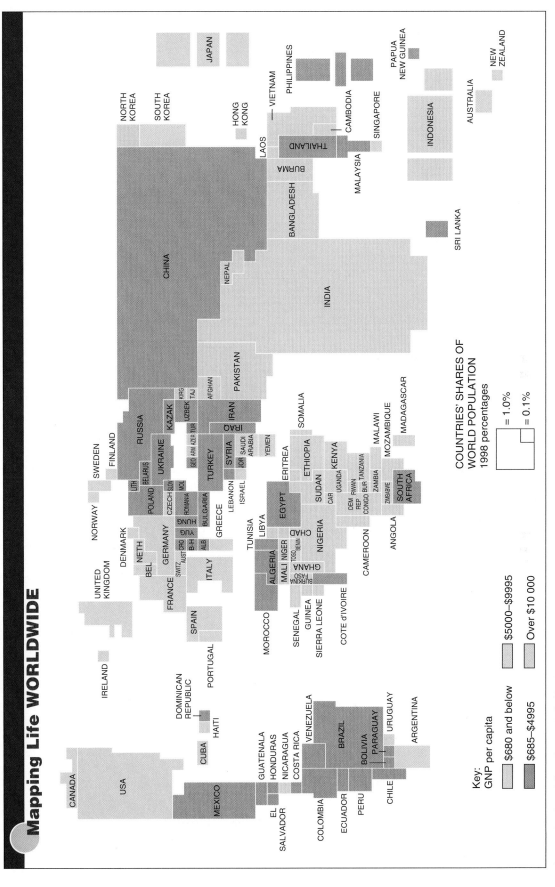

Mapping Life WORLDWIDE

COUNTRIES' SHARES OF
WORLD POPULATION
1998 percentages

☐ = 1.0%
☐ = 0.1%

Key:
GNP per capita

☐ $680 and below
☐ $685–$4995
☐ $5000–$9995
☐ Over $10 000

Sources: Haub and Cornelius 2000; Smith 1999:14–15.

This stylized map reflects the different sizes in population of the world's nations. The colour for each country shows the 2000 estimated *gross national product* (the total value of goods and services produced by the nation in a given year) per capita. As the map shows, some of the world's most populous countries—such as India, Indonesia, Bangladesh, and Pakistan—are among the nations with the lowest standard of living as measured by per capita gross national product.

particularly relevant when it comes to cultural and economic matters. Canada's economy thrives or shrivels substantially depending on what happens in the market south of our border. And our culture, for all its quality and impact, still cannot escape the predominance of American movies and television. The question of whether we are a colony of the United States, in the neocolonial sense of the term, is an ongoing debate.

The economic and political consequences of colonialism and neocolonialism are readily apparent. Drawing on the conflict perspective, sociologist Immanuel Wallerstein (1974, 1979, 1999) views the global economic system as divided between nations that control wealth and those from which wealth-creating resources are taken. Neocolonialism allows industrialized societies to accumulate even more capital. Canada's position essentially as a resource provider to the United States—while at the same time qualifying as a developed, postindustrial nation—is difficult to capture within Wallerstein's model.

Wallerstein has advanced a **world systems analysis** to describe the unequal economic and political relationships in which certain industrialized nations (among them the United States, Japan, and Germany) and their global corporations dominate the *core* of the system. At the *semi-periphery* of the system are countries with marginal economic status, such as Israel, Ireland, and South Korea. Canada falls somewhere in between these two categories. We are included in the former group for recognition of our level of development and our standard of living. At the same time, we do not have the political or economic clout of the other nations at the top of the hierarchy. We are "guest" members of the powerful G8 economic coalition, invited to participate at the insistence of the United States, though with limited status. Wallerstein suggests that the poor developing countries of Asia, Africa, and Latin America are on the *periphery* of the world economic system. Core nations and their corporations control and exploit the developing nations' economies, much as the old colonial empires ruled their colonies (Chase-Dunn and Grimes 1995).

The division between core and periphery nations is significant and remarkably stable. A study by the International Monetary Fund (2000) found little change over the course of the last 100 years for the 42 economies that were studied. The only changes were upward movement into the core by Japan and to lower margins of the semi-periphery by China. However, few economists will deny that China's inclusion or exclusion from the elite group is a matter of choice, and generally assume that within the next two decades China will hold a major role in the global economy.

Wallerstein's world systems analysis is the most widely used version of **dependency theory**. According to this theory, even as developing countries make economic advances, they remain weak and subservient to core nations and corporations within an increasingly intertwined global economy. This allows industrialized nations to continue to exploit developing countries for their own gain. In a sense, dependency theory applies the conflict perspective on a global scale.

In the view of world systems analysis and dependency theory, a growing share of the human and natural resources of developing countries is being redistributed to the core industrialized nations. In part, this is because developing countries owe huge sums of money to industrialized nations as a result of foreign aid, loans, and trade deficits. This global debt crisis has intensified the Third World dependency begun under colonialism, neocolonialism, and multinational investment. International financial institutions are pressuring indebted countries to adopt austerity measures so they can meet their interest payments. The result is that developing nations may be forced to devalue their currencies, freeze workers' wages, increase privatization of industry, and reduce government services and employment.

In addition to their political and economic impact, colonialism and neocolonialism have an important cultural component. The colonized people lose their native values and begin to identify with the culture of the colonial power. People may discard or neglect their native language as they attempt to emulate their colonizers. This process has been characterized by some of those opposed to contemporary neocolonialism as the "Americanization" of global culture. Every consumer product, book, film, or television program designed by a colonial nation is seen as an attack on the traditions and cultural autonomy of the dependent people. Sembene Ousmane, one of Africa's most prominent writers and filmmakers, noted, "[Today] we are more familiar with European fairy tales than with our own traditional stories" (World Development Forum 1990:4).

The antiglobalization movement aims to expose the lack of democracy in the contemporary trend to globalize trade and economic policies. Yet, protesters are accused of being antidemocratic by leaders who meet behind barricades and walls to make decisions that affect people around the world. Naomi Klein, author of *No Logo* and a central figure in the debates on the dangers of globalization, responds: "Democracy does not just happen every four or five years when you vote. Democracy happens in the street. Democracy happens at town hall meetings. It happens in protest" (Klein 2001). She prefers to call the protests a pro-democracy movement.

Multinational Corporations

A key role in neocolonialism today is played by worldwide corporate giants. The term **multinational corporations** refers to commercial organizations that are headquartered in one country but do business throughout the world. Such private trade and lending relationships are not new; merchants have conducted business abroad for hundreds of years, trading gems, spices, garments, and other goods. However, today's multinational giants are not merely buying and selling overseas; they are also *producing* goods all over the world (Wallerstein 1974).

Moreover, today's "global factory" (the factories throughout the developing world run by multinational corporations) now has the "global office" alongside it. Multinationals based in core countries are beginning to establish reservations services, centres to process insurance claims, and data processing centres in the periphery nations. As service industries become a more important part of the international marketplace, many companies have concluded that the low costs of overseas operations more than offset the expense of transmitting information around the world.

Do not underestimate the size of these global corporations. Table 9-1 shows that the total revenues of multinational businesses are on a par with the total value of goods and services exchanged in *entire nations*. Foreign sales represent an important source of profit for multinational corporations, a fact that encourages them to expand into other countries (in many cases, the develop-

ing nations). The economy of Canada is heavily dependent on foreign commerce, much of which is conducted by American multinationals.

Multinational corporations can actually help the developing nations of the world. They bring jobs and industry to areas where subsistence agriculture previously served as the only means of survival. Multinationals promote rapid development through diffusion of inventions and innovations from industrial nations. Viewed from a functionalist perspective, the combination of skilled technology and management provided by multinationals and the relatively cheap labour available in developing nations is ideal for a global enterprise. Multinationals can take maximum advantage of technology while reducing costs and boosting profits.

The international ties of multinational corporations also facilitate the exchange of ideas and technology around the world. They make the nations of the world more interdependent. And these ties may prevent certain disputes from reaching the point of serious conflict. A country cannot afford to sever diplomatic relations, or engage in warfare, with a nation that is the headquarters for its main business suppliers or is a key outlet for exports.

Conflict theorists challenge this favourable evaluation of the impact of multinational corporations. They

Table 9-1 Comparing Multinational Corporations and Nations

Corporation	Revenues ($ millions)	Comparable nations (or city)	Gross national product ($ millions)
1. General Motors (U.S.A.)	176 558	Denmark	175 200
2. Wal-Mart (U.S.A.)	166 809	Norway plus Lebanon	167 000
3. Exxon-Mobil (U.S.A.)	163 881	Venezuela plus Malaysia	163 400
4. Ford Motor (U.S.A.)	162 558	Colombia plus Pakistan	162 200
5. DaimlerChrysler (Germany)	159 985	Hong Kong	158 200
11. Royal Dutch/Shell (Brit./Neth.)	105 366	Israel	96 500
16. IBM (U.S.A.)	87 548	Philippines plus Paraguay	88 100
29. Philip Morris (U.S.A.)	61 751	Pakistan	61 500
30. Sony (Japan)	60 052	Peru	60 500
41. Nestlé (Switzerland)	49 694	Algeria	46 400

Notes: Revenues are generally for 1999. GNP data are for 1998 and are based on local currencies converted to prevailing U.S. dollar equivalencies. Corporations are ranked by their placement on the *Fortune* 500 list of global corporations.

Sources: For corporate data: *Fortune* 2000. For GNP data: World Bank 2000b:9–11.

emphasize that multinationals exploit local workers to maximize profits. Starbucks—the international coffee retailer based in Seattle—gets some of its coffee from farms in Guatemala. But to earn enough money to buy a pound of Starbucks' coffee, a Guatemalan farmworker would have to pick 500 pounds of beans, representing five days of work (Entine and Nichols 1996).

With international trade agreements such as the North American Free Trade Agreement (NAFTA), the pool of cheap labour in the developing world prompts multinationals to move factories out of core countries. An added bonus for the multinationals is that the developing world discourages strong trade unions. Organized labour in industrialized countries insists on decent wages and humane working conditions, but governments seeking to attract or keep multinationals may develop a "climate for investment" that includes repressive antilabour laws restricting union activity and collective bargaining. If labour's demands in factories run by multinational corporations become threatening, the firm will simply move its plant elsewhere, leaving a trail of unemployment behind. Nike, for example, moved its factories from the United States to Korea to Indonesia to Vietnam, seeking the lowest labour costs.

In order to benefit from NAFTA, for example, each country utilizes its comparative advantage. In the case of Mexico, this means it has to expand its unskilled labour industry. One of the consequences of NAFTA has been that agri-businesses have taken over the traditional farming of corn in Mexico, leaving many farmers no choice but to move to the cities in search of work. Their unskilled labour is needed, yet with a greater number of labourers becoming available, there is a tendency for wages to be pushed even lower. Economists claim that trade agreements—such as NAFTA and the proposed Free Trade Area of the Americas (FTAA), which will include Central and South America—work to benefit the economies of poorer nations. But as has been evident in Mexico, "hard working labourers combined with decreasing costs (due to falling wages) does equate to increasing revenue for assembly owners. No, this does not trickle down to the poor" (Wilson 2002). Conflict theorists conclude that, on the whole, multinational corporations have a negative social impact on workers in both industrialized and developing nations.

Workers in core countries are beginning to recognize that their own interests are served by helping to organize workers in developing nations. As long as multinationals can exploit cheap labour abroad, they will be in a strong position to reduce wages and benefits in industrialized countries. With this in mind, in the 1990s, labour unions, religious organizations, campus groups, and other activists mounted public campaigns to pressure companies such as Nike, Starbucks, Reebok, the Gap, and Wal-Mart to improve the wages and working conditions in their overseas operations (Cavanagh and Broad 1996).

Several sociologists have confirmed Homer-Dixon's assessment that the wealth created by globalization does not find its way into the pockets of workers in developing countries. Although it may initially contribute to a host nation's wealth, it eventually increases economic inequality within developing nations. This is true in both income and ownership of land. The upper and middle classes benefit most from economic expansion, while the lower classes are less likely to benefit. Multinationals invest in limited areas of an economy and in restricted regions of a nation. Although certain sectors of the host nation's economy expand, such as hotels and expensive restaurants, this very expansion appears to retard growth in agriculture and other economic sectors. Moreover, multinational corporations often buy out or force out local entrepreneurs and companies, thereby increasing economic and cultural dependence (Bornschier et al. 1978; Chase-Dunn and Grimes 1995; P. Evans 1979; Wallerstein 1979).

Feminist theory also sees the expansion of multinationals as potentially destructive. Women in

As these billboards show, multinational corporations have arrived in Vietnam. Multinationals take advantage of cheap labour in developing countries but they also help diffuse technology to those nations.

Protesters, like this one breaking the window of a Starbucks in Seattle, are demonstrating against what they see as the exploitative practices of large corporations, and the damaging effects they can have on developing nations.

developing countries, who are often powerless, are easier targets for exploitation through the devaluation of their labour by low wages and their lives by dangerous production practices. One of the areas focused upon by feminists interested in the global context (sometimes referred to as global feminists) is the connection between women who work in fast-food restaurants, supermarkets, and agricultural production in Canada, the United States, and Mexico. Some groups, like the Food First Institute for Food and Development Policy, take a critical look at how NAFTA has affected these women and their working conditions in a world that sees consumer demands for exotic flowers dictating that good food-growing soil be turned over to meet the demands for nonfood items, thereby contributing to poverty in places such as Mexico (see Barndt 2000; Rosset 1999; Tiano 1990).

Modernization

Millions of people around the world are witnessing a revolutionary transformation of their day-to-day life. Contemporary social scientists use the term **modernization** to describe the far-reaching process by which peripheral nations move from traditional or less developed institutions to those characteristic of more developed societies.

Wendell Bell (1981a), whose definition of modernization we are using, notes that modern societies tend to be urban, literate, and industrial. They have sophisticated transportation and media systems. Families tend to be organized within the nuclear family unit rather than the extended-family model (see Chapter 13). Members of societies that have undergone modernization shift allegiance from such traditional sources of authority as parents and priests to newer authorities such as government officials.

Many sociologists are quick to note that terms such as *modernization* and even *development* contain an ethnocentric bias. The unstated assumptions behind these terms are that "they" (people living in developing countries) are struggling to become more like "us" (in the core industrialized nations). Viewed from a conflict perspective, such use of these terms perpetuates the dominant ideology of capitalist societies.

There is similar criticism of **modernization theory**, a functionalist approach that proposes that modernization and development will gradually improve the lives of people in developing nations. According to this theory, while countries develop at uneven rates, development in peripheral countries will be assisted by the innovations transferred from the industrialized world. Critics of modernization theory, including feminist and dependency theorists, counter that any such technology transfer only increases the dominance of core nations over developing countries and facilitates further exploitation. One of the key concerns by critics is the pace of change that is now possible using the latest in communications technology.

When we see all the Coca-Cola and IBM signs going up in developing countries, it is easy to assume that economic change is also effecting cultural change. But that is not always the case, researchers note. Distinctive cultural traditions, such as a particular religious orientation or a nationalistic identity, often persist in a developing nation and can soften the impact of modernization (Inglehart and Baker 2000).

Contemporary sociologists emphasize that both industrialized and developing countries are "modern." Current researchers are increasingly viewing modernization as movement along a series of social indicators—among them degree of urbanization, energy use, literacy, political democracy, and use of birth control. Clearly, these are often subjective indicators; even in industrialized nations, not all observers would agree that wider use of birth control represents an example of "progress" (Armer and Katsillis 1992; Hedley 1992).

Current modernization studies generally take a convergence perspective. Using the indicators noted above, researchers focus on how societies are moving closer together despite traditional differences. Initially, such modernization studies emphasized the convergence between Canada and the Asian nations or between capitalist North America and the socialist democracies of Western Europe. Now, however, this convergence perspective increasingly includes the developing countries of the Third World. Researchers recognize the interdependence of core industrialized nations and the developing world—as well as the continuing exploitation of the latter countries by the former. From a conflict perspective, modernization in developing countries often perpetuates their dependence on and continued exploitation by more industrialized nations. Conflict theorists view such a continuing dependence on foreign powers as an example of contemporary neocolonialism (Adelman 1993; C. Kerr 1960; O'Donnell 1992).

Stratification Within Nations: A Comparative Perspective

At the same time that the gap between rich and poor nations is widening, so too is the gap between rich and poor citizens within nations. As discussed earlier, stratification in developing nations is closely related to their relatively weak and dependent position in the global economy. Local elites work hand in hand with multinational corporations and prosper from such alliances. At the same time, the economic system with its prevailing developmental values creates and perpetuates the exploitation of industrial and agricultural workers. That's why foreign investment in developing countries tends to increase economic inequality (Bornschier et al. 1978; Kerbo 1996). As Box 9-1 makes clear, inequality within a society is also evident in industrialized nations such as Japan.

Distribution of Wealth and Income

In at least 15 nations around the world, the most affluent 10 percent of the population receives at least 40 percent of all income: Brazil (the leader at 48 percent), Chile, Colombia, Guatemala, Honduras, Lesotho, Mali, Mexico, Panama, Papua New Guinea, Portugal, Senegal, Sierra Leone, South Africa, and Zimbabwe (World Bank 2000:238–239). Figure 9-2 compares the distribution of income in selected industrialized and developing nations.

The decade of the 1980s was particularly cruel for many developing countries. Some nations—including

Zambia, Bolivia, and Nigeria—saw per capita income plummet as dramatically as it did in the United States during the Great Depression of the 1930s. With these trends in mind, researcher Alan Durning (1990:26) observed that the term "developing nation" has become a cruel misnomer: Many of the world's less affluent nations are disintegrating rather than developing.

Feminist scholars show how difficult life is in developing countries, especially for women. One extreme example is the experience of women living under the Taliban regime in Afghanistan. Karuna Chanana Ahmed, an anthropologist from India who has studied women in developing nations, calls women the most exploited among oppressed people. Women face sex discrimination beginning at birth. They are commonly fed less than male children, are denied educational opportunities, and are often hospitalized only when critically ill. Whether inside or outside the home, women's work is devalued. When economies fail, as they did in Asian countries in the late 1990s and in Argentina in 2001, women are the first to be laid off from work (J. Anderson and Moore 1993; Kristof 1998).

Surveys show a significant degree of *female infanticide* (the killing of baby girls) in China and rural areas of India. Only one-third of Pakistan's sexually segregated schools are for women, and one-third of these schools have no buildings. In Kenya and Tanzania, it is illegal for a woman to own a house. In Saudi Arabia, women are prohibited from driving, walking alone in public, and socializing with men outside their families (C. Murphy 1993). We will explore women's second-class status throughout the world more fully in Chapter 11.

What factors have contributed to the recent difficulties of developing nations? Certainly runaway population growth has hurt the standard of living of many Third World peoples. So, too, has the accelerating environmental decline evident in the quality of air, water, and other natural resources. (We will examine population growth and environmental decline in more detail in Chapter 20.) Still another factor has been the developing nations' collective debt of U.S.$1.3 trillion. If we add to a nation's debt repayment the estimates of money being invested elsewhere by wealthy citizens, the annual outflow of funds may reach U.S.$100 billion (Durning 1990; Kerbo 1996).

Unfortunately, the massive exodus of money from poorer regions of the world only intensifies their destruction of natural resources. From a conflict view, less affluent nations are being forced to exploit their mineral deposits, forests, and fisheries to meet their debt obligations while offering subsistence labour to local workers. The poor turn to the only means of survival available to them: marginal lands. They plow mountain slopes, burn plots in tropical forests, and overgraze grasslands—often knowing that their actions are destructive to the environment. But they see no

FIGURE 9-2

Distribution of Income in Nine Nations

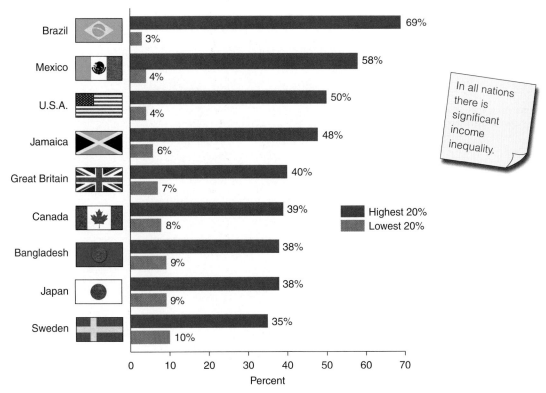

Note: Data are considered comparable although based on statistics covering 1986 to 1999.

Sources: World Bank 1997a:54–56; 2000a:238–239. U.S. data from the Congressional Budget Office cited in Shapiro and Greenstein 1999.

alternative in their agonizing fight for simple survival (Durning 1990; Waring 1988).

Prestige

Sociologists have recognized that comparative research is essential in determining whether observed patterns of stratification are unique to a single nation, are restricted to a particular type of society (such as industrial or developing nations), or are applicable to a wide range of societies (Kalleberg 1988). We have seen that societies as different as Brazil, Mexico, Canada, and Japan all share a marked inequality in the distribution of income (refer to Figure 9-2). But a person's class position, defined largely in economic terms and reflecting his or her level of wealth and income, is but one component of stratification.

p. 206

By ranking the prestige of various occupations, sociologists can gain a deeper understanding of another aspect of inequality. But are perceptions in Canada regarding the prestige of occupations comparable to those held in other societies? In an effort to study stratification from a cross-cultural perspective, sociologist Donald Treiman (1977) examined the reputation that certain jobs had in 53 different nations. People were asked to rate occupations and the results were tabulated along a scale ranging from 0 to 100, with higher scores being more prestigious. Treiman found a high degree of correlation or similarity in all contemporary societies, including both industrialized and nonindustrialized nations.

Treiman's pioneering research inspired subsequent efforts to gather and compare data from many societies using the objective method of measuring stratification differences. In one important study, sociologists Nan Lin and Wen Xie (1988) interviewed a random sample of residents of Beijing, the capital of the People's Republic of China, to study occupational prestige. The researchers recognized the potential bias of sampling those who live in one of China's most cosmopolitan cities. Of the 1,774 respondents questioned, 47 percent were professionals, managers, or administrators—whereas this was true of only 23 percent of residents of other urban areas. Still, given the constraints on acquiring social scientific data in China, this study offers unique insights regarding stratification in the world's most populous nation.

A tourist visiting Japan may at first experience a bit of culture shock after noticing the degree to which everything in Japanese life is ranked: corporations, universities, even educational programs. These rankings are widely reported and accepted. Moreover, the ratings shape day-to-day social interactions: Japanese find it difficult to sit, talk, or eat together unless the relative rankings of those present have been established, often through the practice of *meishi* (the exchange of business cards).

The apparent preoccupation with ranking and formality suggests an exceptional degree of stratification. Yet researchers have determined that Japan's level of income inequality is among the *lowest* of major industrial societies (see Figure 9-2 on page 241). Whereas the pay gap between Japan's top corporate executives and the nation's lowest-paid workers is about 8 to 1, the comparable figure for the United States would be 37 to 1. In addition, Japanese law prohibits the lucrative stock options that are a common perk in North American corporations.

This relative level of income equality in Japanese society is rather recent; it dates back to post-Second World War economic changes, including extensive land reform and the breakup of powerful holding companies. Among the factors that initially contributed to a lower level of inequality in Japan had been an expanding economy combined with a labour shortage. However, during the 1990s the gap between rich and poor began to grow as a result of a severe economic recession and tax laws that let the rich hold on to more of their money.

One factor that still works against inequality is that Japan is rather homogeneous—certainly when compared with Canada and the United States—in terms of race, ethnicity, nationality, and language. Japan's population is 98 percent Japanese. But there is discrimination against the nation's Chinese and Korean minorities, and the *Burakumin* constitute a low-status subculture who encounter extensive prejudice. We will discuss these groups in the next chapter (Box 10-1).

Perhaps the most pervasive form of inequality in Japan is gender discrimination. Japanese girls do not receive the same encouragement to achieve in education that

While women constitute more than 40 percent of Japan's workforce, they are generally restricted to subordinate positions.

boys do. It should be no surprise, then, that Japanese women occupy a subordinate position in higher education. Whereas 80 percent of the nation's male post-secondary students are in four-year universities, two-thirds of female students are in women's junior colleges that promote traditional domestic roles for women. Even when Japanese women enter four-year universities, they often major in home economics, nutrition, or literature.

> **Even in developing countries, women are twice as likely to be managers as in Japan.**

Overall, women earn only about 64 percent of men's wages. Fewer than 10 percent of Japanese managers are female—a ratio that is one of the lowest in the world. Even in developing countries, women are twice as likely to be managers as in Japan.

In 1985, Japan's parliament—at the time, 97 percent male—passed an Equal Employment bill that encourages employers to end sex discrimination in hiring, assignment, and promotion policies. However, feminist organizations were dissatisfied because the law lacked strong sanctions. In a landmark ruling issued in late 1996, a Japanese court for the first time held an employer liable for denying promotions due to sex discrimination. The court ordered a Japanese bank to pay 12 female employees a total of almost $1 million and added that 11 of the women must immediately be promoted to management posts.

On the political front, Japanese women have made progress but remain underrepresented. In a study of women in government around the world, the Inter-Parliamentary Union found that, as of 1999, Japan ranked near the bottom of the countries studied, with less than 5 percent of its national legislators being female.

Let's Discuss

1. What factors contribute to the relatively low level of income inequality in Japan?
2. Describe the types of gender discrimination found in Japan. Why do you think Japanese women occupy such a subordinate social position?

Sources: Abegglen and Stalk 1985; French 2000; Inter-Parliamentary Union 1999; Jordan 1996b; Kerbo 1996; Kristof 1995c; Magnier 1999; Nakane 1970; Sterngold 1992; Strom 2000.

Lin and Xie found that physicians ranked near the top of the occupational hierarchy, while police officers were near the middle, and garbage collectors were close to the bottom—a finding similar to the results of surveys in the United States. Teachers and professors, however, received much lower prestige ratings in China, reflecting the low wages they receive relative to other occupations. The Chinese respondents gave a much higher prestige rating to textile workers than did respondents in the United States. Textile workers in China evidently fare much better relative to other workers than they do in North America or Europe.

p. 212

As one part of their analysis, the researchers compared the prestige rankings of male and female respondents. Although China has officially maintained a national policy of gender equality since 1949, it has not been able to eliminate occupational segregation by gender. Partly as a result, the prestige rankings of Chinese men and women seemed to reflect the structure of occupational opportunity. Males, for example, gave higher ratings than females to such occupations as natural scientist, athlete, driver, and mechanic—all of which are more likely to be held by males. Each gender showed a tendency to rate more highly those occupations most open to it.

Treiman's cross-cultural research reminds us that prestige distinctions are universal; the study of China by Lin and Xie underscores this finding. Even a society that has experienced revolutionary movements and decades of communist party rule still stratifies itself in its ranking of prestigious occupations.

Social Mobility

Mobility in Industrial Nations

Studies of intergenerational mobility in industrialized nations have found the following patterns:

1. There are substantial similarities in the ways that parents' positions in stratification systems are transmitted to their children.
2. As in Canada, mobility opportunities in other nations have been influenced by structural factors, such as labour market changes that lead to the rise or decline of an occupational group within the social hierarchy.
3. Immigration continues to be a significant factor shaping a society's level of intergenerational mobility (Ganzeboom et al. 1991; Haller et al. 1990; Hauser and Grusky 1988).

Cross-cultural studies suggest that intergenerational mobility has been increasing in recent decades, at least among men. Dutch sociologists Harry Ganzeboom and Ruud Luijkx, joined by sociologist Donald Treiman of the United States (1989), examined surveys of mobility in 35 industrial and developing nations. They found that almost all the countries studied had witnessed increased intergenerational mobility between the 1950s and 1980s. In particular, they noted a common pattern of movement away from agriculture-based occupations.

Mobility in Developing Nations

Mobility patterns in industrialized countries are usually associated with intergenerational and intragenerational mobility. However, within developing nations, macro-level social and economic changes often overshadow micro-level movement from one occupation to another. For example, there is typically a substantial wage differential between rural and urban areas, which leads to high levels of migration to the cities. Yet the urban industrial sectors of developing countries generally cannot provide sufficient employment for all those seeking work. When migrants find that they are unable to move upward within the conventional economy, the informal or underground economies described in Box 9-2 become more attractive as a source of employment and financial rewards (Thirlwall 1989:103).

The amount of social movement in a society—both upward and downward—is rather limited in societies characterized by slavery and caste systems of stratification. For example, a study of agricultural households in central India between 1975 and 1983 found that, on average, 84 percent of those who were poor in any year had been poor in the previous year. Over the nine-year period of study, 44 percent of households had been poor for six or more years, and 19 percent were poor in all nine years (World Bank 1990:135).

p. 204

Recent research on social mobility has persuasively pursued a conflict view: Cross-national differences in mobility are influenced by the differing relations of countries to the world economy. Drawing on Wallerstein's world systems analysis, researchers argue that there is likely to be greater inequality and less mobility in the developing countries than in the core industrialized nations (Ries 1992:187).

Gender Differences and Mobility

Only recently, with the development of contemporary feminist theories, have researchers begun to investigate the impact of gender on the mobility patterns of developing nations. Many aspects of the development process—especially modernization in rural areas and the rural-to-urban migration described above—may result in the modification or abandonment of traditional cultural practices and even marital systems. The effects on women's social standing and mobility are not necessarily positive. As a country develops and modernizes, women's vital role in food production deteriorates, jeopardizing both their autonomy and their material well-being. The

9-2 The Informal Economy

Do you know someone who takes in tips and doesn't report the income? Have you traded services with someone—say, a haircut for help with a computer problem? These are aspects of an *informal economy,* the transfer of money, goods, or services that are not reported to the government. Participants in this type of economy avoid taxes, regulations, and minimum wage provisions, as well as expenses incurred for bookkeeping and financial reporting. Anthropologists studying developing nations and preindustrial societies have long acknowledged the existence of informal social networks that make, sell, and trade goods and services. Only recently have these networks been identified as common to all societies.

In industrial societies, the informal economy embraces transactions that are individually quite small but that can be quite significant when taken together. One major segment of this economy involves illegal transactions—such as prostitution, sale of illegal drugs, gambling, and bribery—leading some observers to describe it as an "underground economy." Yet the informal economy also includes unregulated child-care services and the unreported income of craftspeople, street vendors, and employees who receive substantial tips. According to estimates, the informal economy may account for as much as 10 to 20 percent of all economic activity in Canada.

Although these informal economic transactions take place in virtually all societies—both capitalist and socialist—the pattern in developing countries differs somewhat from the informal economy of industrialized nations. In the developing world, governments often set up burdensome business regulations that an overworked bureaucracy must administer.

> When requests for licences and permits pile up, holding up business projects, legitimate entrepreneurs find they need to "go underground" in order to get anything done.

When requests for licences and permits pile up, holding up business projects, legitimate entrepreneurs find they need to "go underground" in order to get anything done. In Latin America, for example, the underground economy is estimated to account for about one-third of the gross domestic product of the area. Informal industrial enterprises, such as textile factories and repair shops, tend to be labour-intensive. Underground entrepreneurs cannot rely on advanced machinery, since a firm's assets can be confiscated for failure to operate within the open economy.

Viewed from a functionalist perspective, the bureaucratic regulations have contributed to the rise of an efficient informal economy in certain countries. Nevertheless, these regulatory systems are dysfunctional for overall political and economic well-being. Since informal firms typically operate in remote locations to avoid detection, they cannot easily expand even when they become profitable. Given the limited protection for their property and contractual rights, participants in the informal economy are less likely to save and invest their income.

Informal economies have been criticized for promoting highly unfair and dangerous working conditions. A study of the underground economy of Spain found that workers' incomes were low, there was little job security, and safety and health standards were rarely enforced. Both the Spanish government and the nation's trade unions seemed to ignore the exploitation of participants in the informal economy. Still, especially in the developing world, the existence of a substantial underground economy simply reflects the absence of an economic system that is accessible to all residents.

Let's Discuss

1. What conditions contribute to the creation of an informal economy?
2. Describe an informal economy that you have observed or been a part of. Which perspective—functionalist, feminist, conflict, or interactionist—do you think best fits the notion of informal economy?

Sources: Ferman et al. 1987; Hershey 1988; Lemkow 1987; Weigard 1992.

---

movement of families to the cities weakens women's ties to relatives who can provide food, financial assistance, and social support (Alam 1985; Boserup 1977; Tiano 1987).

One recent effort to investigate gender and mobility took place in Sri Lanka in Southeast Asia. Researchers examined the impact of foreign aid—in the form of plans to improve agricultural production, irrigation, and rural electrification—on the local population. Virtually all the foreign aid programs were more successful in increasing the incomes of men than of women. Where women's incomes did rise, it was usually in such occupations as rubber and tea cultivation, in which women earn almost 40 percent less than their male counterparts. Overall, foreign aid in Sri Lanka had the unintended consequence of increasing income inequality between male and female workers; similar conclusions were reached in studies

Chinese immigrants at work in a restaurant. Immigrants to industrialized nations may enjoy higher wages but often must accept more menial forms of employment than they had in their native land.

conducted in India and Malaysia (Stoeckel and Sirisena 1988). Studies of the distribution of wealth and income within various countries, comparative studies of prestige, and cross-cultural research on mobility consistently reveal that stratification based on class, gender, and other factors shows up within a wide range of societies. Clearly, a worldwide view of stratification must include not only the sharp contrast between wealthy and impoverished nations but also the layers of hierarchies *within* industrialized societies and developing countries.

Stratification in Mexico: A Case Study

Colonialism, neocolonialism, and the domination and exploitation of a peripheral developing country by a core industrialized nation can be clearly seen in the history of Mexico. In this section we will look in some detail at the dynamics of stratification in this country.

In the 1520s, the Aztecs (known as Indians) that ruled Mexico were overthrown by Spain, and Mexico remained a Spanish colony until the 1820s. In 1836, Texas declared its independence from Mexico, and by 1846, Mexico was at war with the United States. As a result of its defeat, Mexico was forced to surrender over half its territory, including the area of today's California, New Mexico, and northern Arizona. In the 1860s, France sought to turn Mexico into a colony under the Austrian prince Maximilian, but ultimately withdrew after bitter resistance led by a Mexican Indian, Benito Juárez, who served as the nation's president.

Finally, in the twentieth century, as we will explore more fully in this case study, there has been a close cultural, economic, and political relationship between Mexico and the United States, but it has clearly been a relationship in which the United States is the dominant party. According to Wallerstein's analysis, the United States is at the core while neighbouring Mexico is still on the periphery of the world economic system.

As of 2000, Mexico had 99 million residents, making it the eleventh most populous nation in the world. The population is concentrated in the nation's three largest cities: Mexico City (the fifth-largest city in the world), Guadalajara, and Monterrey. Indeed, one of every four Mexicans lives in these urban areas. Population growth is a critical issue in Mexico; by the year 2025, the population is expected to expand to about 125 million. Such rapid growth will inevitably intensify Mexico's already serious economic and environmental problems (Haub and Cornelius 1999; Holt 1999; World Resources Institute et al. 1996).

If we compare Mexico to Canada, the overall differences in the standard of living and in life chances are quite dramatic. The *gross domestic product*—the value of all final goods and services produced within a country—is a commonly used measure of an average resident's economic well-being. In 1997, the gross domestic product per person in Canada came to $22 408; in Mexico, it was a mere $8370. About 95 percent of Canadian youth who are of high-school age are in school, compared to 75 percent in Mexico. At birth, people in Canada can expect to live an average of 79 years, while life expectancy in Mexico is 72 years (United Nations Development Programme 1999; World Bank 2001).

Although Mexico is unquestionably a poor country, the gap between its richest and poorest citizens is one of the widest in the world (refer back to Figure 9-2). In 2000, judged by the standards of the United Nations, 40 percent of the population survived on $2 per day. At the same time, the wealthiest 10 percent of Mexico's people account for 43 percent of the entire nation's income. According to a *Forbes* magazine portrait of the world's wealthiest individuals, Mexico had the fourth-largest number of people on the list—behind only the United

States, Germany, and Japan (Castañeda 1995; World Bank 2000:237, 239).

Political scientist Jorge Castañeda (1995:71) calls Mexico a "polarized society with enormous gaps between rich and poor, town and country, north and south, white and brown (or *criollos* and *mestizos*)." He adds that the country is also divided along lines of class, race, religion, gender, and age. We will examine stratification within Mexico by focusing on race relations and the plight of Mexican Indians, the status of Mexican women, Mexico's economy and environment, and emigration to the United States and its impact on the U.S.–Mexican "borderlands."

Race Relations in Mexico: The Colour Hierarchy

On January 1, 1994, rebels from an armed insurgent group called the Zapatista National Liberation Army seized four towns in the state of Chiapas in Southern Mexico. The rebels—who named their organization after Emiliano Zapata, a farmer and leader of the 1910 revolution against a corrupt dictatorship—were backed by 2000 lightly armed Mayan Indians and peasants. Zapatista leaders declared that they had turned to armed insurrection to protest economic injustices and discrimination against the region's Indian population. The Mexican government mobilized the army to crush the revolt, but was forced to retreat as news organizations broadcast pictures of the confrontation around the world. A ceasefire was declared after only 12 days of fighting, but 196 people had already died. Negotiations between the Mexican government and the Zapatista National Liberation Army collapsed in 1996, with sporadic violence ever since (J. Preston 1998).

The presidential inauguration of Vicente Fox, in December 2000, represented a victory of civilian participation because it overthrew the 70-year ruling party regime of PRI (Institutional Revolutionary Party). Initially, it appeared that Fox might resolve the concerns of the Zapatista who were involved, at the time, in a tour for fulfillment of the 1996 San Andres Agreement (ASA). However, the PAN (National Action Party) legislators showed their discomfort at having to recognize an armed group that had declared war on the Mexican state. In April 2001, the Mexican Senate turned down Fox's proposals for indigenous rights and put forward new legislation. This was rejected by the Zapatista and, to date, the armed insurrection continues (Gutiérrez 2001; Schneider & Silverman 2000).

While many factors contributed to the Zapatista revolt, the subordinate status of Mexico's Indian population throughout the country was surely important. As of early 1996, while accounting for an estimated 15 percent of Mexico's population, Mexican Indians held no important offices in the central government and only a few of the more than 600 seats in the national assembly. Fully 60 percent of Mexican Indians over the age of 12 were unemployed; most of those who did hold jobs earned less than the minimum wage of about $2.50 *per day*. Only 12 percent of Indians complete even a sixth-grade education (DePalma 1995a, 1996; McMahon 1995). The plight of Mexico's Indians is explored further in Figure 9-3.

The subordinate status of Mexico's Indians is but one reflection of the nation's colour hierarchy, which links social class to the appearance of racial purity. At the top of this hierarchy are the *criollos*, the 10 percent of the population who are typically white, well-educated members of the business and intellectual elites with familial roots in Spain. In the middle is the large, impoverished *mestizo* majority, most of whom have brown skin and a mixed racial lineage as a result of intermarriage. At the bottom of the colour hierarchy are the destitute, full-blooded Mexican Indian minority and a small number of blacks, some descended from 200 000 African slaves brought to Mexico. This colour hierarchy is an important part of day-to-day life—enough so

Mexican women mourn the 1994 death of a member of the Zapatista National Liberation Army, an insurgent group protesting economic injustices and discrimination against the Indian population in the state of Chiapas.

FIGURE 9-3

Relative Position of Indians in Mexico, 1990

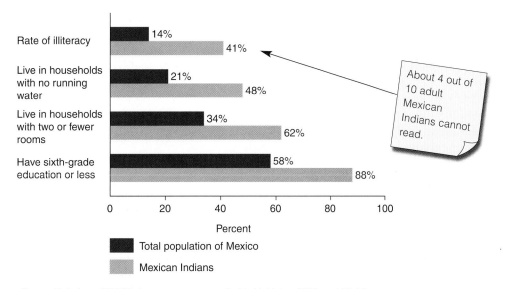

About 4 out of 10 adult Mexican Indians cannot read.

Total population of Mexico

Mexican Indians

Percent

Source: Data from 1990 Mexican census as reported in McMahon 1995; and World Bank 1995.

that some Mexicans in the cities use hair dyes, skin lighteners, and blue or green contact lenses to appear more white and European. Ironically, however, nearly all Mexicans are considered part Indian because of centuries of intermarriage (Castañeda 1995; DePalma 1995a).

Many observers take note of widespread denial of prejudice and discrimination against people of colour in Mexico. Schoolchildren are taught that the election of Benito Juárez, a Zapotec Indian, as president of Mexico in the nineteenth century proves that all Mexicans are equal. In addition, Mexico's National Commission of Human Rights has *never* received a complaint alleging racial discrimination and has no process for handling such a complaint. With such denial in mind, there has been a marked growth in the last decade of formal organizations and voluntary associations representing indigenous Indians. The Zapatista revolt in Chiapas was an even more dramatic indication that those at the bottom of Mexico's colour hierarchy are weary of inequality and injustice (DePalma 1995a, 1996; Stavenhagen 1994).

The Status of Women in Mexico

In 1975, Mexico City hosted the first international conference on the status of women convened by the United Nations. Much of the focus was on the situation of women in developing countries; in that regard, the situation is mixed. Women now constitute 33 percent of the labour force, an increase in the past 20 years but still behind industrial countries. Unfortunately, Mexican

Women account for just a small proportion of elected officials and cabinet ministers in Mexico.

women are even more mired in the lowest-paying jobs than their counterparts in industrial nations. In the political arena, women are rarely seen in top decision-making positions, but they have increased their representation in the national legislature to 18 percent, ranking Mexico at 25th among 179 nations worldwide (Inter-Parliamentary Union 1999; World Bank 2000).

Feminist sociologists emphasize that even when they work outside the home, Mexican women often don't get recognized as active and productive household members, while men are typically viewed as the heads of households. As one consequence, women find it difficult to obtain credit and technical assistance in many parts of the country and to inherit land in rural areas. Within manufacturing and service industries, women generally receive little training and tend to work in the least-automated and least-skilled jobs—in good part because there is little expectation that women will pursue career advancement, organize for better working conditions, or become active in labour unions (Kopinak 1995; Martelo 1996; see also G. Young 1993).

As is true in many developing countries, women in Mexico are more vulnerable than men to contracting the HIV virus and developing AIDS. Their subordinate social and economic position makes it difficult for them to assess their risk of infection from male sexual partners and, even more important, to negotiate taking precautions. Interestingly, abortion is widely available in Mexico. Despite laws prohibiting abortion except in cases of rape or when necessary to save the woman's life, there are an estimated 400 000 abortions each year. Some women obtain abortions from practitioners of folk medicine, but many attempt to self-abort and then seek medical attention to prevent serious injury (Delriozolezzi 1995; Honey 1994).

In recent decades, Mexican women have begun to organize to address an array of economic, political, and health issues. Since women continue to serve as the household managers for their families, even when they work outside the home, they are well aware of the consequences of the inadequate public services in their lower-income urban neighbourhoods. As far back as 1973, women in Monterrey—the nation's third-largest city—began protesting the continuing disruptions of the city's water supply. After individual complaints to city officials and the water authority proved fruitless, social networks of female activists began to emerge. These activists sent delegations to confront politicians, organized protest rallies, and blocked traffic as a means of getting media attention. Their efforts brought improvement in Monterrey's water service, but the issue of reliable and safe water remains a concern in Mexico and many developing countries (V. Bennett 1995).

Mexico's Economy and Environment

Mexico strongly lobbied for acceptance of the North American Free Trade Agreement (NAFTA), which became law on January 1, 1994, the day that the Zapatista began their uprising. NAFTA provided for the dismantling of almost all trade barriers among Canada, the United States, and Mexico. Mexico hoped its struggling economy would receive a major boost from such a favourable linkage to the world's largest consumer market, the United States. Indeed, in 1995 Mexico recorded its first trade surplus with the United States since 1990. Still, any benefit from NAFTA was dramatically undercut in 1994 by the collapse of the *peso,* Mexico's unit of currency. This collapse reflected a widespread loss of confidence as a result of internal political unrest (the Zapatista revolt, discussed earlier) and the assassination of a leading

Vigorous government efforts to control pollution in Mexico City have had some success, but conditions for pollution remain ideal in this large city located in a mountain valley some 2190 metres above sea level.

political figure who had spear-
headed economic reform. Although
investment in Mexico has increased
since the signing of NAFTA, the
implementation of the agreement
has meant little in the day-to-day
economic struggles of the average
Mexican (DePalma 1995b; Robber-
son 1995). We will examine the
impact of NAFTA more fully in
Chapter 17.

Adding to the pressures on low-
income Mexicans, the nation's
Social Security system is in a state of
crisis and could soon go bankrupt.
During the last 50 years, this system
has evolved into a "cradle-to-grave"
security blanket covering hospital
births, child care, lifetime medical
care, retirement pensions, and
funeral costs for 37 million Mexicans. However, the recent economic
crisis has intensified the financial
pressures on the system. It is diffi-

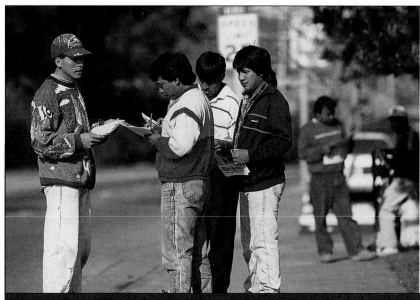

Illegal immigrants from Mexico on a California street, looking for work. The
borderlands along the boundary between the United States and Mexico mix
the cultures of the two countries.

cult in any case to support a population with more older
people than ever before—some of whom need long-term
and expensive hospitalization because of heart disease
and cancer (DePalma 1995c).

Mexico's recession has also hampered efforts to address
the nation's serious environmental problems. Not only was
the government reluctant to introduce new measures, but
citizens could not afford new cars equipped to improve air
quality. At the beginning of the 1990s, air pollutants hit
emergency levels in Mexico City half the year. Despite opposition from oil companies, the government gradually introduced stronger controls. For example, the "Today You Can't
Drive" program took 20 percent of all vehicles without
catalytic converters off the road each weekday.

By 2000 there was reason to be optimistic. Mexico
City was experiencing five emergency pollution days per
year compared to 177 in 1992. This is a dramatic turn-
around, especially since the capital's location in a high
mountain valley provides ideal conditions for the persistence of pollution. Another encouraging development
is that the United States and Mexico signed comprehensive agreements to work together to curb air and water
pollution across their common border, which includes
massive industrial development on the Mexican side
(Saldaña 1999; Smith 2000).

The Borderlands

Air and water pollution are but two of the many ways in
which the problems of Mexico and the United States

intertwine. Growing recognition of the borderlands
reflects the increasingly close and complex relationship
between these two countries. The term ***borderlands*** refers
to the area of a common culture along the border
between Mexico and the United States. Legal and illegal
emigration from Mexico to the United States, day labourers crossing the border regularly to go to jobs in the
United States, the implementation of the North American
Free Trade Agreement, and the exchange of media across
the border all make the notion of separate Mexican and
U.S. cultures obsolete in the borderlands (Heyck 1994).

The economic position of the borderlands is rather
complicated, as we can see in the emergence of the
maquiladoras on the Mexican side. These are foreign
companies that establish operations in Mexico yet are
exempt from Mexican taxes and are not required to provide insurance or benefits for their workers. The
maquiladoras have sucked manufacturing jobs from other
parts of North America to Mexico. As of late 1999, 1 million new jobs had been created in the *maquiladoras,* with
daily wages of $5 to $15 a day. Moreover, since many of
these firms come from the United States and sell their
products to Mexico's vast domestic market, their operations deepen the impact of U.S. consumer culture on
Mexico's urban and rural areas (*Migration News* 1999c;
Wood 1999).

The *maquiladoras* have contributed to Mexico's economic development, but not without some cost. Conflict
theorists note that unregulated growth allows the owners to exploit the workers with jobs that lack security,

possibilities for advancement, and decent wages. Moreover, many of the U.S.-owned companies require female job applicants to take a urine test to screen out those who are pregnant, a violation of Mexican law as well as the NAFTA agreement and the source of numerous cases of sex discrimination. Social activists also complain that tens of thousands of Mexicans work on *maquiladora* assembly lines for much lower wages, such as $1 an hour, raising again the issue of sweatshop labour noted earlier in the chapter (S. Dillon 1998; Dougherty and Holthouse 1999).

When people think about the borderlands, they generally think about immigration. As we'll see in the social policy section of Chapter 10, immigration is a controversial political issue. For its part, Mexico is concerned about the priorities and policies of its powerful northern neighbour. From Mexico's point of view, the United States too often regards Mexico simply as a reserve pool of easily available cheap labour. The United States encourages Mexicans to cross the border when workers are needed but discourages and "cracks down" on immigrants when they are not. Some people, then, see immigration more as a labour market issue than a law enforcement issue. Viewed from the perspective of Immanuel Wallerstein's world systems analysis and dependency theory, this is yet another example of a core industrialized nation exploiting a peripheral developing country.

The social impact of emigration to the United States is felt throughout Mexico. According to sociological research, the earliest emigrants were typically married men of working age who came from the middle of the stratification system. They had enough financial resources to afford the costs and risks of emigration, yet experienced enough financial strain that entering the United States remained attractive. Over time, kinship ties to migrants multiplied and emigration became less class-selective, with entire families making the trek to the United States. More recently, the occupational backgrounds of Mexican emigrants have widened further, reflecting not only changes in U.S. immigration policy but also the continuing crisis in the Mexican economy (Massey 1998).

Many Mexicans who have gone to the United States send some part of their earnings back across the border to family members still in Mexico. This substantial flow of money, sometimes referred to as "remittances" or "migradollars," is estimated by the International Monetary Fund at a minimum of U.S.$6 billion annually and accounts for 3 percent of Mexico's gross domestic product. Sociologist Douglas Massey points out that if these funds went solely into the purchase of consumer goods, this would underscore the view of dependency theory that Mexico's economy is little more than an extension of the economy of the United States. In fact, however, some of these "migradollars" are used by Mexicans to establish and maintain small business enterprises, such as handicraft workshops and farms. Consequently, the transfer of "migradollars" does stimulate the local and national economies of Mexico (Durand et al. 1996; *Migration News* 1999b).

When we examine Native land claims, crises such as the one in Oka, and the military test flights over regions of the North inhabited by Native peoples, we can see similarities between the Mexican history and the story of Canada's First Nations people. These issues will be explored further in Chapter 12.

We now turn to an examination of how social inequality takes on an especially ugly face in the form of human rights abuse.

SOCIAL POLICY AND SOCIAL INEQUALITY WORLDWIDE

Universal Human Rights

The Issue

One October evening in 1999 three men broke into the house of Digna Ochoa y Placido, a human rights lawyer in Mexico. The men tied her up, interrogated her about the members of political and environmental organizations she represented, and threatened her life. When she managed to free herself she found her phone line cut, her gas line open, and her office ransacked. Ochoa had already been abducted several months earlier and received several death threats for her environmental work on behalf of farmer ecologists who opposed logging interests (*Amnesty Now* 2000).

Poised on the third millennium, the world seemed capable of many mighty feats—ranging from explorations of distant solar systems to refinement of tiny genes within human cells. Yet at the same time came constant reminders of how quickly people and their fundamental human rights can be trampled. The end of Soviet dominance of Eastern Europe set off bitter and sometimes violent clashes among racial, ethnic, and religious groups in

Bosnia, Kosovo, Serbia, and former republics of the Soviet Union itself. Under the Taliban rule, fundamentalists in Afghanistan imposed their strict laws on much of their population. Hutus and Tutsis massacred one another in a virulent civil war in Central Africa. Iraq's mistreated Kurdish minority continued to fight for its rights, as did the Mexican peasants of Indian heritage. Ongoing attempts at peace agreements between Israel and the Palestinians did not end hostilities or killings in that troubled area.

Human rights refers to universal moral rights belonging to all people because they are human. The most important elaboration of human rights appears in the Universal Declaration of Human Rights, adopted by the United Nations in 1948. This declaration: prohibits slavery, torture, and degrading punishment; grants everyone the right to a nationality and its culture; affirms freedom of religion and the right to vote; proclaims the right to seek asylum in other countries to escape persecution; and prohibits arbitrary interference with one's privacy and arbitrary taking of a person's property. It also emphasizes that mothers and children are entitled to special care and assistance.

What steps, if any, can the world community take to ensure the protection of these rights? And is it even possible to agree on what those rights are?

The Setting

The 1990s tragically brought the term *ethnic cleansing* into the world's vocabulary. Within the former Yugoslavia, Serbs initiated a policy intended to "cleanse" Muslims from parts of Bosnia-Herzegovina and ethnic Albanians from the province of Kosovo. Hundreds of thousands of people were killed in the fighting in this area, while many others were uprooted from their homes. Moreover, there were reports of substantial numbers of rapes of Muslim, Croatian, and Kosovar women by Serbian soldiers. In 1996 a United Nations tribunal indicted eight Bosnian Serb military and police officers for rape, marking the first time that sexual assault was treated as a war crime under international law (Simons 1996c; see also Fein 1995). In 1999 the International Crimes Tribunal indicted former Yugoslav president Slobodan Milosevic on seven counts of war crimes.

Drawing on the principles of the Universal Declaration of Human Rights, in 1995 the United Nations Human Rights Commission condemned Iraq, Iran, and Sudan for serious human rights violation, including summary executions, cases of torture, and discrimination against women. The commission adopted resolutions expressing concern over human rights abuses in Haiti, Zaire, and Myanmar and only narrowly rejected a resolution to investigate the state of human rights in China (*New York Times* 1995a).

The year 2001 saw protocols set up to outlaw the use of child soldiers (under 18 years of age), the establishment of the International Criminal Court, and continued monitoring of human rights atrocities around the globe, such as those in Chechnya, Congo, Sudan, and East Timor (Human Rights Watch 2002a).

In the initial wake of the September 11 attacks on New York and Washington, the United States government was quick to build a "global alliance" committed to ending terrorism. There was a real desire to fight a cause against attacks that are not legitimate acts of war and that go against all human rights principles about civilians being deliberately slaughtered. Yet, the issue of atrocities against civilians has been largely ignored in other parts of the world, where they have become routine in conflicts (in places such as Angola, Burundi, and Sierra Leone, to name a few).

The United States has, in the past, opposed a binding obligation to the Universal Declaration of Human Rights. The American government feared that the declaration would cause international scrutiny of the nation's own domestic civil rights controversies. And with the war in Afghanistan, the U.S. has come under the watchful eye of human rights organizations with relation to its establishment of "military commissions" to prosecute non-U.S. citizens. It is suspected that these will be used to try people accused of membership in Al Qaeda or "detainees," as President George W. Bush calls those fighters held by U.S. forces at Guantanamo. By most countries' standards, these people would be considered prisoners of war (POWs), with rights under the Geneva Convention, however, the U.S. refuses to grant them POW status (Human Rights Watch 2002b).

Sociological Insights

By its very title, the Universal Declaration of Human Rights emphasizes that such rights should be *universal*. But cultural relativism encourages understanding and respecting the distinctive norms, values, and p. 80 customs of each culture. In some situations, conflicts arise between human rights standards and local social practices that rest on alternative views of human dignity. For example, is India's caste system an inherent violation of human rights? What about the many cultures of the world that view the subordinate status of women as an essential element in their traditions? Should human rights be interpreted differently in different parts of the world?

In a 1993 speech at the World Conference on Human Rights, U.S. Secretary of State Warren Christopher insisted that the Universal Declaration of Human Rights set a single standard for acceptable behaviour around the world. However, in the late 1990s certain Asian and African nations were reviving arguments about cultural relativism in an attempt to block sanctions by the United Nations Human Rights Commission (Crossette 1996b; Donnelly 1989; Sciolino 1993).

It is not often that a nation makes the bold statement that the U.S. did through Christopher. Policymakers more frequently look at human rights issues from an economic perspective. Functionalists would point out how much more quickly we become embroiled in "human rights" concerns when oil is at stake, as in the Middle East, or military alliances come into play, as in Europe. World powers such as the United States are less likely to want to interfere in an area where their economic concerns are modest (as in Africa) or where they are seeking to advance an economic agenda (as in China).

This intersection of economics and human rights issues has led to the creation of a Human Rights Index, using a database that weighs measures of human rights violations in a country against its level of economic development. Human rights abuses include such indicators as the denial of minority and women's rights, the presence of political prisoners, and the use of torture. Because poverty and a position at the periphery of the world economic system make equality difficult to achieve, the index is adjusted to reflect the level of a nation's development. Figure 9-4 highlights the best nations and the worst offenders in this latest index of 195 nations. In this list, Canada is once again in the top 10 of the best nations. By contrast, Israel ranks at 165, and Russia and the United States are tied at 132 (Observer 1999).

The feminist perspective has been particularly useful in unravelling human rights issues. From the perspective of women, the 'single most important international legal instrument'—the Convention on the Elimination of All Forms of Discrimination Against Women (also known as the Convention on the Rights of Women)—was adopted by the UN in 1979 and enforced in 1981 after being ratified by the required 20 governments. This Convention was a reflection of the reality that universally recognized human rights were still not enjoyed equally by women and men. A series of World Conferences was held in Mexico City (1975), Copenhagen (1980), and Nairobi (1985), moving women to the forefront of policy considerations. These conferences served as training grounds for a new leadership by bringing hundreds of women, from around the world, into the public policy process and ensuring, in many countries, the presence of a new mass of women with political clout. The conferences also came to be seen as the birth of global feminism. The NGO Alternative Global Report stated that it was clear, from the growth of conferences and their resolutions, that a global women's movement had been created, setting in motion 'nothing less than a revolution' worldwide (CONGO 2000).

The 1990s saw efforts by the UN system to create an integrated global agenda for development. These were designed to open the eyes of the world to the interconnections among issues such as the environment, human rights, population, and social development. And there was a clear recognition that the goals of the global agenda "are all dependent upon the advancement of women" (United Nations 1995). The Platform for Action developed at the 1995 Fourth World Conference on Women in Beijing has been described by Secretary-General Kofi Annan as "among the most important that we will undertake in this Millennium year," and he put the

FIGURE 9-4

Human Rights Index, 1999

Ten Best

1 Tuvalu
2 Luxembourg
3 San Marino
4 Monaco
5 Finland
6 Netherlands
7 New Zealand
8 Tonga
9 Canada
10 Botswana

Ten Worst

185 Pakistan
186 Yugoslavia (Federal Republic)
187 Indonesia
188 Sudan
189 North Korea
190 Egypt
191 Sierra Leone
192 Algeria
193 Burundi
194 Rwanda
195 Democratic Republic of Congo

Canada is in the top 10 out of 195 nations.

Source: Observer 1999.

world on notice that "the future of this planet depends on women" (United Nations 2000; Pietila 2002).

Policy Initiatives

Human rights come wrapped up in international diplomacy. For that reason, many national policymakers hesitate to interfere in human rights issues, especially if they conflict with what are regarded as more pressing national concerns. Stepping up to fill the gap are international organizations such as the United Nations and nongovernmental organizations (NGOs) like *Médecins sans frontières* and Amnesty International. Most initiatives come from these international bodies.

Médecins sans frontières (Doctors Without Borders), the world's largest independent emergency medical aid organization, won the 1999 Nobel Peace Prize for its work in countries worldwide. Founded in 1971 and based in Paris, the organization has 5000 doctors and nurses working in 80 countries. "Our intention is to highlight current upheavals, to bear witness to foreign tragedies and reflect on the principles of humanitarian aid," explains Dr. Rony Brauman, the organization's president (Spielmann 1992:12; also see Daley 1999).

Among the endangered peoples of the world are many indigenous (native or tribal) peoples whose settlement preceded immigration from other countries and colonialism. They include nomadic Bedouins of the Arabic peninsula, the Inuit of North America, the Sami (or Lapp) of northern Scandinavia, the Ainu of Japan, the Aborigines of Australia, and Brazil's Yanomani Indians. Indigenous peoples are organizing to defend their way of life, assisted by voluntary associations in the core industrialized nations. As one result of this activism, the United Nations has established a working group to draft a Universal Declaration of the Right of Indigenous Peoples (Durning 1993).

Amnesty International monitors human rights violations around the world. Founded in 1966, the organization has chapters in many countries and 67 000 members in Canada alone. It works for the release of men and women detained for their conscientiously held beliefs, their colour, ethnic origin, sex, religion, or language—provided they have neither used nor advocated violence. The winner of the 1977 Nobel Prize for Peace, Amnesty International opposes all forms of torture and capital punishment and advocates prompt trials of all political prisoners.

Women's rights got a boost from the World Conference on Women. In 1995 the conference delegates agreed on a "platform of action" calling on governments around the world to improve the status of girls, better the economic situation of women, and protect women from increasing levels of violence.

In recent years, there has been growing awareness of a sizeable minority of the world's population that continues to be denied the full membership in the human family that the Universal Declaration of Human Rights (UDHR) affirms. Many governments around the world continue to avoid affirming rights for their gay and lesbian citizens. The conspiracy of silence around the abuses and repression of this population is being broken by a vocal movement that has emerged, resulting in some notable achievements. In December 2000, the European Union adopted a Charter of Fundamental Rights, which included sexual orientation among the prohibited grounds of discrimination. In 2001, Netherlands became

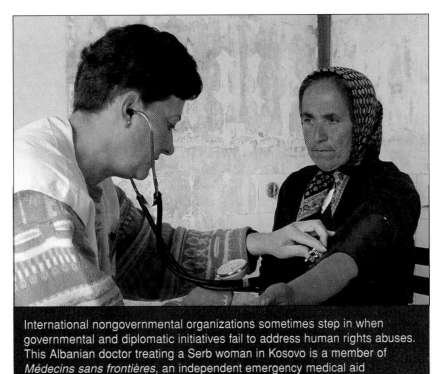

International nongovernmental organizations sometimes step in when governmental and diplomatic initiatives fail to address human rights abuses. This Albanian doctor treating a Serb woman in Kosovo is a member of *Médecins sans frontières*, an independent emergency medical aid organization.

the first state to allow same-sex couples to marry. In Colombia, conjugal visits were granted by the Supreme Court to a lesbian in prison and her partner. A South African court ruled that gay and lesbian couples could adopt children (Human Rights Watch 2002a).

While many countries are now implementing policies to ensure that the UDHR is applied to everyone, this is not universal. For example, in 1994 the United States implemented a "don't ask, don't tell, don't pursue" policy that prohibited discrimination against gays and lesbians in the military. Under the policy, military officials are not allowed to ask about a serviceperson's sexual orientation or to harass those suspected of being gay. However, according to Pentagon figures, there has been an increase rather than a reduction, in anti-gay harassment. From 1994 to 2000, more than 6500 servicemembers were discharged under the policy, with a record number of 1231 during 2000, an average of three to four people every day. This represents an 86 percent increase in dismissals since the "don't ask, don't tell" policy was implemented (Human Rights Watch 2002c).

Amnesty International monitors human rights abuses against sexual orientation and reports on them.

It states that "Lesbian and gay rights belong on the human rights agenda because if we tolerate the denial of rights to any minority, we undermine the whole protective framework of human rights. . . . When governments ignore their responsibility towards one sector of society, then no one's human rights are safe" (Amnesty International 2001). We'll look at lesbian and gay rights in more detail in Chapter 20.

Ethnic cleansing in the former Yugoslavia; human rights violations in Iraq, Iran, and Sudan; persecution of the Aborigines of Australia and other indigenous peoples; violence against women inside and outside the family; governmental torture of lesbians and gay men—all these are vivid reminders that social inequality today can have life-and-death consequences. Universal human rights remain an ideal and not a reality.

Let's Discuss

1. Why are there varying definitions of human rights?
2. Does it surprise you that Canada ranks so highly in human rights compared to the U.S. (Figure 9-4)? Why do you think this is the case?
3. How have feminist groups broadened the debate over universal human rights?

● Chapter Resources

Summary

We can easily see worldwide stratification both in the gap between rich and poor nations and in the inequality *within* countries around the world. This chapter examines stratification within the world economic system, the impact of multinational corporations on developing countries, modernization, and the distribution of wealth and income in various nations.

1. As of 1995, the 140 developing nations accounted for 78 percent of the world's population but only 16 percent of all wealth.
2. Former colonized nations are kept in a subservient position, subject to foreign domination, through the process of *neocolonialism.*
3. Drawing on the conflict perspective, the world systems analysis of sociologist Immanuel Wallerstein views the global economic system as divided between nations that control wealth (*core nations*)

and those from which capital is taken (*periphery nations*).
4. According to *dependency theory,* even as developing countries make economic advances, they remain weak and subservient to core nations and corporations within an increasingly intertwined global economy.
5. *Multinational corporations* bring jobs and industry to developing nations, but they also tend to exploit the workers there in order to maximize profits.
6. Many sociologists are quick to note that terms such as *modernization* and even *development* contain an ethnocentric bias.
7. According to *modernization theory,* development in peripheral countries will be assisted by the innovations transferred from the industrialized world.

8. Social mobility is more limited in developing nations than in the core nations.
9. While Mexico is unquestionably a poor country, the gap between its richest and poorest citizens is one of the widest in the world.
10. The subordinate status of Mexico's Indians is but one reflection of the nation's colour hierarchy, which links social class to the appearance of racial purity.
11. Growing recognition of the *borderlands* reflects the increasingly close and complex relationship between Mexico and the United States.
12. *Human rights* need to be identified and abuses of these rights need to be corrected in all countries, throughout the world.

Critical Thinking Questions

1. In what ways is the informal economy evident in your university community and in the city or town where you grew up? Drawing on the functionalist, feminist, conflict, and interactionist perspectives, analyze the informal economy as you have seen it in these communities.
2. Imagine that you had the opportunity to spend a year in Mexico studying inequality in that nation. How would you draw on the research designs of sociology (surveys, observation, experiments, existing sources) to better understand and document stratification in Mexico?
3. How active should the Canadian government be in addressing violations of human rights in other countries? At what point, if any, does concern for human rights turn into ethnocentrism by failing to respect the distinctive norms, values, and customs of another culture?

Key Terms

Borderlands The area of a common culture along the border between Mexico and the United States. (249)

Colonialism The maintenance of political, social, economic, and cultural dominance over a people by a foreign power for an extended period of time. (234)

Dependency theory An approach that contends that industrialized nations continue to exploit developing countries for their own gain. (236)

Human rights Universal moral rights belonging to all people because they are human. (251)

Informal economy Transfers of money, goods, or services that are not reported to the government. (244)

Modernization The far-reaching process by which peripheral nations move from traditional or less developed institutions to those characteristic of more developed societies. (239)

Modernization theory A functionalist approach that proposes that modernization and development will gradually improve the lives of people in peripheral nations. (239)

Multinational corporations Commercial organizations that, while headquartered in one country, own or control other corporations and subsidiaries throughout the world. (236)

Neocolonialism Continuing dependence of former colonies on foreign countries. (234)

World systems analysis A view of the global economic system as divided between certain industrialized nations that control wealth and developing countries that are controlled and exploited. (236)

Additional Readings

BOOKS

Dollar, David, and Paul Collier. 2001. *Globalization, Growth, and Poverty: Building an Inclusive World Economy.* Toronto: Oxford University Press and World Bank. This report focuses on globalization in terms of growing economic integration resulting from the increased flow of goods, services, people, capital, and information. It is primarily concerned with the effect that this has on economic growth and poverty reduction.

LaFeber, Walter. 1999. *Michael Jordan and the New Global Capitalism.* New York: W.W. Norton. Considers the growing intersection of culture and capital on an international scale.

Teeple, Gary. 2000. *Globalization and the Decline of Social Reform: Into the Twenty-First Century.* Aurora, ON: Garamond Press. This is a study of how globalization negatively impacts and destabilizes the conditions that had once supported social democracy. It delves into the historical background that led to this new agenda.

Waring, Marilyn. 1988. *If Women Counted: A New Feminist Economics.* San Francisco: Harper and Row. Waring, a social scientist from New Zealand, considers how women's labour is overlooked in the global economy.

Weigard, Bruce. 1992. *Off the Books: A Theory and Critique of the Underground Economy.* Dix Hills, N.Y.: General-Hall. An examination of the social consequence of people's participation in activities outside the mainstream economy.

The World Bank. *World Development Report.* New York: Oxford University Press. Published annually by the International Bank for Reconstruction and Development (the United Nations agency more commonly referred to as the World Bank), this volume provides a vast array of social and economic indicators regarding world development.

JOURNALS

Among the journals that consider issues of worldwide stratification, uneven development, and universal human rights are *Holocaust and Genocide Studies* (founded in 1987), *Human Rights Quarterly* (1978), *International Journal of Urban and Regional Research* (1976), *International Labor Review* (1921), *Journal of Developing Areas* (1965), *Latin American Research Review* (1956), *Review of Income and Wealth* (1954), and *World Development* (1973).

Internet Connection

www.mcgrawhill.ca/college/schaefer

*For additional Internet exercises relating to social inequality worldwide, visit the Schaefer Online Learning Centre at **http://www.mcgrawhill.ca/college/schaefer**. Please note that while the URLs listed were current at the time of printing, these sites often change—check the Online Learning Centre for updates.*

Universal human rights have become a major concern for politicians, sociologists, and activist groups. Direct your web browser to (**http://headlines.yahoo.com/Full_Coverage/World/Human_Rights/**) and learn about recent events in the area of human rights.

(a) What news stories dominate the headlines?

(b) Does it appear that human rights are more or less being respected according to these headlines? What examples can you give to support your answer?

(c) According to the Universal Declaration of Human Rights, what rights should all persons enjoy? Can you think of any to add to this list?

(d) Which rights do you feel are the most important? Why?

(e) What examples from your text or from current events show violation of any of these specific human rights?

(f) According to the Human Rights Watch World Report 2000, how well does Canada do in respecting universal human rights? What might improve matters in Canada?

(g) What is Amnesty International? When and why was it founded? What are its goals and mission statements? What are its current campaigns?

(h) What role might television and the Internet play in improving the observance of human rights?

LOOK BEYOND COLOUR

E·R·A·C·I·S·M

Eracism is a community-based program aimed at eliminating racial and ethnic discrimination through education. One of Eracism's initiatives is to raise awareness of March 21 as the International Day for the Elimination of Racial Discrimination.

[M]any Canadians] have shown themselves prepared to own up to sins of intolerance. In a short time, they have built a nation that is multicultural, generous and respected throughout the world. They have done so, in part, by manifesting a willingness to confront racism and hatred and stamp them out in whatever form they appear.

Stamping out white supremacy, anti-Semitism, homophobia and their variants unfortunately will not be easy. At this stage in Canada's history, a number of forces are conspiring to assist racist leaders. Memories, for one, are fading: the horrors of World War Two become increasingly remote with the death of each Holocaust survivor, and Holocaust deniers are attempting to promote a more benign view of past events. In addition, harsh economic realities are crushing the hopes and dreams of a generation—and pushing some of these young people towards the simplistic siren song of hate. Finally, with changing immigration patterns, Canadians are being forced to come to grips with the presence of growing numbers of visible minorities—and they are being asked to accommodate lifestyles and cultural differences that, at first blush, seem strange. The pollsters tell us that all of these things, rightly or wrongly, have left many Canadians feeling insecure, threatened and under siege. And onto the stage have stepped the Klansmen and the neo-Nazis, with their calls for a return to the so-called status quo—and to a time when things were supposedly better for "white" Canadians.

That is not all: racist leaders are aided ironically by advances in technology. With the investment of only a few hundred dollars, they can spread their hateful messages with impunity. They can do so across national and international borders, far from the eyes of police agencies, using computer bulletin boards, fax machines and the like. Increasingly, too, the Canadian ultra-rightists are co-operating with each other. At rallies, conferences and on telephone lines, they are coming together as never before to recruit, attack minorities and propagandize. A good example of the effectiveness of their networking is found in the case of schoolteacher Malcolm Ross. The Moncton resident claims to be a lone dissenting voice in the proverbial wilderness. In fact, he is beneficiary of the attentions of hundreds of neo-Nazis across Canada, the United States and Europe.

Who is susceptible to the recruitment techniques of these hate-mongers? Their numbers include the unemployed, the disenfranchised and, most significantly, the young people who have been marginalized by chronic unemployment and society's increasing selfishness. Among these newcomers to racism we see, for example, the skinheads, who bring a fondness for violence that defies comprehension.

Every citizen of this country must work—and work hard—at maintaining the multicultural society that is Canada. Using the law, using the eduction system, we must remain vigilant. Canadian racist leaders are better organized, better funded and better united than they have been at any time in our history. If we do not fight organized racism for ourselves, then we must do it for our children—because it is the hearts and minds of our children, after all, that the racist leaders are determined to keep. *(Kinsella 1994)* ■

ome people believe that Canada, with its multiculturalism and strong reputation as a haven for refugees, is immune to the kinds of hate-based activities usually associated with the anti-Semitism of the Nazis, the apartheid regimes of South Africa, and the pre–civil rights era in the United States. Warren Kinsella, a Toronto-based lawyer, political consultant, and author of *Web of Hate*, challenges that complacency in his analysis of the growth and persistence of far-right supremacist groups in this country. Kinsella makes it clear that while tolerance may be a defining feature of Canadian society, it is not embraced by all Canadians.

This chapter will focus on the Canadian experience, and the implications of a history dominated by a white, anglo majority. Canada has moved significantly in recent decades to embrace the principles outlined in the first multiculturalism policy set within a bilingual framework in 1971, with important implications for the so-called Charter Groups—French and English—as well as for the myriad of minorities that live in Canada today.

We begin by identifying the basic characteristics of a minority group and distinguishing between racial and ethnic groups. The next section of the chapter will examine the dynamics of prejudice and discrimination. After considering the functionalist, conflict, interactionist, and feminist perspectives on race and ethnicity, we'll take a look at patterns of intergroup relations, particularly in Canada. Finally, the social policy section will explore issues related to immigration worldwide. ■

Minority, Racial, and Ethnic Groups

Sociologists frequently distinguish between racial and ethnic groups. The term ***racial group*** is used to describe a group that is set apart from others because of visible physical differences. Whites, blacks, First Nations people, and Asians are all considered racial groups in Canada. While race does turn on physical differences, it is the culture of a particular society that constructs and attaches social significance to these differences, as we will see later. Unlike racial groups, an ***ethnic group*** is set apart from others primarily because of its national origin or distinctive cultural patterns. In Canada, French Canadians, Jews, and Italian Canadians are all categorized as ethnic groups. As we will learn later in the chapter, ethnic distinctions sometimes reflect the dominant culture's construction of racial categories. For example, white Canadians may classify Chinese, Korean, Japanese, and Vietnamese Canadians as "Asian," thus obscuring the important differences among these groups.

Race and ethnicity are quite different, with one being based on physical biological characteristics and the other being based on cultural distinctions. Yet, as Richard Goldsby stated, sometimes the two go together. For example, Indo-Canadians have visible nonwhite physical characteristics and, for those who continue their traditional practices, they have distinctive cultural attributes as well. But one should not confuse race and ethnicity. Jews, for example, may be described as a race by some, yet it is their religious practices that make them distinctive; therefore, sociologically, they are considered an ethnic group (Goldsby 1977). While the physical characteristics that constitute a race cannot be changed, ethnicity can be altered to a greater degree. As we will see later in the chapter, assimilation occurs when a person takes on the cultural practices of another ethnic group, thereby taking on a new ethnic identity.

Canada is a multicultural society in which members of minority groups are encouraged to maintain their distinctness within the larger national mosaic. This contrasts with the melting pot model in the United States, where minorities are expected to assume the American identity while adding their particular cultural flavour to the pot. Differentiating by race is, therefore, a greater part of the political and social experience in the United States, while Canada's policies focus more on ethnicity and on bilingualism within a multicultural environment.

Minority Groups

A numerical minority is any group that makes up less than half of some larger population. The population of Canada includes thousands of numerical minorities, including television actors, green-eyed people, tax lawyers, and descendants of United Empire loyalists. However, these numerical minorities are not considered to be minorities in the sociological sense; in fact, the number of people in a group does not necessarily determine its status as a social minority (or dominant group). When sociologists define a minority group, they are primarily concerned with the economic and political power, or powerlessness, of that group. A ***minority group*** is a subordinate group whose members have significantly less control or power over their own lives than the

www.mcgrawhill.ca/college/schaefer

members of a dominant or majority group have over theirs.

Sociologists have identified five basic properties of a minority group—unequal treatment, physical or cultural traits, ascribed status, solidarity, and in-group marriage (Wagley and Harris 1958):

1. Members of a minority group experience unequal treatment as compared to members of a dominant group. For example, the management of an apartment complex may refuse to rent to Jamaican or Chinese Canadians. Social inequality may be created or maintained by prejudice, discrimination, segregation, or even extermination.

2. Members of a minority group share physical or cultural characteristics that distinguish them from the dominant group. Each society arbitrarily decides which characteristics are most important in defining the groups.

3. Membership in a minority (or dominant) group is not voluntary; people are born into the group. Thus, race and ethnicity are considered *ascribed* statuses.

p. 117

4. Minority group members have a strong sense of group solidarity. William Graham Sumner, writing in 1906, noted that people make distinctions between members of their own group (the *in-group*) and everyone else (the *out-group*). When a group is the object of long-term prejudice and discrimination, the feeling of "us versus them" can and often does become extremely intense.

p. 144

5. Members of a minority generally marry others from the same group. A member of a dominant group is often unwilling to marry into a supposedly inferior minority. In addition, the minority group's sense of solidarity encourages marriages within the group and discourages marriages to outsiders.

Race

The term *racial group* refers to those minorities (and the corresponding dominant groups) set apart from others by visible physical differences. It is important to remember, however, that while the physical differences may be visible, the concept of race has no basis in science. Studies of the human genome have confirmed that in fact all humans share the same set of biological ancestors. Nonetheless, the social consequences associated with how a culture depicts race are very real. Each society determines which differences are important while ignoring other characteristics that could serve as a basis for social differentiation. In Canada, we see differences in both skin colour and hair colour. Yet people learn

informally that differences in skin colour have a dramatic social and political meaning, while differences in hair colour do not.

When observing skin colour, people in Canada tend to lump others rather casually into such categories as "black," "white," and "Asian." More subtle differences in skin colour often go unnoticed. However, this is not the case in other societies. Many nations of Central America and South America have colour gradients distinguishing people on a continuum from light to dark skin colour. Brazil has approximately 40 colour groupings, while in other countries people may be described as "Mestizo Hondurans," "Mulatto Colombians," or "African Panamanians." What we see as "visible" differences, then, are subject to each society's social definitions.

The largest racial minorities in Canada since the 1800s have comprised three groups: people of Chinese descent, South Asians, and blacks. Figure 10-1 illustrates the changes in the racial and ethnic backgrounds (determined by place of birth) of immigrants to three of Canada's largest cities, from pre-1961 to the early 1990s. By 2001, people of Chinese descent made up 26 percent of all racial minorities in Canada. South Asians and blacks make up 23 percent and 17 percent of the total.

Biological Significance of Race

Viewed from a biological perspective, the term *race* would refer to a genetically isolated group with distinctive gene frequencies. But it is impossible to define or identify such a group scientifically. Contrary to popular belief, there are no "pure races." Nor are there physical traits—whether skin colour or baldness—that can be used to describe one group to the exclusion of all others. If scientists examine a smear of human blood under a microscope, they cannot tell whether it came from a person whose ancestors immigrated to Canada from Kenya or Sweden or Thailand. There is, in fact, more genetic variation *within* races than across them.

Migration, exploration, and invasion have led to intermingling of races. In Canada, the most significant racial exogamy (marriage outside one's own racial or ethnic group), took place in the Red River Valley in what is now Manitoba. There, men of French-Canadian ancestry known as the voyageurs married First Nations women, and the **Metis** were born. While the first of these relationships, begun in the mid-1700s, were the product of economic interdependence, the Metis as a group emerged to take an important place in the exploration and political evolution of the country.

Some people would like to find biological explanations to help social scientists understand why certain peoples of the world have come to dominate others (see the discussion of sociobiology in p. 92

FIGURE 10-1

Percentage of Immigrants from Top 10 Places of Birth

A. Montreal: Pre-1961

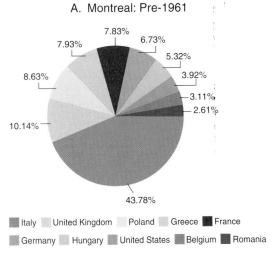

7.83%
6.73%
5.32%
3.92%
3.11%
2.61%
43.78%
10.14%
8.63%
7.93%

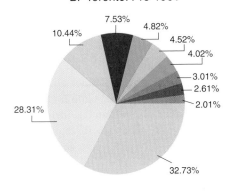

Italy | United Kingdom | Poland | Greece | France
Germany | Hungary | United States | Belgium | Romania

Montreal: 1990s

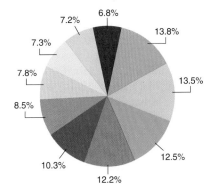

6.8%
13.8%
13.5%
12.5%
12.2%
10.3%
8.5%
7.8%
7.3%
7.2%

Morocco | Romania | Philippines | India | Sri Lanka
Haiti | China | Algeria | France | Lebanon

B. Toronto: Pre-1961

7.53%
4.82%
4.52%
4.02%
3.01%
2.61%
2.01%
32.73%
28.31%
10.44%

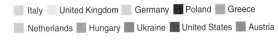

Italy | United Kingdom | Germany | Poland | Greece
Netherlands | Hungary | Ukraine | United States | Austria

Toronto: 1990s

18.6%
17.9%
12.0%
12.0%
11.0%
8.6%
5.5%
5.2%
4.7%
4.5%

Iran | Poland | Guyana | China | India
Philippines | Hong Kong | Sri Lanka | Pakistan | Jamaica

C. Vancouver: Pre-1961

8.24%
4.02%
3.92%
3.72%
3.62%
2.11%
40.60%
14.67%
9.85%
9.25%

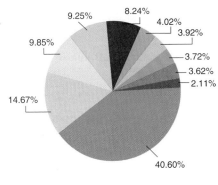

United Kingdom | Germany | Italy | Netherlands | China
Poland | Hungary | United States | Denmark | Austria

Vancouver: 1990s

2.5%
2.5%
2.7%
5.0%
6.0%
10.4%
12.3%
15.4%
19.7%
23.6%

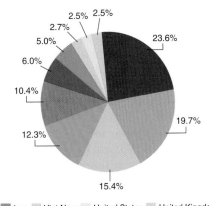

Iran | Viet Nam | United States | United Kingdom | China
Hong Kong | Taiwan | India | Philippines | South Korea

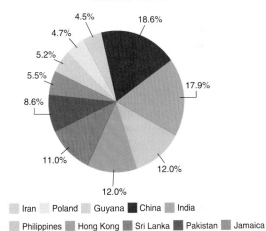

Source: Compiled by Edith Smith based on data from Statistics Canada 2001 Census Tables, 2003a.

Chapter 4). Given the absence of pure racial groups, there can be no satisfactory biological answers for such social and political questions.

Social Construction of Race

Although the characteristics we interpret as race (i.e., skin colour, hair texture, etc.) are genetically determined, culture plays an important role in their implications. In Canada, we have created many racial categories including First Nations, Asian, black, and white. One of the ironies of race as a category is that the majority group that establishes the designations—in the case of Canada, whites—often fails to recognize its own "whiteness" as a racial category. In other words, white Canadians do not have their social identities racialized. At the same time, despite the fact that there are significant differences among the various national and ethnic identities grouped under "First Nations," "Asian," and "black," they are used pervasively in Canadian society. On the eastern edge of the Pacific Rim, for example, Asian countries have populations as physically and culturally distinct from one group to another as Italians are from Swedes. Obscuring these differences to create a single category labelled "Asians" reflects a white bias.

The debate over the biological validity of race has raged for centuries. A number of different theories have emerged claiming distinct origins for peoples who share certain physical characteristics. Just recently, however, the Human Genome Project finished mapping the human genetic profile, and scientists have gathered clear evidence that we all share a common set of ancestors. This confirms that race is indeed a social construction. However, the fact that the term *race* is socially constructed and has limitations does not diminish its social significance.

A dominant or majority group has the power not only to define itself legally but to define a society's values. Sociologist William I. Thomas (1923), an early critic of theories of racial and gender differences, saw that the "definition of the situation" could mould the personality of the individual. To put it another way, Thomas, writing from the interactionist perspective, observed that people respond not only to the objective features of a situation or person but also to the *meaning* that situation or person has for them. Thus, we can create false images or stereotypes that become real in their consequences. *Stereotypes* are unreliable generalizations about all members of a group that do not recognize individual differences within the group.

In the last 30 years, critics have pointed out the power of the mass media to perpetuate false racial and ethnic stereotypes. Television is a prime example: Almost all the leading dramatic roles are cast as whites, even in urban-based programs like *Friends*. Blacks tend to be featured mainly in crime-based dramas. In Canada, one example of the media's role in distorting reality is its portrayal of the Doukhobor culture as discussed in Box 10-3, on page 286.

Self-Fulfilling Prophecy

In certain situations, we may respond to stereotypes in such a way that false definitions end up being accurate. In this phenomenon, called the *self-fulfilling prophecy*, a person or group that is described as having particular characteristics begins to display those very traits. When teachers and counsellors tell a bright child from a working-class family that he would make a good carpenter or mechanic, for instance, they may discourage him from thinking of university or a profession. Seeing himself through their eyes as a tradesperson, he may well grow up to become a blue-collar worker. In assessing the impact of self-fulfilling prophecies, we can refer back to labelling theory, which emphasizes how a person comes to be labelled as deviant and even to accept a self-image of deviance. p. 179

Caribana, which takes place each year in Toronto, is one of the largest celebrations of West Indian culture and arts in North America. The 18-day festival concludes with a massive tribute to the islands and their peoples on the first Monday in August.

Self-fulfilling prophecies can be especially devastating for minority groups (see Figure 10-2). The dominant group in a society believes that subordinate group members lack the ability to perform in important and lucrative positions. So it denies them the training needed to become scientists, executives, or physicians, effectively locking the subordinate group into society's inferior jobs. The false definition has become real: in terms of employment, the minority has become inferior because it was originally defined as inferior and was prevented from achieving equality.

Because of this vicious circle, talented people from minority groups may come to see the worlds of entertainment and professional sports as their only hope for achieving wealth and fame. It is no accident that successive waves of Irish, Jewish, Italian, black, and Hispanic performers and athletes have made their mark on North American society. Unfortunately, these very successes may convince the dominant group that its original stereotypes are valid—that these are the *only* areas of society in which minorities can excel (Allport 1979; Merton 1968).

Minorities do not always passively accept harmful stereotypes and self-fulfilling prophecies. In the 1960s and 1970s, many subordinate minorities in the United States rejected traditional definitions and replaced them with feelings of pride, power, and strength. "Black is beautiful" and "Red power" movements among Blacks and Native Americans were efforts to take control of their own lives and self-images. However, although a minority can make a determined effort to redefine a situation and resist stereotypes, the definition that remains most important is the one used by a society's powerful groups. In this sense, the historic white, Anglo-Saxon, Protestant norms

of Canada still shape the definitions and stereotypes of racial and ethnic minorities. The power of race to be a defining characteristic even shows up in societies that seem outwardly homogeneous, as Box 10-1 shows.

Ethnicity

Whereas race is attributed on the basis of physical features, ethnicity is a reflection of cultural affiliation. An ethnic group may share language, religion, and/or cultural practice. As with race, ethnicity is subjectively assigned by one group to another, or assumed by a group as an identity. Canadian sociologist John Porter (1965) was one of the first to recognize the limiting potential when distinct ethnic identities compose a single society.

As noted earlier, the distinction made between racial and ethnic minorities is not always clear. For example, citizens of Canada who are labelled as racially "black" do not share a common culture. Some come from the developing nations of Africa and the Caribbean, while others come from the more technologically advanced societies like the United States and England. The physical characteristics that have led them to be assigned to a racial group have no impact on their ethnic heritage, the cultural standards to which they were socialized. This is an ethnically diverse population. However, the consequences of being perceived as a member of a minority racial group are clear. Members of racial minorities have less access to both opportunity and status.

Another example in Canada relates to peoples from Asia, some of whom are referred to collectively as Indo-Canadians, while others are designated simply as coming from Asian cultural heritage. Both designations

FIGURE 10-2

The Self-Fulfilling Prophecy

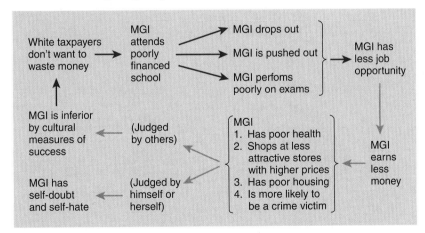

The self-validating effects of definitions made by the dominant group are shown in this figure. A minority group individual attends a poorly financed school and is left unequipped to perform jobs that offer high status and high pay. He or she then gets a low-paying job and must settle for a lifestyle far short of society's standards. Since the person shares these standards, he or she may begin to feel self-doubt and self-hatred. This last phase of the cycle has been called into question in recent research.

Note: MGI stands for "minority group individual." Arrows represent direction of negative cumulative effect.

Source: Schaefer 2000:21.

Sociology in the Global Community

10-1 Social Construction of Race and Ethnicity in Japan

To those who watched the 1998 Winter Olympics in Nagano, those who tour Japan, and those who do business there from abroad, Japan seems very homogeneous, with outward civility to all races or nationalities.

This picture of tolerance, however, disguises significant inequality along racial and ethnic lines in Japan. These distinctions may be difficult to discern because, after all, 96 percent of the population is Japanese, but for the racial and ethnic minorities, the historical and contemporary discrimination is very real. The largest minority is the Burakumins, followed by resident Koreans. The 2 million Burakumins represent an interesting case because physically they are indistinguishable from the Japanese. Their ancestors were part of the lowest group in a quasi-caste system originating four centuries ago, and they have lived in segregated communities ever since. Identified by their station in life and viewed as a distinct socially constructed race, the Burakumins continue to face discrimination in marriage, employment, and education, as well as other areas. One study showed that one-third declared their rights were being violated in such areas as work, school, or choosing a marriage partner. It is not unusual for employers or families to hire private detectives if they suspect a prospective employee or in-law is a Burakumin. In 1969, the Japanese government passed legislation

to counter discrimination and provided special incentives to increase the numbers of Burakumins continuing their schooling. Despite these efforts, a variety of groups today find it necessary to work on behalf of the Burakumins. Some use established policymaking channels, while others take much more militant positions.

> It is not unusual for employers or families to hire private detectives if they suspect a prospective employee or in-law is a Burakumin.

There has also been growing controversy concerning Japan's treatment of its Korean minority—a more visible subordinate group to outsiders. About 700 000 Koreans live in Japan, of whom more than 85 percent were born there. It is not easy for Koreans to obtain Japanese citizenship; without citizenship, they cannot vote, cannot work as teachers or government officials, and must carry alien registration cards at all times. Only about half of the Korean males finish high school, compared to 97 percent of the general population.

Koreans in Japan disproportionately work for low wages, without safety standards, and without any real hope of advancement. Moreover, because discrimination is so common,

fewer than 5 percent of Koreans use their own names in business circles. Similarly, many young Koreans use Japanese aliases to conceal their heritage in schools.

Over time, the government of Japan has taken a more conciliatory attitude toward resident Koreans. In 1993, after years of bitter debate, Japan's parliament agreed to end the mandatory fingerprinting of most Koreans and other foreign residents required under the nation's Alien Registration Law. Nevertheless, Korean residents—many of whose families have lived in Japan for generations—still have no right to work in government jobs or to learn about their heritage in public schools. The nation's Supreme Court did rule in 1995 that local governments could permit resident Koreans to vote. Though this step was hailed as a major victory, there is little movement to make it a national policy.

Let's Discuss

1. Has anyone in your family ever been denied a job or an education because of his or her race or ethnicity? If so, explain the circumstances.

2. Did one of your ancestors ever change the family surname to escape discrimination based on ethnicity? If so, when and under what circumstances? Did the change make a difference in your family's social standing?

Sources: Kerbo and McKinstry 1998; T. Neary 1997; Sugimoto 1997.

encompass a variety of religious, linguistic, and cultural standards. While grouping them all under one label is a convenient classification, as we will see shortly, it encourages stereotyping and obscures important differences. As well, it fails to show the reality that many Canadians are of mixed ethnic ancestry. Table 10-1 profiles the top 25 ethnic origins in Canada according to the 2001 Census,

which asked people to provide their ethnic origins. One could choose more than one response to the question. The table illustrates that the ethnic groups that have intermingled the most tend to be from Western and Northern Europe, while the populations from Asia and Southern Europe tended to give single responses to the question on ethnic origins.

Table 10-1 Top 25 Ethnic Origins in Canada, Single and Multiple Responses, 2001 Census

Total population = 29 639 035

Ethnic origins	Total responses	Single responses	Multiple responses
1. Canadian	11 626 680	6 748 135	4 934 550
2. English	5 978 875	1 479 520	4 499 355
3. French	4 668 410	1 060 755	3 607 655
4. Scottish	4 157 210	607 235	3 549 975
5. Irish	3 822 660	496 865	3 325 800
6. German	2 742 765	705 595	2 037 170
7. Italian	1 270 370	726 275	544 090
8. Chinese	1 094 700	936 210	158 490
9. Ukrainian	1 071 060	326 200	744 860
10. North American Indian	1 000 890	455 805	545 085
11. Dutch (Netherlands)	923 310	316 220	607 090
12. Polish	817 085	260 415	556 670
13. East Indian	713 330	581 665	131 665
14. Norwegian	363 760	47 230	316 530
15. Portuguese	357 690	252 853	104 855
16. Welsh	350 365	28 445	321 925
17. Jewish	348 605	186 475	162 130
18. Russian	337 960	70 890	267 070
19. Filipino	327 545	266 140	61 410
20. Métis	307 845	72 210	235 635
21. Swedish	282 760	30 440	252 320
22. Hungarian (Magyar)	267 255	91 795	175 460
23. American (USA)	250 010	25 200	224 805
24. Greek	215 105	143 780	71 320
25. Spanish	213 100	66 545	146 555

Source: Statistics Canada, 2003i.

In his 1965 classic, *The Vertical Mosaic*, Porter characterized the diversity of Canadian society as a mosaic resembling a tiled floor, in which each piece is distinct, but nonetheless forms part of a larger whole. Porter characterized the Canadian mosaic as "vertical," by which he implied that the ethnic distinctions that define Canadians make it easy to discriminate against minorities. In other words, encouraging immigrants to Canada to maintain their ethnic distinctiveness makes it easier to slot them into one of the lower levels of the mosaic.

Characteristics of Ethnicity

Beyond the basic elements of shared customs, religion, language, and ancestry, ethnicity has four significant characteristics.

1. *Ethnic affiliation is handed down from generation to generation.* An ethnic group must have the capacity to pass on its standards of behaviour and moral and ethical foundations, as well as its material culture. The stronger the ties within the group, the better the ability of its members to instill in their children the beliefs and expectations of their culture.

2. *Ethnicity is an ascribed status.* A child is born with a cultural identity defined by the ethnicity of his or her parents. And while it may be possible to change one's citizenship, it is difficult to change one's ethnicity. Even though it is possible to abandon cultural origins, as in the case of someone who renounces the religion practised by his or her parents, original ethnic linkage remains part of one's identity.

3. *The structures of an ethnic community—its institutions, roles, and distribution of power—evolve over many generations*, and are the product of social interaction and interdependence. Particularly important to the survival of any ethnic group is its capacity to provide for its members.

    Institutional completeness refers to the degree to which an ethnic community is able to provide for its own institutional needs, particularly in the key areas of religion, education, and social welfare. History has shown that those groups that have been able to remain institutionally independent have a better chance of maintaining the integrity of their community.

4. *Ethnic identity can only be established if its institutions and standards are different enough from other groups to provide members with a sense of distinctiveness.* The concept of **social distance** refers to the amount

of difference that exists between two cultures. For example, there is very little social distance between the cultures of the United States and Canada. The more established the ethnicity, the clearer are those lines of demarcation, and, as a consequence, the easier it is to define membership. The fact that both the U.S. and Canada derive from the same source—Anglo-Saxon, Christian, British traditions—explains their similarities and lack of social distance.

Social Construction of Ethnicity

We have already talked about how race is socially constructed. Ethnicity is effected by a similar process. The designation of a particular group as "ethnic" can be as much a function of that group's treatment within a given society as it is of any real or imagined cultural divide. A number of such groups have emerged in Canada, including the Doukhobors. While they are a Christian group from Eastern Europe, not unlike many others who came to Canada in the late 1800s and early 1900s to settle the land in the West, these Russian immigrants have been singled out for harsh treatment by authorities because of their fervent adherence to religious doctrine. As with race, ethnicity is important within a society only when the dominant culture makes it so.

Despite categorization problems, sociologists continue to feel that the distinction between racial groups and ethnic groups is socially significant. That is because in most societies, including Canada, physical differences tend to be more visible than ethnic differences. Partly as a result of this fact, stratification along racial lines is more resistant to change than stratification along ethnic lines. Members of an ethnic minority sometimes can become, over time, indistinguishable from the majority—although this process may take generations and may never include all members of the group. By contrast, members of a racial minority find it much more difficult to blend in with the larger society and to gain acceptance from the majority.

Prejudice and Discrimination

As the full impact of the events of September 11, 2001, began to sink in, people in the Western world, and Americans in particular, responded with calls for retribution. To their credit, public figures warned against rash responses. President George W. Bush was among the first to remind his country that terrorist acts had been carried out by extremists who did not represent the majority of Muslims. Despite the president's caution, attacks on Muslims, or even people thought to be Muslims, occurred. In one instance, a man wearing a turban,

mistaken by his attackers to be Muslim, was beaten to death. In Canada, concerns about similar acts of violence led Keith Norton, Chief Commissioner of the Ontario Human Rights Commission, to issue a statement reminding Ontarians that discrimination is against the law in that province. He urged people to guard against backlash, and to "... build bridges of goodwill and understanding" (Ontario Human Rights Commission 2001).

Prejudice is a negative attitude toward an entire category of people. The group may be race-based, ethnicity-based, or labelled as a social category defined by some other culturally relevant characteristic. A *social category* is a group defined by some culturally relevant characteristic; that is, one that has an impact on a person's status within a society. For example, your career puts you in a social category. If you are a doctor, you may be approached differently than if you are a labourer. Even seemingly trivial characteristics can have an effect. If you refuse to eat meat, you may be placed in a category that influences the way people perceive or treat you. Prejudice perpetuates inaccurate and often damaging characterizations, and is frequently the product of insufficient information.

When a prejudice involves the negative evaluation of someone based on an ethnic affiliation, it can be a product of *ethnocentrism*—the tendency to assume that one's own culture is better than all others. From this perspective, an individual evaluates other cultures by comparing them negatively to his or her own. In effect, the holder of the prejudice is saying: The standards of my culture are the right ones, and my beliefs and my morality are superior. This prejudice becomes discrimination when it translates into action.

One important and widespread form of prejudice is *racism*. Despite the obvious implications of the word, racism is not directed solely toward those with different skin colour or other physically distinguishing characteristics. It can also be based on ethnic indicators such as language and dress, informing an attitude that judges members as less deserving or less capable than those belonging to the dominant group (Stasiulis 1990).

As illustrated earlier, despite its image as a safe haven for international refugees, Canada is not without its hate groups that promote distrust and negative stereotypes of racial and ethnic minorities. The Ku Klux Klan has actively recruited new members in Canada for decades. In the 1920s, KKK membership in Saskatchewan was estimated at several thousand. Today, some of the leading figures of this organization have become visible in the media, including Jim Keegstra, the Alberta high school social studies teacher who taught Holocaust denial, and Wolfgang Droege, head of the ultra-right Heritage Front.

Muslim men stop to pray in the midst of a Muslim Day parade in Manhattan, New York. The Muslim population in the United States has increased dramatically over the past two decades, but is often misunderstood and stereotyped by the media.

In sum, it is clear from these findings that educational achievement at any level fails to protect persons of visible minority background from being disadvantaged in terms of the income they receive (Lian and Matthews 1997:475)

The study found that some groups have seen improvement in return on educational investment. For instance, by the early 1990s after 200 years as a significant majority in their own province of Quebec yet a significant minority in Canada, French Canadians finally reached a position of earning more than their counterparts of British heritage for the same level of education. The data also revealed a similar pattern for ethnic groups from Italy, Germany, and other parts of Europe.

However, Lian and Matthews found, such advances have not been enjoyed by all minority Canadians. Outcomes for those groups identified as "visible minorities with a racial identifier" were quite different. When compared to the non-visible minority population, Asians and individuals from the Middle East all gained less from having bachelor's, master's, or Ph.D. degrees. Even further down the return-on-human-capital scale were First Nations people, who remained at the bottom of the Canadian income hierarchy. Figure 10-3 shows the impact of one's racial group (RG) on income. University-educated Aboriginal people and visible minorities who are foreign-born (F-B) are almost twice as likely to be in the bottom income quintile as are whites and visible minorities born in Canada (C-B). At the other end of the income scale we see that whites are three times as likely to be in the top income quintile.

The conclusions reached by Lian and Matthews cast some doubt on Canadians' claim that our multiculturalist society is without racism. The study suggests that while Canadians may be tolerant of difference, that tolerance is conditional. We are apparently willing to accept cultural variation from diverse European sources, but are less willing to accept difference if it is expressed as skin colour or as greater social distance. Beginning with the question "Does the vertical mosaic still exist?", the researchers ended with another, more troubling query: "Is Canada a racist society?"

Whereas prejudice can be seen as an attitude, discrimination can be characterized as behaviour. ***Discrimination*** is the denying of opportunities and equal

While the activity of hate groups in Canada seems limited, with some estimates indicating that membership in hate organizations is less than 1000 for the whole country (Barrett 1987), there is growing concern about the potential threat posed by an explosion of Internet sites devoted to spreading race- and ethnicity-based prejudice. Websites on the Internet advocating hatred numbered at least 2000 as of 1999. Among these are the Zundelsite, promoting hatred of Jews, and the Heritage Front Resource Center, which offers an array of material in support of white nationalism. Court challenges to these sites have had varied success. In January 2002, the Canadian Human Rights Commission ordered the Zundelsite removed from the World Wide Web.

Particularly troubling are those sites disguised as video games for young people, or as "educational sites" about crusaders against prejudice, like Martin Luther King, Jr. The technology of the Internet has allowed race-hate groups to expand far beyond their traditional base in the southern United States (J. Sandberg 1999). It has also provided a platform for the worldwide distribution of material produced by anti-immigrant groups in Europe.

Discriminatory Behaviour

In 1997, Jason Lian and David Matthews published a study questioning whether John Porter's vertical mosaic still existed in Canada. The two researchers, from McMaster University and the University of British Columbia, respectively, came to the following conclusion:

FIGURE 10-3

Impact of Racial Group on Income

Percent of Racial Groups with University Level Education in Bottom 20 Percent and Top 20 Percent of the Income Scale (people aged 25-64), 1996

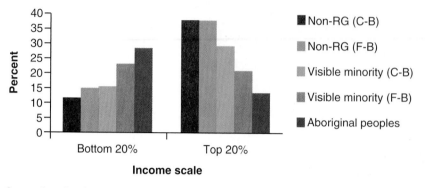

Source: Canadian Council on Social Development, 2000.

rights to individuals and groups based on their membership in a particular social category. It is important to recognize that this process has an opposite effect on those who are not discriminated against. This is ***privilege***—access to opportunities provided to people as a direct result of their membership in a particular societal group. White Anglo-Saxon males in Canadian society have been the beneficiaries of such privilege since before Confederation. Feminist scholar Peggy McIntosh (1988) lists advantages that come from 'white privilege.' They include:

1. Avoiding having to spend time with people you were trained to mistrust or who have learned to mistrust your kind
2. Being considered financially reliable whenever using cheques, credit cards, or cash
3. Never having to speak for all the people in your racial group
4. Taking a job without having co-workers suspect you got it because of race
5. Being able to worry about racism without being regarded as self-serving.

There are two important expressions of discrimination that are of interest to sociologists: those that affect an individual's ability to participate in the economic opportunities available to most members of a particular society, and those that arbitrarily impose social segregation. Both of these types of discrimination are examples of ***marginalization***—the process by which an individual, as a result of her or his minority status, is provided no access or only partial access to opportunities given to the average member of society. The Lian and Matthews study demonstrated that visible minorities in Canada are indeed marginalized.

It is not surprising that prejudice often leads to discrimination. Suppose that you are a human resources manager for a large company, and you dislike people of a certain minority because of a *stereotype*—an unreliable generalization that all members of a group are the same and that, therefore, individual differences need not, or should not, be taken into consideration. This is a prejudice. However, if you refuse to offer a particular candidate a job because she belongs to a group about which you hold a stereotype, it is discrimination. As long as stereotypes exist, they have the potential to influence behaviour, but that link is not inevitable.

Prejudiced attitude should not be equated with discriminatory behaviour. Although the two are generally related, they are not identical, and either condition can be present without the other. A prejudiced person, perhaps because of social pressure or out of convenience, does not always act on his or her biases. As a human resources manager, you might feel pressure from your boss, company policy, or your fellow workers to provide an opportunity for our hypothetical minority applicant. Or, you might find her résumé so outstanding that you cannot let her go to the competition. In these cases, prejudice does not lead to discrimination. On the other hand, if the only reason you refused to hire this minority applicant was out of fear that your company's biggest client—a bigot—would take his business elsewhere, that would be discrimination without prejudice.

Discrimination persists even for those minority group members who are well educated, highly qualified, and come from the most advantaged family backgrounds. Despite their talents and experiences, they sometimes encounter attitudinal or organizational bias that prevents them from reaching their full potential. The term ***glass ceiling*** refers to an invisible barrier that blocks the promotion of a qualified individual in a work environment because of the individual's gender, race, or ethnicity (Schaefer 2000; H. Yamagata et al. 1997).

Studies have shown that the existence of this glass ceiling results principally from the fears and prejudices of many middle- and upper-level white male managers, who believe that the inclusion of women and minority group men in management circles will threaten their own prospects for advancement (Department of Labour 1995a, 1995b). Box 10-2 shows that even though more and more women of colour are entering the political arena, they must overcome greater obstacles than their

There is a perception held by many women of colour, and supported by research, that they are members of a double minority, a situation that puts them at a distinct disadvantage in their efforts to participate in the mainstream of Canadian society. McGill University's Jerome Black examined the reality of this marginalization in his study *"Entering the Political Elite in Canada: The Case of Minority Women as Parliamentary Candidates and MPs."* In his findings, based on participation in the 1993 Canadian federal election, Black concludes that, despite efforts to compensate for the double set of obstacles faced by these women, "inequity continues to characterize the process of political elite access in Canada" (Black 2000).

Black suggests that Canadian women of colour are disadvantaged even in comparison with their counterparts in the United States. He argues that decades of visibility at the forefront of the American civil rights movement, as well as their positions of leadership in religious and other community organizations, have given black women a public status that has served them well in their efforts to invade the "bastions of male political dominance."

When contrasting the experiences of minority women and females of English and/or French ancestry, Black found that minority women appeared to face more rigorous qualifying criteria in their attempts to enter federal politics. For instance, in a comparison of successful candidates for the 35th Canadian parliament, minority women were found to have higher levels of accomplishment in both education and career attainments. One hundred percent of the visible minority women and 50 percent of women from Southern European countries in the study had earned advanced degrees. This surpassed the 30 percent of women from English or French ancestry who achieved equivalent credentials. The same pattern held true for undergraduate degrees.

> **Canadian women of colour are disadvantaged even in comparison with their counterparts in the United States.**

Besides the overachievement in credentials, the study revealed that this same group also appeared to have to work harder at establishing themselves within the party structure. It is customary for potential candidates to devote time to party activities as a volunteer. This practice intensifies as the election draws closer, particularly in the last month before nomination meetings. While all groups participate in this process, minority women, perhaps because of their awareness of the compounded disadvantage they face, contributed significantly more time to these activities than did either male or female majority aspirants. Half of the minority women candidates participated in this process, while only a third of other female candidates did.

The study also found factors that served to benefit minority women, although not always within the formal structure. On average, women were found to have better support from their personal and professional networks than did men. Minority women in all situations were found to have received more support for their political ambitions from family, friends, and their community. Within the formal partisan structure, minority women, more so than majority women or men, were encouraged by their parties to run for office. That encouragement carried over into the actual nomination process, in which three-quarters of the minority MPs examined in the study had achieved their candidacy via acclamation.

Let's Discuss

1. Do you think enough has been done, or is being done, to encourage the participation of minority women at all levels of Canadian politics?
2. Is gender a factor when your family discusses political candidates? What about your circle of friends?

Source: Black 2000.

white, male counterparts. In the past decade, more and more of these women have made it past traditional political party gatekeepers and through glass ceilings to become elected representatives in parliament and the provincial legislatures.

Institutional Discrimination

Discrimination is practised not only by individuals in one-to-one encounters but also by institutions in their daily operations. Social scientists are particularly concerned with the ways in which structural factors such as employment, housing, health care, and government operations maintain the social significance of race and ethnicity. *Institutional discrimination*, sometimes referred to as 'systemic discrimination', refers to the denial of opportunities and equal rights to individuals and groups that results from the normal operations of a society. This kind of discrimination consistently affects certain racial and ethnic groups more than others.

Changes to the *Canadian Citizenship Act* in 1967 introduced a new set of criteria for allowing immigrants into the country. While the previous standards had focused on race and ethnicity, the new Act evaluated applicants on their ability to contribute to the Canadian economy. This method of evaluation became known as the "points system." While nonwhites had been allowed in previously, the circumstances were narrowly defined and self-serving—blacks as slaves, Chinese as railway workers, minority women to be domestics or nannies. From the earliest days of immigration, Canada's policies restricted entrance on the basis of race and ethnicity, and that restrictive approach was further emphasized by the *Immigration Act* of 1952, which gave government the power to restrict the entry of individuals arbitrarily based solely on their ethnic or racial status (Pigler Christensen 2001). This policy reflected Ottawa's long-term strategy of institutional discrimination, in which exclusion was accomplished through proscriptive guidelines, avoiding formal policies that explicitly barred entry to ethnic and racial

In November 1999, *Lethal Weapon* star Danny Glover charged the city of New York with discrimination after several municipally licensed cabs passed him by. A former cab driver himself, Glover declared that the Big Apple's cabbies needed diversity training.

minorities. But perhaps the single most blatant act of institutional discrimination in Canadian history was the 60 years of residential schooling imposed on First Nations children and their families (Haig-Brown 1988).

The argument is often heard that since the *Charter of Rights and Freedoms* was entrenched in the repatriated *Constitution Act* of 1982, Canadian institutions have been unable to discriminate. The good intentions of those who wrote the Charter cannot be questioned, but the claim that discrimination has been eradicated certainly is open to debate.

Discrimination in educational institutions is seen as particularly punitive because of its potential for long-term impact on the life chances of the individuals against whom it is perpetrated. Henry et al. (1995) examined the implications of a "sacrosanct" curriculum in our universities, citing a Queen's University report that identified Eurocentric characteristics in its course offerings. The report identified:

- The need for course names that reflect their content (e.g., "The History of Political Thought" should be renamed "The History of Western Political Thought")
- The need for core courses that include more than just the Eurocentric issues
- The need for mandatory antiracist courses in the curriculum
- The need to hire faculty who can teach courses that do not have a Eurocentric focus
- The need to introduce more interdisciplinary studies, such as black studies and First Nations studies
- The need to develop supplementary programs for minority students that would help them meet academic standards.

These vestiges of European privilege are not unique. Across Canada, schools at all levels are working to identify and eliminate similar shortcomings.

In Canada, we often point south of the border when discrimination in the enforcement or judicial arms of the justice system is the topic. The overrepresentation of blacks in American jails is a repeated theme among those fighting for racial equality. However, as the case below illustrates, Canadian authorities have faced similar charges.

The *Canadian Human Rights Advocate* reported the case of the discriminatory treatment of a black man by Victoria police in the late 1980s. The man, a Canadian citizen with a graduate-level education, went to a local restaurant to eat. His order was taken by the server, but then as he waited for his meal, he was approached by another employee and told that he would have to move so that she could seat two people at the table he was occupying. As no other seats were available at the time, he refused. The Victoria police were summoned, and on arriving, questioned the man pointedly about his citizenship, threatened him with deportation, and took him off to jail in handcuffs. He was held there for eight hours. The man subsequently complained to the provincial Human Rights Council, which concluded that he had been the victim of racial discrimination, and awarded damages (Kallen 1990). The argument could be made that this type of incident is more a reflection of the prejudices of the individual police officers; however, in their position as representatives of the state, it is the state that must be held accountable for their behaviour.

Institutional discrimination can also be found in the Canadian housing market. University of Calgary professor James Frideres points out that First Nations people in particular are subject to barriers when it comes to either buying or renting a home. Even though the *Charter of Rights and Freedoms* has discouraged landlords from overt racism in approving tenants, overt behaviour has been replaced by more subtle tactics. When they try to purchase a home, First Nations home buyers are often discouraged by realtors trying to protect the existing racial composition of a neighbourhood. Real estate companies worry that property values will drop if First Nations people move into a community, with an attendant loss in revenue and commissions (Bolaria 1995). As a result, First Nations people are discouraged from looking for a home in predominantly white neighbourhoods.

Since the enactment of the Charter, Canadians have enacted other laws against institutional discrimination. The attempt to provide access to equal treatment across the social landscape has been effective for most Canadians most of the time, yet discriminatory practices continue to pervade nearly all areas of life in Canada today. In part, this is because various individuals and groups actually benefit from racial and ethnic discrimination in terms of money, status, and influence. Discrimination permits members of the dominant group to enhance their wealth, power, and prestige at the expense of others. Less qualified people may get jobs and promotions simply because they are members of the dominant group. Such individuals and groups will not surrender these advantages easily. We will now take a closer look at this functionalist analysis of discrimination, as well as the conflict, feminist, and interactionist perspectives.

Studying Race and Ethnicity

Relations among racial and ethnic groups lend themselves to analysis from the four major perspectives of sociology. Viewing race from the macro level, functionalists observe that racial prejudice and discrimination serve

positive functions for dominant groups, whereas conflict theorists see the economic structure as a central factor in the exploitation of minorities. Some feminist perspectives, on the other hand, examine how gender, race, and class intersect to produce multiple degrees of inequality. The micro-level analysis of interactionist researchers stresses the manner in which everyday contact between people from different racial and ethnic backgrounds contributes to tolerance or leads to hostility.

Functionalist Perspective

What possible use could racial bigotry have for society? Functionalist theorists, while agreeing that racial hostility is hardly to be admired, point out that it indeed serves positive functions for those practising discrimination.

Anthropologist Manning Nash (1962) has identified three functions that racially prejudiced beliefs have for the dominant group:

1. Such views provide a moral justification for maintaining an unequal society that routinely deprives a minority of its rights and privileges. Before the change in Canadian immigration policy allowing nonwhites to apply for entrance, the discrimination against visible minorities was justified by claiming that there was only a limited number of menial jobs for which they were qualified (Satzewich 1991). It was reasonable to expect, therefore, that increasing the numbers of immigrants from those groups would only lead to unemployment and a drain on the welfare rolls.

2. Racist beliefs discourage the subordinate minority from attempting to question its lowly status, which would be to question the very foundation of society. It is not difficult to imagine that an immigrant would hesitate to challenge the values of a society he or she has chosen as a new home.

3. Racial myths encourage support for the existing order by introducing the argument that any major societal change (such as the end of discrimination) would only bring greater poverty to the minority and lower the majority's standard of living. As a result, Nash suggests, racial prejudice grows when a society's value system is being threatened. A good example of this is the thriving Japanese fishing community on the West Coast prior to the Second World War, which was subsequently interned during the war.

Although racial prejudice and discrimination may serve the interests of the powerful, such unequal treatment can also be dysfunctional to a society and even to its dominant group. Sociologist Arnold Rose (1951) outlines four dysfunctions associated with racism:

1. A society that practises discrimination fails to use the resources of all individuals. Discrimination limits the search for talent and leadership to the dominant group.

2. Discrimination aggravates social problems such as poverty, delinquency, and crime and places the financial burden to alleviate these problems on the dominant group.

3. Society must invest a good deal of time and money to defend its barriers to full participation of all members.

4. Racial prejudice and discrimination often undercut goodwill and friendly diplomatic relations between nations.

Conflict Perspective

Conflict theorists would certainly agree with Arnold Rose that racial prejudice and discrimination have many harmful consequences for society. Sociologists such as Oliver Cox (1948), Robert Blauner (1972), and Herbert M. Hunter (2000) have used the *exploitation theory* (or *Marxist class theory*) to explain the basis of racial subordination in the United States and Canada. As we saw in Chapter 8, Karl Marx viewed the exploitation of the lower class as a basic part of the capitalist economic system. From a Marxist point of view, racism keeps minorities in low-paying jobs, thereby supplying the capitalist ruling class with a pool of cheap labour. Moreover, by forcing racial minorities to accept low wages, capitalists can restrict the wages of *all* members of the proletariat. Workers from the dominant group who demand higher wages can always be replaced by minorities who have no choice but to accept low-paying jobs.

The conflict view of racial and ethnic relations seems persuasive in a number of instances. As we will see, Canada's history with immigration was built on the needs of its capitalist groups, on capitalist accumulation through the labour of immigrants. Japanese Canadians were able to establish themselves and create a thriving community in and around Vancouver until the white population began to see them as an economic threat. Similarly, Canada recruited Chinese workers, first to work in the gold fields of the 1850s, and subsequently to serve as labour on the construction of the Canadian Pacific Railway line. But, when the gold dried up and the rail construction was finished, the government imposed a head tax intended to stem the flow of immigrants from China.

However, the exploitation theory is too limited to explain prejudice in its many forms. Not all minority groups have been economically exploited to the same extent. In addition, many groups (such as the First Nations and the Mormons) have been victimized by

prejudice for other than economic reasons. Still, as Gordon Allport (1979:210) concludes, the exploitation theory correctly "points a sure finger at one of the factors involved in prejudice, . . . rationalized self-interest of the upper classes."

Feminist Perspectives

Given the great diversity of feminist perspectives, it is perhaps not surprising to discover differences among these theories in their analysis of race and ethnicity. Some early feminists have taken the problematic dominant stance where white, middle-class, heterosexual women's experiences are viewed as the norm, while ignoring "the specificity of black, native, and other ethnic and cultural experiences" (Elliot and Mandell 1998:14). While perspectives such as radical feminism treat women as a uniform, undifferentiated group whose major source of oppression is sexism, other perspectives have strenuously challenged this point of view (Grant 1991; Brand 1993). Global and antiracist feminism point out that gender is not the sole source of oppression because gender, race, and class intersect to produce multiple degrees of inequality. Unlike white middle-class women, immigrant women, visible minority women, and First Nations women experience the compounded effects of inequality associated with their race and class, as well as their gender.

Patricia Hill Collins (1998) uses the term "outsiders-within" to describe the condition of black women situated in academic, legal, business, and other communities. As "outsiders-within," Collins argues, these women are members of a given community but at the same time are dually marginalized in that community as women and as blacks; they find themselves unable to access the knowledge and possess the full power granted to others in the community.

Canadian sociologist Roxana Ng has written extensively on the experience of grassroots and community activism in helping immigrant women in Canada to find meaningful employment. In particular, Ng points to the role of the government in providing state funding for doubly marginalized immigrant women (Ng 1990). Box 10-2 discussed some of the intersections of race, class, and gender for women in Canada's political parties.

Interactionist Perspective

A Jamaican woman working in a Southern Ontario automotive plant is transferred from a job on an assembly line to a similar position working next to a white man. At first, the white man is patronizing, assuming that she must be incompetent. She is cold and resentful; even when she needs assistance, she refuses to admit it. After a week, the

IVANA FILICE:
Independent Educator, Researcher and Consultant

Ivana Filice, a daughter of Italian immigrant parents, received her M.A. in Sociology at Carleton University in Ottawa. While she began her career in law enforcement, she ultimately became fascinated by her sociology classes in theory, health and immigration, and refugee and population movements.

As a student, she was offered a research position at the Research Resource Division for Refugees. Currently, Ivana is continuing the work she did as a research associate and graduate student: consulting, speaking to university classes, and presenting reports at national and international conferences in the areas of human rights, violence against women and children, and health care issues.

She expanded her academic sociological training into the community through her activities with the Centre for Immigrant and Visible Minority Women Against Abuse, with emphasis on cross-cultural sensitivity and accessibility issues. Ivana also became involved in research and public education programs with the National Organization of Immigrant and Visible Minority Women in Canada and the Canadian Council of Muslim Women.

During the early 1990s, Ivana, along with other concerned and committed feminists in the community, identified a need to educate the public on the human rights violations and health conditions faced by refugee women and children during the Bosnian and Somali civil wars. Ivana is one of the co-founders and coordinators of the Women's Health Project in Ottawa, established with the specific intent of educating the public, fundraising, and supporting health projects for women and children in Bosnia and Somalia. The Project continues today and has been expanded into the Kashmir area with future plans to support projects in Afghanistan and other war-torn areas.

Ivana states that "sociology has enabled me to see beyond what is presented as fact and truth and instead to ask questions about how human conditions and situations come to be. But most importantly, it has taught me how to engage in society to facilitate change and promote health and human rights."

---

growing tension between the two leads to a bitter quarrel. Over time, however, each slowly comes to appreciate the other's strengths and talents. A year after they begin working together, these two workers become respectful friends. This is an example of what interactionists call the *contact hypothesis* in action.

The **contact hypothesis** states that interracial contact between people of equal status in cooperative circumstances will cause them to become less prejudiced and to abandon previous stereotypes. People begin to see one another as individuals and discard the broad generalizations characteristic of stereotyping. Note the factors of *equal status* and *cooperative circumstances*. In the example above, if the two workers had been competing for one vacancy as a supervisor, the racial hostility between them might have worsened (Allport 1979; Schaefer 2000b; Sigelman et al. 1996).

As blacks, Asians, and other minorities gain access to better paying and more responsible jobs, the contact hypothesis may take on even greater significance. The trend in our society is toward increasing contact between individuals from dominant and subordinate groups. This may be one way of eliminating—or at least reducing—racial and ethnic stereotyping and prejudice. Another may be the establishment of interracial coalitions, an idea suggested by sociologist William Julius Wilson (1999b).

To work, such coalitions would obviously need to be organized so that all members have an equal role.

Contact between individuals occurs on the micro level. We turn now to a consideration of intergroup relations on a macro level.

Patterns of Intergroup Relations

Racial and ethnic groups can relate to one another in a wide variety of ways, ranging from friendships and intermarriages to genocide, from behaviours that require mutual approval to behaviours imposed by the dominant group.

One devastating pattern of intergroup relations is **genocide**—the deliberate, systematic killing of or blatant disregard for the well-being of an entire people or nation. This term describes the killing of 1 million Armenians by Turkey beginning in 1915 (Melson 1986). It is most commonly applied to Nazi Germany's extermination of 6 million European Jews, as well as gays, lesbians, and the Romani people ("Gypsies"), during the Second World War. The term *genocide* is also appropriate in describing the United States' policies toward Aboriginal people in the nineteenth century. In 1800, the Aboriginal population of that country was about 600 000; by 1850, it had

Ethnic Albanian women mourn the death of a man killed by Serbs in the province of Kosovo. Such "ethnic cleansings" have met with worldwide condemnation.

been reduced to 250 000 through warfare with the cavalry, disease, and forced relocation to inhospitable environments.

While the treatment of Aboriginal groups within the territory that came to be known as Canada was not as extreme as that inflicted by American settlers, the disappearance of at least one Aboriginal group can be directly attributed to policies of exclusion and genocide perpetrated by newcomers from Europe. The Beothuks of Newfoundland and Labrador were decimated by new diseases, such as smallpox and typhus, that were carried by the settlers. As a result, the last member of the Beothuks, a woman who lived in the white community for years after her family died, passed away in 1829 (Beaujot and McQuillan 1982).

The *expulsion* of a people is another extreme means of acting out racial or ethnic prejudice. In 1979, Vietnam expelled nearly 1 million ethnic Chinese, partly as a result of centuries of hostility between Vietnam and neighbouring China. In a more recent example of expulsion (which had aspects of genocide), Serbian forces began a program of "ethnic cleansing" in 1991 in the newly independent states of Bosnia and Herzegovina. Throughout the former nation of Yugoslavia, the Serbs drove more than 1 million Croats and Muslims from their homes. Some were tortured and killed, others abused and terrorized, in an attempt to "purify" the land for the remaining ethnic Serbs. In 1999, Serbs were again the focus of worldwide condemnation as they sought to "cleanse" the province of Kosovo of ethnic Albanians.

Genocide and expulsion are extreme behaviours. More typical intergroup relations as they occur in North America and throughout the world follow four identifiable patterns: (1) amalgamation, (2) assimilation, (3) segregation, and (4) multiculturalism. Each pattern defines the dominant group's actions. The minority groups' responses can be categorized as either acceptance or rejection responses. The acceptance response involves cooperation with assimilation and integration efforts. The rejection response can take the form of rebellion or avoidance designed to frustrate the goals of the dominant group. Intergroup relations are rarely restricted to only one of the four patterns, although invariably one does tend to dominate. Therefore, think of these patterns primarily as ideal types.

Amalgamation

Amalgamation happens when a majority group and a minority group combine to form a new group. Through intermarriage over several generations, various groups in the society combine to form a new group. This can be expressed as A + B + C → D, where A, B, and C represent different groups present in a society, and D signifies the end result, a unique cultural–racial group unlike any of the initial groups (Newman 1973).

The Metis represent the closest thing to ideal amalgamation that we can identify in Canadian society. The group was created when the voyageurs seeking furs and establishing posts for the Northwest Company moved into the Red River Valley in the 1700s. These traders established close relations with the local Cree and ultimately married into that group. The resultant families and their descendants have been recognized as a valid ethnic group since at least 1869, when Louis Riel, a seminary-educated member of the group, incited an uprising to prevent the transfer of their homeland from the Hudson's Bay Company to the new nation of Canada (Finlay et al. 1979). The Metis assumed aspects of both ancestral lines, continuing to live in the territory of their First Nations mothers, and adopting the knowledge and some of the skills traceable to their French roots.

Assimilation

Many Hindus in India complain about Indian citizens who copy the traditions and customs of the British. In Australia, Aborigines who have become part of the dominant society refuse to acknowledge their darker-skinned grandparents on the street. ***Assimilation*** is the process by which a person forsakes his or her own cultural tradition to become part of a different culture. Generally, it is practised by a minority group member who wants to conform to the standards of the dominant group. Assimilation can be described as an ideology in which A + B + C → A. The majority A dominates in such a way that members of minorities B and C imitate A and attempt to become indistinguishable from the dominant group (Newman 1973).

Assimilation can strike at the very roots of a person's identity as he or she seeks to blend in with the dominant group. Alphonso D'Abuzzo, for example, changed his name to Alan Alda, and the British actress Joyce Frankenberg changed her name to Jane Seymour. Name changes,

"Ho, ho, ho" apparently works in any language. As Japanese people assimilated the norms and values of mainstream North American culture, they created their own "Shogun Santa." This one can be found in the Little Tokyo neighbourhood of Los Angeles.

switches in religious affiliation, and dropping of native languages can obscure one's roots and heritage. Moreover, assimilation does not necessarily bring acceptance for the minority group individual. A Chinese Canadian may speak flawless English, attend a Protestant church faithfully, and know the names of all members of the Hockey Hall of Fame. Yet he or she is still *seen* as different and may therefore be rejected as a business associate, a neighbour, or a marriage partner.

Segregation

Segregation refers to the physical separation of two groups of people in terms of residence, workplace, and social events. Generally, a dominant group imposes it on a minority group. Segregation is rarely complete, however. Intergroup contact inevitably occurs even in the most segregated societies.

In North America, the term *segregation* tends to bring to mind the rules against interracial commingling associated with the Southern United States prior to the 1970s. Images of "black" or "white" water fountains and hooded Klansmen blockading schools against integration by black students are powerful reminders of segregation at its worst. In Canada, the kind of overt, formal, legislated segregation associated with the American South has been uncommon, but not unheard of. Certainly, the internment of Japanese Canadians during the Second World War qualifies as segregation in its crudest form. However, minority groups have frequently chosen to establish their own enclaves, particularly in the large metropolitan areas. This is ***self-segregation***—the situation that arises when members of a minority deliberately develop residential, economic, and/or social network structures that are separate from those of the majority population. Jewish immigrants have been among the most active groups in establishing their own neighbourhoods in Canada, and unlike some others that have disappeared over time, these have endured. Most major Canadian cities also have a "Chinatown" area where the ancestors of many early Asian immigrants settled, and which flourish as economically vibrant areas today. Recent immigrant populations including those from Southern Europe and Asia have indicated a preference for self-segregation (Kalbach 1990).

From 1948 (when it received its independence) to 1990, the Republic of South Africa severely restricted the movement of blacks and other nonwhites by means of a wide-ranging system of segregation known as ***apartheid***. Apartheid even included the creation of homelands where blacks were expected to live. However, decades of local resistance to apartheid, combined with international pressure, led to marked political changes in the 1990s. In 1994, a prominent black activist, Nelson Mandela, was elected as South Africa's president, the first election in which blacks (the majority of the nation's population) were allowed to vote. Mandela had spent almost 28 years in South African prisons for his anti-apartheid activities. His election was widely viewed as the final blow to South Africa's oppressive policy of apartheid.

Multiculturalism

In a pluralistic society, a subordinate group does not have to forsake its lifestyle and traditions. **Pluralism** is based on mutual respect for one another's cultures among various groups in a society. It allows a minority group to express its own culture and still participate without prejudice in the larger society. Earlier, we described amalgamation as A + B + C → D, and assimilation as A + B + C → A. Using this same approach, we can conceive of pluralism as A + B + C → A + B + C. All of the groups are able to coexist in the same society (Newman 1973).

In Canada, the ideal of pluralism was entrenched in law by the *Multiculturalism Act* of 1988. The Act and its subsequent revisions have created a social environment in which minorities are not only permitted to engage in their distinct cultural expressions, but are encouraged to do so, through such initiatives as the federal government's funding of ethnic arts programs and the creation of cultural programming on community access television.

From the outset, the Canadian style of pluralism focused on two goals. First, the government wanted to quell the growing dissent in Quebec. The rise of the political wing of the separatist movement had been causing concern in Ottawa, and the government felt that unless the French language was given official status, and the French-Canadian culture given protection and support, the people of Quebec would follow their nationalist leaders out of Confederation (Li 2000). The report of the Royal Commission on Bilingualism and Biculturalism contributed to the establishment of the *Official Languages Act* in 1969, which clearly recognized French as one of Canada's two official languages. But at the same time, it also recognized the contribution of other ethnic groups to the cultural enrichment of Canada, thereby opening the way for others.

The second goal of the government was to bring the burgeoning minority population into the political fold. Since the major changes to Canadian immigration policy that introduced the "points system" in 1967, the proportion of new Canadians from nontraditional sources had increased dramatically (Keely et al. 1981). This group now represented a significant voting block, and the government was aware of its potential (Hawkins 1988).

Regardless of the motives behind the legislation, multiculturalism as a national policy has provided recognition of the value of minority cultures. For example, in 1988, the Canadian government and the National Asso-

ciation of Japanese Canadians signed the Japanese Canadian Redress Agreement. Under the terms of the agreement, the federal government promised to create a Canadian Race Relations Foundation (CRRF), which would 'foster racial harmony and cross-cultural understanding and help to eliminate racism.' In 1996, the government proclaimed the *Canadian Race Relations Foundation Act* into law. The aim of the CRRF is reflected in its goal to build a national framework for the fight against racism in Canadian society. "We will: shed light on the causes and manifestations of racism; provide independent, outspoken national leadership; and act as a resource and facilitator in the pursuit of equity, fairness and social justice" (CRRF 2002).

Race and Ethnicity in Canada

Few societies have a more diverse population than Canada, a truly multiracial, multi-ethnic community. Of course this has not always been the case. The population of what is now Canada changed dramatically with the arrival of the first French settlers along the north shore of the St. Lawrence River in the early 1600s. Prior to that time, the continent had been peopled exclusively by First Nations groups for thousands of years, and while it was culturally diverse, it was racially monolithic. Since then, the Battle of the Plains of Abraham and the steady flow of immigration to this land have been the two critical forces in the formation of Canada's ethnic and racial landscape.

Canada's diversity is evident from the statistical profile presented in Table 10-1, and that diversity, particularly with regard to race, has been increasing dramatically in recent years. Between the pre–points system days of the early 1960s and the 1990s, there was a gradual shift away from Europe and towards Asia as the source of the majority of immigrants to Canada (Statistics Canada 2003a). Figure 10-1 showed this change in the immigrant population of Canada's three largest cities.

That diversity, so obvious in statistics profiling the general population, is not evident in media representations, particularly on television. A study by Perigoe and Lazar (1992) monitored national evening news programs to determine the representations of people of colour. What they found was a skewed portrayal, where visible minorities were seldom included unless a given story involved members of their own racial community. In other types of programming, they made up less than 3 percent of the total participants.

Racial Groups

The 2001 Canadian census form specified 10 categories of race, with an eleventh option for "Other." The rationale for the reintroduction of the race question was that data produced by using other census information such as mother tongue has proven less accurate in determining race. Among the groups identified on the form are Chinese, South Asian (which includes East Indian, Pakistani, Punjabi, and Sri Lankan), Black (which includes African, Haitian, Jamaican, and Somali), Latin American, and Japanese. Interestingly, there is no "First Nations" category on the long form that is to be sent to one in five Canadian households.

First Nations People

"We have proved that we will not be assimilated. We have demonstrated that our culture has a viability that cannot be suppressed." So said Grand Chief John Kelly in 1970 (Kelly 1970). In his 1997 bestseller, *Reflections of a Siamese Twin: Canada at the End of the Twentieth Century,* John Ralston Saul suggests that Canada, rather than being a duality of French and English peoples, is in fact a "triangular reality" with the First Nations community as the third leg of the national foundation. He argues that for 300 years, until the middle of the nineteenth century, First Nations people were in fact in positions equal or superior to those of European settlers (Ralston Saul 1997:91).

Ralston Saul makes the point that Europeans were dependent upon First Nations peoples' knowledge and skills for their survival during this period. After a brief initial hostility, a period during which the doomed Beothuks found themselves attacked, the new immigrants realized the value of making alliances with First Nations people. Subsequent relations involved collaboration among the groups, which peaked during the boom years of the fur trade. Ultimately, First Nations people found themselves abandoning their traditional economy and material culture, as the demand for their furs provided greater access to European goods and ideas (Palmer Patterson 1972).

By the mid-1800s, the relationship between the British-based authority and First Nations people reflected the dwindling autonomy of the latter. In 1857, the government gave up all pretence of recognizing First Nations peoples' right to self-determination, and passed the *Gradual Civilization Act* aimed at assimilation (Royal Commission on Aboriginal Peoples 1994). Perhaps the most atrocious aspect of this legislation was its approval of government funding of the residential schools that appeared in the 1840s in Upper Canada (now Ontario). Attendance at these institutions became mandatory in 1920. Despite the reports of horrors that took place in these institutions, and the fact that they served the assimilation agenda poorly, residential schools remained a facet of First Nations childhood into the 1960s. Only in 1973, after strong representations from the National Indian Brotherhood, did parliament completely rescind the policy, and then it adopted a policy of First Nations local control of education.

In 1876, 20 years after authorities had begun to move First Nations peoples onto reservations, the *Indian Act* placed them under the formal protection and administration of the federal government (Mawhiney 2001). This pivotal event relieved First Nations people of their status as self-governing, autonomous populations and transformed them into just another minority.

This status remained effectively unchanged until after the Second World War, when First Nations people adopted a more active political presence in Canadian society. They rebelled against their treatment, instigating a series of changes, including gaining the franchise in all Canadian provinces between 1949 and 1969, and the right to vote federally in 1960 (Satzewich 1990). In June 1969, after a year of consultation with First Nations leaders, Ottawa published a white paper entitled *Statement of the Government of Canada on Indian Policy.* The paper repealed the 1876 *Indian*

The ethnic mosaic of the Canadian community has marginalized First Nations peoples. In recent years, the Assembly of First Nations and local Native groups have had great success in focusing attention on the ongoing discrimination to which they are subjected.

Act, terminating the special status of First Nations people, and demonstrated to them that they would have to be even more politically proactive in their pursuit of self-government and treaty rights. That effort was rewarded finally in December 1997, when the Supreme Court of Canada handed down the Delgamuukw decision, which recognizes that First Nations people must be consulted whenever the integrity of their quality of life is threatened (Mawhiney 2001).

Today, Canada's First Nations population—those claiming to be Aboriginal as either a single or multiple response to the census question on ancestry—totals 976 305, or 3.3 percent of Canada's population (Statistics Canada 2003b). Figure 10-4 shows the breakdown of the First Nations population into those who responded to the labels of North American Indian, Metis, and Inuit. One-fourth of the total Aboriginal population lives off-reserve in large cities, with the largest concentration in Winnipeg. They are younger than the general Aboriginal population by an average of 10 years, a phenomenon caused by the tendency of the young to leave reservation life in favour of the big city. More than half of their number is poor, compared with 21.2 percent of other Canadians (Lee 1999). And, they are overrepresented in our penal institutions, making up 17 percent of all those in federal custody (Daily June 1/00).

After a century and a half of degradation, Canada's First Nations people are poised to regain their former status as independent, self-determining peoples. On December 13, 1999, ratification by the House of Commons officially marked the successful conclusion of treaty negotiations with the Nisga'a of Northern British Columbia, and established a precedent for First Nations claims for land and political autonomy (see Figure 10-5 for the sovereign indigenous nations' territorial boundaries within British Columbia). The Delgamuukw decision, giving First Nations persons authority over resources on traditional lands, is also evidence of this resurgence of Canada's Aboriginal groups.

Asian Canadians

The 2001 census found that there were almost 2 million (1 964 500) Canadians whose origins could be traced to Asia. Over 1 million (1 029 400) of those people claimed Chinese heritage either as immigrants from or as descendants of immigrants from China, or as ethnic Chinese from such places as Vietnam.

The Chinese represent the second largest racial minority in the country after the First Nations population. A century and a half after their ancestors began arriving on the West Coast to take up jobs as labourers and small-business owners servicing the Fraser River gold rush of the 1850s, members of the Chinese Canadian community have attained middle-class status, many as

professionals (Nguyen 1982; Reitz 1980). It has been a difficult and sometimes painful process.

Having established themselves as diligent and productive workers during the gold rush, Chinese people were actively recruited by the government of the day to provide the labour necessary to complete the last and most dangerous phase of the transcontinental Canadian Pacific Railway, through the Rocky and Selkirk mountains. In the early 1880s, 14 000 Chinese nationals were given five- to ten-year contracts, and put to work at a fraction of the wage white workers earned (Creese et al. 1991; Lampkin 1985).

In 1885, with the railway completed and white workers' groups lobbying politicians to protect jobs, the federal government imposed the first of a series of head taxes designed to discourage Chinese immigrants. The initial tax was $50, but when it became clear that the amount was not a deterrent, Ottawa raised the amount to $100 in 1900, and then again to $500 in 1903, an amount equal to a year's wages (Finkel et al. 1993).

This was not the first time the federal government had discriminated against Chinese immigrants. In 1875, two decades after the gold rush, Canada disenfranchised them (Tarnopolsky 1991). In later periods, the institutional discrimination took other, sometimes more punitive forms such as the *Chinese Immigration Act*—also known as the *Chinese Exclusion Act*—of 1923, which completely barred them from entering Canada. The same piece of legislation prevented those Chinese already in the country from holding public office or voting, and from sitting on juries (Naiman 1997). At the same time, in different parts of the country, governments at both the provincial and municipal levels sought ways to further marginalize their visible minority populations. This was especially the case in British Columbia, where the

FIGURE 10-4

First Nations People, 2001

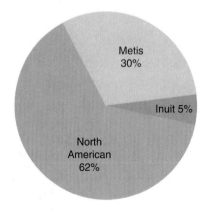

Source: Statistics Canada, 2003b.

FIGURE 10-5

Sovereign Indigenous Nations' Territorial Boundaries in British Columbia

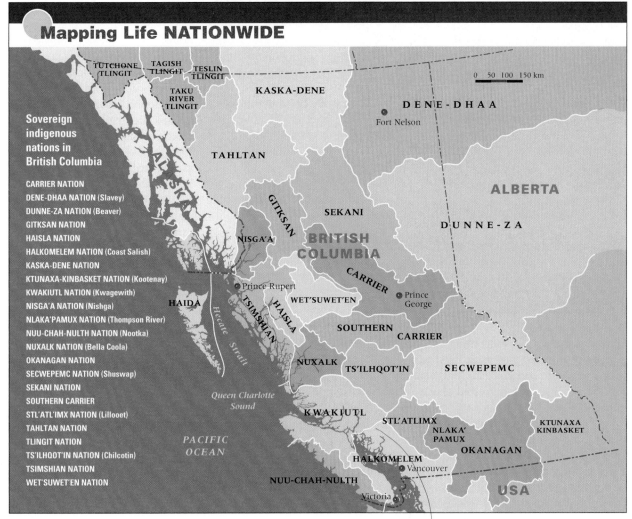

Source: Compiled by the Union of BC Indian Chiefs. Published by the Technical Support Section, Surveys and Resource Mapping Branch, Ministry of the Environment, Lands, and Parks. Victoria, 1991.

This map shows the traditional lands of the First Nations of British Columbia. The province has 65 independent nations, more than the rest of Canada combined.

majority of the Chinese immigrants had first found work and settled. Here, the legislature tried to keep Chinese children out of the public school system (Henry et al. 1995).

Gradually, through the latter part of the twentieth century, Chinese Canadians have emerged from this imposed segregation. For the first time, in 1962, changes to the *Immigration Act* allowed them to apply for entry into Canada as independent rather than sponsored candidates. In 1976, the government finally replaced country of origin as the criterion for entry into Canada with

family reunification and workforce eligibility. During the decades of the 1980s and 1990s, Chinese nationals and ethnics were one of the minority groups that benefited most from this new, less biased system.

Other immigrant groups from Asia have endured similar injustices. Certainly for the Japanese, the struggle to become accepted members of this society has been exacerbated by racist actions and institutional or systemic discrimination. The most destructive race riot in British Columbia's history occurred when a ship carrying over 1000 Japanese and some Sikh immigrants

Immigrants from China, initially denied membership in the communities within which they settled, ultimately established their own neighbourhoods. Chinatowns, like this one in Vancouver, have subsequently become cultural havens for their populations.

arrived at the port of Vancouver in 1907. It was met by a mob organized by the Asiatic Exclusion League, established to incite working-class sentiment against immigration because of a perceived threat to job security (Adachi 1976).

Then, two decades later, those of Japanese origin were again the target of attack, only this time by the government itself. In 1941, against the advice of some of its most senior security officials, parliament suspended the rights of all residents of Japanese descent, and ordered them rounded up and detained, and their property confiscated (Sunahara 1981). For the next four years, almost 14 000 people, many of whom were Canadian-born, were confined to camps constructed at sites such as British Columbia's Arrow Lakes.

For Indo-Canadians, no memory is more hurtful than that of the *Komagata Maru*. The story is similar to a number of other racist events in the country's history. The ship, carrying 400 passengers from Calcutta, India, arrived in Vancouver in the spring of 1914, on the eve of the First World War. Public protest and government ambivalence resulted in the ship remaining anchored in English Bay for three months, while debate raged, fuelled by racist rhetoric, and conditions onboard deteriorated. Finally, the captain was refused berth, and the ship was forced to return to India.

In 1939, the Supreme Court of Canada ruled that discrimination on the basis of race was legally enforceable (Henry et al. 1995). That ruling remained in place until the enactment of the multiculturalism policy sought to end institutional discrimination. However, vestiges of prejudice remain within Canadian society even now, decades later.

Asian Canadians are, as we pointed out at the beginning of this chapter, a diverse group, and in recent decades have been the fastest-growing segment of Canada's immigrant population. Among the many groups included in this catch-all label are those from Japan, Hong Kong, and mainland China, as well as Taiwan, Korea, Thailand, and Vietnam.

Asian Canadians are often held up as a model or ideal immigrant minority, supposedly because, despite past suffering from prejudice and discrimination, they have succeeded economically, socially, and educationally without resorting to confrontations with the white, Anglo-Saxon majority. From a functionalist perspective, the existence of a model minority seems to reaffirm the notion that anyone can get ahead in Canada with talent and hard work, and implies that the failure of some minorities to match those successes has more to do with personal inadequacies than it does with any systemic discrimination. Viewed from a conflict perspective, this becomes yet another instance of "blaming the victims" (Hurh and Kim 1998).

Of course, the concept of a model minority ignores critical factors that can go a long way toward explaining discrepancies in outcomes for other minorities. It ignores, for example, the fact that immigrants from Hong Kong are more likely to speak English, at least as a second language, than are new arrivals from other Asian nations. They are also more familiar with the material and interpersonal aspects of Western culture. In addition, the stereotyping ignores the diversity within groups. There are rich, poor, and middle-class individuals in each of the nationalities that make up the "Asian" category of Canadian.

Ethnic Groups

Unlike racial minorities, members of subordinate ethnic groups are generally not hindered by physical differences from assimilating into the dominant culture of Canada. However, as pointed out earlier, even 35 years after he coined the phrase Porter's image of the vertical mosaic is an accurate depiction of the stratification that continues to exist within Canadian society.

French Canadians

John Porter coined the label "charter groups" for settlers who establish themselves in a territory and claim the right to screen subsequent arrivals. Canada has two charter groups: the French and the English. The relative status of the two groups, however, has been unequal since the British defeated the French in a farmer's field outside Quebec City in 1759. The dominance of the English-speaking elite began four years later with the Treaty of Paris, which awarded them dominion over all the former French colonial lands in North America, with the exception of St Pierre and Miquelon, and continued all but unchallenged until the 1960s. In the interim, Canada's francophone population lived an isolated, marginalized existence, either in Quebec or in pockets of francophones in other provinces (such as those in French communities in Manitoba). Yet, as the history of French Canadians shows, this group (which represents almost a quarter of Canada's people), has been the greatest threat to the country's unity.

The *Quebec Act* of 1774 recognized the integrity of the community's Catholic roots and language, and the authority of French civil law (Russell 1993). This Act was an effort by British governors to forestall rebellion. Aware of growing discontent to the south in the New England colonies, Britain understood the potential for French settlers, unhappy about the English victory, to join the looming American Revolution. The transfer of significant institutional authority to the Roman Catholic Church was made in exchange for a promise by Rome to control the population's aspiration to independence. While the transfer ensured the continued existence of a distinct French community, it did little to empower the people (Li 2000).

French rights were further entrenched in 1791 when the *Constitution Act* created Upper and Lower Canada, and recognized the special status of francophones. This status was confirmed again in the *Confederation Act* of 1867. However, recognition did not provide equality. Throughout the next century, francophones continued to lag behind their English compatriots in terms of education, income, and access to positions of influence in government and business. When voters finally threw out the Church-supported *Union nationale* party in 1959, it was time for a change.

The following year, the new Liberal government began to institute a series of reforms intended to move the education of French-speaking Quebecers away from its parochial roots. The result was a sophisticated and university-trained generation of young people dissatisfied with their place in a province where they were part of a subservient majority (Milner 1978). The Quiet Revolution, a peaceful revolt by the Québécois intelligentsia, protested the historical second-class status of francophones in their own province. The Revolution spawned a period of social and economic reform, and a vigorous separatist movement that in turn produced the 40 years of political unrest that has followed.

The "quiet" aspect of the revolution was soon ended by the terrorist activities of the *Front de libération du Québec* (FLQ) and other extremist groups, culminating in the 1970 October Crisis and the invocation of the *War Measures Act* by Prime Minister Pierre Elliott Trudeau. The momentum initiated by a generation of young, educated Québécois, however, was destined to change the place of their ethnic group within Canadian society.

In 1969, the *Official Languages Act*, a response to the findings of the Royal Commission of Bilingualism and Biculturalism, recognized French as one of the country's two official languages. The result was the creation of a national program to make French part of the daily lives of Canadians—all government communications were

After 200 years of subjugation to the dominant English majority, French Canadians rejected their second-class status during the Quiet Revolution of the 1960s, ultimately electing a separatist government to lead Quebec out of Confederation.

now available in both French and English, and all products carried bilingual labels. The French minority had at last become visible, not to mention audible, partners in Confederation.

Francophones had managed to overcome 200 years of marginalization and reestablish their status as a legitimate force at the national level. As support grew steadily, the political arm of movement, the Parti Québécois (PQ), finally won the 1976 provincial election and formed a majority government in the National Assembly. A year later, with popular support surging, they launched Bill 101, the *Charter of the French Language*, to protect Quebec's linguistic heritage from further erosion. With this act, the French citizens of Canada reclaimed their influence on the national stage, and demonstrated that independence was more than empty rhetoric. Four years later in the first of two referenda on sovereignty, the PQ government asked the people of Quebec if they wanted to redefine their association with the rest of Canada. Quebec voters turned down the idea of sovereignty association by a substantial margin. Then, again in 1995, another Parti Québécois government posed a similar question in a second referendum. This time the count was much closer. The separatists lost by less than 1 percentage point in the final tally. Since that time, the electorate of Quebec has apparently put aside *l'independence* as an option for the time being. While it seems unlikely that there will be another vote on separation in the near future, there are still those fighting to keep alive the movement for Quebec nationhood, thereby continuing to threaten Canada's unity.

Europeans

According to the 2001 Census, Canadians claiming European origins represented 42 percent of the total population. Yet, the perception often associated with multiculturalism is that it is a policy intended to provide non-European or nonwhite ethnic and racial groups equal participation in Canadian society. What is frequently ignored is that the status of Europeans in this country has never been homogeneous. There are the two charter groups—the French and the English—but beyond those is a spectrum of national and ethnic minorities that have suffered discrimination, both interpersonal and institutional.

The majority of immigrants to Canada in the seventeenth century and the first half of the eighteenth century were settlers from France. Then, following the defeat of the French on the Plains of Abraham, arrivals from France ceased and were replaced by newcomers from England, and then Scotland, and finally from Ireland. The Scots seem to have arrived early enough to receive a warm reception as Anglos needed to balance the French majority. The Irish were not so lucky. Arriving in huge numbers during the Irish Potato Famine of the 1840s in their home country, the Irish immigrants were seen as less than desirable, and were subject to both workplace and residential discrimination. As a result, many headed for the American border. In 1848, as many as two-thirds of the Irish newcomers stepped off the boat and immediately headed to New England. Those who chose to remain in Canada found themselves relegated to poor neighbourhoods, such as the Pointe Charles area of Montreal.

The treatment of the Irish in Canada was a foretaste of the nation's future public attitudes and policy decisions about immigration. Immigration legislation passed by parliament through the latter part of the nineteenth century and well into the twentieth century was utilitarian. As we can see from the experience of the Chinese, discussed earlier in this chapter, it served Canada's economic interests and ignored the needs of those who were recruited. The experience of the Chinese and the Irish was repeated with other minority groups during the waves of immigration that followed over the next century.

Shortly after Confederation, politicians and the business community recognized that a declaration of

This could be almost any urban street in Canada, despite the fact that it is populated almost exclusively by an ethnic minority. Can you guess from which country these people and their ancestors emigrated to settle in Canada?

Canadian nationhood was not likely to be respected by the American pioneers who were moving across the country by the tens of thousands. A simple geographic fact caused this concern: the Rocky Mountains. The pioneers had moved rapidly en masse across the flat prairie of the American Midwest, establishing farms and communities along the way. The problem was that once this mass of land-hungry humanity reached the mountains, they would have two choices: one, struggle to get their wagons and animals over the craggy obstacle, or two, turn right and expand their settlement to the north. The issue facing the government of Canada was how to prevent the second option from being exercised.

The response was to send agents to recruit Europeans previously seen as undesirable. Government representatives were dispatched to middle and eastern parts of the continent to find "agriculturists"—or farmers (Henripin et al. 1974). As a result, during the 1880s and 1890s, thousands of Germans and Ukrainians and other nontraditional immigrants were brought to Canada, put on the newly completed railroad, and shipped off to the land beyond the Red River Valley to establish a Canadian presence. Conditions were harsh, the climate inhospitable, and the tools primitive, but most of these settlers survived, and the farming communities they established thrived. However, this imposed isolation physically segregated these new arrivals from the national mainstream. Their marginalization would impact on the ability of these minorities to integrate into the general society for generations to come.

Other, more infamous incidents of discrimination against these ethnic minorities occurred throughout the twentieth century. One particularly distressing event took place in the summer of 1939 when, at the height of Hitler's "Final Solution," the *St. Louis*, a boat carrying Jewish refugees from Europe, was turned away at Halifax Harbour. Ultimately, the ship was forced to return to its port of departure, and its passengers were handed back to the waiting German authorities.

In the case of the Doukhobors, a religious sect that fled to Canada to escape persecution in Russia, the colour of their skin failed to protect them from having their children apprehended by the state. Following a prolonged argument with British Columbian officials about their desire for religious education to be integrated into the curriculum, the RCMP raided the community and took all school-aged children into the custody of the province. The children were shipped off to camps that had been used for the Japanese internment during the Second World War, almost 100 miles away. The children were held there for several years with only limited and supervised access provided to their parents. See Box 10-3 for a description of how the media has portrayed the Doukhobors over the last 100 years.

During that same period following the Second World War, when the majority of immigrants were coming from the Southern European countries of Italy, Greece, and Portugal, the attitude of the government remained exclusionary. These formerly restricted nationalities were given entry to the country as a gesture of good will acknowledging that they had suffered substantially during the war, and were under extreme fiscal pressures as a result of their disrupted economies. Nevertheless, Canadian officials were concerned about diluting the national culture (Beaujot and McQuillan 1982). As a consequence, the opportunities open to these new arrivals in both employment and housing were restricted. By the end of the twentieth century, Canadians of European ancestry were no longer considered the newcomers, and their status as a marginal population had all but disappeared.

In many respects, the plight of white ethnics raises the same basic issues as that of other subordinate people in Canada: How ethnic can people be—how much can they deviate from an essentially white, Anglo-Saxon, Protestant norm—before society punishes them for a willingness to be different? Despite our pride in our multicultural policies, our society does seem to reward people for assimilating. Yet, as we have seen, assimilation is no guarantee of equality or freedom from discrimination. In the social policy section that follows, we will focus on immigrants, people who inevitably face the question of whether to strive for assimilation.

10-3 The Doukhobors and the Canadian Media

The history of immigrants to Canada has, for the most part, been documented by a biased public press. Portrayals of the dangers presented by each successive wave of newcomers have been an integral part of the representations in the popular Canadian press. From the shiploads of poor Irish people who arrived during the famines of the 1840s to the Chinese miners and railways workers, the Japanese fishers, and the dispossessed Doukhobors, each group has had its reputation sullied by the perpetuation—and sometimes even the creation—of unfortunate stereotypes here in Canada. While most of these groups have gone on over time to establish a certain amount of power and influence, not to mention their own media in Canadian society, the small and isolated Doukhobor communities have not. In an article in the journal *Canadian Ethnic Studies*, researcher Larry Ewashen traces the treatment of the Doukhobors by the mainstream press, from their arrival in the late 1800s to the present.

Ewashen tells how the Doukhobors arrived in Halifax in January 1899, as religious refugees from Russia. Ironically, unlike many other immigrant groups, the Doukhobors were welcomed by Canadians and characterized in the local press as hardworking, Christian victims of tyranny. The new arrivals soon left the Maritimes, eventually settling along the shores of the Columbia River in the East Kootenay region of British Columbia. Despite the promising start, however, the over 2000 original settlers were soon to fall into disfavour. One of the major factors in their demonization was the behaviour of a tiny but very visible breakaway faction known as the Sons of Freedom. The sensational acts of public resistance including nudity and arson appealed to the media's appetite for eye-catching headlines, and thus it was on this group that the media focused for nearly a century. As recently as the summer of 2001, articles about the Doukhobors in the Canadian press continued to focus on the stereotype that

the Sons of Freedom splinter group had created for the whole population.

The consequences of these negative portrayals have dogged the Doukhobor community for decades, overshadowing the peaceful and productive lives of the majority of the group's members.

> **The sensational acts of public resistance including nudity and arson appealed to the media's appetite for eye-catching headlines.**

However, it appears that finally, a century after their arrival in Canada, the media image of the Doukhobor people may be changing. Considerable attention has been given in recent years by both print and broadcast journalists to the suffering endured by Doukhobor families in Castlegar, British Columbia, at the hands of authorities during the 1950s. When the Doukhobors' request that religious instruction be included in the curriculum was ignored, they protested by keeping their children home from school. In a series of incidents that seem more indicative of a

police state than a developed democracy, the provincial government's Department of Child Welfare and the RCMP physically wrested the community's school-aged children from their homes and incarcerated them in internment camps. As might be expected, the actions were defended in the local press at the time—the incidents were not deemed important enough for national coverage—as a last resort against people who refused to send their children to school. Now, 40 years later, the horrific details of the seizures and the long-term consequences for both parents and children are being brought to the attention of Canadians.

Let's Discuss

1. Why do you think the media were so quick to adopt and sustain a negative stereotype of the Doukhobors?
2. Do you think that the Canadian media are free from prejudicial characterizations? Can you think of a minority group within your own community that has been subjected to negative portrayals in the media?

This monument to the Doukhobor struggle acknowledges the multiculturalism of Canadian society. Functionalists would see the Doukhobors' protests as a necessary contribution to social stability in an ethnically diverse country.

Source: Ewashen 1995.

SOCIAL POLICY AND RACE AND ETHNICITY

Global Immigration

The Issue

Worldwide immigration is at an all-time high. Each year, 2 to 4 million people move from one country to another. As of the mid-1990s, immigrants totalled about 125 million, representing 2 percent of the global population (Martin and Widgren 1996). In Canada, during the five-year period between 1991 and 1995, immigration accounted for more than half the country's population growth for the first time in our history. This trend to greater dependence on immigration has heightened the stakes in our ongoing debate as to whether immigrants represent a net benefit or a net cost to Canada: do they provide a benefit by bringing skills, education, and a solid work ethic, or do they represent a net cost because they use social services and displace Canadian workers from their jobs? These questions point to troubling issues, not just for Canada, but for many of the world's economic powers. Who should be allowed in? At what point should immigration be curtailed?

The Setting

The migration of people is not uniform across time or space. At certain times, wars or famines may precipitate large movements of people, either temporarily or permanently. Sometimes the reasons for a large migration cannot be clearly discerned, as in the period between 1931 and 1941, when more people emigrated from Canada than immigrated to the country, a phenomenon that has not been repeated since. Temporary dislocations occur when people leave and then wait until it is safe to return home. However, more and more migrants who cannot make an adequate living in their home nations are moving permanently to developed nations. Figure 10-6 shows the destinations of the major migration streams: into North America, the oil-rich areas of the Middle East, and the industrial economies of Western Europe and Asia. Currently, seven of the world's wealthiest nations (including Canada, Germany, France, the United Kingdom, and the United States) shelter about one-third of the world's migrant population, but less than one-fifth of the total world population. As long as there are disparities in job opportunities among countries, there is little reason to expect this international migration trend to end.

Countries such as Canada that have long been a destination for immigrants have a history of policies to determine who is given preference to enter. Often, clear racial and ethnic biases are built into these policies. In the early twentieth century, Canadian immigration policy excluded non-Europeans, and, while the law was directed mainly at restricting Asians from entering the country, it also was intended to discourage blacks emigrating from the United States and the Caribbean. During the late 1930s and early 1940s, the federal government refused to lift or loosen restrictive immigration quotas in order to allow Jewish refugees to escape the terror of the Nazi regime. In line with this policy, the SS *St. Louis,* mentioned earlier in this chapter, was denied permission to land in Halifax in 1939. This ship was forced to sail back to Europe, where it is estimated that at least a few hundred of the 900 Jewish refugees onboard later died at the hands of the Nazis (Morse 1967; G. Thomas and Witts 1974).

Since the 1960s, policies in Canada have encouraged the immigration of people with relatives here as well as people who have needed skills, or capital to invest. Changes to the *Immigration Act* in 1962 removed "nation of origin" as a condition of eligibility. This has significantly altered the pattern of source nations. While European nations were previously the major source of immigration, in the last 40 years, immigrants have come primarily from Asia and some other countries (see Table 10-2). This means that an ever-growing proportion of Canada is of Chinese or Iranian or Indian heritage. To a large degree, fear and resentment of this growing racial and ethnic diversity is a key factor in opposition to immigration. In many nations, people are very concerned that the new arrivals do not reflect the cultural and racial heritage of the country.

Sociological Insights

Despite people's fears about immigration, it provides many valuable functions. For the receiving society, it alleviates labour shortages, such as Canada is currently experiencing in the areas of health care and technology. Though Canada does not have a specific classification for skilled potential immigrants, the *Immigration and Refugee Protection Act* does provide special status for

FIGURE 10-6

Major Migration Patterns of the 1990s

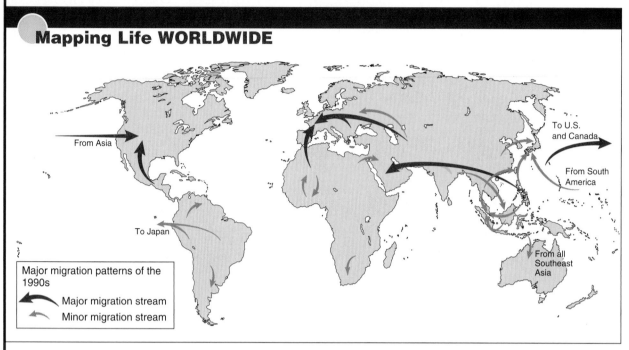

Mapping Life WORLDWIDE

Major migration patterns of the 1990s

← Major migration stream
← Minor migration stream

From Asia
To Japan
To U.S. and Canada
From South America
From all Southeast Asia

Source: Martin and Widgren 1996:21.

applicants who are deemed to have a demonstrable ability to become financially independent. For the sending nation, emigration can relieve economies unable to support large numbers of people. Another important consideration is the large amount of money that expatriates send *back* to their home nations. For example, worldwide emigrants from Portugal alone send more than $6 billion annually back to their home country (World Bank 1995).

There has been considerable research on the impact of immigration on a country's economy. Studies generally show that it has a positive impact on the economy, although areas experiencing high concentrations of immigrants may find it difficult to meet short-term social service needs. When migrants with skills or educational potential leave developing countries, it can be dysfunctional for those nations. No amount of money sent to relatives back at home can make up for the loss of valuable human resources from poor nations (Martin and Midgley 1999).

Conflict theorists note how much of the debate over immigration is phrased in economic terms. But this debate is intensified when the arrivals are of different racial and ethnic background from the host population. For example, Europeans often refer to "foreigners," but the term does not necessarily mean one of foreign birth. In Germany,

"foreigners" refers to people of non-German ancestry, even if they were born in Germany; it does not refer to people of German ancestry born in another country who may choose to come to their "mother country." Fear and dislike of new ethnic groups divide countries throughout the world. In 1998, the One Nation Party of Australia sought office on a platform of removing all illegal immigrants and seizing their property to cover deportation costs (Martin and Widgren 1996; *Migration News* 1998b).

Policy Initiatives

During the summer of 1999, the long and rugged British Columbia coastline became the focus of Canada's fight against illegal immigration when four boatloads of Chinese nationals attempted to land in isolated areas. A year later, a report entitled *Refugee Protection and Border Security: Striking a Balance,* issued by the Department of Citizenship and Immigration, called for changes to the *Immigration Act.* The government responded with Bill C-11 in 2001. A set of core changes to the Act involved alterations to the section on human smuggling. The new legislation increased the fines and the jail terms for those convicted under its provisions—up to $1 million and life in prison. The changes also created a new offence category to cover those who used force to

Table 10-2 Top 10 Places of Birth for Immigrants Arriving Before 1961 and Recent Immigrants to Canada, 2001 Census

Immigrated before 1961

	Number	Percent
Total	1 054 930	100.0
United Kingdom	265 575	25.2
Italy	161 730	15.3
Germany	107 270	10.2
Netherlands	88 810	8.4
Poland	57 820	5.5
United States	45 050	4.3
Hungary	33 215	3.1
Ukraine	27 640	2.6
Greece	21 555	2.0
People's Republic of China	17 545	1.7

Recent immigrants

	Number	Percent
Total	1 830 680	100.0
People's Republic of China	197 360	10.8
India	156 120	8.5
Philippines	122 010	6.7
Hong Kong	118 385	6.5
Sri Lanka	62 590	3.4
Pakistan	57 990	3.2
Taiwan	53 755	2.9
United States	51 440	2.8
Iran	47 080	2.6
Poland	43 370	2.4

Source: Statistics Canada 2001a; 2003a.

(1) Nonpermanent residents are not included in this table.

(2) Recent immigrants are those who immigrated in the 1990s.

This table contains data selected from Catalogue No. 93F0023XDB96003 in the Nation Series.

coerce foreign nationals into coming to Canada, or attempted to disembark people at sea.

The events of September 11, 2001, have also resulted in changes to the way Canada views its borders.

The Department of Foreign Affairs and International Trade has entered into an agreement with the United States to establish a "North American Zone of Confidence" with the creation of a "smart border" (Department of Foreign Affairs 2001). This new collaborative arrangement is intended to set up a continental security zone that would allow for the continued free flow of people and goods across the longest undefended border in the world, while at the same time addressing concerns about terrorist infiltration.

The entire world feels the overwhelming impact of economic globalization on immigration patterns. Europe is also wrestling with policy initiatives. The European Union agreement of 1997 gave the governing commission authority to propose Europe-wide legislation on immigration beginning in 2002. However, the policies must be accepted unanimously, which seems unlikely. An EU policy that would allow immigrants to live and work in one EU country would allow them to work anywhere. The immigration issue is expected to complicate efforts by the sending nations (such as Turkey) to become members of the EU (Light 1999; Sassen 1999).

The intense debate over immigration reflects deep value conflicts in the cultures of many nations. One strand of our culture, for example, has traditionally emphasized egalitarian principles and a desire to help people in their time of need. At the same time, however, hostility to potential immigrants and refugees—whether Irish in the 1840s, Chinese in the 1880s, European Jews in the 1930s and 1940s, or Vietnamese and Jamaican immigrants today—reflects not only racial, ethnic, and religious prejudice, but also a desire to maintain the dominant culture of the in-group by keeping out those viewed as outsiders.

Let's Discuss

1. Did you or your parents or grandparents immigrate to Canada from another nation? If so, when and from where did your family come, and why? Did they face discrimination?

2. Do you live, work, or study with recent immigrants to Canada? If so, are they well accepted in your community, or do they face prejudice and discrimination?

3. Do you think that the concept of a "Zone of Confidence" is a positive step towards controlling access to North America by undesirable foreign nationals? What do you think the impact might be on legitimate refugees and immigrants?

Chapter Resources

Summary

The social dimensions of race and ethnicity are important factors in shaping people's lives in Canada and other countries. In this chapter, we examine the meaning of race and ethnicity and study the major racial and ethnic minorities of Canada.

1. A *racial group* is set apart from others by visible physical differences deemed socially significant, whereas an *ethnic group* is set apart primarily because of national origin or distinctive cultural patterns.

2. When sociologists define a *minority group*, they are primarily concerned with the economic and political power, or powerlessness, of the group.

3. There is no biological basis for the concept of race, and there are no physical traits that can be used to describe one *racial group* to the exclusion of all others.

4. The meaning that people give to the physical differences between races gives social significance to race, leading to *stereotypes*.

5. *Prejudice* often leads to *discrimination*, but the two are not identical, and each can be present without the other.

6. *Institutional or systemic discrimination* results when the structural components of a society create and/or foster differential treatment of groups.

7. Functionalists point out that discrimination is both functional and dysfunctional in society. Conflict theorists explain racial subordination by *exploitation theory*. Perspectives such as global or antiracist feminists point out that gender is not the sole source of oppression, and that gender, race, and class intersect to produce multiple degrees of inequality. Interactionists focus on the micro level of race relations, posing

the *contact hypothesis* as a means of reducing prejudice and discrimination.

8. Four patterns describe typical intergroup relations in North America and elsewhere: *amalgamation, assimilation, segregation*, and *multiculturalism*.

9. In Canada, the ideal pattern of intergroup relations is *multiculturalism*. In our country, there is an ongoing debate over whether the ideal is in fact the reality of life for most minority Canadians.

10. After a century and half of degradation, Canada's First Nations are poised to reclaim their status as an independent, self-determining people, as the legitimate third leg of John Ralston Saul's "triangular reality."

11. French Canadians were marginalized for most of the last 400 years, segregated in the rural countryside of Quebec. It was only after the Quiet Revolution of the 1960s, and the subsequent separatist movement, that Canada's first European settlers reclaimed their status as equal partners in Confederation.

12. Europeans who came neither from France nor England commonly found themselves stereotyped and marginalized by mainstream Canadian society. The Irish, the Ukrainians, and later the Italians all suffered discrimination in the early years of their particular wave of immigration.

13. Porter's "vertical mosaic" is as accurate a portrayal of Canadian multiculturalism today as it was in 1965. While significant progress has been made towards making Canada a truly pluralistic society, stratification on the basis of race and ethnicity still exists.

14. The increase in immigration worldwide has raised questions in individual nations about how to control the process.

Critical Thinking Questions

1. How is institutional or systemic discrimination even more powerful than individual discrimination? How would functionalists, conflict theorists, feminists and interactionists examine this kind of discrimination?

2. The textbook discusses that in Canada, multiculturalism might be more of an ideal than a reality. Can the community in which you grew up and the university you attend be viewed as genuine examples of

multiculturalism? Examine the relations between dominant and subordinate racial and ethnic groups in your hometown and your university.

3. What place in our society do you see Canada's First Nations peoples occupying in the twenty-first century? Do you think they will become more integrated into the mainstream culture, or distance themselves from it by reestablishing their traditional communities?

Key Terms

Amalgamation   The process by which a majority group and a minority group combine through intermarriage to form a new group. (276)

Apartheid   The policy of the South African government designed to maintain the separation of blacks and other nonwhites from the dominant whites. (277)

Assimilation   The process by which a person forsakes his or her own cultural tradition to become part of a different culture. (277)

Contact hypothesis   An interactionist perspective that states that interracial contact between people of equal status in cooperative circumstances will reduce prejudice. (275)

Discrimination   The process of denying opportunities and equal rights to individuals and groups because of prejudice or for other arbitrary reasons. (269)

Ethnic group   A group that is set apart from others because of its national origin or distinctive cultural patterns. (261)

Ethnocentrism   The tendency to assume that one's own culture and way of life are superior to all others. (268)

Exploitation theory   A Marxist theory that views racial subordination such as that in the United States and Canada as a manifestation of the class system inherent in capitalism. (274)

Genocide   The deliberate, systematic killing of or blatant disregard for the well-being of an entire people or nation. (275)

Glass ceiling   An invisible barrier that blocks the promotion of a qualified individual in a work environment because of the individual's gender, race, or ethnicity. (270)

Institutional completeness   The degree to which an ethnic community provides for its own institutional needs, particularly in the key areas of religion, education, and social welfare. (267)

Institutional discrimination   The denial of opportunities and equal rights to individuals and groups that results from the normal operations of a society. (271)

Marginalization   The process by which an individual, as a result of her or his minority status, is provided only partial access to opportunities. This discrimination is often more intense in the case of women. (270)

Metis   The group of people formed when French male fur traders married First Nations women in the Red River Valley area of Manitoba. (262)

Minority group   A subordinate group whose members have significantly less control or power over their own lives than the members of a dominant or majority group have over theirs. (261)

Pluralism   The process by which all groups are able to coexist in the same society because of mutual respect for one another's cultures. (278)

Prejudice   A negative attitude toward an entire category of people, such as a racial or ethnic minority. (268)

Privilege   Access to opportunities provided to people as a direct result of their membership in a particular societal group. (270)

Racial group   A group that is set apart from others because of visible physical differences. (261)

Racism   The belief that one race is supreme and all others are innately inferior. (268)

Segregation   The act of physically separating two groups; often imposed on a minority group by a dominant group. (277)

Self-fulfilling prophecy   The tendency of people to respond to and act on the basis of stereotypes, leading to validation of false definitions. (264)

Self-segregation   The situation that arises when members of a minority deliberately develop residential, economic, and/or social network structures that are separate from those of the majority population. (277)

Social category   A group defined by some culturally relevant characteristic; that is, one that has an impact on a person's status within a society. (268)

Social distance   The degree of difference between cultures, which can vary from slight (e.g., the Canadian and American cultures) to great (e.g., the Canadian culture and that of the Mongols of Northern China). (268)

Stereotypes   Unreliable generalizations about all members of a group that do not recognize individual differences within the group. (264)

Additional Readings

Day, Richard J. F. 2000. *Multiculturalism and the History of Canadian Diversity.* Toronto: U of T Press. The author contends that formal legislation cannot resolve culture-based issues. Day criticizes the federal policy as fantasy, arguing that equality is a myth in a society as diverse as Canada's.

Kalbach, Madeline A., and Warren E. Kalbach, eds. 2000. *Perspectives on Ethnicity in Canada: A Reader.* Toronto: Harcourt Brace. Respected observers of Canada's experiment in pluralism analyze the effects of almost 30 years of multiculturalism.

O'Hearn, Claudine Chiawei, ed. 1998. *Half and Half: Writers on Growing Up Biracial and Bicultural.* New York: Parthenon Books. Eighteen essayists address the difficulties of fitting into, and the benefits of being part of, two worlds.

Schaefer, Richard T. 2002. *Racial and Ethnic Groups.* 9th ed. Upper Saddle River, NJ: Prentice Hall. Comprehensive in its coverage of race and ethnicity, this text also discusses women as a subordinate minority and examines dominant–subordinate relations in Canada, Northern Ireland, Israel and the Palestinian territory, Mexico, and South Africa.

JOURNALS

Among the journals that focus on issues of race and ethnicity are *Canadian Journal of Native Studies* (founded in 1981), *Currents: Readings in Race Relations* (1983), *Ethnic and Racial Studies* (1978), *Études inuit/Inuit Studies* (1977), *Journal of Refugee Studies* (1988), *Native Studies Review* (1984), and *Race and Society* (1997). Local publications produced by racial and ethnic communities are also useful.

Internet Connection

www.mcgrawhill.ca/college/schaefer

For additional Internet exercises relating to exclusionary policies and work by diverse Canadian artists, visit the Schaefer Online Learning Centre at **http://www. mcgrawhill.ca/college/schaefer**. *Please note that while the URLs listed were current at the time of printing, these sites often change—check the Online Learning Centre for updates.*

Sometimes referred to as "The Other" or "Forgotten" Holocaust, the conflicts in Nanking, China, which began in 1937, have recently become the subject of historical debate and interest. Masato Kajimoto offers an online documentary entitled *The Nanking Atrocities* (**http://web.missouri.edu/ ~jschool/nanking/**). On the site, visitors will find text, photographs, and videos to explore.

(a) What historical and social forces played a part in the "Nanking Atrocities"? Which groups and individuals were involved?

(b) What were some of the experiences of Chinese citizens living in Nanking at that time under Japanese military authority?

What was the Chinese "scorched earth policy" and how did that affect citizens?

(c) How many people died during these times described on the site? Why is it hard for researchers to agree upon a precise figure?

(d) What role did members of the media play before and after these events, according to the site?

(e) What was the IMTFE? When and where did the postwar trials occur? What arguments were presented by the prosecution and the defense? Ultimately, who was found responsible and what were the punishments?

(f) Had you ever heard of these events before visiting the site? What impact did the stories and images have on you?

(g) How can the sociological theories in this chapter add to our understanding of the causes and consequences of this tragic form of intergroup relations?

CBC Video

Visit the Schaefer Online Learning Centre at **http://www.mcgrawhill.ca/college/schaefer** to view the CBC video segment "The Prairie Porter: The Treatment of Blacks in Western Canada" and answer related questions.

STRATIFICATION BY GENDER

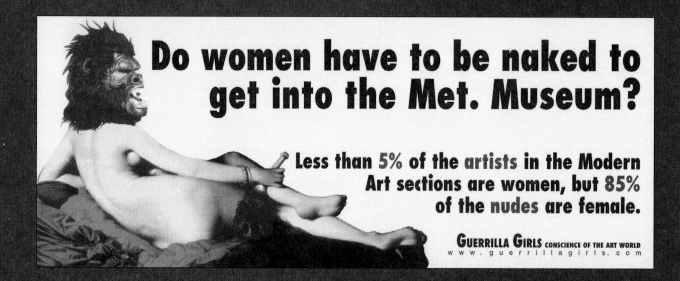

In 1989 a group called the Guerrilla Girls called attention to sexism in the art world with this poster, which protests the underrepresentation of female artists at the world-famous Metropolitan Museum of Art in New York City. This poster and others dealing with sexism in the arts can be viewed at www.guerrillagirls.com.

At last, after a long silence, women took to the streets. In the two decades of radical action that followed the rebirth of feminism in the early 1970s, Western women gained legal and reproductive rights, pursued higher education, entered the trades and the professions, and overturned ancient and revered beliefs about their social role. A generation on, do women feel free?

The affluent, educated, liberated women of the First World, who can enjoy freedoms unavailable to any women ever before, do not feel as free as they want to. And they can no longer restrict to the subconscious their sense that this lack of freedom has something to do with—with apparently frivolous issues, things that really should not matter. Many are ashamed to admit that such trivial concerns—to do with physical appearance, bodies, faces, hair, clothes—matter so much. But in spite of shame, guilt, and denial, more and more women are wondering if . . . something important is indeed at stake that has to do with the relationship between female liberation and female beauty.

The more legal and material hindrances women have broken through, the more strictly and heavily and cruelly images of female beauty have come to weigh upon us. . . .

During the past decade, women breached the power structure; meanwhile, eating disorders rose exponentially and cosmetic surgery became the fastest-growing medical specialty. During the past five years, consumer spending doubled, pornography became the main media category, ahead of legitimate films and records combined, and thirty-three thousand American women told researchers that they would rather lose ten to fifteen pounds than achieve any other goal. More women have more money and power and scope and legal recognition than we have ever had before; but in terms of how we feel about ourselves *physically,* we may actually be worse off than our unliberated grandmothers. Recent research consistently shows that inside the majority of the West's controlled, attractive, successful working women, there is a secret "underlife" poisoning our freedom; infused with notions of beauty, it is a dark vein of self-hatred, physical obsessions, terror of aging, and dread of lost control. *(Wolf 1992:9–10)* ∎

In this excerpt from Naomi Wolf's book, *The Beauty Myth*, a feminist confronts the power of a false ideal of womanhood. Though in recent decades North American women have broken legal and institutional barriers that once limited their educational opportunities and career advancement, Wolf writes, psychologically they are still enslaved by unrealistic standards of appearance. The more freedom women have gained, in fact, the more obsessed they seem to have become with the ideal of the emaciated super-model—an ideal that few women can ever hope to attain without jeopardizing their health or resorting to expensive cosmetic surgery.

Wolf implies that the beauty myth is a societal control mechanism that is meant to keep women in their place—as subordinates to men at home and on the job. Indeed, the term *trophy wife* reduces the conventionally beautiful woman to the role of status symbol of a successful man. But men too are captive to unrealistic expectations regarding their physical appearance. In hopes of attaining the brawny, muscular physique characteristic of body builders and professional wrestlers, more and more men are now taking steroids or electing to undergo cosmetic surgery.

The beauty myth is but one example of how cultural norms may lead to differentiation based on gender. Such differentiation is evident in virtually every human society about which we have information. We saw in Chapters 8, 9, and 10 that most societies establish hierarchies based on social class, race, and ethnicity. This chapter will examine the ways in which societies stratify their members on the basis of gender.

We will begin by looking at how various cultures, including our own, assign women and men to particular social roles. Then we will consider sociological explanations for gender stratification.

Next, the chapter will focus on the diverse experiences of women as an oppressed majority. It will analyze the social, economic, and political aspects of women's subordinate position and consider the consequences of gender stratification for men and minority women. The chapter will also examine the emergence of the contemporary feminist movement, its goals and its contradictions. Finally, the social policy section will analyze links between abortion, new reproductive technology, and women's reproductive choices. ■

Social Construction of Gender

Gender is such a routine part of our everyday activities that we typically take it for granted and only take notice when someone deviates from conventional behaviour and expectations. How many air passengers do you think feel a start when the captain's voice from the cockpit belongs to a female? Or consider another example: A father announces that he will be late for work because his son has a routine medical checkup. We are likely to wonder how he found himself in this situation. Is he a single father struggling to bring up his son by himself? Could his wife have such pressing business that she cannot adjust her schedule to perform the appropriate parental duties? Consciously or unconsciously, we are likely to assume that these parental duties are, in fact, *maternal* duties.

Although a few people begin life with an unclear sexual identity, the overwhelming majority begin with a definite sex and quickly receive societal messages about how to behave. Many societies have established social distinctions between females and males that do not inevitably result from biological differences between the sexes (such as women's reproductive capabilities).

In studying gender, sociologists are interested in the gender-role socialization that leads females and males to behave differently. In Chapter 4, **gender roles** were defined as expectations regarding the proper behaviour, attitudes, and activities of males and females. The application of traditional gender roles leads to many forms of differentiation between women and men. Both sexes are physically capable of learning to cook and sew, yet most Western societies determine that these tasks should be performed by women. Both men and women are capable of learning to weld and fly airplanes, but these functions are generally assigned to men.

Gender roles are evident not only in our work and behaviour but in how we react to others. We are constantly "doing gender" without realizing it. If the father discussed above sits in the doctor's office with his son in the middle of a workday, he will receive approving glances from the receptionist and from other patients. "Isn't he a wonderful father?" runs through their minds. But if the boy's mother leaves *her* job and sits with the son in the doctor's office, she will not receive such silent applause.

We socially construct our behaviour so that male–female differences are either created or exaggerated. For

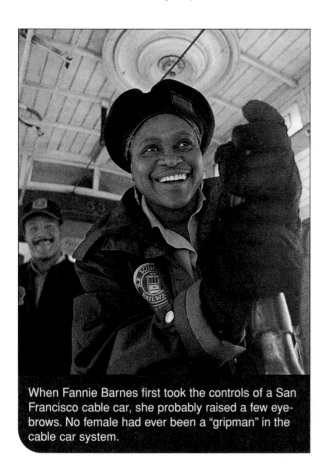

When Fannie Barnes first took the controls of a San Francisco cable car, she probably raised a few eyebrows. No female had ever been a "gripman" in the cable car system.

Gender Roles in North America

Gender-Role Socialization

Male babies get blue blankets, while females get pink ones. Boys are expected to play with trucks, blocks, and toy soldiers; girls are given dolls and kitchen goods. Boys must be masculine—active, aggressive, tough, daring, and dominant—whereas girls must be feminine—soft, emotional, sweet, and submissive. These are all traditional gender-role patterns that have been influential in the socialization of children in North America.

An important element in traditional views of proper "masculine" and "feminine" behaviour is fear of homosexuality. In Chapter 5, we defined ***homophobia*** as fear of and prejudice against homosexuality. Homophobia contributes significantly to rigid gender-role socialization, since many people stereotypically associate male homosexuality with femininity and lesbianism with masculinity. Consequently, men and women who deviate from traditional expectations about gender roles are often presumed to be gay. Despite the advances made by the gay liberation movement (which will be explored in Chapter 21), the continuing stigma attached to homosexuality in our culture places pressure on all males (whether gay or not) to exhibit only narrow "masculine" behaviour and on all females (whether lesbian or not) to exhibit only narrow "feminine" behaviour (Seidman 1994; see also Lehne 1995).

example, men and women come in a variety of heights, sizes, and ages. Yet traditional norms regarding marriage and even casual dating tell us that in heterosexual couples, the man should be older, taller, and wiser than the woman. As we will see throughout this chapter, such social norms help to reinforce and legitimize patterns of male dominance.

In recent decades, women have increasingly entered occupations and professions previously dominated by men. Yet our society still focuses on "masculine" and "feminine" qualities as if men and women must be evaluated in these terms. Clearly, we continue to "do gender," and this social construction of gender continues to define significantly different expectations for females and males (Lorber 1994; L. Rosenbaum 1996; C. West and Zimmerman 1987).

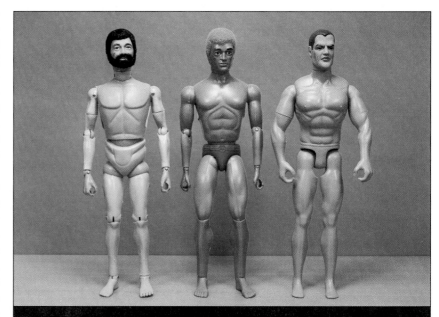

Society often exaggerates male–female differences in appearance and behaviour. In 1964, the G.I. Joe doll (left) had a realistic appearance, but by 1992 (middle) it had begun to acquire the exaggerated muscularity characteristic of professional wrestlers (right). The change intensified the contrast with ultra-thin female figures, like the Barbie doll (Angier 1998).

It is *adults,* of course, who play a critical role in guiding children into those gender roles deemed appropriate in a society. Parents are normally the first and most crucial agents of socialization. But other adults, older siblings, the mass media, and religious and educational institutions also exert an important influence on gender-role socialization in Canada and elsewhere. Researchers Sandnabba and Ahlberg (1999) found that in Finland, parents' responses to children's cross-gender behaviour varied with the child's gender. Girls who engaged in "boyish" behaviour were more accepted than boys whose behaviour was seen as "girlish."

p. 94

It is not hard to test how rigid gender-role socialization can be. Just try transgressing some gender norms— say, by smoking a cigar in public if you are female or carrying a purse if you are male. That is exactly the assignment given to a group of sociology students when their professors asked them to behave in ways that they thought violated norms of how a man or woman should act. The students had no trouble coming up with gender norm "transgressions" (see Table 11-1), and they kept careful notes on how others reacted to their behaviour, with responses ranging from amusement to disgust (Nielsen et al. 2000).

Gender Role Socialization and Social Class Location

The movie "Billy Elliott," released in 2000, portrays the life and gender socialization of a young boy growing up in a British mining town. Billy's father and older brother are both coal miners who are on strike. They discover that Billy has dropped out of boxing lessons and is now, secretly, attending ballet classes. Billy's behaviour causes his father great concern and displeasure, because he sees his son's dancing as a lack of conformity to gender role expectations. The father actively attempts to discourage him from pursuing his love for dance, until he comes to the realization that Billy possesses great talent. At that point, even though his son is defying cultural norms and community standards of appropriate male behaviour, the father begins to support and encourage Billy's dream of becoming a professional dancer.

Research shows that patterns of gender socialization are not homogeneous, but rather, they vary according to one's social class. Working-class parents tend to be more concerned with their children's outward conformity to society's norms and roles (Kohn et al. 1986). Middle-class parents, on the other hand, tend to be more concerned with their children's motivation for certain behaviours, and focus on developing qualities such as self-expression and self-control (Langman 1987). Upper-middle-class families are most likely to support more egalitarian gender relations and thus, socialize their children accordingly (Langman 1987; Lips 1993). Children whose families include middle-class, career-oriented mothers tend to hold more egalitarian attitudes toward women's and men's roles (Tuck et al. 1994).

Women's Gender Roles

How does a girl come to develop a feminine self-image whereas a boy develops one that is masculine? In part, they do so by identifying with females and males in their families and neighbourhoods and in the media. If a young girl regularly sees female characters on television working as defence attorneys and judges, she may believe that she herself can become a lawyer. And it will not hurt if women that she knows—her mother, sister, parents' friends, or neighbours—are lawyers. By contrast, if this young girl sees women portrayed in the media only as models, nurses, and secretaries, her identification and self-image will be quite different. Even if she does become a professional, she may secretly regret falling short of the media stereotype—a shapely, sexy young woman in a bathing suit (Wolf 1992).

Television is far from being alone in stereotyping women. Studies of children's books published in North

Table 11-1 An Experiment of Gender Norm Violations by University Students

Norm violations by women	Norm violations by men
Send men flowers	Wear fingernail polish
Spit in public	Needlepoint in public
Use men's bathroom	Throw Tupperware party
Buy jock strap	Cry in public
Buy/chew tobacco	Have pedicure
Talk knowledgeably about cars	Apply to babysit
Open doors for men	Shave body hair

Based on class projects, sociology students were asked to behave in ways that might be regarded as violating gender norms. This is a sample of their actual choices over a seven-year period. Do you agree that these actions test the boundaries of conventional gender behaviour?

Source: Nielsen et al. 2000:287.

America in the 1940s, 1950s, and 1960s found that females were significantly underrepresented in central roles and illustrations. Virtually all female characters were portrayed as helpless, passive, incompetent, and in need of a strong male caretaker. By the 1980s, there was somewhat less stereotyping in children's books, with some female characters shown to be active. Nevertheless, boys were still shown engaged in active play three times as often as girls (Kortenhaus and Demarest 1993).

Social research on gender roles reveals some persistent differences between men and women in North America and Europe. Women experience a mandate both to marry and to be a mother. Often, marriage is viewed as the true entry into adulthood. And women are expected not only to become mothers but to *want* to be mothers. Obviously, men play a role in these events, but they do not appear to be as critical in identifying the life course for a man. Society defines men's roles by economic success. While women may achieve recognition in the labour force, it is not as important to their identity as it is for men (Doyle and Paludi 1998; Russo 1976).

Traditional gender roles have most severely restricted females. Throughout this chapter, we will see how women have been confined to subordinate roles within the political and economic institutions of Canada and elsewhere. Yet it is also true that gender roles have restricted males.

Men's Gender Roles

> During the game I always played the outfield. Right field. Far right field. And there I would stand in the hot sun wishing I was anyplace else in the world (Fager et al. 1971).

This is the childhood recollection of a man who, as a boy, disliked sports, dreaded gym classes, and had particular problems with baseball. Obviously, he did not conform to the socially constructed male gender role and no doubt paid the price for it.

Men's roles are socially constructed in much the same way as women's roles are. Family, peers, and the media all influence how a boy or a man comes to view his appropriate role in society. Robert Brannon (1976) and James Doyle (1995) have identified five aspects of the male gender role:

- Antifeminine element—show no "sissy stuff," including any expression of openness or vulnerability
- Success element—prove one's masculinity at work and sports
- Aggressive element—use force in dealing with others
- Sexual element—initiate and control all sexual relations
- Self-reliant element—keep cool and unflappable.

No systematic research has established all these elements as a common aspect among boys and men, but specific studies have confirmed individual elements.

Being antifeminine is basic to men's gender roles. Males who do not conform to the socially constructed gender role face constant criticism and even humiliation both from children when they are boys and from adults as men. It can be agonizing to be treated as a "chicken" or a "sissy"—particularly if such remarks come from one's father or brothers. At the same time, boys who successfully adapt to cultural standards of masculinity may grow up to be inexpressive men who cannot share their feelings with others. They remain forceful and tough—but as a result they are also closed and isolated (Faludi 1999; McCreary 1994; G. Sheehy 1999).

In the last 35 years, inspired in good part by the contemporary feminist movement (examined later in the chapter), increasing numbers of men in North America have criticized the restrictive aspects of the traditional male gender role. Some men have taken strong public positions in support of women's struggle for full equality and have even organized voluntary associations such as the White Ribbon Campaign, founded in Canada in 1991 to end men's violence against women. Nevertheless, the traditional male gender role remains well entrenched as an influential element of our culture (Messner 1997; NOMAS 1999).

One recent reflection of the persistence of traditional gender roles has been the rise of the Promise Keepers, an evangelical Christian men's ministry that in the mid-1990s drew more than 700 000 men to stadiums across North America to hear inspirational messages. At Promise Keeper events, men "promise" to return to the home and assume their "rightful" place as head of the household. The Promise Keepers have been criticized for their reassertion of male dominance and their exclusion of women and gay men.

Many of the same criticisms have been directed against the October 1995 Million Man March on Washington, D.C., organized by controversial minister Louis Farrakhan of the Nation of Islam. The march encouraged African American men to accept responsibility for their families and communities; it received strong support in black communities around the United States. For some, the Promise Keepers and the Million Man March represent welcome efforts to reassess the traditional male role; for others, they represent an unwelcome return to conventional norms of male dominance (Miller and Schaefer 1998).

Cross-Cultural Perspective

To what extent do actual biological differences between the sexes contribute to the cultural differences associated with gender? This question brings us back to the debate p. 94 over "nature versus nurture." In assessing the alleged and real differences between men and women, it is useful to examine cross-cultural data.

The research of anthropologist Margaret Mead points to the importance of cultural conditioning—as opposed to biology—in defining the social roles of males and females. In *Sex and Temperament,* Mead (1963, original edition 1935; 1973) describes typical behaviours of each sex in three different cultures in New Guinea:

> In one [the Arapesh], both men and women act as we expect women to act—in a mild parental responsive way; in the second [the Mundugumor], both act as we expect men to act—in a fierce initiating fashion; and in the third [the Tchambuli], the men act according to our stereotypes for women—are catty, wear curls, and go shopping—while the women are energetic, managerial, unadorned partners (Mead 1963: preface to 1950 ed.).

Cultural conditioning is important in the development of gender role differences. This sister and brother from Sudest Island in Papua New Guinea expect women to be the honorary heads of the family.

If biology determined all differences between the sexes, then cross-cultural differences, such as those described by Mead, would not exist. Her findings confirm the influential role of culture and socialization in gender-role differentiation. There appears to be no innate or biological reason to designate completely different gender roles for men and women.

In any society, gender stratification requires not only individual socialization into traditional gender roles within the family, but also the promotion and support of these traditional roles by other social institutions such as religion and education. Moreover, even with all major institutions socializing the young into conventional gender roles, every society has women and men who resist and successfully oppose these stereotypes: strong women who become leaders or professionals, gentle men who care for children, and so forth. It seems clear that differences between the sexes are not dictated by biology. Indeed, the maintenance of traditional gender roles requires constant social controls—and these controls are not always effective.

Explaining Stratification by Gender

Cross-cultural studies indicate that societies dominated by men are much more common than those in which women play the decisive role. Sociologists have turned to all the major theoretical perspectives to understand how and why these social distinctions are established. Each approach focuses on culture, rather than biology, as the primary determinant of gender differences. Yet, in other respects, there are wide disagreements between advocates of these sociological perspectives.

The Functionalist View

Functionalists maintain that gender differentiation has contributed to overall social stability. Sociologists Talcott Parsons and Robert Bales (1955) argued that to function most effectively, the family requires adults who will specialize in particular roles. They viewed the traditional arrangement of gender roles as arising out of this need to establish a division of labour between marital partners.

Parsons and Bales contended that women take the expressive, emotionally supportive role and men the instrumental, practical role, with the two complementing each other. *Instrumentality* refers to emphasis on tasks, focus on more distant goals, and a concern for the external relationship between one's family and other social institutions. *Expressiveness* denotes concern for maintenance of harmony and the internal emotional affairs of the family. According to this theory, women's interest in expressive goals frees men for instrumental tasks, and vice versa. Women become "anchored" in the family as wives, mothers, and household managers; men are anchored in the occupational world outside the home. Of course, Parsons and Bales offered this framework in the 1950s, when many more women were full-time home-makers than is true today. These theorists did not explicitly endorse traditional gender roles, but they implied that dividing tasks between spouses was functional for the family unit.

Given the typical socialization of women and men in North America, the functionalist view is initially persuasive. However, it would lead us to expect girls and women with no interest in children to become babysitters and mothers. Similarly, males who love spending time with children might be "programmed" into careers in the business world. Such differentiation might harm the individual who does not fit into prescribed roles, while also depriving society of the contributions of many talented people who are confined by gender stereotyping. Moreover, the functionalist approach does not convincingly explain why men should be categorically assigned to the instrumental role and women to the expressive role.

The Conflict Response

Viewed from a conflict perspective, this functionalist approach masks underlying power relations between men and women. Parsons and Bales never explicitly presented the expressive and instrumental tasks as unequally valued by society, yet this inequality is quite evident. Although social institutions may pay lip service

to women's expressive skills, it is men's instrumental skills that are most highly rewarded—whether in terms of money or prestige. Consequently, according to feminists and conflict theorists, any division of labour by gender into instrumental and expressive tasks is far from neutral in its impact on women.

Conflict theorists contend that the relationship between females and males has traditionally been one of unequal power, with men in a dominant position over women. Men may originally have become powerful in preindustrial times because their size, physical strength, and freedom from childbearing duties allowed them to dominate women physically. In contemporary societies, such considerations are not so important, yet cultural beliefs about the sexes are long established, as anthropologist Margaret Mead and feminist sociologist Helen Mayer Hacker (1951, 1974) both stressed. Such beliefs support a social structure that places males in controlling positions.

In this sense, traditional gender roles do not simply assign various qualities and behaviours to females and males. They also send messages about these roles. Feminist author Letty Cottin Pogrebin (1981:40) suggests that the two crucial messages of gender-role stereotypes are that "boys are better" and "girls are meant to be mothers." In order for a system of male dominance to maintain itself, she argues, children must be socialized to accept traditional gender-role divisions as natural and just. Sociologist Barbara Bovee Polk (1974:418), in describing the "conflicting cultures approach" to gender differences, observes that "masculine values have higher status and constitute the dominant and visible culture of the society. They . . . provide the standard for adulthood and normality." According to this view, women are oppressed because they constitute an alternative subculture that deviates from the prevailing masculine value system.

Thus, conflict theorists see gender differences as a reflection of the subjugation of one group (women) by another group (men). pp. 13, 18 If we use an analogy to Marx's analysis of class conflict, we can say that males are like the bourgeois, or capitalists; they control most of the society's wealth, prestige, and power. Females are like the proletarians, or workers; they can acquire valuable resources only by following the dictates of their "bosses." Men's work is uniformly valued, while women's work

Conflict theorists emphasize that men's work is uniformly valued, while women's work (whether unpaid labour in the home or wage labour) is devalued. These women are making tents in a factory.

(whether unpaid labour in the home or wage labour) is devalued.

Feminist Perspectives

While some feminist perspectives can be categorized as outgrowths of conflict theory and interactionist approaches, others stand on their own as unique frameworks within which to study the conditions of women's lives. Despite their diversity, they share the belief that women have been subordinated, undervalued, underrepresented, and excluded in male-dominated societies, which, in practical terms, means most of the world. Feminist perspectives encompass a wide-ranging and diverse group of theories focusing on gender inequality, its causes, and its solutions.

Liberal feminists believe that sexism is the root cause of gender inequality, and that women's equality can only be obtained through the extension of equality of opportunity. Rather than advocating structural societal changes, this approach assumes that extending women's opportunities in education and employment, for example, will result in greater gender equality. The 1970 Report of the Royal Commission on the Status of Women in Canada was based on the principles of liberal feminism.

Marxist feminists place the system of capitalism at fault for the oppression of women. If the capitalist economy—with its private ownership of resources and unequal class relations—were to be replaced with a socialist system, economic inequality between the sexes would also change. They believe that women are not oppressed by sexism or lack of opportunity, but rather by a system of economic production that is based upon unequal gender relations (Tong 1984).

Radical feminists disagree that the subordination of women will be eradicated with the abolition of capitalism. Rather, they argue that the subordination of women occurs in all societies, regardless of whether they are capitalist, communist, or socialist. The root of all women's oppression, according to radical feminism, is embedded in patriarchy (Code 1993). Some radicals have focused on reproduction, arguing that women's freedom from reproduction (i.e., through technological developments) will lead to their overall emancipation (Firestone 1970).

Gender relations, according to socialist feminists, are shaped by both patriarchy and capitalism. They claim that the elimination of class distinctions will not bring about gender equality because patriarchy's grip occurs in the home as well as in the public sphere. Class and patriarchal gender relations are inextricably connected, thus equality for women implies that both the system of capitalism and the ideology of patriarchy must be challenged and eliminated (Luxton 1980).

Standpoint feminists (also known as global feminists) look at the diversity and differences (e.g., class, race, sexuality, etc.) in women's experiences that cannot be easily expressed as a single account of "women's experiences." They challenge other feminist theories that attempt to lay the blame for women's oppression in one cause, thus ignoring the wide range of diversity in women. Given the differences in women's lives, standpoint perspectives acknowledge that no *one* standpoint will represent the lives of *all* women (Comack 1996).

This perspective is in line with what Angela Miles refers to as "integrative feminism." Claiming that women are oppressed just because they are women, for example, does little to account for the differences in their lived experience. We need to integrate all aspects of women's lives (class, race, religion, geographic location, sexuality, etc.) into the basis of theory and practice in feminism, according to Miles (2001, 2000).

Another theorist in this perspective is Judith Butler, whose work is representative of "queer theory." Butler (1990) argues that feminism has made a mistake in viewing women as a group with common characteristics and interests. That merely reinforces a binary view of gender relations in which humans are divided into two clear-cut groups: women and men. Instead, she says, gender should be seen as a fluid variable that shifts and changes in different contexts and at different times. In other words, a woman does not necessarily feel feminine all the time, any more than a man feels masculine all the time. Viewing women as a unified homogenous group eliminates them as unique individuals with many divisive differences between them.

While there has been an explosion in the growth of feminist perspectives, including the use of the term "feminism," since the 1960s, the critique of women's position in society and culture goes back to some of the earliest works that have influenced sociology. Among the most important are Mary Wollstonecraft's *A Vindication of the Rights of Women* (originally published in 1792), John Stuart Mill's *The Subjection of Women* (originally published in 1869), and Friedrich Engels's *The Origin of Private Property, the Family, and the State* (originally published in 1884).

Engels, a close associate of Karl Marx, argued that women's subjugation coincided with the rise of private property during industrialization. Only when people moved beyond an agrarian economy could males "enjoy" the luxury of leisure and withhold rewards and privileges from women.

Feminist sociologists would find little with which to disagree in the conflict theorists' perspective. But feminist perspectives would argue that the very discussion of women and society has been distorted by the exclusion of women from academic thought, including sociology. Perhaps, one of the most illustrative examples of this exclusion of women from academic sociology is that of the American sociologist Jane Addams (1860–1935). Although Addams made significant contributions to sociology through her work on women and the family, urban settlements, and working-class immigrants, she was viewed by mainstream sociology as an outsider and not a legitimate member of academia. Her work focused on what we would now call applied sociology and social work. At the time, her efforts, while valued as humanitarian, were seen as unrelated to the research and conclusions being reached in academic circles, which, of course, were male academic circles (M. Andersen 1997).

For most of the history of sociology, studies were conducted on male subjects or about male-led groups and organizations, and the findings were generalized to all people. For example, for many decades studies of urban life focused on street corners, neighbourhood taverns, and bowling alleys—places where men typically congregated. While the insights were valuable, they did not give a true impression of city life because they overlooked the areas where women were likely to gather (L. Lofland 1975).

Since men and women have had different life experiences, the issues they approach are different, and even when they choose similar concerns, they approach them from different perspectives. For example, women who enter politics today typically do so for different reasons than do men. Men often embark on a political career to make business contacts or build on them, a natural extension of their livelihood; women generally become involved because they want to help. This difference is relevant to the likelihood of their future success. The areas in which women achieve political recognition revolve around such social issues as daycare, the environment, education, and child protection—areas that do not attract a lot of big donors. Men focus on tax policies, business regulation, and trade agreements—issues that do excite big donors. Sometimes women do become concerned with these issues, but then they must constantly reassure voters that they are still concerned about "family issues." Male politicians who occasionally focus on the "bread and butter" issues, however, are seen as enlightened and ready to govern (G. Collins 1998).

Feminist theorists emphasize that male dominance goes far beyond the economic sphere. On the surface, economic inequality may look like a separate measure of gender inequality, but it is inextricably related to spousal abuse, sexual harassment, and sexual assault—issues addressed in other chapters of this textbook. Violence towards women by men is a major component of many interrelated experiences that contribute to women's inequality in Canada and around the world.

Both functionalist and conflict theorists acknowledge that it is not possible to change gender roles drastically without dramatic revisions to a culture's social structure. Functionalists perceive potential for social disorder, or at least unknown social consequences, if all aspects of traditional gender stratification are disturbed. Yet, for conflict theorists, no social structure is ultimately desirable if it is maintained by oppressing a majority of its citizens. These theorists argue that gender stratification may be functional for men—who hold power and privilege—but it is hardly in the interests of women (R. Collins 1975; Schmid 1980).

The Interactionist Approach

While functionalist, conflict, and some feminist theorists studying gender stratification typically focus on macro-level social forces and institutions, interactionist researchers often examine gender stratification on the micro level of everyday behaviour. As an example, studies show that men initiate up to 96 percent of all interruptions in cross-sex (male–female) conversations. Men are more likely than women to change topics of conversation, to ignore topics chosen by members of the opposite sex, to minimize the contributions and ideas of members of the opposite sex, and to validate their own contributions. These patterns reflect the conversational (and, in a sense, political) dominance of males. Moreover, even when women occupy a prestigious position, such as that of physician, they are more likely to be interrupted

Studies show that as many as 96 percent of all interruptions in cross-sex (male–female) conversations are initiated by men.

than are their male counterparts (A. Kohn 1988; Tannen 1990; C. West and Zimmerman 1983).

In certain studies, all participants are advised in advance of the overall finding that males are more likely than females to interrupt during a cross-sex conversation. After learning this information, men reduce the frequency of their interruptions, yet they continue to verbally dominate conversations with women. At the same time, women reduce their already low frequency of interruption and other conversationally dominant behaviours.

These findings regarding cross-sex conversations have been frequently replicated. They have striking implications when one considers the power dynamics underlying likely cross-sex interactions—employer and job seeker, professor and student, husband and wife, to name only a few. From an interactionist perspective, these simple, day-to-day exchanges are one more battleground in the struggle for sexual equality—as women try to "get a word in edgewise" in the midst of men's interruptions and verbal dominance (Tannen 1994a, 1994b).

Nordic countries have the highest proportion of female political representatives in the world. In March 1996, Swedish Prime Minister Goran Persson posed with members of his new government, half of whom were women.

Women: The Oppressed Majority

Many people—both male and female—find it difficult to conceive of women as a subordinate and oppressed group. Yet take a look at the political structure of Canada: Women remain noticeably underrepresented. The past decades have brought many firsts for women in Canadian public life: Kim Campbell as the first female prime minister in 1993, Catherine Callbeck of PEI as the first elected female premier (1993), Beverly McLachlin as the first woman to serve as Chief Justice of the Supreme Court of Canada (2000). Yet, women remain underrepresented in both federal and provincial politics. For example, in mid-2001, none of the provincial premiers in Canada was female. And in 2000, women made up 51 percent of the total population, but only 20 percent of those elected to the federal House of Commons. (We will examine women's involvement in politics and government in more detail in Chapter 16.)

This lack of women in decision-making positions is evidence of women's powerlessness in Canada. In Chapter 10, we identified five basic properties that define a minority or subordinate group. If we apply this model to the situation of women in this country, we find that a numerical majority group fits our definitions of a subordinate minority (Dworkin 1982; Hochschild 1973).

1. Women experience unequal treatment. In 2001, the average income for year-round, male workers was $49 250; for comparable female workers, it was only $35 258 (Statistics Canada 2003e). Though they are not segregated from men, women are the victims of prejudice and discrimination in the paid labour force, in the legal system, and in other areas of society. Moreover, women are increasingly dominating the p. 211 ranks of the impoverished, leading to what has been called the *feminization of poverty*.

2. Despite their diversity, women obviously share physical and cultural characteristics that distinguish them from the dominant group (men).

3. Membership in this subordinate group is involuntary.

4. Through the rise of contemporary feminism, women are developing a greater sense of group solidarity, as we will see later in the chapter.

5. Women are not forced to marry within the group, yet many women feel that their subordinate status is most irrevocably defined within the institution of marriage and family. Even when women are employed outside the home, they are still usually responsible for the care of their homes and families. As a result, they experience higher levels of stress and have less time for leisure activities than do their male partners (Statistics Canada 2000).

Sexism and Sex Discrimination

Just as visible minorities in Canada are victimized by racism, women suffer from the sexism of our society. *Sexism* is the ideology that one sex is superior to the other. The term is generally used to refer to male prejudice and discrimination against women. In Chapter 10, we noted that visible minorities can suffer from both individual acts of racism and institutional discrimination. *Institutional discrimination* was defined as the denial of opportunities and equal rights to individuals or groups that results from the normal operations of a society. In the same sense, women suffer both from individual acts of sexism (such as sexist remarks and acts of violence) and from institutional sexism.

It is not simply that particular men in Canada are biased in their treatment of women. All the major institutions of our society—including the government, armed forces, large corporations, the media, the universities, and the medical establishment—are controlled by men. These institutions, in their "normal," day-to-day operations, often discriminate against women and perpetuate sexism. For example, if the central office of a nationwide bank sets a policy that single women are a bad risk for loans—regardless of their incomes and investments—the institution will discriminate against women as a group. It will do so even at bank branches in which loan officers hold no personal biases concerning women, but are merely "following orders." We will examine institutional discrimination against women within the educational system in Chapter 15.

Our society is run by male-dominated institutions, yet with the power that flows to men come responsibility and stress. Men have higher reported rates of certain types of mental illness, shorter lifespans, and greater likelihood of death due to heart attacks or strokes (see Chapter 18). The pressure on men to succeed—and then to remain on top in a competitive world of work—can be especially intense. This is not to suggest that gender stratification is as damaging to men as it is to women. But it is clear that the power and privilege men enjoy are no guarantee of well-being.

The Status of Women Worldwide

The Hindu society of India makes life especially harsh for widows. When Hindu women marry, they join their husband's family. If the husband dies, the widow is the "property" of that family. In many cases, she ends up working as an unpaid servant; in others she is simply abandoned and left penniless. Ancient Hindu scriptures portray widows as "inauspicious" and advise that "a wise man should avoid her blessings like the poison of a snake" (J. Burns 1998:10). Such attitudes die slowly in the villages, where most Indians live.

Though Westerners tend to view Muslim societies as being similarly harsh toward women, that perception is actually an overgeneralization. Muslim countries are exceedingly varied and complex, and do not often fit the stereotypes created by the Western media. For a detailed discussion of the status of Muslim women today, see Box 11-1.

These are but a few reflections of women's second-class status throughout the world. It is estimated that women grow half of the world's food, but they rarely own land. They constitute one-third of the world's paid labour force but are generally found in the lowest-paying jobs. Single-parent households headed by women—which appear to be on the increase in many nations—are typically found in the poorest sections of the population. Indeed, the feminization of poverty has become a global phenomenon. As in Canada, women worldwide are underrepresented politically.

A detailed overview of the status of the world's women, issued by the United Nations in 1995, noted that "too often, women and men live in different worlds—worlds that differ in access to education and

Women have second-class status around the world. These women are processing raw silk by hand in India.

11-1 The Head Scarf and the Veil: Complex Symbols

"My mother wears a *djellabah* [a robelike outergarment] and a veil. I have never worn them. But so what? I still cannot get divorced as easily as a man, and I am still a member of my family group and responsible to them for everything that I do. What is the veil? A piece of cloth" (Fernea and Fernea 1979:77).

The Moroccan woman who made this comment to a Western scholar several decades ago worked as a linguist and bought her clothes in Paris. She was saying, in essence, that despite a dramatic change in the clothing many Moroccan women wore, their roles and their status in the family had not changed. She was right about the strong cultural continuity in Moroccan society; for her and for millions of other Muslim women, traditions were much the same then as they had been for centuries. But as interactionists would point out, the veil is much more than a piece of cloth. Like a flag, it represents values that are sacred to Islamic society.

The wearing of a veil or head scarf, which is common to many but not all Middle Eastern societies, is based on a verse from the Koran: "Prophet, enjoin your wives, your daughters and the wives of true believers to draw their veils close round them . . . so that they may be recognized and not molested." The injunction to cover one's body in the presence of men to whom one is not closely related is based on a view of women as bearers of the family's honour. To protect their chastity from men's predatory sexual advances, women must keep themselves out of harm's way. Wearing a veil in public is intended to do just that, to signal others that they are not to touch the wearer. A man who ignores that signal does so at his peril, for his action shames not just the woman, but her whole family.

The veil is also a way of maintaining a family's social status. Unlike rich families, poor families depend on their wives' and daughters' presence in the fields and markets, where a veil and robe can hamper a woman's ability to work. Thus in some regions of North Africa, Muslim women have never worn the veil. Nor do women veil themselves in small communities, where everyone knows everyone else. Only in the city is a woman required to wear a veil.

> In effect, the veil represents a rejection of the beauty myth, which is so prevalent in Western societies.

In effect, the veil represents a rejection of the beauty myth, which is so prevalent in Western societies. While a Muslim woman's beauty is valued, it is not to be seen or exploited by the whole world. By covering themselves almost completely, Muslim women assure themselves and their families that their physical persons will not play a role in their contacts outside the family. Rather, these women will be known only for their faith, their intellect, and their personalities.

In the twentieth century, the veil was politicized by modernization movements that pitted Western cultural values against traditional Islamic values. In Turkey, for instance, the rise to power of Mustafa Attaturk in 1923 sparked a process of sweeping social change, in which government officials attempted to subordinate traditional ethnic and religious influences to their nationalistic goals. They substituted Latin for Arabic in written documents, and purged the spoken language of Persian and Arabic words. Though women weren't forbidden to wear the veil, they were not allowed to veil themselves in public places like schools. Not surprisingly, many Muslims resented these forced social changes.

In Turkey, however, a modified version of the veil has recently become the symbol of militant feminists. Among educated young women who study at the universities, the new veil signifies an intention to transcend the traditional roles of wife and mother. Women who are professionals, writers, intellectuals, and activists wear it as a public statement of their aspirations.

Westerners may think the Turkish feminists' adoption of the veil is strange. Together with some Muslim feminists, people from the West tend to see the veil as a symbol of women's second-class status. But to many Muslim women it makes sense. The veil allows young women to leave their homes in the countryside and mix with strange men in the great universities of the city, without violating Islamic custom. To many Muslim women, the veil is no less than a means of liberation.

Let's Discuss

1. Consider life in a society in which women wear veils. Can you see any advantages, from the woman's point of view? From the man's?
2. Do you find the Western emphasis on physical beauty oppressive? If so, in what ways?

Sources: C. Cancel 1997; Fernea 1998; Fernea and Fernea 1977, 1979; N. Gole 1997; Read and Bartkowski 1999.

greater financial rewards and prestige than women's jobs. For example, in 1999, women made up approximately 46 percent of the paid labour force of Canada. Yet they constituted only 26.8 percent of senior managers, 19.6 percent of those employed in the natural science, engineering, and mathematics fields, and 6.2 percent in trades, transport, and construction. Canadian women, however, have made gains in the areas of business and finance, medicine, and dentistry, where they now account for almost half of all professionals in these previously male-dominated fields (see Table 11-2). In Box 11-2, we consider unique situations that run *against* sex-typing: male nurses and female hockey players.

Women from all groups, particularly those from visible minorities or those from older age groups, are at increased risk of encountering attitudinal or organizational bias that prevents them from reaching their full potential. As we saw in Chapter 10, the term **glass ceiling** refers to an invisible barrier that blocks the promotion of a qualified individual in a work environment because of the individual's gender, race, or ethnicity. A recent study of the *Fortune* 1000 largest corporations in the United States showed that only 9 percent of the seats on their boards of directors were held by women. Indeed, 16 percent of these corporations still did not have even one woman on the board (Catalyst 1999).

Table 11-2 Canadian Women in Selected Occupations, 1999

Women as percentage of total employed in occupation	
Underrepresented	
Trades, transport, and construction	6.2%
Natural sciences, engineering, mathematics	19.6%
Senior management	26.8%
Overrepresented	
Nursing, therapy, other health-related	86.5%
Clerical and administrative	75.3%
Teaching	62.1%
Sales and service	58.7%
Roughly equally represented	
Business and finance	49.4%
Doctors, dentists, other health occupation	47.1%
Artistic, literary, recreational	54.8%

Source: Statistics Canada 1999f.

One response to the "glass ceiling" and other gender bias in the workplace is to start your own business and work for yourself. This route to success, traditionally taken by men from immigrant and racial minority groups, has become more common among women as they have increasingly sought paid employment outside the home. Women entrepreneurs are a rapidly growing employment category in Canada. As of 1995, women represented 30 percent of the self-employed, up from 24 percent in 1985. An international report comparing 140 nations reports that Canadian women start businesses at a rate three times that of men, and their success rate is twice the rate of men (Neft and Levine 1997).

The workplace patterns described here have one crucial result: Women earn much less money than men in the paid labour force of Canada. In 1999, the median weekly earnings of full-time female workers were about 70 percent of those for full-time male workers. Given these data, it is hardly surprising to learn that many women are living in poverty, particularly when they must function as heads of households. In the discussion of poverty in Chapter 8, we noted that female heads of households and their children accounted for most of the nation's poor people living in families. Yet not all women are in equal danger of experiencing poverty. As will be discussed more fully later in the chapter, women who are members of racial and ethnic minorities suffer from "double jeopardy": stratification by race and ethnicity as well as by gender.

Social Consequences of Women's Employment

"What a circus we women perform every day of our lives. It puts a trapeze artist to shame." These words by the writer Anne Morrow Lindbergh attest to the lives of women today who try to juggle their work and family lives. This situation has many social consequences. For one thing, it puts pressure on child care facilities and on public financing of daycare and even on the fast-food industry, which provides many of the meals women used to prepare during the day. For another, it raises questions about what responsibility male wage earners have in the household.

Who does the housework when women become productive wage earners? Studies indicate that there continues to be a clear gender gap in the performance of housework, although the differences are narrowing. Still, as shown in Figure 11-3, the most recent study finds women doing more housework and spending more time on child care than men, whether it be on a workday or when off work. Taken together, then, a woman's workday on and off the job is much longer than a man's. When calculating the total of paid and unpaid work hours, Canadian women worked approximately 80 hours more per year than men did, in 1998 (Statistics Canada 1999a). In

SOCIAL POLICY AND GENDER STRATIFICATION

Abortion and Sex Selection: The "New Eug

The Issue

A woman's decision to have an abortion in Canada today is usually made in consultation with her doctor, based on factors related to her overall health and well-being. However, with the emergence of new reproductive and genetic technologies, referred to collectively as "reprogenetics" (McTeer 1999), the twinning of abortion and reprogenetics presents new ethical and moral considerations. The results of this combination have led to what some sociologists are calling the "new eugenics"—a movement to promote the reproduction of those with particular characteristics, while attempting to limit or control the reproduction of others. Thus, abortion becomes not simply a choice a woman makes on the basis of her health and well-being, but potentially, with reprogenetics, an instrument of social control, controlling what "type" of person is to be reproduced.

The Setting

In 1892, Canada's first Criminal Code made "procuring or performing an abortion a crime punishable by life imprisonment" (McTeer 1999:32). With amendments to the Criminal Code in 1968, legal abortion became permissible

Advocates on both sides see abortion as a life-and-death issue. Pro-life advocates regard the fetus as a life, while pro-choice supporters express outrage at violent attacks on abortion clinics and abortion providers.

under certain
a special com
to take place
tals and prov
committee a
unavailable c
particularly th
changed in 1
pregnant wor
her doctor" (N

In 1993,
formed in Ca
Differences i
relate to the
For example,
1995 were p
and 24 (Stat

In the la
lished a Roy
tive technolo
assisted repr
fertilization,
(one woman
and prenatal
fication of th
these techno
as a society
treated (e.g.
female fetus
ductive righ
(McTeer 199

In 1996
C-47, a legis
mercial surr
than those
linked here
ban 13 diff
died "on the
was called.

Sociolog

Sociologist
defining the
conflict ove

Ever
all the
degrees,
problem
family li
graduate
business
asked if t
cessful
family.
respond
Yet 53 p
tioned s
their job
family o
of those
left the p
(Swiss a

Mo
care, an
time act
men per
ever, s
(1996) v
ences in
about th
with 25
more in
associat
involvec
likely to
become
they fai

A s
Susan S
ways in
ically, n
activitie
"work."
women'
freedom
care. Ch
than wc

The
ety is sh
done by
(Pleck
work w
retirem
and tha
Implici
and ste
2002).
greater

Research in Action   11-2 Female Hockey Players and Male Nurses

When you sit down to watch hockey, you expect to watch men playing. When you are being assisted by a nurse, you expect it to be a woman. And, indeed, in almost every case you would be correct, but not always.

In Canada, about 5 percent of all registered nurses are male (Canada Census 1996). Sociologist E. Joel Heikes (1991) wondered what characteristics male nurses exhibit when entering a traditionally female occupation; consequently, he conducted in-depth interviews with male registered nurses employed in hospital settings. Heikes reports that male nurses felt more visible than female nurses and typically responded by overachieving. Although they did not feel polarized from the female nurses, they did feel socially isolated as "tokens" in the workplace. Typically, they were excluded from traditionally female gatherings, such as female nurses' baby and bridal showers. Such social isolation did not reduce the male nurses' skills training, but it excluded them from informal interactions in which they could have "networked" with female nurses and learned more about the day-to-day workings of the hospital.

Stereotyping was also evident: Male nurses were commonly mistaken for physicians. Even though being mistaken for someone of higher status may appear to be advantageous, it can often have negative connotations for the male nurse. It is a constant reminder of his deviant position in a traditionally female occupation. The implicit message is that men should be doctors rather than nurses. Indeed, when correctly identified as nurses, men face a much more serious form of stereotyping. Because of the persistence of traditional gender roles, it is assumed that all male nurses must be gay. Many male nurses told Heikes that they felt a need to deny this stigmatized identity.

More recently, sociologist Christine

Williams (1992, 1995) examined the underrepresentation of men in four predominantly female professions: nursing, elementary school teaching, librarianship, and social work. Drawing on in-depth interviews with 99 men and women in these professions, Williams found that the experience of tokenism is very different for women and men. While men in these traditionally female professions commonly experience negative stereotyping, they nevertheless benefit from hidden *advantages* stemming from their status as men, such as receiving early and disproportionate encouragement to become administrators. By contrast, women in traditionally male professions often find that their advancement is limited and their token status is hardly an asset.

> Like male nurses, female hockey players are rare specimens, although they have actually been around almost as long as male players.

Like male nurses, female hockey players are rare specimens, although they have actually been around almost as long as male players. A photograph of the daughter of Lord Stanley, founder of the coveted Stanley Cup given to the champions in professional hockey, shows her playing the sport in 1890. A rivalry between U.S. and Canadian women's teams goes back to 1916. But women were never taken very seriously as hockey players—until quite recently. In 1998, women made their first appearance on the rink in the Olympics, where the U.S. team took a gold medal. Then, in 2002, the Canadian team reciprocated and took gold in the Salt Lake City Olympics.

While increasing numbers of women have come into their own in

hockey, they still are put down for not being as "tough and strong" as male hockey players. Hockey rules do not allow women to body check, which calls for shoving an opponent hard into the boards on the side of the rink. Their game relies more on finesse than strength. Using both observation and interviews, sociologist Nancy Theberge (1997) studied a female Canadian league. She found that while the players generally acknowledge that the game is more skill-oriented without body checking, they favour including body checking in women's hockey to make the sport more professional. They reason that if they can make a living at the sport, then they should accept the risk of injury that comes with "hard checks." Ironically, their willingness to accept a more intense level of the game comes at a time when many people feel that men's professional hockey has become too physical and too violent; hard body checking leads to the fights that accompany many games.

Theberge found that even without body checking, injury and pain were routine features of the lives of female hockey players. She notes, "For these athletes, overcoming injury and pain is a measure of both ability and commitment." Some observers, however, find it troubling that as women's involvement in ice hockey grows, the pressure increases to develop a system that normalizes injury and pain in the sport.

Let's Discuss

1. Have you ever played a sport or worked in a job that was stereotyped as being more appropriate for the opposite sex? If so, how comfortable were you with your role?

2. Do you think women's hockey rules should be amended to allow body checking? Why or why not? Should men's hockey rules be amended to discourage checking?

Sources: Bureau of the Census 1999a; DeSimone 2000; Elliot 1997; Heikes 1991; Lillard 1998; Theberge 1997; Zimmer 1988.

FIG

Gen
and

Paid

Unpa
H

C

Sour

Taking Sociology to Work

PRUDENCE HANNIS:
Research and Community
Quebec Native Women

Prudence Hannis is an Abenati First Nations woman who is responsible for the women's health portfolio in the Quebec Native Women organization. Her job entails organizing and facilitating activities such as a seminar on sexual abuse in local communities, and producing a resource booklet on the subject for community members. Prudence also works for the Centre of Excellence on Women's Health, Consortium Université de Montreal, where she focuses on First Nations women's health issues, such as HIV–AIDS, prostitution, poverty, sexual discrimination, drug and alcohol abuse, and family violence.

Hannis
ment, and
op
soc
me
the
"S
of
Na
wh
ters, and
empower

add
thei
expr
"Me
the
coo
to"

wo
repe
ill fa
care
per
Two
forc

the
wo
wo
equ
tio

iN

Figure 11-5 illustrates, these women also earned considerably less than men (Statistics Canada 2001a; 2001c).

Feminists have addressed themselves to the particular needs of minority women. The question for First Nations and other visible minority women appears to be whether they should unify with their "brothers" against racism or challenge them for their sexism. One answer is that, in a truly just society, both sexism and racism must be eradicated.

The discussion of gender roles among visible minorities has always provoked controversy. Advocates

of black
only dis
struggle
among b
commun
ety. By
argue, in
maintain
society.
portray
as illiter
forth.
We
not agre
ing for s
racial an
ity can I
pioneer
before t
tisan ob
twin bat
men wil
America

FIGURE 11-5

Average Earnings By Sex and Minority Status,
Full-Time/Full-Year Employment, 2001

Visible minority women	$43 758
Nonvisible minority women	$45 820
Visible minority men	$54 173
Nonvisible minority men	$58 250

Source: Human Resources Development Canada 2003.

Internet Connection

www.mcgrawhill.ca/college/schaefer

For additional Internet exercises relating to gender stratification, visit the Schaefer Online Learning Centre at **http://www.mcgrawhill.ca/college/schaefer**. *Please note that while the URLs listed were current at the time of printing, these sites often change—check the Online Learning Centre for updates.*

Political decisions made at the federal and provincial levels of government often have a gendered impact. Visit PAR-L's "The Policy Shop" (**http://www.unb.ca/par-l/policy1.htm**) for resources on gender and policymaking in Canada.

(a)   Identify some "hot issues" relating to gender at the federal level of government.

(b)   Identify some "hot issues" relating to gender at the provincial level of government.

(c)   Identify some "hot issues" related to gender at the international level.

(d)   Describe what a "gender-based" analysis of policymaking would involve.

(e)   What kinds of efforts are being made at the federal level to ensure that Canada has a voice in international discussions on gender related issues?

(f)   What policy or policies do you think currently has/have the greatest differential impact on the genders?

CBC Video

Visit the Schaefer Online Learning Centre at **http://www.mcgrawhill.ca/college/schaefer** to view the CBC video segment "Military Women: Fighting for Fairness" and answer related questions.

STRATIFICATION BY AGE

The theme of this poster, "a society for all ages," was chosen to promote 1999 as the United Nations' International Year of Older Persons. In April 2002, recognizing that soon every third person will be over 60, the Second World Assembly on Ageing was held in Madrid, Spain. UN members focused on strategies to ensure that everyone, regardless of age, will have an active role to play in building society.

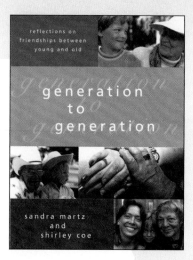

On bad days, I wish I'd never answered the phone that Tuesday night.

It was a fluke we were home in the first place. Manny was in the car, within seconds of tooting the horn at me, while I rummaged through my desk looking for the tickets to the travelogue we were late for. *If only I hadn't forgotten the tickets; if only I'd cleaned my desk the week before; if only . . .*

It solved nothing to think of the *if onlys.* I was in the house, the phone rang, I answered it. And our lives were changed. . . .

"Mom, Jake's left! He's gone. Sarah's crying, Jon threw up, and the soup boiled over. I can't deal with it, Mom. Can I bring the kids over? Please?"

I stopped looking for the tickets. I heard Manny toot the horn. We wouldn't be late for the travelogue. We weren't going.

"Bring them over," I said.

That was nine months ago.

To be perfectly honest—a trait that is more and more dear to me—if we had missed that particular phone call, there would've been another. Life-changing phone calls are persistent and inevitable.

On good days I look at our grandchildren, Sarah and Jonathan, and smile at the fine job they're doing coloring their pictures or setting the table. And when they climb into my lap at night and nuzzle their downy cheeks against mine, I praise God for the love He brought into our lives.

This dizzying combination of regret and gratitude is natural now. The tranquility of our retirement years has been replaced by the chaos and tedium of raising two small children. Loud voices. Rigid schedules.

It's harder on Manny. Even though I'd long ago left behind thoughts of homework and skinned knees, I was infinitely more prepared to take on the responsibility of our grandchildren than he was. He'd never witnessed the day-to-day dealings of broken shoelaces and sack lunches with our own daughter. He'd been at work. But work was over for him. He paid his dues, and his lofty dreams of retirement—our lofty dreams—were cut short as we backtracked twenty years to the sights and sounds of parenthood. . . .

The children are no longer visitors. Their Barbie dolls and race cars are at home on the shelves in the family room, right next to my needlepoint and Manny's fishing magazines. There is an odd comfort in the sounds of their footfalls. Their laughter weaves its way through the rungs of the chairs and echoes in the cookie jar. They belong here. They are ours. *(N. Moser 1998:158, 159, 160)* ■

s this excerpt suggests, the distinctions between generations are getting more and more blurred. We are not automatically "old" when we turn 60 or when we become grandparents, as Nancy Moser discovered. She and her husband Manny saw the years fall away when they reassumed the responsibilities of parenthood in raising their grandchildren. At the same time they had to put their retirement dreams on hold. Her essay, which appears in the anthology *Generation to Generation,* is aptly titled "Wishing for Maybes." While the Mosers' situation is not typical of people their age, it is certainly not unusual. There are almost 1.5 million grandparents raising their grandchildren in Canada today (Smith 2000).

People are becoming increasingly aware that age—like race or gender—is socially constructed. We tend to view age as an ascribed status, and this view dominates our perceptions of others. Rather than simply suggesting that a particular driver is not competent, someone may say, "Those old codgers shouldn't be on the road." In such instances, senior citizens are categorized by age in a way that obscures individual differences. Many social observers today feel that stereotypical attitudes toward age and aging won't change until we look at the life course as a continuum, rather than a series of finite stages with predictable consequences.

This chapter looks at the process of aging in terms of the life course. It examines aging around the world but focuses primarily on the position of older people within the age stratification system of Canada. After exploring various theories to explain the impact of aging on the individual and society, we will take a look at role transitions throughout the life course, including the role of the "sandwich generation," which finds itself caring for both children and parents. We will pay particular attention to the effects of prejudice and discrimination on older people and the rise of a political consciousness among senior citizens. Finally, the social policy section examines the controversy surrounding the issue of "the right to die." ■

Aging and Society

The Sherpas—a Tibetan-speaking, Buddhist people in Nepal—live in a culture that idealizes old age. Almost all senior members of the Sherpa culture own their homes, and most are in relatively good physical condition. Typically, older Sherpas value their independence and prefer not to live with their children. Among the Fulani of Africa, however, older men and women move to the edge of the family homestead. Since this is where people are buried, the seniors sleep over their own graves, for they are already viewed as socially dead. Like gender stratification, age stratification varies from culture to culture. One society may treat older people with great reverence, while another sees them as unproductive and "difficult" (M.C. Goldstein and Beall 1981; Stenning 1958; Tonkinson 1978).

It is understandable that all societies have some system of age stratification and associate certain social roles with distinct periods in one's life (see Box 12-1). Some of this age differentiation seems inevitable; it would make little sense to send young children off to war or to expect most older citizens to handle physically demanding tasks such as loading goods at shipyards. However, as is the case with the social construction of gender, age stratification in North America goes far beyond the physical constraints of human beings at different ages.

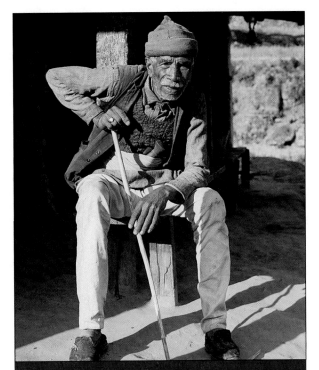

This Sherpa living in Nepal is honoured among his people for his age. Not all old people are so lucky—in many cultures being old is considered next to dead.

12-1 Aging Worldwide: Issues and Consequences

An electric water kettle is wired so that people in another location can determine if it has been used in the previous 24 hours. This may seem a zany bit of modern technology, but it symbolizes a change taking place around the globe—the growing needs of an aging population. Welfare Network Ikebukuro Honcho has installed these wired hot pots in Japan so that volunteers can monitor if senior citizens have used the devices to prepare their morning tea. An unused pot initiates contacts to see if the older person needs help. This technological monitoring system is an indication of the tremendous growth of Japan's senior population and, of particular social significance, the increasing numbers who live *alone*.

In 2002, the United Nations held its Second World Assembly on Ageing in Madrid, Spain. Release of demographic data shows that around the world, there are more than 600 million people aged 65 or over; they represent about 10 percent of the world population. And as illustrated in Figure 12-1, when one examines world population aging over three generations, we see that within 100 years, seniors will represent almost one-third of the world's population.

> **An unused pot initiates contacts to see if the older person needs help.**

Through the efforts of both national governments and international agencies, many societies have drastically reduced the incidence of diseases and their rates of death. Consequently, these nations—especially the industrialized countries of Europe and North America—have increasingly higher proportions of older members.

Figure 12-2 provides a projected regional breakdown of changes in population aging over the next 50 years. We see that Europe has, and will continue to have, the largest percentage of seniors. The overall population of Europe is older than that of any other continent. As the proportion of older people in Europe continues to rise, many governments that have long prided themselves on their social welfare programs are examining ways to shift a larger share of the costs of caring for older people to the private sector and charities. Germany and France have instituted or are weighing plans to raise the age at which retirees will qualify for pensions.

In most developing countries, people over 60 are likely to be in poorer health than their counterparts in industrialized nations. Yet few of these nations are in a position to offer extensive financial support to seniors.

International studies and conferences have examined social and economic policies dealing with the "oldest

Sources: Crossette 1996; Hani 1998; Haub and Cornelius 1999; Longworth 1996; M. Specter 1998; Strom 2000a.

"Being old" is a master status that commonly overshadows all others in our society. The insights of labelling theory help us analyze the consequences of aging. Once people are labelled "old," this designation has a major impact on how others perceive them and even on how they view themselves. Negative stereotypes of senior citizens contribute to their position as a minority group subject to discrimination, as we'll see later in the chapter.

p. 179

The model of five basic properties of a minority or subordinate group (introduced in Chapter 10) can be applied to older people in Canada to clarify their subordinate status:

p. 262

1. Senior citizens experience unequal treatment in employment and may face prejudice and discrimination.

2. Seniors share physical characteristics that distinguish them from younger people. In addition, their cultural preferences and leisure-time activities often differ from those of the rest of society.

3. Membership in this disadvantaged group is involuntary.

4. Older people have a strong sense of group solidarity, as is reflected in the growth of senior citizens' centres, retirement communities, and advocacy organizations.

5. Older people generally are married to others of comparable age.

There is one crucial difference between older people and other subordinate groups, such as racial and ethnic minorities or women: *All* of us who live long enough will

FIGURE 12-1

Three Centuries of World Population Aging

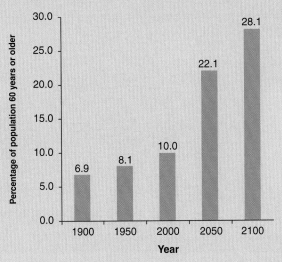

Source: Long-Range World Population Projections: Based on the 1998 Revision. The Population Division, Department of Economic and Social Affairs, United Nations Secretariat.

FIGURE 12-2

Percentage Increase in Age 60 and Over by Region, 2000–2050

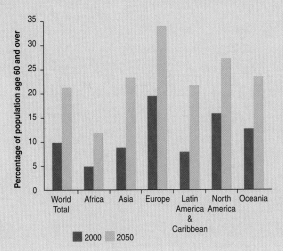

Source: "World Population Prospects, The 1998 Revision, Volume II: Sex and Age." The Population Division Department of Economic and Social Affairs, United Nations Secretariat.

old"—those people aged 80 and over. This rapidly growing group deserves special attention. First, the oldest old in both industrialized and developing countries will probably have to depend for their security on a declining proportion of the population that is of working age. Second, in their search for support systems from either family or government, the oldest old may be forced to migrate, which will affect the immigration policies of many nations. Finally, the needs of the oldest old may intensify the pressures on their children (older workers) to postpone retirement for 5 or 10 additional years.

Let's Discuss

1. For an older person, how might life in Pakistan differ from life in France?
2. Do you know an aged person who lives alone? What arrangements have been made (or should be made) for care in case of emergency?

eventually assume the ascribed status of being an older person (M. Barron 1953; J. Levin and Levin 1980; Wagley and Harris 1958).

Explaining the Aging Process

Aging is one important aspect of socialization—the lifelong process through which an individual learns the cultural norms and values of a particular society. There are no clear-cut definitions for different periods of the aging cycle in Canada. Thus, while *old age* has typically been regarded as beginning at 65, which corresponds to the retirement age for many workers, not everyone accepts this definition. The senior population is not a homogeneous group. According to Health Canada, people aged 65 to 74 resemble those under age 65 much more closely than they do those aged 85 and over. Meanwhile, the middle range (75 to 84 years) is considered to be in a period of transition. With life expectancy being extended, writers are beginning to refer to people in their 60s as the "young old" to distinguish them from those in their 80s and beyond (the "old old").

The particular problems of senior citizens have become the focus for a specialized area of research and inquiry known as gerontology. *Gerontology* is the scientific study of the sociological and psychological aspects of aging and the problems of the aged. It originally developed in the 1930s, as an increasing number of social scientists became aware of seniors' plight.

Gerontologists rely heavily on sociological principles and theories to explain the impact of aging on the individual and society. They also draw upon the disciplines of psychology, anthropology, physical education,

A. DAVID ROBERTS:
Social Worker

Dave Roberts admits to being a "people person," a trait that sociology courses fostered by showing how "everybody has differences; there are little bits of different cultures in all of us." He also had the benefit of "a lot of great teachers", including Dr. Jill Quadagno in an "Aging" course. It was this class that sparked his interest in aging issues, which led to a certificate in gerontology in addition to a sociology degree in 1998. He realized that there was a good job market in working with the aging baby boom generation.

Volunteer work with the Meals on Wheels program steered him toward working with seniors. Today Roberts is a social worker in a nursing home, where he is responsible for patients' care plans. In the course of this work, he meets regularly with patients, family members, and medical residents.

Roberts finds that the concept of teamwork he learned in group projects in university has helped him in this job. Also, the projects he had to do in school taught him to work on a schedule. Perhaps most importantly, sociology has helped him "to grow as a person to explore different angles, different theories. . . . I'm a better person."

His advice for sociology students: "Just give it a chance; they throw everything into an intro course. Don't get overwhelmed; take it as it comes."

counselling, and medicine in their study of the aging process. Two influential views of aging—disengagement theory and activity theory—can be best understood in terms of the sociological perspectives of functionalism and interactionism, respectively. The conflict and feminist perspectives also contribute to our sociological understanding of aging.

Functionalist Approach: Disengagement Theory

Elaine Cumming and William Henry (1961) introduced an explanation of the impact of aging during one's life course known as *disengagement theory*. This theory, based on a study of older people in good health and relatively comfortable economic circumstances, contends that society and the aging individual mutually sever many of their relationships. In keeping with the functionalist perspective, disengagement theory emphasizes that passing social roles on from one generation to another ensures social stability.

According to this theory, the approach of death forces people to drop most of their social roles—including those of worker, volunteer, spouse, hobby enthusiast, and even reader. Younger members of society then take on these functions. The aging person, it is held, withdraws into an increasing state of inactivity while preparing for death. At the same time, society withdraws from seniors by segregating them residentially (retirement homes and communities), educationally (programs designed solely for senior citizens), and recreationally (senior citizens' social centres). Implicit in disengagement theory is the view that society should *help* older people to withdraw from their accustomed social roles.

Since it was first outlined more than three decades ago, disengagement theory has generated considerable controversy. Some gerontologists have objected to the implication that older people want to be ignored and "put away"—and even more to the idea that they should be encouraged to withdraw from meaningful social roles. Critics of disengagement theory insist that society *forces* seniors into an involuntary and painful withdrawal from the paid labour force and from meaningful social relationships. Rather than voluntarily seeking to disengage, older employees find themselves pushed out of their jobs—in many instances, even before they are entitled to maximum retirement benefits (Boaz 1987).

Although functionalist in its approach, disengagement theory ignores those with postretirement employment. Some move into a "bridge job"—employment that bridges the period between the end of a person's career and his or her retirement. Unfortunately, seniors can easily be victimized in such "bridge jobs." Psychologist Kathleen Christensen (1990), warning of "bridges over troubled water," emphasizes that older employees do not want to end their working days as minimum-wage jobholders engaged in activities unrelated to their career jobs (Doeringer 1990; Hayward et al. 1987).

Interactionist Approach: Activity Theory

Often seen as an opposing approach to disengagement theory, *activity theory* argues that seniors who remain active and socially involved will be best-adjusted. Proponents of this perspective acknowledge that a 70-year-old person may not have the ability or desire to perform various social roles that he or she had at age 40. Yet they contend that old people have essentially the same need for social interaction as any other group.

The improved health of older people—sometimes overlooked by social scientists—has strengthened the arguments of activity theorists. Illness and chronic disease are no longer quite the scourge of the senior population that they once were. The recent emphasis on fitness, the availability of better medical care, greater control of infectious diseases, and the reduction of fatal strokes and heart attacks have combined to mitigate the traumas of growing old. Accumulating medical research also points to the importance of remaining socially involved. Among those who decline in their mental capacities later in life, deterioration is most rapid in old people who withdraw from social relationships and activities (Liao et al. 2000; National Institute on Aging 1999b).

Admittedly, many activities open to seniors involve unpaid labour, for which younger adults may receive salaries. Such unpaid workers include hospital volunteers (versus aides and orderlies), drivers for charities such as the Red Cross (versus chauffeurs), tutors (as opposed to teachers), and craftspeople for charity bazaars (as opposed to carpenters and dressmakers). As noted in Chapter 6, in 2000, 18 percent of Canadians aged 65 and over were involved in unpaid volunteer activities (Hall et al. 2001). Some companies have recently initiated programs to hire retirees for full-time or part-time work. For example, about 130 of the 600 reservationists at the Days Inn motel chain are over 60 years of age. In Britain, Hot House Flowers found that older workers had a higher rate of retention and the company now makes a point of hiring people over the age of 55. In Japan, over 71 percent of men aged 60 and over are employed. Silver Human Resource Centres, established initially in Tokyo in 1975, contract out services whereby retirees perform tasks that benefit their communities, such as translation, gardening, carpentry, and providing home help and other services to older people (Marshall and Clarke 1996).

Disengagement theory suggests that older people find satisfaction in withdrawal from society. Functionally speaking, they conveniently recede into the background and allow the next generation to take over. Proponents of activity theory view such withdrawal as harmful for both seniors and society and focus on the potential contributions of older people to the maintenance of society. In their opinion, aging citizens will feel satisfied only when they can be useful and productive in society's terms— primarily by working for wages (Civic Ventures 1999; Dowd 1980; Quadagno 1999).

The Days Inn motel chain hires many retirees to work full- or part-time as reservationists. *Activity theory* argues that the older person who remains active will be best adjusted.

The Conflict Approach

Conflict theorists have criticized both disengagement theory and activity theory for failing to consider the impact of social structure on patterns of aging. Neither approach, they say, attempts to question why social interaction "must" change or decrease in old age. In addition, these perspectives, in contrast to the conflict perspective, often ignore the impact of social class on the lives of older people.

The privileged position of the upper class generally leads to better health and vigour and to less likelihood of dependency in old age. Affluence cannot forestall aging indefinitely, but it can soften the economic hardships faced in later years. Although pension plans, retirement packages, and insurance benefits may be developed to assist older people, those whose wealth allows them access to investment funds can generate the greatest income for their later years.

By contrast, working-class jobs often carry greater hazards to health and a greater risk of disability; aging will be particularly difficult for those who suffer job-related injuries or illnesses. Working-class people also depend more heavily on government benefits and pension programs. During inflationary times, their relatively fixed incomes from these sources barely keep pace with escalating costs of food, housing, utilities, and other necessities (Atchley 1985).

Conflict theorists have noted that the transition from agricultural economies to industrialization and capitalism has not always been beneficial for senior citizens. As a society's production methods change, the traditionally valued role of older people within the economy tends to erode. Their wisdom is no longer relevant.

According to the conflict approach, the treatment of older people in Canada reflects the many divisions in our society. The low status of older people is seen in prejudice and discrimination against them, age segregation, and unfair job practices—none of which are directly addressed by either disengagement or activity theory.

Feminist Approaches

With the view that society is gendered by nature, feminist theories analyze how gender defines social interactions and experiences of aging, concluding that men and women experience aging differently. Feminist theorists criticize other theories on aging for failing to focus on women's experiences. For example, Neysmith (1995) says that gerontologists tend to use men's experience as a yardstick to evaluate women's experience. The failure can also be seen in research on life stages and its inability to identify stages and issues that mark women's lives (Jones et al. 1990).

In previous decades, women's aging was seen almost exclusively in the context of marriage and family development (Nelson and Robinson 1999). Moreover, studies on family life often contain an agist bias, as they adopt the perspective of middle-aged adults while treating the aged as passive members of families (Eichler 2001). This results in a failure to recognize that aging family members, particularly women, not only receive care but also give care to the younger members. Thus, they are not solely dependent, but interdependent members of the family (Connidis 1989).

Feminist research in aging has focused on many issues, such as power relationships and elder abuse, widowhood, wife assault in old age, women's retirement, the organization of informal health care, the double standard with regard to the portrayal of senior men and women, and differences in the experience of aging for men and women (Novak and Campbell 2001). Feminist theories have made distinct contributions to gerontology. First, they have drawn attention to the importance of individual characteristics and diverse backgrounds, to show that aging does not manifest itself in everyone in a universal manner. Rather, age intersects with gender, class, race, ethnicity, and sexual orientation to produce different patterns and conditions and experiences. Second, they present a more inclusive picture of aging and older adults, by focusing on issues that are relevant to the majority of the older population—women. Third, feminist theories challenge the androcentric focus found in traditional theories. And they also challenge the agist biases in "mainstream" feminist theories that ignore issues of age (Novak and Campbell 2001).

The four perspectives considered here take different views of senior citizens. Functionalists portray them as socially isolated with reduced social roles; interactionists see older people as involved in new networks of people in a change of social roles; conflict theorists regard older people as victimized by social structure, with their social roles relatively unchanged but devalued; and feminist perspectives have challenged the androcentricity implicit in many explanations of women's aging. Feminist perspectives draw attention to how aging intersects with gender, class, race, ethnicity, and sexual orientation. Table 12-1 summarizes these perspectives.

Table 12-1   Theories of Aging

Sociological perspective	View of aging	Social roles	Portrayal of seniors
Functionalist	Disengagement	Reduced	Socially isolated
Interactionist	Activity	Changed	Involved in new networks
Conflict	Competition	Relatively unchanged	Victimized, organized to confront victimization
Feminist theories	Challenge androcentric bias and assumptions of homogeneity	Socially constructed, diverse according to class, ethnicity, race, and sexual orientation	Double standard, whereby men gain status and women lose status

Role Transitions Throughout the LifeCourse

p. 89 As we have seen in Chapter 4 and throughout this textbook, socialization is a lifelong process. We simply do not experience things the same way at different points in the life course. For example, one study found that even falling in love differs depending on where we are in the life course. Young unmarried adults tend to treat love as a noncommittal game or else as an obsession characterized by possessiveness and dependency. People over the age of 50 are much more likely to see love as involving commitment, and they tend to take a practical approach to finding a partner who meets a set of rational criteria. The life course, then, affects the manner in which we relate to one another (Montgomery and Sorell 1997).

How we move through the life course varies dramatically, depending on the individual. Some people, for instance, start their own households in their early 20s, while others are well into their 30s before beginning a permanent relationship with someone else. Still, it is possible to identify a series of developmental periods, with critical transitions between the various stages, as shown in the model devised by psychologist Daniel Levinson (Figure 12-3). In the following sections, we will focus on major transitions associated with the later stages of the life course: the sandwich generation, retirement, and death and dying.

The Sandwich Generation

The first transitional period identified by Levinson begins at about age 17 and extends to age 22. It marks the time at which an individual gradually enters the adult world, perhaps by moving out of the parental home, beginning a career, or entering a marriage. The second transitional period, the midlife transition, typically begins at about age 40. Men and women often experience a stressful period of self-evaluation, commonly known as the *midlife crisis*, in which they realize that they have not achieved basic goals and ambitions and have little time left to do so. Thus, Levinson (1978, 1996) found that most adults surveyed experienced tumultuous midlife conflicts within the self and with the external world.

Not all the challenges at this time of life come from career or one's partner. During the late 1990s growing attention focused on the *sandwich generation*—adults who simultaneously try to meet the competing needs of their parents and of their own children. Caregiving goes in two directions: (1) to children who even as young adults may still require significant direction and (2) to aging parents whose health and economic problems may demand intervention by their adult children. A 1999

FIGURE 12-3

Developmental and Transitional Periods in Adulthood

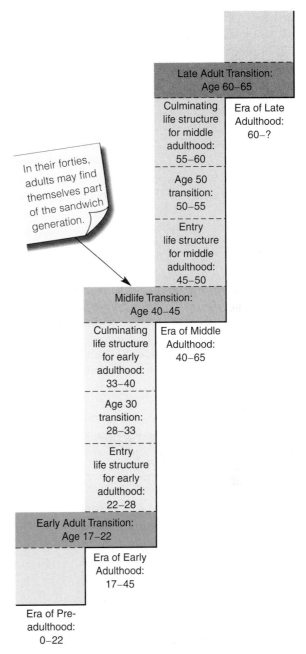

Source: D. Levinson 1996:18.

Conference Board of Canada study found that almost one in four households provides care or support in some form to an older family member or friend. The average time spent on elder care is approximately 28 hours per month, although those who provide more personal care (bathing, dressing, feeding, etc.) report spending as many as 60 hours per month giving care to a senior citizen. It is understandable that elder care constitutes a significant amount of time for the 15 percent of caregivers who also have children at home (MacBride-King 1999).

The last major transition identified by Levinson occurs after age 60, and this is a time when dramatic changes take place in people's everyday lives, as we will now see.

Adjusting to Retirement

Retirement is a rite of passage that marks a critical transition from one phase of a person's life to another. Typically, there are symbolic events associated with this rite of passage, such as retirement gifts, a retirement party, and special moments on the "last day on the job." The pre-retirement period itself can be emotionally charged, especially if the retiree is expected to train his or her successor (Atchley 1976).

For both men and women in Canada, the overall age of retirement has declined steadily. In 2000, 40 percent of all workers retired before they were 60; the average retirement age is 61.7 years for men and 60.1 years for women. At the same time, longevity has increased: in 2001 there were more that 900 000 people aged 80 and over in Canada, up from less than 200 000 in 1971. According to the research report "Seniors in Canada," most seniors report that their overall health is good, and the number of seniors living in hospitals or institutions has fallen in recent decades (Health Canada 2002; Statistics Canada 2002; BC Stats 2001).

Gerontologist Robert Atchley (1976) has identified several phases of the retirement experience:

- *Preretirement,* a period of anticipatory socialization as the person prepares for retirement
- *The near phase,* when the person establishes a specific departure date from his or her job
- *The honeymoon phase,* an often-euphoric period in which the person pursues activities that he or she never had time for before
- *The disenchantment phase,* in which retirees feel a sense of letdown or even depression as they cope with their new lives, which may include illness or poverty
- *The reorientation phase,* which involves the development of a more realistic view of retirement alternatives
- *The stability phase,* a period in which the person has learned to deal with life after retirement in a reasonable and comfortable fashion
- *The termination phase,* which begins when the person can no longer engage in basic, day-to-day activities such as self-care and housework

As this analysis demonstrates, retirement is not a single transition but rather a series of adjustments that vary from one person to another. The length and timing of each phase will vary for each individual, depending on such factors as his or her financial and health status. In fact, a person will not necessarily go through all the phases identified by Atchley. For example, people who were forced to retire or who face financial difficulties may never experience a "honeymoon phase." A number of seniors continue to participate in the paid labour force. In 2000, 9 percent of men and 3 percent of women over the age of 65 years were part of the workforce. More than half of them were self-employed and 43 percent were employed on a part-time basis (Health Canada 2002).

Like other aspects of life in Canada, the experience of retirement varies according to gender, race, and ethnicity. White males are most likely to benefit from a structure of retirement wages as well as to have participated in a formal retirement preparation program. As a result, anticipatory socialization for retirement is most systematic for white men.

Three generations in this family celebrate their March birthdays together. While we all move through the life course in individual ways, it is possible to identify certain developmental periods with critical transitions between the stages.

Death and Dying

Among the role transitions that typically (but not always) come later in life is death. Until recently, death was viewed as a taboo topic in North America. However, psychologist Elisabeth Kübler-Ross (1969) through her pioneering book *On Death and Dying* has greatly encouraged open discussion of the process of dying.

Drawing on her work with 200 cancer patients, Kübler-Ross identified five stages of the experience of dying that a person may undergo:

1. When people finally realize that they are dying, they first *deny* the truth to themselves, their families, and their friends.

2. When denial can no longer be maintained, it is followed by a period of *anger,* which can be directed at almost anyone or anything.

3. In the stage of *bargaining*—often relatively brief—people talk about the unfulfilled goals they will pursue if they somehow recover. In effect, they are hoping to bargain with God for additional time.

4. When people realize that these deals are not realistic, they enter a stage of *depression* and experience a pervasive sense of loss.

5. The final stage, *acceptance,* is not always reached by the dying patient. Those who accept death are not happy about the prospect, but have come to terms with their fate and are ready to die in peace.

Coffins in Ghana sometimes reflect the way the dead lived their lives. This Methodist burial service is for a woman who died at age 85, leaving behind 11 children, 82 grandchildren, and 60 great-grandchildren. Her coffin, designed as a mother hen, features 11 chicks nestling between the wings (Secretan 1995).

As Kübler-Ross (1969:113) notes: "It is as if the pain had gone, the struggle is over, and there comes a time for 'the final rest before the long journey' as one patient phrased it."

Despite its continued popular appeal, the Kübler-Ross five-stage theory of dying has been challenged. Researchers often can't substantiate these stages. Moreover, this model relies on an assumption that the dying person clearly recognizes that death is nearing. But an array of chronic, debilitative, degenerative diseases can mask death. Finally, critics of Kübler-Ross emphasize that even if this five-stage model is accurate for North America, it does not apply to other cultures that deal with death quite differently (Marshall and Levy 1990; Retsinas 1988).

Functionalists would see those who are dying as fulfilling distinct social functions. Gerontologist Richard Kalish (1985) lists among the tasks of the dying: completing unfinished business, such as settling insurance and legacy matters; restoring harmony to social relationships and saying farewell to friends and family; dealing with medical care needs; and making funeral plans and other arrangements for survivors after death occurs. In accomplishing these tasks, the dying person actively contributes to meeting society's needs for smooth intergenerational transitions, role continuity, compliance with medical procedures, and minimal disruption of the social system despite loss of one of its members.

This functionalist analysis brings to mind the cherished yet controversial concept of a "good death." One researcher described a "good death" among the Kaliai, a people of the South Pacific, in which the dying person "called all his kinsmen to gather around him, disposed of his possessions after repaying the obligations owed by him and forgiving any obligations of others to him, and then informed those gathered that it was time for him to die" (Counts 1977:370).

The "good death" among the Kaliai has its parallel in Western societies, where we may refer to a "natural death," an "appropriate death," or a "death with dignity." In the Western ideal of a "good death," friends and family surround the dying person, there is minimal technological interference with the natural dying process, the dying person's pain and discomfort are controlled, and there is an orderly and meaningful closure for the dying person and his or her loved ones. While this Western ideal makes the experience of dying as positive as possible, some critics fear that acceptance of the "good death" concept may direct individual efforts and social resources away from attempts to extend life. Some people do argue that fatally ill older people should not only passively accept death but should forgo further treatment in order to reduce health care expenditures. As we will see in the social policy section, such issues are at the heart of current debates over the "right to die" and physician-assisted suicide (Kearl 1989; Marshall and Levy 1990).

Recent studies suggest that, in many varied ways, people have broken through the historic taboos about death and are attempting to arrange certain aspects of the idealized "good death." For example, bereavement practices—once highly socially structured—are becoming increasingly varied and therapeutic. More and more people are actively addressing the inevitability of death by making wills, leaving "living wills" (health care proxies that explain their feelings about the use of life-support equipment), donating organs, and providing instructions for family members about funerals, cremations, and burials. Given medical and technological advances and a breakthrough in open discussion and negotiation regarding death and dying, it is more possible than ever that "good deaths" can become a social norm in North America (M. LaGanga 1999; J. Riley 1992).

Table 12-2   Population of Canada, Aged 65 and Over

Year	People aged 65 and over			As a percent of the Canadian population
	Men	Women	Total	
	(thousands)			
1921	215.0	205.3	420.2	4.8
1931	294.6	281.5	576.1	5.6
1941	390.9	376.9	767.8	6.7
1951	551.3	535.0	1086.3	7.8
1961	674.1	717.0	1391.1	7.6
1971	790.3	972.0	1762.3	8.0
1981	1017.2	1360.1	2377.3	9.6
1986	1147.6	1589.3	2737.0	10.4
1991	1349.8	1867.4	3217.2	11.4
1996	1515.3	2066.7	3582.0	12.1
1998	1587.4	2142.3	3729.8	12.3
2000	1645.4	2204.4	3849.9	12.5
2001	1671.8	2216.7	3888.5	13.0
Projections				
2016	2521.2	3181.2	5702.4	16.6
2021	2989.6	3681.1	6670.6	18.9
2026	3515.5	4237.4	7753.0	21.4
2031	3950.2	4705.9	8656.1	23.6
2036	4132.7	4934.0	9066.7	24.4
2041	4197.1	5035.8	9232.9	24.9
2046	4231.4	5087.2	9318.7	25.2
2051	4257.5	5108.9	9366.4	25.4

Source: Statistics Canada 2002; Health Canada 2001a.

Age Stratification in Canada

The "Aging of Canada"

As noted earlier, as the number of seniors in society increases, gerontologists are showing that having a broad category to include anyone over 65 fails to take into consideration that seniors are not a homogenous group. Analysts today tend to differentiate between 'young', 'middle' and 'senior' or 'old' seniors.

In a similar vein, when looking at aging of the global population, the United Nations uses an index of aging that also classifies countries into three possible categories: young, mature, or aged populations. A country is considered 'young' on the aging index if its proportion of those 65 years of age and over is under 4 percent of the total population. A 'mature' country's proportion of older adults is between 4 and 8 percent, and an 'aged' country has more than 8 percent of the total population in the senior age bracket (McVey and Kalbach 1995).

As Table 12-2 illustrates, Canada was a 'mature' population from the early 1900s until 1971, when those 65 and over represented 8 percent of the population, officially placing Canada into the UN's 'aged' population category. Today, seniors represent one the fastest-growing groups in Canada. In 2001, more than 13 percent of the population was over 65 years of age. When compared to 9.6 percent in 1981, one can see that the senior population grew about twice as fast as the overall population in that time period (Statistics Canada 2002; Health Canada 2001a). Statistics Canada has projected that the growth will continue, to 20 percent by the early 2020s and then peaking at 25 percent in approximately 2050 (Health Canada 2001a).

Averages such as this, however, mask the great diversity among Canada's seniors as relates to age, region, gender, and race or ethnicity. For example, if we break up the number of seniors into age groups, we see that the 'old' seniors (those 85 years of age and over) are the fastest-growing category. "In fact, about one in 10 Canadian seniors is now 85 or over, up from one in 20 in the early 1920s" (Health Canada 2001b). As seen in Figure 12-4, Statistics Canada projects that number will be 4 percent in 2041.

While Canada's seniors account for a substantial population of all provinces, there are differences in the proportion of the older age group. Using the UN categories, most of the provinces would have an 'aged' population but the Northwest Territories and Yukon would be considered 'mature,' with seniors representing 4.4 percent and 6 percent of their populations, while Nunavut is the 'young' area, with seniors representing only 2.2 percent of its total population. Saskatchewan

has the oldest population, with 15.1 percent of its population 65 years of age and over (Statistics Canada 2002; Health Canada 2002). Map 12-1 shows these variations within Canada in 2001 and the projected changes by 2021, suggesting that although the overall trend toward an aging population is occurring, regional responses to the form of specialized housing, health care, care-giving services, and other social services may vary.

Gender differences sharply punctuate overall rates of aging in Canadian society. "At the turn of the century there were 105 men for every 100 women aged 65 and over. In the mid-1950s, older men still outnumbered older women, but by the 1960s, the pattern reversed itself" (Novak & Campbell 2001:64). Women make up less than half of the population under age 55, but in 2001 they represented 51 percent of those aged 55 to 64, and 57 percent of all people over 65 (Health Canada 2001d). When looking at categories of seniors, however, we can see the differences that the rapid increase in women's life expectancy make. In 2001, women made up 53 percent of 'young' seniors (65 to 74 years of age), 60 percent of the 'middle' group (75 to 84 years), and 70 percent of 'old' seniors (85 years and over) (Health Canada 2001d; Health Canada 2002).

A relatively large proportion of seniors in Canada are immigrants. Health Canada's Division of Aging and Seniors reports that one in four seniors was born outside of Canada. However, most of them (three out of five) arrived in Canada more than 35 years earlier, when they were children or young adults. Only 3 percent of

FIGURE 12-4

Seniors By Age Subgroups, as Percent of the Total Population, Canada, 1921–2041

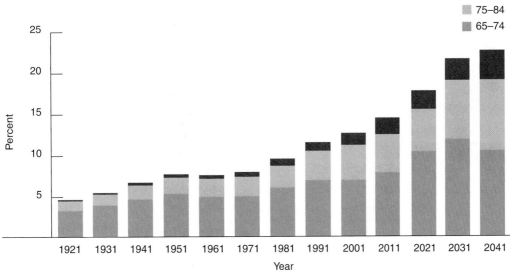

Source: Health Canada 2002:3.

MAP 12-1

Percentage of Seniors in Each Canadian Province and Territory

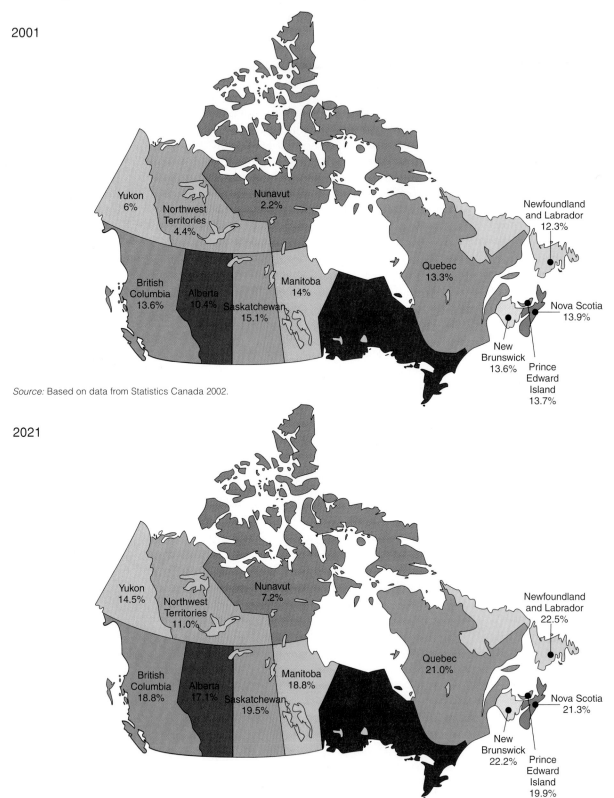

2001

Yukon
6%

Northwest
Territories
4.4%

Nunavut
2.2%

Newfoundland
and Labrador
12.3%

British
Columbia
13.6%

Alberta
10.4%

Saskatchewan
15.1%

Manitoba
14%

Quebec
13.3%

Nova Scotia
13.9%

New
Brunswick
13.6%

Prince
Edward
Island
13.7%

Source: Based on data from Statistics Canada 2002.

2021

Yukon
14.5%

Northwest
Territories
11.0%

Nunavut
7.2%

Newfoundland
and Labrador
22.5%

British
Columbia
18.8%

Alberta
17.1%

Saskatchewan
19.5%

Manitoba
18.8%

Quebec
21.0%

Nova Scotia
21.3%

New
Brunswick
22.2%

Prince
Edward
Island
19.9%

Source: Health Canada 2002:7.

immigrants arrive in Canada each year as seniors (Health Canada 2002). Visible minorities make up just 6 percent of Canada's seniors, and of these 40 percent are Chinese and 19 percent are South Asian. The smallest percentage of visible minority seniors is from Southeast Asia, Latin America, and Korea (Health Canada 2001e).

Seniors make up a much smaller proportion of Canada's Aboriginal population. In 1996, only 4 percent of First Nations people were aged 65 and over. Though the prevalence of certain diseases and health conditions among Aboriginal seniors is double or triple the rate reported by seniors in general, Aboriginal seniors are living longer today than ever before. Their numbers are expected to grow rapidly in the next few decades, and the Royal Commission on Aboriginal Peoples estimated that the numbers of seniors will triple by 2016 (Health Canada 2002; Health Canada 2001f).

While Canada is noticeably aging, the nation's older citizens are in a sense getting younger, owing to improved health and nutrition. In fact, Canadians tend to live their later years in better health than ever before. In "Canada's Aging Population," Health Canada reports on a 1997 study, which found that more than three-quarters of seniors living at home viewed their health as good, very good, or excellent. Only 6 percent reported their health as poor, as Figure 12-5 shows (Health Canada 2002).

Clearly, the aging of Canada is a phenomenon that can no longer be ignored—either by social scientists or by government policymakers. Groups advocating on behalf of seniors have emerged and spoken out on a wide range of issues (as we will see later in the chapter). Politicians court the votes of older people, since they are the age group most likely to vote. In fact, they are the only age group that has actually increased its turnout rate over the last 25 years (L. Feldman 1999; LaGanga 2000).

Wealth and Income

Canada's seniors have lower incomes, on average, than people in most other age groups, and yet, the typical senior citizen enjoys a standard of living that is higher than at any point in the nation's past. In fact, the incomes of our seniors have risen faster than other group's in the past few decades. In 1998, seniors had an average income of just over $21 000 compared to the national average of $28 500 for those under 64 years of age (Health Canada 2002; Health Canada 2001g). And as in society in general, senior men have higher incomes than senior women—$26 800 compared to $16 900 in 1998 (Health Canada 2001h).

Class differences among senior citizens remain evident but tend to narrow somewhat: Those older people who enjoyed middle-class incomes while younger tend to remain better off after retirement than those who previously had lower incomes, but the financial gap lessens a bit (Arber and Ginn 1991; Duncan and Smith 1989).

To some extent, older people owe their overall improved standard of living to a greater accumulation of wealth—in the form of home ownership, private pensions, and other financial assets. Much of the improvement is the result of the 'maturation of the public pension system.' Pension plans, whether public (Old Age Security and Canada/Quebec Pension Plans) or private—including employer sponsored pension plans and individual registered retirement savings plans (RRSPs)—account for approximately 75 percent of the income for seniors (Health Canada 2002). Women rely much more heavily on public sources, while private employment related sources contribute more to men's income.

There is variance, however, that is not revealed through these figures. In 1998, one in five seniors in Canada lived in a low-income situation, with an income below Statistics Canada's low income cut-offs (as discussed in Chapter 8). While seniors are more likely than adults under the age of 64 to have low incomes, this has fallen sharply in the past few decades. In 1980, one in three seniors was considered poor (Health Canada 2001i).

As noted earlier, women account for 57 percent of people in Canada aged 65 years and over and 70 percent of those 85 and over. Older women experience a double burden: They are female in a society that favours males, and they are aged in a society that values youth. The social inequities that women experience throughout their

FIGURE 12-5

Most Canadian Seniors* Rate Their Health Positively, 1996–1997

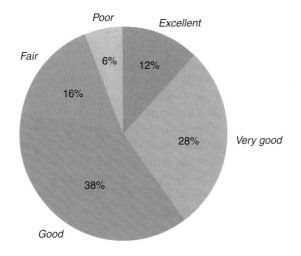

*Seniors living in private households only.
Source: Health Canada 2002:9.

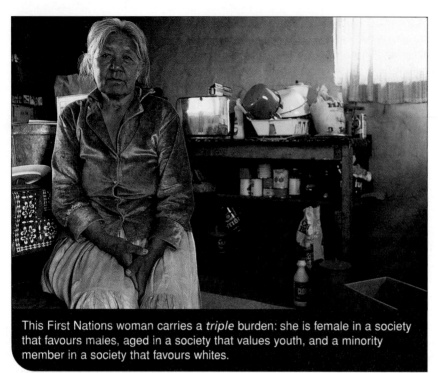

This First Nations woman carries a *triple* burden: she is female in a society that favours males, aged in a society that values youth, and a minority member in a society that favours whites.

lifetimes, as noted earlier in the chapter, only intensify as they age. As a result, in 1998 about half of older women living alone received some form of public assistance. Unattached senior women (widowed, divorced, single) are most at risk of poverty. This is a reflection of their historically lower participation in the paid labour force and their lower wages when compared to men. However, with increased participation rates since the early 1970s, it is anticipated that improvements will soon be seen in the incomes of all senior women.

Viewed from a conflict perspective, it is not surprising that older women experience a double burden; the same is true of senior First Nations people and visible minorities. Economic inequality is not a static condition, for people move in and out of poverty. Race and ethnicity, however, are ascribed characteristics. And while people may move up and down the social ladder, those who *begin* life with greater resources have more opportunities to acquire additional resources. Women and minorities, and especially minority women, are less likely to accumulate savings or even have adequate pension plans for their older years. (See Box 12-2.)

Agism

It "knows no one century, nor culture, and is not likely to go away any time soon." This is how physician Robert Butler (1990:178) described prejudice and discrimination against senior citizens, which he called *agism*. Agism reflects a deep uneasiness among young and middle-aged

people about growing old. For many, old age symbolizes disease, disability, and death; seeing older people serves as a reminder that *they* may someday become old and infirm. Agism was popularized by Maggie Kuhn, a senior citizen who took up the cause of seniors' rights after she was forced to retire from her position at the United Presbyterian Church. Kuhn formed the Gray Panthers in 1971, an American organization dedicated to the fight against age discrimination. Later in this chapter, we'll look at other successful efforts of senior citizens to organize (R. Thomas 1995).

With agism all too common in North America, it is hardly surprising that older people are barely visible on television. A content analysis of 1446 fictional American television characters revealed that only 2 percent were aged 65 and over— even though this age group accounts for about 13 percent of the nation's population. A second study found older women to be particularly underrepresented on television (Robinson and Skill 1993; Vernon et al. 1990).

Feminist perspectives have drawn attention to the social construction of gender as it relates to agism in North American society. While men's aging is seen as a sign of wisdom and experience, women's aging is seen as a sign of decline and diminishing status. Standards of beauty, in our society, are based on women's youth and sexual attractiveness and are often narrowly defined and frequently impossible to achieve (Abu-Labau and McDaniel 1995). Aging women, therefore, are seen as a departure from our culture's norms of physical beauty and sexual attractiveness. The culture, through messages transmitted by mass media, encourages us to "steal beauty back from the ravages of time" (Nelson and Robinson 1999:464). Thus, a multibillion-dollar beauty industry of cosmetics, fashion, fitness, and cosmetic surgery is flourishing (Wolf 1991) in the midst of an aging population in an agist culture.

Competition in the Labour Force

A trend that Canada shares with much of the industrialized world is that of early retirement. In Canada, the past few decades have seen the median age of retirement reduced by three years for men (from 64.5 to 61) and by five years for women (from 65 to 60) (Health Canada 2002). Another trend is that of the number of seniors in the paid labour

Steve, a white male, grew up in a middle-class family. His parents, while not well off, were able to send him through university. Steve worked nights to pay his way through graduate school and obtained a master's degree in business. He joined a brokerage business and worked his way up the corporate ladder. By the time he retired at 65 as a vice-president of the company, Steve had accumulated a nest egg of savings through stock and bond purchases, owned a house in an affluent suburb, and could look forward to substantial monthly pension payments as well as receiving money from the Canada Pension Plan.

Contrast Steve's life course with that of James, an Aboriginal male. James was raised by a single mother, who generally depended on welfare payments to put food on the table. James actually liked the structure of school but felt pressure to contribute income to the family, so he dropped out of high school to work as an inventory clerk in a warehouse for little more than minimum wage. When the warehouse closed he bounced around from job to job, with long periods of unemployment. Health problems also sidelined him. James was never able to save money or to buy a home or an apartment; he felt lucky just to make the rent each month. He never worked anyplace long enough to earn a pension. In his old age James must make do with whatever government pension and other old age income he is entitled to.

> **While senior citizens as a group have made economic strides, members of some minorities have not kept pace.**

James's story illustrates the increasing inequality faced by aging racial and ethnic group members as a result of diminished life chances. While senior citizens as a group have made economic strides, members of some minorities have not kept pace. Sociologist Angela O'Rand has advanced the notion of *cumulative disadvantage* over the life course to explain what is happening. Two biases work against minority group members: First, they are less likely than whites to have steady work histories, which would allow them to accumulate wealth (such as a home) that can serve as a valuable nest egg in later years. The second bias is related to the first. Members of minorities are less likely than white males to be served by private pension programs that provide steady income during retirement.

In short, those who are advantaged early in life have more opportunity to receive formal schooling, to obtain a job that leads to advancement up the ladder, to save for retirement, and to have access to dependable retirement savings programs. Their *advantages* accumulate over the life course, while the *disadvantages* suffered by racial and ethnic groups accumulate.

Let's Discuss

1. How did your grandparents' life chances affect the quality of life in their later years?
2. Would a conflict theorist agree with the notion of cumulative disadvantage? Why or why not?

Sources: Oliver and Shapiro 1995; A. O'Rand 1996.

---

force. In 1999, only 6.6 percent of Canadians over the age of 65 were employed, a rate comparable to those of Australia and the United Kingdom. Other countries such as France and Spain have lower labour force participation rates for seniors, at 2.8 percent and 1.8 percent respectively. The United States has a rate of 13 percent, and in Japan, 25 percent of the senior population is employed full-time. In each of these countries, part-time senior workers are in addition to these figures. These numbers have been declining for most countries; in Canada, for example, 10 percent of seniors were employed in 1975, compared to 6.6 percent 24 years later (Statistics Canada 2000). Despite these falling percentages, younger adults continue to view older workers as "job stealers," a biased p. 269 judgment similar to that directed against illegal immigrants. This mistaken belief not only intensifies age conflict but leads to age discrimination.

While firing people simply because they are old violates federal laws, courts have upheld the right to lay off older workers for economic reasons. Critics contend that later the same firms hire young, cheaper workers to replace the experienced, older workers. Norman Matloff (1998), a computer science professor at the University of California, finds rampant age discrimination in the computer software industry, supposedly an understaffed field. Employers shove aside mid-career programmers because they command higher salaries than recent university graduates. Companies defend their actions on the grounds that the older workers lack skills in the latest software programs.

In contrast to the negative stereotypes, researchers have found that older workers can be an *asset* for employers. According to a study issued in 1991, older workers can be retrained in new technologies, have lower rates of

Older job applicants must deal with negative stereotypes, despite the fact that older workers are often found to be a good investment for a company: they can learn new technologies, are absent less often than younger employees, and have proven to be effective in sales.

country, advocating "student power," collectively demanded a role in the governance of educational institutions. In the following decade, the 1970s, many older people became aware that *they* were being treated as second-class citizens and also turned to collective action.

One prominent organization representing Canada's seniors is the Canadian Association of Retired Persons (CARP), founded in 1984 by a group of seniors having a discussion around a kitchen table. Some of CARP's services involve discounts and insurance for its 400 000 members, but the organization also functions as a powerful lobby group. Its website states that it "is never a matter of just 'carping' about concerns, but rather offering practical alternatives regarding the social, economic, financial, and political issues we raise" (**www.50plus.com**).

People grow old in many different ways. Not all seniors face the same challenges or enjoy the same resources. While CARP lobbies to protect seniors in general, other groups work in more specific ways. For example, in 1978 the Alzheimer Society was established to provide help for people with Alzheimer Disease and their caregivers. The society helps people to find programs and services they need, as well as promotes public education and awareness. Some organizations are established mainly for research and advocacy purposes (i.e., Council on Aging) and others are dedicated to providing direct services to seniors (i.e., Senior Citizens' Council). Every province and territory has departments that deal with issues related to aging and seniors.

Still another manifestation of the new awareness of older people is the formation of organizations for senior homosexuals. One such group, Senior Action in a Gay Environment (SAGE), was established in New York City in

absenteeism than younger employees, and are often more effective salespeople. The study focused on two corporations based in the United States and a British retail chain—all of which have long-term experience in hiring workers aged 50 and over. An official of the private fund that commissioned the study concluded, "We have here the first systematic hard-nosed economic analysis showing older workers are good investments" (Telsch 1991:A16).

Senior Citizens: Emergence of a Collective Consciousness

During the 1960s, students at colleges and universities across the

Members of SAGE, Senior Action in a Gay Environment, take part in a gay pride demonstration in New York City. This organization focuses on the special needs of gay seniors.

1978 and now oversees a nationwide network of local community groups. At the same time, SAGE must deal with special concerns. Many gay couples find that nursing homes won't allow them to share a room. In addition, nearly 90 percent of gay seniors today have no children, and more than two-thirds live alone—twice the percentage of heterosexual seniors. It's not surprising that SAGE has surfaced to deal with these large-scale special needs (R. Bragg 1999; SAGE 1999). Other groups such as Prime Timers (1987) and Golden Threads (1985) were established to help gay and lesbian seniors end the isolation and loneliness they experience as double-jeopardy minorities.

Seniors in Canada are better off today financially and physically than ever before. Many of them have strong financial assets that will take care of most of their needs. But, as we have seen, another segment is impoverished, faced with the prospect of declining health and mounting medical bills. And some older people may now have to add being aged to a lifetime of discrimination. As in all other stages of the life course, the aged constitute a diverse group in Canada and around the world.

We will now turn to a topic that many older persons find of intense interest—the right to die. But as we will see, this issue is highly controversial.

SOCIAL POLICY AND AGE STRATIFICATION

The Right to Die Worldwide

The Issue

On August 4, 1993, Dr. Jack Kevorkian, a retired pathologist, helped a 30-year-old Michigan man with Lou Gehrig's disease commit suicide in a van. Thomas Hyde, Jr., died after inhaling carbon monoxide through a mask designed by Dr. Kevorkian; in doing so, he became the 17th person to commit suicide with Kevorkian's assistance. The physician was openly challenging a Michigan law (aimed at him) that makes it a felony crime—punishable by up to four years in jail—to assist in a suicide. Since then Kevorkian has assisted in numerous other suicides, but it was not until he did it on television in 1998 that charges brought against him resulted in a guilty verdict (see Box 12-3).

In 1993, Sue Rodriguez, a British Columbia woman with Lou Gehrig's disease, challenged Canada's Criminal Code prohibition against assisted suicide. Her case went to the Supreme Court of Canada, which upheld the law, although by a narrow five to four margin. The four dissenting judges found that she was discriminated against on the grounds of disability: the option of suicide, which is legally available to anyone, was not available to her because of her inability, physically, to commit suicide (Lavery and Singer 1997). The following year, Rodriguez followed through with her belief in a "right to choose," and, with the help of an anonymous doctor and NDP MP Svend Robinson (a right-to-choose advocate), she chose to die.

Another event in Canada in 1993 raised other issues on the right to die. Robert Latimer is a Saskatchewan farmer whose 12-year-old daughter, Tracy, was severely and painfully handicapped. After years of watching her suffer, Latimer chose to end her life with the help of carbon monoxide. He was found guilty of second-degree murder, which carries a minimum penalty of 10 years in prison with no parole (Lane 2001). On January 18, 2001, the Supreme Court declined his request to consider creating a new category of compassionate homicide; Latimer would have to serve his sentence.

The issues of the right to die and of physician-assisted suicide (PAS) are part of the larger debate in Canada and elsewhere over the ethics of suicide and euthanasia. The term **euthanasia** has been defined as "the deliberate act undertaken by one person with the intention of ending the life of another in order to relieve that person's suffering" (Senate 1995). Other definitions speak of the use of "painless methods" to relieve a "terminally-ill or severely debilitated person" (Duhaime 1996). This type of "mercy killing" reminds us of the ideal of "good death" discussed earlier in the chapter. The debates over euthanasia and assisted suicide often focus on cases involving older people, though it can involve younger adults with terminal and degenerative diseases, as in the cases of Tracy Latimer or Thomas Hyde, Jr.

The Setting

Many societies are known to have practised **senilicide**—"killing of the old"—because of extreme difficulties in providing basic necessities such as food and shelter. In a study of the treatment of senior citizens in 41 nonindustrialized

12-3 Death by Doctor on Television

In 1998, the television newsprogram *60 Minutes*, known for its pathbreaking visual stories, created a stir when it aired a videotape made by Dr. Jack Kevorkian that shows him assisting the suicide of Thomas Youk. Youk, 52 years old, was suffering from incurable Lou Gehrig's disease and was terrified of choking to death in the course of his illness. The tape shows the doctor administering a lethal injection of potassium chloride, which Kevorkian calls his "medicide." It produces death by stopping the heart.

> The tape shows the doctor administering a lethal injection of potassium chloride, which Kevorkian calls his "medicide."

The CBS show, which drew huge ratings, brought the issue of physician-assisted "mercy killing" right into people's homes. Some media observers questioned the wisdom of showing the tape provided by Kevorkian. The "in-your-face" publicity tactic led to a successful prosecution of Kevorkian by the state of Michigan, after four earlier attempts to find him guilty failed.

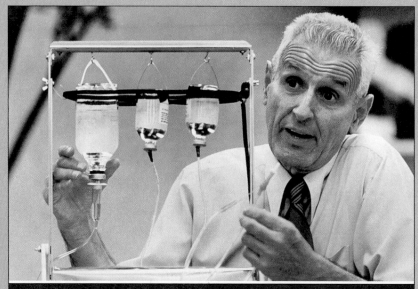

Dr. Jack Kevorkian with the apparatus that administers a lethal injection to those who want assistance in suicide.

Kevorkian's medical licence was revoked by the state in June 1998, and he is now awaiting the outcome of his appeal.

Let's Discuss

1. If you were the producer of *60 Minutes*, would you air Dr. Kevorkian's videotape? Why or why not?

2. Thomas Youk signed a consent form for the doctor to carry out the lethal injection. Should that be enough to shield Kevorkian from prosecution by the state?

Source: P. Belluck 1999

---

societies, Anthony Glascock (1990) found that some form of "death-hastening" behaviour was present in 21 of them. Killing of seniors was evident in 14 of these societies, while abandoning of older people was evident in 8 societies. Typically, such death-hastening occurs when older people become decrepit and are viewed as "already dead." Death-hastening in these nonindustrialized cultures is open and socially approved. Family members generally make decisions, often after open consultation with those about to die.

Currently, laws in Canada do not permit *active euthanasia* (such as a deliberate injection of lethal drugs to a terminally ill patient) or physician-assisted suicide.

Although suicide itself is no longer a crime, assisting suicide is illegal. There is greater legal tolerance today for *passive euthanasia* (such as disconnecting life-support equipment from a comatose patient).

Sociological Insights

While formal norms concerning euthanasia may be in flux, informal norms seem to permit mercy killings. One of the reasons for this appears to be definitions. Many doctors argue that acts of withholding or withdrawing a life-support system are fundamentally different from acts of euthanasia, because withholding treatment is merely allowing death to occur naturally, while euthanasia is causing

344

death. "There are 3 practices along the spectrum of end-of-life care: palliative care, decisions to forgo treatment, and euthanasia and assisted suicide. The first 2 are ethically uncontroversial, legally permissible and part of quality medical care. The third is ethically controversial and clearly illegal" (Lavery and Singer 1997:405–6). The Special Senate Committee on Euthanasia and Assisted Suicide heard many testimonies from medical witnesses over the 14-month study. They reported that doctors do not use the term "euthanasia" for care that involves withholding or withdrawing life-saving medical care or "pulling the plug," but, according to Professor Arthur Schafer of the Centre for Professional and Applied Ethics at the University of Manitoba, tens of thousands of Canadians die every year by this form of passive euthanasia, arranged between doctors, patients, and families (Senate 1995). In a period in which AIDS-related deaths are common, an AIDS underground is known to share information and assistance regarding suicide (Gibbs 1993; Martinez 1993).

Conflict theorists ask questions about the values raised by such decisions. By endorsing physician-assisted suicide, are we devaluing the disabled through an acceptance of their premature death? Critics note that we all are only temporarily able-bodied; disease or a speeding automobile can place any one of us among the disabled. By establishing a precedent for ending the lives of selected disabled people, we may unwittingly contribute to negative social views and labelling of all disabled people. Further reflecting the conflict perspective, gerontologist Elizabeth Markson (1992:6) argues that the "powerless, poor or undesirable are at special risk of being 'encouraged' to choose assisted death."

Critics of euthanasia charge that many of its supporters are guilty of agism and other forms of bias. In a society that commonly discriminates against seniors and people with disabilities, medical authorities and even family members may decide too quickly that such people should die "for their own good" or (in a view somewhat reminiscent of disengagement theory) "for the good of society." It is also feared that society may use euthanasia to reduce healthcare costs—rather than striving to make life better for those near the end. Older people may even feel compelled to end their lives (prematurely) to ease the emotional and financial burdens on family members and friends (Glascock 1990:45; *New York Times* 1993b; Richman 1992).

Policy Initiatives

In the industrialized world, euthanasia is legally practised only in the Netherlands. In 2000, the Dutch parliament approved a law to legalize it. The legislation allows a doctor to administer a lethal drug under six strict criteria: (1) the patient's request must be voluntary and well-considered; (2) the patient must be suffering unbearable and unremitting pain; (3) the patient must have a clear understanding of the situation and prognosis, but doesn't have to be terminally ill; (4) the doctor and patient must decide that there is no reasonable and acceptable alternative; (5) the physician must consult at least one other independent doctor; and (6) the physician must carry out the termination of life in a medically appropriate manner (*Washington Post* 2000).

In 1996, the Northern Territory of Australia legalized euthanasia but the law was struck down the following year by Australia's federal parliament in Canberra (Richburg 2000). Despite this, 78 percent of Australians agree that a doctor should be able to provide a lethal substance to a patient in the same condition as those in the Netherlands' law. National polls in Britain show that a strong majority (up to 82 percent) are in favour of legalizing voluntary euthanasia.

In the United States, the only state to pass a law permitting assisted suicide is Oregon, with its *Death with Dignity Act* in 1997. While only 15 terminally ill people have ended their lives with lethal medication under Oregon's law, the legislation has encountered sharp opposition. In 1999, the U.S. Congress passed a measure that effectively overruled Oregon's law by preventing federally controlled drugs from being used to end a life. But the law allows for use of drugs to control pain, which could hasten death (Pear 1999; Verhovek 1999).

In Canada, a number of events have raised issues and led to many Canadians considering end-of-life choices. Court decisions have established the right of individuals to make decisions about their own medical treatment. For example, in 1992, Quebec's Superior Court granted Nancy B. (a competent woman suffering from an incurable neurological disease that left her incapable of movement) the right to choose when to have her respirator disconnected. The Rodriguez and Latimer cases of 1993, mentioned earlier, focused the attention of Canadians on euthanasia. A 1994 National Angus Reid Poll found that 74 percent of Canadians believed a doctor should be allowed, legally, to assist a terminally ill patient end his or her life if desired.

The Special Committee set up by the Senate of Canada in 1994 undertook a wide-ranging study of attitudes toward assisted suicide and euthanasia. The committee reported growing support for the right to choose, and while its final report put forth a number of important recommendations regarding pain control and palliative care in general, the committee concluded by recommending that no changes should be made to the Criminal Code (Senate 1995). A more recent survey, reported in 2001, was conducted by the Institute for Social Research at York University. The findings indicated that 69 percent of those surveyed approved when presented with a scenario of passive euthanasia, and 61 percent approved of active euthanasia. Respondents were asked about their support of the right to choose—including the right to die—versus the sanctity of human life, and 58 percent supported the right to choose. A substantial majority (65 percent) believed there should be a free vote in the House of Commons on the legalization of euthanasia (Pollard 2001).

Advances in technology allow us to prolong life in ways that were unimaginable decades ago. But should people be forced or expected to prolong lives that are unbearably painful or that are, in effect, "lifeless"? Unfortunately, medical and technological advances cannot provide answers to complex ethical, legal, and political questions.

Let's Discuss

1. Why do you think "death-hastening" behaviour is common in nonindustrialized countries?
2. In what ways are conflict theory and disengagement theory relevant in the debate over the "right to die"?
3. Do you think someone should be allowed to choose to die? Why or why not?

Chapter Resources

Summary

Age, like gender and race, is an ascribed status that forms the basis for social differentiation. This chapter examines theories regarding the aging process, role transitions in the life course, age stratification in Canada, the growing political activism of the nation's senior population, and controversy surrounding the right to die.

1. Like other forms of stratification, age stratification varies from culture to culture.
2. "Being old" is a master status that seems to overshadow all others in our society.
3. The particular problems of the aged have become the focus for a specialized area of research and inquiry known as *gerontology*.
4. *Disengagement theory* implicitly suggests that society should help older people withdraw from their accustomed social roles, whereas *activity theory* argues that the senior who remains active and socially involved will be best-adjusted.
5. From a conflict perspective, the low status of older people is reflected in prejudice and discrimination against them and unfair job practices.

6. Feminist theories on aging have made distinct contributions to gerontology by drawing attention to the importance of individual characteristics and diverse backgrounds. In challenging the androcentric focus of previous research, they provide a more inclusive picture of aging, showing that it does not manifest itself in a universal manner in every person. Rather age intersects with gender, class, race, ethnicity, and sexual orientation to produce different patterns and experiences.
7. As we age, we go through role transitions, including the role of the sandwich generation, adjustment to retirement, and preparation for death.
8. An increasing proportion of the population of Canada is composed of older people.
9. *Agism* reflects a deep uneasiness on the part of younger people about growing old.
10. The Canadian Association of Retired Persons (CARP) works as a powerful lobbying group backing legislation that will benefit senior citizens.
11. The "right to die" often entails physician-assisted suicide, a very controversial issue worldwide.

Critical Thinking Questions

1. Are senior citizens students at your university? How are they treated by younger students and by faculty members? Is there a subculture of older students? How do younger students view faculty members in their fifties and sixties?

2. Is age segregation functional or dysfunctional for older people in Canada? Is it functional or dysfunctional for society as a whole? What are the manifest functions, the latent functions, and the dysfunctions of age segregation?

3. Imagine that you were asked to study political activism among older people. How might you employ surveys, observations, experiments, and existing sources to better understand such activism?

Key Terms

Activity theory An interactionist theory of aging that argues that seniors who remain active and socially involved will be best-adjusted. (330)

Agism Prejudice and discrimination against senior citizens. (340)

Disengagement theory A functionalist theory of aging that contends that society and the aging individual mutually sever many of their relationships. (330)

Euthanasia The deliberate act undertaken by one person with the intention of ending the life of another in order to relieve that person's suffering. (343)

Gerontology The scientific study of the sociological and psychological aspects of aging and the problems of the aged. (329)

Midlife crisis A stressful period of self-evaluation that begins at about age 40. (333)

Sandwich generation The generation of adults who simultaneously try to meet the competing needs of their parents and their own children. (333)

Senilicide The killing of the old. (343)

Additional Readings

BOOKS

Dychtwald, Ken. 1999. *Age Power: How the 21st Century Will Be Ruled by the New Old*. New York: Putnam. A gerontologist projects social patterns and aging into the future.

McPherson, Barry. 1998. *Aging As a Social Process*. Scarborough: Nelson Thomson Learning. A theoretical examination of the discipline of gerontology that focuses on the interplay between the aging individual, a changing social structure, the physical environment, and a variety of cultural contexts.

McTeer, Maureen A. 1999. *Tough Choices: Living and Dying in the 21st Century*. Toronto: Irwin Law. The author examines the ways in which science and technology are influencing medical practice and our society's choices about life and death.

Novak, Mark and Lori Campbell. 2001. *Aging & Society: A Canadian Perspective*. 4th edition. Scarborough: Nelson Thomson Learning. A presentation of current issues in aging within the context of Canada's history and social life. It provides facts and commentary that facilitate an understanding of the issues that surround aging today.

Quadagno, Jill. 1999. *Aging and the Life Course: An Introduction to Social Gerontology*. New York: McGraw-Hill. A sociological overview not only of senior citizens but of the entire process of aging.

JOURNALS

Among the journals that focus on issues of aging and age stratification are *Canadian Journal on Aging* (founded in 1975), *Ageing and Society* (1981), *Ageing International* (1994), *Contemporary Gerontology* (1994), *Journal of Aging and Ethnicity* (1996), *Journal of Women and Aging* (1989), *Journal of Cross-Cultural Gerontology* (1986), *Research on Aging* (1979) and *Youth and Society* (1968).

Internet Connection

www.mcgrawhill.ca/college/schaefer

For additional Internet exercises relating to stratification by age, visit the Schaefer Online Learning Centre at **http://www.mcgrawhill.ca/college/schaefer.** *Please note that while the URLs listed were current at the time of printing, these sites often change—check the Online Learning Centre for updates.*

Debate rages around the world regarding euthanasia and physician-assisted suicide. Religious Tolerance.org offers multiple perspectives and statistics on the issue (**http://www.religioustolerance.org/euthanas.htm**).

(a) What does the term "euthanasia" mean? Where did it originate?

(b) What is the difference between passive euthanasia, active euthanasia, physician-assisted suicide, and involuntary euthanasia, according to the site?

(c) How do various religious organizations view the issue?

(d) What are some of the arguments offered by those on differing sides of this issue?

(e) What is the "Death with Dignity Law" in the state of Oregon? What is its current status? Under what circumstances and conditions can a person seek to end his or her life? What were the demographics of those who exercised their right to die?

(f) According to polls, what attitudes do Canadians hold toward euthanasia and physician-assisted suicide?

(g) What is your opinion of the issue in general? Why do you hold that opinion?

(h) Use your sociological imagination and discuss/compare how a functionalist and a conflict theorist would view such a law.

(i) What is the legal standing of euthanasia in Australia, Colombia, the Netherlands, Nigeria, and Japan?

CBC Video

Visit the Schaefer Online Learning Centre at **http://www.mcgrawhill.ca/college/schaefer** to view the CBC video segment "How Old is 'Old'?: Re-Thinking our Views on Mandatory Retirement" and answer related questions.

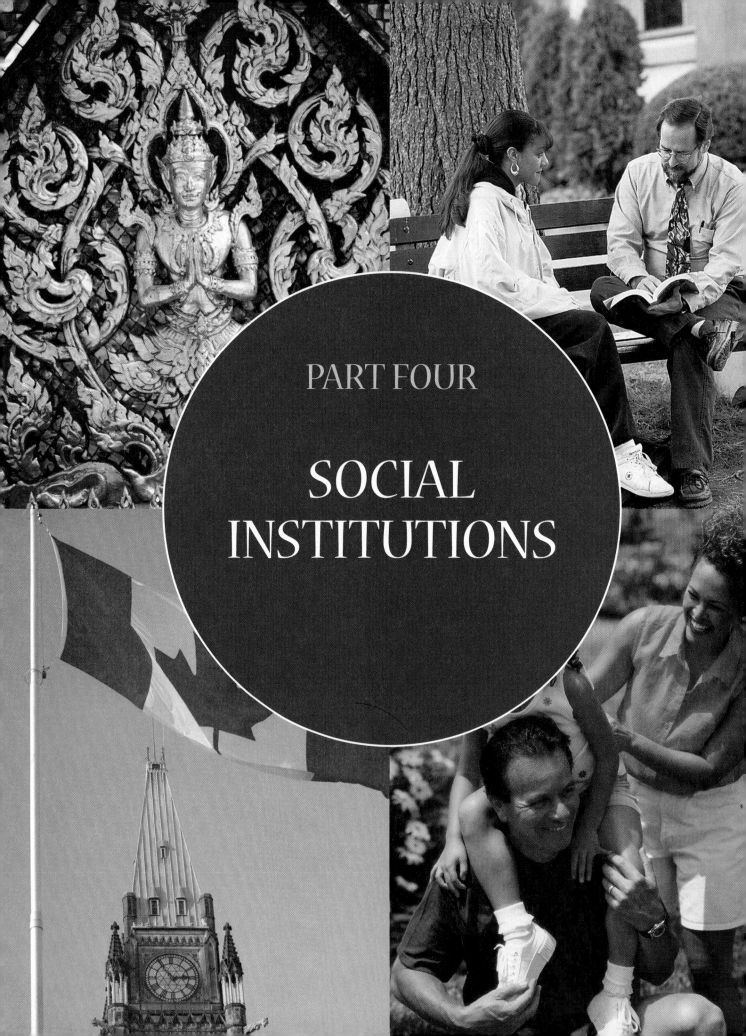

PART FOUR

SOCIAL INSTITUTIONS

Part Four considers sociological analysis of major social institutions, including the family, religion, education, government, the economy, and the health-care system. As noted earlier in the text, *social institutions* are organized patterns of beliefs and behaviour centred on basic social needs.

Chapter 13 focuses on the functions of the family and intimate relationships and their importance as cultural universals. Chapter 14 discusses the dimensions, functions, and organization of religion, and Chapter 15 considers the functions of education, schools as social organizations, and recent trends in education. Chapter 16 looks at government and politics, with particular emphasis on types of governments. Chapter 17 examines economic systems, aspects of work, and the changing economy. Chapter 18 analyzes sociological perspectives on health and illness, the health-care system, and mental illness.

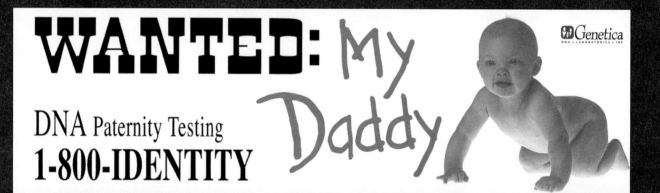

New technology has sparked a demand for testing services to determine who is and who is not the father of a child. When billboards advertising these services appeared in 1997, some people found them amusing while others perceived them as further evidence of the problems confronting the family.

From the time of the breakdown of my marriage to Cliff's mother in 1979 to my marriage to Elleni in 1990, I was forced to deal with a difficult but nonetheless standard set of problems. My ex-wife was awarded custody of two-year-old Cliff and then decided to move to Atlanta. I had no recourse, legal or otherwise. And yet in my struggle to build a close relationship with my son, I now had to cope with an almost impossible set of barriers. Hundreds of miles separated me from Cliff, and I had limited visitation rights—a few specified weekends during the year plus three months in the summer. Besides which, what would I do with my son during our precious time together? My bachelor homes did not provide a supportive context for a four-year-old or a nine-year-old—there were no kids on the block, no basketball hoop in the back yard. But I wrestled with these problems and over time developed a strategy that worked, albeit imperfectly.

I hit upon this great solution for the summers. I would take Cliff back to Sacramento, back to the loving, child-centered home that had been so good to me and my siblings a generation ago. It required a lot of stretching and bending of the rules, but I organized life so that I really could take two and a half months out of the year. It meant postponing book deadlines and taming an almost impossible travel schedule, but it was well worth it. Those summers in Sacramento stand out like jewels in my memory. My parents' home turned out to be a profoundly healing place in which Cliff and I could reach out to one another. It provided the deeply needed (and yet so hard to contrive) rhythms and routines of normal family life. Three meals a day; regular bedtimes; clean clothes; a bevy of cousins—Kahnie, Phillip and Phyllis, Cornel and Erika—just around the corner, on tap for casual play; bicycles and baseball gear in the garage all ready to be put to use whenever a grownup was available. And hovering in the backgrounds, loving, eagle-eyed grandparents. . . . The evening meal was particularly important, as all three generations gathered for a cookout in the backyard. Conversation and laughter flowed, advice was sought and help was freely offered, jokes and stories were traded, and the children, spellbound, hung on the edges, absorbing the spirit and the meaning of family life.

The rest of the year was a struggle. I maintained regular telephone contact with Cliff, calling him several times a week just to hear his voice and shoot the breeze. But in the rushed, tantalizing visits around Thanksgiving, Christmas, and Easter, it was always hard not to lapse into the role of being a "good-time dad," showering gifts on him in an attempt to make up for real time or a deeper agenda. *(Hewlett and West 1998: 21–22)* ∎

In this excerpt from *The War Against Parents*, philosophy scholar Cornel West underscores how deeply family life has been altered by divorce, one of many social factors that have gradually but inevitably turned the traditional nuclear family on its head. The family of today is not what it was a century ago or even a generation ago. New roles, new gender distinctions, and new child-rearing patterns have all combined to create new forms of family life. Today, for example, we are seeing more and more women take the breadwinner's role, whether married or as a single parent. Blended families—the result of divorces and remarriages—are almost the norm. And many people are seeking intimate relationships outside marriage, whether it be in gay partnerships or in cohabiting arrangements.

This chapter addresses family and intimate relationships in Canada as well as in other parts of the world. As we will see, family patterns differ from one culture to another and even within the same culture. A *family* can be defined as a set of people related by blood, marriage (or some other agreed-upon relationship), or adoption who share the primary responsibility for reproduction and caring for members of society.

While this definition is generally agreed upon from a sociological point of view, "official" definitions are more specific, depending on their purpose. Statistics Canada has a definition of family that it uses when gathering census data on everyone in Canada. A census family is defined as: "a now-married couple, a common-law couple or a lone-parent with or without children under the age of 25 . . . living in the same household" (Statistics Canada 2002B). This definition of family officially includes only heterosexual couples. In the 2001 census, for the first time, Statistics Canada had a category for same-sex common-law couples. While reporting that 34 200 couples live in this type of household, all further analyses of families in the report on Canada's 2001 census one again excluded them, thus failing to capture the true diversity of families today.

In this chapter, we will see that the family is universal—found in every culture—however varied in its organization. We will look at the family and intimate relationships from the functionalist, conflict, interactionist, and feminist points of view and at the variations in marital patterns and family life, including different family forms of child rearing. We'll pay particular attention to the increasing number of people in dual-income or single-parent families. We will examine divorce in Canada and consider such diverse lifestyles as cohabitation, remaining single, lesbian and gay relationships, and marriage without children. The social policy section will look at controversial issues surrounding the use of reproductive technology. ■

Global View of the Family

Among Tibetans, a woman may be simultaneously married to more than one man, usually brothers. This system allows sons to share the limited amount of good land. A Hopi woman may divorce her husband by placing her belongings outside the door. A Trobriand Island couple signals marriage by sitting in public on a porch eating yams provided by the bride's mother. She continues to provide cooked yams for a year while the groom's family offers in exchange such valuables as stone axes and clay pots (W. Haviland 1999).

As these examples illustrate, there are many variations in "the family" from culture to culture. Yet the family as a social institution is present in all cultures. Moreover, certain general principles concerning its composition, kinship patterns, and authority patterns are universal.

Composition: What Is the Family?

If we were to take our information on what a family is from what we see on television, we might come up with some very strange scenarios (see Box 13-1). The media don't always help us get a realistic view of the family. Moreover, many people still think of the family in very narrow terms—as a married couple and their unmarried children living together, like the family in the old *Cosby Show* or *Family Ties* or *Growing Pains*. However, this is but one type of family, what sociologists refer to as a **nuclear family**. The term *nuclear family* is well chosen, since this type of family serves as the nucleus, or core, upon which larger family groups are built. Most people in Canada see the nuclear family as the preferred family arrangement. Yet, as Figure 13-1 shows, by 2001 only about 44 percent of the nation's family households fit this model.

In wedding ceremonies in Sumatra, Indonesia, the bride's headdress indicates her village and her social status—the more elaborate the headdress, the higher her status. After she is married, the bride and her groom live with her maternal family, and all property passes from mother to daughter.

The proportion of households in Canada composed of married couples with children at home has decreased steadily over the last 30 years, and this trend is expected to continue. At the same time, there have been increases in the number of single-parent households (see Figure 13-1). Similar trends are evident in other industrialized nations, including the United States, Great Britain, and Japan (see Figure 13-2). As noted earlier, Statistics Canada's official definition of family does not include same-sex couples. When "two persons of the same sex identify themselves on the census form as living in a gay or lesbian relationship, the information is retained but not included in the published data on families" (Statistics Canada 2002c). Therefore, when viewing graphs such as Figure 13-1, keep in mind that same-sex households are not included in the figures, either as two-parent families or as common-law couples.

A family in which relatives—such as grandparents, aunts, or uncles—live in the same home as parents and their children is known as an *extended family.* While not the norm in Canada overall, extended families are fairly common in First Nations communities and in some Canadian ethnic groups. The structure of the extended family offers certain advantages over that of the nuclear family. Crises such as death, divorce, and illness put less strain on family members, since there are more people who can provide assistance and emotional support. In addition, the extended family constitutes a larger economic unit than the nuclear family. If the family is engaged in a common enterprise—a farm or a small business—the additional family members may represent the difference between prosperity and failure.

In considering these differing family types, we have limited ourselves to the form of marriage that is characteristic of Canada—monogamy. The term *monogamy* describes a form of marriage in which one woman and one man are married only to each other. Some observers, noting the rate of divorce in Canada, have suggested that "serial monogamy" is a more accurate description of the form that monogamy takes in Canada. Under *serial monogamy*, a person may have several spouses in his or her life but only one spouse at a time. Once again, definitions exclude same-sex couples. Many gays and lesbians are in monogamous relationships, often of a long-term duration, but since their unions are not recognized as marriage, they are excluded from definitions of monogamy.

Some cultures allow an individual to have several husbands or wives simultaneously. This form of marriage

FIGURE 13-1

Types of Family Households in Canada, 1981 and 2001

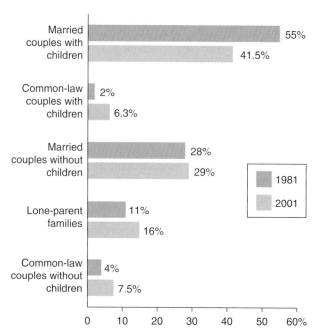

Married couples with children: 55% (1981), 41.5% (2001)
Common-law couples with children: 2% (1981), 6.3% (2001)
Married couples without children: 28% (1981), 29% (2001)
Lone-parent families: 11% (1981), 16% (2001)
Common-law couples without children: 4% (1981), 7.5% (2001)

Note: Due to official definitions, couples and families are made up of men and women. Data on same-sex couples collected by StatsCan are not included in these numbers.

Source: Statistics Canada 1997b, 2002e.

Eye on the Media

13-1 The Family in TV Land

Put an alien creature from outer space in front of a television, and it would have no idea of what family life is like in North America. It would conclude that most adults are men, most adults are not married, almost no one is over age 50, very few adults have children, most mothers don't work for pay, and child care is simply not an issue. When parents are depicted, they are either not around for the most part or they are clueless. The baby boomers in *Everybody Loves Raymond* treat their parents like meddling invaders, which is also how the teenage generation treats its boomer parents in *Dawson's Creek*.

The fact is that *Friends, Frasier, Sports Night, Ally McBeal,* and similar programs present fantasy lives that most households find fascinating, but not exactly true to their lives. Eight out of 10 adults in the United States think that almost no TV family is like their own; nearly half find no TV family like theirs.

These conclusions come out of a content analysis of prime-time TV programming conducted by Katharine Heintz-Knowles, a communications professor at the University of Washington and the mother of three children, who knows first-hand what a work–family conflict looks like. She has had to deal with finding sitters on short notice, taking children to work with her when a sitter was unavailable, and missing meetings to tend to a sick child. In fact, she acknowledges that her "life today is one big work–family conflict" (Gardner 1998:13). But when she watched television, she didn't see much of her life reflected on the screen.

Her study, called "Balancing Acts: Work/Family Issues on Prime-Time TV," carried out content analysis of 150 episodes of 92 different programs on commercial networks over a two-week period. She found that of the 820 TV

	Adult TV characters	Adult population
Women	38%	51%
Over age 50	14%	38%
Parents of minor children	15%	32%

Television Reality versus Social Reality

characters studied, only 38 percent were women, only 15 percent could be identified as parents of minor children, and only 14 percent were over age 50 (see the table for how these percentages compare to the adult U.S. population). Only 3 percent of the TV characters faced recognizable conflicts between work and family, and no TV family made use of a child-care centre. Commenting on this study, TV personality Rosie O'Donnell (1998) noted, "Television may bring the realities of violence

> **Eighty percent of the characters on Canadian television, both in French and English shows, appear in American productions.**

and natural disaster into our lives, but it rarely captures the reality of work and family life. . . . And heaven forbid a person over the age of 30 and bigger than a size four ever showed up on Melrose Place."

Canadians are presented with strikingly similar images of work–family roles, since 80 percent of characters on Canadian television, in both French and English, appear in U.S. productions (Graydon 2001). Canadian research has revealed that women with young families are critical of television's portrayal

of poor role models; they express a desire to have children exposed to positive portrayals of women successfully coping with a variety of situations and lifestyles (ComQuest Research Group 1993).

Because television is the major storyteller in our lives today, its programs can shape our attitudes and beliefs. Unfortunately, television gives a distorted view of family life, not only to our hypothetical alien, but also to viewers at home and in other societies on planet Earth. If very few shows depict real-life challenges in family life and possible solutions, then viewers may well go away thinking their own problems are unique and insoluble. By confronting these issues, television could call attention to what needs to be changed—both on an individual level and on a societal level—and offer hope for solutions. It appears, however, that most TV programmers offer up a fantasy world in order to satisfy people who seek entertainment and escape from their everyday lives.

Let's Discuss

1. How well does television portray the social reality of your family life?
2. Take the role of a television producer. What kind of show would you create to reflect family life today?

Sources: Blanco 1998; ComQuest Research Group 1993; Graydon 2001; National Partnership for Women and Families 1998; O'Donnell 1998.

FIGURE 13-2

The Nuclear Family in Industrialized Nations, 1960 and 1990

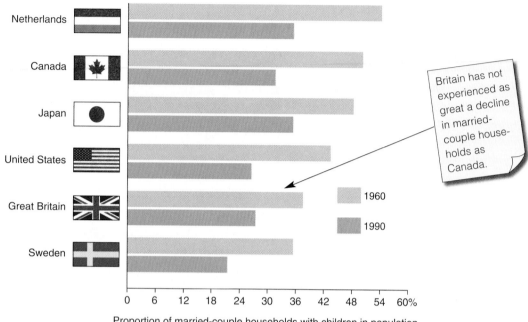

Proportion of married-couple households with children in population

Source: Bureau of Labor Statistics data in Sorrentino 1990 and author's estimate.

is known as ***polygamy.*** In fact, most societies throughout the world, past and present, have preferred polygamy to monogamy. Anthropologist George Murdock (1949, 1957) sampled 565 societies and found that more than 80 percent had some type of polygamy as their preferred form. While polygamy steadily declined through most of the twentieth century, it continues to be practised in many African and South Asian countries, as well as by certain groups (i.e., Mormons) in North America (Population Reference Bureau 1996).

There are two basic types of polygamy. According to Murdock, the most common—endorsed by the majority of cultures he sampled—was *polygyny.* ***Polygyny*** refers to the marriage of a man to more than one woman at the same time. The various wives are often sisters, who are expected to hold similar values and have already had experience sharing a household. In polygynous societies, relatively few men actually have multiple spouses. Most individuals live in typical monogamous families; having multiple wives is viewed as a mark of status.

The other principal variation of polygamy is ***polyandry,*** under which some women have more than one husband at the same time. This is the case in the culture of the Todas of Southern India. Polyandry, however, tends to be exceedingly rare in the world today. It has been accepted by some extremely poor societies that practise female infanticide (the killing of baby girls) and

thus have a relatively small number of women. Like many other societies, polyandrous cultures devalue the social worth of women.

In 1999 controversy over polygamy erupted in Russia. The president of the Russian republic of Ingushetia signed a decree legalizing polygyny for the mostly Islamic population. It allows men whose wives didn't produce sons or were childless to take on additional wives. The president pointed out that each additional marriage must be approved by all spouses and the wives' relatives, and that the system is advantageous for women who might not otherwise find a husband. But women in other parts of Russia were deeply offended by the decree. One female democratic activist claimed it "plays into the hands of those who have always considered Russia to be a barbaric country" (R. Paddock 1999:A28). Another problem is that polygyny is incompatible with the Russian Constitution, which prohibits the practice but provides for no penalty.

Kinship Patterns: To Whom Are We Related?

Many of us can trace our roots by looking at a family tree or listening to senior family members tell us about their lives—and about the lives of ancestors who died long before we were even born. Yet a person's lineage is more than simply a personal history; it also reflects societal patterns that govern descent. In every culture, children encounter relatives to whom they are expected to show an emotional attachment. The state of being related to others is called **kinship.** Kinship is culturally learned and is not totally determined by biological or marital ties. For example, adoption creates a kinship tie that is legally acknowledged and socially accepted.

The family and the kin group are not necessarily the same. While the family is a household unit, kin do not always live together or function as a collective body on a daily basis. Kin groups include aunts, uncles, cousins, in-laws, and so forth. In a society such as Canada, the kinship group may come together only rarely, as for a wedding or funeral. However, kinship ties frequently create obligations and responsibilities. We may feel compelled to assist our kin and feel free to call upon relatives for many types of aid, including loans and babysitting.

Smile—it's family reunion time! The state of being related to others is called kinship. Kin groups include aunts, uncles, cousins, and so forth, as shown in this family from Slovakia.

How are kinship groups identified? The principle of descent assigns people to kinship groups according to their relationship to an individual's mother or father. There are three primary ways of determining descent. Canada generally follows the system of **bilateral descent,** which means that both sides of a person's family are regarded as equally important. For example no higher value is given to the brothers of one's father as opposed to the brothers of one's mother.

Most societies—according to Murdock, 64 percent—give preference to one side of the family or the other in tracing descent. **Patrilineal descent** (from Latin *pater,* "father") indicates that only the father's relatives are important in terms of property, inheritance, and emotional ties. Conversely, in societies that favour **matrilineal descent** (from Latin *mater,* "mother") only the mother's relatives are significant.

New forms of reproductive technology (discussed in the policy section) will force a new way of looking at kinship. Today a combination of biological and social processes can "create" a family member, requiring that more distinctions be made about who is related to whom (C. Cussins 1998).

Authority Patterns: Who Rules?

Imagine that you have recently married and must begin to make decisions about the future of your new family. You and your spouse face many questions. Where will you live? How will you furnish your home? Who will do the cooking, the shopping, the cleaning? Whose friends will be invited to dinner? Each time a decision must be made, an issue is raised: Who has the power to make the decision? In simple terms, who rules the family? The conflict perspective examines these questions in the context of traditional gender stratification, under p. 203 which men have held a dominant position over women.

Societies vary in the way that power within the family is distributed. If a society expects males to dominate in all family decision making, it is termed a **patriarchy.** Frequently, in patriarchal societies, such as Iran, the eldest male wields the greatest power, although wives are expected to be treated with respect and kindness. A woman's status in Iran is typically defined by her relationship to a male relative, usually as a wife or daughter. In many patriarchal societies women find it more difficult to obtain a divorce than a man does (G. Farr 1999). By contrast, in a **matriarchy,** women have greater authority than men. Matriarchies, which are very uncommon, emerged among Native American tribal societies and in nations in which men were absent for long periods of time for warfare or food gathering.

A third type of authority pattern, the **egalitarian family,** is one in which spouses are regarded as equals. This does not mean, however, that each decision is shared in such families. Wives may hold authority in some spheres, husbands in others. Some sociologists believe that the egalitarian family has begun to replace the patriarchal family as the social norm in Canada, but there is substantial debate on the issue.

Studying the Family

Do we really need the family? A century ago, Friedrich Engels (1884), a colleague of Karl Marx, described the family as the ultimate source of social inequality because of its role in the transfer of power, property, and privilege. More recently, conflict and feminist theorists have argued that the family contributes to societal injustice, denies opportunities to women that are extended to men, and limits freedom in sexual expression and selection of a mate. By contrast, the functionalist perspective focuses on the ways in which the family gratifies the needs of its members and contributes to the stability of society. The interactionist view considers more intimate, face-to-face relationships.

Functionalist View

There are six paramount functions performed by the family, first outlined more than 60 years ago by sociologist William F. Ogburn (Ogburn and Tibbits 1934):

1. **Reproduction.** For a society to maintain itself, it must replace dying members. In this sense, the family contributes to human survival through its function of reproduction.

2. **Protection.** Unlike the young of other animal species, human infants need constant care and economic security. The extremely long period of dependency for children places special demands on older family members. In all cultures, it is the family that assumes ultimate responsibility for the protection and upbringing of children.

3. **Socialization.** Parents and other kin monitor a child's behaviour and transmit the norms, values, and language of a culture to the child (see Chapters 3 and 4).

4. **Regulation of sexual behaviour.** Sexual norms are subject to change over time (for instance, changes in customs for dating) and across cultures (Islamic Saudi Arabia compared with more-permissive Denmark). However, whatever the time period or cultural values in a society, standards of sexual behaviour are most clearly defined within the family circle. The structure of society influences these standards. In male-dominated societies, for example, formal and informal norms generally permit men to express and enjoy their sexual desires more freely than women may.

5. **Affection and companionship.** Ideally, the family provides members with warm and intimate relationships and helps them feel satisfied and secure. Of course, a family member may find such rewards outside the family—from peers, in school, at work—and may perceive the home as an unpleasant place. Nevertheless, unlike other institutions, the family is obligated to serve the emotional needs of its members. We expect our relatives to understand us, to care for us, and to be there for us when we need them.

6. **Provision of social status.** We inherit a social position because of the "family background" and reputation of our parents and siblings. The family unit presents the newborn child with an ascribed status of race and ethnicity that helps to determine his or her place within a society's stratification system. Moreover, family resources affect children's ability to pursue certain opportunities such as higher education and specialized lessons.

The family has traditionally fulfilled a number of other functions, such as providing religious training, education,

We inherit our social status from our family. It is not hard to guess that this young man has a big step up the social and economic ladder compared with a child from a disadvantaged family.

and recreational outlets. Ogburn argued that other social institutions have gradually assumed many of these functions. Although the family once played a major role in religious life—with the reading of the Bible and the singing of hymns commonly taking place at home—this function has largely shifted to churches, synagogues, and other religious organizations. Similarly, education once took place at the family fireside; now it is the responsibility of professionals working in schools, colleges, and universities. Even the family's traditional recreational function has been transferred to outside groups such as Little Leagues, athletic clubs, and Internet chat rooms.

Conflict View

Conflict theorists view the family not as a contributor to social stability, but as a reflection of the inequality in wealth and power found within the larger society. Feminist theorists and conflict theorists note that the family has traditionally legitimized and perpetuated male dominance. Throughout most of human history—and in a very wide range of societies—husbands have exercised overwhelming power and authority within the family. Indeed, not until the "first wave" of contemporary feminism in the mid-1800s was there a substantial challenge to the historic status of wives and children as the legal property of husbands.

p. 18

While the egalitarian family has become a more common pattern in Canada in recent decades—owing in good part to the activism of feminists beginning in the late 1960s and early 1970s—male dominance within the family has hardly disappeared. Sociologists have found that women are significantly more likely to leave their jobs when their husbands find better employment opportunities than men are when their wives receive desirable job offers (Bielby and Bielby 1992). And unfortunately, as discussed later in the chapter, many husbands reinforce their power and control over wives and children through acts of domestic violence. (Box 13-2 on page 373 considers cross-cultural findings about violence within the home.)

Conflict theorists also view the family as an economic unit that contributes to societal injustice. The family is the basis for transferring power, property, and privilege from one generation to the next. North America is widely viewed as a "land of opportunity," yet social mobility is restricted in important ways. Children "inherit" the privileged or less-than-privileged social and economic status of their parents (and, in some cases, of earlier generations as well). As conflict theorists point out, the social class of their parents significantly influences children's socialization experiences and the protection they receive. This means that the socioeconomic status of a child's family will have a marked influence on his or her nutrition, health care, housing,

p. 221

educational opportunities, and, in many respects, life chances as an adult. For that reason, conflict theorists argue that the family helps to maintain inequality.

Interactionist View

Interactionists focus on the micro level of family and other intimate relationships. They are interested in how individuals interact with one another, whether they are cohabiting partners, long-time married couples, or gay and lesbian couples. For example, studies have shown that it is the nature of family interactions and the quality of the relationship (i.e., parental conflict, parenting stress, love between parents and for children), rather than the parents' sexual orientation, that strongly predict children's behavioural adjustment (Chan et al. 1998).

Another interactionist study might examine the role of the step-parent. The increased number of single parents who remarry has sparked an interest in those who are helping to raise other people's children. While no young girl or boy may dream about one day becoming a stepmom or stepdad, this is hardly an unusual occurrence today. Studies have found that stepmothers are more likely to accept the blame for bad relations with their stepchildren, whereas stepfathers are less likely to accept responsibility. Interactionists theorize that stepfathers (like most fathers) may simply be unaccustomed to interaction directly with children when the mother isn't there (Bray and Kelly 1999; Furstenberg and Cherlin 1991).

Feminist Views

No single theory represents how feminist theories conceptualize the family. Views on the topic are as diverse as feminist theories themselves. They do, however, share certain assumptions in their study of family and kinship. For example, they reject the belief in the "naturalness" of family (Luxton 2001). Instead, they argue that the family is a socially constructed institution, and thus, it varies over time and place. In other words, families are diverse, flexible, and changeable, rather than being "monolithic" or the same. Feminist theorists especially challenge the functionalist view of family, when they raise the question "for whom and in whose interests is the family functional?"

While feminist views on the family do share an understanding of the important need to consider women's experiences, including their inequality and discrimination in the family, global and antiracist feminists argue that these too vary according to class, race, and ethnicity. What similarities are there in the discrimination faced by a stay-at-home married mother and a lesbian mother in a same-sex relationship? How does the experience of being a grandmother in a First Nations community compare to being an older white woman in a seniors' home in a large city? How does the experience of being the wife of an immigrant compare to that of a woman born in Canada? Questions such as these reveal that it is obvious that one's position in the family varies when other things are taken into consideration, even though each question asks about the experience of women within a family.

Margrit Eichler (2001), a Canadian feminist theorist, argues that the ways in which sociologists have traditionally studied the family often contain biases. She names seven ways in which the research has been biased, including:

1. *Monolithic bias*, which is a tendency to assume that "the family" is uniform, the same, rather than recognizing its diversity
2. *Conservative bias*, which treats recent changes in the family (including new forms of family) as fleeting; this also leads to ignoring and/or viewing some of the more ugly sides of family life as rare (e.g., family violence)
3. *Agist bias*, which regards children and the aged only as passive members of families

4. *Sexist bias*, which is exhibited in patterns such as double standards for female and male members of a family, as well as gender insensitivity in that all members are treated the same and assumed to experience family in the same way
5. *Microstructural bias*, which overemphasizes micro-level variables, failing to see how the institution of the family fits into society, and affects/is affected by other social structures
6. *Racist bias*, which explicitly or implicitly assumes the superiority of the family form of the dominant group, and ignores race/racism when relevant
7. *Heterosexist bias*, which either ignores same-sex families, or treats them as problematic and deviant.

Marriage and Family

Though there has been a decline in marriage rates in the past few decades, more than 70 percent of Canadians over the age of 15 either were, or have been, married at some point (Statistics Canada 2002). Historically, the most consistent aspect of family life in this country has been the high rate of marriage. In fact, despite an increase in divorce rates in the 1970s and '80s, Canada's rate of divorce is lower than those in many other countries. For example, whereas almost one in two U.S. marriages ends in divorce, in Canada the rate is 37 percent (Vanier Institute of the Family 2000a). Marriage is so highly valued in Canadian society that remarriage is now a norm. Of those who do divorce, 63 percent of males and 57 percent of females will remarry (McDaniel & Tepperman 2000).

In this part of the chapter, we will examine various aspects of love, marriage, and parenthood in Canada and contrast them with cross-cultural examples. We're used to thinking of romance and mate selection as strictly a matter of individual preference. Yet, sociological analysis tells us that social institutions and distinctive cultural norms and values also play an important role.

Courtship and Mate Selection

"My rugby mates would roll over in their graves," says Tom Buckley of his online courtship and subsequent marriage to Terri Muir. But Tom and Terri are hardly alone these days in turning to the Internet for matchmaking services. By the end of 1999 more than 2500 websites were helping people find mates. You could choose from oneandonly.com or 2ofakind.com or cupidnet.com, among others. One service alone claims 2 million subscribers. Tom and Terri carried on their romance via e-mail for a year before they met. According to Tom, "E-mail made it easier to communicate because neither

When fathers interact regularly with their children, it's a win/win situation. The fathers get close to their offspring, and studies show that the children end up with fewer behaviour problems.

one of us was the type to walk up to someone in the gym or a bar and say, 'You're the fuel to my fire' " (B. Morris 1999:D1).

Internet romance is only the latest courtship practice. In the Central Asian nation of Uzbekistan and other traditional cultures that favour arranged marriages, courtship is defined largely through the interaction of two sets of parents. They arrange spouses for their children. Typically, a young Uzbekistani woman will be socialized to eagerly anticipate her marriage to a man whom she has met only once, when he is presented to her family at the time of the final inspection of her dowry. In Canada, by contrast, courtship is conducted primarily by individuals who may have a romantic interest in each other. In our culture, courtship often requires these individuals to rely heavily on intricate games, gestures, and signals. Despite such differences, courtship—whether in Canada, Uzbekistan, or elsewhere—is influenced by the norms and values of the larger society (C. J. Williams 1995).

Take our choice of a mate. Why are we drawn to a particular person in the first place? To what extent are these judgments shaped by the society around us?

Aspects of Mate Selection

Many societies have explicit or unstated rules that define potential mates as acceptable or unacceptable. These norms can be distinguished in terms of endogamy and exogamy. *Endogamy* (from the Greek *endon*, "within") specifies the groups within which a spouse must be found and prohibits marriage with others. For example, in Canada, many people are expected to marry within their own racial, ethnic, or religious group and are strongly discouraged or even prohibited from marrying outside the group. Endogamy is intended to reinforce the cohesiveness of the group by suggesting to the young that they should marry someone "of our own kind."

By contrast, *exogamy* (from the Greek *exo*, "outside") requires mate selection outside certain groups, usually one's own family or certain kinfolk. The *incest taboo*, a social norm common to virtually all societies, prohibits sexual relationships between certain culturally specified relatives. For people in Canada, this taboo means that we must marry outside the nuclear family. We cannot marry our siblings, and it's often recommended that we do not marry our first cousins.

Endogamous restrictions may be seen as preferences for one group over another. In the United States, such preferences are most obvious in racial barriers. Until the 1960s, some states outlawed interracial marriages. This practice was challenged by Richard Loving (a white man) and Mildred Jeter Loving (a part-black, part-Native American woman), who married in 1958. Eventually, in 1967, the Supreme Court ruled that it was unconstitutional to prohibit marriage solely on the basis of race. The decision struck down statutes in Virginia and 16 other states.

In Canada there is evidence to suggest that the longer they reside in Canada, the more likely Canadians are to marry someone outside of their own ethnic group. While 11 percent of immigrants to this country report more than one ethnic background, approximately one-third of those born in Canada had a mixed ethnic background (Howell, in Baker 2001).

Variations in the rates of intermarriage exist based on the length of time that different ethnic groups have been in Canada. Northern, Western and Eastern Europeans have the highest rates of intermarriage, while Asians, Africans, and Latin Americans have the lowest. Despite the efforts of the Canadian government to promote the ideology and policies of multiculturalism, Canadian families are beginning to resemble one another more through increased intermarriage among various ethnic groups.

Interracial unions force a society to reconsider its definitions of race and ethnicity. In Chapter 10, we noted that race is socially constructed in p. 262 Canada and around the world. As increasing proportions

Interracial unions, which are becoming increasingly common and accepted, are blurring definitions of race. Would the children of this interracial couple be considered black or white?

of children in this country come from biracial or multiracial backgrounds, traditional definitions of race and ethnicity will no longer be as relevant. The sensitive issue of racial labels became a legislative concern in the mid-1990s, when the U.S. Bureau of the Census considered how to ask people about their racial backgrounds in the 2000 census. Several voluntary associations representing mixed-race children requested that the census offer a new category of "multiracial" or "biracial" so that they would no longer be forced to define themselves as solely "white," "black," "Asian," or "American Indian." In the end it was decided to let people check off several categories they felt applied to them but not to provide the "multiracial" or "biracial" classification (R. Schaefer 2000).

The Love Relationship

Whatever else "love" is, most people would agree it is complicated. Listen to what a university student has to say on the subject:

> Love isn't in the air these days, at least not in New Haven . . . my peers and I find ourselves in a new world of romance, and we're feeling a little out of our league. We are children of the Age of Divorce, born into the AIDS crisis, reared on Madonna, *Friends*, and *Beverly Hills 90210*. No wonder we're confused. We know we want this thing called love. More than previous generations, though, we're unsure of what love is and how to get it— and we're not so sure that finding it will be worth the trouble (Rodberg 1999:1–2).

Another student claims that "love, like everything else, must be pondered, and we have too many other things to ponder—no matter how much we profess to want love" (quoted in Rodberg 1999:4).

For a variety of reasons, hinted at in these quotations, this generation of students seems more likely to "hook up" or cruise in large packs than engage in the romantic dating relationships of their parents and grandparents. Still, at some point in their adult lives the great majority of today's students will meet someone they "love" and enter into a long-term relationship that focuses on creating a family.

In Canada, love is important in the courtship process. Living in their own home makes the affectional bond between husband and wife especially important. The couple is expected to develop its own emotional ties, free of the demands of other household members for affection. Sociologist William Goode (1959) observed that spouses in a nuclear family have to rely heavily on each other for the companionship and support that might be provided by other relatives in an extended-family situation.

Parents in Canada tend to value love highly as a rationale for marriage, and they encourage their children to develop intimate relationships based on love and affection. In addition, songs, films, books, magazines, television shows, and even cartoons and comic books reinforce the theme of love. At the same time, our society expects parents and peers to help a person confine his or her search for a mate to "socially acceptable" members of the opposite sex.

Traditional gender-role socialization has made it easier for women to express love and other feelings of social intimacy than it is for men. The qualities identified with intimacy—emotional warmth, expressiveness, vulnerability, and sensitivity—are associated with the female but not the male gender role. Studies show that men are more likely than women to base their perceptions of love and intimacy on sex, on providing practical help, and on simply being in the presence of a loved one (Cancian 1986; L. Thompson and Walker 1989).

Most people in Canada may take the importance of falling in love for granted, but love-and-marriage is by no means a cultural universal. In fact, in many cultures (both today and in the past) love and marriage are unconnected and are sometimes at odds with one another. For example, feelings of love are not a prerequisite for marriage among the Yaruros of inland Venezuela or in other cultures where there is little freedom for mate selection. The Yaruro male of marriageable age doesn't engage in the kind of dating behaviour so typical of young people in Canada. Rather, he knows that, under the traditions of his culture, he must marry one of his mother's brothers' daughters or one of his father's sisters' daughters. The young man's choice is further limited because one of his uncles selects the eligible cousin that he must marry (Freeman 1958; Lindholm 1999).

Many of the world's cultures give priority in mate selection to factors other than romantic feelings. In societies with *arranged marriages,* often engineered by parents or religious authorities, economic considerations play a significant role. The newly married couple is expected to develop a feeling of love *after* the legal union is formalized.

Even within Canada, some subcultures carry on the arranged marriage practices of their native cultures. Young people among the Sikhs and Hindus who have immigrated from India and among Islamic Muslims and Hasidic Jews allow their parents or designated matchmakers to find spouses within their ethnic community. As one young Sikh declared, "I will definitely marry who my parents wish. They know me better than I know myself" (Segall 1998:48). It has been suggested that in countries such as Canada, practices of arranged marriage may be changing due to cultural pressures from the larger society. Young people who have emigrated without their families often turn to the Internet to find partners who share their background and goals. Matrimonial ads for the Indian community run on such websites as SuitableMatch.com and INDOLINK.com. Speaking of arranged marriages, one Hasidic Jewish woman noted that "the system isn't perfect, and it doesn't work for everyone, but this is the system we know and trust, the way we couple, and the way we learn to love. So it works for most of us" (p. 53).

Variations in Family Life and Intimate Relationships

Within Canada, social class, race, ethnicity, and sexual orientation create variations in family life. Understanding these variations will give us a more sophisticated understanding of contemporary family styles in our country.

Social Class Differences

Various studies have documented the differences in family organization among social classes in North America. The upper class emphasizes lineage and maintenance of family position. If you are in the upper class, you are not simply a member of a nuclear family but rather a member of a larger family tradition. As a result, upper-class families are quite concerned about what they see as "proper training" for children.

Lower-class families do not often have the luxury of worrying about the "family name"; they must first struggle to pay their bills and survive the crises often associated with life in poverty. Such families are more likely to have only one parent in the home, creating special challenges in child care and financial needs. Children in lower-class families typically assume adult responsibilities—including marriage and parenthood—at an earlier age than children of affluent homes. In part, this is because they may lack the money needed to remain in school.

Social class differences in family life are less striking than they once were. In the past, family specialists agreed that there were pronounced contrasts in child-rearing practices. Lower-class families were found to be more authoritarian in rearing children and more inclined to use physical punishment. Middle-class families were more permissive and more restrained in punishing their children. However, these differences may have narrowed as more and more families from all social classes have turned to the

same books, magazines, and even television talk shows for advice on rearing children (M. Kohn 1970; Luster et al. 1989).

Among the poor, women often play a significant role in the economic support of the family. Men may earn low wages, may be unemployed, or may be entirely absent from the family. In 1998, 42 percent of all families headed by women with no husband present were below the government poverty line. This compared with only 7.3 percent for married couples (Vanier Institute of the Family 2000b).

Many racial and ethnic groups appear to have distinctive family characteristics. However, racial and class factors are often closely related. In examining family life among racial and ethnic minorities, keep in mind that certain patterns may result from class as well as cultural factors.

Racial and Ethnic Differences

The subordinate status of Canada's First Nations people and the other ethnic minorities in Canada has profound effects on their family life. The ways in which race, ethnicity, gender, and class intersect contribute to the diversity of Canadian families.

First Nations people are a heterogeneous group with different histories, geographies, languages, economies, and cultures. Their families, which include those who are kin as well as those who come together for a common community purpose, have been fundamentally disrupted

Korean family ties often provide a huge economic boost. Not only do family members work together in family businesses as do the husband and wife pictured here; they also contribute financial resources through a rotating credit association known as a kye.

by hundreds of years of European domination. For example, the Montagnais–Naskapi of the Eastern Labrador Peninsula underwent major changes in family structure and gender relations as they moved away from traditional hunting and fishing, to trapping introduced by Europeans. The sexual division of labour became more specialized and families became smaller, approaching the size of the nuclear family (Leacock 2001).

The families of Canada's First Nations people have been devalued and undermined by the Canadian government and religious institutions. Children have been removed from their homes, to be taken to residential schools where they were punished for speaking their own language and expressing their culture. Those who ran the schools—the very people who had been assigned to be the children's guardians—often also subjected them to sexual and physical abuse. In addition, many First Nations children were put up for adoption and adopted by, most often, white families in Canada and the U.S., rather than by those from their own band (Eichler 1997). Today, after years of cultural oppression under government control, First Nations families are plagued by problems of domestic abuse, youth suicide, and substance abuse.

The links between race, class, and gender are also demonstrated by research carried out in Nova Scotia and Toronto on black families (Calliste 2001). Significantly more women head black families, compared to nonblack families; these single female-headed black families earn approximately half of the income of their married couple-headed black counterparts, who in turn earn less than their married couple-headed nonblack counterparts. The study concludes that the high rate of teenage pregnancy and the feminization of poverty need to be addressed by black community groups and government, in the form of education, employment equity, sex education, and parenting sessions (Calliste 2001:417). Some similarities exist between African-Canadian and African-American families, as the effects of race, class, and gender intersect to produce inequality for families in both countries.

Child-Rearing Patterns in Family Life

The Nayars of Southern India acknowledge the biological role of fathers, but the mother's eldest brother is responsible for her children (Gough 1974). By contrast, uncles play only a peripheral role in child care in Canada. Caring for children is a universal function of the family, yet the ways in which different societies assign this function to family members can vary significantly. Even within Canada, child-rearing patterns are varied. We'll take a look here at parenthood and grandparenthood, adoption, dual-income families, single-parent families,

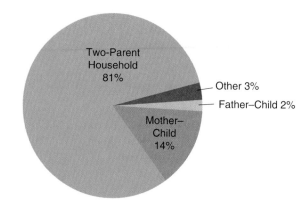

FIGURE 13-3

Living Arrangements of Children in Canada by Type of Family, 1998

Source: National Council of Welfare 2000.

and stepfamilies. (See Figure 13-3 for an idea of how children in Canada are distributed by type of family as defined by Statistics Canada.)

Parenthood and Grandparenthood

The socialization of children is essential to the maintenance of any culture. Consequently, parenthood is one of the most important (and most demanding) social roles in Canada. Sociologist Alice Rossi (1968, 1984) has identified four factors that complicate the transition to parenthood and the role of socialization. First, there is little anticipatory socialization for the social role of caregiver. The normal school curriculum gives scant attention to the subjects most relevant to successful family life—such as child care and home maintenance. Second, only limited learning occurs during the period of pregnancy itself. Third, the transition to parenthood is quite abrupt. Unlike adolescence, it is not prolonged; unlike socialization for work, you cannot gradually take on the duties of caregiving. Finally, in Rossi's view, our society lacks clear and helpful guidelines for successful parenthood. There is little consensus on how parents can produce happy and well-adjusted offspring—or even on what it means to be "well-adjusted." For these reasons, socialization for parenthood involves difficult challenges for most men and women.

One recent development in family life in North America has been the extension of parenthood, as adult children continue to (or return to) live in their parents' home. In 2001, 52 percent of women and 64 percent of men aged 20 to 24 lived in their parents' home. When compared with the 1981 numbers of 33 percent and 51 percent, we see a substantial increase in 20 years (Boyd and Norris 1999; Statistics Canada 2002e). Some of these adult children are still pursuing an education, but in many instances, financial difficulties are at the heart of these living arrangements. While rents and real estate

prices skyrocketed in the 1990s, salaries for younger workers did not keep pace, and many found themselves unable to afford their own homes. Moreover, with many marriages now ending in divorce—most commonly in the first seven years of marriage—divorced sons and daughters are returning to live with their parents, sometimes with their own children.

Is this living arrangement a positive development for family members? Social scientists have just begun to examine this phenomenon, sometimes called the "boomerang generation," the "revolving door," or the "full-nest syndrome" in the popular press. One survey in the U.S. seemed to show that neither the parents nor their adult children were happy about continuing to live together. The children often felt resentful and isolated, but the parents also suffered: Learning to live without children in the home is an essential stage of adult life and may even be a significant turning point for a marriage (Berkeley Wellness Letter 1990; Mogelonsky 1996).

As life expectancy increases in North America, more and more parents are becoming grandparents and even great-grandparents. After interviewing many grandparents, sociologists Andrew Cherlin and Frank Furstenberg Jr. (1992) identified three principal styles of grandparenting:

1. More than half (55 percent) of grandparents surveyed functioned as "specialists in recreational caregiving." They enriched their grandchildren's lives through recreational outings and other special activities.

2. More than one-fourth (29 percent) carried on a "ritualistic" (primarily symbolic) relationship with their grandchildren. In some instances, this was because the grandparents lived far away from their grandchildren and could see them only occasionally.

3. About one-sixth (16 percent) of grandparents surveyed were actively involved in everyday routine care of their grandchildren and exercised substantial authority over them.

Even though parenthood is a crucial social role, society generally provides few clear guidelines for successful parenting. Shown here are some successes: a Canadian mother with her children and a family boating on a river in India.

Later in this chapter, we will look further at the increasing number of households where children are raised by a grandparent.

Adoption

In a legal sense, *adoption* is a "process that allows for the transfer of the legal rights, responsibilities, and privileges of parenthood" to a new legal parent or parents (E. Cole 1985:638). In many cases, these rights are transferred from a biological parent or parents (often called birth parents) to an adoptive parent or parents.

Viewed from a functionalist perspective, government has a strong interest in encouraging adoption. Policymakers, in fact, have both a humanitarian and a financial stake in the process. In theory, adoption offers a stable family environment for children who otherwise might not receive satisfactory care. Moreover, government data show that unwed mothers who keep their babies tend to be of lower socioeconomic status and often require public assistance to support their children. Government can lower its social welfare expenses if children are transferred to economically self-sufficient families. From a conflict perspective, however, such financial considerations raise the ugly specter of adoption's serving as a means whereby affluent (often infertile) couples "buy" the children of the poor (C. Bachrach 1986).

As noted earlier, in Canada, for decades many First Nations children were adopted by white families in this country and the United States. This has since been identified as a form of cultural genocide (Johnson 1983).

As women gained greater access to legal contraception and abortion since the 1960s, the rates of unplanned births declined. This has resulted in the decrease of available Canadian infants for adoption. As well, with changing societal attitudes, more single mothers opted to keep their babies and support them through earnings or with social assistance. Currently, the goals of family preservation in Canadian child welfare, and the preference of Canadians to adopt infants and younger children, make international adoptions (most often from developing countries) more compelling (Baker 2001). Some Canadian couples have adopted orphans from Romania, for example, or Chinese babies (especially girls, who may be unwanted due to the one-child policy). A number of controversies exist about this practice, not the least of which is the practice of children being held by "adoption agencies" that demand more and more fees from the adopting parents (McDaniel and Tepperman 2000). This supports the conflict view of the wealthy, more powerful countries' control over the poorer, less powerful countries. In this case, it involves the "purchase" of children.

Dual-Income Families

The idea of a family consisting of a wage-earning husband and a stay-at-home wife has largely given way to the *dual-income household.* In 1990, among married people, 90 percent of the men and 65 percent of the women were in the labour force. While the rates for married men did not change substantially over the next 10 years (rising by only 1 percent), in 2000, 72 percent of married women with children were in the paid labour force (Sauve 2002). Why has there been such a rise in the number of dual-income couples? A major factor is economic need.

Raising children in urban centres, where the majority of Canadians live, is expensive. The Vanier Institute of the Family (1999) estimated the cost of raising a child from birth to age 18 to be almost $160 000. The percentage of household income spent by two-income families on child-rearing costs was as high as 18 percent of gross earnings in Ontario (Douthitt & Fedyk 1990:29).

In 1999, the median income for households with both partners employed was 80 percent more than in households in which only one person was working outside the home ($54 100, compared with $30 000 if the husband was the sole earner) (Statistics Canada 2001). Of course, not all of a family's second wage is genuine additional income because of such work-related costs as child care. Other factors contributing to the rise of the dual-income model include the nation's declining birth rate (see Chapter 18), the increase in the proportion of women with a post-secondary education, the shift in the economy from manufacturing to service industries, and the impact of the feminist movement in changing women's consciousness.

Dual-income families raise issues about quality of life—marital relationships, child care, and standard of living. Television programming hasn't aided the process. As we saw in Box 13-1, real-life work–family conflicts are rarely portrayed. Sociologist Arlie Hochschild (1989, 1990) has used the phrase "second shift" to describe the double burden—work outside the home followed by child care and housework—that many women carry and few men share equitably. More recently, Hochschild has referred to the failure of corporate and public policies to ease the work–family dilemma as the "stalled revolution." As noted in the social policy section of Chapter 4, there is still not enough quality daycare available.

p. 357

p. 107

Single-Parent Families

In recent decades, the stigma attached to "unwed mothers" and other single parents has significantly diminished. *Single-parent families,* in which there is only one parent present to care for the children, can hardly be viewed as a rarity in Canada. In 2001, 16 percent of families in Canada were headed by a lone parent (up from 11 percent in 1981), and the overwhelming majority of these were female-headed. Variation and diversity exist among single-parent families. For example, the percentage of female-headed black families was over three times that of female-headed nonblack families. The intersection of

Dad takes breakfast duty while Mom rushes off to work in this "dual-income" family. An increasing proportion of couples in Canada reject the traditional nuclear family model of husband as breadwinner and wife as homemaker.

Drawing on two decades of social science research, sociologist Kristin Luker (1996:11) observes:

> The short answer to why teenagers get pregnant and especially to why they continue those pregnancies is that a fairly substantial number of them just don't believe what adults tell them, be it about sex, contraception, marriage, or babies. They don't believe in adult conventional wisdom.

Why might low-income teenaged women wish to have children and face the obvious financial difficulties of motherhood? Viewed from an interactionist perspective, these women tend to have low self-esteem and limited options; a child may provide a sense of motivation and purpose for a teenager whose economic worth in our society is limited at best. Given the barriers that many young women face because of their gender, race, ethnicity, and class, many teenagers may believe that they have little to lose and much to gain by having a child.

What about single fathers who do not head the household? This is typically an understudied group for sociological purposes, but a study of low-income unmarried fathers in Philadelphia came up with some unexpected findings. When asked what their lives would be like without having children, they responded that they would be dead or in jail. This was true even of those fathers who had very little to do with their children. Apparently, the mere fact of fathering children prompts men to get jobs, stay in the community, and stay healthy. Many of these men were upset that they have to hand over money without having a say in how it is spent or in some cases even having legal access to their offspring (P. Cohen 1998).

Countries belonging to the Organization of Economic Cooperation and Development (OECD) have all experienced an increase in single-parent families since the early 1970s, with the greatest increase occurring in the U.S. (Baker 2001). However, poverty rates of these families vary among industrialized countries, depending on the availability of social welfare programs, rates of male/female unemployment, government disincentives to work while receiving social assistance, availability of social welfare programs, and child care.

Despite the current concern over the increase in the number of single-parent families, this form of family has existed for over 100 years in Canada. In 1901, the ratio of

race, class, and gender is evident in patterns of black family structure (Calliste 2001).

While marital dissolution is the major cause of the increase in single-parent families, never-married lone parents are growing in number. The children of these unions often live with both parents, not just one (Marcil-Gratton 1999). This trend reflects the growing trend of non-legal relationships in Canada, as well as in most industrialized countries. In Quebec, for example, 38 percent of all children and 48 percent of first births are categorized as "out-of-wedlock," but 90 percent of these children were born to parents living together (Le Bourdais & Marcil-Gratton 1994).

The lives of single parents and their children are not inevitably more difficult than those of traditional nuclear families. It is as inaccurate to assume that a single-parent family is necessarily "deprived" as it is to assume that a two-parent family is always secure and happy. Nevertheless, life in a single-parent family can be extremely stressful, in both economic and emotional terms.

Economic inequality and poverty are striking characteristics of single-parent families. When compared to two-parent families, female-led single-parent families in North America are the most vulnerable to poverty, contributing to the phenomenon known as the feminization of poverty. Again, race, class, and gender intersect to produce varying patterns of inequality among these families.

A family headed by a single mother faces especially difficult problems when the mother is a teenager.

KARLA JESSEN WILLIAMSON:
Executive Director,
The Arctic Institute of North America

Karla Jessen Williamson is a *kalaaleq*, a Greenland Inuk, born in Appamiut. She completed her bachelor's and master's degrees in education at the University of Saskatchewan, and is working on her Ph.D. in sociology from the University of Aberdeen, Scotland. Her master's thesis focused on child-raising practices in the community of Pangnirtung, Nunavut, while her doctoral dissertation concentrates on Inuit gender relations in the postcolonial Greenland Inuit community.

Presently, Williamson holds the position of executive director of the Arctic Institute of North America, a multidisciplinary research institute mandated to study Canada's North. She oversees the functioning of the Institute, which includes research, teaching, and information dissemination related to the North. Her back-

ground in sociology provides grounding to her understanding of such issues as cultural preservation, cultural diversity, and socioeconomic development in Northern communities.

Prior to taking this position, she held teaching appointments at the University of Saskatchewan, and was the editor of the *Journal of Indigenous Studies*. Williamson states that her own pursuit of the social sciences has been greatly shaped by her Inuit cultural background, in particular by her maternal grandmother, whose intellectual curiosity is based on Inuit *sitarsuaat*. According to Williamson, this refers to a concept that includes the capacity to understand the forces behind all intellects and how they "have been integrated, animating the environment, the universe, and the spirit."

Sources: American Association for the Advancement of Science 2000; University of Calgary Gazette 2000.

---

single-parent families to two-parent families was only slightly lower than today's ratio. The primary difference is the reason for the family having only one parent: whereas in the past this occurred due to the death of a spouse, today it is more likely to be the result of divorce. A major interdisciplinary study, carried out at the University of Victoria and based on 1901 census data, concluded that the family has always been a variable and flexible institution. "There was much more volatility and shifting of marital status than anyone was prepared to admit at the state level" (Lepp 2001).

Blended Families/Stepfamilies

Recent figures show that more than one-third of marriages in Canada involve at least one partner who has been married before. In almost half of these marriages, both spouses have been married at least once (Milan 2000). These numbers are more than double what they were in the 1960s. Remarriage after divorce is common enough today to be considered normative. The rising rates of divorce and remarriage have led to a noticeable increase in blended families and stepfamily relationships.

Stepfamilies are an exceedingly complex form of family organization. Here is how one 13-year-old boy described his family.

> Tim and Janet are my stepbrother and sister. Josh is my stepdad. Carin and Don are my real parents, who are divorced. And Don married Anna and together they had Ethan and Ellen, my half-sister and brother. And

Carin married Josh and had little Alice, my half-sister (Bernstein 1988).

The exact nature of these blended families has social significance for adults and children alike. Certainly resocialization is required when an adult becomes a step-parent or a child becomes a stepchild and stepsibling. Moreover, an important distinction must be made between first-time stepfamilies and households where there have been repeated divorces, breakups, or changes in custodial arrangements.

In evaluating the rise of stepfamilies, some observers have assumed that children would benefit from remarriage because they would be gaining a second custodial parent and potentially would enjoy greater economic security. However, after reviewing many studies on stepfamilies, sociologist Andrew Cherlin (1999:421) concluded that "the well-being of children in stepfamily households is no better, on average, than the well-being of children in divorced, single-parent households." Stepparents can play valuable and unique roles in their stepchildren's lives, but their involvement does not guarantee an improvement.

Domestic Violence in Canada

The mass media and other institutions often portray the family as a source of comfort, security, and safety—as a place where members can escape the trials of the day in the public world of work or school. Lasch (1977) wrote about the social construction of the family as a "haven in a heartless world," which obscures the reality for many who experience the family as a source of conflict and, possibly, danger. Sociologists Gelles and Straus point out that, "You are more likely to be physically assaulted, beaten, and killed in your own home at the hands of a loved one than anyplace else, or by anyone else in society" (1988:18). Domestic violence includes forms such as spousal violence, violence against women, violence against children, sibling violence, and violence against elders (DeKeseredy 2001).

The Canadian Centre for Justice Statistics reports that the rate of wife assault in Canada declined from 12 percent in 1993 to 8 percent in 1999 (CCJS 2001:26). The official definition of spousal "violence" or "assault" includes being beaten, slapped, choked, pushed, threatened with a gun, knife, or other object, or being forced to have unwanted sexual activity. It has been suggested that the overall decline in wife assault in the six-year period of the report may be due to factors such as:

- Increased availability of shelters for abused women
- Increased reporting to police by victims of abuse
- Mandatory arrest policies for men who assault their wives
- Growth in the number, and use, of support services by women
- Growth in treatment programs for violent men
- Changes in the economic and social status of women, which allow them to leave violent relationships more easily, and
- More effective public education leading to changes in society's attitudes and recognition of spousal assault as a crime (CCJS 2001).

Figures 13-4 and 13-5 appear to support the suggestions since both reports to police and use of social services have increased substantially for the six year period of the study.

Many people assume that spousal violence ends after the breakup of the marriage and they wonder, "Why doesn't she just leave?" However, violence often continues after

FIGURE 13-4

Increased Reporting to Police by Female Spousal Violence Victims, 1993 to 1999

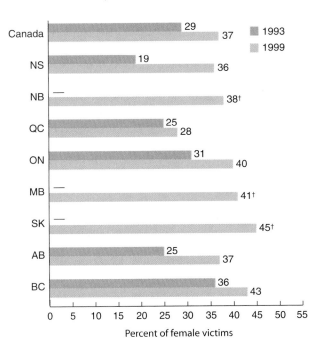

— Amount too small to be expressed.

† Coefficient of variation is high (16.6% to 33.3%).

Figures for Prince Edward Island and Newfoundland and Labrador are too small to be expressed.

Source: CCJS 2001:27; Statistics Canada, catalogue no. 85-224.

FIGURE 13-5

Increased Use of Social Services by Female Spousal Violence Victims, 1993 to 1999

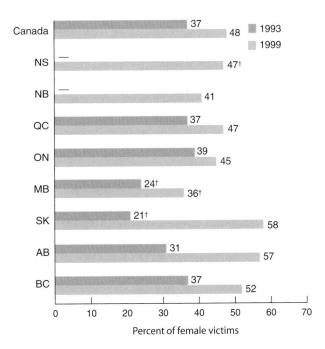

— Amount too small to be expressed.

† Coefficient of variation is high (16.6% to 33.3%).

Figures for Prince Edward Island and Newfoundland and Labrador are too small to be expressed.

Source: CCJS 2001:27; Statistics Canada, catalogue no. 85-224.

the couple separates, and in some cases only begins at that point. In 1999, approximately 63 000 women and 35 000 men in Canada were assaulted for the first time after their marriage was over (CCJS 2001). Male 'proprietariness' or male sexual jealousy has often been used to explain patterns of male violence toward female ex-partners, particularly in acts of killing (Gartner et al. 2001).

While spousal violence occurs in all cultures worldwide (see Box 13-2), in Canada First Nations women run a greater risk of being harmed in episodes of domestic violence. During the period 1993–1999, 25 percent of First Nations women were assaulted by a current or former spouse. This was twice the rate of First Nations men and three times the rate of non-Aboriginal women (CCJS 2001).

Canadian children and youth who die from homicide are most likely killed by family members. Between 1974 and 1999, family members were responsible for 63 percent of solved homicides of children and youth, as recorded by police in Canada. The majority of substantiated cases of violence towards children in 1998 involved inappropriate punishment, while touching and fondling of genitals was the most common form of child sexual abuse. Children are also mistreated emotionally, in particular when they are exposed to other forms of violence in the family, such as hearing or seeing one parent assault the other (CCJS 2001).

Divorce

"Do you promise to love, honour, and cherish . . . until death do you part?" Every year, people of all social classes and racial and ethnic groups make this legally binding agreement. Yet an increasing number of these promises shatter in divorce. While rates may vary among provinces, divorce is a nationwide phenomenon.

Statistical Trends in Divorce

Just how common is divorce? Surprisingly, this is not a simple question; divorce statistics are difficult to interpret.

The media frequently report that one out of every three marriages ends in divorce. But this figure is misleading, since many marriages last for decades. It is based on a comparison of all divorces that occur in a single year (regardless of when the couples were married) against the number of new marriages in the same year. And, since same-sex relationships are not counted in marriage statistics, breakups in gay and lesbian unions are not reflected in divorce statistics either, adding to the misleading figures.

The divorce rate in Canada, and many other countries, began to increase in the late 1960s but then started to level off and even decline in the late 1980s. In 1998, the divorce rate in Canada rose by a few percentage points for the first time in four years, and currently 37.7 percent of marriages are expected to end in divorce (Bélanger 1999; Statistics Canada 2003h). It is suggested that the rates declined partly because of the aging of the baby boomer population, the corresponding decline in the proportion of people of marriageable age, and the rise in cohabitation, which doesn't show up in divorce statistics if the union breaks up.

Getting divorced obviously does not sour people on marriage, however. About 57 percent of divorced women and 63 percent of divorced men eventually remarry. Women are less likely than men to remarry because many retain custody of children after a divorce, which complicates establishing a new adult relationship (Bianchi and Spain 1996; McDaniel and Tepperman 2000).

Some people regard the nation's high rate of remarriage as an endorsement of the institution of marriage, but it does lead to the new challenges of a remarriage kin network composed of current and prior marital relationships. This network can be particularly complex if children are involved or if an ex-spouse remarries.

There is no question that the divorce rate has increased substantially in Canada since 1968 when the *Divorce Act* took effect. In the year preceding the Act, the divorce rate was 54.8 per 100 000 population. In the year following the legislation, the rate more than doubled to 124.2 per 100 000. That was not a surprise since those Canadians who were already separated could now legally dissolve their marriages. Figure 13-6 shows the divorce rate in comparison with the declining marriage rate since 1967. The steady incline in the divorce rate peaked in 1987, and then began to decline slightly each year until 1998, when it rose again, slightly (Baker 2001; Ambert 1998; Statistics Canada 2000). The current divorce rate is not the result of a sudden explosion; rather, signs of such a tendency showed up early in the nation's history.

Factors Associated With Divorce

Perhaps the most important factor in the increase in the divorce rate throughout the twentieth century has been the greater social *acceptance* of divorce. It's no longer considered necessary to endure an unhappy marriage. Most importantly, various religious denominations have relaxed negative attitudes toward divorce, and most religious leaders no longer treat it as a sin. The growing acceptance of divorce is a worldwide phenomenon. In 1998, a few months after a highly publicized divorce by pop superstar Seiko Matsuda, the prime minister of Japan released a survey showing that 54 percent of those polled supported uncontested divorce, compared to 20 percent in 1979 (Kyodo News International 1998a).

A few other factors deserve mention:

- Canada has adopted more liberal divorce laws in the last three decades. No-fault divorce laws,

Sociology in the Global Community

13-2 Domestic Violence

"It's the same every Saturday night. The husband comes home drunk and beats her." This is how Tania Kucherenko describes her downstairs neighbours in Moscow after turning a deaf ear to the screams of terror and the sounds of furniture being overthrown and glass breaking. "There's nothing we can do. It's best not to interfere." Contempt for women runs deep in Russia, where women who dare to leave their husbands risk losing their legal status, a place to live, and the right to work (Bennett 1997:A1).

Wife battering, child abuse, abuse of seniors, and other forms of domestic violence are an ugly reality of family life across the world. In Japan, Tanzania, and Chile, more than half of women report physical abuse by a partner. While estimates are difficult to find on a topic so hidden from public view, an estimate in 2000 concluded that around the world one-third of all women have been beaten, or coerced into sex, or otherwise physically abused in their lifetime.

Drawing on studies conducted throughout the world, we can make the following generalizations:

- Women are most at risk of violence from the men they know.
- Violence against women is evident in all socioeconomic groups.
- Violence in the family is at least as dangerous as assaults committed by strangers.
- Though women sometimes exhibit violent behaviour toward men, often in the process of defending themselves from violence by men, most acts of violence that cause injury are perpetrated by men against women.
- Violence within intimate relationships tends to escalate over time.
- Emotional and psychological abuse can be at least as debilitating as physical abuse.
- Use of alcohol exacerbates family violence but does not cause it.

This billboard in Poland featuring the bruised face of a child reads, "Because he had to let off steam." It is a reminder to Poles that domestic violence is a serious problem in their country, affecting both wives and children.

Using the conflict and feminist models, researchers have found that in relationships where the inequality is greater between men and women, the likelihood of assault on wives increases dramatically. This suggests that much of the violence between intimates, even when sexual in nature, is about power rather than sex.

> **The situation of battered women is so intolerable that it has been compared to that of prison inmates.**

The situation of battered women is so intolerable that it has been compared to that of prison inmates. Criminologist Noga Avni (1991) interviewed battered women at a shelter in Israel and found that their day-to-day lives with their husbands or lovers shared many elements of life in an oppressive total institution, as described by Erving Goffman (1961). Physical barriers are imposed on these women; by threatening further violence, men are able to restrict women to their homes, damaging both their self-esteem and their ability to cope with repeated abuse. Moreover, as in a total institution, these battered women are cut off from

external sources of physical and emotional assistance and moral support. But worst of all, unlike prison inmates, battered women don't have an end to their "sentence." In Avni's view, society could more effectively aid victims of domestic violence if it better p. 98 understood the essential imprisonment of these women. Women in these situations have few economic alternatives, and they fear that their children may also be victimized if they don't submit to the abuse.

The family can be a dangerous place not only for women but also for children and seniors. Canada, for example, has established a child abuse telephone hotline called the Kids Help Phone Line (1-800-668-6868) for children needing help or support (DeKeseredy 2001). An Ontario study surveying 9953 residents in that province found that 31.2 percent of males aged 15 and older reported physical abuse while growing up; 21.1 percent of females of the same age reported experiencing abuse (MacMillan et al. 1997).

Many studies have documented the existence and the nature of abuse of seniors, but few have collected data on its prevalence. In addition, definitions of elder abuse vary. However, some studies have reported rates of 4 percent of seniors being abused in Canada, compared to 3 percent in Australia, Norway, and the United States, and a reported high of 20 percent in France (Health Canada 1999).

Let's Discuss

1. How does the degree of equality in a relationship correlate to the likelihood of domestic violence? How might conflict theorists explain this?

2. Do you know of a family that experienced domestic violence? Did the victim(s) seek outside help, and was that help effective?

Sources: American Bar Association 1999; CCJS 2001; DeKeseredy 2001; Gelles and Cornell 1990; Heise et al. 1999; MacMillan et al. 1997; National Center on Elder Abuse 1998; Straus 1994.

FIGURE 13-6

Marriage and Divorce Rates in Canada, 1967-1998

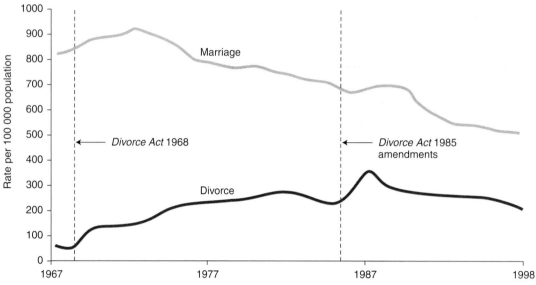

Source: Statistics Canada: Divorces (1987-1988, 1990, 1991, 1992, 1993, 1994, 1995, 1996-1997, 1998), from Baker 2001:218.

allowing a couple to end the marriage without fault on either side (such as specifying adultery), accounted for a surge in the divorce rate after they were introduced in 1985, although they appear to have had little effect beyond that.

- Divorce has become a more practical option in newly formed families, since they now tend to have fewer children than in the past.
- A general increase in family incomes, coupled with the availability of free legal aid for some poor people, has meant that more couples can afford costly divorce proceedings.
- As society provides greater opportunities for women, more and more wives are becoming less dependent on their husbands—both economically and emotionally. They may then feel more able to leave if the marriage seems hopeless.

Impact of Divorce on Children

Divorce is traumatic for all involved, as Cornel West made clear in the excerpt that opened this chapter. But it has special meaning for children, more than 60 000 of whom in Canada were involved in custody disputes in 1996 (Driedger 1998; Robinson 1998). Of course, for some of these children, divorce signals the welcome end of being witness to a very dysfunctional relationship. An American study conducted by sociologists Paul Amato and Alan Booth (1997) found that in about a third of divorces, the children benefit from parental separation because it

lessens their exposure to conflict. But in about 70 percent of all divorces, they found that the parents engaged in a low level of conflict; in these cases, the realities of divorce appear to be harder for the children to bear than living with the marital unhappiness. Other researchers, using differing definitions of conflict, have found greater unhappiness for children living in homes with marital differences. Still, it would be simplistic to assume that children are automatically better off following the breakup of their parents' marriage. Clearly, the interests of the parents do not necessarily serve children well.

Divorce can obviously be a painful experience for both female and male children, but we should avoid labelling young people as "children of divorce" as if this *parental* experience is the singular event defining the life of a girl or boy. Large-scale studies in the United States and Great Britain have shown that some of the alleged negative effects of divorce actually resulted from conditions (such as poverty) that existed *before* the parental separation. Moreover, if divorce does not lower children's access to resources and does not increase stress, its impact on children may be neutral or even positive. Divorce does not ruin the life of every child it touches, though its effect on a child is not always benign (Cherlin 1999). Divorces involving children also have an impact on family members beyond the nuclear family. In Box 13-3, we consider recent research on the role of grandparents in divorce.

Since women's wages are lower and they are more likely to be awarded child custody, children of divorced parents often encounter serious economic consequences.

Research in Action   13-3 Grandparents and Divorce

When a couple with children gets divorced, an important legal decision must be made as to legal custody. Who has the right to make important decisions about the children and to have legal responsibility for them? While joint custody between the mother and father is growing in popularity, the social reality is that most children remain in the care of their mother most of the time. About one-quarter of divorced fathers see their children weekly, but an almost equal proportion have not seen their children in over a year.

Add to this picture sporadic contact with grandparents. If many parents rarely see their children following divorce, what is the likelihood that grandparents can maintain the type of contact they would like? While data on this subject are not complete, it seems that kinship ties become even more fragile beyond the immediate family following a breakup. Indeed, if children are young at the time of divorce and remarriage soon occurs, the new step-grandparents often come to view the children as their own grandchildren. Obviously, this creates tension and jealousy on the part of the natural grandparents, who now view the family scene from a distance.

Yet sometimes they are successful in maintaining stronger ties than even their own adult son or daughter has with the children. There is a growing trend in North America for families to be *maintained* by grandparents. In the U.S. in 1998, 5.6 percent of all children lived in households maintained by a grandparent. Grandparents raised the children without either parent present in 37 percent of these households.

> There is a growing trend in North America for families to be maintained by grandparents.

What do we know about the families solely maintained by grandparents? They face many of the challenges of parent–child households. In the majority of cases, a grandparent is working and has to juggle work and home responsibilities. But in some ways the challenges are even greater than in parent–child families. These grandparents had been through child rearing at a much younger age and presumably were not anticipating doing it again. Since they are past their prime earning years, their households tend to be poorer, and to receive more public

assistance than comparable families with children. They tend to raise older children—children who are at least six years of age.

This growing phenomenon of grandparent-maintained families raises some important issues. First, sociologists need to assess quality-of-life issues and the parenting skills of grandparents unexpectedly parenting again. In the meantime, grandparents and their grandchildren would benefit greatly from the extension of policies and programs intended to help traditional parent–child families in times of need. The welfare policies that require recipients to get jobs have spawned employer-based or subsidized child care and family-friendly policies. These now need to be extended to grandparents who care for their grandchildren. Unfortunately, most agencies are currently ill-equipped to deal with the grandparent-maintained household.

Let's Discuss

1. Why is the number of grandparent-maintained households increasing?
2. How do grandparent-maintained households differ from parent-maintained households? In what ways are they similar?

Sources: Cherlin and Furstenberg 1992; Coontz 1997; Hall and Jerding 1999.

Canadian studies show that while men experience moderate increases in their level of economic well-being after divorce, women experience a drop in income of approximately 40 percent. "Even three years after divorce, women's income remains far below what they had during marriage and far below their ex-husbands' current income" (Ambert 1998:8).

Family Diversity

Marriage is no longer the presumed route from adolescence to adulthood. In fact, it has lost much of its social significance as a rite of passage. The nation's marriage rate

has dipped by approximately 40 percent since 1950 because people are postponing marriage until later in life and more couples, including same-sex couples, are deciding to form partnerships without marriage (Milan 2000).

Cohabitation

The apostle Paul wrote, "It is better to marry than to burn." However, as journalist Tom Ferrell (1979) has suggested, more people than ever "prefer combustible to connubial bliss." One of the most dramatic trends of recent years has been the tremendous increase in male–female couples who choose to live together without marrying, thereby engaging in what is commonly called *cohabitation.*

This young couple in England is cohabiting, an increasingly popular alternative to marriage in many countries today.

In 2001, 14 percent of Canadian couples were cohabiting; as seen in Figure 13-1, that was more than double the rate in 1981. Younger Canadians are choosing cohabitation over marriage as their first union at increasing rates. Of those living as a couple in 2001, approximately 43 percent of 20- to 29-year-olds, and 3 percent of couples over 60 years of age, were cohabiting (Statistics Canada 2002d; Wilson 2001). As we will see shortly, the norm for new couples in Quebec is cohabitation.

We can also find increases in cohabitation in the United States, France, Sweden, Denmark, and Australia. Data released in Great Britain indicate that more than 12 percent of people aged 18 to 24 are cohabiting. One report notes that in Sweden it is almost universal for couples to live together before marriage. Demographers in Denmark call the practice of living together *marriage without papers*. In Australia, these couples are known as *de factos* (Blanc 1984; Levinson 1984; O'Donnell 1992; Thomson and Colella 1992).

Some countries have governmental policies that do not encourage marriage. For example, Sweden offers no married-couple allowance for tax purposes, no tax deduction for raising children, and no way for couples to file their income taxes jointly. Not surprisingly, many Swedish couples choose to cohabit rather than to marry. About half of the babies in Sweden are born to unmarried mothers—although there are proportionately many fewer unmarried *teenage* mothers in Sweden than in the United States (*Economist* 1995).

Like Sweden, Quebec stands out in its low rate of marriage and high rate of cohabitation. It has the lowest

marriage rate among the provinces. In fact, it has one of the lowest rates of marriage worldwide (Wilson 2001). Quebec residents are increasingly turning away from traditional institutions such as the church and state in the establishment of their families, and common-law unions were accepted and adopted in Quebec sooner than in the other provinces. In every age group, we find that Quebec women were more likely to begin their conjugal life through a common-law relationship than through marriage. For example, among women aged 30 to 39 in a marital relationship in 2001, 70 percent began with common law, while the numbers for the same age group in other provinces is 40 percent. And only one-third will marry their common-law partner (compared to more than twice as many in the other provinces) (Statistics Canada 2002d). Moreover, couples in Quebec are more inclined than those in other provinces to have children in common-law relationships. Cohabitation is the norm for first unions in Quebec, and having children does not encourage couples to marry, as it does in other provinces. And while common-law relationships are more stable in Quebec than elsewhere, the rates of separation are similar. Common-law unions are twice as likely to separate as marriage unions (55.3 percent compared to 26.8 percent) (Statistics Canada 2002d).

Census data have documented increases in cohabitation among older people in Canada. Older couples may choose cohabitation rather than marriage for many reasons: because of religious differences, to preserve the full pension benefits they receive as single people, out of fear of commitment, to avoid upsetting children from previous marriages, because one partner or both are not legally divorced, or because one or both have lived through a spouse's illness and death and do not want to experience that again. But some older couples simply see no need for marriage and report being happy living together as they are.

Remaining Single

Looking at TV programs today, as Box 13-1 pointed out, you would be justified in thinking that most households are composed of singles. While this is not the case, it is true that more and more people in Canada are *postponing* entry into first marriages. In 2000, 29 percent of Canadians over 15 years of age had never married, compared to 23 percent in 1981 (Statistics Canada 2002; Beaujot et al., 1995). As well as the postponement of marriage and the increase in common-law relationships, Canadians are experiencing a decline in any form of heterosexual union (Fox 2001).

The trend toward maintaining a single lifestyle for a longer period of time is related to the growing economic independence of young people. This is especially significant for women. Freed from financial needs, women don't necessarily have to marry to enjoy a satisfying life.

p. 309 ◀

There are many reasons why a person may choose not to marry. Singleness is an attractive option for those who do not want to limit their sexual intimacy to one lifetime partner. Also, some men and women do not want to become highly dependent on any one person—and do not want anyone depending heavily on them. In a society that values individuality and self-fulfillment, the single lifestyle can offer certain freedoms that married couples may not enjoy.

Remaining single represents a clear departure from societal expectations; indeed, it has been likened to "being single on Noah's Ark." A single adult must confront the inaccurate view that he or she is always lonely, is a workaholic, is immature, and is automatically affluent. These stereotypes help support the traditional assumption in Canada and most other societies that to be truly happy and fulfilled, a person must get married and raise a family. To help counter these societal expectations, singles have formed numerous support groups, such as Alternative to Marriage Project (www.unmarried.org).

Lesbian and Gay Relationships

We were both raised in middle-class families, where the expectation was we would go to college, we would become educated, we'd get a nice white-collar job, we'd move up and own a nice house in the suburbs. And that's exactly what we've done (*New York Times* 1998:B2).

Sound like an average family? The only break with traditional expectations in this case is that the "we" described here is a gay couple.

The lifestyles of lesbians and gays vary as greatly as those of heterosexual couples. Some live in long-term, monogamous relationships. Some couples live with children from former heterosexual marriages or adopted children. Some live alone, others with roommates. Others remain married and do not publicly acknowledge their homosexuality.

Recognition of same-sex partnerships is not uncommon in Europe, including Denmark, Holland, Switzerland, France, Belgium, and parts of Germany, Italy, and Spain. In 2001, the Netherlands converted its "registered same-sex partnerships" into full-fledged marriages, with divorce provisions (S. Daley 2000).

Gay activist organizations emphasize that despite the passage of laws protecting the civil rights of lesbians and gays, lesbian and gay couples are prohibited from marrying—and therefore from gaining traditional partnership benefits. With such inequities in mind, some jurisdictions have passed legislation allowing for registration of domestic partnerships. A ***domestic partnership*** may be defined as two unrelated adults who reside together, agree to be jointly responsible for their dependants, basic living expenses, and other common necessities, and share a mutually caring relationship. Domestic partnership benefits can apply to such areas as inheritance, parenting, pensions, taxation, housing, immigration, workplace fringe benefits, and health care. While the most passionate support for domestic partnership legislation has come from lesbian and gay activists, the majority of those eligible for such benefits would be cohabiting heterosexual couples (ACLU 1999).

Domestic partnership legislation, however, faces strong opposition from conservative religious and political groups. In the view of opponents, support for domestic partnership undermines the historic societal preference for the nuclear family. Advocates of domestic partnership counter that such relationships fulfill the same functions for the individuals involved and for

In 2001, a lesbian couple in Halifax became the first same-sex couple in Canada to register their relationship as a "domestic partnership."

society as the traditional family and should enjoy the same legal protections and benefits. The gay couple quoted at the beginning of this section consider themselves a family unit, just like the nuclear family that lives down the street in their suburb. They cannot understand why they have been denied a family membership at their municipal swimming pool and why they have to pay more than a married couple (*New York Times* 1998).

In 2001, after a decade of court challenges and demonstrations over the rights of same-sex couples, Nova Scotia became the first jurisdiction in Canada to register same-sex and common-law relationships as legal domestic partnerships. This change will allow same-sex couples many of the rights accorded to married couples in that province: equal division of property and spousal support if the relationship dissolves, and full spousal benefits and pensions to partners. The registration of domestic partnerships, however, is not considered "marriage." While some gays and lesbians pushed for Nova Scotia to become the first province to allow same-sex marriage and joint adoption of children, the provincial government insisted that such legislation would not pass. Instead, a change to the *Vital Statistics Act* in Nova Scotia, allowing the registration of same-sex couples as domestic partners, was introduced and passed with little controversy (Cox 2001).

In 2002 Quebec passed the *Civil Union Act* giving all couples, including gays and lesbians, the choice of registering their union with the province rather than the church. An Ontario Superior Court went further in July of 2002. The three judges unanimously ruled that Canada's definition of marriage as a union between a man and a woman is discriminatory and unconstitutional. Their judgment was made in the case of eight same-sex couples who applied for civil marriage licences in Toronto in 2002 and were denied registration of their licences by the province. The judges called the restriction against same-sex marriage in Canada "an offense to the dignity of lesbians and gays" who, like heterosexual couples, are "entitled to full and equal recognition, and the law must therefore be adapted accordingly" (cited in EGALE Canada 2002). The Ontario judges opened the door for the federal government to extend the common-law definition of marriage to include same-sex couples. However, two weeks later, Justice Minister Martin Cauchon issued a statement that the government would appeal the landmark Ontario court decision. This appeal is expected to take years, buying time for the government to come up with a solution to clarifying the definition of marriage, in a social climate of heated debates on the issue.

Marriage is an emotionally charged issue among the gay and lesbian communities. Some believe that it represents a sign of legitimacy and normalization to their already established relationships. Others believe that marriage, given its history of patriarchy and oppression, is not an institution to be emulated by gay and lesbian couples. Alison Kemper and Joyce Barnett are Anglican ministers and one of the couples involved in the Ontario case. Upon hearing that the federal government was appealing the Ontario decision, Kemper stated: "What we wanted was not just a gold star of approval, but also a sense that what we had made a difference to the world around us and that the world around us needed to support us as well" (Jaimet 2002:A2).

Marriage Without Children

There has been a modest increase in childlessness in Canada. According to the General Social Survey, 12 percent of women and 14 percent of men aged 20 to 39 state that they do not intend to have any children (Dupuis 1998). Rates of actual childlessness began to increase for women born in the 1940s, as they had easier access to contraception when it became legal in the late 1960s. These women entered young adulthood at a time when additional options in advanced education and job opportunities for women were expanding.

Childlessness within marriage has generally been viewed as a problem that can be solved through such means as adoption and artificial insemination. Some couples, however, choose not to have children and regard themselves as child-free, not childless. They do not believe that having children automatically follows from marriage, nor do they feel that reproduction is the duty of all married couples.

Economic considerations have contributed to this shift in attitudes; having children has become quite expensive. As noted earlier, findings in 1999 were that the average middle-class family will spend $160 000 to feed, clothe, and shelter a child from birth to age 18. If the child attends university, that amount could rise substantially, depending upon which campus is chosen. Aware of the financial pressures, some couples are having fewer children than they otherwise might, and others are weighing the advantages of a child-free marriage (Vanier Institute of the Family 1999).

Despite changing attitudes, Canadian women today continue to "pay a price in the labour market for marriage and motherhood, and shoulder more responsibility for housework and child care at home than men" (Fox 2001:164). This contributes to the trend of women postponing marriage or never marrying, and postponing childbearing or remaining childless. Meanwhile, some childless couples who desperately want children are willing to try any means necessary to get pregnant and/or adopt. The social policy section that follows explores the controversy surrounding recent advances in reproductive technology.

SOCIAL POLICY AND THE FAMILY

Reproductive Technology

The Issue

The 1997 feature film *Gattaca* told the story of a future in which genetic engineering enhanced people's genes. Those who were not "enhanced" in the womb—principally those whose parents could not afford the treatments—suffered discrimination and social hurdles throughout their lives. To borrow a line from the movie, "Your genes are your résumé."

Far-fetched? Perhaps, but today we are witnessing common aspects of reproductive technology that were regarded as so much science fiction just a generation ago. "Test tube" babies, frozen embryos, surrogate mothers, sperm and egg donation, and cloning of human cells are raising questions about the ethics of creating and shaping human life. How will these possibilities change the nature of families and the definitions we have of motherhood and fatherhood? To what extent should social policy encourage or discourage innovative reproductive technology?

The Setting

In an effort to overcome infertility, many couples turn to a recent reproductive advance known as in vitro fertilization (IVF). In this technique, an egg and sperm are combined in a laboratory dish. If the egg is fertilized, the resulting embryo (the so-called test tube baby) is transferred into a woman's uterus. The fertilized egg could be transferred into the uterus of the woman from whom it was harvested, or of a woman who has not donated the egg but who plays the role of surrogate (i.e., substitute). A surrogate mother carries the pregnancy to term and then transfers the child to the social mother. After this occurs, depending on the agreement between the social mother and the surrogate mother, the child may or may not be a part of the surrogate mother's life.

These possibilities, and many more, make the definition and responsibilities of motherhood complicated and somewhat murky. How should motherhood be defined—as providing gestation, as providing care for the child, as providing the egg, or all or some combination of these?

Sociological Insights

Replacing personnel is a functional prerequisite that the family as a social institution performs. Obviously,

advances in reproductive technology allow childless couples to fulfill their personal and societal goals. The new technology also allows opportunities not previously considered. A small but growing number of same-sex couples is using donated sperm or eggs to have genetically related children and fulfill the desire to have children and a family (Bruni 1998).

p. 125

As mentioned earlier, sometimes it is difficult to define relationships. For example, in 1995, one California couple, John and Luanne Buzzanca, hired a married woman to carry a child to term for them—a child conceived of the sperm and egg of anonymous, unrelated donors. One month before the birth, John filed for divorce and claimed that he had no parental responsibilities, including child support. Eventually the court ruled that the baby girl had no legal parents; she is temporarily living with Luanne, who may seek to adopt the baby. While this is an unusual case, it suggests the type of functional confusion that can arise in trying to establish kinship ties (Weiss 1998).

Canadian feminist sociologist Margrit Eichler has developed a typology of motherhood in this age of new reproductive technology. She states that there can be up to 25 types of mothers, considering that mothers can now be "partial biological mothers—genetic but not gestational, or gestational but not genetic" (Eichler 1997:80). Her list of possible types of mothers includes:

1. Genetic and gestational but not social mothers (mothers who have given up their children for adoption)
2. Genetic, non-gestational, and not social mothers (those who provide an egg)
3. Non-genetic, but gestational, social, exclusive, full mothers (those who receive an egg)
4. Dead mother whose egg has been fertilized (mother #1), implanted in a carrier (mother #2), and handed to a third woman (mother #3).

Eichler adds that new reproductive technologies have had a far less dramatic impact on fatherhood, for which the most noticeable change has come in the form of what she calls "post-mortem biological fathers" (1997:72). This term refers to fatherhood that occurs after a man's death, when his sperm is harvested and used to impregnate a woman.

In the future depicted in *Gattaca,* the poor were at a disadvantage in being able to control their lives genetically. The conflict perspective would note that in the world today, the technologies available are often accessible only to the most affluent.

In addition, a 1993 report of the Royal Commission on New Reproductive Technologies warned that these technologies could potentially be used for commercial purposes (i.e., surrogacy), making women of lower classes vulnerable to exploitation. Thus, in Canada today there is a voluntary ban on the use of many technologies that could be used commercially, ones that would enable those with resources to "buy" a reproductive service from those with fewer resources but the ability to "sell" the services in demand.

Interactionists observe that the quest for information and social support connected with reproductive technology has created new social networks. Like other special-interest groups, couples with infertility problems band together to share information, offer support to one another, and demand better treatment. They develop social networks—sometimes through voluntary associations or Internet support groups—where they share information about new medical techniques, insurance plans, and the merits of particular physicians and hospitals. One Internet self-help group, Mothers of Supertwins, offers supportive services for mothers but also lobbies for improved counselling at infertility clinics to better prepare couples for the demands of many babies at one time (MOST 1999).

Policy Initiatives

In Japan, some infertile couples have caused a controversy by using eggs or sperm donated by siblings for in vitro fertilization. This violates an ethical (though not legal) ban on "extramarital fertilization," the use of genetic material from anyone other than a spouse for conception. While opinion is divided on this issue, most Japanese agree that there should be government guidelines on reproductive technology. Many nations, including England and Australia, bar payments to egg donors, resulting in very few donors in these countries. Even more countries limit how many times a man can donate sperm. Because the United States has no such restrictions, infertile foreigners who can afford the costs view this country as a land of opportunity (Efron 1998; Kolata 1998).

The legal and ethical issues connected with reproductive technology are immense. Many people feel we

The possibility of cloning humans in the future, eerily foreshadowed in Andy Warhol's *The Twenty Marilyns*, poses major ethical dilemmas.

should be preparing for the possibility of a human clone. At this time, however, industrial societies are hard-pressed to deal with present advances in reproductive technology, much less future ones. Already, reputable hospitals are mixing donated sperm and eggs to create embryos that are frozen for future use. This raises the possibility of genetic screening as couples choose what they regard as the most "desirable" embryo—a "designer baby" in effect. Couples can select (some would say adopt) a frozen embryo that matches their requests in terms of race, sex, height, body type, eye colour, intelligence, ethnic and religious background, and even national origin (S. Begley 1998; Rifkin 1998).

Let's Discuss

1. What are some of the innovations in reproductive technology in recent years? What ethical and legal issues do they raise?

2. How do these technologies change the definition of motherhood and fatherhood?

3. If you were writing legislation to regulate reproductive technology, what guidelines (if any) would you include?

Chapter Resources

Summary

The *family,* in its many varying forms, is present in all human cultures. This chapter examines the state of marriage, the family, and other intimate relationships in Canada and considers alternatives to the traditional nuclear family.

1. There are many variations in the family from culture to culture and even within the same culture.

2. The structure of the *extended family* can offer certain advantages over that of the *nuclear family*.

3. We determine kinship by descent from both parents (*bilateral descent*), from the father (*patrilineal descent*), or from the mother (*matrilineal descent*).

4. Sociologists do not agree on whether the *egalitarian family* has replaced the *patriarchal family* as the social norm in Canada.

5. Sociologists have identified six basic functions of the family: reproduction, protection, socialization, regulation of sexual behaviour, companionship, and the provision of social status.

6. Conflict theorists argue that the family contributes to societal injustice and denies opportunities to women that are extended to men.

7. Interactionists focus on the micro level—on how individuals interact in the family and other intimate relationships.

8. Feminist theorists expand on the conflict theorists' notions of denied opportunities by analyzing the social construction of the family and the inherent biases in traditional research on family.

9. Mates are selected in a variety of ways. Some marriages are arranged. Some people are able to choose their mates. Some societies require choosing a mate within a certain group (*endogamy*) or outside certain groups (*exogamy*).

10. In Canada, there is considerable variation in family life associated with social class, race, and ethnic differences.

11. Currently, the majority of all married couples in Canada have two partners active in the paid labour force.

12. The family can also be a dangerous place. Domestic violence includes forms such as spousal violence, violence against children, sibling violence, and violence against elders.

13. Among the factors that contribute to the current divorce rate in Canada are the greater social acceptance of divorce and the liberalization of divorce laws in many states.

14. More and more people are living together without marrying, thereby engaging in what is called *cohabitation*. People are also staying single longer in general or deciding not to have children within marriage.

15. While Nova Scotia has passed *domestic partnership* legislation, such proposals continue to face strong opposition from conservative religious and political groups elsewhere in the country.

16. Reproductive technology has advanced to such an extent that ethical questions have arisen about the creation and shaping of human life.

Critical Thinking Questions

1. Recent political discussions have focused on the definition of "family." Should governments continue to promote the model of family that includes only opposite-sex couples? Are there ways in which "family" might be defined other than on the basis of sexual orientation? What groups in society would be most opposed to such a change? Why?

2. In an increasing proportion of couples in Canada, both partners work outside the home. What are the advantages and disadvantages of the dual-income model for women, for men, for children, and for the society as a whole?

3. Given the current rate of divorce in Canada, is it more appropriate to view divorce as dysfunctional or as a normal part of our marriage system? What are the implications of viewing divorce as normal rather than as dysfunctional?

Key Terms

Adoption   In a legal sense, a process that allows for the transfer of the legal rights, responsibilities, and privileges of parenthood to a new legal parent or parents. (368)

Bilateral descent   A kinship system in which both sides of a person's family are regarded as equally important. (359)

Cohabitation   The practice of living together as a male–female couple without marrying. (375)

Domestic partnership   Two unrelated adults who have chosen to share one another's lives in a relationship of mutual caring, who reside together, and who agree to be jointly responsible for their dependants, basic living expenses, and other common necessities. (377)

Egalitarian family   An authority pattern in which the adult members of the family are regarded as equals. (359)

Endogamy   The restriction of mate selection to people within the same group. (363)

Exogamy   The requirement that people select mates outside certain groups. (363)

Extended family   A family in which relatives—such as grandparents, aunts, or uncles—live in the same home as parents and their children. (356)

Family   A set of people related by blood, marriage (or some other agreed-upon relationship), or adoption who share the responsibility for reproducing and caring for members of society. (355)

Incest taboo   The prohibition of sexual relationships between certain culturally specified relatives. (363)

Kinship   The state of being related to others. (359)

Matriarchy   A society in which women dominate in family decision making. (359)

Matrilineal descent   A kinship system that favours the relatives of the mother. (359)

Monogamy   A form of marriage in which one woman and one man are married only to each other. (356)

Nuclear family   A married couple and their unmarried children living together. (355)

Patriarchy   A society in which men dominate family decision making. (359)

Patrilineal descent   A kinship system that favours the relatives of the father. (359)

Polyandry   A form of polygamy in which some women have more than one husband at the same time. (358)

Polygamy   A form of marriage in which an individual can have several husbands or wives simultaneously. (358)

Polygyny   A form of polygamy in which a husband can have several wives at the same time. (358)

Serial monogamy   A form of marriage in which a person can have several spouses in his or her lifetime but only one spouse at a time. (356)

Single-parent families   Families in which there is only one parent present to care for children. (368)

Social institutions   Organized patterns of beliefs and behaviour centred on basic social needs. (352)

Additional Readings

BOOKS

Baker, Maureen (ed.). 2001. *Families: Changing Trends in Canada.* 4th edition. Toronto: McGraw-Hill Ryerson. An edited collection of chapters by sociologists, examining such areas as family violence, ethnic families, biases in family literature, and marriage and divorce.

Coontz, Stephanie. 1997. *The Way We Really Are: Coming to Terms with America's Changing Families.* New York: Basic Books. A family historian considers how much and how little family organization has changed in the United States.

Eichler, Margrit. 1997. *Family Shifts: Families, Policies, and Gender Equality.* Toronto: Oxford University Press. A sociologist outlines the ways in which our concept of family has not kept pace with recent developments in reproductive technologies.

Hochschild, Arlie Russell. 1997. *Time Bind: When Work Becomes Home and Home Becomes Work.* New York: Metropolitan Books, Henry Holt. The author of *The Second Shift* describes the crunch that is taking place in time commitments to work and home and the social consequences it can have on both.

Milan, Anne. 2000. "One Hundred Years of Families" in *Canadian Social Trends.* Ottawa: Statistics Canada. Catalogue No. 11-008, Spring, 2000:2–13. This article provides a demographic overview of the changing Canadian family.

Salinger, Adrienne. 1999. *Living Solo.* Kansas City, MO: Andrews McMeel Publishing. A photojournalist examines the lives of single people, investigating their inner lives, dwelling places, and somewhat eccentric indulgences.

JOURNALS

Among the journals focusing on the family are *Family Planning Perspectives* (founded in 1969), *Family Relations* (1951), *International Family Planning Perspectives* (1975), *International Journal of Sociology of the Family* (1971), *Journal of Comparative Family Studies* (1970), *Journal of Family Issues* (1980), *Journal of Family Violence* (1986), and *Journal of Marriage and the Family* (1938).

Internet Connection

www.mcgrawhill.ca/college/schaefer

For additional Internet exercises relating to the family and intimate relationships, visit the Schaefer Online Learning Centre at **http://www.mcgrawhill.ca/college/schaefer.** *Please note that while the URLs listed were current at the time of printing, these sites often change—check the Online Learning Centre for updates*

The Stepfamily Network at **http://www.stepfamily. net/index.htm** aims to educate members of stepfamilies and professionals. Click on "Article" and "Forum" to read current and past offerings.

(a) What are some of the unique challenges faced by stepfamilies regarding such issues as discipline and vacation time?

(b) How do step-parents deal with holidays such as Mother's and Father's Day?

(c) If you come from a blended family, do you recognize some of the issues presented on this Internet site? If you do not come from a blended family, how does your home life compare? Are some of the challenges and issues applicable to all families?

(d) Visit the "Kids Corner" and explore the artwork of stepchildren. What themes are found in the art?

(e) What emotions are the children trying to express through their work?

(f) How do these drawings relate to this book's discussion of children of divorced parents and the rise of stepfamilies?

In this billboard distributed by Volkswagen of France, the figure of Jesus at the Last Supper says to his apostles, "Rejoice, my friends, for a new Golf is born." While an image of Jesus is sacred for Christians, it is used here in a secular manner—to advertise cars.

I am the grandson of the late Joseph Michael Augustine.

My grandfather was a devout Catholic. He was baptized Catholic, raised by strong Christian beliefs and ascended into heaven shortly after our parish priest stood over his bedside to read him his last rites

I record this religious aspect of his life in the home of one of his daughters—Aunt Madeline to me—where today I write from within a small, antiquated room in her basement. On each surrounding wall hang large, life-like portraits of religious figures with names like Pontifex Pius X and Leo XIII and His Holiness Pope John XXIII. As was my grandfather, my aunt is a member of the Catholic Church.

With such strong ties to the Catholic religion, should I not feel ashamed of the fact that I do not even understand why each of these figures looming above me is holding the same pose, with right hand raised in the air and two fingers pointing upwards, obviously communicating to the observer something of righteous significance?

Or should I be ashamed that I choose not to understand the righteous significance of these men with all their symbolic gestures, and how they seemingly stare right through me, from every direction of this room, as if God might strike me down for recording such thoughts on religion.

I do not wish to be disrespectful, for my grandfather did not raise us in this way. I respect the Catholic religion, and my family for practising its teachings. However, I was raised in the generation where aboriginal culture and spiritual traditions have since been reawakened, and despite being born into a strong Catholic family, I choose to honour our Great Spirit—God—through the practices and ceremonies originally given to the First Peoples of this land.

Rather than going to church, I attend a sweat lodge; rather than accepting bread and toast from the Holy Priest, I smoke a ceremonial pipe to come into Communion with the Great Spirit; and rather than kneeling with my hands placed together in prayer, I let sweetgrass be feathered over my entire being for spiritual cleansing and allow smoke to carry my prayers into the heavens. I am a Mi'kmaq, and this is how we pray. (*Augustine 2000*) ■

This excerpt from Noah Augustine's article "Grandfather Was a Knowing Christian" contrasts his grandfather's religious beliefs to his own. Augustine, a Mi'kmaq, came to practise Aboriginal spiritual traditions—attending a sweat lodge and smoking a ceremonial pipe—even though he had been born into what he calls a "strong Catholic family." His grandfather, however, who was also a Mi'kmaq, practised Catholicism and was never "reawakened" by the spiritual traditions of his Aboriginal heritage. Noah Augustine's reawakening represents a growing trend among First Nations people in Canada in which Aboriginal spirituality is again being expressed, after years of suppression by the dominant culture.

Religion plays a major role in people's lives, and religious practices of some sort are evident in every society. That makes religion a **cultural universal,** along with other general practices found in every culture such as dancing, food preparation, the family, and personal names. At present, an estimated 4 billion people belong to the world's many religious faiths (see Figure 14-1).

p. 64

When religion's influence on other social institutions in a society diminishes, the process of **secularization** is said to be underway. During this process, religion may survive in the private sphere of individual and family life; it may even thrive on a personal level. But, at the same time, other social institutions—such as the economy, politics, and education—maintain their own sets of norms independent of religious guidance (Stark and Iannaccone 1992).

This chapter focuses on religion as it has emerged in modern industrial societies. It begins with a brief overview of the approaches that sociologists have used in studying religion. We will explore religion's role in societal integration, social support, social change, and social control. We'll examine three important dimensions of religious behaviour—belief, ritual, and experience—as well as the basic forms of religious organization. We will pay particular attention to the emergence of new religious movements. Finally, the social policy section will examine the controversy over religion in public schools. ■

The Sociological Approach to Religion

If a group believes that it is being directed by a "vision from God," sociologists will not attempt to prove or disprove this revelation. Instead, they will assess the effects of the religious experience on the group. What sociologists are interested in is the social impact of religion on individuals and institutions (M. McGuire 1981:12).

Émile Durkheim was perhaps the first sociologist to recognize the critical importance of religion in human societies. He saw its appeal for the individual, but—more important—he stressed the *social* impact of religion. In Durkheim's view, religion is a collective act and includes many forms of behaviour in which people interact with others. As in his work on suicide, Durkheim was not so interested in the personalities of religious believers as he was in understanding religious behaviour within a social context.

p. 389

In line with that tradition, we can define **religion** as a social institution involving a unified system of beliefs and practices relative to sacred things. Religion involves a set of beliefs and practices that are uniquely the property of religion—as opposed to other social institutions and ways of thinking. Durkheim (1947, original edition 1912) argued that religious faiths distinguish between certain events that transcend the ordinary and the everyday world. He referred to these realms as the *sacred* and the *profane.*

The **sacred** encompasses elements beyond everyday life that inspire awe, respect, and even fear. People become a part of the sacred realm only by completing some ritual, such as prayer or sacrifice. Believers have faith in the sacred; this faith allows them to accept what they cannot understand. By contrast, the **profane** includes the ordinary and commonplace. It can get confusing, however, because the same object can be either sacred or profane depending on how it is viewed. A normal dining room table is profane, but it becomes sacred to Christians if it bears the elements of communion. For Confucians and Taoists, incense sticks are not mere decorative items; they are highly valued offerings to the gods in religious ceremonies marking new and full moons.

Contemporary sociologists view religions in two different ways. They study the norms and values of religious faiths through examination of their substantive religious beliefs. For example, it is possible to compare the degree to which Christian faiths literally interpret the Bible, or Muslim groups follow the Koran (or Qur'an), the sacred book of Islam. At the same time, sociologists examine

FIGURE 14-1

Religions

Mapping Life WORLDWIDE

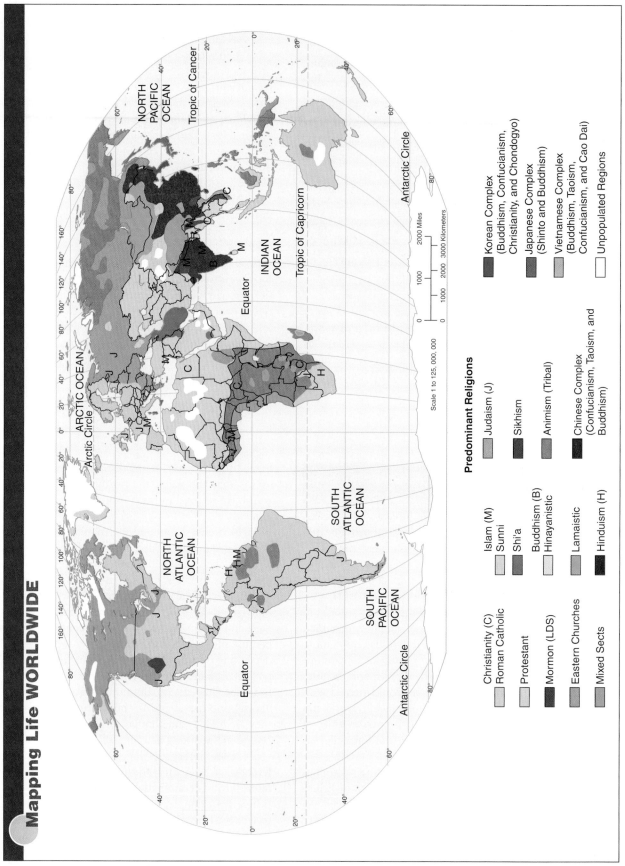

Predominant Religions

Christianity (C)
Roman Catholic

Protestant

Mormon (LDS)

Eastern Churches

Mixed Sects

Islam (M)
Sunni

Shi'a

Buddhism (B)
Hinayanistic

Lamaistic

Hinduism (H)

Judaism (J)

Sikhism

Animism (Tribal)

Chinese Complex
(Confucianism, Taoism, and Buddhism)

Korean Complex
(Buddhism, Confucianism, Christianity, and Chondogyo)

Japanese Complex
(Shinto and Buddhism)

Vietnamese Complex
(Buddhism, Taoism, Confucianism, and Cao Dai)

Unpopulated Regions

Scale 1 to 125, 000, 000

0   1000   2000   3000 Kilometers
0   1000   2000 Miles

Source: Allen 1996:12–13.

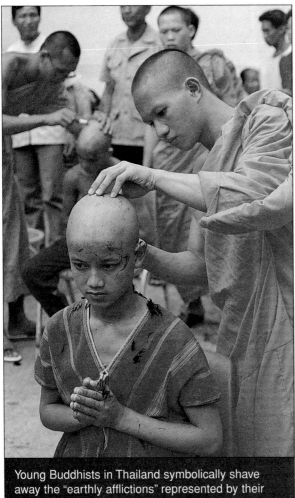

Young Buddhists in Thailand symbolically shave away the "earthly afflictions" represented by their hair.

religions in terms of the social functions and dysfunctions they fulfill, such as providing social support or reinforcing the norms of the status quo. By exploring both the beliefs and the functions of religion, we can better understand its impact on the individual, on groups, and on society as a whole.

Theories on the Role of Religion

Since religion is a cultural universal, it is not surprising that it plays a basic role in human societies. In sociological terms, these include both manifest and latent functions. Among its *manifest* (open and stated) functions, religion defines the spiritual world and gives meaning to the divine. Religion provides an explanation for events that seem difficult to understand, such as our relationship to what lies beyond the grave.

p. 17

The *latent* functions of religion are unintended, covert, or hidden. Even though the manifest function of

church services is to offer a forum for religious worship, they might at the same time fulfill a latent function as a meeting ground for unmarried members.

Each of the four theoretical perspectives we've applied throughout this textbook evaluates religion's impact as a social institution on human societies. We'll consider Durkheim's functionalist view of religion's role in social integration and social support, Weber's thesis on religion's role in promoting social change, and then we'll look at religion as a means of social control from the conflict and feminist perspectives. Note that, for the most part, religion's impact is best understood from a macro-level viewpoint, oriented toward the larger society. The social support function is an exception: it is best viewed on the micro level, directed toward the individual.

Social Integration and Social Support: Durkheim's Theories

The Integrative Function of Religion

Émile Durkheim viewed religion as an integrative power in human society—a perspective reflected in functionalist thought today. As we have seen in previous chapters, Durkheim sought to answer a perplexing question: "How can human societies be held together when they are generally composed of individuals and social groups with diverse interests and aspirations?" In his view, religious bonds often transcend these personal and divisive forces. Durkheim acknowledged that religion is not the only integrative force—nationalism or patriotism may serve the same end.

How does religion provide this "societal glue"? Religion, whether it be Buddhism, Islam, Christianity, or Judaism, offers people meaning and purpose for their lives. It gives them certain ultimate values and ends to hold in common. Although subjective and not always fully accepted, these values and ends help a society to function as an integrated social system. For example, funerals, weddings, bar and bat mitzvahs, and confirmations serve to integrate people into larger communities by providing shared beliefs and values about the ultimate questions of life.

The integrative power of religion can be seen in the role that churches, synagogues, temples, and mosques have traditionally played and continue to play, especially for immigrant groups in Canada. For example, Roman Catholic immigrants may settle near a parish church that offers services in their native language, such as Polish or Spanish. Similarly, Korean immigrants may join a Presbyterian church with many Korean Canadian members and with religious practices like those of churches in Korea. Like other religious organizations, these Roman Catholic and Presbyterian churches help to integrate immigrants into their new homeland.

Although same-sex marriage is not legal in Canada, some churches, such as the Metropolitan Community Church in Toronto, perform "holy union" ceremonies joining same-sex couples.

Yet another example of the integrative impact of religion is provided by the Universal Fellowship of Metropolitan Community Churches. It was established in the United States in 1968 to offer a welcoming place of worship for lesbians and gays. This spiritual community is especially important today, given the many organized religions openly hostile to homosexuality. Currently, the Metropolitan Community Church has 42 000 members in its local churches in 15 countries including Canada, with three such churches in Toronto alone. As part of its effort to support lesbian and gay rights, the Metropolitan Community Church performs same-sex marriages, which it calls "holy union ceremonies" (L. Stammer 1999).

In some instances, religious loyalties are *dysfunctional;* they contribute to tension and even conflict between groups or nations. During the p. 17 Second World War, the German Nazis attempted to exterminate the Jewish people; approximately 6 million European Jews were killed. In modern times, nations such as Lebanon (Muslims versus Christians), Israel (Muslims versus Jews as well as Orthodox versus secular Jews), Northern Ireland (Roman Catholics versus Protestants), and India (Hindus versus Muslims and, more recently, Sikhs) have been torn by clashes that are in large part based on religion.

In the 1990s, religious tensions contributed to bloody conflict in the former Yugoslavia. Serbia, Macedonia, and Montenegro are dominated by the Orthodox Church, and Croatia and Slovenia by the Catholic church; the embattled republic of Bosnia–Herzegovina has a 40 percent Islamic plurality. In many of these areas, the dominant political party is tied into the most influential church.

Religious conflict (though on a less violent level) is evident in Canada as well. Christian fundamentalists, conservative Catholics, and Orthodox Jews have joined forces in many communities in a battle against their liberal counterparts for control of the secular culture. The battle for power in controlling social norms can be widely seen with an array of familiar social issues, among them multiculturalism, child rearing (Chapter 4), abortion (Chapter 11), educational funding (Chapter 15), and gay and lesbian rights (Chapter 21). p. 208

One of the most obvious examples of religion and conflict for control comes from the history of Canada's Aboriginal people. As we will see in the next chapter, dominant European religions in Canada played a large role in the attempt to assimilate Aboriginal children into the mainstream through residential schools. By denying these students the right to speak their own language and practise their own spiritual traditions, Christian religious institutions have a responsibility for the loss of cultural history in First Nations communities. In 1991, Doug Crosby, then president of the Oblate Conference of Canada, issued an apology before 20 000 people at a traditional pilgrimage in Alberta. In it, he stated that sociological insights led to an understanding of the depth of damage that was caused by the "religious superiority complex" that considered Aboriginal sacred practices as pagan and superstitious. He acknowledged his organization's role in threatening religious traditions of First Nations people and the social consequences of this imperialism.

> "We recognize that many of the problems that beset native communities today—high unemployment, alcoholism, family breakdown, domestic violence, spiralling suicide rates, lack of healthy self-esteem—are not so much the result of personal failure as they are the result of centuries of systemic imperialism. Any people stripped of its traditions as well as of its pride falls victim to precisely these social ills" (Crosby 1991:1).

When speaking of the role of residential schools in this process, Crosby stated that the physical and sexual abuses in the schools were horrific but the "biggest abuse was not what happened in the schools, but that the schools themselves happened" (Crosby 1991). As described in the case of Noah Augustine in the chapter opener, a growing trend in First Nations communities is a reawakening of the Aboriginal spirituality that was almost extinguished by the dominant culture's religions.

Religion and Social Support

Most of us find it difficult to accept the stressful events of life—death of a loved one, serious injury, bankruptcy, divorce, and so forth. This is especially true when something "senseless" happens. How can family and friends come to terms with the death of a talented student, not even 20 years old, from a terminal disease?

Did somebody say McDonald's? Probably not among the Orthodox Jews in Israel. They object to the fact that the establishment is open on Friday night and Saturday (the Jewish Sabbath). Secular Jews living in Jerusalem, on the other hand, have no objections. This is but a small skirmish amid intense conflicts between Orthodox and secular Jews in Israel today.

Through its emphasis on the divine and the supernatural, religion allows us to "do something" about the calamities we face. In some faiths, adherents can offer sacrifices or pray to a deity in the belief that such acts will change their earthly condition. At a more basic level, religion encourages us to view our personal misfortunes as relatively unimportant in the broader perspective of human history—or even as part of an undisclosed divine purpose. Friends and relatives of the student may see this death as being "God's will" and as having some ultimate benefit that we cannot understand. This perspective may be much more comforting than the terrifying feeling that any of us can die senselessly at any moment—and that there is no divine "answer" as to why one person lives a long and full life, while another dies tragically at a relatively early age.

Faith-based community organizations have taken on more and more responsibilities in the area of social assistance. In fact, as part of an effort to cut back on government-funded welfare programs, government leaders have advocated shifting the social "safety net" to private organizations in general and to churches and religious charities in particular.

Social Change: Weber's Thesis

Max Weber (1958a, original edition 1904) carefully examined the connection between religious allegiance and capitalist development. His findings appeared in his pioneering work *The Protestant Ethic and the Spirit of Capitalism,* first published in 1904.

Weber noted that in European nations with both Protestant and Catholic citizens, an overwhelming number of business leaders, owners of capital, and skilled workers were Protestant. In his view, this was no mere coincidence. Weber pointed out that the followers of John Calvin (1509–1564), a leader of the Protestant Reformation, believed that God had preordained that some people would live their afterlife in heaven, some in hell, and it was impossible to know in which group one was. To alleviate their anxiety, they searched for signs of favour from God. One of those signs of divine blessing was prosperity, so there was a drive toward a disciplined work ethic, which should lead to accumulation of wealth that could be reinvested to increase that prosperity. The wealth was not to be used frivolously, for self-indulgence, and it was also not to be shared with those who had less, because poverty was a sign of God's displeasure of those in that condition. This rational orientation to life has become known as the **Protestant ethic** and it fits very well into a capitalist mode of thinking—work hard, accumulate profits, be thrifty, and don't waste. This "spirit of capitalism," to use Weber's phrase, contrasted with the moderate work hours, leisurely work habits, and lack of ambition that he saw as typical of the times (Winter 1977; Yinger 1974).

Few books on the sociology of religion have aroused as much commentary and criticism as *The Protestant Ethic and the Spirit of Capitalism.* It has been hailed as one of the most important theoretical works in the field and as an excellent example of macro-level analysis. Like Durkheim, Weber demonstrated that religion is not solely a matter of intimate personal beliefs. He stressed that the collective nature of religion and living one's beliefs has social consequences for society as a whole.

Weber provides a convincing description of the origins of European capitalism. But this economic system has subsequently been adopted by non-Calvinists in many parts of the world. Apparently, the "spirit of capitalism" has become a generalized cultural trait rather than a specific religious tenet (Greeley 1989).

Conflict theorists caution that Weber's theory—even if it is accepted—should not be regarded as an analysis of mature capitalism as reflected in the rise of multinational corporations that cross national boundaries. p. 236 The primary disagreement between Max Weber and Karl Marx concerned not the origins of capitalism but its future. Unlike Marx, Weber believed that capitalism could endure indefinitely as an economic system. He added, however, that the decline of religion as an overriding force in society opened the way for workers to express their discontent more vocally (R. Collins 1980).

Social Control: A Marxist View, Liberation Theology and Feminist Perspectives

A Marxist View

Karl Marx saw the traditional role of the church in a more negative fashion than Weber. In his view, religion *impeded* social change by encouraging oppressed people to focus on other-worldly concerns rather than on their immediate poverty or exploitation. Marx described religion as an "opiate" particularly harmful to oppressed peoples. He felt that religion often drugged the masses into submission by offering a consolation for their harsh lives on earth: the hope of salvation in an ideal afterlife. For example, as noted earlier, First Nations children housed in residential schools in Canada were forbidden to practise their own forms of spirituality, and were forced to adopt the Christian religion. Christianity taught First Nations people that obedience would lead to salvation and eternal happiness in the hereafter. Viewed from a conflict perspective, Christianity pacified certain oppressed groups and blunted the rage that often fuels rebellion (M. McGuire 1992; Yinger 1970).

Marx acknowledged that religion plays an important role in propping up the existing social structure. The values of religion, as already noted, reinforce other social institutions and the social order as a whole. From Marx's perspective, however, religion's promotion of stability within society only helps to perpetuate patterns of social inequality. In a society with several religious faiths, the dominant religion will represent the ruling economic and political class. Marx was concerned that religion would reinforce social control within an oppressive society. He argued that religion's focus on heavenly concerns diverted attention from earthly problems and from needless suffering created by unequal distribution of valued resources (Harap 1982).

According to Marx, religion reinforces the interests of those in power. For example, India's traditional caste system defined the social structure p. 204 of that society, at least among the Hindu majority. The caste system was almost certainly the creation of the priesthood, but it also served the interests of India's political rulers by granting a certain religious legitimacy to social inequality. Contemporary Christianity, like the Hindu faith, reinforces traditional patterns of behaviour that call for the subordination of the powerless.

One very prominent contemporary example is the consequence of giving extraordinary power to leaders in a church, such as the respect given to priests in the Roman Catholic church. Reports of abuse of that power, in the form of physical and sexual abuse, have come to light over many years, as in the charges of child abuse by priests in the Mount Cashel orphanage in Newfoundland, and sexual abuse by religious brothers in Quebec orphanages. However, it has been argued that for many years, the Catholic church ignored the complaints or dealt with priests internally, rather than having the secular laws applied. In practical terms, that meant that priests were shuffled from one parish to another, with no record of their behaviour accompanying them. Then, in 2002, a scandal of incredible proportions broke out when, initially, as many as 50 charges of sexual abuse were laid against one priest from Boston, and parishioners accused the church of covering up any knowledge it had of the behaviour of its priests. After the Boston case was broadcast in the media, other charges against other priests in other cities began to surface in large numbers, causing some to charge the church itself with systemic sexual abuse. The U.S. cardinals were called to the Vatican for meetings with the Pope, in an attempt to determine the extent of the problem and formulate a united response to it. The meetings did not result in admissions of a cover-up, however, they did result in a uniform policy regarding intolerance of abuse in the future. Many people remain unhappy with the results of the Vatican meetings and continue to call for more serious action against the charged priests.

The scandal in the Catholic church is an example of the abuse of power by those in a position of control over others in a religious context. The respect and the fear that the church instilled in its practitioners kept many from reporting abuses experienced. This same social control of religion can be seen in other areas as well. From a Marxist perspective, religion also functions as an "agent of

When Raedora Steward-Dodd found out that the American Baptist Church ordains women, she decided to exchange her Texas police officer badge for the robes of a Baptist minister. Female clergy don't often have an easy time, however. They are more likely to serve in subsidiary pastoral roles and to wait longer for desirable assignments than male clergy.

de-politicization" (J. Wilson 1973). In simpler terms, religion keeps people from seeing their lives and societal conditions in political terms—for example, by obscuring the overriding significance of conflicting economic inter-

p. 207 ests. Marxists suggest that by inducing a "false consciousness" among the disadvantaged, religion lessens the possibility of collective political action that can end capitalist oppression and transform society.

Liberation Theology

Sometimes the clergy can be found in the forefront of activism. Many religious activists, especially in the Roman Catholic church in Latin America, support **liberation theology**—the use of a church in a political effort to eliminate poverty, discrimination, and other forms of conflict and social injustice evident in a secular

society. Advocates of this religious movement usually sympathize with Marxism. Many believe that radical change, rather than economic development in itself, is the only acceptable solution to the desperation of the masses in impoverished developing countries. Activists associated with liberation theology believe that organized religion has a moral responsibility to take a strong public stand against the oppression of the poor, racial and ethnic minorities, and women (C. Smith 1991).

The term *liberation theology* dates back to the 1973 publication of the English translation of *A Theology of Liberation*. This book was written by a Peruvian priest, Gustavo Gutierrez (1990), who lived in a slum area of Lima during the early 1960s. After years of exposure to the vast poverty around him, Gutierrez concluded that "in order to serve the poor, one had to move into political action" (R.M. Brown 1980:23).

Politically committed Latin American theologians came under the influence of social scientists who viewed the domination of capitalism and multinational corporations as central to the hemisphere's problems. One result was a new approach to theology that rejected the models developed in Europe and the United States and instead built on the cultural and religious traditions of Latin America.

While many worshippers support liberation theology, religious leaders in the Roman Catholic church are not happy with the radical movement. The official position of Pope John Paul II and others in the church hierarchy is that clergy should adhere to traditional pastoral duties and keep a distance from radical politics. The Pope specifically came out against church activists in his 1999 visit to Mexico City (S. Pagani 1999).

Liberation theory is also seen as dysfunctional. Some Roman Catholics have come to believe that by focusing on opposing political and governmental injustice, the clergy are no longer putting their energy and attention into addressing the personal and spiritual needs of their parishioners. Partly as a result of such disenchantment, some Catholics in Latin America are converting to mainstream Protestant faiths or to Mormonism.

Feminist Perspectives

Feminists view the study of spirituality and religions as essential to revealing ways in which male-dominated political systems maintain control over both women and men. "Gendered religious symbols continue to reflect and influence cultural and political assumptions" (Stuckey 1998:268). Feminist theologians work from within established religious traditions as well as from outside. They agree that traditions in all major religions have devalued and often betrayed women. For too long, they claim, the study of religions has meant the study of male religious roles, male understanding of spirituality, and male symbols. For most religious scholars, half the human population has not existed.

Feminists concentrate on a number of interconnected issues in their analysis of the world's religions and women's roles in them. For example, feminist research in religion focuses on: the sexism inherent in both sacred texts and religious organizations; the problems caused by male god language, symbols, and images; and the shortage of female leadership in religious institutions (Stuckey 1998).

For some feminist theologians, replacing male language with gender-neutral language is a satisfactory means of producing correct interpretations of the messages at the core of religions. Others believe that it is necessary to expose the parts of the tradition that are sexist, and to alter language and symbols to include female imagery. A third group pushes for inclusion of language, imagery, and ritual from other traditions such as the goddess spirituality, while a fourth group rejects traditional religions as irreparable and has set out to create a new spiritual tradition.

Religiosity refers to the intensity of an individual's commitment to a belief system as indicated by attendance at religious services and volunteering in the organization's activities, knowledge of and belief in religious doctrine, and having beliefs direct daily behaviour. Despite the patriarchal nature of religious traditions, women have, historically, shown greater religious devotion. Polls indicate that: more women than men consider religion to be important in their lives; women have more confidence in organized religion than men do; and more women believe that religion can answer today's problems (Renzetti and Curran 1992). Though a majority of Canadians report an affiliation with a religious denomination, women are more likely to attend religious services regularly. In 1999, while 20 percent of Canadians reported attending some sort of religious activity on a weekly basis, women were more likely to participate than men (23 percent of women compared to 17 percent of men) (CCJS 2001).

Yet, women find it difficult to achieve leadership positions in traditional religions. For example, only 25 percent of ordained ministers in the United Church in Canada and approximately 10 percent of Anglican priests are female (Nason-Clark 1993). Female clergy more often serve in subsidiary pastoral roles and wait longer for desirable assignments. While women play a significant role as volunteers in community churches, men continue to make the major theological and financial judgments for nationwide church organizations.

Among Canada's First Nations, on the other hand, women have traditionally been granted roles of spiritual leadership.

Like Marx, feminist theorists argue that to whatever extent religion actually does influence social behaviour, it reinforces existing patterns of patriarchical dominance and inequality, makes this seem spiritually ordained, and thus religion acts as the opiate of masses of women.

Religious Behaviour

All religions have certain elements in common, yet these elements are expressed in the distinctive manner of each faith. The patterns of religious behaviour, like other patterns of social behaviour, are of great interest to sociologists, since they underscore the relationship between religion and society.

Religious beliefs, religious rituals, and religious experience all help to define what is sacred and to differentiate the sacred from the profane. Let us now examine these three dimensions of religious behaviour.

Belief

Some people believe in life after death, in supreme beings with unlimited powers, or in supernatural forces. *Religious beliefs* are statements to which members of a particular religion adhere. These views can vary dramatically from religion to religion.

The Adam and Eve account of creation found in Genesis, the first book of the Old Testament, is an example of a religious belief. Many people in Canada strongly adhere to this biblical explanation of creation. They are also the ones who are the greatest supporters of different social roles based on gender. It is believed that this social arrangement was prescribed by God after Eve tempted Adam with the apple, thus leading him into sin. These people, known as *creationists,* are worried by the secularization of society and oppose teaching that directly or indirectly questions biblical scripture.

Ritual

Religious rituals are practices required or expected of members of a faith. Rituals usually honour the divine power (or powers) worshipped by believers; they also remind adherents of their religious duties and responsibilities. Rituals and beliefs can be interdependent; rituals generally involve the affirmation of beliefs, as in a public or private statement confessing a sin (Roberts 1995). Like any social institution, religion develops distinctive normative patterns to structure people's behaviour. Moreover, there are sanctions attached to religious rituals, whether rewards (bar mitzvah gifts) or penalties (expulsion from a religious institution for violation of norms).

In Canada, rituals may be very simple, such as saying grace at a meal or observing a moment of silence to

Research in Action   14-1 Doing Religion

More than 100 people in a black congregation are packed into the living room of an old house. Led by the pastor's wife and four dancing women, the worshippers are singing, dancing, and waving their arms. The church is rocking, and the pace doesn't stop for three hours. Across town a white congregation is singing the same hymns, but no one is dancing. The mood is mellow and the drummer looks almost embarrassed to be there. Sharon Bjorkman uncovered these contrasting styles in the course of fieldwork researching forms of worship in churches in the Chicago area. This observation research was part of a nationwide study conducted by the Hartford Institute for Religion Research.

Bjorkman was interested in going beyond the doctrinal background of a particular church and observing the physical actions of the people attending services and those conducting them. As Durkheim noted, defining what is sacred in a religion is a collective act. Using the interactionist perspective, Bjorkman took notes on what happened at services, who participated, and what or who motivated them to do so.

The first thing that she discovered was the disadvantage of being an outsider. For example, not "knowing the ropes," she was unprepared for the strenuous physical activity in the black church. In the churches she visited she didn't know whether to carry a Bible or what version to use. As Bjorkman notes, you need to be socialized to know what is expected of you in a church service. Depending on the socialization church members receive, usually through example and reprimand, they will be active or passive, loud or quiet, meditative or demonstrative.

> The church is rocking, and the pace doesn't stop for three hours.

The church leader plays a key role in shaping the congregation's actions. Leaders decide the format of services, including what songs are sung, what instruments are used, and how much to involve the worshippers. In services that call for testimonies from the congregation, the leader would actively solicit certain members and badger

them if need be. The same tactic applied to "altar calls" where congregants would come forward to confess sins or seek blessings.

As important as church leaders are, they would have little influence if the individual members chose not to cooperate. Worship styles, then, are jointly developed by leaders and members. Generally, Bjorkman found, leaders would take small incremental steps to "train" their members to accept a particular style of service.

This study illustrates the crucial part that human relations play within formal organizations. Religious rituals are not just dry formal procedures dictated by a rote program of service. They evolve out of the active participation of leaders and members "doing religion" together.

Let's Discuss

1. What accounts for differing forms of church rituals, even within the same denomination?
2. Do you attend a church regularly? What style of worship does the church leader set? How does that affect your feelings about your religion?

Sources: Bjorkman 1999; Ammerman et al. 1998.

---

commemorate someone's death. Yet certain rituals, such as the process of canonizing a saint, are quite elaborate. Most religious rituals in our culture focus on services conducted at houses of worship. Thus, attendance at a service, silent and spoken reading of prayers, and singing of spiritual hymns and chants are common forms of ritual behaviour that generally take place in group settings. From an interactionist perspective, these rituals serve as important face-to-face encounters in which people reinforce their religious beliefs and their commitment to their faith. One way to think of religious rituals is as how people "do religion" together, as Box 14-1 describes.

For Canadian Aboriginals, spirituality is a total way of life rather than a specific set of rituals or practices. It is not based on a division into sacred and secular realms but

rather on a fundamental connection of all forms of creation (from humans and animals to fish and rivers to rocks, trees, and mountains). All of the created world is seen as alive and sacred in that it is filled with spiritual power. That is why Aboriginal peoples offer thanksgiving whenever they take something from another living thing, such as water from a river, or during a hunt when they take the skins and meat from the animals killed (Hoxie 1996; Solomon and Stonechild 1999).

Ceremonies are the primary means of religious expression, and ceremonies performed by different Aboriginal groups have some commonalities. For example, the sweat lodge is a purifying and worship ceremony, usually preceding spiritual quests. It is carried out in a hole in the earth, with a covering, where the "hole" is considered the womb of Mother Earth. A sweat lodge is built from willow branches covered with canvas tarps; in a shallow pit in the centre of the structure are the red-hot rocks brought into the lodge from a fire outside. As small amounts of water are poured onto the rocks, creating steam, participants sit in the dark and pray and sing and smoke a pipe, usually for a few hours (Solomon and Stonechild 1999; McKenzie 2001).

The pipe is considered an instrument of choice for prayers in many ceremonies. The prayers are transmitted in the smoke of the burning plant material (usually tobacco or red willow shavings) in the bowl of the pipe. Before the pipe is lit, sweet grass is burned as an incense to purify the worshippers, with the smoldering grass being drawn to the face four times, then passed to the next participant. The pipe is lit by the elder (either male or female), and offered to each of the four directions representing the four sacred medicine powers before it is passed from person to person at the ceremony. Aboriginal spirituality is distinct in its communitarian nature and purpose; even when an individual asks for personal assistance through ceremonies, it is being done for the ultimate benefit of the whole community (Hoxie 1996; Solomon and Stonechild 1999).

For Muslims, a very important ritual is the *hajj,* a pilgrimage to the Grand Mosque in Mecca, Saudi Arabia. Every Muslim who is physically and financially able is expected to make this trip at least once. Each year 2 million pilgrims go to Mecca during the one-week period indicated by the Islamic lunar calendar. Muslims from all over the world make the *hajj,* including those in Canada, where many tours are arranged to facilitate this ritual.

Some rituals induce an almost trancelike state. The First Nations of the American plains eat or drink peyote, a cactus containing the powerful hallucinogenic drug mescaline. Similarly, the ancient Greek followers of the god Pan chewed intoxicating leaves of ivy in order to become more ecstatic during their celebrations. Of course, artificial stimulants are not necessary to achieve a religious "high." Devout believers, such as those who practise the Pentecostal Christian ritual of "speaking in tongues," can reach a state of ecstasy simply through spiritual passion.

Candidates for the priesthood prostrate themselves prior to ordination in Notre Dame Cathedral in Paris. Prostration signifies that the initiate has separated himself from his old life and humbled himself sufficiently to accept a higher authority. Such examples of "doing religion" help people solidify their faith in face-to-face encounters.

Experience

In sociological study of religion, the term ***religious experience*** refers to the feeling or perception of being in direct contact with the ultimate reality, such as a divine being, or of being overcome with religious emotion. A religious experience may be rather slight, such as the feeling of exaltation a person receives from hearing a choir sing Handel's "Hallelujah Chorus." But many religious experiences are more profound, such as a Muslim's experience on a *hajj.* In his autobiography, the late African American activist Malcolm X (1964:338) wrote of his *hajj* and how deeply moved he was by the way that Muslims in Mecca came together across lines of race and colour. For Malcolm X, the colour blindness of the Muslim world "proved to me the power of the One God."

Still another profound religious experience is being "born again"—that is, at a turning point in one's life making a personal commitment to Jesus as lord and saviour. According to a 1999 national survey, more than 46 percent of people in the United States claimed that they had a born-again Christian experience at some time in their lives. An earlier survey found that Baptists (61 percent) were the most likely to report such experiences; by contrast, only 18 percent of Catholics and 11 percent of Episcopalians stated that they had been born again. In Canada, 10 percent of Canadians have stated that they are born again (CBC 2000). The collective nature of religion, as emphasized by Durkheim, is evident in these statistics.

The representation of religion can take many forms. This motorcycle club organizes itself as a strong Christian group, even though its attire and lifestyle may be objectionable to many Christians.

The beliefs and rituals of a particular faith can create an atmosphere either friendly or hostile to this type of religious experience. Thus, a Baptist would be encouraged to come forward and share such experiences with others, whereas an Episcopalian who claimed to have been born again would receive much less support (Princeton Religious Research Center 1998).

Religious Organization

The collective nature of religion has led to many forms of religious association. In modern societies, religion has become increasingly formalized. Specific structures such as churches, temples, and synagogues are constructed for religious worship; individuals are trained for occupational roles within various fields. These developments make it possible to distinguish clearly between the sacred and secular parts of one's life—a distinction that could not be made in earlier societies in which religion was largely a family activity carried out in the home.

Sociologists find it useful to distinguish among four basic forms of organization: the ecclesia, the denomination, the sect, and the new religious movement or cult. We can see differences among these types of organizations in such factors as size, power, degree of commitment expected from members, and historical ties to other faiths.

Ecclesiae

An *ecclesia* (plural, *ecclesiae*) is a religious organization that claims to include most or all of the members of a society and is recognized as the national or official religion. Since virtually everyone belongs to the faith, membership is by birth rather than conscious decision. Examples of ecclesiae include the Lutheran church in Sweden, the Catholic church in Spain, Islam in Saudi Arabia, and Buddhism in Thailand. However, there can be significant differences even within the category of *ecclesia*. In Saudi Arabia's Islamic regime, leaders of the ecclesia hold vast power over actions of the state. By contrast, the Lutheran church in contemporary Sweden has no such power over the Riksdag (parliament) or the prime minister.

Generally, ecclesiae are conservative in that they do not challenge the leaders of a secular government. In a society with an ecclesia, the political and religious institutions often act in harmony and mutually reinforce each other's power over their relative spheres of influence. Within the modern world, ecclesiae tend to be declining in power.

Denominations

A *denomination* is a large, organized religion not officially linked with the state or government. Like an ecclesia, it tends to have an explicit set of beliefs, a defined system of authority, and a generally respected position in society (Doress and Porter 1977). Denominations claim as members large segments of a population. Generally, children accept the denomination of their parents and give little thought to membership in other faiths. Denominations also resemble ecclesiae in that generally few demands are made on members. However, there is a critical difference between these two forms of religious organization. Although the denomination is considered respectable and is not viewed as a challenge to the secular government, it lacks the official recognition and power held by an ecclesia (Doress and Porter 1977).

Canada is marked by greater diversity in religious denominations than most countries in the world. With the exception of the First Nations, we are a country of immigrants and Canadian religious diversity reflects patterns of multiculturalism, immigration, and population change.

As Table 14-1 shows, the majority of Canadians claim affiliation with some kind of religion, and while this has declined since 1981, more than 70 percent of the population is affiliated with either the Catholic or Protestant denominations. But we can also see the changes that have come with the influx of immigrants from non-Christian countries. While Catholic, Protestant, Eastern Orthodox, and Jewish denominations have seen their membership decline in the past few decades, there has been growth in denominations such as Islam, Buddhist, Hindu, Sikh, Baha'i, and other Eastern religions. In 1981, only 1.2 percent of Canadians had an affiliation with these faiths, but by 2001, the number of adherents had more than quadrupled to 4.9 percent. And the percentage of Canadians who claim to have no religious affiliation has also grown substantially: from 7.4 percent in 1981 to 16.2 percent by 2001 (CCJS 2001; Statistics Canada 1993; 2003g).

Attendance at religious services in Canada tends to vary according to age, rural/urban setting, immigrant status, and family status. In 1998, married couples aged 25 to 44 with young children were more likely to worship regularly than those who were of the same age but childless. Seniors aged 75 and over had the highest rates of attendance. However, attendance rates over the period 1988–1998 declined for adults in all age groups.

Those born in Canada were less likely to be regular attendees of religious services than were immigrants (31 percent of Canadian-born versus 43 percent of immigrants). Approximately 50 percent of Asian immigrants who entered Canada between 1994 and 1998 attended worship services regularly, compared to approximately 20 percent of European immigrants who entered the country during the same period (Statistics Canada 2000).

According to the 1998 General Social Survey by Statistics Canada, residents of rural areas and small towns attended religious services more than city dwellers. The survey also showed that people who attend religious services regularly were more likely to feel a strong sense of belonging to their community (Statistics Canada 2000). Reginald Bibby surveys Canadians on their religious practices and beliefs. Despite declining attendance rates, Bibby reports that 81 percent of Canadians still believe in God, and 90 percent expect to be baptized, married, and buried in church services (Bibby 1995).

In the last 20 years, some distinctions among denominations have started to blur. Certain faiths have even allowed members of other faiths to participate in some of their most sacred rituals, such as communion. Even more dramatic has been the appearance of *megachurches*—large congregations that often lack direct ties to a worldwide denomination, as described in Box 14-2 (p. 400).

Sects

A *sect* can be defined as a relatively small religious group that has broken away from some other religious organization to renew what it considers to be the original vision of the faith.

Table 14-1   Religious Affiliation in Canada, 1981–2001

Religious group	Includes:	1981	1991	2001
Some kind of affiliation		92.5	87.3	83.8
Catholic	Roman, Ukrainian, Polish, other	47.3	45.7	43.2
Protestant	United, Presbyterian, Lutheran, Anglican, Baptist, Jehovah's Witness, Pentecostal, Mormon, other	41.2	36.2	31.6
Eastern Orthodox	Greek, Ukrainian, Russian, other	1.5	1.4	1.6
Other Eastern	Islam, Buddhist, Hindu, Sikh, Baha'i, etc.	1.2	2.8	4.9
Jewish		1.2	1.2	1.1
Other	Atheist, Free Thinker, Humanist, New Age, Scientology, New Thought, Native Indian, Inuit, etc.	0.2	0.1	1.4
No religion		7.4	12.5	16.2

Source: Compiled by Smith, based on data from CCJS 2001; Statistics Canada 1993; 2003g.

PAT DUFFY HUTCHEON: Secular Humanist

Pat Duffy Hutcheon is a secular humanist or, according to her own definition, "a non-believer in supernatural beings" (Todd 2001). Hutcheon is a retired University of British Columbia sociologist who, in 2000, won the Canadian Humanist of the Year Award. She is also a recipient of the American 2001 Humanist Distinguished Service Award (others who have received this award include Harvard paleontologist Stephen Jay Gould and zoologist Edward O. Wilson.) Growing up in the Prairies and attending churches there, she began to question how people could believe in religion. Hutcheon came to believe that people must rely on themselves to protect the world, not supernatural beings. She says, "My emphasis is on morality—and how human beings are the only ones responsible for it" (Todd 2001). In 1999, she published her book, *Building Character and Culture*, in which she outlines how to build ethical character based on virtues such as honesty, courage, nonviolence, perseverance, responsibility, and respect for human dignity. Hutcheon's basic message is the belief that one does not have to be religious to be ethical.

Source: Hutcheon 1999; Todd 2001.

Many sects, such as that led by Martin Luther during the Reformation, claim to be the "true church" because they seek to cleanse the established faith of what they regard as extraneous beliefs and rituals (Stark and Bainbridge 1985). Max Weber (1958b:114, original edition 1916) termed the sect a "believer's church," because affiliation is based on conscious acceptance of a specific religious dogma.

Sects are fundamentally at odds with society and do not seek to become established national religions. Unlike ecclesiae and denominations, sects require intensive commitments and demonstrations of belief by members. Partly owing to their "outsider" status in society, sects frequently exhibit a higher degree of religious fervour and loyalty than more established religious groups do. Recruitment focuses mainly on adults, and acceptance comes through conversion. One current-day sect is called the People of the Church, a movement within the Roman Catholic Church that began in Vienna, Austria. This sect has called for reforms of Catholicism, such as the ordination of women, local election of bishops, and optional celibacy for priests (*Religion Watch* 1995).

Sects are often short-lived. But those that are able to survive may over time become less antagonistic to society and begin to resemble denominations. In a few instances, sects have been able to endure over several generations while remaining fairly separate from society. Sociologist J. Milton Yinger (1970: 226–73) uses the term **established sect** to describe a religious group that is the outgrowth of a sect, yet remains isolated from society. The Hutterites, Jehovah's Witnesses, Seventh-Day Adventists, and Amish are contemporary examples of established sects in Canada.

New Religious Movements or Cults

The Branch Davidians began as a sect of the Seventh-Day Adventist church, basing their beliefs largely on the biblical book of Revelation and its doomsday prophecies. In 1984, the Davidians' sect split, with one group emerging as a cult under the leadership of David Koresh. In 1993, violence erupted at their compound near Waco, Texas. After a 51-day standoff against federal authorities, Koresh and 85 of his followers died when the U.S. Federal Bureau of Investigation (FBI) attempted to seize control of the compound and its arsenal of weapons. Between 1994 and 1997, 74 members of the Order of the Solar Temple died in a series of murder/suicides by forming a cross and setting themselves on fire in Quebec, Switzerland, and France. The first group of 50 deaths occurred simultaneously in the three countries, while the others have taken place a few at a time. In 1997, 38 members of the Heaven's Gate cult were found dead in Southern California after a mass suicide timed to occur with the appearance of the Hale–Bopp comet. They believed that the comet hid a spaceship on which they could catch a ride once they had broken free of their "bodily containers."

Partly as a result of the notoriety generated by such groups, the popular media have stigmatized the word *cult* by associating cults with the occult and the use of intense and forceful conversion techniques. The stereotyping of cults as uniformly bizarre and unethical has led sociologists to abandon the term and refer to a cult instead as a *new religious movement (NRM)*. While some NRMs, like the Branch Davidians, exhibit strange behaviour, many do not. They attract new members just like any other religion and often follow teachings similar

14-2 The Emergence of the Megachurch

The Yoido Full Gospel Church in Seoul, South Korea, has six daily services in a facility with 13 000 seats. Unable to serve all of its 700 000 members, the church reaches 30 000 other worshippers via closed-circuit television, and 50 000 tune in from 20 satellite congregations across the metropolitan area. Worshippers listen to the sermons of Pastor David Cho and join in with 11 choirs, accompanied by a pipe organ or a 24-piece orchestra.

Not as large but still impressive is the Harvest Christian Fellowship in Riverside, California, which attracts up to 20 000 churchgoers. Clear glass and modern music have replaced stained glass windows and hymns. While Christian, the sermons are just as likely to make references to Elvis and Oprah as to Jacob and Abraham.

The 6000-seat temple of the Protestant Works and Mission Church near Abidjan, Ivory Coast, is as impressive as any modern structure in Africa. The mix of Baptist and Jehovah's Witness teachings has found a reception among locals in a largely Muslim nation.

These are just three examples of the growing emergence worldwide of megachurches, large worship centres only loosely affiliated, if at all, with existing denominations. Megachurches that begin with denominational ties frequently break them when they become financially self-sufficient. They often break away not so much on the basis of doctrinal issues as from a desire to be viewed as unique and to be free of church hierarchy.

Sociologists have observed the significant impact on religious organizations of these megachurches, whose growth is sometimes defined by the size of the parking lot. Their size often provokes hostility from more traditional churches that fear being overwhelmed or, in some cases, from the preexisting dominant faith (such as Buddhism in South Korea and Islam in the Ivory Coast). Some people view the megachurch as the latest intrusion of European/North American culture into the local landscape, especially in Latin America and Africa.

> **The sermons are just as likely to make references to Elvis and Oprah as to Jacob and Abraham.**

Megachurches appeal particularly to younger people, who seem prepared to shop around for religious faith just as they would a university or automobile. The very size of the megachurch facility may attract someone used to working in large bureaucracies or dealing with huge supermarkets or large medical clinics or shopping malls. People comfortable in these settings may find the anonymity of a huge religious place of worship preferable to the intimacy of a small church with 50 to 100 members genuinely interested in getting to know them as individuals.

In addition, these megachurches in North America and developing nations often attract the growing number of self-identified born-again or charismatic Christians who do not feel welcome in more traditional faiths. Their size allows these megachurches to offer programs that cater to specific needs, such as those of singles or people with chronic health issues. Perhaps most importantly, the megachurch is willing to use the latest marketing tools, multimedia presentations, and motivational techniques to reach out to those who feel disenchanted with traditional denominations.

Let's Discuss

1. What impact are the megachurches having on other religious organizations?
2. What advantages would megachurches have over more traditional churches with smaller congregations? What would be the disadvantages?

Sources: Carey and Mosemak 1999; M. Luo 1999; Maxwell 1992; Ostling 1993; Schaller 1990.

to established Christian denominations, but with less ritual.

It is difficult to distinguish sects from cults. A *new religious movement (NRM)* or *cult* is a generally small, secretive religious group that represents either a new religion or a major innovation of an existing faith. NRMs are similar to sects in that they tend to be small and are often viewed as less respectable than more established faiths.

However, unlike sects, NRMs normally do not result from schisms or breaks with established ecclesiae or denominations. Some cults, such as those focused on UFO sightings, may be totally unrelated to the existing faiths in a culture. Even when a cult does accept certain fundamental tenets of a dominant faith—such as belief in Jesus as divine or Muhammad as a messenger of God—it will offer new revelations or new insights to justify its claim to be a more advanced religion (Stark and Bainbridge 1979, 1985).

Like sects, NRMs may undergo transformation over time into other types of religious organizations. An example is the Christian Science church, which began as a new religious movement under the leadership of Mary Baker Eddy. Today, this church exhibits the characteristics of a denomination. NRMs tend to be in the early stages of what may develop into a denomination, or they may just as easily fade away through loss of members or weak leadership (Richardson and van Driel 1997).

Case Studies on Cults: Aum Supreme Truth and Falun Gong

Cults have a long history and are global in scope. Two cults in Asia are currently attracting worldwide attention—the Aum in Japan and the Falun Gong in China.

Few people, even in Japan, had heard of the Aum Supreme Truth (or *Shinrikyo*) before March 1995. That was when Aum supporters released deadly nerve gas in the Tokyo subway system, killing 12 and injuring more than 5000 people. Aum's charismatic leader, Shoko Asahara, studied Buddhism and Hinduism in the Himalayas before founding his own religion in Japan in 1987, combining Buddhist elements with Christianity. He promises his followers that they will develop supernatural powers, but they must submit to arbitrary and strict rules of behaviour described as being part of an ancient tradition.

The Aum cult manifests a siege mentality: It is convinced that

outside groups are intent on destroying the organization. Asahara called on his followers to join in a final world revolution against Japan's enemies. To prepare for this Armageddon, the group built chemical factories and stockpiled various lethal chemicals, including the sarin gas used in the Tokyo subway. The Aum group has been accused as well of other gas attacks and assorted murders. Many Aum followers have been convicted, while Asahara is still on trial for being the mastermind of the doomsday cult's crimes.

Membership in the cult has fallen off from a peak of 10 000 to about 2100 today, and the cult has had to declare bankruptcy. In September 1999 the cult announced that it was suspending external activities, and in December a spokesman for the cult apologized, for the first time, for its attacks. Meanwhile, the Japanese government passed legislation late in 1999 that will enable it to conduct surveillance of groups whose members attempted or carried out indiscriminate murders in the past 10 years—in effect, specifically targeting the Aum cult (Gaouette 1999; Takahara 1999; *New York Times* 1999b).

While Japan has been dealing with its cult problem, China has been encountering its own version—although on the face of it, one that is far more innocent. To the casual observer, the followers of Falun Gong (literally, "the Law of the Wheel Breathing Exercise") simply perform slow-motion exercises to music from a tape recorder. But the Falun Gong (pronounced *fah-luhn gung*) is essentially a religious movement that borrows heavily from Buddhist and Taoist philosophies and styles itself as a school of qigong (pronounced *chee-gong*), a

Practitioners of Falun Gong combine meditation with martial arts exercises, borrowing from Buddhist and Taoist philosophies. Falun Gong's phenomenal growth in China has raised alarms among the Communist leadership, which wants no competition for the control of the masses.

traditional Chinese practice that uses meditation and martial arts exercises to channel unseen forces and improve health. Founded in 1992 by Li Hongzhi, its adherents—primarily middle-aged women, retirees, and students—number in the tens of millions today.

The group's rapid growth and strong appeal have worried the Communist Chinese leadership. The Communist party mistrusts any group whose value system it cannot control. In addition, since Marxism is basically the state "religion," the Chinese authorities might be seeing Falun Gong as a form of liberation theology, meant to rouse the masses. These fears seemed confirmed when 10 000 members of Falun Gong suddenly materialized in Beijing in April of 1999 to demand official recognition from the government. Several months later the government banned the group, put its exiled leader on the most wanted list, and began arresting, detaining, or dispersing thousands of people caught practising Falun Gong (Platt 1999; Eckholm 1999; McCarthy 1999). One of those arrested was sculpture professor Zhang Kunlun, who immigrated to Canada in 1989 and became a Canadian national in 1995 while maintaining his Chinese nationality. Zhang returned to China in 1996 to continue his teaching career and was arrested in the fall of 2000. He claims that he and other Falun Gong followers have been repeatedly tortured and forced to write letters of confession denouncing Falun Gong. Human rights groups report that close to 100 adherents have died while in detention in China; authorities admit that several deaths have occurred but say that most resulted from suicide or illness. (CNN.com 2001). Apparently, all traces of the organized movement are to be stamped out.

Comparing Forms of Religious Organization

How can we determine whether a particular religious group falls into the sociological category of ecclesia, denomination, sect, or NRM? As we have seen, these types of religious organizations have somewhat different relationships to society. Ecclesiae are recognized as national churches; denominations, although not officially approved by the state, are generally widely respected. By contrast, sects as well as NRMs are much more likely to be at odds with the larger culture.

Still, ecclesiae, denominations, and sects are best viewed as ideal types along a continuum rather than as mutually exclusive categories. Table 14-2 summarizes some of the primary characteristics of these ideal types. Since Canada has no ecclesiae, sociologists studying this country's religions have naturally focused on the denomination and the sect. These religious forms have been

Table 14-2   Characteristics of Ecclesiae, Denominations, Sects, and New Religious Movements

Characteristic	Ecclesia	Denomination	Sect	New religious movement (or cult)
Size	Very large	Large	Small	Small
Wealth	Extensive	Extensive	Limited	Variable
Religious services	Formal, little participation	Formal, little participation	Informal, emotional	Variable
Doctrines	Specific, but interpretation may be tolerated	Specific, but interpretation may be tolerated	Specific, purity of doctrine emphasized	Innovative, pathbreaking
Clergy	Well-trained, full-time	Well-trained, full-time	Trained to some degree	Unspecialized
Membership	By virtue of being a member of society	By acceptance of doctrine	By acceptance of doctrine	By an emotional commitment
Relationship to the state	Recognized, closely aligned	Tolerated	Not encouraged	Ignored or challenged

Source: Adapted from G. Vernon 1962; see also Chalfant et al. 1994.

pictured on either end of a continuum, with denominations accommodating to the secular world and sects making a protest against established religions. NRMs have also been included in Table 14-2 but are outside the continuum because they generally define themselves as a new view of life rather than in terms of existing religious faiths (Chalfant et al. 1994).

Advances in electronic communications have led to still another form of religious organization: the electronic church. Facilitated by cable television and satellite transmissions, *televangelists* (as they are called) direct their messages to more people—especially in the United States—than are served by all but the largest denominations. While some televangelists are affiliated with religious denominations, most give viewers the impression that they are disassociated from established faiths. While they claim to be nondenominational, they also present a message that their "television ministry" relies on its viewers to keep it on the air, offering gifts from coffee cups to books to anyone who will send in an "offering" to contribute to the enormous amount of money needed to support them. The more successful these televangelists are at selling their message, the more profitable they become, and the greater their influence in the conservative political arena of the U.S. In Canada, their success has been much more limited. Bibby's 1998 study of religion in Canada reported that fewer than 5 percent of Canadians watch religious services regularly today, compared to 29 percent who did in the 1950s.

At the close of the 1990s, the electronic church had taken on yet another dimension—the Internet. One research group estimated that in 1999, 25 million people used the Internet for religious purposes. Another estimate projects that by 2010, 10 to 20 percent of the U.S. population may be relying primarily or exclusively on the Internet for religious input (Barna Research Group 1998).

Much of the spiritual content on the Internet is tied to organized denominations. People use cyberspace to

By Kevin Rechin, USA TODAY

learn more about their faith or even just the activities of their own place of worship. But, as more and more people are discovering, the "church" we locate on the World Wide Web exists only in *virtual* reality. For some purposes, virtual religious experience simply will not do. For example, a minyan, a set quorum for Jewish prayers, requires 10 Jews gathered in one space; cyberspace doesn't count at this point. While Muslims can view the Kaaba, or the Holy Shrine, in Mecca on the Net, they cannot fulfill their religious obligations except by actual pilgrimage there. The Internet, then, isn't suitable for some forms of religious and spiritual expression, but it certainly has added a new dimension to religious behaviour (G. Zelizer 1999).

Religion in the Schools

The Issue

Should public schools be allowed to sponsor organized prayers in the classroom? Should the Lord's Prayer be part of the agenda at weekly school assemblies? How about reading Bible verses? Or just a collective moment of silence? Can public school athletes offer up a group prayer in a team huddle? Should students be able to initiate voluntary prayers

at school events? Should a school be allowed to post the Ten Commandments in a hallway? Each of these situations has been an object of great dissension among those who see a role for prayer in public schools and those who want to maintain a strict separation of church and state.

Another area of controversy centres on the teaching of theories about the origin of humans and of the universe. Mainstream scientific thinking theorizes that humans evolved over billions of years from one-celled organisms, and that the universe came into being 15 billion years ago as a result of the "Big Bang." But these theories are challenged by people who hold to the biblical account of the creation of humans and the universe some 10 000 years ago—a viewpoint known as **creationism.** Creationists want their theory taught in the schools as the only one or, at the very least, as an alternative to the theory of evolution.

Who has the right to decide these issues? And what is the "right" decision? Religion in public schools constitutes one of the thorniest issues in Canadian public policy today.

The Setting

Both of the issues just described go to the heart of the Canadian Charter of Rights and Freedoms' provisions on religious freedom. On the one hand, the government is required to protect the right to practise one's religion but, on the other hand, it cannot take any measures that would seem to "establish" one religion over another (the church/state separation). Both the Charter and the Canadian Constitution protect the rights and privileges held by denominational schools since the time of Confederation in 1867. This has meant that some provinces fund Catholic school education and others, such as Quebec, fund Protestant education.

In 1997, the Quebec government set up a task force to investigate the place of religion in schools. Its report, "Religion in Secular Schools," was submitted in 1999 with 14 recommendations to redefine the place of religion in schools. Among them were recommendations to enact legislation that would establish a secular system of school, thus revoking the status held by the current denominational schools. In other words, the Catholic and Protestant status for public schools should be abolished and replaced with "secular" public schools.

In the case of these nondenominational or "secular" schools, where explicit religious affiliation is not established, the issue of religious content in the form of prayers and Bible readings has become a contentious one. Quebec is not the only province to experience these tensions in secular schools. In 1999, Saskatchewan became the fourth province in Canada to oppose prayer in public schools. Stemming from a complaint by nine Saskatoon parents in 1993, the hundred-year-old tradition of encouraging public school teachers to say the Lord's Prayer in classrooms and assemblies was challenged. The *Saskatchewan Act*, part of the provincial constitution, permitted prayer and Bible readings in the public schools.

The group of Saskatoon parents included Muslims, Jews, Unitarians, and atheists. They complained that this practice violated the Saskatchewan Human Rights Code. More specifically, they argued that it violated their children's (and others') right to freedom of conscience, and that students were being denied the right to enjoy an education without discrimination because of creed or religion. As a result, in 1999, a board of inquiry ruled that it was discriminatory to require recitation of the Lord's Prayer in Saskatoon classrooms and assemblies.

While the explicit practices of religious prayers or of dividing schools along two Christian denominational lines have been challenged, that does not mean that religion has no place in Canadian schools. In 1988, when the Ontario Court of Appeal struck down sections of the legislation that allowed public schools to open or close the day with religious exercises from a particular faith, the court elaborated on the differences between education and indoctrination. For example, it stated that schools could sponsor the *study* of religion but not the *practice* of it, or that the approach should be *academic* rather than *devotional* (Ontario Ministry of Education 1994). This distinction ensured that students would be exposed to all religious viewpoints in courses on religion. Quebec's Task Force took a similar stance in recommending that schools provide the study of religions from a cultural perspective. They are not suggesting that schools have no business teaching religion, but rather that the perspective must change.

Lois Sweet, author of *God in the Classroom: The Controversial Issue of Religion in Canada's Schools*, agrees. In a recent speech at an Ontario university, she stated that while the classroom is no place for prayer, it is a place for developing "religious literacy." Sweet represents those who believe that schools should teach the facts of many religions and help develop critical thinking about faith systems—that is, religious literacy (Petricevic 2002).

Sociological Insights

Supporters of school prayer and of creationism feel that strict court rulings force too great a separation between what Émile Durkheim called the *sacred* and the *profane*. They insist that use of nondenominational prayer can in no way lead to the establishment of an ecclesia in Canada. Moreover, they believe that school prayer—and the teaching of creationism—can provide the spiritual guidance and socialization that many children today do not receive from parents or regular church attendance. Many communities also believe that schools should transmit the dominant culture of Canada by encouraging prayer (Coeyman 1999).

According to a 1998 General Social Survey, 55 percent of adults in the United States disapprove of a Supreme Court ruling against the required reading of the Lord's Prayer or Bible verses in public schools. A national survey in 1999 showed that 68 percent of the public favours teaching creationism along with evolution in public schools, and 40 percent favours teaching *only* creationism. No other Western society has such a large body of opinion supporting views that depart so much from contemporary scientific understanding. Perhaps this is a reflection of a deep-rooted and enduring strain of religious fundamentalism in the United States, and the fact that religious belief in general is stronger in the United States than in Canada and other Western societies (Davis and Smith 1999; G. Johnson 1999; Lewis 1999).

Opponents of school prayer and creationism argue that a religious majority in a community might impose religious viewpoints specific to its faith, at the expense of religious minorities. Viewed from a conflict perspective, organized school prayer could: reinforce the religious beliefs, rituals, and interests of the powerful; violate the rights of the powerless; increase religious dissension; and threaten the multiculturalism of Canada. These critics question whether school prayer can remain truly voluntary. Drawing on the interactionist perspective and small-group research, they suggest that children will face enormous social pressure to conform to the beliefs and practices of a religious majority.

Policy Initiatives

School education is fundamentally a local issue, so most initiatives and lobbying have taken place at the local school board or the provincial level. The case involving the Saskatoon Board of Education provides a good example of how policymakers in some communities are trying to find a compromise between those who want prayer in schools and those who do not. In 2001, two years after the Lord's Prayer was removed from the daily routine of public schools, the Saskatoon Public School Board is considering a Christian education program for children of religious parents (*National Post* Feb. 9/01). Modelled after the Logos Christian Education program, which is already in place in Edmonton public schools, students from Christian families would receive instruction in a separate classroom, with a religious environment. Those who feel that the Logos program would be divisive, dividing students along religious lines and undermining the basis of the public school system, have raised opposition to the proposal.

The activism of religious fundamentalists in the nation's public school system raises a more general question: Whose ideas and values deserve a hearing in classrooms? Critics see this campaign as one step toward sectarian religious control of public education. They worry that, at some point in the future, teachers may not be able to use books, or make statements, that conflict with fundamentalist interpretations of the Bible. For advocates of a liberal education who are deeply committed to intellectual (and religious) diversity, this is a genuinely frightening prospect.

Let's Discuss

1. Was there any organized prayer in the school you attended? Do you think promoting religious observance is a legitimate function of the social institution of education?

2. How might a conflict theorist view the issue of organized school prayer?

3. In what ways have Christian fundamentalists and their allies attempted to reshape public education in Canada?

● Chapter Resources

Summary

Religion is a cultural universal, found throughout the world, although in varied forms. This chapter examines the dimensions and functions of religion and types of religious organizations.

1. Émile Durkheim stressed the social impact of religion and attempted to understand individual religious behaviour within the context of the larger society.
2. Religion serves the functions of integrating people in a diverse society and providing social support in time of need.
3. Max Weber saw a connection between religious allegiance and capitalistic behaviour through a religious orientation known as the *Protestant ethic.*
4. From a Marxist point of view, religion serves to reinforce the social control of those in power. It lessens the possibility of collective political action that can end capitalist oppression and transform society.

5. *Liberation theology* uses the church in a political effort to alleviate poverty and social injustice.
6. Feminist theologians point to the social control of women through the sexism inherent in religions that use male god language, symbols, and images. While women are largely absent as leaders in religious institutions, they exhibit greater *religiosity* than men.
7. Religious behaviour is expressed through *beliefs, rituals,* and *religious experience.*
8. Sociologists have identified four basic types of religious organization: the *ecclesia,* the *denomination,* the *sect,* and the *new religious movement (NRM)* or *cult.* Advances in communication have led to a new type of church organization—the electronic church.
9. How much religion—if any—should be permitted in the schools is a matter of debate in Canadian society today.

Critical Thinking Questions

1. From a conflict point of view, explain how religion could be used to bring about social change.
2. What role do new religious movements (or cults) play in the organization of religion? Why are they so often controversial?

3. Compare Aboriginal spiritual ceremonies with religious services in the dominant culture's churches or synagogues. In what ways are they similar?

Key Terms

Creationism A literal interpretation of the Bible regarding the creation of humanity and the universe used to argue that the theory of evolution should not be presented as established scientific fact. (404)

Cultural universal A general practice found in every culture. (387)

Denomination A large, organized religion not officially linked with the state or government. (397)

Ecclesia A religious organization that claims to include most or all of the members of a society and is recognized as the national or official religion. (397)

Established sect A religious group that is the outgrowth of a sect, yet remains isolated from society. (399)

Liberation theology The use of a church in a political effort to eliminate poverty, discrimination, and other

forms of conflict and social injustice evident in a secular society. (393)

Megachurches Large congregations that often lack direct ties to a worldwide denomination. (398)

New religious movement (NRM) or **cult** A generally small, secretive religious group that represents either a new religion or a major innovation of an existing faith. (401)

Profane The ordinary and commonplace elements of life, as distinguished from the sacred. (387)

Protestant ethic Max Weber's term for the disciplined work ethic, this-worldly concerns, and rational orientation to life emphasized by John Calvin and his followers. (391)

Religion A social institution involving a unified system of beliefs and practices relative to sacred things. (387)

Religiosity The intensity of an individual's commitment to a belief system (394)

Religious beliefs Statements to which members of a particular religion adhere. (394)

Religious experience The feeling or perception of being in direct contact with the ultimate reality, such as a divine being, or of being overcome with religious emotion. (396)

Religious rituals Practices required or expected of members of a faith. (394)

Sacred Elements beyond everyday life that inspire awe, respect, and even fear. (387)

Sect A relatively small religious group that has broken away from some other religious organization to renew what it considers to be the original vision of the faith. (398)

Secularization The process through which religion's influence on other social institutions diminishes. (387)

Additional Readings

BOOKS

Bibby, Reginald W. 2002. *Restless Gods: The Renaissance of Religion in Canada.* Toronto: Stoddart Publishing Co. Ltd. Using completely updated statistics on subjects such as church attendance, the role of organized religion in our culture, and the views of religious and secular Canadians concerning the place of God in their lives, Bibby draws conclusions about our spiritual restlessness today.

King, Ursula, ed. 1995. *Religion and Gender.* Oxford, Eng.: Blackwell. A professor of religious studies offers a collection of articles on women's portrayal of and participation in religion, drawing on contributions from feminists, anthropologists, and others.

Stark, Rodney, and William Sims Bainbridge. 1996. *Religion, Deviance, and Social Control.* New York: Routledge. An examination of religion as a source of social control and religion's impact on deviance, beginning with Durkheim's work on suicide and continuing with such contemporary issues as drugs, alcohol, cults, and mental illness.

Zellner, William W., and Marc Petrowky, eds. 1999. *Sects, Cults, and Spiritual Communities: A Sociological Analysis.* Westport, CT: Praeger. A collection of essays profiling religious groups outside the mainstream of American spiritual organizations. Included are treatments of the Jesus People, Santería, and Scientology.

JOURNALS

The sociological study of religion is reflected in the *Journal for the Scientific Study of Religion* (founded in 1961), *Religion Watch* (monthly newsletter, 1986), *Review of Religious Research* (1958), *Social Compass* (1954), and *Sociology of Religion* (1940).

 ## Internet Connection

www.mcgrawhill.ca/college/schaefer

For additional Internet exercises relating to sociology and religion, visit the Schaefer Online Learning Centre at **http://www.mcgrawhill.ca/college/schaefer**. *Please note that while the URLs listed were current at the time of printing, these sites often change—check the Online Learning Centre for updates.*

Sociologists who utilize the interactionist perspective focus on the meaning of symbols. Religious holiday celebrations are an obvious source of symbolism. The following website affords the opportunity to learn more about religious holidays and observances: (**http://dir.yahoo.com/Society_and_Culture/Religion_and_Spirituality/Holidays_and_Observances/**). Visit this site and choose an unfamiliar religious group and holiday/observance. Now, activate your sociological imagination.

(a) What is the name of the holiday? With which religious group is it associated?

(b) During what time of the year does the event occur? Is the timing of the event important?

(c) How many days does it last?

(d) What is the purpose of the celebration or observation?

(e) What are its origins?

(f) Has the holiday changed over time?

(g) What are the various roles played by members during ceremonies or rituals?

(h) What specific symbols and items are used by participants? What do those symbols/items represent?

(i) Does the holiday reflect important beliefs and values of the religion? How so?

(j) Does the holiday you just examined have any features in common with holidays or celebrations practised by other religious groups with which you are familiar?

Government of Canada   Gouvernement du Canada

connecting canadians   Spring 2002

SchoolNet

MAGAZINE   *Making a Difference with ICT*

Featuring...

E-learning According to the Experts: What Students Are Saying

Pioneer Sees Bright Future for ICT in Education

A Window on Innovation in Nova Scotia

1755536

Canada

On March 30, 1999, Canada became the first country in the world to connect its public schools, including First Nations schools, and public libraries to the Information Highway, through Canada's SchoolNet. One of its resources is SchoolNet Magazine, designed to help teachers integrate the Internet into classroom teaching.

In Room 16, on the second floor of Vancouver's Grace Elementary School, sat Karen Riley's class of grades 3 and 4 students. Having two grades in one class has been one of the improvements in some inner city schools since the late 1980s; the theory being that a teacher is able to follow a child's development for longer than just one year. Directly across the hall were large paintings by Riley's pupils celebrating those things society has decided amount to good manners. A couple of weeks earlier, the staff had decided the school's children needed a good dose of etiquette. . . . They adopted a 1942 British book on manners (someone just happened to have one, said a teacher) as their guide, and for two weeks the kids were expected to open doors for teachers, say please, excuse me, and thank you whenever proper etiquette dictated. . . .

As Riley waved me into her classroom, the children sat in five straight rows, their heads lowered, eyes fixed on the tops of their desks. Riley sat at her desk on the opposite side of the room, facing the door. She told me to settle down at the back and only a head or two looked up as I made my way down the middle aisle. I sat down and a curious sensation touched me that had little to do with the miniature chair I had balanced myself on. I felt I had disrupted a sacred ritual. In a monotonous, hypnotizing drone, a woman's voice on a tape recorder at the side of the classroom conducted a math drill. The children had a script of the plotline and filled in the blanks at each pause.

"6 times 4 equals. . . 7 times 8 equals. . . 2 times 2 equals. . . ."

A pause and then: "Isn't this fun?" the disembodied voice asked. . . .

Plastered all over the classroom walls were directives; variations of the socialist realism billboards that line the streets of some totalitarian countries. At the front of the class under the heading "OUR GOALS" was written: "Excellent work habits/ Self-control/ Quiet work manners/ Organization/ Positive attitudes/ Think before you act/ Smiling faces/ Honesty/ Responsibility/ Self-respect/ Independently working hard with maturity and a good attitude/ Well groomed."

"1 times 8 equals. . . ."

. . . The Voice: "Be brave, you're almost there." It ended a moment later and a couple of kids let out a muffled shout of joy, "Yaahh."

The Voice: "Well, congratulations. You did it. Doesn't it feel good?"

For a husky boy at the front the end couldn't have come too soon. He stood up and shook his right hand wildly, trying desperately to regain the flow of blood. Riley examined the drill sheet of a child with freckles. He had one wrong answer. She said, "Oh, that's too bad." Then she told him to do the whole drill over. She looked at me and smiled. "I just feel so badly for him but that's the name of the game."

At the front of the class, another poster: "Our word for this week is/ FRIENDLINESS.". . .

"At times I wonder what the motivation is in the child," said Riley. "I'm always astonished at how if I say, 'stand up,' they all stand up. Nobody says, 'No, I'm not going to.'" Well, at least not out loud. Besides, conformity has little to do with motivation and much more to do with the exercise of power. Riley has it; the children don't. *(Contenta 1993:3–6)* ∎

n the prosperous 1980s Sandro Contenta, the author of this passage from *Rituals of Failure: What Schools Really Teach*, toured public schools across Canada. He found that there were many almost invisible ways in which schools were "breaking the spirits" of the students. As we will see later in the chapter, these are part of the "hidden curriculum." Using storytelling, classroom vignettes, and analysis, Contenta challenges the Canadian educational system to restructure schools and provide education for social change with a more holistic understanding of the world.

Education, like the family and religion, is a *cultural universal.* As such it is an important aspect of socialization—the lifelong process of learning the attitudes, values, and behaviour considered appropriate to members of a particular culture. As we saw in Chapter 4, socialization can occur in the classroom or at home, through interactions with parents, teachers,

friends, and even strangers. Exposure to books, films, television, and other forms of communication also promotes socialization. When learning is explicit and formalized—when some people consciously teach, while others adopt the role of learner—the process of socialization is called *education.* But students learn far more about their society at school than what is included in the curriculum.

This chapter focuses in particular on the formal systems of education that characterize modern industrial societies. We will begin with a discussion of four theoretical perspectives on education: functionalist, conflict, interactionist, and feminist. As we will see, education can both perpetuate the status quo and foster social change. An examination of schools as formal organizations—as bureaucracies and subcultures of teachers and students—follows. Two types of education that are becoming more common in Canada today—adult education and home schooling—merit special mention. The chapter closes with a social policy discussion of controversial school choice programs. ■

Sociological Perspectives on Education

Education has become a vast and complex social institution throughout the world. It prepares citizens for the various roles demanded by other social institutions, such as the family, government, and the economy. The functionalist, conflict, interactionist, and feminist perspectives offer distinctive ways of examining education as a social institution.

Education is a major industry in Canada. In the last few decades, an increasing proportion of people has obtained a high school diploma, and at least some post-secondary education. Of those aged 25 to 54, the proportion of people with less than high school education has decreased, while the proportion of post-secondary education graduates has increased. For example, 17 percent of females and 18 percent of males over the age of 25 had not completed high school in 1998, compared to 26 percent and 27 percent respectively in 1990. When looking at those in the same age group who have a post-secondary education, we see the numbers go up. In 1998, 53 percent of females and 54 percent of males had completed higher educational degrees, compared to 40 percent and 44 percent in 1990 (CESC 2000).

Aboriginal youth are the least likely to complete high school when compared with visible minorities and nonracialized groups. Though their rates are improving, according to the 2001 Census, 39 percent of those 25

years of age and under had not completed high school, although that is an improvement from the 57 percent who had not completed secondary school in 1991. They are also the group with the least likelihood of attending and/or completing university education, with a rate of approximately 8 percent compared to rates of 28 percent and 21 percent for visible minorities and nonracialized groups born in Canada. And again, one sees an increase in enrolment since 1991 when the number of completed university degrees for Aboriginals was too small a sample to provide a reliable estimate, according to the Canadian Race Relations Foundation (CRRF 2000, Statistics Canada 2003d).

While there have been increasing levels of enrolment in education around the globe, vast regional and country differences exist in this overall trend. Figure 15-1 shows international comparisons of Canada and selected OECD countries. We see from this figure that Canada has the highest participation rate in post-secondary education. While the United States has a higher rate of university degree attainment (28 percent in the U.S. versus 20 percent in Canada), and Norway's university completion rate is also higher than Canada's (26 percent), when the 21 percent rate of attending nonuniversity post-secondary education (college, trade vocational, etc.) is included it brings Canada's rate to 41 percent, the highest of the OECD countries.

FIGURE 15-1

Percentage of the Population Aged 25 to 64 That Has Completed Post-Secondary Education, OECD Countries, 2000

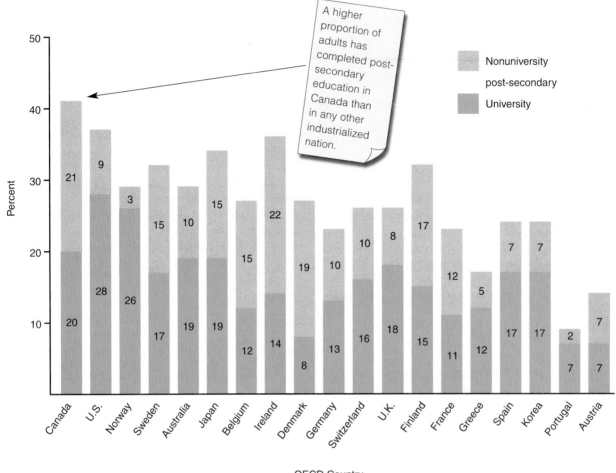

Source: Education at a Glance: OECD Indicators *2000*.

When examining less-developed regions as a whole, we see that while progress has been made, only 57 percent of males and 48 percent of females were enrolled in secondary education in the mid-to-late 1990s (Population Reference Bureau 2000). Most girls in less-developed countries receive less education than boys, and in some of the world's poorest countries, fewer than half of young women receive the basic seven years of schooling. As the UN document "State of World Population Report 2000" stated, girls and women throughout the world continue to be denied access to education routinely (Population Reference Bureau 2000).

Functionalist View

Like other social institutions, education has both manifest (open, stated) and latent (hidden) functions. The most basic *manifest* function of education is the transmission

of knowledge. Schools teach students how to read, speak foreign languages, and repair automobiles. Education has another important manifest function: bestowing status. Because many believe this function to be performed inequitably, it will be considered later, in the section on the conflict view of education.

In addition to these manifest functions, schools perform a number of *latent* functions: transmitting culture, promoting social and political integration, maintaining social control, and serving as agents of change.

Transmitting Culture

As a social institution, education performs a rather conservative function—transmitting the dominant culture. Schooling exposes each generation of young people to the existing beliefs, norms, and values of their culture. In our society, we learn respect for social control and reverence for established institutions, such as religion, the family,

Behaviour Technician/Counsellor

With a very general goal of wanting to "contribute to the human cause," Sarah Humphrey completed her bachelor of social science degree in sociology at the University of Ottawa. She found that it covered perspectives rarely encountered in other fields, and every perspective showed a different way to "understand, listen, and learn from people."

When considering how best to utilize her newly acquired skills, Sarah initially turned to the social services area and worked as a counsellor in a group home for teenaged girls. After a while and wanting a new challenge, Sarah approached her local elementary school board to offer her services as a "quasi-counsellor" outside the classroom. Because a degree in sociology was seen as being very general, the principal was apprehensive about hiring her, but after two weeks of Sarah's volunteer work, the principal saw how sociological skills could be used to help children with a variety of social and behavioural problems. She hired Sarah as a behaviour technician to deal, in part, with perpetrators and victims of behaviours such as bullying, violence, and racism.

"The knowledge and skills learned in sociology trained me not to judge immediately but to look at the larger picture. They have helped me to see how some behaviour is learned through the school but other times it is due to the circumstances of the parents and the broader social environment, and therefore solutions need to be found on those levels, not just on an individual basis. Having taken a more specific degree designed to work with schoolchildren might have prevented me from seeing situations from every angle."

---

and the government. Of course, this is true in many other cultures as well.

In Great Britain, the transmission of the dominant culture in schools goes far beyond learning about monarchs and prime ministers. In 1996, the government's chief curriculum adviser—noting the need to fill a void left by the diminishing authority of the Church of England—proposed that British schools socialize students into a set of core values. These include honesty, respect for others, politeness, a sense of fair play, forgiveness, punctuality, nonviolent behaviour, patience, faithfulness, and self-discipline (Charter and Sherman 1996).

Sometimes nations need to reassess their ways of transmitting culture. When an economic crisis hit Asian countries in 1997 and 1998, many Asian students who had been studying abroad could no longer afford to do so. South Korea, for example, had sent 42 000 university students to the United States alone in 1998. Now it had to figure out how to accommodate thousands more students pursuing higher education at home. South Koreans also began to question the content of the curriculum. Their schools traditionally teach Confucian values with a focus on rote memorization. This leads to an emphasis on accumulating facts as opposed to using reasoning. Entrance to university turns on a highly competitive exam that tests knowledge of facts. Once in university, a student has virtually no opportunity to change his or her program, and the classes continue to rely on memorization. The combination of an economic crisis and growing complaints about the educational process has caused government officials to re-evaluate the educational structure. Moreover, growth in juvenile crime, although low by North American standards, has led the government to introduce a new civic education program emphasizing honesty and discipline (Institute of International Education 1999; Woodard 1998).

Throughout the education system in Canada, there continues to be controversy surrounding the curricula's exclusion of authors and historical figures who do not represent the dominant culture. Critics charge that standard academic curricula have failed to represent the important contributions of women, people of colour, immigrants, and First Nations people to history, literature, and other fields of study. The underlying questions raised by this debate, still to be resolved, are: Which ideas and values are essential for instruction? Which cultures should be transmitted by the schools and post-secondary institutions in Canada?

Promoting Social and Political Integration

Many universities require their first- and second-year students to live together on campus in order to foster a sense of community among diverse groups. Education serves the latent function of promoting social and political integration by transforming a population composed of diverse racial, ethnic, and religious groups into a society whose members share—to some extent—a common identity (Touraine 1974). Schools have historically played an important role in socializing the children of immigrants into the norms, values, and beliefs of the dominant culture. From a functionalist perspective, the common identity and social integration fostered by education contribute to societal stability and consensus.

One of the most extreme Canadian examples of attempts to promote social integration through education is that of residential schools. These institutions were established by the Canadian government, and operated by the Roman Catholic, Anglican, United, and Presbyterian churches up until the middle of the twentieth century, for the purpose of assimilating First Nations children to the dominant culture. First Nations children were taken from their homes and forced to speak a common language—one that was foreign to them. In residential schools, children learned the values and norms of the dominant European groups while, at the same time, learning that their own culture was inferior and needed to be replaced. This process of promoting conformity to the dominant culture resulted in the emotional, physical, and sexual abuse of many Aboriginal children by those who operated the schools. Today, many First Nations adults are still living lives traumatized by their experiences as children in residential schools.

Maintaining Social Control

In performing the manifest function of transmitting knowledge, schools go far beyond teaching such skills as reading, writing, and mathematics. Like other social institutions, such as the family and religion, education prepares young people to lead productive and orderly lives as adults by introducing them to the norms, values, and sanctions of the larger society.

Through the exercise of social control, schools teach students various skills and values essential to their future positions within the labour force. They learn punctuality, discipline, scheduling, and responsible work habits, as well as how to negotiate their way through the complexities of a bureaucratic organization. As a social institution, education reflects the interests of the family and in turn prepares young people for their participation in yet another social institution—the economy. Students are being trained for what is ahead, whether it be the assembly line or a physician's office. In effect, then, schools serve as a transitional agent of social control—between parents and employers in the life cycle of most individuals (Bowles and Gintis 1976; M. Cole 1988).

Schools direct and even restrict students' aspirations in a manner that reflects societal values and prejudices. School administrators may allocate funds for athletic programs while giving much less support to music, art, and dance. Teachers and guidance counsellors may encourage male students to pursue careers in the sciences but steer equally talented female students into careers as early childhood teachers. Such socialization into traditional gender roles can be viewed as a form of social control. p. 182

Serving as an Agent of Change

So far, we have focused on conservative functions of education—on its role in transmitting the existing culture, promoting social and political integration, and maintaining social control. Yet education can also stimulate or bring about desired social change. Sex education classes were introduced in public schools in response to higher rates of sexual activity among teens. Special "girls only" science and mathematics classes were created in response to the low participation rates of females in fields such as science and engineering. Antiracism programs in schools have responded to the problem of racism in schools themselves, and in society in general.

Education also promotes social change by serving as a meeting ground where distinctive beliefs and traditions can be shared. The number of international post-secondary students coming to Canada has increased slightly in recent years to a

This bilingual adult education class in Long Beach, California, is helping to integrate immigrant mothers and their children into mainstream society. While they are learning English, students also absorb the norms, values, and beliefs of the dominant culture.

In response to rising rates of teen sexual activity, many schools have begun to offer sex education courses. When schools attempt to remedy negative social trends, they are serving as an agent of social change.

total of 27 500 in 1998, representing 3.1 percent of all students enrolled in Canadian universities (AUCC 1999). Cross-cultural exchanges between these visitors and Canadian citizens ultimately broaden the perspective of both the hosts and their guests. The same is certainly true when students from Canada attend schools in Europe, Latin America, Africa, or the Far East.

Numerous sociological studies have revealed that increased years of formal schooling are associated with openness to new ideas and more liberal social and political viewpoints. Sociologist Robin Williams points out that better-educated people tend to have greater access to factual information, more diverse opinions, and the ability to make subtle distinctions in analysis. Formal education stresses both the importance of qualifying statements (in place of broad generalizations) and the need at least to question (rather than simply accept) established truths and practices. As we saw in Chapter 2, the scientific method relies on *testing* hypotheses and on in-depth understanding, and it reflects the questioning spirit that characterizes modern education (R. Williams et al. 1964).

Conflict View

Sociologist Christopher Hurn (1985) has compared the functionalist and conflict views of schooling. According to Hurn, the functionalist perspective portrays contemporary education as basically benign. For example, it argues that schools rationally sort and select students for future high-status positions, thereby meeting society's need for talented and expert personnel. By contrast, the conflict perspective views education as an instrument of elite domination. Schools convince subordinate groups of their inferiority, reinforce existing social class inequality, and discourage alternative and more democratic visions of society.

Criticizing the functionalist view, conflict theorists argue that the educational system socializes students into values dictated by the powerful, that schools stifle individualism and creativity in the name of maintaining order, and that the level of change promoted by education is relatively insignificant. From a conflict perspective, the inhibiting effects of education are particularly apparent in the "hidden curriculum," creation of standards for entry into occupations, the differential way in which status is bestowed, and the treatment of women in education.

The Hidden Curriculum

Schools are highly bureaucratic organizations (as we will see later). Many teachers rely on the rules and regulations of schools to maintain order, as we saw in the example of Karen Riley's class (in the chapter opener). Unfortunately, the need for control and discipline can take precedence over the learning process. Teachers may focus on obedience to the rules as an end in itself. If this occurs, students and teachers alike become victims of what Philip Jackson (1968) has called the *hidden curriculum* (see also P. Freire 1970).

The term **hidden curriculum** refers to standards of behaviour that are deemed proper by society and are taught subtly in schools. According to this curriculum, children must not speak until the teacher calls on them and must regulate their activities according to the clock or bells. In addition, they are expected to concentrate on their own work rather than assist other students who learn more slowly. A hidden curriculum is evident in schools around the world. For example, Japanese schools offer guidance sessions during lunch that seek to improve the classroom experience but also to develop healthy living skills. In effect, these sessions instill values and encourage behaviour useful for the Japanese business world, such as self-discipline and openness to group problem solving and decision making (Okano and Tsuchiya 1999).

In a classroom overly focused on obedience, value is placed on pleasing the teacher and remaining quiet—

rather than on creative thought and academic learning (Leacock 1969). Habitual obedience to authority may result in the type of distressing behaviour documented by Stanley Milgram in his classic obedience studies (see Chapter 7).

Credentialism

Fifty years ago, a high school diploma was a minimum requirement for entry into the paid labour force; today, a post-secondary degree is virtually the bare minimum. This change reflects the process of *credentialism*—a term used to describe the increase in the lowest level of education needed to enter a field.

In recent decades, the number of occupations viewed as professions has risen. Credentialism is one symptom of this trend. Employers and occupational associations typically contend that such changes are a logical response to the increasing complexity of many jobs. However, in many cases, employers raise degree requirements for a position simply because all applicants have achieved the existing minimum credential (R. Collins 1979; Dore 1976; Hurn 1985).

In Tokyo's public schools, students learn adult responsibilities early on. In this classroom, classmates take turns serving the lunch.

Conflict theorists observe that credentialism may reinforce social inequality. Applicants from poor and minority backgrounds are especially likely to suffer from the escalation of qualifications, since they lack the financial resources needed to obtain degree after degree. In addition, upgrading credentials serves the self-interest of the two groups most responsible for this trend. Educational institutions profit from prolonging the investment of time and money that people make by staying in school. Moreover, as Hurn (1985) has suggested, current jobholders have a stake in raising occupational requirements. Credentialism can increase the status of an occupation and is crucial to demands for higher pay. Max Weber anticipated such possibilities as far back as 1916, concluding that the "universal clamor for the creation of educational certificates in all fields makes for the formation of a privileged stratum in businesses and in offices" (Gerth and Mills 1958:240–41).

Bestowal of Status

Both functionalist and conflict theorists agree that education performs the important function of bestowing status. As noted earlier, an increasing proportion of people in Canada is obtaining a high school diploma, post-secondary certificate, degree, diploma, or advanced professional degree. From a functionalist perspective, this widening bestowal of status is beneficial not only to particular recipients but to society as a whole. In the view of Kingsley Davis and Wilbert Moore (1945), society must distribute its members among a variety of social positions. Education can contribute to this process by sorting people into appropriate levels and courses of study that will prepare them for appropriate positions within the labour force depending on their socioeconomic background.

p. 17

Conflict sociologists are far more critical of the *differential* way in which education bestows status. They stress that schools sort pupils according to social class background. Although the educational system helps certain poor children to move into middle-class professional positions, it denies most disadvantaged children the same educational opportunities afforded children of the affluent. In this way, schools tend to preserve social class inequalities in each new generation (Giroux 1988; Labaree 1986; Mingle 1987).

Money contributes to this disparity. For the most part, local property taxes finance public schools in the United States. Since the total value of property tends to be lower in areas with many low-income families, these school districts generally have less money available for education. For instance, in affluent Beverly Hills High School, students who qualify have a choice of 14 advanced placement courses that carry extra weight in college admissions. But in poor neighbourhoods nearby, black and Latino students have a choice of only three such courses (Coeyman 1999; Sappenfield 1999).

Studies conducted since 1987 suggest that the funding inequities between richer and poorer districts have actually widened in recent years. Educational expenses have increased across the nation, but less-affluent districts have been unable to keep pace. In recent years, there has been a growing number of legal challenges to the district-by-district school financing inequities within various states (Glaub 1990).

Statistics Canada's Pan-Canadian Education Indicators Program reports on the many facets of education in Canada. One finding of the research has to do with educational attainment and family socioeconomic status, as measured by quartiles. When assessing the background of those who completed high school, the data indicate that 34 percent of those in the lowest quartile had not completed high school, compared with 23 percent of those in the upper quartile. At the same time, a gap exists in university participation rates between persons from the lowest to the highest quartile. Fewer than 20 percent of young people from the lowest quartile attend university, compared with 40 percent of those from the highest quartile (CESC 2000).

Attendance rates are later reflected in labour market earnings, which serve to perpetuate socioeconomic inequality further. For most Canadians, getting more education results in higher earnings. As Table 15-1 indicates, both males and females with a university degree earn, on average, more than those who have not completed high school (Statistics Canada 2003e).

Even a single school can reinforce class differences by putting students in tracks. The term ***tracking*** (or streaming) refers to the practice of placing students in specific curriculum groups on the basis of test scores and other criteria. Tracking begins very early in the classroom, often in reading groups during first grade. These tracks can reinforce the disadvantages that children from less affluent families may face if they haven't been exposed to reading materials and computers and other forms of educational stimulation in their homes during early childhood years.

Studies conducted since 1987 suggest that the funding inequities between richer and poorer school districts have actually widened in recent years.

A national study released in 1992 found that ability grouping worsens the academic prospects of lower-achieving students while it fails to improve the prospects of higher-achieving students. Moreover, tracking appears to lessen the likelihood that students will learn about and interact with others from different racial backgrounds, since ability grouping often contributes to segregation within schools (Oakes 1985).

Tracking and differential access to higher education are evident in many other nations around the world. Japan's educational system mandates equality in school funding and insists that all schools use the same textbooks. Nevertheless, it is only the more affluent Japanese families who can afford to send their children to *juku*, or cram schools. These afternoon schools prepare high school students for examinations that determine admission into prestigious colleges (Efron 1997).

According to a study of teachers' attitudes toward students in the "outback" in rural Australia—an area where sheep vastly outnumber people—students are being prepared to stay in the "bush." Indeed, only a small minority seeks out electives geared toward preparation for post-secondary institutions. However, beginning in the 1980s, parents questioned this agriculture-oriented curriculum in view of rural Australia's declining employment base (M. Henry 1989).

Table 15-1 Mean Earnings by Gender and Educational Achievement, 2000		
Education	**Men**	**Women**
High school or less	$38 900	$27 600
Completed post-secondary	46 700	32 800
University completed	76 000	50 000

Source: Extracted from Statistics Canada 2003j.

Conflict theorists hold that the educational inequalities resulting from funding disparities and streaming or tracking are designed to meet the needs of modern capitalist societies. Samuel Bowles and Herbert Gintis (1976) argue that capitalism requires a skilled, disciplined labour force and that the educational system is structured with this objective in mind. Citing numerous studies, they offer support for what they call the **correspondence principle.**

According to this approach, schools with students from different social classes promote the values expected of individuals in each class and perpetuate social class divisions from one generation to the next. Thus, working-class children, assumed to be destined for subordinate positions, are more likely to be placed in high school vocational and general tracks, which emphasize close supervision and compliance with authority. By contrast, young people from more affluent families are largely directed to university entrance tracks, which stress leadership and decision-making skills—corresponding to their likely futures. While the correspondence principle continues to be persuasive, researchers have noted that the impact of race and gender on students' educational experiences may even overshadow that of class (M. Cole 1988).

Interactionist View

In George Bernard Shaw's play *Pygmalion*, later adapted into the hit Broadway musical *My Fair Lady*, flower seller Eliza Doolittle is transformed into a "lady" by Professor Henry Higgins. He changes her manner of speech and teaches her the etiquette of "high society." When she is introduced into society as an aristocrat, she is readily accepted. People treat her as a "lady" and she responds as one.

The labelling approach and the concept of the self-fulfilling prophecy suggest that if pp. 179, 264 we treat people in particular ways, they may fulfill our expectations. Children labelled as "troublemakers" come to view themselves as delinquents. A dominant group's stereotyping of racial minorities may limit their opportunities to break away from expected roles.

Can this labelling process operate in the classroom? Because of their focus on micro-level classroom dynamics, interactionist researchers have been particularly interested in this question. Howard Becker (1952) studied public schools in low-income and more affluent areas of Chicago. He noticed that administrators expected less of students from poor neighbourhoods, and he wondered if teachers were accepting this view. Subsequently, in *Pygmalion in the Classroom,* psychologist Robert Rosenthal and school principal Lenore Jacobson (1968) documented what they referred to as a **teacher-expectancy effect**—the impact that a teacher's expectations about a student's performance may have on the student's actual achievements. This appears to be especially true in lower grades (through Grade 3) (Brint 1998).

Between 1965 and 1966, children in a San Francisco elementary school were administered a verbal and reasoning pretest. Rosenthal and Jacobson then *randomly* selected 20 percent of the sample and designated these students as "spurters"—children of whom teachers were told to expect superior performance. On a later verbal and reasoning test, the spurters were found to score significantly higher than before. Moreover, teachers evaluated them as more interesting, more curious, and better-adjusted than their classmates. These results were striking. Apparently, teachers' perceptions that these students were exceptional led to noticeable improvements in performance.

Studies have revealed that teachers wait longer for an answer from a student believed to be a high achiever and are more likely to give such children a second chance. In one experiment, teachers' expectations were even shown to have an impact on students' athletic achievements. Teachers obtained better athletic performance—as measured in the number of sit-ups or push-ups performed—from those students of

Although the Chinese government is attempting to address educational inequalities, girls continue to receive less education than boys—especially in rural areas.

whom they *expected* higher numbers (R. Rosenthal and Babad 1985).

The teacher-expectancy effect has been confirmed in a rather surprising setting: a training base for the Israeli army. Instructors for a combat command course were purposely given incorrect information about the "command potential" of 105 men about four days before the trainees arrived. Once the course began, the trainees who had been labelled "high in potential" did indeed learn more than others. These trainees also looked on the combat command course more favourably than the other recruits did (Eden and Shani 1982).

Despite these findings, some researchers continue to question the accuracy of this self-fulfilling prophecy because of the difficulties in defining and measuring teacher expectancy. Further studies are needed to clarify the relationship between teacher expectations and actual student performance. Nevertheless, interactionists emphasize that ability alone may not be so completely predictive of academic success as one might think (Brint 1998).

Feminist Views

In *A Room of One's Own* (1928), Virginia Woolf advocated the value of educational reform so that a female student could "live and write her poetry" (Woolf, 1928:123). She contended that even if one had to struggle in "poverty and obscurity" to bring about educational reform on behalf of females, it was worthwhile. Although contemporary feminist perspectives on education are diverse, many share the view that educational institutions must attempt to resolve the gendered inequality found in society, and prevent it from being perpetuated in the classroom.

Treatment of Women in Education

The educational system of Canada, like many other social institutions, has long been characterized by discriminatory treatment of women. In 1849, after formal appeal to the lieutenant-governor of New Brunswick, women were admitted to a teachers' college. However, the principal of the school set up special rules governing their behaviour. For example, Martha Hamm Lewis had to wear a veil, enter the classroom ten minutes before the other students, sit alone at the back of the room, leave before the lecture ended, and be sure never to speak to the male students (Guppy et al. 1987). While there are no explicit rules for differential treatment of females in Canadian schools today, many women still feel like outsiders.

Feminist perspectives on the treatment of women in education focus on a wide range of areas from the historical exclusion of girls and women in education to the persistent "chilly climate" of educational institutions.

While Canadian women have access to all universities across the country today, many feminist sociologists have written about the lack of warmth or encouragement female students and faculty claim to receive in classes and outside of them (Chilly Collective 1995). When race/ethnicity and sexuality are added to the fact of being female, the chilliness increases substantially (Carty 1991; Bannerji 1991). The university is a chilly environment where many females experience a sense of being treated as "outsiders," which then affects their self-esteem.

In the twentieth century, sexism in education shows up in many ways—in textbooks with negative stereotypes of women, counsellors' pressure on female students to prepare for "women's work," and unequal funding for women's and men's athletic programs. But perhaps nowhere has educational discrimination been more evident than in the employment of teachers. The positions of university professor and college administrator, which hold relatively high status in Canada, generally are filled by men. Public school teachers, who earn much lower salaries, are largely female.

Women have made great strides in one area: the proportion of women continuing their schooling. As was detailed in Chapter 11, women's access to graduate education and to medical, dental, and law schools has increased dramatically in the last few decades. Pressure from the feminist movement played a major role in opening the doors of these institutions.

In cultures where traditional gender roles remain as social norms, women's education suffers appreciably. For example, in rural China, a school with several hundred students often has only a handful of girls. Although the central government is attempting to address such inequality, the typical five- or six-year-old girl in a Chinese village is engaged in farmwork rather than schoolwork. In 1995, China's State Education Commission estimated that the nation had nearly 10 million school dropouts, most of them girls (P. Tyler 1995).

The same gender disparities can be seen in many other countries. Worldwide, illiteracy is generally below 30 percent of the adult population, except in Africa, the Arab States, and Southern Asia (see Table 15-2). Yet women account for more than 60 percent of illiterate adults in every region except Latin America/Caribbean and North/South America (UNESCO 1999).

Schools as Formal Organizations

In many respects, today's schools, when viewed as an example of a formal organization, are similar to factories, hospitals, and business firms. Like these organizations, schools do not operate autonomously; they are influenced by the market of potential students. This is especially true

Table 15-2   Illiteracy Rate By Major Region and Gender, 2000

Country/ region	Percent of total	Male	Female	Female as percent of total
World	20.6	14.7	26.4	64.3
Developed	1.1	0.9	1.3	63.6
Developing	26.3	18.6	34.2	64.3
Africa	40.3	31.3	49.1	61.5
Arab States	38.8	27.1	51.0	64.7
Americas:				
North & South	7.3	6.7	7.9	54.5
Latin & Caribbean	11.7	10.8	12.6	54.8
Asia	24.9	16.8	33.2	65.7
East Asia	13.4	7.3	19.7	72.4
South Asia	45.8	33.4	59.0	62.5
Europe	1.3	0.9	1.5	62.5
Oceania	4.6	3.4	5.8	63.6

Source: Data compiled from estimates in UNESCO 1999.

of private schools, but could have broader impact if acceptance of voucher plans and other types of school choice programs increases (see the social policy section at the end of this chapter). The parallels between schools and other types of formal organizations will become more apparent as we examine the bureaucratic nature of schools, teaching as an occupational role, and the student subculture (Dougherty and Hammack 1992).

Bureaucratization of Schools

It is simply not possible for a single teacher to transmit culture and skills to children of varying ages who will enter many diverse occupations. The growing number of students being served by individual schools and school systems as well as the greater degree of specialization required within a technologically complex society have combined to bureaucratize schools.

Max Weber noted five basic characteristics of bureaucracy, all of which are evident in the p. 150 vast majority of schools, whether at the elementary, secondary, or even university level.

1. **Division of labour.** Specialized experts teach particular age levels of students and specific subjects.

Public elementary and secondary schools now employ instructors whose sole responsibility is to work with children with learning disabilities or physical impairments. In a university sociology department, one professor may specialize in sociology of religion, another in marriage and the family, and a third in industrial sociology.

2. **Hierarchy of authority.** Each employee of a school system is responsible to a higher authority. Teachers must report to principals and assistant principals and may also be supervised by department heads. Principals are answerable to a superintendent of schools, and the superintendent is hired and fired by a board of education. Even the students are hierarchically organized by grade and within clubs and organizations.

3. **Written rules and regulations.** Teachers and administrators must conform to numerous rules and regulations in the performance of their duties. This bureaucratic trait can become dysfunctional; the time invested in completing required forms could instead be spent in preparing lessons or conferring with students.

4. **Impersonality.** As was noted in Chapter 6, the university has been portrayed as a giant, faceless bureaucracy that cares little for the uniqueness of the individual. As class sizes have swelled at schools and universities, it has become more difficult for teachers to give personal attention to each student. In fact, bureaucratic norms may actually encourage teachers to treat all students in the same way despite the fact that students have distinctive personalities and learning needs.

5. **Employment based on technical qualifications.** At least in theory, the hiring of teachers and professors is based on professional competence and expertise. Promotions are normally dictated by written personnel policies; people who excel may be granted lifelong job security through tenure. Teachers have achieved these protections partly

because of the bargaining power of unions (Borman and Spring 1984; W. Tyler 1985).

Functionalists take a generally positive view of the bureaucratization of education. Teachers can master the skills needed to work with a specialized clientele, since they no longer are expected to cover a broad range of instruction. The chain of command within schools is clear; students are presumably treated in an unbiased fashion because of uniformly applied rules. Finally, security of position protects teachers from unjustified dismissal. In general, then, functionalists observe that bureaucratization of education increases the likelihood that students, teachers, and administrators will be dealt with fairly—that is, on the basis of rational and equitable criteria.

By contrast, conflict theorists argue that the trend toward more centralized education has harmful consequences for disadvantaged people. The standardization of educational curricula, including textbooks, will generally reflect the values, interests, and lifestyles of the most powerful groups in our society and may ignore those of racial and ethnic minorities. In addition, the disadvantaged, more so than the affluent, will find it difficult to sort through complex educational bureaucracies and to organize effective lobbying groups. Therefore, in the view of conflict theorists, low-income and minority parents will have even less influence over citywide and regional educational administrators than they have over local school officials (Bowles and Gintis 1976; Katz 1971). The experiences of parents in many developing countries seem to support this view of centralized education; see Box 15-1.

A significant countertrend to the bureaucratization of schools is the availability of education over the Internet. Increasingly, colleges and universities are reaching out via the Web, offering entire courses and even majors to students in the comfort of their homes. Online curricula provide flexibility for working students and others who may have difficulty attending conventional classes because of distance or disability. Research on this type of learning is just beginning, so the question of whether teacher–student contact can thrive online remains to be settled. Computer-mediated instruction may also have an impact on instructors' status as employees, which we will discuss next, as well as on alternative forms of education like adult education and home schooling.

Teachers: Employees and Instructors

Whether they serve as instructors of preschoolers or graduate students, teachers are employees of formal organizations with bureaucratic structures. There is an inherent conflict in serving as a professional within a bureaucracy. The organization follows the principles of hierarchy and expects adherence to its rules; professionalism demands the individual responsibility of the practitioner. This conflict is very real for teachers, who experience all the positive and negative consequences of working in bureaucracies (refer back to Table 6-2 on page 150).

A teacher undergoes many perplexing stresses every day. While teachers' academic assignments have become more specialized, the demands on their time remain diverse and contradictory. There are conflicts inherent in serving as an instructor, a disciplinarian, and an employee of a school district at the same time. For university professors, different types of role strain arise. While formally employed as teachers, they are expected to work on committees and are encouraged to conduct scholarly research. In many colleges and universities, security of position (tenure) is based primarily on the publication of original scholarship. As a result, instructors must fulfill goals that compete for time.

University professors rarely have to take on the role of disciplinarian,

A professor takes time to confer with a student. In large classes, it is difficult for instructors to give personal attention to individual students.

15-1 Schooling in Vietnam

For many people, Vietnam is still a painful memory, a distant place devastated by civil war and a long and destructive bombing campaign. Yet this country, unified following the withdrawal of U.S. troops in the 1970s, is now a peaceful and independent nation determined to rebuild its society. Like neighbouring countries, Vietnam is struggling to provide its citizens basic services, including formal education. The government of Vietnam spends less than 3 percent of the gross national product on education—about half the proportion spent by industrial countries like Canada and Great Britain. Less than half of all high school-aged children in Vietnam attend school (compared to over 80 percent in Canada), and girls make up only a quarter of high school enrolments there (compared to more than half in Canada).

Despite these differences, Vietnamese parents' concerns are similar to those of North American parents. According to the World Bank, surveys of Vietnamese households show that parents of school-aged children are significantly less satisfied with the quality of the education their children are receiving than are school administrators and local government officials.

Parents, analysts suspect, may be more concerned with the outcome of their children's schooling than are school administrators, who may focus more on the quality of the services they deliver. Similar differences of opinion regarding the quality of education can be heard at school board meetings in communities across Canada.

> Less than half of all high school-aged children in Vietnam attend school (compared to over 80 percent in Canada), and girls make up only a quarter of high school enrolments there.

In Vietnam as in Canada, school administration tends to be centralized. In such systems, parents are often frustrated in their efforts to influence educators and hold them accountable for children's learning. Under extreme conditions, students may learn very little of the prescribed curriculum. For example, in Ghana and Kenya, testing showed that a significant percentage of grade school pupils could score little better than if they had guessed on

measures of their learning. Together with parental disenchantment, such results have prompted a search for alternatives to centralized educational systems.

One response has been a move toward community-managed schools. In Nicaragua, school reform has given parents, teachers, and principals greater power over decisions regarding the staffing and educational methods used in local schools. While the results have been mixed, in general student achievement has improved. In El Salvador, a similar program has brought noticeable improvements in the quality of schooling. Parental monitoring of community-managed schools, for example, has halved the rate of teacher absenteeism there.

Let's Discuss

1. Has the quality of the public schools in your community become a subject of debate? If so, what are parents complaining about at school board meetings and other public forums?
2. Do parents in your community have any control over the kind of education their children receive? If so, how do they exercise that control?

Sources: J. Knowles et al. 1998; World Bank 1999a, 1999b.

but this task has become a major focus of schoolteachers' work in countries such as Canada and the United States. Order is needed to establish an environment in which students can actually learn. Many observers sense that schools have been the scene of increasingly violent misbehaviour in recent years, although these concerns may be overblown (see Box 15-2).

The fact that Canada has increasingly become a "schooled society" (Guppy and Davies 1998) will contribute to the employment prospects of students wishing to become teachers. The growing proportion of our population between the ages of 5 and 19, the increase in the

number of schools, and overall increases in the highest level of schooling all contribute to this trend (McVey and Kalbach 1995). As reflective of our aging population, a changing composition of teachers means that a greater number of retiring teachers will need to be replaced. This trend is also occurring in the United States where, due to teacher shortages in some regions, American school boards are advertising for, and recruiting, teachers in Canada.

The status of any job reflects several factors, including the level of education required, financial compensation, and the respect given the occupation within society. The teaching profession (see Table 8-1, page 212) is feeling pressure in all three of these areas. First, the amount of formal schooling required for teaching remains high, but the public has begun to call for new competency examinations for teachers. Second, the statistics cited above demonstrate that teachers' salaries are significantly lower than those of many professionals and skilled workers. Finally, as we have seen, the overall prestige of the teaching profession has declined in the last decade. Many teachers have become disappointed and frustrated and have left the educational world for other careers in other professions. Many are simply "burned out" by the severe demands, limited rewards, and general sense of alienation that they experience on the job.

The Student Subculture

An important latent function of education relates directly to student life: Schools provide for students' social and recreational needs. Education helps young children develop interpersonal skills that are essential during adolescence and adulthood. During high school and university years, students may meet future partners and may establish lifelong friendships.

When people observe high schools, community colleges, or universities from the outside, students appear to constitute a cohesive, uniform group. However, the student subculture is actually much more complex and diverse. High school cliques and social groups may crop up based on race, social class, physical attractiveness, placement in courses, athletic ability, and leadership roles in the school and community. In his classic community study of "Elmtown," August Hollingshead (1975) found some 259 distinct cliques in a single high school. These cliques, which on average included five people, were centred on the school itself, on recreational activities, and on religious and community groups.

We can find a similar diversity at the post-secondary level. Burton Clark and Martin Trow (1966) and, more recently, Helen Lefkowitz Horowitz (1987) have identified distinctive subcultures among post-secondary students. Here are four ideal types of subcultures that come out of their analyses:

1. The *collegiate* subculture focuses on having fun and socializing. These students define what constitutes a "reasonable" amount of academic work (and what amount of work is "excessive"

and leads to being labelled as a "grind"). Members of the collegiate subculture have little commitment to academic pursuits.

2. By contrast, the *academic* subculture identifies with the intellectual concerns of the faculty and values knowledge for its own sake.

3. The *vocational* subculture is primarily interested in career prospects and views education as a means of obtaining degrees that are essential for advancement.

4. Finally, the *nonconformist* subculture is hostile to the institution's environment and seeks out ideas that may or may not relate to studies. It may find outlets through campus publications or issue-oriented groups.

Each student is eventually exposed to these competing subcultures and must determine which (if any) seems most in line with his or her feelings and interests.

The typology used by these researchers reminds us that school is a complex social organization—almost like a community with different neighbourhoods. Of course, these four subcultures are not the only ones evident on campuses. For example, one might find subcultures of mature students and part-time students.

Sociologist Joe Feagin has studied a distinctive collegiate subculture: black students at predominantly white American universities. These students must function academically and socially within universities where there are few black faculty members or black administrators, where harassment of blacks by campus police is common, and where the curricula place little emphasis on black contributions. Indeed, Feagin (1989:11) suggests that "for

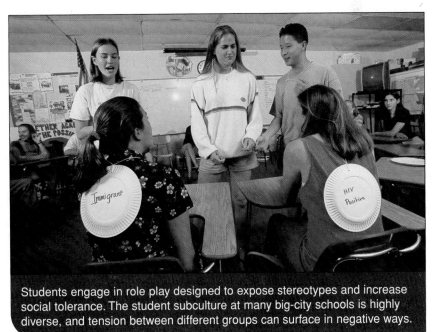

Students engage in role play designed to expose stereotypes and increase social tolerance. The student subculture at many big-city schools is highly diverse, and tension between different groups can surface in negative ways.

Erfurt in Germany, Littleton (Colorado) in the United States, and Taber (Alberta) in Canada were relatively un-noteworthy locations before they became associated with school killings. Now, they resonate with the sound of gunshots, of kids killing kids on school grounds. In addition to killings, school-based violence can take the form of minor discipline problems (i.e., disobedience, taunting, and teasing), obscenity, verbal and physical threats, aggression, bullying, assault (with or without a weapon), vandalism, extortion, and gang-related activities (Day et al. 1995).

In Canada, we have seen the consequences of bullying in cases such as the 1997 British Columbia incident resulting in the killing of Reena Virk by seven of her schoolmates, or the recent suicides of young people from Nova Scotia and BC who chose to die rather than continue being bullied. In Eastern Ontario, a 16-year-old was arrested and held in a detention centre for over a month, due to fears by the school personnel and other parents when he presented a paper written for a drama class. In it, he describes a fictional account of violent action taken in a high school. It was discovered that a speech impediment played a role in his subjection to bullying and his subse-

quent feelings being put on paper. People no longer perceive schools as safe havens. But how accurate is this impression?

There is a growing concern on the part of school officials in Canada about the problem of violence in schools. Many researchers, however, disagree with school officials about its prevalence. There are those who suggest that violence in our schools is relatively low key, and that we should not assume that what is happening in schools in the U.S. is happening here (West 1993).

> **A child has only a one-in-a-million chance of being killed at school.**

Some studies suggest that school-based violence is actually decreasing (Fitzpatrick 1994; West 1993). On the other hand, some studies point to an increase in certain forms of school-based violence. One study, conducted by the Ontario Teachers Federation, surveyed 881 schools and reported a 150 percent increase in incidents such as biting, kicking, punching, and the use of weapons over the period 1987–1990 (Roher 1993).

As well, research on the problem of school-based violence indicates great

regional variation. For example, students in Nova Scotia and in the Niagara region of Ontario did not consider it to be a particular problem (Rodgers 1993; Robb 1993). However, one observation does not seem to be disputed: there is a greater scope and severity of youth violence spilling over into schools in the United States than in Canada.

However, studies of school violence in the United States put the recent spate of school killings in perspective:

- A child has only a one-in-a-million chance of being killed at school.
- The number of people shot and killed in school in the 1997–1998 school year was 40 (including adults), about average over the last six years.
- According to the U.S. Center for Disease Control, 99 percent of violent deaths of school-aged children in 1992–1994 occurred *outside* school grounds.
- Fewer students are now being found with guns in school.
- Data from the National School Safety Center at Pepperdine University in the U.S. suggest that there has been a 27 percent decline in school-associated violent deaths from 1992 through the 1997–1998 school year.

Source: Bowles 1999; Day et al. 1995; Department of Education 1999; National Center for Education Statistics 1998; S. Schaefer 1996; West 1993.

minority students life at a predominantly white college or university means long-term encounters with *pervasive whiteness.*" In Feagin's view, African American students at such institutions experience blatant and subtle racial discrimination, which has a cumulative impact that can seriously damage the students' confidence (see also Feagin et al. 1996).

Sometimes schools can seem overwhelmingly bureaucratic, with the effect of stifling rather than nourishing intellectual curiosity in students. This concern has led many parents and policymakers to push for school choice programs—allowing parents to choose the school that suits their children's needs and forcing schools to

compete for their "customers." We'll take a look at this issue in the social policy section at the end of the chapter.

Adult Education

Picture a "university student." Most likely, you will imagine someone under 25 years of age. This reflects the belief that education is something experienced and completed during the first two or three decades of life and rarely supplemented after that. However, many post-secondary institutions have witnessed a dramatic increase in the number of older students pursuing higher education. These older students are more likely to be female—and are

- Twenty-three times more children are killed in gun *accidents* than in school killings.

Schools, then, are safer than neighbourhoods, but people still are unnerved by the perception of an alarming rise in schoolyard violence that has been generated by heavy media coverage of the recent incidents. Some conflict theorists object to the huge outcry about recent violence in schools. After all, they note, violence in and around city schools has a long history. It seems that only when middle-class white children are the victims does school violence become a plank on the national policy agenda. When violence hits the middle class, the problem is viewed not as an extension of delinquency, but as a structural issue in need of remedies.

Meanwhile, feminists observe that virtually all the offenders are male and, in some instances, the victims are disproportionately female. The precipitating factor for violence is often a broken-off dating relationship—yet another example of violence of men against women (or, in this case, boys against girls).

Increasingly, efforts to prevent school violence are focusing on the ways in which the socialization of young people contributes to violence. For example,

the *Journal of the American Medical Association* published a study of Second Step, a violence prevention curriculum for elementary school students that teaches social skills related to anger management, impulse control, and empathy. The study evaluated the impact of the program on urban and suburban elementary school students and found that it appeared to lead to a moderate decrease in physically aggressive behaviour and an increase in neutral and prosocial behaviour in school.

A national study, providing a snapshot of violence prevention programs in Canadian schools, concluded that the school board's response to school violence must be one in which students are themselves involved in the development of policies (Day et al. 1995). The study concluded that school boards must not take the view that certain youth are "out of control"; rather, boards must make a strong effort to promote a prosocial environment, develop comprehensive

policies, establish developmentally appropriate consequences for certain behaviours, and institute a multifaceted violence prevention program (on both the macro and micro levels).

Let's Discuss

1. Has a violent episode ever occurred at your school? If so, how did students react? Do you feel safer at school than at home, as experts say you are?
2. What steps have administrators at your school taken to prevent violence? Have they been effective, or should other steps be taken?

more likely to be visible minorities—than is the typical 19- or 20-year-old student. Viewed from a conflict perspective, it is not surprising that women and minorities are overrepresented among older students; members of these groups are the most likely to miss out on higher education the first time around (F. Best and Eberhard 1990).

According to the 1998 Adult Education and Training Survey (AETS), close to 28 percent of Canadians participated in adult education and training activities in 1997. The majority of them (75 percent) took courses for job-related purposes (Statistics Canada 2001a). In 2000, 26 percent of the students enrolled in Canadian universities were over 25 years of age (Statistics Canada 2001b).

Obviously, sociological models of the post-secondary subculture will have to be revised significantly in light of such changes. Moreover, as the age of the "typical" student increases, there will be a growing need for on-campus child care.

It should be noted that the nation's universities *need* older students. Given the expected decrease in population in the age group 18 to 24 years old over the period 2010 through 2050, institutions of higher learning will have to find new consumers for their services in order to survive financially. This need has led educational institutions across Canada to develop adult education programs.

One explanation for the adult education boom is that society is changing rapidly in an age of technological innovation, and a growing knowledge-based economy. Business firms have come to accept the view of education as lifelong and may encourage (or require) employees to learn job-related skills. Thus, secretaries are sent to special schools to be trained to use the latest computer software. Realtors attend classes to learn about alternative forms of financing for home buyers. In occupation after occupation, long-time workers and professionals are going back to school to adapt to the new demands of their jobs.

Taking a conflict perspective, Canadian sociologist David Livingstone argues that despite Canadians' growing technological proficiency and growing levels of training and education, employers are failing to utilize their skills fully, thus contributing to "underemployment" (1999).

Not all adult education is at the formal level. The 1998 General Social Survey reported that more than 6 million Canadians over the age of 25 were engaged in "informal" learning during the previous month. This type of learning involves self-directed activity done at the learner's own time and pace, with an aim to "enrich their ability to function within their communities and homes, to deal with family issues and enjoy their leisure time. Increasingly, people are also encouraged to view lifelong learning as a means of combating the mental deterioration associated with aging" (Silver et al 2001:19). Although gender had little effect on one's likelihood to study informally, gendered patterns of subject interest were found to exist. Women were more likely to study health and child care than men, who were more likely to study trade-related subjects (Silver et al. 2001).

Home Schooling

When most people think of school, they think of bricks and mortar and the teachers, administrators, and other employees who staff school buildings. But for an increasing number of students in Canada, home is the classroom and the teacher is a parent. Estimates of the number of children being home-schooled in Canada vary. Statistics Canada reported 19 114 registered home-schooled students in 1997 but warned that the figures underestimate the total number since many home schools are not registered. The Home School Legal Defense Association (HSLDA) estimates the number to be 80 000 (Wake 2000).

In the past, families that taught their children at home lived in isolated environments or held strict religious views at odds with the secular environment of public schools. But today, home schooling is attracting a broader range of families not necessarily tied to organized religion. Poor academic quality, school strikes, peer pressure, and school violence are motivating many parents to teach their children at home (*Education Week* 1999; Schnaiberg 1999b). In addition, the growing presence of computers and availability of educational resources online have been very helpful to parents who were interested in educating their children at home. Rates of home schooling in Canada have increased every year since 1980. The greatest increases were experienced in Western Canada, where the number of registered home schoolers grew by 10 percent between 1995–96 and 1996–97 (Wake 2000).

While supporters of home schooling feel that children can do just as well or better in home schools as in public schools, critics counter that because home-schooled children are isolated from the larger community, they lose an important chance to improve their socialization skills. But proponents of home schooling claim that their children benefit from contact with others besides their own age group. They also see home schools as a good alternative for children who suffer from

Many adults return to school in later life to obtain further education, advance their careers, or change their line of work. These adults are studying microbiology.

As greater numbers of Canadian children are being home schooled with the aid of computers, parents must oversee their children's computer use.

attention deficit disorder (ADD) and learning disorders (LDs). Such children often do better in smaller classes, which present fewer distractions to disturb their concentration (National Homeschool Association 1999).

Given the lack of regulation of home schools, quality control is an issue. Canada's provincial governments require that parents register their children, but this does not always happen. For example, in Alberta, where home schooling is particularly popular, estimates are high regarding the numbers of unregistered children—children whose curricular and academic achievement the government cannot monitor. Many of these children are from families where the motivating factor to home-school is religion. They believe that the secular school system does not reflect their values, particularly those that concern abortion, homosexuality, and evolution. In 1988, Canada's Supreme Court ruled that the province of Alberta had a "compelling interest" in ensuring that the children of that province were properly educated (*Globe and Mail*, Feb. 2/99). This would mean making sure that home-schooled children followed a government-approved curriculum, and that they were tested annually according to provincial standards. Despite the court ruling, many Christian parents continue to believe that the government has no business monitoring their children's education, and that the values of secular education are not those to which they want their children exposed. Home schooling works, particularly for those who have made a commitment to it (*Education Week* 1999; Schnaiberg 1999a).

Who are the people who are running home schools? In general, they tend to have higher-than-average incomes and educational levels. Most are two-parent families, and their children watch less television than average—both factors that are likely to support superior educational performance. The same students, with the same type of family and the same support from their parents, would probably do just as well in the public schools. As research has repeatedly shown, small classes are better than big classes, and strong parental and community involvement is key (Schnaiberg 1999a).

Home schooling, then, gives those parents who are willing to make the effort an alternative to traditional education. So do voucher programs and school choice, the subjects of the next section.

SOCIAL POLICY AND EDUCATION

School Choice Programs

The Issue

Imagine a school where classes are small, and where teachers are chosen by the school, not assigned to it; where children from all backgrounds are taught with an explicit goal of turning them into high achievers. Where teachers respect students and students respect teachers. Problems with discipline are rare, the average student's performance is high, and failure rates are very low. This school is purported to have the longest waiting list to join it. Foundations for the Future Charter Academy is one of ten charter schools opened in Alberta since 1995, as part of the province's experiment with public education reform. Seven out of ten of the charter schools are located in either Calgary or Edmonton. The enrolments are as low as 75 and as high as 480, with a total of more than 2000 students attending charter schools. Other provinces are watching Alberta closely, with great interest in charter schools as a "solution" to their public education problems.

Charter schools do not exist in Alberta alone. In the United States, there were over 1700 public charter schools in 2000. In Britain, charter schools are called grant maintained schools (GM schools). They were initiated in 1988 when the Thatcher government passed legislation to allow regular public schools to "opt out" of the traditional system and turn to a governing body of trustees for their daily governance. There are over 1100 operating GM schools today. On October 1, 1989, all New Zealand public schools became charter schools as a part of a national educational reform process (Dobbin 1997).

This is the world of the school choice movement, which is increasingly pitting parents against public school proponents. How far should school choice go? For example, should public funds be used to send children to private and parochial schools? Should charter schools be allowed to skim the best students off the public schools? What role should the government play in promoting school choice and in improving public education in general?

The Setting

The term *school choice programs* refers to various types of educational experiments under which parents can choose where to send their children. The notion of choice is not new—historically, Canadians have had a number of options, including choice among private schools, choice between public and private schools, and choice among public schools. The Canadian Teachers' Federation (CTF) suggests that parents can choose from a "wide variety of programs (such as fine arts, remedial education, the International Baccalaureate program,

Charter schools have become so popular that some of them have long waiting lists. While parents are happy with the educational results of these schools, critics are concerned that the most motivated students are being lured away from the regular public schools.

Montessori programs) geared toward a diversity of students (at-risk students, talented students, older students, First Nations students)" (CTF 2002:2).

One proposed form of school choice involves the use of *education vouchers*. The Ontario government introduced the voucher idea in the form of tax credits. Quebec, Manitoba, and British Columbia either have or are planning similar policies. Education vouchers provide for the transfer of public funds to a public or private school of the parents' choice. Since the funds follow the child, it is hoped that voucher plans will stimulate the local schools to perform better in order to keep their students.

One of the most recent school choice developments has been the *charter school movement*, which allows parents and private educators (or anyone who has an idea for a school) to create and control a school that is chartered by the province and funded by public money. The Canadian Charter Schools Centre explains that charter schools offer the mandated provincial curriculum and are required to fulfill all the terms of the contract in order to have their charter renewed. "While held fully accountable to a publicly elected government body, they control their own budget, staffing, programs, and services to better meet the needs of their students" (CCSC 2002).

Proponents of school choice often rely on the work of economists for support (Tucker 1993). The use of school vouchers, for example, was first advanced by economist Milton Friedman in his book *Capitalism and*

Freedom (1962). The idea is to set up a sort of free-market system of education: Parents shop for the school they want, which receives that child's portion of the school budget ($6000 in Alberta, for example). The schools that are most popular thrive, and those that are not picked must improve to compete or else close their doors (McCarthy 2001; Tashman 1992).

Support for school choice comes from a diverse sampling of the "consumers of education": liberals who oppose compulsory school assignments for their children and seek more freedom of choice, nonpolitical parents disillusioned by schools that have become too impersonal and bureaucratized, and religious fundamentalists who view religious education as a means of combating growing secularization. A study conducted on Alberta's charter schools found that parents were very satisfied with the schools: 82 percent intended to keep their children enrolled in the charter school (Bosetti et al. 2000). However, a public opinion poll conducted in Ontario found that 67 percent of those polled opposed the proposed tax credit for private schools and only 15 percent of parents would consider switching their children to a private school if the "voucher" system were implemented (OSSTF 2001).

Sociological Insights

Many criticisms have been aimed at school choice programs. The analogy to business competition within a free-market economy seems deceptive to some observers. They argue that while a successful business such as Coca-Cola can expand into new markets across North America and the world, an elementary school has a limited potential for expanding its customer base. Rather than expanding, an outstanding school will become ever more selective as parents compete to enrol their children. Most charter schools in Alberta are so oversubscribed that they have lengthy waiting lists. Every day, another dozen or so are added to the list, including babies whose parents hope to be first in line for 2006 (Wente 2001). There is concern, too, about the state of public schools whose most motivated or talented students are skimmed off by school choice programs. They are often left with disproportionately high numbers of poorly motivated students and students with severe learning difficulties.

The divisive religious issue underlying the voucher policy also troubles critics of choice programs. According to the Canadian Association of Independent Schools, about two-thirds of Ontario's independent schools (including the private schools that would benefit from the proposed tax credit) have a specific religious focus. Since charter schools do not charge tuition (and therefore would not be eligible for a tax credit voucher), they are to maintain the principles of public education, which includes not offering religious instruction. However, that is often not clear, as seen by their supporters in British Columbia, where the campaign for charter schools is funded by right-wing think tanks and led by Christian fundamentalists. The Ontario Federation of Independent Schools explains that a religious dimension in education includes values, morals, ethics, and attitudes based on some belief system that should be decided on by parents and not government (Dobbin 1997).

For opponents of vouchers and tuition tax credits, any government aid to parochial education—whether direct (payments to the schools) or indirect (tuition grants to students or tax credits)—violates the nation's historic separation of church and state. Moreover, drawing on the functionalist perspective, critics of school choice point out that education in Canada has traditionally promoted social and political integration. Such integration is undermined when students attend private and parochial schools and do not interact with peers across class, racial, ethnic, and religious lines (Bracey 1993; Lines 1985; V. Martinez et al. 1994).

Viewed from a conflict perspective, the social class and religious implications of school choice programs are a matter of concern—especially when such programs provide financial support for families to send children to private and parochial schools. Studies of existing choice programs suggest that the more affluent households and those with highly educated parents are especially likely to take advantage of these experiments. In part, this is because vouchers and tax credits may not cover the full cost of private school and therefore may not be useful for less affluent families.

Research has just begun on the impact of school choice programs, since they are relatively new. A University of Calgary study of Alberta charter schools found that while there is evidence that the majority of these schools "reflect improved student improvement," there is a need for better development of specific benchmarks and methods of tracking student performance over the long term (Bosetti et al. 2000:2).

In the U.S., an evaluation of Cleveland's school voucher program found that the program was popular with parents surveyed and that it raised the scores of students tested at the end of the first year (Chaddock 1999; Greene et al. 1997a).

Studies of Britain's GM schools show that they have begun to select students on the basis of performance, which makes comparisons of achievement deceptive. As well, the research shows that rather than modernizing the curriculum, education reform in Britain has meant a trend toward "reinvented traditionalism." Research on New Zealand's charter school system suggests that little has changed, although only short-term assessments have been done. However, that country has experienced mass resignations of teachers and principals due to stress related to the added tasks of "running schools," and this has had a detrimental impact on students and their learning environment (Dobbin 1997).

Policy Initiatives

As interest in school choice grows, the controversy that surrounds the programs grows as well. In 2001, the Ontario Ministry of Education announced its Equity in Education Tax Credit, which provides parents a tax credit of up to $3500 for fees paid to send their children to independent schools. The debates that raged around the plan came from many groups. People for Education, a non-profit parent organization, called for the $300 million set aside for the tax credit to be spent on the public education system. The Fraser Institute stated that the tax credit would ensure that public schools stop their in-fighting and focus on serving parents rather than fighting the government. The Canadian Jewish Congress, along with other non-Catholic Christian and Muslim school advocates, supported the credit. While the Catholic school board has been subsidized since the 1867 *British North America Act*, these other religious groups have been fighting for decades to achieve equity in funding for their schools. But those who believe in a separation between church and state are opposed. They also argue that funding all religious schools ultimately leads to isolation by dividing students along ethnic and religious lines (Reid 2001). Teachers' unions strongly oppose the legislation and call for its repeal. The Ontario Secondary School Teachers' Federation believes the credit will produce inequities by "politically funding special interests, creating a two-tier educational system with public funds and driving educational policy on fiscal policy, rather than student need" (OSSTF 2001).

Teachers' unions have also been opposed to charter schools on similar grounds. Robertson found that charter schools in the U.S. reported that "increasing educational choice is increasing the separation of students by race, social class, and cultural background" (Robertson 1997). In Britain, opponents to the GM schools have focused their struggle on the national curriculum and tests. These

tests were proposed as a way to help diagnose the learning needs of students but have become a way to rank schools based on student performance. Claiming that they are used to polarize students and schools, teachers, backed by their unions, began to boycott them. It began with a few schools and escalated into a national movement of enough schools boycotting tests that the government could not process the results (Miner 1997). Earlier we saw that New Zealand teachers are protesting the charter school system by resigning in large numbers.

So far, in Canada, school choice policy decisions have been made only at the provincial level. As of 2002, there were only 11 charter schools in Canada, all in Alberta. Other provinces such as British Columbia and New Brunswick have organizations that are working to get their provincial legislatures to provide for the implementation of charter schools. While no province has an education voucher system like that of the U.S., Ontario is not the only province to provide educational tax credits. Using public dollars for independent schools has been going on for decades. Alberta, British Columbia, and Manitoba provide grants directly to the independent schools, while Saskatchewan supports selected independent high schools (Reid 2001).

In the U.S. in 2000, only five public voucher programs were operating—in Milwaukee, Cleveland, and in the states of Florida, Minnesota, and Arizona. Some 25 other state legislatures were thinking of using public money to pay for private and parochial school tuition, however. In Great Britain, New Zealand, and Sweden, policymakers have given parents a measure of freedom in selecting their children's schools, and government financing of schools is based on enrolment figures. In Australia, Denmark, and the Netherlands, there has been increasing governmental financial support for private schools (*The Economist* 1994).

Let's Discuss

1. Would you send your child to a private or charter school if the government offered you a tax credit? Why or why not?
2. What do you think of the idea that public schools should be able to compete with private schools? What difficulties might they face that private schools do not?
3. Which is more important, maintaining the separation of church and state or fostering educational choice by allowing students to attend religious schools at public expense? Justify your position.

Chapter Resources

Summary

Education is a cultural universal, found throughout the world, although in varied forms. This chapter examines sociological views of education and analyzes schools as an example of formal organizations.

1. Transmission of knowledge and bestowal of status are manifest functions of education. Among its latent functions are transmitting culture, promoting social and political integration, maintaining social control, and serving as an agent of social change.
2. In the view of conflict theorists, education serves as an instrument of elite domination by creating standards for entry into occupations, bestowing status unequally, and subordinating the role of women in education.
3. Teacher expectations about a student's performance can sometimes have an impact on the student's actual achievements.

4. Today, most schools in Canada are organized in a bureaucratic fashion. Weber's five basic characteristics of bureaucracy are all evident in schools.
5. For over three decades, the proportion of adults enrolled in Canadian post-secondary institutions has been rising steadily, in part because of sweeping changes in business, industry, and technology. For many Canadians, education has become a lifelong pursuit.
6. Home schooling has become a viable alternative to traditional public and private schools. An estimated 19 000 Canadian children are now educated at home.
7. School choice and tuition voucher programs are having a direct effect on public education, forcing some schools to compete or go out of business.

Critical Thinking Questions

1. What are the functions and dysfunctions of tracking in schools? Viewed from an interactionist perspective, how would tracking of high school students influence the interactions between students and teachers? In what ways might tracking have positive and negative impacts on the self-concepts of various students?

2. Are the student subcultures identified in the text evident on your campus? What other student subcultures are present? Which subcultures have the highest (and the lowest) social status? How might functionalists, conflict theorists, feminists, and interactionists view the existence of student subcultures on a college campus?

Key Terms

Correspondence principle   The tendency of schools to promote the values expected of individuals in each social class and to prepare students for the types of jobs typically held by members of their class. (418)

Credentialism   An increase in the lowest level of education required to enter a field. (416)

Cultural universal   A general practice found in every culture. (411)

Education   A formal process of learning in which some people consciously teach while others adopt the social role of learner. (411)

Hidden curriculum   Standards of behaviour that are deemed proper by society and are taught subtly in schools. (415)

Teacher-expectancy effect   The impact that a teacher's expectations about a student's performance may have on the student's actual achievements. (418)

Tracking   The practice of placing students in specific curriculum groups on the basis of test scores and other criteria. (417)

Additional Readings

BOOKS

Ballantine, Jeanne H. 1997. *The Sociology of Education : A Systematic Analysis*. 4th ed. Englewood Cliffs, N.J.: Prentice Hall. A comprehensive approach to education that includes theoretical frameworks, current educational issues, and the process and structure of education systems.

Gaskell, Jane and Arlene McLaren. 1991. *Women and Education*. 2nd edition. Calgary: Detselig Enterprises Limited. By exploring the questions raised by female educational experiences, the book makes knowledge of women in education available, while introducing new ways of thinking about education and society in general.

Ghosh, Ratna and Douglas Ray. 1995. *Social Change and Education in Canada*. 3rd edition. Toronto: Harcourt Brace & Company Canada. This is a collection of essays examining critical issues affecting the relationship between education and social change. This edition focuses on the rights of diverse communities to be served by the educational system and on the policies devoted to protecting these rights.

Sadker, Myra, and David Sadker. 1995. *Failing at Fairness: How America's Schools Cheat Girls*. New York: Touchstone. The authors present a history of women's education in the United States and then critically examine the contemporary treatment of females from elementary school through graduate school.

Wotherspoon, Terry. 1998. *The Sociology of Education in Canada: Critical Perspectives*. Toronto: Oxford University Press. Using a critical perspective, the author traces the historical development and organization of Canadian education, and describes sociological theories and analysis of education.

JOURNALS

The sociology of education is reflected in *Educational Record* (founded in 1920), *Education and Urban Society* (1968), *Education Week* (1981), the *Harvard Educational Review* (1974), *Journal of Contemporary Education* (1984), *Journal of Educational Finance* (1975), *Phi Delta Kappan* (1915), and *Sociology of Education* (1927).

 Internet Connection

www.mcgrawhill.ca/college/schaefer

For additional Internet exercises relating to sociology and education, visit the Schaefer Online Learning Centre at **http://www.mcgrawhill.ca/college/schaefer**. *Please note that while the URLs listed were current at the time of printing, these sites often change—check the Online Learning Centre for updates.*

Bully B'ware is an organization in British Columbia, the purpose of which is to raise awareness on bullying and how to take action against it. Visit its website at **www.bullybeware.com/moreinfo.html** and then answer the following questions.

(a) What can schools do to eliminate bullying?

(b) What role can students play in an anti-bullying campaign?

(c) Do you think students might consider reporting acts of bullying as "ratting"?

(d) Why is reporting bullying considered to be a social taboo in many schools?

CBC Video

Visit the Schaefer Online Learning Centre at **http://www.mcgrawhill.ca/college/schaefer** to view the CBC video segments "Children Having Children: Teen Pregnancy and the Politics of Sex Education" and "Our Minds Are Not For Sale: The Commercialization of Public Education" and answer related questions.

GOVERNMENT

Voter turnout has been on the decline in Canada and other Western democracies. A clothing store in the United States offered this public service advertisement to encourage citizens to vote.

Now at the peak of what should be its key citizenship years, Nexus is confronting two challenges to the definition of what it means to be a citizen. First, the boundaries of the common good are becoming fuzzy. We've described how globalization is slowly eroding the foundations of the old, insular Canadian welfare state and replacing it with a more outward-looking "competition state." For Nexus, this process is having two polarizing effects.

On the one hand, the generation has reacted to sweeping global forces by turning inward, to embellish its own personal identity with something distinct from whatever fad seems to be sweeping the world. Often, as in the case of Nexus Québécois, the inward pull manifests itself in a return to cultural identity groups, where there is a strong sense of difference. Other times, it means the creation of new and smaller tribes, where members can find an authentic sense of community. Snowboarders and squeegee kids are obvious examples. These more local attachments help to combat the feeling of "rootlessness" that globalization can bring. In the words of Nexus journalist and political commentator Irshad Manji, "As institutional and geographic borders lose their legitimacy, our search for belonging intensifies."

On the other hand, Nexus is fearful of being left behind in a global economy and is therefore turning its gaze outward. Globalization is diverting Nexus loyalties to larger collectives—to North America, to the G7, or to the Western world—rather than keeping her eyes fixed on the traditional nation-state. Today, members of this generation are actively encouraged to study in the U.S. or abroad and often find themselves working in the foreign offices of global Canadian companies or for multinational corporations. Perhaps the most poignant example of shifting loyalties was the 1998 NHL All-Star Game. In what was once "Canada's game," Nexus saw *North America* pitted against the world. Another bastion of Canadianism sacrificed on the altar of global competition. *(Barnard, Cosgrave, and Welsh 2000:214–215)* ■

As part
be taken
this prot

n *Chips and Pop: Decoding the Nexus Generation*, Barnard, Cosgrave, and Welsh look at the forces that were impacting on young people (18- to 30-year-olds, also called Generation X) in Canadian society at the end of the twentieth century. It is not difficult to see their point that contemporary young adults are being pulled in different directions by the forces of a local and global culture that seems beyond their control. As governments struggle to maintain both their political and economic relevance in a world increasingly dominated by transnational corporations, their message is largely ignored by youth caught up in the pervasive consumerism of globalization. As they bounce from individualism to corporatism, these young people are left unsure of their own place in a new culture that offers no clear messages about expectations for their participation. The result for the Nexus generation is a sense of exclusion, confirmed by a life experience of minimum-wage employment and governments with no apparent interest in addressing their concerns.

Within the framework of any political system, be it local, provincial, national, or international, there is a power elite made up almost exclusively of middle-aged men who reflect the standards of the dominant, contemporary culture. By **political system**, sociologists mean the social institution with accepted structures and processes used for implementing and achieving society's goals, such as the allocation of valued resources. Like religion and the family, the political system is a cultural universal: It is found in every society. In Canada, the political system holds the ultimate responsibility for addressing the social policy issues examined in this textbook: child care, the AIDS crisis, sexual harassment, poverty, and so forth.

This chapter will present a sociological analysis of the impact of government on people's lives. We will begin with a macro-level analysis of the sources of power in a political system, and the three major types of authority. We will see how politics works in Canada, with particular attention to political socialization, citizens' participation in politics, the changing role of women in politics, ongoing negotiations for Aboriginal self-government, and the influence of interest groups on political decision making. We'll also look at two models of power in democracies: the elite and the pluralist models. Finally, the social policy section will explore the evolving role of women in Canadian public life, and their struggles in achieving gender equality. ■

of 1972, w
mote the
In other w
that mem
Canadian
    Withi
vided rec
ments of
protectior
affiliation
these grou
nificant r
entrenche
who claim
membersh
several hu
imagine a

Politics and Government

An economic system does not exist in a vacuum. Someone or some group makes important decisions about how to use resources and how to allocate goods, whether it be a tribal chief or a parliament or a dictator. A cultural universal common to all economic systems, then, is the exercise of power and authority. The struggle for power and authority inevitably involves *politics*, which political scientist Harold Lasswell (1936) tersely defined as "who gets what, when, and how." While power and authority are most commonly analyzed in terms of their economic and political applications, there is another area where they are just as critical. ***Ideological power and authority*** is the ability to change attitudes or agendas by controlling people's perceptions and beliefs. Capitalism and democracy work because the populations that live under these systems are convinced that they are the best forms available. In their study of politics and government, sociologists are concerned with social interactions among individuals and groups and their impact on the larger political and economic order.

Power

p. 208

Power is at the heart of a political system. According to Max Weber, **power** is the ability to exercise one's will over others. To put it another way, whoever can control the behaviour and outcomes of others is exercising power. Power relations can involve large organizations, small groups, or even people in an intimate association.

There are three basic sources of power within any political system—force, influence, and authority. ***Force*** is the actual or threatened use of coercion to impose one's will on others. When leaders imprison or even execute political dissidents, they are applying force; so, too, are terrorists when they seize or bomb an embassy or assassinate a political leader (see Box 16-1 on p. 439). ***Influence***, on the other hand, refers to the exercise of power through a process of persuasion. A person may reconsider his or her choice of career because of comments made by peers, the advice of school guidance counsellors, or a passionate description of a profession by someone recruiting talented youth. In each case, sociologists would view such efforts to persuade people as examples

Table 16-2   Progress of Women's Rights in Canada

1916 — First provinces give women right to vote — Alberta, Saskatchewan, and Manitoba

1918 — Women are given full federal right to vote

1920 — Women are given right to be elected to parliament

1921 — First woman elected to the House of Commons

1928 — Supreme Court of Canada decides that women are not "persons" and cannot be appointed to the Senate of Canada

1929 — British Privy Council overturns Supreme Court decision

1930 — First woman senator

1952 — First province enacts equal pay legislation — Ontario

1955 — Restrictions on the employment of married woman in the federal public service are removed

1956 — Legislation is enacted guaranteeing equal pay for equal work within federal jurisdiction

1957 — First woman cabinet minister

1961 — *Canadian Bill of Rights* is passed

1977 — *Canadian Human Rights Act* forbids discrimination on the basis of sex and ensures equal pay for work of equal value for women: *Canadian Labour Code* is similarly amended and provides for 17 weeks of maternity leave

1978 — *Canadian Labour Code* is amended, eliminating pregnancy as a basis for lay-off or dismissal

1982 — *Canadian Charter of Rights and Freedoms*, Section 28, is enacted — Charter guarantees apply equally to men and women

1983 — *Canadian Human Rights Act* is amended to prohibit sexual harassment and to ban discrimination on the basis of pregnancy and family or marital status

1984 — First woman governor general

1984 — Canadian Constitution is amended to affirm that Aboriginal and treaty rights are guaranteed equally to both men and woman

1985 — Section 15 of the *Canadian Charter of Rights and Freedoms* comes into effect, guaranteeing equality for all Canadians before and under law and equal protection and benefit of law

1985 — Court Challenges Program expanded to address equality rights cases

1985 — *Indian Act* is amended, restoring status and right to band membership to Indian women who had lost such status through marriage to a non-Indian

1986 — *Employment Equity Act* is introduced, applicable to Crown corporations and federally regulated business, aimed at redressing historic and systemic discrimination of "target group" populations

1993 — Guidelines on women refugee claimants are instituted for the Immigration and Refugee Board

1994 — Funding for equality test cases is reinstated as Charter Law Development Program

1995 — Gender-based analysis of legislation and policies is adopted by the federal government

Source: Status of Women Canada 1995:5.

Of course, not all social theorists believe that gender inequality should be addressed through proactive measures by the government. Functionalists, for example, suggest that these types of interventions may have a negative effect on society by unsettling the natural balance created by tradition and precedent. For these sociologists, the slow and self-generating process of social evolution can be relied on, over time, to make changes that will be beneficial to the community as a whole.

Most sociologists though—and especially conflict theorists—view gender equity policies as an attempt to reduce inequality embedded in the social structure, by increasing opportunities of women that have been deprived in the past.

Policy Initiatives

Canada's commitment to gender equality extends to its partnerships with other countries, particularly those that receive significant amounts of foreign aid. The Canadian International Development Agency (CIDA) has established clear policy guidelines outlining its expectations that gender be taken into consideration in all projects—that treatment of girls and women be given attention. Within the limitations imposed by recognizing cultural diversity and national autonomy, there has been some success in convincing developing countries that progress in the twenty-first century must include full participation by women.

CIDA's policy is intended to establish gender-neutral political and economic environments that reflect equal status for men and women. It has done this by convincing participating states that the well-being of the country is tied inevitably to the well-being of all its citizens. This policy (CIDA 1999) incorporates the following principles:

1. Gender equality must be considered as an integral part of all CIDA policies, programs and projects
2. Achieving gender equality requires the recognition that every policy, program, and project affects women and men differently
3. Achieving gender equality does not mean that women become the same as men
4. Women's empowerment is central to achieving gender equality, and
5. Promoting the equal participation of women as agents of change in economic, social, and political processes is essential to achieving gender equality (Simpson 1999).

Given its positive profile on the global stage, Canada represents a model to be imitated by many underdeveloped nations. Using the leverage provided by its international relief and development arms, Canada has a unique and important role to play in advocating for the increased inclusion of women in those countries still striving to achieve economic and political stability.

Let's Discuss

1. Do you think the focus should be for women to gain equality in the home or in the workplace? Why?
2. If you could draft a law that would provide equality for women in Canadian society, what provisions would it include?
3. Do men and women get equal treatment in your university? Is there any particular area where inequality is still an issue? What can you do to help change this?

● Chapter Resources

Summary

1. Every society must have a *political system* in order to have recognized procedures for the allocation of valued resources.
2. There are three basic sources of *power* within any political system: *force, influence,* and *authority.*
3. Max Weber identified three ideal types of authority: *traditional, legal–rational,* and *charismatic.*
4. The principal institutions of *political socialization* in Canada are the family, schools, and the media.
5. Political participation makes government accountable to its citizens, but there is a great deal of apathy in both Canada and other countries.

6. Women are still underrepresented in office but are becoming more successful at winning elections to public office.
7. One of the most important political issues in Canada today is the pursuit of First Nations communities to restore their inherent right to self-government. There are currently 80 different groups negotiating with their individual provinces and/or territories to regain control over their land and resources, with the goal to return to the self-sufficiency that they had when they met the first European explorers that came to their land.
8. Sometimes people band together in **interest groups** to influence public policy.
9. Advocates of the **elite model** of the power structure of Canada see the country as being ruled by a small group of individuals who share common political and economic interests (a **power elite**), whereas advocates of a **pluralist model** believe that power is more widely shared among conflicting groups.
10. The struggle for women's equality in Canada has been ongoing through the past 100 years. There have been significant improvements in women's access to political and economic opportunities in the past 40 years, but the goal of a gender-neutral environment is not yet achieved. Through its foreign aid and international relations policies and programs, Canada has also begun to work for women's inclusion in other parts of the world.

Critical Thinking Questions

1. The plight of the Nexus generation outlined at the beginning of the chapter suggests that people of university age are marginalized by the political powers in Canada. Do you agree or disagree with this portrayal? Base your answer on the information and ideas contained in this chapter.
2. Who really holds power in the university you attend? Describe the distribution of power at your school, drawing on the elite and pluralist models where they are relevant.
3. Imagine that you have a summer job working for your local representative in provincial politics. She wants you to work on a project that is trying to find solutions to the problem of youth participation in the democratic process in your province. How could you use what you have learned about sociology to conceptualize the problem? What types of research would you suggest to the project team?

Key Terms

Authority   Power that has been institutionalized and is recognized by the people over whom it is exercised. (438)

Charismatic authority   Power made legitimate by a leader's exceptional personal or emotional appeal to his or her followers. (440)

Elite model   A view of society as ruled by a small group of individuals who share a common set of political and economic interests. (449)

Force   The actual or threatened use of coercion to impose one's will on others. (437)

Ideological power and authority   The ability to change attitudes or agendas by controlling people's perceptions and beliefs. (437)

Influence   The exercise of power through a process of persuasion. (437)

Interest group   A voluntary association of citizens who attempt to influence public policy. (448)

Legal–rational authority   Power made legitimate by law. (438)

Majority government   A government where one party controls more than half the seats in a legislative house. (442)

Military–industrial complex   The close association between the government, the military, and defence industries. (450)

Pluralist model   A view of society in which many competing groups within the community have access to government so that no single group is dominant. (450)

Political action committee (PAC)   A political committee established by an interest group—say, a national bank, corporation, trade association, or cooperative or membership association—to solicit contributions for candidates or political parties. (448)

Political socialization   The process by which individuals acquire political attitudes and develop patterns of political behaviour. (440)

Political system   The social institution that relies on a recognized set of procedures for implementing and achieving the goals of a group. (437)

Politics   In Harold D. Lasswell's words, "who gets what, when, and how." (437)

Power   The ability to exercise one's will over others. (437)

Power elite   A small group of military, industrial, and government leaders who control the fate of the country. (449)

Terrorism   The use or threat of violence against random or symbolic targets in pursuit of political aims. (439)

Traditional authority   Legitimate power conferred by custom and accepted practice. (438)

Additional Readings

BOOKS

Bashevkin, Sylvia. 1998. *Women on the Defensive: Living Through Conservative Times.* Toronto: University of Toronto Press. Bashevkin traces the fate of contemporary feminism through the ideological and policy debates of the 1980s under the leadership of Ronald Reagan, Brian Mulroney, and Margaret Thatcher. By examining the policies and goals of feminists in all three countries, she follows their collision courses with conservative administrations.

Enloe, Cynthia. 1990. *Bananas, Beaches, and Bases: Making Feminist Sense of International Politics.* Berkeley: University of California Press. Enloe studied the lives of women on military bases and of diplomatic wives as part of her examination of the male-dominated agenda of international politics.

Zweigenhaft, Richard L., and G. William Domhoff. 1998. *Diversity in the Power Elite.* New Haven: Yale University Press. A psychologist and a sociologist team up to consider why, although women and minorities have made inroads, the overwhelming majority of the elite of the nation continues to be white and male.

JOURNALS

Among the journals that focus on issues of government are the *American Political Science Review* (founded in 1906), *Canadian Journal of Political Science* (1958), *Canadian Parliamentary Review* (1978), T*he Hill Times, Insurgent Sociologist* (1969), *Social Policy* (1970), and *Today on Parliament Hill.*

 ## Internet Connection

www.mcgrawhill.ca/college/schaefer

For additional Internet exercises relating to sociology and government, visit the Schaefer Online Learning Centre at **http://www.mcgrawhill.ca/college/schaefer**. *Please note that while the URLs listed were current at the time of printing, these sites often change—check the Online Learning Centre for updates.*

Max Weber's writings have been crucial in expanding sociologists' understanding of the workings of political institutions, government, and bureaucracies. In particular, his work on types of authority helps to frame the relationship of those in power to the people they lead. First direct your web browser to an Internet search engine such as Google (**www.google.ca**) or AltaVista (**www.altavista.com**). Second, think of a leader from politics, religion, or history that you always wanted to learn more about. If you need an idea,

just flip through your textbook and you will find pictures and names of many such leaders. Search for that person's name and visit links dedicated to her or his life.

(a)   Which person did you choose? Why did you select her or him?

(b)   When did this person live? What group or nation did this person lead? What role has this person played in history?

(c)   What type of authority did he or she have over followers? Was it traditional, legal–rational, or charismatic authority, or some combination? What reasons/examples can you give to support your choice?

(d)   Did the person you studied ever use force to exert or maintain power over others? Did the person ever use influence? How so?

(e)   What is your opinion of this leader in light of all you have learned?

This poster from 1991 calls for blocking the lowering of trade barriers with the United States. The fear was that Canadians would lose jobs (symbolized by the empty factory in the background). The controversy over trade barriers continues today worldwide, reflecting the concern that national economies are giving way to a single global economy.

Technology, Jobs and Your Future

The Decline of the Global Labor Force and the Dawn of the Post-Market Era

Percy Barnevik is the chief executive officer of Asea Brown Boveri, a 29-billion-dollar-a-year Swiss–Swedish builder of electric generators and transportation systems, and one of the largest engineering firms in the world. Like other global companies, ABB has recently re-engineered its operations, cutting nearly 50,000 workers from the payroll, while increasing turnover 60 percent in the same time period. Barnevik asks, "Where will all these [unemployed] people go?" He predicts that the proportion of Europe's labor force employed in manufacturing and business services will decline from 35 percent today to 25 percent in ten years from now, with a further decline to 15 percent twenty years down the road. Barnevik is deeply pessimistic about Europe's future: "If anybody tells me, wait two or three years and there will be a hell of a demand for labor, I say, tell me where? What jobs? In what cities? Which companies? When I add it all together, I find a clear risk that the 10% unemployed or underemployed today could easily become 20 to 25%." . . .

For some, particularly the scientists, engineers, and employers, a world without work will signal the beginning of a new era in history in which human beings are liberated, at long last, from a life of back-breaking toil and mindless repetitive tasks. For others, the worker-less society conjures up the notion of a grim future of mass unemployment and global destitution, punctuated by increasing social unrest and upheaval. On one point virtually all of the contending parties agree. We are, indeed, entering into a new period in history—one in which machines increasingly replace human beings in the process of making and moving goods and providing services. . . .

Most workers feel completely unprepared to cope with the enormity of the transition taking place. The rash of current technological breakthroughs and economic restructuring initiatives seem to have descended on us with little warning. Suddenly, all over the world, men and women are asking if there is a role for them in the new future unfolding across the global economy. Workers with years of education, skills, and experience face the very real prospect of being made redundant by the new forces of automation and information. What just a few short years ago was a rather esoteric debate among intellectuals and a small number of social writers around the role of technology in society is now the topic of heated conversation among millions of working people. They wonder if they will be the next to be replaced by the new thinking machines. . . .

The new high-technology revolution could mean fewer hours of work and greater benefits for millions. For the first time in modern history, large numbers of human beings could be liberated from long hours of labor in the formal marketplace, to be free to pursue leisure-time activities. The same technological forces could, however, as easily lead to growing unemployment and a global depression. *(Rifkin 1995a:11–13)* ■

n this book *The End of Work,* social activist Jeremy Rifkin takes a look at what the economic world will look like after automation and high technology make human labour more and more obsolete. Economic forces have a huge impact on our lives—from something as basic as whether we can put food on the table to more soul-searching concerns such as "How can I be productive?" Rifkin's view is that we must be prepared to deal with the inevitable dysfunctions and dislocations that accompany a major transformation of the global economic system.

The term **economic system** refers to the social institution through which goods and services are produced, distributed, and consumed. As with social institutions such as the family, religion, and government, the economic system shapes other aspects of the social order and is, in turn, influenced by them. Throughout this textbook, you have been reminded of the economy's impact on social behaviour—for example, individual and group behaviour in factories and offices. You have studied the work of conflict and feminist theorists, who emphasized that the economic system of a society can promote social inequality. And you learned that foreign investment in developing countries can intensify inequality among residents.

p. 18

p. 18

This chapter will present a sociological analysis of the impact of the economy on people's lives. We begin with macro-level analysis of capitalism and socialism as ideal types of economic systems. Next we examine aspects of work, including types of jobs, alienation in the workplace, and worker satisfaction. Then we take a look at the changing nature of the North American economy and the global economic structure and process as we begin the twenty-first century. Finally, the social policy section explores the controversy over employment equity, an issue that focuses on unequal opportunities. ■

Economic Systems

The sociocultural evolution approach developed by Gerhard Lenski categorizes preindustrial societies according to the way in which the economy is organized. The principal types of preindustrial societies, as you recall, are hunting-and-gathering societies, horticultural societies, and agrarian societies.

p. 130

As noted in Chapter 5, the *Industrial Revolution*—which began in England during the period 1760 to 1830—brought about changes in the social organization of the workplace. People left their homesteads and began working in central locations such as factories. As the Industrial Revolution proceeded, a new form of social structure emerged: the **industrial society**, a society that depends on mechanization to produce its goods and services.

p. 131

Two basic types of economic systems distinguish contemporary industrial societies: capitalism and socialism. As described in the following sections, capitalism and socialism serve as ideal types of economic systems. No nation precisely fits either model. Instead, the economy of each individual country represents a mixture of capitalism and socialism, although one type or the other is generally useful in describing a society's economic structure. China's economy, for example, is primarily socialistic, while the U.S. economy reflects the capitalist ideal. Canada's economic model lies somewhere between the two, incorporating aspects of both capitalism and socialism.

Capitalism

In preindustrial societies, land functioned as the source of virtually all wealth. The Industrial Revolution changed all that. It required that certain individuals and institutions be willing to take substantial risks in order to finance new inventions, machinery, and business enterprises. Eventually, bankers, industrialists, and other holders of large sums of money, known as *capital*, replaced landowners as the most powerful economic force. These people invested their funds in the hope of realizing even greater profits and thereby became owners of *the means of production*.

The transition to private ownership of business was accompanied by the emergence of the capitalist economic system. **Capitalism** is an economic system in which capital, primarily in the form of currency, is used as a tool to create wealth. In this model, the means of production are largely in private hands and the main incentive for economic activity is the accumulation of profits. In practice, capitalist systems vary in the degree to which the government regulates private ownership and economic activity (Rosenberg 1991).

p. 207

Immediately following the Industrial Revolution, the prevailing form of capitalism was what is termed **laissez-faire** ("leave alone"). Under the principle of laissez-faire, as expounded and endorsed by British economist Adam Smith (1723–1790), people could compete freely with minimal government intervention in the economy. Business retained the right to regulate itself and essentially

Policy Initiatives

By the early 1990s, employment equity had emerged as an increasingly important issue in both provincial and federal legislatures. Generally, discussion focused on the use of quotas (or the "Q word," as it came to be known) in hiring practices. Supporters of the policy argue that removing barriers to participation for designated groups does not exclude truly qualified candidates from any group. Opponents insist that hiring targets exist as quotas that lead to reverse discrimination. In *Employment Equity: Myths and Realities* (HRDC 2001b), the government responds by stating that the Act means "everyone has equal employment opportunities—not just a select group."

Provincial employment equity policies are quite varied. Eight provinces have some sort of policy in place; the exceptions are Newfoundland and Labrador and Alberta. With the exception of Quebec, provincial policies apply only to the public sector. In Quebec, the Act applies to all public bodies with 100 or more employees in the municipal sector and in the education, health, and social service systems (HRDC 2001a).

Canada is not alone in its efforts to compensate minority group members for generations of inequality. In fact, Canada is recognized as a world leader in welcoming diversity and including all groups in the nation's economic life. While we have one piece of legislation covering four designated groups, most other industrialized countries have more fragmented legislation.

Australia, for example, has a series of laws protecting the rights of its disadvantaged groups: racial minorities (including Aboriginal people), women, and persons with disabilities. Great Britain also has three pieces of legislation in its platform for equal opportunities, covering groups based on race, sex, and ability. The same three categories are covered in Sweden's legislation. The Netherlands' equality legislation is focused on improvement of the representation of women, ethnic minorities, and disabled people in the workplace, and its programs tend to be quite specific. The affirmative action programs in the United States are designed to protect women, individuals over 40 years of age, persons with disabilities, war veterans, and racial minorities. Their programs are fragmented and the complaint system is court-oriented. While legislation has been in place since the late 1960s, progress in the U.S. is considered very uneven (HRDC 2001a).

South Africa is an example of a country that passed affirmative action legislation modelled after the Canadian *Employment Equity Act*. After dismantling the system of apartheid that favoured whites economically and socially, the Republic of South Africa is now trying to level the playing field. Inequality is stark: 88 percent of the nation's population is nonwhite, yet this group accounts for only 4 percent of the managerial ranks. The South African government has chosen the term "affirmative action" for its policy to encourage the hiring of blacks in management positions where none existed before. Because the gaps are much greater than in Canada, there has been a virtual hiring frenzy in the limited pool of black South African managers and professionals. The subject of affirmative action in this nation almost always splits along racial lines: blacks are infuriated that there is so much injustice for which to make up, while whites are reluctant to embrace the program meant to redress inequality. The specifics may be different from Canada, but the concerns and impatience seen in South Africa are familiar (Daley 1997).

The First National Bank in South Africa has made an effort to hire blacks for management positions. South Africa has used a policy named affirmative action to help close a gap in which 88 percent of the population is nonwhite but only 4 percent of this group fills the managerial ranks.

Let's Discuss

1. Would a conflict theorist support employment equity? Why or why not?
2. Do you think claims of reverse discrimination have any validity? What should be done about them?
3. If you were to draft legislation either supporting or abolishing employment equity, what provisions would it include?

Chapter Resources

Summary

The **economic system** of a society has an important influence on social behaviour and on other social institutions.

1. As the Industrial Revolution proceeded, a new form of social structure emerged: the **industrial society.**
2. Economic systems of **capitalism** vary in the degree to which the government regulates private ownership and economic activity, but all emphasize the profit motive.
3. The basic objective of a **socialist** economic system is to eliminate economic exploitation and meet people's needs.
4. Marx believed that **communism** would naturally evolve out of the socialism stage.
5. In most societies today the trend is toward an increase in jobs providing services and a rise in the number of occupations that aspire to be a **profession.**
6. Industrial jobs can lead to a sense of **alienation** in the workplace. Karl Marx expected that powerless workers would eventually overthrow the capitalist system.
7. The nature of the Canadian economy is changing. Sociologists are interested in the changing face of the workforce, the effects of **deindustrialization,** increased use of a contingency workforce, and the emergence of e-commerce.
8. Despite numerous recent **employment equity** programs, white males continue to hold the overwhelming majority of prestigious and high-paying jobs in Canada.

Critical Thinking Questions

1. North America has long been put forward as the ultimate capitalist society. Drawing on material in earlier chapters of the textbook, discuss the values and beliefs that have led people in Canada to cherish a laissez-faire, capitalist economy. To what degree did these values and beliefs change during the twentieth century? What aspects of socialism are now evident in the nation's economy? Have there been basic changes in our values and beliefs to support certain principles traditionally associated with socialist societies?
2. Describe some of the service workers in the university that you attend. Do any issues point toward alienation in the workplace? Does your school make much use of a contingent workforce, especially among students?
3. Imagine that you have been assigned to study possible changes in the economy of the nearest city. How could you use surveys, observation research, experiments, and existing sources to complete this task?

Key Terms

Affirmative action   Term used in some countries to refer to positive efforts to recruit minority group members or women for jobs, promotions, and educational opportunities. (476)

Alienation   The situation of being estranged or disassociated from the surrounding society. (465)

Capitalism   An economic system in which capital, primarily in the form of currency, is used as a tool to create wealth. In this model, the means of production are largely in private hands, and the main incentive for economic activity is the accumulation of profits. (461)

Communism   As an ideal type, an economic system under which all property is communally owned and no social distinctions are made on the basis of people's ability to contribute to the economy. (463)

Crown Corporation   A company that is owned by the government but operates as an independent financial entity. (462)

Deindustrialization   The systematic, widespread withdrawal of investment in basic aspects of productivity such as factories and plants. (470)

Downsizing   Reductions taken in a company's workforce as part of deindustrialization. (471)

E-commerce   Numerous ways that people with access to the Internet can do business from a computer. (472)

Economic system   The social institution through which goods and services are produced, distributed, and consumed. (461)

Employment equity   Plans and programs to identify and eliminate workplace barriers to four designated groups, including women, Aboriginal Peoples, persons with disabilities, and visible minorities. (476)

Industrial society   A society that depends on mechanization to produce its goods and services. (461)

Laissez-faire   A form of capitalism under which people compete freely, with minimal government intervention in the economy. (461)

Monopoly   Control of a market by a single business firm. (462)

Oligopoly   Control of a market by a small group of companies. (462)

Profession   An occupation requiring extensive knowledge that is governed by a code of ethics. (464)

Social democracy   An economy that is dominated primarily by private businesses operating within a political framework that is responsible for the redistribution of wealth. (462)

Socialism   An economic system under which the means of production and distribution are collectively owned. (462)

Trade unions   Organizations that seek to improve the material status of their members, all of whom perform a similar job or work for a common employer. (471)

Additional Readings

BOOKS

Fernandez, John P. 1998. *Race, Gender and Rhetoric.* New York: McGraw-Hill. A scholar of management theory looks at the changes taking place in organizations as they become more diverse and more representative of women in decision-making positions.

Gleick, James. 1999. *Faster: The Acceleration of Just About Everything.* New York: Pantheon Books. A journalistic look at the ever-increasing pace of life in the workplace and throughout the lives of people in industrial nations.

Krahn, Harvey J. and Graham S. Lowe. 2002. *Work, Industry, and Canadian Society.* 4th Edition. Toronto: Nelson Thomson Learning. Using a Canadian focus, the authors study the ramifications of work, and how individual, societal, national, and global issues shape work.

Molot, Maureen Appel, and Fen Osler Hampson, ed. 2000. *Canada Among Nations, 2000: Vanishing Borders.* Toronto: Oxford University Press. The authors analyze the impacts of the North American Free Trade Agreement as it has effectively removed the national barriers between Canada and the United States and Mexico.

Rogers, Jackie Krasas. 2000. *Temps: The Many Faces of the Changing Workplace.* Ithaca, NY: Cornell University Press. An examination of the growing use of temporary workers in both low- and high-skill jobs.

JOURNALS

Among the journals focusing on the economy are *Industrial and Labor Relations Review* (founded in 1947), *Insurgent Sociologist* (1969), *Journal of Social, Political and Economic Studies* (1981), *Labour/ Travailleur* (1976), and *Work and Occupations* (1974).

Internet Connection

For additional Internet exercises relating to the economy and work, visit the Schaefer Online Learning Centre at **http://www.mcgrawhill.ca/college/schaefer**. *Please note that while the URLs listed were current at the time of printing, these sites often change—check the Online Learning Centre for updates.*

The History Place: Child Labor in America 1908–1912 offers a virtual look at the photographs of Lewis W. Hine. Hine used his camera as a tool to document social issues and injustices such as child labour in the United States. Visit the website (**www.historyplace. com/unitedstates/childlabor/ index.html**), examine the photos, and read the text accompanying the pictures.

(a) How old are the children in Hine's photos?

(b) What variety of work did these children perform?

(c) What were the challenges and dangers in their jobs?

(d) Are there gender differences in terms of who did what job?

(e) What kinds of emotions do you see on the faces of the children? What feelings do you have while looking at these pictures?

(f) Ask a grandparent or older relative if he or she worked as a child, or if his or her parents worked under such conditions. How do their experiences compare with those of the children in the photo essay? How did your own childhood compare?

(g) Are there still countries today with child labour?

(h) Compare the experiences in Hine's photos with that of children from another website (**www.freethechildren.org**), which discusses contemporary child labour. Does child labour exist in Canada today?

(i) What surprised you most about the photographs and the text in the two websites? Why?

Ⓣ Ontario

Health • Santé

Anne Nicole Gilbert
3821 • 694 • 372 • AM

BORN / NÉ(E)
1966 • 12 • 05
YR. / AN.   MO. / M.   DAY / J.

SEX / SEXE
F

VALID / VALIDE
1995 • 12 • 05 ▶2000 • 12 • 05
YR. / AN.   MO. / M.   DAY / J.   YR. / AN.   MO. / M.   DAY / J.

Anne Gilbert

The condition of medicare has become a major concern for Canadians, with public debates and private discussions focusing on whether the present system requires restructuring or dismantling. The Ontario health card, necessary for health care in that province, can also be used in other provinces, illustrating the *Canada Health Act*'s principle of portability.

PART FIVE

CHANGING SOCIETY

hroughout this textbook, we have been reminded that sociologists are vitally concerned with changes in cultures, social institutions, and social behaviour. Part Five will focus more directly on change as a characteristic aspect of human societies.

Chapter 19 describes changes in human communities, with particular emphasis on urbanization and metropolitan growth. This chapter also examines the diversity of suburban and rural communities. Chapter 20 considers changing patterns of population growth and their social consequences in Canada and throughout the world. The chapter then turns to the environmental issues that confront our planet as we move through the twenty-first century, with special emphasis on technological changes and the ways in which they are reshaping our future. Chapter 21 presents sociological analysis of social movements and how this collective behaviour contributes to social change.

The homeless are among the socially overlooked poor in urban centres around the world. In 1990, an artists' collective collaborated with activists in Chicago to create personalized billboards covered with the signatures of homeless people who lived nearby. The poignant message of the signs acknowledged the homeless as individuals, raising their profile in the community.

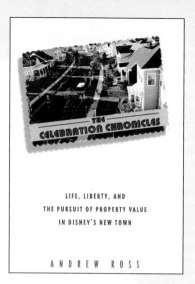

LIFE, LIBERTY, AND
THE PURSUIT OF PROPERTY VALUE
IN DISNEY'S NEW TOWN

A N D R E W   R O S S

Of all the amenities Celebration would offer—summarized in the five cornerstones of Place, Health, Education, Community, and Technology—the promise of a "sense of community" is the least easy to plan, guarantee, or put a price on. Hiring professionals to deliver the promise and ensure its upkeep is the natural offshoot of a corporate society where layers of experts are added yearly to monitor and manage activities that people used to do for themselves. The corporate concept of a community manager would have been as bizarre as a bug-eyed Martian to the idealized small towns of yore, whose close-knit civic virtue and neighborliness Celebration was designed to restore. Nowadays, there are managers for everything, even things that are supposed to have been lost, like our fabled sense of community.

"Community" is one of the most emotionally ubiquitous and versatile touchstones of American life. As a result, it is one of the more overused words in our daily lexicon, relentlessly mined for all sorts of social, religious, and commercial purposes, and in most instances no more meaningful than a sugary advertising cliché. . . .

In the last twenty years, "community" has become a competitive feature in the consumer housing industry, where developers bundle it into the package of amenities on offer. Customers can buy into a "strong" community where others appear to be weak or disorganized or in decline. Community then acquires value as a therapeutic asset that can be purchased by those who, among all the groups in society, probably have least need for its restorative virtues. Celebration's planners set out to raise the bar in the industry by offering a deluxe, next-generation version of the all-inclusive community package, far beyond the "enclaving" model that promised a safe retreat from the hustle and bustle of the city, and the "lifestyle" model that threw in golf and other sports. Celebration's packaging was expected to set the new standard for community-in-depth models of marketing. The demand for such a place rests on the perception that community is everywhere else an endangered species, especially in the nowhere of suburbia. Move to a real town, goes the pitch, and you'll see the difference it makes in your social life. *(Ross 1999:218–220)* ∎

In this excerpt from *The Celebration Chronicles,* Andrew Ross, a professor of American Studies, debunks the promise of prepackaged community used to market the Disney-planned town called Celebration. A brand-new place, built from the ground up in a cypress swamp in Florida, Celebration is designed to resemble an old-fashioned home town, from its Victorian-style houses with their front porches clustered close to the street to its quaint-looking shops in the downtown business district. Similar building trends are happening in Canada as developers are being pressed to bring back a twentieth-century feel to neighbourhoods across the country. Families nostalgic for the small-town life their grandparents once knew are flocking to these places, some of them moving hundreds of miles or leaving good jobs and thriving businesses behind. But community is an elusive concept, an intangible that cannot necessarily be manufactured overnight. Ross reports that the teenagers who live in Celebration have taken to miming Disney's robotic theme-park characters in front of visitors who come to admire the town (Grief 2000).

This chapter explores the important role that communities of all sorts—from planned towns like Celebration to suburbs and big-city neighbourhoods—play in people's lives. Communities give people the feeling that they are a part of something larger than themselves—or sometimes, as in the case of Celebration's teens, the feeling that they are just going through the motions. In sociological terms, a *community* may be formally defined as a spatial or political unit of social organization that gives people a sense of belonging. That sense of belonging can be based either on shared residence in a particular city or neighbourhood or on a common identity, like that of gays and lesbians (Dotson 1991; see also Hillery 1955).

Anthropologist George Murdock (1949) has observed that there are only two truly universal units of human social organization: the family and the community. This chapter explores the importance of communities from a sociological perspective. We will begin with the successive development of early communities, preindustrial cities, and industrial and post-industrial cities. We will examine the dramatic urbanization evident around the world in the twentieth century, and contrast two different views of urban growth. Then we'll look at the three types of communities found in Canada—central cities, suburbs, and rural areas. Later in the chapter, we will consider a new type of community brought about by technological change: the online community. Finally, in the social policy section, we will analyze the distressing phenomenon of homelessness in Canada and elsewhere. ■

In the Disney-planned town of Celebration, Florida, homes are clustered close together, inviting neighbours to socialize over the traditional white picket fences.

How Did Communities Originate?

Early Communities

For most of human history, people used very basic tools and knowledge to survive. They satisfied their need for an adequate food supply through hunting, foraging for fruits or vegetables, fishing, and herding. In comparison with later industrial societies, early civilizations were much more dependent on the physical environment and much less able to alter that environment to their advantage. The emergence of horticultural societies, in which people actually cultivated food rather than

p. 131

merely gathering fruits and vegetables, led to many dramatic changes in human social organization.

Significantly, it was no longer necessary to move from place to place in search of food. Because people had to remain in specific locations to cultivate crops, more stable and enduring communities began to develop. Ultimately, as agricultural techniques became more and more sophisticated, a cooperative division of labour involving both family members and others developed. It gradually became possible for people to produce more food than they actually needed for themselves. They could give food, perhaps as part of an exchange, to others who might be involved in nonagricultural labour. This transition from subsistence to surplus represented a critical step in the emergence of cities.

Eventually, people produced enough goods to cover both their own needs and those of people not engaged in agricultural tasks. Initially, the surplus was limited to agricultural products, but it gradually evolved to include all types of goods and services. Residents of a city came to rely on community members who provided craft products and means of transportation, gathered information, and so forth (Lenski et al. 1995).

With these social changes came an even more elaborate division of labour, as well as a greater opportunity for differential rewards and privileges. So long as everyone was engaged in the same tasks, stratification was limited to such factors as gender, age, and perhaps the ability to perform the task (a skilful hunter could win unusual respect from the community). However, the surplus allowed for expansion of goods and services, leading to greater differentiation, a hierarchy of occupations, and social inequality. Therefore, surplus was a precondition not only for the establishment of cities but also for the division of members of a community into social classes (see Chapter 8). The ability to produce goods for other communities marked a fundamental shift in human social organization.

Preindustrial Cities

It is estimated that, beginning at about 10 000 B.C., permanent settlements free from dependence on crop cultivation emerged. Yet, by today's standards of population, these early communities would barely qualify as cities. The **preindustrial city**, as it is termed, generally had only a few thousand people living within its borders and was characterized by a relatively closed class system and limited mobility. Status in these early cities was usually based on ascribed characteristics such as family background, and education was limited to members of the elite. All the residents relied on perhaps 100 000 farmers and their own part-time farming to provide them with the needed agricultural surplus. The Mesopotamian city of Ur had a

This painting shows twelfth-century traders in a port city on the Mediterranean Sea. Such early settlements represented one type of preindustrial city.

population of about 10,000 and was limited to roughly 220 acres of land, including the canals, the temple, and the harbour.

Why were these early cities so small and relatively few in number? A number of key factors restricted urbanization:

- *Reliance on animal power (both humans and beasts of burden) as a source of energy for economic production.* This limited the ability of humans to make use of and alter the physical environment.

- *Modest levels of surplus produced by the agricultural sector.* Between 50 and 90 farmers may have been required to support one city resident (Davis 1995, originally published in 1949).

- *Problems in transportation and storage of food and other goods.* Even an excellent crop could easily be lost as a result of such difficulties.

- *Hardships of migration to the city.* For many peasants, migration was both physically and economically impossible. A few weeks of travel was out of the question without more sophisticated techniques for food storage.

- *Dangers of city life.* Concentrating a society's population in a small area left it open to attack from outsiders, as well as more susceptible to extreme damage from plagues and fires.

Gideon Sjoberg (1960) examined the available information on early urban settlements of medieval Europe, India, and China. He identified three preconditions of city life: advanced technology in both agricultural and nonagricultural areas, a favourable physical environment, and a well-developed social organization.

For Sjoberg, the criteria for defining a "favourable" physical environment are variable. Proximity to coal and iron helps only if a society knows how to use these natural resources. Similarly, proximity to a river is particularly beneficial only if a culture has the means to transport water efficiently to the fields for irrigation and to the cities for consumption.

A sophisticated social organization is also an essential precondition for urban existence. Specialized social roles bring people together in new ways through the exchange of goods and services. A well-developed social organization ensures that these relationships are clearly defined and generally acceptable to all parties. Admittedly, Sjoberg's view of city life is an ideal type, since inequality did not vanish with the emergence of urban communities.

Industrial and Postindustrial Cities

Imagine how life could change by harnessing the energy of air, water, and other natural resources to power society's tasks. Advances in agricultural technology led to dramatic changes in community life, but so did the process of industrialization. The *Industrial Revolution*, which began in the middle of the eighteenth century, focused on the application of nonanimal sources of power to labour tasks. Industrialization had a wide range of effects on people's lifestyles as well as on the structure of communities. Emerging urban settlements became centres not only of industry but also of banking, finance, and industrial management.

The factory system that developed during the Industrial Revolution led to a much more refined division of labour than was evident in early preindustrial cities. The many new occupations that were created produced a complex set of relationships among workers. Thus, the *industrial city* was not merely more populous than its preindustrial predecessors; it was also based on very different principles of social organization. Sjoberg outlined the contrasts between preindustrial and industrial cities, as summarized in Table 19-1.

In comparison with preindustrial cities, industrial cities have a more open class system and more mobility. After initiatives in industrial cities by women's rights groups, labour unions, and other political activists, formal education gradually became available to many children from poor and working-class families. While ascribed characteristics such as gender, race, and ethnicity

remained important, a talented or skilled individual had a greater opportunity to better his or her social position. In these and other respects, the industrial city is genuinely a "different world" from the preindustrial urban community.

In the latter part of the twentieth century, a new type of urban community emerged. The **postindustrial city** is a city in which global finance and the electronic flow of information dominate the economy. Production is decentralized and often takes place outside of urban centres, but control is centralized in multinational corporations whose influence transcends urban and even national boundaries. Social change is a constant feature of the postindustrial city. Economic and spatial restructuring seems to occur each decade if not more frequently. In the postindustrial world, cities are forced into increasing competition for economic opportunities, which deepens the plight of the urban poor (E. Phillips 1996; D. Smith and Timberlake 1993).

Sociologist Louis Wirth (1928, 1938) argued that a relatively large and permanent settlement leads to distinctive patterns of behaviour, which he called **urbanism**. He identified three critical factors contributing to urbanism: the size of the population, population density, and the heterogeneity (variety) of the population. A frequent result of urbanism, according to Wirth, is that we become insensitive to events around us and restrict our attention to primary groups to which we are emotionally attached. Today, people living in postindustrial cities are developing new types of attachments through the use of electronic communication: see the case study of the Blacksburg Electronic Village, pages 534–535.

Urbanization

The decade between the 1921 and 1931 census counts saw the first time Canada's urban population surpassed its rural counterpart (Statistics Canada 1999). In 1996 three out of every four Canadians lived in urban centres, most of them in one of four broad regions: the Golden Horseshoe of Southern Ontario, Montreal and its adjacent regions, the Lower Mainland of British Columbia, and the Calgary–Edmonton corridor. In fact, by 2001, 50.2 percent of the people in Canada lived in one of nine cities with a size of half a million people or more (Statistics Canada 2002). It is obvious that urbanization has become a central aspect of life in Canada.

Urbanization shows up throughout the world. In 1920, only 14 percent of the world's people lived in urban areas, but by 2000 that proportion had risen to 45 percent, and by the year 2025 it is expected to be as high as 61 percent (Haub and Cornelius 2000; World Resources Institute et al. 1996). Historian Kenneth Jackson (1996:E15) notes,

Table 19-1 Comparing Types of Cities

Preindustrial cities (through eighteenth century)	Industrial cities (eighteenth through mid-twentieth century)	Postindustrial cities (beginning late twentieth century)
Closed class system—pervasive influence of social class at birth	Open class system—mobility based on achieved characteristics	Wealth based on ability to obtain and use information
Economic realm controlled by guilds and a few families	Relatively open competition	Corporate power dominates
Beginnings of division of labour in creation of goods	Elaborate specialization in manufacturing of goods	Sense of place fades, transitional networks emerge
Pervasive influence of religion on social norms	Influence of religion limited to certain areas as society becomes more secularized	Religion becomes more fragmented; greater openness to new religious faiths
Little standardization of prices, weights, and measures	Standardization enforced by custom and law	Conflicting views of prevailing standards
Population largely illiterate, communication by word of mouth	Emergence of communication through posters, bulletins, and newspapers	Emergence of extended electronic networks
Schools limited to elites and designed to perpetuate their privileged status	Formal schooling open to the masses and viewed as a means of advancing the social order	Professional, scientific, and technical personnel are increasingly important

Sources: Based on Sjoberg 1960:323–328; E. Phillips 1996:132–135.

At the turn of the century, only 14 percent of us called a city home and just 11 places on the planet had a million inhabitants. Now there are 400 cities with populations of at least one million and 20 megacities of more than 10 million.

During the nineteenth and early twentieth centuries, rapid urbanization occurred primarily in European and North American cities; however, since the Second World War, there has been an urban "explosion" in the world's developing countries (see Figure 19-1). Such rapid growth is evident in the rising number of "squatter settlements," areas occupied by the very poor on the fringe of cities, described in Box 19-1.

Some metropolitan areas have spread so far that they have connected with other urban centres. Such a densely populated area, containing two or more cities and their suburbs, has become known as a *megalopolis*. An example of this is the huge urban area known as the Golden Horseshoe of Southeast Ontario, consisting of the urban centres of Oshawa and Toronto down to Hamilton and St. Catharines–Niagara and north to Kitchener, Guelph, and

Barrie. This area accounted for 59 percent of Ontario's population and 22 percent of the nation's in 2001

FIGURE 19-1

Urbanization Around the World, 2000.

Mapping Life WORLDWIDE

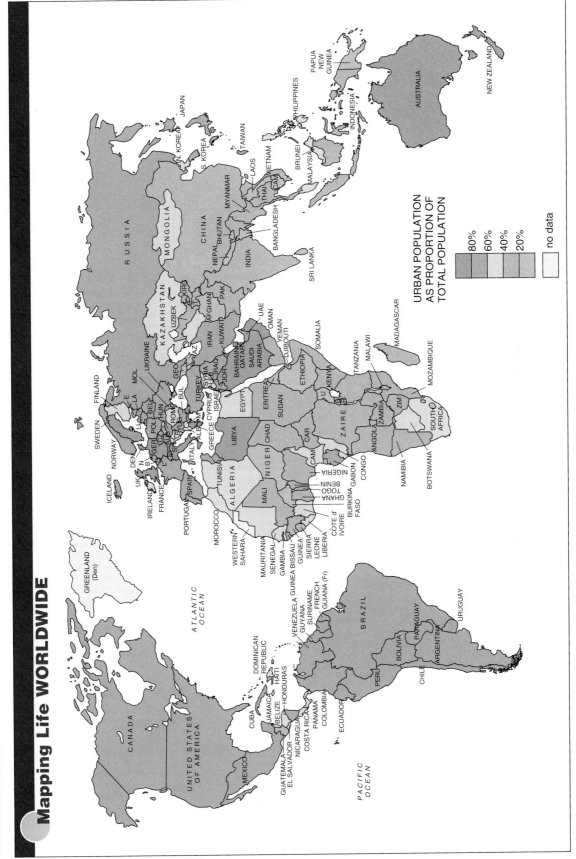

URBAN POPULATION
AS PROPORTION OF
TOTAL POPULATION

80%
60%
40%
20%

no data

Source: Based on data in Haub and Cornelius 2000

Sociology in the Global Community

19-1 Squatter Settlements

ariadas, favelas, bustees, kampungs, and *bidonvilles:* The terms vary depending on the nation and language, but the meaning is the same— "squatter settlements." In **squatter settlements**, areas occupied by the very poor on the fringe of cities, housing is constructed by the settlers themselves from discarded material, including crates from loading docks and loose lumber from building projects. While the term "squatter settlement" has wide use, many observers prefer to use a less pejorative term, such as "autonomous settlements."

This type of settlement is very typical of cities in the world's developing nations. In such countries, new housing has not kept pace with the combined urban population growth resulting from births and migration from rural areas. In addition, squatter settlements are swelled by city dwellers forced out of housing by astronomical jumps in rent. By definition, squatters living on vacant land are trespassers and can be legally evicted. However, given the large number of poor people who live in such settlements (by UN estimates, 40 or 50 percent of inhabitants of cities in many developing nations), governments generally look the other way.

Obviously squatters live in substandard housing, yet this is only one of the many problems they face. Residents do not receive most public services, since their presence cannot be legally recognized. Police and fire protection, paved streets, and sanitary sewers are virtually nonexistent. In some countries, squatters may have trouble voting or enrolling their children in public schools.

> Squatter settlements are not always as bleak as they may appear from the outside.

Despite such conditions, squatter settlements are not always as bleak as they may appear from the outside. Rather than disorganized collections of people, you can often find a well-developed social organization. A thriving "informal economy" typically develops: residents establish small, home-based businesses such as grocery stores, jewellery shops, and the like. Rarely, however, can any but the most ambitious entrepreneurs climb out of poverty through success in this underground economy.

Local churches, men's clubs, and women's clubs are often established in specific neighbourhoods within the settlements. In addition, certain areas may form governing councils or membership associations. These governing bodies may face the usual problems of municipal governments, including charges of corruption and factional splits. Yet, in many cases, they seem to serve their constituents effectively. In Peru, squatters hold annual elections, whereas the rest of the nation has not held local elections for more than 70 years.

Squatter settlements remind us that respected theoretical models of social science in Canada may not directly apply to other cultures. The various ecological models of urban growth, for example, would not explain metropolitan expansion that locates the poorest people on the urban fringes. Furthermore, solutions that are logical for a highly industrialized nation may not be relevant in the developing nations. Planners in developing nations, rather than focusing on large-scale solutions to urban problems, must think in terms of basic amenities, such as providing water taps or electrical power lines to the ever-expanding squatter settlements.

Let's Discuss

1. Do you know of any "squatters" in your own community? If so, describe them and the place where they live.
2. Given the number of homeless people in Canada, why aren't there more squatters?

Sources: Castells 1983; Patton 1988; Yap 1998.

(Statistics Canada 2002). Even when it is divided into autonomous political jurisdictions, the megalopolis can be viewed as a single economic entity. The megalopolis is also evident in Great Britain, Germany, Italy, Egypt, India, Japan, and China.

Functionalist View: Urban Ecology

Human ecology is concerned with the interrelationships between people and their spatial setting and physical environment. Human ecologists have long been interested in how the physical environment shapes people's lives (for example, rivers can serve as a barrier to residential expansion) and also how people influence the surrounding environment (central heating has facilitated settlement in the Arctic). **Urban ecology** focuses on such relationships as they emerge in urban areas. Although the urban ecological approach examines social change in cities, it is nevertheless functionalist in its orientation because it emphasizes that different elements in urban areas contribute to stability.

Early urban ecologists such as Robert Park (1916, 1936) and Ernest Burgess (1925) concentrated on city life but drew on the approaches used by ecologists in studying plant and

522

www.mcgrawhill.ca/college/schaefer

animal communities. With few exceptions, urban ecologists trace their work back to the **concentric-zone theory** devised in the 1920s by Burgess (see Figure 19-2). Burgess proposed a theory for describing land use in industrial cities. At the centre, or nucleus, of such a city is the central business district. Large department stores, hotels, theatres, and financial institutions occupy this highly valued land. Surrounding this urban centre are succeeding zones that contain other types of land use and that illustrate the growth of the urban area over time.

Note that the creation of zones is a *social* process, not the result of nature alone. Families and business firms compete for the most valuable land; those possessing the most wealth and power are generally the winners. The concentric-zone theory proposed by Burgess also represented a dynamic model of urban growth. As urban growth proceeded, each zone would move even farther from the central business district.

Because of its functionalist orientation and its emphasis on stability, the concentric-zone theory tended to understate or ignore certain tensions apparent in metropolitan areas. For example, the growing use by the affluent of land in a city's peripheral areas has been uncritically approved despite the displacement of poor and minority families who have, for decades, occupied these historically less expensive neighbourhoods. Moreover, the urban ecological perspective gave little thought to gender inequities, such as the establishment of men's softball and golf leagues in city parks without any programs for women's sports. Consequently, the urban ecological approach has been criticized for its failure to address issues of gender, race, and class.

By the middle of the twentieth century, urban populations had spilled beyond the traditional city limits. No longer could urban ecologists focus exclusively on *growth* in the central city, for large numbers of urban residents were abandoning the cities to live in suburban areas. As a response to the emergence of more than one focal point in some metropolitan areas, C.D. Harris and Edward Ullman (1945) presented the **multiple-nuclei theory** (see Figure 19-2). In their view, all urban growth does not radiate outward from a central business district. Instead, a metropolitan area may have many centres of development, each of which reflects a particular urban need or activity. Thus, a city may have a financial district, a manufacturing zone, a waterfront area, an entertainment centre, and so forth. Certain types of business firms and certain types of housing will naturally cluster around each distinctive nucleus (Schwab 1993).

The rise of suburban shopping malls is a vivid example of the phenomenon of multiple nuclei within metropolitan areas. Initially, all major retailing in cities was located in the central business district. Each residential neighbourhood had its own grocers, bakers, and butchers, but people travelled to the centre of the city to make major purchases at department stores. However, as major metropolitan areas expanded and the suburbs became more populous, an increasing number of people began to shop nearer their homes. Today, the suburban mall is a significant retailing and social centre for communities across Canada.

In a refinement of multiple-nuclei theory, contemporary urban ecologists have begun to study what journalist Joel Garreau (1991) has called "edge cities." These

FIGURE 19-2

Comparison of Ecological Theories of Urban Growth

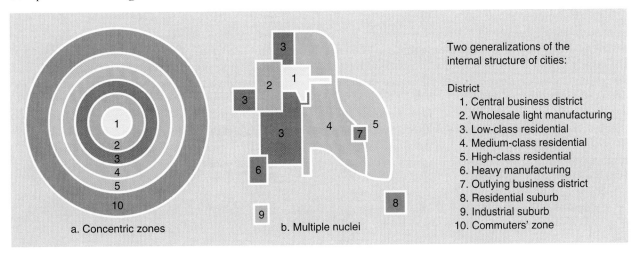

Two generalizations of the internal structure of cities:

District
1. Central business district
2. Wholesale light manufacturing
3. Low-class residential
4. Medium-class residential
5. High-class residential
6. Heavy manufacturing
7. Outlying business district
8. Residential suburb
9. Industrial suburb
10. Commuters' zone

a. Concentric zones   b. Multiple nuclei

Source: C. Harris and Ullmann 1945:13.

Though the African country of Kenya is mostly rural, Nairobi, a city with almost a million residents, is a modern urban area with international business connections. According to world systems analysis, the cities of developing nations exist on the periphery of the global economy, controlled and exploited by the more powerful industrialized nations.

communities, which have grown up on the outskirts of major metropolitan areas, are economic and social centres with identities of their own. By any standard of measurement—height of buildings, amount of office space, presence of medical facilities, presence of leisure-time facilities, or, of course, population—edge cities qualify as independent cities rather than large suburbs.

Conflict View: New Urban Sociology

While acknowledging the descriptive value of urban ecological models, contemporary sociologists point out that metropolitan growth is not governed by waterways and rail lines, as a purely ecological interpretation might suggest. From a conflict perspective, communities are human creations that reflect people's needs, choices, and decisions—but some people have more influence over these decisions than others. Drawing on conflict theory, an approach called the **new urban sociology** considers the interplay of local, national, and worldwide forces and their effect on local space, with special emphasis on the impact of global economic activity (Gottdiener and Hutchison 2000).

New urban sociologists note that ecological approaches typically have avoided examining the social forces, largely economic in nature, that have guided urban growth. For example, central business districts may be upgraded or abandoned, depending on whether urban

policymakers grant substantial tax exemptions to developers. The suburban boom in the post–Second World War era was fuelled by federal housing policies that channelled investment capital into the construction of single-family homes rather than to affordable rental housing in the cities. Similarly, while some observers suggest that the growth of sun-belt cities in the American South is due to a "good business climate," new urban sociologists counter that this term is actually a euphemism for hefty state and local government subsidies and antilabour policies intended to draw manufacturers (Gottdiener and Feagin 1988; M. Smith 1988).

The new urban sociology draws generally on the conflict perspective and more specifically on sociologist Immanuel Wallerstein's **world systems analysis**.

p. 236

Wallerstein argues that certain industrialized nations (among them, the United States, Japan, and Germany) hold a dominant position at the *core* of the global economic system. At the same time, the poor developing countries of Asia, Africa, and Latin America are on the *periphery* of the global economy, where they are controlled and exploited by core industrialized nations. Countries like Canada and Sweden, while technologically and economically advanced to the same level as core countries, do not have the same level of global influence. These countries are referred to as *semi-peripheral*, indicating their proximity to, but marginalization from, the core of power.

Through use of world systems analysis, new urban sociologists consider urbanization from a global perspective. They view cities not as independent and autonomous entities but rather as the outcome of decision-making processes directed or influenced by a society's dominant classes and by core industrialized nations. New urban sociologists note that the rapidly growing cities of the world's developing countries have been shaped by the historical impact of colonialism followed by a global economy controlled by core nations and multinational corporations (Gottdiener and Feagin 1988; D. Smith 1995).

The urban ecologists of the 1920s and 1930s were not ignorant of the role that the larger economy played in urbanization, but their theories emphasized the impact of local rather than national or global forces. By contrast, through a broad, global emphasis on social inequality

Residential neighbourhoods in Las Vegas sprawl across the desert to the foothills. Like other urban areas in the United States, this sunbelt city has mushroomed in size through the construction of mostly single-family suburban homes.

and conflict, new urban sociologists are interested in such topics as the existence of an underclass (refer back to Chapter 8), the power of multinational corporations (refer back to Chapter 9), and deindustrialization (refer back to Chapter 17), as well as issues to be examined later in this chapter, such as urban fiscal crises, residential segregation, and homelessness.

In an illustration of the new urban sociology, Joe Feagin has likened urban development to a game in which powerful elites play Monopoly with real money. Feagin (1983:2) points out that class conflict has always been part of the dynamics of urban life:

> On the one side we have the progressive city councils and the urban grass-roots peoples movements opposing unbridled growth and development. On the other side, we have the class of profit-oriented developers, bankers, landowners, and industrial executives who buy, sell, and develop land and buildings in cities just like they do with other for-profit commodities.

Developers, builders, and investment bankers are not especially interested in urban growth when it means providing housing for middle- or low-income people. This lack of interest contributes to the problem of homelessness, which will be discussed in the social policy section at the end of the chapter. These urban elites counter that the nation's housing shortage and the plight of the homeless are not their fault—and insist that they do not have the capital needed to construct and support such housing. But

affluent people *are* interested in growth and *can* somehow find capital to build new shopping centres, office towers, and ballparks.

Why, then, can't they provide the capital for affordable housing, ask new urban sociologists? Part of the answer is that developers, bankers, and other powerful real estate interests view housing in quite a different manner from tenants and most homeowners. For a tenant, an apartment is shelter, housing, a home. But for developers and investors—many of them large (and sometimes multinational) corporations—an apartment is simply a housing investment. These financiers and owners are primarily concerned with maximizing profit, not with solving social problems (Feagin 1983; Gottdiener and Hutchison 2000).

As we have seen throughout this textbook—in studying such varied issues as deviance, race and ethnicity, and aging—no single theoretical approach necessarily offers sociologists the only valuable perspective. As is shown in Table 19-2, urban ecology and new urban sociology offer significantly different ways of viewing urbanization that enrich our understanding of this complex phenomenon.

Types of Communities

Communities vary substantially in the degree to which their members feel connected and share a common identity. Ferdinand Tönnies (1988, original edition 1887) used the term *Gemeinschaft* to describe p. 128 close-knit communities where social interaction among people is intimate and familiar. A small town with a single coffee shop, where when anyone enters, people stop talking, assuming they know whoever walks through the door, is a good example of a *Gemeinschaft*. A shopper at the small grocery store in this town would expect to know every employee, and probably every customer as well. By contrast, the ideal type of *Gesellschaft* describes modern urban life, in which there is little sense of commonality, and social relationships often develop as a result of interactions focused on immediate tasks, such as purchasing a product. Contemporary city life in Canada generally resembles a *Gesellschaft*.

The following sections will examine different types of communities found in Canada, focusing on the

Table 19-2   Comparing Approaches to Urbanization

	Urban ecology	New urban sociology
Theoretical perspective	Functionalist	Conflict
Primary focus	Relationship of urban areas to their spatial setting and physical environment	Relationship of urban areas to global, national, and local forces
Key source of change	Technological innovations such as new methods of transportation	Economic competition and monopolization of power
Initiator of actions	Individuals, neighbourhoods, communities	Real estate developers, banks and other financial institutions, multinational corporations
Allied disciplines	Geography	Political science
	Architecture	Economics

distinctive characteristics and problems of central cities, suburbs, and rural communities.

Central Cities

In terms of land, Canada is the second-largest nation in the world, covering nearly 7 percent of the Earth's surface. Yet is has only one-half of one percent of the world's population, and only 10 percent of Canada itself has ever been permanently settled. In 2001, almost 24 million people—accounting for 79 percent of the nation's population—lived in **Metropolitan Influence Zones** (MIZs), which, as we will see later, are areas outside of large metropolitan population centres, but still influenced by them. These territories account for just 4 percent of Canada's landmass and are contained within a narrow strip less than 150 kilometres wide, along the American border. Even those who live outside central cities, such as residents of suburban and rural communities, find that urban centres heavily influence their lifestyles (Statistics Canada 2002, 1998).

Urban Dwellers

Many urban residents are the descendants of European immigrants—Irish, Italians, Jews, Poles, and others—who came to Canada in the nineteenth and early twentieth centuries. The cities socialized these newcomers to the norms, values, and language of their new homeland and gave them an opportunity to work their way up the economic ladder. In addition, a substantial number of Canadians who had been born and raised on farms came to the cities from rural areas in the period following the Second World War.

Even today, cities in Canada are the destinations of immigrants from around the world—including Vietnam, Jamaica, India, and China. Yet, unlike those who came to this country 100 years ago, current immigrants are arriving at a time of growing urban decline. This makes it more difficult for them to find employment and decent housing.

Urban life is noteworthy for its diversity, so it would be a serious mistake to see all city residents as being alike. Sociologist Herbert J. Gans (1991) has distinguished between five types of people found in our cities:

1. *Cosmopolites.* Such residents remain in cities to take advantage of the unique cultural and intellectual benefits. Writers, artists, and scholars fall into this category.
2. *Unmarried and childless people.* Such people choose to live in cities because of the active nightlife and varied recreational opportunities.
3. *Ethnic villagers.* These urban residents prefer to live in their own tight-knit communities. Typically, immigrant groups isolate themselves in such neighbourhoods to avoid resentment from well-established urban dwellers.
4. *The deprived.* Very poor people and families have little choice but to live in low-rent, and often run-down, urban neighbourhoods.
5. *The trapped.* Some city residents wish to leave urban centres but cannot because of their limited

Many racial and ethnic minorities, like this Indo-Canadian community, live in close-knit urban neighbourhoods.

business advertisements all serve to define an area and distinguish it from nearby communities.

In some cases, a neighbourhood must literally defend itself. Plans for urban renewal or a superhighway may threaten to destroy an area's unique character and sense of attachment. In resisting such changes, a neighbourhood may use the strategies and tactics of community organization developed by pioneering organizer Saul Alinsky (1909–1972). Like many conflict sociologists, Alinsky was concerned with the ways in which society's most powerful institutions protect the privileges of certain groups (such as real estate developers) while keeping other groups (such as slum dwellers) in a subservient position. Alinsky (1946) emphasized the need for community residents to fight for power in their localities. In his view, it was only through the achievement and constructive use of power that people could better themselves (Horwitt 1989).

The Canadian courts have repeatedly upheld the rights of communities to restrict the freedoms of individuals living within them. Age restrictions, prohibitions against pets, and limitations on the size, and design of exterior decoration have all been in place in different communities for some time. While each of these is defended as necessary to maintain the look or feel of a particular neighbourhood, there is a fine line distinguishing discrimination based on these criteria from that based on less socially acceptable criteria such as race, gender, or ethnicity. Sometimes a neighbourhood maintains its distinctive identity by excluding those who are deemed different or threatening. Defended neighbourhoods with physical barriers have become more common across Canada because of the growing number of "gated communities" (see Box 19-2).

Issues Facing Cities

People and neighbourhoods vary greatly within any large city. Yet they all face common problems associated with crowded conditions in limited space. High incidence of crime, air pollution, overcrowded transportation arteries, noise—these unpleasant realities and others are an increasing feature of contemporary urban life. Yet for all the shared experience, there are competing interests among the various populations that inhabit the downtown core. Beginning with the farm-to-factory boom of the early twentieth century, there

economic resources and prospects. Gans includes the "downward mobiles" in this category—people who once held higher social positions but who are forced to live in less prestigious neighbourhoods owing to loss of a job, death of a wage earner, or old age. Both elderly individuals living alone and families may feel "trapped" in part because they resent changes in their communities. Their desire to live elsewhere may reflect their uneasiness with unfamiliar immigrant groups who have become their neighbours.

These categories remind us that the city represents a choice (even a dream) for certain people and a nightmare for others. Gans's work underscores the importance of neighbourhoods in contemporary urban life. Ernest Burgess, in his study of life in Chicago in the 1920s, had given special attention to the ethnic neighbourhoods of that city. Many decades later, residents in such districts as Chinatowns or Greektowns continue to feel attached to their own ethnic communities rather than to the larger unit of a city. Even outside ethnic enclaves, a special sense of belonging can take hold in a neighbourhood.

In a more recent study in Chicago, Gerald Suttles (1972) coined the term ***defended neighbourhood*** to refer to people's definitions of their community boundaries. Neighbourhoods acquire unique identities because they are viewed by residents as geographically separate—and socially different—from adjacent areas. The defended neighbourhood, in effect, becomes a sentimental union of similar people. Neighbourhood phone directories, community newspapers, school and parish boundaries, and

The poet Robert Frost wrote that "good fences make good neighbors"; locked doors, walls, and fences have been features of shelter in Canada for generations. However, in recent decades, there has been a growing interest in isolating entire communities from those who otherwise would be neighbours. Political scientist Evan McKenzie (1994) uses the term *privatopia* to describe the emergence of a new type of artificial utopia: private communities within cities and suburbs.

In some cases, the communities are gated, sealed off from surrounding neighbourhoods. There are three categories of gated communities:

- *Lifestyle communities,* including retirement communities, golf and country club leisure developments, and suburban new towns.
- *Prestige communities,* where gates symbolize distinction and stature, including enclaves of the rich and famous, developments for high-level professionals, and executive home developments for the middle class.
- *Security zones,* motivated by fear of crime and outsiders.

The private developers who build these generally "upscale" communities create homeowners' associations to establish rules and to contract for such services as security, garbage collection, and even education. The associations build community parks, recreation centres, swimming pools, and golf courses—all of which are restricted to association members and their guests.

Some gated communities and homeowners' associations have banned display of political signs, prohibited the distribution of newspapers, and barred political meetings or rallies in public areas. Many residents of private communities defend such restrictions as essential for maintaining property values and believe that relinquishing a bit of personal freedom is worthwhile so they may be protected from improper behaviour by their neighbours.

> **The message is clear: These streets are for members only.**

From a conflict perspective, there is particular concern about the symbolism of gated communities, which currently house about 4 million people in the United States. While there are not nearly as many gated communities in Canada as in the United States, we are beginning to see them spreading into our suburbs (Lister 2000). The residents of gated communities are overwhelmingly white and affluent. Gated communities are vividly separated from adjoining neighbourhoods; their gates, walls, and entry doors are monitored 24 hours a day by uniformed private security guards. The message is clear: These streets are for members only.

The emergence of homeowners' associations and gated communities is troubling because it suggests an even sharper segregation of our society, with the "haves" hidden in their private fortresses and walled off from the "have-nots." Moreover, as people become isolated in private communities, they may care less and less about the deterioration of public services *outside* their communities, in nearby cities and counties. With this in mind, Evan McKenzie refers to the shift toward privatopia as "secession by the successful," with affluent individuals and families seceding from the rights and responsibilities of citizenship in a larger society.

Let's Discuss

1. Is there a gated community near you? If so, is it a lifestyle community, a prestige community, or a security zone?
2. What do you think of people who live in gated communities? Would you want to live in one yourself (or if you already do, would you want to stay)?

Sources: Blakely and Snyder 1997; Egan 1995; E. McKenzie 1994; Vanderpool 1995.

---

was a prolonged period of urban growth during which downtown neighbourhoods flourished.

The reversal of this process began with the advent of the suburbs following the boom in automobile sales after the Second World War. During this period, core areas of major cities were rapidly abandoned by middle-class Canadians looking for detached, single-family homes. In an ever-widening circle, peripheral neighbourhoods emerged. As this demographic moved out of the city centres, it was replaced by other members of society eager to take advantage of lower rents created by the exodus. This group was, for the most part, transient and often without full-time employment. Gradually, city centre neighbourhoods deteriorated, becoming infamous for their association with crime.

Then, during the early 1990s, an odd reversal took place, and those wealthier individuals who had left the cities, now tired of commuting, began to return to the core with their children. **Gentrification** refers to the process of resettlement of low-income city neighbourhoods by prosperous families and business firms. This tends to transform a community from a home for those at the bottom of the socioeconomic ladder to an upscale collection of condominiums and boutiques. Older buildings, which offered low-income families and individuals affordable rent, are degraded, demolished, or renovated and upgraded for a new class of resident. Rising in their place are exclusive condos or apartments well beyond the reach of existing area residents.

According to *The Impact of Urban Growth on Affordable Housing*, a study funded by a grant from the Alberta Real Estate Foundation, housing affordability decreases as the density and numbers of city dwellers increase. The pace of urban growth, combined with the devolution of housing responsibilities from federal to provincial to municipal governments, has created a situation where a housing crisis is seen as imminent. A similar process has taken place in American cities where the separation of people on the basis of race, ethnicity, or socioeconomic status has become a serious problem. The segregation has resulted from the policies of financial institutions, the business practices of real estate agents, the actions of home sellers, and even urban planning initiatives (for example, in decisions about where to locate public housing).

Sociologists Douglas Massey and Nancy Denton (1993) have used the term "American apartheid" to refer to the residential patterns of that nation. In their view, segregation is no longer perceived as a problem but rather is accepted as a feature of the urban landscape. For subordinate minority groups, segregation means not only limited housing opportunities but also less access to employment, retail outlets, and medical services.

Another critical problem for the cities has been mass transportation. Since 1950, the number of cars in Canada has multiplied twice as fast as the number of people. As a result, there has been growing traffic congestion in metropolitan areas, and many cities have recognized a need for safe, efficient, and inexpensive mass transit systems. However, the federal government has traditionally given much more assistance to highway programs than to public transportation. Conflict theorists note that such a bias favours the relatively affluent (automobile owners) as well as corporations such as auto manufacturers, tire makers, and oil companies. Meanwhile, poor residents of metropolitan areas, who are much less likely to own cars than are members of the middle and upper classes, face higher fares on public transit along with deteriorating service (Mason 1998).

"Over the last few years, government's role in transportation has been redefined and the economic regulatory framework has been lessened, paving the way for a significantly greater role for market forces" (Transport Canada 1998). This quote from Transport Canada's 1997 Annual Report demonstrates changing federal priorities. Of particular interest is the choice of the word "paving," which reflects an apparent preference for an infrastructure designed to facilitate the use of the private automobile over public transit.

The increased emphasis on building roads and highways is reflected in recent spending reports, which indicate that total government spending on roads reached $12.5 billion in 1999/2000 while spending on transit was a mere $2.5 billion (Transport Canada 2000). What these figures reveal is a bias in favour of an emerging elite within Canadian society—those able to afford a private automobile at a time when vehicle prices and fuel costs have climbed dramatically in recent years. Those Canadians using public transit systems are disproportionately from the lower income group, and because of economic circumstances they have no choice but to rely on transit.

The same skewed spending patterns are found in the budgets of the provinces. For example, in 2000,

Although many cities claim that they do not have enough money to pay for essential public services, they nevertheless seem willing to use valuable resources to attract or keep professional sports teams.

provincial governments spent 75 percent of their transportation dollars on highways, and less than 13 percent on transit (Transport Canada 2000). Despite irrefutable evidence linking the private automobile with increased levels of air pollution in metropolitan areas, governments at all levels seem determined to facilitate its use.

Ironically, while many communities are insisting that they cannot afford to maintain public services and are shifting them to the private sector, some nevertheless find substantial funds to attract professional sports franchises. The most prominent Canadian example of this is Toronto's Skydome, a stadium built specifically to maintain the economic viability of professional American baseball. It beats out Montreal's Olympic Stadium, the Big 'O', a facility that costs millions of dollars more simply because it was constructed originally as a venue for amateur sport. Local politicians and business leaders claim that winning a sports franchise provides a significant boost to the local economy and enhances community spirit. But critics counter that professional sports teams build profits for a wealthy few—and offer tax write-offs to corporations that maintain lavish luxury boxes—without genuinely revitalizing neighbourhoods, much less an entire city. Consequently, the use of significant public funds to attract professional sports franchises has been derided as "stadium welfare." They counter the pro-stadium lobby's estimates of generated revenue by suggesting that those dollars, had they not gone to pay for hockey or baseball tickets, would have been spent elsewhere in the community.

Some developers and bankers are less interested in providing affordable housing than in building new ballparks, preferably with government subsidies. Yet subsidized sports complexes rarely yield the employment opportunities they promise.

Suburbs

The term *suburb* derives from the Latin *sub urbe*, meaning "under the city." Until recent times, most suburbs were just that—tiny communities totally dependent on urban centres for jobs, recreation, and even water.

Today, the term *suburb* defies any simple definition. The term generally refers to any community near a large city—however, the term has not been used by Statistics Canada. Instead, it has traditionally made the distinction between urban and rural populations. The 2001 Census identifies populations in one of four categories:

1. *Census Metropolitan Areas* (CMAs) Urban, suburban, and rural areas of more than 100 000 people, which are socially and economically integrated
2. *Census Areas* (CAs) The same as CMAs, but with a population threshold of only 10 000
3. *Metropolitan Influence Zones* (MIZs) The areas outside CMAs, classified into one of four categories reflecting the degree of influence the CMAs have on them
4. *Census Area Influence Zones* (also known as MIZs) Those areas outside of CAs, classified into one of four categories reflecting the degree of influence the CAs have on them.

Three social factors differentiate suburbs from cities. First, suburbs are generally less dense than cities; in the newest suburbs, there are often no more than two dwellings on an acre of land. Second, the suburbs consist almost exclusively of private space. Private ornamental lawns replace common park areas for the most part. Third, suburbs have more exacting building design codes than cities, and these codes have become increasingly precise in the last decade. While the suburbs may be diverse in terms of population, such design standards give the impression of uniformity (Peterson 1996).

It can also be difficult to distinguish between suburbs and rural areas. Certain criteria generally define suburbs: Most people work at urban (as opposed to rural) jobs, and local governments provide services such as water supply, sewage disposal, and fire protection. In rural areas, these services are less common, and a greater proportion of residents is employed in farming and related activities (Baldassare 1992).

Suburban Expansion

Whatever the precise definition of a suburb, it is clear that suburbs have expanded. In fact, suburbanization has been the most dramatic population trend in Canada throughout the twentieth century. Suburban areas grew at first along railroad lines, then at the termini of streetcar tracks, and by the 1950s along the nation's growing systems of highways and expressways. The suburban boom has been especially evident since the Second World War.

Suburbanization is not necessarily prompted by expansion of transportation services to the fringe of a city. The 1923 earthquake that devastated Tokyo encouraged decentralization of the city. Until the 1970s, dwellings were limited to a height of 102 feet. Initially, the poor were relegated to areas outside municipal boundaries in their search for housing; many chose to live in squatter-type settlements. With the advent of a rail network and rising land costs in the central city, middle-class Japanese began moving to the suburbs after the Second World War (P. Hall 1977).

Proponents of the new urban sociology contend that factories were initially moved from central cities to suburbs as a means of reducing the power of labour unions. Subsequently, many suburban communities induced businesses to relocate by offering them subsidies and tax incentives. As sociologist William Julius Wilson (1996) has observed, federal housing policies contributed to the suburban boom by withholding mortgage capital from inner-city neighbourhoods, and by offering favourable mortgages to new home buyers to assist in the rapid development of massive amounts of affordable tract housing in the suburbs. Moreover, federal funding for provincial construction of new roads provided a substantial boost for highway systems (which made commuting to the cities much easier), while undermining urban communities by building highway networks through the hearts of cities.

All of these factors contributed to the movement of Canadians out of the core cities and into the suburbs. However, whereas the American experience was initiated as a segregation process with whites in the suburbs and nonwhites in inner cities, the Canadian model was founded more on class considerations. In Canada, suburbanization was fuelled more by the availability of affordable housing than it was by a desire to flee the city.

Neighbourhoods like this one began springing up around Canadian cities during the 1950s and 1960s. Today, the suburbs still provide less expensive land for developers marketing homes to families.

Diversity in the Suburbs

In the U.S., as whites moved to suburban tracts, they left behind a black population that grew to dominate the vacated space. In Canada, that same process saw the predominantly white, working class playing "musical neighbourhoods," with the members of each stratum upgrading their living arrangements on the heels of the socioeconomic group ahead of them. Visible minority populations like the Chinese tended to remain isolated in their traditional urban pockets.

Suburbs in Canada remained relatively homogeneous for many years, in part because of immigration laws restricting access for nonwhite applicants. Those people of colour allowed entry to Canada were almost exclusively from the "sponsored" category, which meant they were required to live with family members or friends, most of whom lived in the segregated, urban neighbourhoods. As the immigration laws changed and individuals were able to qualify for landed immigrant status on their own, the option of choosing to live in suburban areas became more feasible. As a result, the population profile of these communities changed. Even in the United States, where the large nonwhite population was deliberately discouraged from expanding beyond its core by racist mortgage policies and real estate agents conscious of devaluing properties, urban neighbourhood integration has occurred.

Over the past 20 years, suburban diversification has taken place and it is probably a safe assumption to say that there are some parallels between the Canadian and

American experiences. Data from the U.S. indicates that the segregation that characterized race and ethnic relations in the big city is not being mirrored in the suburbs. This is not to say that the suburbs are completely integrated, but that the separations that exist are based more on socioeconomic factors than on race or ethnicity. Studies in both countries have demonstrated that the composition of neighbourhoods, while essentially reflecting the presence of visible minorities within the population as a whole, shows no signs of class integration. In fact, it appears that white, Asian, Indo-Canadian, and other groups share neighbourhoods that are defined on the basis of family income.

Suburban settlements have become so diverse that even the collective term *suburbs* gives undue support to the stereotype of suburban uniformity. Pollster Louis Harris has divided suburbs into four distinct categories based on income level and rate of growth. Higher-income suburbs are categorized as either affluent bedroom or affluent settled. *Affluent bedroom communities* rank at the highest levels in terms of income, proportion of people employed in professional and managerial occupations, and percentage of homeowners. *Affluent settled communities* tend to be older and perhaps even declining in population. They are more likely to house business firms and do not serve mainly as a place of residence for commuters.

Harris has recognized that certain suburban areas are composed of individuals and families with low or moderate incomes. *Low-income growing communities* serve as the home of upwardly mobile blue-collar workers who have moved from the central cities. *Low-income stagnant communities* are among the oldest suburbs and are experiencing the full range of social problems characteristic of the central cities. As well, one of the consequences of this uneven distribution of socioeconomic status within communities is the difference in services available. Lower property values in low-income communities may mean that lower taxes are paid, but this results in fewer, or poorer quality, services (i.e., health facilities, schools) and reduced power in municipal governments. As is true of Gans's model of city residents, Harris emphasizes the diversity found within the general category of suburbia (*Time* 1971).

Clearly, not all suburban residents appreciate the diversity of the suburbs—especially if it means that less affluent families, or members of racial and ethnic minorities, will be moving into their communities. **Zoning laws** are enacted, in theory, to ensure that certain standards of housing construction are satisfied; these laws generally stipulate land use and architectural design of housing. Zoning laws can also separate industrial and commercial enterprises from residential areas. Thus, a suburb might wish to prevent a factory from moving to a quiet residential neighbourhood. However, some zoning laws have served as thinly veiled efforts to keep low-income people out of a suburb and have been attacked as "snob statutes." By requiring that a person own a certain number of square feet of land before he or she can build a home— or by prohibiting prefabricated or modular housing—a community can effectively prevent the construction of any homes that lower-class families might be able to afford. The courts have generally let such exclusionary zoning laws stand, even when charges have been made that their enactment was designed to keep out racial minorities and new immigrants with large families (Salins 1996).

Some urban and suburban residents are moving to communities even more remote from the central city or to rural areas altogether. As we will see in the next chapter, one of the noticeable trends in Canada is an increase in young families choosing to live and raise their children away from the core cities, but within commuting distances (similar to the move to the suburbs a few decades ago). Regina, for example, has had a decline of 1.2 percent in population while the municipalities around it have increased by 10 percent (Statistics Canada 2002). In the United States, a similar phenomenon is occurring, and initial evidence suggests that this move to rural areas is only furthering the racial disparities in metropolitan areas (U.S. Bureau of the Census 1997b; Holmes 1997).

Rural Communities

As we have seen, the people of Canada live mainly in urban areas. Yet millions of Canadians live in towns of 2500 people or less that are not adjacent to a city. As is true of the suburbs, it would be a mistake to view rural communities as fitting into one set image. Turkey farms, coal mining towns, cattle ranches, and gas stations along isolated stretches of the Trans Canada Highway are all part of the rural landscape in Canada.

The urbanization that swept Europe during the early stages of the Industrial Revolution took somewhat longer to affect population distributions in North America, simply because of the easy availability of land. However, the transition from rural-based peoples to an urban society is all but complete. At the beginning of the twentieth century, the majority of Canadians lived in what would be classified as a rural setting. During the hundred years since, that proportion has dropped dramatically, from 80 percent in 1901 to 20 percent in 2001 (Statistics Canada 2002). The obvious consequence of this change in urban/rural distribution of Canada's population is that some parts of the country have experienced greater impact than others.

While Canada's primary economic foundations are solidly set in its people's reputation as hewers of wood, miners, and grain growers, all of these activities have been declining in importance to the nation's bottom line. When jobs in farming, mining, and logging disappear, the rural populations who want to remain economically self-sufficient face special problems. Jobs, never in overabundance in rural areas, become even more scarce, and those available tend to pay low wages, in sharp contrast to the substantial union wages that once characterized the primary staples sector.

The sharp drop in rural numbers also has an impact on the social fabric of those communities substantially dependent on farming. Ninety-eight percent of Canadian farms are family owned (Department of Health & Welfare Canada 1973). This means that the economic disruption will also lead to upheavals in the home. Under these circumstances, changing jobs becomes much more than just moving from one employer to another, or changing career paths. It means that the family's day-to-day existence will be dramatically altered.

Rural business activities have accounted for just 29 percent of Canada's economy in recent years (Beshiri 2001). But even that apparently low figure does not reflect the true decline in traditional rural enterprises. Like the rest of Canada, over the last decade small towns have seen most of the job growth in the service and wholesale sectors.

Two other factors play a particularly important role in the struggle for survival being experienced by many rural communities in Canada. Outside of the relatively stable farm regions of the Prairies, where a vulnerable but nonetheless sustained economic structure has been alive for the past century, Canada's small towns and surrounding districts are almost exclusively dependent on single-employer enterprises. Mines and large sawmills have become the economic backbone of these places. As world markets become more competitive and the resources on which these industries rely become more expensive to extract, or run out altogether, towns and villages are watching their job pool evaporate.

The coal mining community of Tumbler Ridge, in Northeastern British Columbia, is an example of just such a process. The town, built in the 1980s by a provincial government keen to take advantage of the growing global demand for coal, has seen that demand dry up, and its employer leave. While some success has been achieved in recasting the remote community as an ideal retirement site—inexpensive housing and a year-round natural playground at your door—it is doubtful that it can return to its former level of activity.

Ironically, while one set of problems is being created by businesses leaving rural communities, another set, perhaps just as threatening, is being created by businesses arriving. The names "Wal-Mart" and "Canadian Tire" have the potential to strike terror into the hearts of small town merchants. Many residents welcome the new employment opportunities, as well as the convenience and savings associated with these discount stores. However, the owner of the town's long-time hardware or clothing store is intimidated at the prospect of a formidable 200 000-square-foot competitor with a national reputation. Even when such discount stores provide a boost to a town's economy (and this is not always the case), they can undermine the community's sense of identity and shared destiny (Curtius 1999).

Compounding the challenges faced by the residents of rural Canada are inadequacies associated with access to services. Amenities such as affordable daycare, taken for granted in large cities, are seldom found outside municipalities. Even services thought of as essential have been impacted. Health

Abandoned buildings are a common feature in small, single-industry towns where market dynamics or a depleted resource resulted in the employer leaving. Once-thriving rural communities are on the decline throughout Canada and the United States.

care provision is a perfect example. As the whole nation struggles with the economic realities of a public medical care system, some provinces, such as Saskatchewan and Ontario, have trimmed the number of facilities situated in rural locations. The argument that the service is still available within an hour's drive provides little solace to families with an emergency, or with someone in acute care whom they wish to visit.

Government fiscal policies, aimed primarily at balancing budgets, have found the sparsely populated countryside an easy target for program restraint. As rural communities decline from a loss of residents and economic base, policymakers have been confronted with an unpleasant task: deciding which ailing towns and counties to support with economic development funds and which rural communities will be allowed to die. New schools, health clinics, and roads can help salvage a declining area, but budgetary realities will not allow governments to invest in every region. This is not a new problem. The provincial legislature in Newfoundland faced an identical dilemma four decades ago when it came to the conclusion that many of its outport villages were simply too remote to sustain.

In a similar vein, Canadians living outside urban centres have historically been poor cousins when it came to housing. A study released by the Canada Mortgage and Housing Corporation in February 2001 concluded that almost one-third of all the homes in rural Canada failed to meet minimum standards for amenities and quality of construction.

On a more positive note, advances in electronic communication, particularly those involving satellite services, have provided rural residents with a level of connectedness that few could imagine even a decade ago. Though use of computers in the home and at work has lagged behind, the proportion of farms and small town homes with a computer has started to catch up with the rates of usage in larger cities. Critical to this improvement was the federal government's commitment to getting rural Canada online.

No matter where people make their homes—whether in city, suburb, or country village—economic and technological change will have an impact on their quality of life.

Community and Technological Change: A Case Study

Like many other aspects of modern society, the concept of community is evolving in response to technological change. Many people now speak of communities or neighbourhoods on the Internet, for example. We saw in our discussion of Table 19-1 that several of the changes communities and urban areas have undergone in recent years can be traced to the growth of electronic information networks. A case in point is the city of Blacksburg, Virginia, which offers a glimpse into the future of many other cities.

Blacksburg is a small American college town whose population swells each year with the influx of students

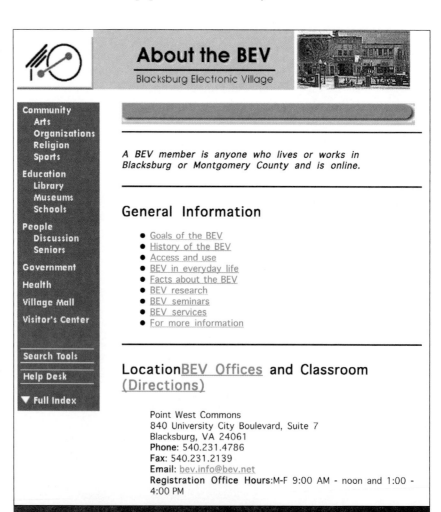

The home page of Blacksburg Electronic Village (www.bev.net), one of the world's first online communities.

returning from summer break. It lies in the Appalachian Mountain range. This rural community, at first glance no different from any other small town, has acquired an international reputation as an electronic village, one of the first of its kind. Foreigners visiting Washington, D.C., frequently seek out the town, which they expect will look something like Las Vegas. Andrew Cohill, a professor at Virginia Polytechnic Institute and State University, says he frequently hears from visitors eager to see the electronic village. He tells them there's nothing to see (Yaukey 1997).

Blacksburg Electronic Village (www.bev.net) is an online community that connects 85 percent of Blacksburg's residents and 75 percent of its businesses. The network began in 1987, when Virginia Tech invested $16 million in a high-speed voice and data network for use throughout the university. By the early 1990s university administrators were talking with Blacksburg officials and representatives of Bell Atlantic about providing affordable high-speed Internet access to everyone in town. In 1993 universal Internet access became a reality. The majority of residents have modems in their homes; schools, libraries, and the senior centre offer public access to those who don't. Citizens of Blacksburg can now communicate with city hall, schools, and businesses via e-mail. Soon they will be able to pay their bills, register their cars, and license their dogs online.

BEV has had a positive effect on the town, users agree. An enhanced sense of community is the most pervasive outcome. Seniors have greeted the new service enthusiastically: The senior centre houses 10 computers, and a special service tailored to the needs of elders has 180 subscribers. The strengthening of local bonds has surprised some, perhaps because it runs counter to the conventional wisdom that the Internet will unite people from around the world in a global online community. One retired physicist didn't think BEV would catch on, but was pleasantly surprised by the speed with which residents adopted it.

BEV has also brought some noticeable economic benefits to the town. Some residents, like the proprietor of Green Dreams, an online retailer of homemade vinegars, have seized the opportunity to become online

entrepreneurs. And a corporate research centre at the edge of town has been attracting more and more startup ventures, bringing new jobs and income to the college town. CEOs of the innovative new companies like the fresh air, low crime rate, and cutting-edge intellectual climate of Blacksburg. One, the head of Blue Ridge Interactive, an online purveyor of magazines, raves about the supportive atmosphere in the town (Clark 1999; Yaukey 1997; Zajac 1999).

The wider implications of the electronic village are only beginning to become clear. If the installation of universal high-speed access to the Internet can draw new companies away from more heavily populated areas like Northern Virginia, it may contribute to the decay of older urban areas, worsening the plight of inner-city residents. And BEV users are concerned about the fact that not all families in rural Montgomery County can afford to tap into the network, which requires an in-home computer and a small monthly connection fee. Roger Ehrich, a professor of computer science at Virginia Tech, believes the best way to level the playing field is to provide Internet access to children at school, wherever they live (Zajac 1999). Canada has been a leader in this area—on March 30, 1999, Canada became the first of the OECD countries to reach its goal of having every school in the country connected to the Internet.

Finally, the advent of the electronic community has the potential to revolutionize not just communities, but the way in which sociological research on communities is done. Automatic electronic monitoring of online response rates may someday replace telephone surveys and the distribution, collection, and coding of paper questionnaires. In the future, scholars may be able to visit far-flung electronic communities without leaving the comfort of their offices, and to travel safely through otherwise dangerous villages.

In the next and concluding section of this chapter, we will discuss a pressing social policy issue: the growing community of homeless people, both in Canada and abroad. What can be done to improve the lives of the homeless, who seem to have been bypassed by the Information Revolution that is benefiting so many others?

SOCIAL POLICY AND COMMUNITIES

Seeking Shelter Worldwide

The Issue

A chance meeting brought two old classmates together. In late 1997, Prince Charles encountered Clive Harold during a tour of the offices of a magazine sold by the

homeless in London. But while Prince Charles can call several palaces home, Harold is homeless. This modern-day version of the "The Prince and the Pauper" intrigued many people with its message that "it can happen to

In a story the press dubbed "The Prince and the Pauper," Prince Charles was surprised to run into an old classmate while visiting the office of a magazine sold by the homeless—and was even more surprised to learn that the fellow was himself homeless.

anyone." Harold had been a successful author and journalist until his marriage fell apart and alcohol turned his life inside out (*Chicago Tribune* 1997b).

The issue of inadequate shelter manifests itself in many ways, for all housing problems can be considered relative. For a middle-class family in Canada, it may mean a somewhat smaller house than they need because that is all they can afford. For a single working adult in Tokyo, it may mean having to commute two hours to a full-time job. For many people worldwide, however, the housing problem consists of merely finding shelter of any kind that they can afford, in a place where anyone would reasonably wish to live. Prince Charles of Buckingham Palace and Clive Harold, homeless person, are extreme examples of a continuum present in all communities in all societies. What can be done to ensure adequate shelter for those who can't afford it?

The Setting

Homelessness is evident in both industrialized and developing countries. One of the problems with determining the numbers of homeless people has to do with lack of consistent definitions of the problem. Just as we saw in Chapter 8 with definitions of poverty, there are degrees

of homelessness. "*Absolute homelessness* refers to people living on the streets with no physical shelter, while *relative homelessness* refers to those who live in spaces that do not meet basic health and safety standards" (Hargrave 1999:1). The substandard housing of the latter group includes poorly maintained, often overcrowded, vermin-infested makeshift accommodations that most of us would not consider "housing." Most people define homelessness in North America by its most limited and narrow sense: those using emergency shelters and those living in the street (Pohl 2001).

According to researchers such as those at the Centre for Applied Research at the University of Toronto, there have been only a handful of attempts to count Canada's homeless population. Estimates may range from 25 000 to more than 300 000 when we include relative homelessness in the count, but finding an accurate list is both difficult and expensive. Given the limited space in public shelters, at a minimum tens of thousands of people in Canada are homeless and without adequate shelter. Estimates in the United States in 1999 indicate that its homeless population is at least 700 000 and may be as high as 3 million (Kilborn 1999).

In Great Britain, some 175 000 people are accepted as homeless by the government and are given housing. An even larger number, perhaps 1 million people, are turned away from government assistance or are sharing a household with relatives or acquaintances but want separate accommodations. While an accurate figure is not available, it is estimated that 1 percent of Western Europeans are homeless; they sleep in the streets, depend on night shelters and hostels, or live in precarious accommodations (B. Lee 1992; Platt 1993; Stearn 1993).

In Japan, the problem of homelessness is just as serious. A single protest drew roughly 6000 homeless people to Tokyo in 1998. The Japanese usually hide such misfortune, thinking it shameful, but a severe economic downturn had victimized many formerly prosperous citizens, swelling the numbers of the homeless. A chronic space shortage in the heavily populated island nation, together with opposition to the establishment of homeless shelters in residential neighbourhoods, compounds the problem (Hara 2000).

In developing countries, rapid population growth has outpaced the expansion of housing by a wide margin, leading to a rise in homelessness. For example, estimates of homelessness in Mexico City range from 10 000 to 100 000, and these estimates do not include the many people living in caves or squatter settlements (see Box 19-1). By 1998, 600 million people around the world were either homeless or inadequately housed in urban areas alone (G. Goldstein 1998; Ross 1996).

Sociological Insights

Both in Canada and around the world, being homeless functions as a master status that largely defines a person's position within society. In this case, homelessness tends to mean that in many important respects, the individual is *outside* society. Without a home address and telephone, it is difficult to look for work or even apply for public assistance. Moreover, the master status of being homeless carries a serious stigma and can lead to prejudice and discrimination. Poor treatment of people suspected of being homeless is common in stores and restaurants, and many communities have reported acts of random violence against homeless people.

p. 118

There has been a significant change in the profile of homelessness during the last 20 years. In the past, homeless people were primarily older white males living as alcoholics in skid-row areas. However, best estimates suggest that today's homeless are comparatively younger. Studies done in the 1950s revealed that the average age of the homeless was near 50, while today the homeless are more often in their early thirties. As with counting the overall number of homeless Canadians, calculating their age in any precise way is extremely difficult. Along with the prominence of younger males among those without housing, there are also many more homeless women and families today—reports from shelters, advocacy groups, and governments show that around 30 percent of those using emergency shelters are women and more than 10 percent are children (Pohl 2001; Hargrave 1999).

The diversity of the homeless also extends to race and ethnicity. First Nations people, refugees and ethnic minorities are overrepresented among the homeless. The literature indicates quite clearly that First Nations people are more at risk of falling victim to homelessness than other groups. Studies indicate that the problem among First Nations people is "endemic" both on and off reserves, and in both rural and urban settings. At particular risk are young Aboriginal women in Western Canada, who outnumber males on the street in our large Prairie cities (Hargrave 1999).

Changing economic and residential patterns account for much of this increase in homelessness. As discussed earlier, in recent decades, the process of urban renewal has included a noticeable boom in *gentrification*. In some instances, city governments have promoted gentrification by granting lucrative tax breaks to developers who convert low-cost rental units into luxury apartments and condominiums. Conflict theorists note that although the affluent may derive both financial and emotional benefits from gentrification and redevelopment, the poor often end up being thrown out on the street. Between the early 1970s and mid-1990s, the process of gentrification resulted in a net loss of 250 000 affordable housing units in Canada's four major cities (Pohl 2001).

There is an undeniable connection between the nation's growing shortage of affordable housing and the rise in homelessness (Elliot and Krivo 1991). Yet sociologist Peter Rossi (1989, 1990) cautions against focusing too narrowly on housing shortage while ignoring structural factors, such as the decline in the demand for manual labour in cities and the increasing prevalence of chronically unemployed young men among the homeless. Rossi contends that structural changes have put everyone in extreme poverty at higher risk of becoming homeless—especially poor people with an accumulation of disabilities (such as drug abuse, bad health, unemployment, and criminal records). Being disabled in this manner forces the individual to rely on family and friends for support, often for a prolonged period. If the strain on this support network is so great that it collapses, homelessness may result. While many researchers accept Rossi's theory, the general public often prefers to "blame the victim" for becoming homeless (B. Lee 1992).

The stereotype that overlooks the impact of homelessness on Aboriginals also fails to recognize the degree to which women in Canada are affected by this condition. One of the difficulties faced by service providers seeking to assist this population is their relative invisibility. Research done in both Canada and the United States indicates that women's homelessness is often disguised in an attempt to limit others' perceptions of their vulnerability. Women on the street are, for obvious reasons, more susceptible to violence. Another significant factor contributing to this phenomenon is the fact that

In Japan in 1998, as many as 6000 homeless people marched on the Tokyo Metropolitan Office to protest the lack of shelter facilities. This biting cartoon from the *Japan Times* acknowledges their plight.

homeless females are often involved in prostitution. This finding correlates with information that identifies these women as generally younger than their male counterparts. Finally, homeless women have a profile that distinguishes them in many ways from men. Proportionately, they are more likely to be dealing with a mental illness, less likely to be alcoholics, more likely to have dependent children, and more likely to have maintained some social network. Anthropologist Elliot Liebow conducted a five-year, participant-observation study of single homeless women living in emergency shelters. Liebow (1995:112) concludes that

> Homeless women are mainly from working-class and lower-class families that can no longer support them or from families whose members can no longer live together as husband and wife or parent and child. The weakest one (wife, mother, daughter) gets pushed out.

Sociologists attribute homelessness in developing nations not only to income inequality but also to population growth and an influx of people from rural areas and areas experiencing natural disaster, famine, or warfare. A major barrier to constructing decent, legal, and affordable housing in the urban areas of these developing nations is the political power of large-scale landowners and small-scale land speculators—anyone buying a few lots as investment. In the view of conflict theorists, these groups conspire to enhance their own financial investment by making the supply of legally buildable land scarce. (This problem is not unknown in the cities of

North America, but a World Bank survey shows that the increase in the cost of land is twice as great in developing nations as in industrial countries.) In many cases, residents who can afford building materials have no choice but to become squatters. Those who can't are likely to become homeless.

Policy Initiatives

Thus far, policymakers have often been content to steer the homeless toward large, overcrowded, unhealthful shelters. Many neighbourhoods and communities have resisted plans to open large shelters or even smaller residences for the homeless, often raising the familiar cry of "Not in my backyard!" (or "NIMBY", as is often heard).

The federal government used to finance and build nonprofit and cooperative housing to the point where it represented 6 percent of Canada's housing stock. Then, in the name of budget constraints, it cancelled funding for all new developments in 1994. At that point, it turned over responsibility for public housing to individual provinces, which also cut back on the number of new low-income units built each year, looking instead to municipalities for solutions (Hargrave 1999). In 1998, in an attempt to pressure the federal government to take a more active role, the mayors of the 10 largest cities in Canada passed a resolution declaring homelessness "a national disaster" (Pohl 2001).

During the summer of 1999, the federal government's representatives visited 15 communities in Canada and consulted with agencies and organizations that provide services for homeless people and those at risk. This led to the launch of the *National Homelessness Initiative (NHI)*, a program that provides $753 million in funding over three years "to ensure community access to programs, services, and support for reducing and alleviating homelessness in urban and rural regions across all the provinces and territories" (HRDC 2002). The intention was to work through partnerships with local governments in the 10 Canadian cities that represent 80 percent of the documented "significant absolute homeless problem." The funding was intended to develop affordable stable housing as alternatives to the streets and emergency shelters. The main goals of the NHI were:

1. To ensure that no one is forced to live on the street
2. To reduce the numbers of Canadians dependent on shelters, transition, and supportive housing, and
3. To help the homeless achieve self-sufficiency.

Recently we are seeing a hardening of attitudes toward the homeless. Some elected officials openly refer to them as "pests," "intimidators," or "thugs." A number of cities have passed by-laws restricting public begging or automobile windshield washing by "squeegee kids" (Pohl 2001). A survey called Canadians' Attitudes Toward Homelessness, conducted by the Canada Mortgage and Housing Corporation in 2000, shows some recognition that the problem is not going away. It tells us that most Canadians believe the number of people living without stable accommodation to be increasing, with a recognition that there are more homeless women and families. We also understand that make-do responses such as temporary shelters and food banks are not capable of dealing with the challenges facing this population—what is needed is affordable housing and more of it (CMHC 2000).

Despite occasional media spotlights on the homeless and the booming economy of the 1990s, affordable housing has become harder to find. Two out of three low-income renters receive no housing allowance, and most spend a disproportionately large share of their income to maintain their shelter. Research shows that this worsening of the affordable housing situation stems from a substantial drop in the number of unsubsidized low-cost rental housing units in the private market and a growing number of low-income renter households. (Daskal 1998).

Developing nations have special problems. They have understandably given highest priority to economic productivity as measured by jobs with living wages. Unfortunately, even the most ambitious economic and social programs may be overwhelmed by minor currency fluctuations, a drop in the value of a nation's major export, or an influx of refugees from a neighbouring country. Some of the reforms implemented have included promoting private (as opposed to government-controlled) housing markets, allowing dwellings to be places of business as well, and loosening restrictions on building materials.

All three of these short-term solutions have shortcomings. Private housing markets invite exploitation; mixed residential/commercial use may only cause good housing to deteriorate faster; and the use of marginal building materials leaves low-income residential areas more vulnerable to calamities such as floods, fires, and earthquakes. Large-scale rental housing under government supervision, the typical solution in North America and Europe, has been successful only in economically advanced city-states like Hong Kong and Singapore (Strassman 1998).

In sum, homeless people both in Canada and abroad are not getting the shelter they need, and they lack the political clout to corral the attention of policymakers.

Let's Discuss

1. Have you ever worked as a volunteer in a shelter or soup kitchen? If so, were you surprised by the types of people who lived or ate there? Has anyone you know ever had to move into a shelter?
2. Is gentrification of low-income housing a problem where you live? Have you ever had difficulty finding an affordable place to live?
3. What kind of assistance is available to homeless people in the community where you live? Does the help come from the government, from private charities, or both? What about housing assistance—such as rent subsidies—for people with low incomes; is assistance available?

Chapter Resources

Summary

A *community* is a spatial or political unit of social organization that gives people a sense of belonging, based either on shared residence in a particular place or on a common identity. This chapter explains how communities originated and analyzes the process of urbanization from both the functionalist and conflict perspectives. It describes various types of communities, including the central cities, the suburbs, and rural communities, and it introduces the new concept of an electronic community. The chapter closes with an analysis of public policy toward the community of the homeless.

1. Stable communities began to develop when people stayed in one place to cultivate crops; surplus production enabled cities to emerge.
2. Gideon Sjoberg identified three preconditions of city life: advanced technology in both agricultural and nonagricultural areas, a favourable physical environment, and a well-developed social organization.
3. There are important differences between the *preindustrial city*, the *industrial city*, and the *postindustrial city.*
4. Urbanization is evident not only in Canada but throughout the world; by 2000, 45 percent of the world's population lived in urban areas.
5. The *urban ecological* approach is functionalist because it emphasizes that different elements in urban areas contribute to stability.
6. Drawing on conflict theory, *new urban sociology* considers the interplay of a community's political and economic interests as well as the impact of the global economy on communities in Canada and other countries.
7. Many urban residents are immigrants from other nations and tend to live in ethnic neighbourhoods.
8. In the last three decades, cities have confronted an overwhelming array of economic and social problems, including crime, unemployment, and the deterioration of schools and public transit systems.
9. Suburbanization was the most dramatic population trend in Canada throughout the twentieth century. In recent decades, suburbs have witnessed increasing diversity in race and ethnicity.
10. Farming, mining, and logging have all been in decline in the rural communities of Canada.
11. Technological advances like electronic information networks are changing the economy, the distribution of population, and even the concept of community. Online communities can both strengthen social ties in rural cities like Blacksburg, Virginia, and undermine the economies of the central cities.
12. Soaring housing costs, unemployment, cutbacks in public assistance, and rapid population growth have all contributed to rising homelessness around the world. Most social policy is directed toward sending the homeless to large shelters.

Critical Thinking Questions

1. How can the functionalist and conflict perspectives be used in examining the growing interest among policymakers in privatizing public services presently offered by cities and other communities?
2. How has your home community (your city, town, or neighbourhood) changed over the years you have lived there? Have there been significant changes in the community's economic base and in its racial and ethnic profile? Have the community's social problems intensified or lessened over time? Is unemployment currently a major problem? What are the community's future prospects in the twenty-first century?
3. Imagine that you have been asked to study the issue of homelessness in the largest city in your province. How might you draw on surveys, observation research, experiments, and existing sources to help you study this issue?

Key Terms

Community A spatial or political unit of social organization that gives people a sense of belonging, based either on shared residence in a particular place or on a common identity. (517)

Concentric-zone theory A theory of urban growth devised by Ernest Burgess that sees growth in terms of a series of rings radiating from the central business district. (523)

Defended neighbourhood A neighbourhood that residents identify through defined community borders and a perception that adjacent areas are geographically separate and socially different. (527)

Gentrification The resettlement of low-income city neighbourhoods by prosperous families and business firms. (528)

Human ecology An area of study concerned with the interrelationships between people and their spatial setting and physical environment. (522)

Industrial city A city characterized by relatively large size, open competition, an open class system, and elaborate specialization in the manufacturing of goods. (519)

Megalopolis A densely populated area containing two or more cities and their surrounding suburbs. (520)

Metropolitan Influence Zones (MIZs) Areas outside of large metropolitan population centres, but still influenced by them. (526)

Multiple-nuclei theory A theory of urban growth developed by Harris and Ullman that views growth as emerging from many centres of development, each of which may reflect a particular urban need or activity. (523)

New urban sociology An approach to urbanization that considers the interplay of local, national, and worldwide forces and their effect on local space, with special emphasis on the impact of global economic activity. (524)

Postindustrial city A city in which global finance and the electronic flow of information dominate the economy. (519)

Preindustrial city A city with only a few thousand people living within its borders and characterized by a relatively closed class system and limited mobility. (518)

Squatter settlements Areas occupied by the very poor on the fringes of cities, in which housing is often constructed by the settlers themselves from discarded material. (522)

Urban ecology An area of study that focuses on the interrelationships between people and their environment in urban areas. (522)

Urbanism A term used by Wirth to describe distinctive patterns of social behaviour evident among city residents. (519)

World systems analysis A view of the global economic system that sees it as divided between certain industrialized nations and the developing countries that they control and exploit. (524)

Zoning laws Legal provisions stipulating land use and architectural design of housing, often employed as a means of keeping racial minorities and low-income people out of suburban areas. (532)

Additional Readings

BOOKS

Duany, Andres, Elizabeth Plater-Zybert, and Jeff Speck. 2000. *Suburban Nation: The Rise of Sprawl and the Decline of the American Dream.* New York: North Point Press. A critical look at most post-Second World War suburban development, both residential and commercial.

Dunier, Mitchell. 1999. *Sidewalk.* New York: Farrar, Straus and Giroux. Joined by photographer Ovie Carter, a sociologist looks at street life in New York's Greenwich Village, with a special focus on the experiences of sidewalk vendors.

Mitchell, William J. 1999. *E-topia.* Cambridge: MIT Press. A futuristic view of what the world's cities might look like in an age of cybernetics. Written by a dean of architecture, the book predicts a variety of cityscapes based on different cultural traditions, all unified by a global digital network. Visit the author's website (**http://mitpress.mit.edu/e-books/City_of_Bits/**) for his companion book *City of Bits* (Cambridge: MIT Press, 1996).

Murphy, Barbara. 2000. *On the Street: How We Created the Homeless.* Winnipeg: J. Gordon Shillingford Publ. In Canada there are more people living below the poverty line than ever before. The author outlines the reasons, starting with the middle class reclaiming the housing market in the inner cities, and examining the problem of mentally ill Canadians moving to local communities that do not have resources or special housing to accommodate them.

Phillips, E. Barbara. 1996. *City Lights: Urban–Suburban Life in the Global Society.* New York: Oxford University Press. Drawing upon all the social sciences, a sociologist looks at the urban–global network of the twentieth century and at alternative urban–suburban futures.

JOURNALS

Among the journals that focus on community issues are *Community Development Journal* (founded in 1966), *Journal of Developing Societies* (1985), *Journal of Urban Affairs* (1979), *Rural Sociology* (1936), *Urban Affairs Quarterly* (1965), and *Urban Studies* (1964).

Internet Connection

www.mcgrawhill.ca/college/schaefer

For additional Internet exercises relating to communities and urbanization, visit the Schaefer Online Learning Centre at **http://www.mcgrawhill.ca/college/schaefer**. *Please note that while the URLs listed were current at the time of printing, these sites often change—check the Online Learning Centre for updates.*

Have you ever wondered what causes homelessness—what social forces and life circumstances separate those who have shelter from those who don't? Hobson's Choice (**http://www.realchange news.org/ hobsons/index.html**) is an online game that helps people understand this complex issue better. At the start of the game, players find themselves in a particular economic situation and are asked to make choices, each of which leads to a new situation or problem. Log on to the site and play the game four times.

(a) In how many games were you able to escape homelessness? In how many did you find yourself on the street, without shelter?

(b) Reflect on the choices you made. Was there a pattern to them? Which situations seemed to lead toward homelessness and which away from it?

(c) Did you feel frustrated by the results of any of your choices? What choices would you have made differently, and why?

(d) What is a Hobson's choice, and why it is applicable to the issue of homelessness?

(e) What do you think are the most important social causes of homelessness? What can be done, in practical terms, to alleviate the worldwide need for shelter?

CHAPTER
20

POPULATION, THE ENVIRONMENT, AND TECHNOLOGY

In India, pollution is becoming a controversial political issue. This billboard graphically suggests the harmful effect of pollution on public health.

COLLECTIVE BEHAVIOUR, SOCIAL MOVEMENTS, AND SOCIAL CHANGE

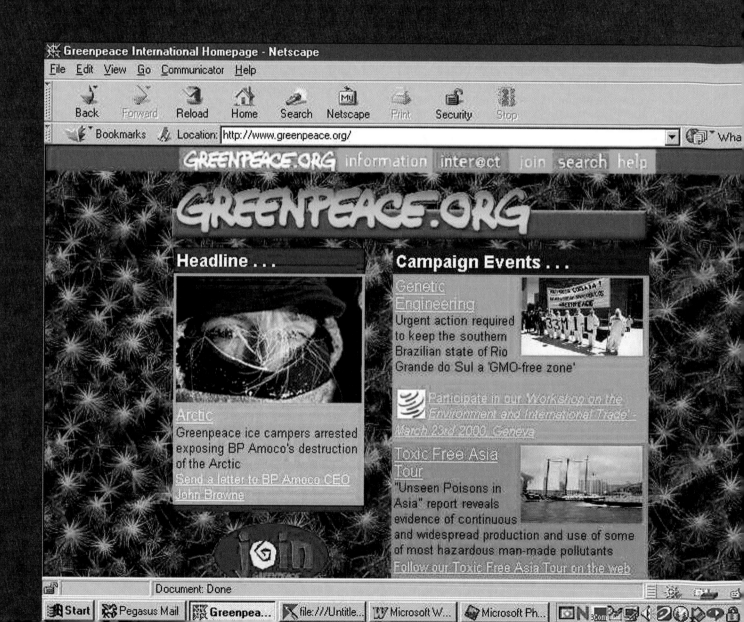

Social activism today has gone beyond pamphlets, buttons, bumper stickers, and public service ads. Now the World Wide Web offers a new opportunity to post concerns about any social issue anywhere in the world.

If somebody at Bowling Green State University of Ohio had talked to somebody at the University of San Diego in California in October of 1998, both schools could have avoided a lot of unnecessary panic. Based on the stories sweeping their respective campuses at the time, a conversation between our imaginary students might have gone something like this:

Bowling Green Student: You're never going to believe what's happening here! People are freaking out.

San Diego Student: You think you're freaking out there, you should see what's going on here! . . . There's this psychic guy—he's supposed to be the most famous psychic in the world, he predicted the Oklahoma City bombing—and he went on Oprah Winfrey's show and predicted there was going to be a mass murder on Halloween at an H-shaped residence hall, and guess what, *we* have an H-shaped residence hall at USD. . . .

(There's a long pause.)

SD: What's the matter?

BG: I don't know what you're talking about, because the psychic who was on *Oprah* didn't say anything about an H-shaped building. He said the massacre was going to take place at a state college in the Midwest and he even mentioned Bowling Green as one of the possibilities, and that's why people are freaking out here!

SD: I don't get it. Did you see the show when the guy was on?

BG: Um, no. Did you?

SD: No, I didn't see it either. What's going on here?

The reason neither of our mythological students saw the psychic's appearance is that there has never been such a segment of *Oprah*. . . .

Nevertheless, the feelings of fear on the campuses of the University of San Diego and Bowling Green State University in the fall of 1998 were very palpable. A story published on Oct. 31 in the *San Diego Union–Tribune* said that "most residents [of the H-shaped hall] were looking for somewhere else to spend the weekend" due to the spreading of a "classic urban legend." . . .

Meanwhile, similar rumors circulated through the University of Michigan, Kent State University, the University of Iowa, and the University of Illinois. Patient spokespeople for Oprah's show explained again that nothing even remotely resembling such an incident had ever happened. . . .

Students at San Diego, Bowling Green, et al., soon realized the scare was borne of pure fiction, but that certainly won't stop the class of '00 or later from going through the whole thing again. The psychic-on-the-talk-show story has been around for years. *(Roeper 1999:91–94)* ■

ractically everyone has a tale to tell of an out-landish rumour or prank that they read about or saw on TV or learned of in an e-mail. Richard Roeper, a journalist, has collected many such stories in his book *Urban Legends.* Rumours (such as "the psychic on the talk show") and public opinion (for example, the reaction in the press and on the college campuses) are two forms of collective behaviour. Practically all behaviour can be thought of as collective behaviour, but sociologists have given distinct meaning to the term. Neil Smelser (1981:431), a sociologist who specializes in this field of study, has defined **collective behaviour** as the "relatively spontaneous and unstructured behaviour of a group of people who are reacting to a common influence in an ambiguous situation."

This chapter begins with an examination of a number of theories used by sociologists to better understand collective behaviour, including the emergent-norm, value-added, and assembling perspectives. Particular attention is given to certain types of collective behaviour, among them crowd behaviour, disaster behaviour, fads and fashions, panics and crazes, rumours, and public opinion. Sociologists study collective behaviour because it incorporates activities in which we all engage on a regular basis.

Moreover, contemporary sociology acknowledges the crucial role that social movements can play in mobilizing discontented members of a society and initiating social change.

Social change has been defined as significant alteration over time in behaviour patterns and culture (Moore 1967). But what constitutes a "significant" alteration? Certainly the dramatic rise in formal education documented in Chapter 15 represents a change that has had profound social consequences. Other social changes that have had long-term and important consequences include the Industrial Revolution (Chapters 5 and 19), the increased participation of women in the paid labour forces of Canada, the United States, and Europe (Chapter 11), and the worldwide population explosion (Chapter 20).

Efforts to explain long-term social changes have led to the development of theories of change, four of which will be considered: the evolutionary, functionalist, conflict, and feminist approaches to change. We will see how vested interests can block changes that they see as threatening. Collective behaviour and social movements have played an important role in promoting social change, and how they have been assisted by communication technology is explored. Finally, in the social policy section, we focus on the role that the social movement for lesbian and gay rights plays in promoting change in Canada and worldwide. ■

Theories of Collective Behaviour

In 1989, when thousands of soccer fans forced their way into a stadium to see the semifinals of the English Cup, more than 90 people were trampled to death or smothered. In 1991, three young people died of suffocation *inside* an arena in Salt Lake City as a crowd surged forward to get the best vantage point to hear the heavy metal group AC/DC (J. Gross 1991; D. L. Miller 2000; see also R. Pogrebin 1996).

Collective behaviour is usually unstructured and spontaneous. This fluidity makes it more difficult for sociologists to generalize about people's behaviour in such situations. Nevertheless, sociologists have developed various theoretical perspectives that can help us to study—and deal with in a constructive manner—crowds, riots, fads, and other types of collective behaviour.

Emergent-Norm Perspective

The early writings on collective behaviour imply that crowds are basically ungovernable. However, this is not always the case. In many situations, crowds are effectively governed by norms and procedures, including queuing, or waiting in line. We routinely encounter queues when we await service, as in a fast-food restaurant or bank, or when we wish to enter or exit, as in a movie theatre or hockey arena. Normally, physical barriers, such as guardrails and checkout counters, help to regulate queuing. When massive crowds are involved, ushers or security personnel may also be present to assist in the orderly movement of the crowd. Nevertheless, there are times when such measures prove inadequate, as the examples above and the one below demonstrate.

On December 28, 1991, people began gathering outside the City College gymnasium in New York City to see a heavily promoted charity basketball game featuring rap stars and other celebrities. By late afternoon, more than 5000 people had gathered for the 6:00 P.M. game, even though the gym could accommodate only 2730 spectators. Although the crowd was divided into separate lines for ticket holders and those wishing to buy tickets at the door, restlessness and discontent swept through both lines and sporadic fights broke out. The arrival of

Collective behaviour can sometimes have fatal results. Nine young men and women died and 29 were injured in 1991 when a crowd surged through this stairwell to gain entrance to a celebrity-studded charity basketball game at City College in New York.

celebrities only added to the commotion and the crowd's tension.

Doors to the gymnasium were finally opened one hour before game time, but only 50 people were admitted to the lobby at a time. Once their tickets had been taken, spectators proceeded down two flights of stairs, through a single unlocked entrance, and into the gym. Those further back in the crowd experienced the disconcerting feeling of moving forward, then stopping for a period of time, then repeating this process again and again. Well past the publicized starting time, huge crowds were still outside, pressing to gain entrance to the building.

Finally, with the arena more than full, the doors to the gym were closed, As rumours spread outside the building that the game was beginning, more than 1000 frustrated fans, many with valid tickets, poured through the glass doors into the building and headed for the stairs. Soon the stairwell became a horrifying mass of people surging against locked metal doors to the gym and crushed against concrete walls. The result was a tragedy: 9 young men and women eventually died, and 29 were injured through the sheer pressure of bodies against one another and against walls and doors (Mollen 1992).

Sociologists Ralph Turner and Lewis Killian (1987) have offered a view of collective behaviour that is helpful in assessing a tragic event like this one. It begins with the assumption that a large crowd, such as a group of rock or soccer fans, is governed by expectations of proper behaviour just as much as four people playing doubles tennis.

But during the episode of collective behaviour a definition of what behaviour is appropriate or not emerges from the crowd. Turner and Killian call p. 581 this the ***emergent-norm perspective***. Like other social norms, the emergent norm reflects shared convictions held by members of the group and is enforced through sanctions. These new norms of proper behaviour may arise in what seem at first to be ambiguous situations. There is latitude for a wide range of acts, yet within a general framework established by the emergent norms (for a critique of this perspective, see McPhail 1991).

Using the emergent-norm perspective, we can see that fans outside the charity basketball game found themselves in an ambiguous situation. Normal procedures of crowd control, such as orderly queues, were rapidly dissolving. A new norm was simultaneously emerging: It is acceptable to push forward, even if people in front protest. Some members of the crowd—especially those with valid tickets—may have felt that this push forward was justified as a way of ensuring that they would get to see the game. Others pushed forward simply to relieve the physical pressure of those pushing behind them. Even individuals who rejected the emergent norm may have felt afraid to oppose it, fearing ridicule or injury. Thus, conforming behaviour, which we usually associate with highly structured situations, was evident in p. 182 this rather chaotic crowd, just as it had been at the soccer game in England. It would be misleading to assume that these fans acted simply as a united, collective unit in creating a dangerous situation.

Value-Added Perspective

Neil Smelser (1962) proposed still another sociological explanation for collective behaviour. He used the ***value-added model*** to explain how broad social conditions are transformed in a definite pattern into some form of collective behaviour. This model outlines six important determinants of collective behaviour: structural conduciveness, structural strain, generalized belief, a precipitating factor, mobilization for action, and the exercise of social control.

Initially, in Smelser's view, certain elements must be present for an incident of collective behaviour to take place. He uses the term *structural conduciveness* to indicate that the organization of society can facilitate the emergence of conflicting interests. Structural conduciveness was evident in the former East Germany in 1989, just a year before the collapse of the ruling communist party and the reunification of Germany. The government was extremely unpopular, and there was growing freedom to publicly express and be exposed to new and challenging viewpoints. Such structural conduciveness makes collective behaviour possible, though not inevitable.

The second determinant of collective behaviour, *structural strain,* occurs when the conduciveness of the social structure to potential conflict gives way to a perception that conflicting interests do, in fact, exist. The intense desire of many East Germans to travel to or immigrate to Western European countries placed great strain on the social control exercised by the communist party. Such structural strain contributes to what Smelser calls a *generalized belief*—a shared view of reality that redefines social action and serves to guide behaviour. The overthrow of communist rule in East Germany and other Soviet-bloc nations occurred in part as a result of a generalized belief that the communist regimes were oppressive and that popular resistance *could* lead to social change.

Smelser suggests that a specific event or incident, known as a *precipitating factor,* triggers collective behaviour. The event may grow out of the social structure, but whatever its origins, it contributes to the strains and beliefs shared by a group or community. For example, studies of race riots have found that interracial fights or arrests and searches of minority individuals by police officers often precede disturbances. The 1992 riots in South Central Los Angeles, which claimed 58 lives, were sparked by the acquittal of four white police officers charged after the videotaped beating of Rodney King, a black construction worker.

According to Smelser, the four determinants identified above are necessary for collective behaviour to occur. However, in addition to these factors, the group must be *mobilized for action.* An extended thundershower or severe snowstorm may preclude such a mobilization. People are also more likely to come together on weekends than on weekdays, in the evening rather than during the daytime.

The manner in which *social control is exercised*—both formally and informally—can be significant in determining whether the preceding factors will end in collective behaviour. Stated simply, social control may prevent, delay, or interrupt a collective outburst. In some instances, those using social control may be guilty of misjudgments that intensify the severity of an outbreak. Many observers, for example, believe that the use of pepper spray by the RCMP at the Vancouver APEC summit

in 1997 contributed to the violence by demonstrators at subsequent meetings of global leaders in Quebec City, Ottawa, Genoa, and Halifax.

Sociologists have questioned the validity of both the emergent-norm and value-added perspectives because of their imprecise definitions and the difficulty of testing them empirically. For example, they have criticized the emergent-norm perspective for being too vague in defining what constitutes a norm and have challenged the value-added model for its lack of specificity in defining generalized belief and structural strain. Of these two theories, the emergent-norm perspective appears to offer a more useful explanation of societywide episodes of collective behaviour, such as crazes and fashions, than the value-added approach (M. Brown and Goldin 1973; Quarantelli and Hundley 1975; K. Tierney 1980).

Smelser's value-added model, however, represents an advance over earlier theories that treated crowd behaviour as dominated by irrational, extreme impulses. The value-added approach firmly relates episodes of collective behaviour to the overall social structure of a society (for a critique, see McPhail 1994).

Assembling Perspective

Sociologists have studied the phenomenon of sports riots that spill into the streets of major cities. Sometimes it takes the form of a protest riot, such as the rampage that took place in Moscow following a loss to Japan in the World Cup in 2002, where two people died and many others were injured. Other times, fans end up rioting as part of an exuberant victory celebration; this happened when the Montreal Canadiens won the Stanley Cup in 1993, or when the Chicago Bulls basketball team won numerous championships in the 1990s. One particular study involved football fans in Austin, Texas (Snow et al. 1981). Some participants actively tried to recruit passersby for the celebrations by thrusting out open palms "to get five" or by yelling at drivers to honk their horns. In fact, encouraging still further assembling became a preoccupation of the celebrators. Whenever spectators were absent, those celebrating were relatively quiet. As we have seen, a key determinant of collective behaviour is mobilization for action. How do people come together to undertake collective action?

Clark McPhail, perhaps the most prolific researcher of collective behaviour in the last three decades, sees people and organizations consciously responding to one another's actions. Building on the interactionist approach, McPhail and Miller (1973) introduced the concept of the assembling process. The *assembling perspective* sought for the first time to examine how and why people move from different points in space to a common location.

Marche mondiale des femmes

2000

World March of Women

Marcha mundial de las mujeres

The World March of Women in the Year 2000, initiated by Fédération des femmes du Québec (http://ffq.qc.ca/marche2000), took place on or around October 17, 2000 in hundreds of countries around the world. It was aimed at bringing about concrete change in the struggles with poverty and violence faced by women around the world.

A basic distinction has been made between two types of assemblies. *Periodic assemblies* include recurring, relatively routine gatherings of people such as work groups, university classes, and season ticket holders of an athletic series. These assemblies are characterized by advance scheduling and recurring attendance of the majority of participants. For example, members of an introductory sociology class may gather together for lectures every Monday, Wednesday, and Friday morning at 10 A.M. By contrast, **nonperiodic assemblies** include demonstrations, parades, and gatherings at the scene of fires, accidents, and arrests. Such assemblies result from casually transmitted information and are generally less formal than periodic assemblies.

These three approaches to collective behaviour give us deeper insight into relatively spontaneous and unstructured situations. Although episodes of collective behaviour may seem irrational to outsiders, norms emerge among the participants and organized efforts are made to assemble at a certain time and place.

Forms of Collective Behaviour

Do you remember Cabbage Patch kids? Did you collect Beanie Babies or *Star Wars* toys when you were young? Any bell-bottom pants lurking in your closets? These are all fads and fashions that depend on collective behaviour. Using the emergent-norm, value-added, and assembling perspectives along with other aspects of sociological examination, sociologists have looked at many forms of collective behaviour—not only fads and fashions but also crowds, disaster behaviour, panics and crazes, rumours, public opinion, and social movements.

Crowds

Crowds are temporary groupings of people in close proximity who share a common focus or interest. Spectators at a baseball game, participants at a pep rally, and rioters are all examples of crowds. Sociologists have been interested in what characteristics are common to crowds. Of course, it can be difficult to generalize, since the nature of crowds varies dramatically. Think about how hostages on a hijacked airplane might feel as opposed to participants in a religious revival.

Like other forms of collective behaviour, crowds are not totally lacking in structure. Even during riots, participants are governed by identifiable social norms and exhibit definite patterns of behaviour. Sociologists Richard Berk and Howard Aldrich (1972) analyzed patterns of vandalism in 15 cities in the United States during the race riots of the 1960s. They found that stores of merchants perceived as exploitative were likely to be attacked, while private homes and public agencies with positive reputations were more likely to be spared. Apparently, looters had reached a collective agreement as to what constituted a "proper" or "improper" target for destruction.

The emergent-norm perspective suggests that during urban rioting a new social norm is accepted (at least temporarily) that basically condones looting. The norms of respect for private property—as well as norms involving obedience to the law—are replaced by a concept of all goods as community property. All desirable items, including those behind locked doors, can be used for the "general welfare." In effect, the emergent norm allows looters to take what they regard as properly theirs (Quarantelli and Dynes 1970; see also McPhail 1991).

Disaster Behaviour

Newspapers, television reports, and even rumours bring us word of many disasters around the world. The term *disaster* refers to a sudden or disruptive event or set of events that overtaxes a community's resources so that outside aid is necessary. Traditionally, disasters have been catastrophes related to nature, such as earthquakes, floods, and fires. Yet, in an industrial age, natural disasters have now been joined by such "technological disasters" as airplane crashes, industrial explosions, nuclear meltdowns, and massive chemical poisonings.

Sociologists have made enormous strides in disaster research, despite the problems inherent in this type of investigation. The work of the Disaster Research Center at the University of Delaware has been especially important. The centre has teams of trained researchers prepared to leave for the site of any disaster on four hours' notice. Their field kits include identification material, recording equipment, and general interview guidelines for use in various types of disasters. En route to the scene, these researchers try to get informed about the conditions they may encounter. Upon arrival, the team establishes a communication post to coordinate fieldwork and maintain contact with the centre's headquarters.

Since its founding, the Disaster Research Center has conducted more than 600 field studies of natural and technological disasters in a number of nations. Its research has been used to develop effective planning in such areas as delivery of emergency health care, establishment and operation of rumour-control centres, coordination of mental health services after disasters, and implementation of disaster-preparedness and emergency-response programs. The centre has provided training and field research for graduate students. These students maintain a professional commitment to disaster research and often go on to work for disaster service organizations such as the Red Cross and civil defence agencies (Disaster Research Center 2000; D. L. Miller 2000; Quarantelli 1992).

Remarkably, in the wake of many natural and technological disasters, there is increased structure and organization rather than chaos. Disasters are often followed by the creation of an emergency "operations group" that coordinates public services and even certain services normally carried out by the private sector. This was very evident in the aftermath of September 11, 2001, when services such as temporary food distribution centres were set up to feed the thousands of search volunteers, and information centres were established to collect photos and medical documents from families who were looking for missing members as well as to provide updates to them. In instances such as these, decision making often becomes more centralized than in normal times, with few objections (Dynes 1978).

Fads and Fashions

An almost endless list of objects and behaviour patterns seems temporarily to catch the fancy of adults and children. Think about silly putty, hula hoops, the Rubik's cube, break dancing, *The Simpsons* T-shirts, Nintendo games, and mosh pits. Fads and fashions are sudden movements toward the acceptance of some lifestyle or particular taste in clothing, music, or recreation (Aguirre et al. 1988; R. Johnson 1985).

Fads are temporary patterns of behaviour involving large numbers of people; they spring up independently of preceding trends and do not give rise to successors. By contrast, *fashions* are pleasurable mass involvements that feature a certain amount of acceptance by society and have a line of historical continuity (Lofland 1981, 1985). Thus, punk haircuts would be considered a fashion, part of the constantly changing standards of hair length and style, whereas doing the Macarena would be considered a fad of the mid-1990s.

Typically, when people think of *fashions*, they think of clothing, particularly women's clothing. In reality, fads and fashions enter every aspect of life where choices are not dictated by sheer necessity—vehicles, sports, music, drama, beverages, art, and even selection of pets. Any area of our lives that is subject to continuing change is open to fads and fashions. There is a clear commercial motive behind these norms of collective behaviour. For example, in about seven months of 1955, over U.S.$100 million of Davy Crockett items were sold (think what that would be worth in today's dollars!), including coonskin caps, toy rifles, knives, camping gear, cameras, and jigsaw puzzles. This was dwarfed by the well over U.S.$5 billion Nintendo took in from the 1999 Pokémon fad, ranging from virtual pets to compact discs (Javna 1986; King 1999).

Fads and fashions allow people to identify with something different from the dominant institutions and symbols of a culture. Members of a subculture can break with tradition while remaining "in" with a significant reference group of peers. Fads are generally short-lived and tend to be viewed with amusement or lack of interest by most nonparticipants. Fashions, by contrast, often have wider implications because they can reflect (or give the impression of) wealth and status.

Panics and Crazes

Panics and crazes both represent responses to some generalized belief. A *craze* is an exciting mass involvement that lasts for a relatively long period of time (Lofland 1981, 1985). For example, in late 1973, a press release from a United States congressman described how the federal bureaucracy had failed to contract for enough toilet paper for government buildings. Then, on December 19,

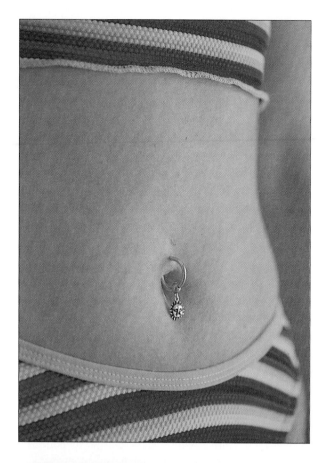

as part of his nightly monologue, then *Tonight Show* host Johnny Carson suggested that it would not be strange if the entire nation experienced a shortage of toilet paper. Millions of people took his humorous comment seriously and immediately began stockpiling this item out of fear that it would soon be unavailable. Shortly thereafter, as a consequence of this craze, a shortage of toilet paper actually resulted. Its effects were felt into 1974 (Malcolm 1974; *Money* 1987).

By contrast, a **panic** is a fearful arousal or collective flight based on a generalized belief that may or may not be accurate. In a panic, people commonly think there is insufficient time or inadequate means to avoid injury. Panics often occur on battlefields, in overcrowded burning buildings, or during stock market crashes. The key distinction between panics and crazes is that panics are flights *from* something whereas crazes are movements *to* something.

One of the most famous cases of panic was touched off by a media event: the 1938 Halloween eve radio dramatization of H.G. Wells's science fiction novel *The War of the Worlds.* This CBS broadcast realistically told of an invasion from Mars, with interplanetary visitors landing in Northern New Jersey and taking over New York City 15 minutes later. The announcer indicated at the beginning of the broadcast that the account was fictional, but about 80 percent of the listeners tuned in late.

Many listeners became frightened by what they assumed to be a news report. However, some accounts have exaggerated the extent of people's reactions to *The War of the Worlds.* One report concluded that "people all over the United States were praying, crying, fleeing frantically to escape death from the Martians." In contrast, a CBS national survey of listeners found that only 20 percent were genuinely scared by the broadcast. Although perhaps a million people *reacted* to this program, many reacted by switching to other stations to see if the "news" was being carried elsewhere. This "invasion from outer space" set off a limited panic, rather than mass hysteria (R.W. Brown 1954; Cantril 1940; Houseman 1972). On the fiftieth anniversary of the dramatization, in 1988, a Portuguese radio station rebroadcast the program, and once again, there was panic in that country.

Fads and fashions of the new millennium. Navel rings can be thought of as a fashion, a new form of body adornment. The Dennis Rodman poster decorates the back of a "tap tap," a passenger truck used for transport in Haiti. Famous sports and pop stars have become the new fad in tap-tap decorations, replacing popular religious and voodoo figures.

It is often believed that people engaged in panics or crazes are unaware of their actions, but this is certainly not the case. As the emergent-norm perspective suggests, people take cues from one another as to how to act during such forms of collective behaviour. Even in the midst of an escape from a life-threatening situation, such as a fire in a crowded theatre, people do not tend to run in a headlong stampede. Rather, they adjust their behaviour on the basis of the perceived circumstances and the conduct of others who are assembling in a given location. To outside observers studying the events, people's decisions may seem foolish (pushing against a locked door) or suicidal (jumping from a balcony). Yet, for that individual at that moment, the action may genuinely seem appropriate—or the only desperate choice available (Quarantelli 1957).

Rumours

The e-mail carried the subject line "Travelers Beware!" Its message was to warn those planning on going to Mardi Gras in New Orleans in 1997 that a highly organized crime ring there was drugging tourists, removing organs from their bodies, and selling them on the black market. The rumour circulated the country via e-mail and fax, causing an avalanche of calls to the New Orleans Police Department. Of course, an investigation turned up absolutely no evidence of an organ-snatching ring. The Department finally set up a website to quash the rumours.

Similar stories targeted visitors to other cities. It was said that a visitor to Las Vegas woke up one morning in a bathtub full of ice, and minus one kidney. Some version of the organ-snatching tale has swept through numerous countries, repeated by thousands of people. And there has never been one person to verify the story or to offer proof of its truth (Emery 1997).

Not all rumours we hear are so astonishing as the kidney snatchers or the college dormitory Halloween massacre (see the chapter opening). But none of us is immune to hearing or starting rumours. A ***rumour*** is a piece of information gathered informally that is used to interpret an ambiguous situation. Rumours serve a function by providing a group with a shared belief. As a group strives for consensus, members eliminate those rumours that are least useful or credible. Sociologist Tamotsu Shibutani (1966) sees this as something akin to the survival of the "fittest" or strongest rumour. Rumours are also a means of adapting to change. If a business is about to be taken over by another firm, rumours usually abound as to the significance that the move will have for personnel. Gradually, such rumours are either verified or discarded, but the very exchange of rumours allows people to cope with changes over which they have little

control. Scary rumours probably spread the fastest because fear induces stress and stress is reduced by sharing the fear with others. Moreover, some people enjoy provoking fear in others (R. Berk 1974; Emery 1997; Rosnow and Fine 1976).

Although some people may start rumours with specific intent to spread a falsehood, Jean-Noël Kapferer (1992:53), a professor of communication in France, suggests that rumours are typically "spontaneous social products, devoid of ulterior motives and underlying strategies." Kapferer argues that the existence and spreading of rumours reflect natural processes within groups. In his view, it is misleading to project the responsibility for a rumour outside the group that hears the rumour, finds it meaningful, and mobilizes to pass it on.

Spreading rumours about celebrities—whether politicians, movie stars, members of royal families or notorious criminals—has long been a popular pastime around the world. Modern communication technology facilitates the rapid dissemination of rumours. For example, despite a media publication ban on information about the killings of Leslie Mahaffy and Kristin French during the 1993 Bernardo and Homolka trials, rumour had it that graphic details were available on the Internet. Due to the nature of the World Wide Web, there are no controls over whether or not information is factual or just rumour.

A good way to get a rumour started is to broadcast it on a daytime talk show, like this one hosted by Jenny Jones. Rumours about celebrities also get spread on television through entertainment "gossip" programs and even news shows—as well as on radio, in print media, and over the Internet.

Natural disasters also tend to be a common subject for rumours. For example, after California was shaken (literally and figuratively) in 1992 by a series of powerful earthquakes and aftershocks, rumours abounded that the long-dreaded "big one" was imminent. According to one unfounded account, the California Institute of Technology in Pasadena—the site of the top seismology laboratory in the area—had ordered all its employees to leave town (*New York Times* 1992; Rosnow 1991).

Like celebrities, business firms find that rumours can be damaging, especially ill-founded charges of contamination or that a company is using its profits for evil purposes. For example, throughout the 1980s, Procter and Gamble had to counter persistent and unfounded rumours that the company was engaged in satanic activities and that its distinctive corporate trademark was a symbol of Satanism. Businesses can also be hurt by rumours about alleged political activism on controversial issues. In 2000, KFC, formerly known as Kentucky Fried Chicken, defended itself against rumours that it had to change its name because the company was no longer selling the meat of real chickens (Koenig 1985; University of New Hampshire 2000).

Publics and Public Opinion

The least organized and most individualized form of collective behaviour is represented by publics. The term *public* refers to a dispersed group of people, not necessarily in contact with one another, who share interest in an issue. As the term is used in the study of collective behaviour, the public does not include everyone. Rather, it is a collective of people who focus on some issue, engage in discussion, agree or disagree, and sometimes dissolve when the issue has been decided (Blumer 1955, 1969; R. Turner and Killian 1987).

The term *public opinion* refers to expressions of attitudes on matters of public policy that are communicated to decision makers. The last part of this definition is particularly important. Theorists of collective behaviour see no public opinion without both a public and a decision maker. In studying public opinion, we are not concerned with the formation of an *individual's* attitudes on social and political issues. Instead, we focus on the ways in which a public's attitudes get communicated to decision makers and on the ultimate outcome of the public's attempts to influence policymaking (R. Turner and Killian 1987).

Polls and surveys play a major role in assessing public opinion. Using the same techniques for developing reliable questionnaire and interview schedules, survey specialists conduct studies of public opinion for business firms (market analyses), the government, the mass media (ratings of programs), and,

p. 40

of course, politicians. Survey data have become extremely influential not only in preselecting the products we buy but in determining which political candidates are likely to win an election or how Canadians feel about issues such as Quebec separatism, gun control, same-sex marriage, pollution, or health care.

The earliest political polls were not always reliable. In a famous example of unscientific and misleading polling, the magazine *Literary Digest* sent 18 million postcard ballots across the United States to assess voters' opinions on the 1936 presidential election. The 2 million replies indicated that Republican candidate Alf Landon would defeat Democratic incumbent Franklin D. Roosevelt. *Literary Digest* predicted a Landon victory, yet Roosevelt was re-elected in a landslide.

Today we would regard this method of polling as completely unreliable. The magazine took its original sample from automobile registration lists and telephone books. Yet, in 1936, in the midst of the Depression, those people with enough money to own a car or a private telephone were hardly a representative cross-section of the nation's voters. Instead, those polled tended to be prosperous citizens who might be likely to support Republican candidates (Squire 1988). Current political polls are more precise and use representative sampling techniques. As a result, their projections of federal elections often fall within a few percentage points of the actual vote.

While political polling has improved dramatically since the *Literary Digest*'s 1936 fiasco, misleading surveys are still with us. Telephone companies have marketed call-in "polls" using 1-900 area code numbers. Television viewers or newspaper readers are asked to call one number to register an opinion on an issue, or a second number to register an alternative opinion. There are many problems inherent in this type of "polling." The sample that emerges is hardly representative since it includes only those people who happened to p. 36 see the commercial or advertisement for the poll and who feel strongly enough about the issue to spend the typical charge of $1 for a 900 call.

By the 1990s, surveys of public opinion had become a global phenomenon. With coordinated polling, the opinions of people in countries around the world can be compared. While surveys of public opinion have become more common in many diverse countries, social scientists and polling professionals are well aware that sophisticated sampling techniques are not always used. Exit polling—surveying voters as they leave the polls—has been a fact of political life in Western democracies for more than a decade. While it has been successfully conducted in certain developing countries, notably Mexico, use of exit polls in recent elections in Russia has served as a reminder that poor sampling procedures lead to unreliable data (Corning 1993; Specter 1996b).

Social Movements

Social movements are the most all-encompassing type of collective behaviour, because they may include aspects of other types such as crowds, rumours, publics, and public opinion. Although such factors as physical environment, population, technology, and social inequality serve as sources of change, it is the *collective* effort of individuals organized in social movements that ultimately leads to change.

Sociologists use the term **social movements** to refer to organized collective activities to bring about or resist fundamental change in an existing group or society (Benford 1992). Herbert Blumer (1955:19) recognized the special importance of social movements when he defined them as "collective enterprises to establish a new order of life."

In many nations, including Canada, social movements have had a dramatic impact on the course of history and the evolution of social structure. Consider the actions of Quebec separatists, suffragists, and the Metis rebellion of 1837. Members of each social movement stepped outside traditional channels for bringing about social change and yet had a noticeable influence on public policy. Equally dramatic collective efforts in Eastern Europe helped to topple communist regimes in a largely peaceful manner, in nations that many observers had felt were "immune" to such social change (Ramet 1991).

Social movements imply the existence of conflict, but we can also analyze their activities from a functionalist perspective. Even when unsuccessful, social movements contribute to the formation of public opinion. Initially, the ideas of Margaret Sanger and other early advocates of birth control were viewed as "radical," yet contraceptives are now widely available in Canada and the United States. Moreover, functionalists view social movements as training grounds for leaders of the political establishment. Such heads of state as Cuba's Fidel Castro and South Africa's Nelson Mandela came to power after serving as leaders of revolutionary movements. More recently, Poland's Lech Walesa, Russia's Boris Yeltsin, and Czech playwright Vaclav Havel led protest movements against communist rule and subsequently became leaders of their countries' governments.

How and why do social movements emerge? Obviously, people are often discontented with the way things

Two views on abortion among social movements in France: In the top photo, members of the pro-choice movement take to the streets. One sign states, "A child if I want it, when I want it." In the bottom photo, a member of the pro-life movement wears a T-shirt that states, "To abort is to kill."

are. But what causes them to organize at a particular moment in a collective effort to work for change? Sociologists rely on two explanations for why people mobilize: the relative-deprivation and resource-mobilization approaches.

Relative Deprivation

Those members of a society who feel most frustrated and disgruntled by the social and economic conditions of their lives are not necessarily "worst off" in an objective sense. Social scientists have long recognized that what is most significant is how people *perceive* their situation. Karl Marx pointed out that although the misery of the workers was important in reflecting their oppressed state, so was their position *relative* to the capitalist ruling class (Marx and Engels 1955, original edition 1847).

The term ***relative deprivation*** is defined as the conscious feeling of a negative discrepancy between legitimate expectations and present actualities (J. Wilson 1973). In other words, things aren't as good as you hoped they would be. Such a state may be characterized by scarcity rather than complete lack of necessities (refer back to the distinction between absolute and p. 214 relative poverty in Chapter 8). A relatively deprived person is dissatisfied because he or she feels downtrodden relative to some appropriate reference group. Thus, blue-collar workers who live in townhouses with little lawn space—though hardly at the bottom of the economic ladder—may nevertheless feel deprived in comparison with corporate managers and professionals who live in lavish and exclusive suburbs.

In addition to the feeling of relative deprivation, two other elements must be present before discontent will be channelled into a social movement. People must feel that they have a *right* to their goals, that they deserve better than what they have. For example, the struggle against European colonialism in Africa intensified when growing numbers of Africans decided that it was legitimate for them to have political and economic independence. At the same time, the disadvantaged group must perceive that it cannot attain its goals through conventional means. This belief may or may not be correct. Whichever is the case, the group will not mobilize into a social movement unless there is a shared perception that it can end its relative deprivation only through collective action (Morrison 1971).

Critics of this approach have noted that an increase in feelings of deprivation is not always necessary before people are moved to act. In addition, this approach fails to explain why certain feelings of deprivation are transformed into social movements, whereas in other similar situations, there is no collective effort to reshape society. Consequently, in recent years, sociologists have given increasing attention to the forces needed to bring about the emergence of social movements (Alain 1985; Finkel and Rule 1987; Orum 1989).

Resource Mobilization

It takes more than desire to start a social movement. It helps to have money, political influence, access to the media, and volunteers. The term ***resource mobilization*** refers to the ways in which a social movement utilizes such resources. The success of a movement for change will depend in good part on how effectively it mobilizes its resources (see also Gamson 1989; Staggenborg 1989a, 1989b).

Sociologist Anthony Oberschall (1973:199) has argued that to sustain social protest or resistance, there must be an "organizational base and continuity of leadership." As people become part of a social movement, norms develop to guide their behaviour. Members of the movement may be expected to attend regular meetings of organizations, pay dues, recruit new adherents, and boycott "enemy" products or speakers. The emergence of a new social movement can be evident from the rise of special language or new words for familiar terms. In recent years, social movements have been responsible for such new terms of self-reference as *senior citizens* (used to replace *old folks*), *gays* (used to replace *homosexuals*), and *people with disabilities* (used to replace *the handicapped*).

Leadership is a central factor in the mobilization of the discontented into social movements. Often, a movement will be led by a charismatic figure, such as Rene Levesque or Louis Riel. As Max Weber described it in 1904, charisma is that quality of an individual that sets him or her apart from ordinary people. Of course, charisma can fade abruptly; this helps p. 440 account for the fragility of certain social movements.

Yet many social movements do persist over long periods of time because their leadership is frequently well organized and ongoing. Ironically, as Robert Michels (1915) noted, political movements fighting for social change eventually take on bureaucratic forms of organization. Leaders tend to dominate the p. 150 decision-making process without directly consulting followers.

Why do certain individuals join a social movement whereas others who are in similar situations do not? Some of them are recruited to join. Karl Marx recognized the importance of recruitment when he called on workers to become *aware* of their oppressed status and develop a class consciousness. In agreement with the contemporary resource-mobilization approach, Marx held that a social movement (specifically, the p. 13 revolt of the proletariat) would require leaders to sharpen the awareness of the oppressed. They must help workers to overcome feelings of *false consciousness*, or attitudes that do not reflect workers' objective position, in order to organize a revolutionary movement. Similarly, one of the challenges faced by women's liberation activists of the late 1960s and early 1970s was to convince women that they were being deprived of their rights and of socially valued resources.

Unlike the relative-deprivation approach, the resource-mobilization perspective focuses on strategic difficulties facing social movements. Any movement for fundamental change will almost certainly arouse opposition; effective mobilization will depend in part on how the movement deals with resistance to its activities.

Gender and Social Movements

Sociologists point out that gender is an important element in understanding the development of social movements. In our male-dominated society, women have traditionally found it more difficult to hold leadership positions in social movement organizations, and have often disproportionately served as volunteers in them. In these positions, their work was not always recognized, nor were their voices as easily heard as men's. However, women's positions within social movements are changing so that women now assume much more of a leadership role. For example, Maude Barlow, a former politician, now holds the position of Chair of the Council of Canadians, an organization that lobbies government on issues of economic justice, social programs, alternatives to free trade, and the environment. However, gender bias still causes the real extent of women's influence to be overlooked.

Traditional examination of the sociopolitical system tends to focus on such male-dominated corridors of power as legislatures and corporate boardrooms to the neglect of more female-dominated domains, such as households, community-based groups, or faith-based networks. But efforts to influence family values, child rearing, relationships between parents and schools, and spiritual values are clearly significant to a culture and society (Ferree and Merrill 2000; Noonan 1995). For this reason, we have organizations such as the National Action Committee on the Status of Women (NAC). NAC, as the largest feminist organization in Canada, is a coalition of more than 700 member groups and has been fighting for women's concerns for 27 years.

Scholars of social movements now realize that gender can affect even the way we view organized efforts to bring about or resist change. For example, an emphasis on using rationality and an adversarial approach to achieve goals helps to obscure the importance of passion and cooperation in successful social movements. Calls for a more serious study of the role of cooperation are

frequently seen as applying only to the women's movement, because they are traditionally thought of as feminine traits. Yet it would be difficult to find any movement—from labour battles to voting rights to animal rights—where passion was not part of the consensus-building force (Ferree and Merrill 2000; Taylor 1995).

Spillover Effects

Can one social movement grow from another? In the early 1980s, after a period of inactivity, a peace movement re-emerged in a more vibrant form, one that bore many resemblances to the ongoing feminist movement. In fact, noting these similarities, political scientist David Meyer and sociologist Nancy Whittier suggest that social movements have "spillover effects" on other social protest movements. In their view, social movements "grow from and give birth to other movements, work in coalition with other movements, and influence each other indirectly through their effects on the larger cultural and political environment" (1994:277).

Meyer and Whittier argue that the form and content of the peace movement in the early 1980s reflected the far-reaching impact of the "second wave" of feminism. Indeed, coalitions between feminist, environmental, and peace organizations (sometimes referred to as "ecofeminism") became increasingly common as a response to what each group viewed as a hostile political climate.

The influence of the women's movement was evident in four distinct areas:

- *Ideological messages.* Peace activists successfully linked traditional themes about war and peace (the dangers of militarism contrasted with women's special caring for life) with feminist themes (analysis of the arms race as a reflection of the larger evils of men's patriarchal rule over women).
- *Tactics.* The activism of women's peace groups drew on feminist traditions of protest, such as sewing and coordinating quilts for large "peace ribbons."
- *Leadership.* Many women active in the peace movement of the 1980s brought their skills and insights directly from years of feminist activism.
- *Organizational structure.* Drawing on the ideals and values of "feminist process," various organizations of the peace movement established decentralized organizational structures that emphasized egalitarian participation by all members, consensus decision making, and rotation of key roles among members. There was often an aversion to hierarchy and a strong attachment to "local self-determination."

Meyer and Whittier conclude that a social movement can go beyond its expressly articulated goals to influence the larger sector of social movements. Consequently, the "spillover effects" of a particular social movement can persist over time, even in the face of policy defeats and the demise of movement organizations.

New Social Movements

The most recent effort to analyze social movements has come from European social scientists, who observed that, beginning in the late 1960s, there was a change in both the composition and the targets of emerging social movements. Previously, traditional social movements had focused on economic issues, often led by people sharing the same occupation or by labour unions. However, many social movements that have become active in recent decades—including the contemporary women's movement, the lesbian and gay rights movement, and the environmental movement—did not have the social class roots typical of the labour protests in Canada, the United States, and Europe over the preceding 100 years (Tilly 1993).

The term *new social movements* was introduced to refer to organized collective activities that promote autonomy and self-determination as well as improvements in the quality of life. These movements may be involved in developing collective identities, have complex agendas that go beyond a single issue, and often cross national boundaries. Educated, middle-class people are significantly represented in some of these new social movements, such as the women's movement and the movement for Quebec's independence. However, marginalized people are also involved in new social movements; as one example, some homeless people create communities of squatters who take over abandoned buildings and fight efforts to evict them (Buechler 1995).

New social movements generally do not view government as their ally in the struggle for a better society. While they typically do not seek to overthrow the government, they may criticize, protest, or harass public officials. Researchers have found that members of new social movements show little inclination to accept established authority, even scientific or technical authority. This is especially evident in the environmental and anti-nuclear power movements, where movement activists present their own experts to counter those of government or big business (Garner 1996; A. Scott 1990).

Although new social movement theory was developed in industrialized nations, its applications are worldwide. Box 21-1 describes Manisha Desai's research into collective behaviour, which led to a new social movement in rural India in the 1980s to bring more power to rural areas. Researchers emphasize that many new social movements have become national and even global in their scope. This development is not surprising, given the growing interdependence of people around the world within a global economy and the dramatic advances in communication technology. p. 66

The environmental social movement is one of many new movements that have adopted a worldwide focus. In their efforts to reduce air and water pollution, curtail global warming and protect species at risk, environmental activists have realized that strong regulatory measures within a single country are not sufficient. Similarly, labour union leaders and human rights advocates cannot adequately address exploitative sweatshop conditions in a developing country if a multinational corporation can simply move the factory to another country where it pays workers even less. Whereas traditional views of social movements tended to emphasize resource mobilization on a local level, new social movement theory offers a broader, global perspective on social and political activism. However we view it, collective behaviour in the form of social movements has contributed greatly to social change.

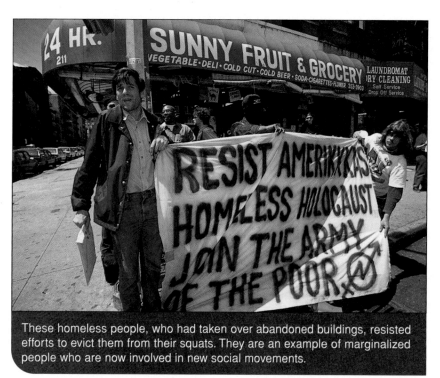

These homeless people, who had taken over abandoned buildings, resisted efforts to evict them from their squats. They are an example of marginalized people who are now involved in new social movements.

21-1 A New Social Movement in Rural India

In the mid-1980s, 5000 striking textile workers came home from Bombay to mobilize support in their rural villages and to gather food for strikers in the city. As the strike persisted, some strikers stayed in their villages and sought employment on governmental drought-relief projects. However, there were not even enough jobs for rural residents, much less for these new migrants from Bombay.

This was the origin of a new social movement described in Manisha Desai's examination of collective behaviour in India. Through her research into these strikes, she saw how, with unemployment now confronting an expanded population in rural areas, activists formed a movement that came to be called *Shoshit, Shetkari, Kashtakari, Kamgar, Mukti Sangharsh (SSKKMS)*, which means "exploited peasants, toilers, workers liberation struggle." The initial goal of the movement was to provide drought relief for villagers, but the deeper goal was to bring more power to the rural areas.

When Desai compared the SSKKMS movement with other social movements in India, she noticed a distinct difference: about half of its participants and many of its leaders were women. This was no accident, for the movement also sought to address gender inequities in the nation. For example, at a meeting seeking support in 1986, Indutai Patankar—a pioneer in the rural women's movement—declared:

We have gathered here to discuss our problems as women and a rural poor. . . . Not only do we work twice as hard as men but we also do not get equal wages, no child care. . . . We have to organize as women with the other oppressed toilers in urban and rural areas (Desai 1996:214).

Women and men from the movement were equally involved in many forms of political activism, including such direct-action tactics as blocking roads with carts and people until more government projects were approved.

> The initial goal of the movement was to provide drought relief for villagers, but the deeper goal was to bring more power to the rural areas.

In addition to addressing issues of gender stratification, the SSKKMS movement openly confronted the pervasive inequities associated with *dalit*. This term refers to oppressed people from lower castes (previously called "untouchables"). Movement activists insisted that both women and landless peasants (most of whom are *dalits*) should have equal access to water once dams were completed. This is a critical issue in the lives of rural Indian women, who typically must spend many hours a day in search of good drinking water.

In the analysis of her research into the SSKKMS movement, sociologist Manisha Desai (1996) emphasizes that the movement does not have a single focus, but is committed to multiple struggles for social and economic justice. Desai views the SSKKMS as an example of a new social movement because it incorporates concrete, material targets as well as broad ideological goals.

As with any social movement, there are contradictions in the SSKKMS movement. A middle-class leadership core generally articulates goals for the many exploited villagers in the mass movement. While in one rural area all local assemblies must be at least 30 percent female—a goal rarely achieved in Canada—rural women sometimes simply serve as fronts for the hidden agendas of their male relatives. Nevertheless, Desai's study of the SSKKMS movement underscores the fact that social movements in general, and new social movements in particular, are found *throughout* the world and not solely in industrialized nations.

Let's Discuss

1. Why do you think so many women participated in the SSKKMS movement? Describe their goals.
2. What would happen if "powerless" people in Canada formed a similar movement? Would it succeed? Why or why not?

Theories of Social Change

A new millennium provides the occasion to offer explanations of social change, but this is clearly a challenge in the diverse and complex world we inhabit today. Nevertheless, theorists from several disciplines have sought to analyze social change. In some instances, they have examined historical events to arrive at a better understanding of contemporary changes. We will review four theoretical approaches to change—evolutionary, functionalist,

conflict, and feminist theories—and then take a look at global change today.

Evolutionary Theory

Charles Darwin's (1809–1882) pioneering work in biological evolution contributed to nineteenth-century theories of social change. According to his approach, there has been a continuing progression of successive life forms. For example, since human beings came at a later stage of evolution than reptiles, we represent a "higher" form of life. Social theorists sought an analogy to this biological model and originated *evolutionary theory*, which views society as moving in a definite direction. Early evolutionary theorists generally agreed that society was inevitably progressing to a higher state. As might be expected, they concluded in ethnocentric fashion that their own behaviour and culture were more advanced than those of earlier civilizations.

August Comte (1798–1857), a founder of sociology, was an evolutionary theorist of change. He saw human societies as moving forward in their thinking from mythology to the scientific method. Similarly, Émile Durkheim (1933, original edition 1893) maintained that society progressed from simple to more complex forms of social organization.

The writings of Comte and Durkheim are examples of *unilinear evolutionary theory*. This approach contends that all societies pass through the same successive stages of evolution and inevitably reach the same end. English sociologist Herbert Spencer (1820–1903) used a similar approach: Spencer likened society to a living body with interrelated parts that were moving toward a common destiny. However, contemporary evolutionary theorists such as Gerhard Lenski are more likely to picture social change as multilinear than to rely on the more limited unilinear perspective. *Multilinear evolutionary theory* holds that change can occur in several ways and that it does not inevitably lead in the same direction (Haines 1988; J. Turner 1985).

Multilinear theorists recognize that human culture has evolved along a number of lines. For example, the theory of demographic transition graphically demonstrates that population change in developing nations has not necessarily followed the model evident in industrialized nations. Sociologists today recognize that events do not necessarily follow in a single or several straight lines but instead are subject to disruptions—a topic we will consider later in the discussion of global social change.

Functionalist Theory

Functionalist sociologists focus on what *maintains* a system, not on what changes it. This might seem to suggest that functionalists can offer

little of value to the study of social change. Yet, as the work of sociologist Talcott Parsons demonstrates, functionalists have made a distinctive contribution to this area of sociological investigation.

Parsons (1902–1979), a leading proponent of functionalist theory, viewed society as naturally being in a state of equilibrium. By "equilibrium," he meant that society tends toward a state of stability or balance. Parsons would view even prolonged labour strikes or civilian riots as temporary disruptions in the status quo rather than as significant alterations in social structure. Therefore, according to his *equilibrium model*, as changes occur in one part of society, there must be adjustments in other parts. If this does not take place, the society's equilibrium will be threatened and strains will occur.

Reflecting an evolutionary approach, Parsons (1966) maintained that four processes of social change are inevitable. The first, *differentiation,* refers to the increasing complexity of social organization. A change from "medicine man" to physician, nurse, and pharmacist is an illustration of differentiation in the field of health. This process is accompanied by *adaptive upgrading,* whereby social institutions become more specialized in their purposes. The division of labour among physicians into obstetricians, internists, surgeons, and so forth is an example of adaptive upgrading.

The third process identified by Parsons is the *inclusion* of groups into society that were previously excluded

Visible minorities are now accepted in many exclusive golf clubs that were previously restricted, illustrating the process of *inclusion* described by Talcott Parsons. The phenomenal success of pro golfer Tiger Woods has helped the process along.

because of such factors as gender, race, and social class background. Medical schools have practised inclusion by admitting increasing numbers of women and visible minorities. Finally, Parsons contends that societies experience *value generalization,* the development of new values that tolerate and legitimate a greater range of activities. The acceptance of preventive and alternative medicine is an example of value generalization; our society has broadened its view of health care. All four processes identified by Parsons stress consensus—societal agreement on the nature of social organization and values (B. Johnson 1975; R. Wallace and Wolf 1980).

Parsons's approach explicitly incorporates the evolutionary notion of continuing progress. However, the dominant theme in his model is balance and stability. Society may change, but it remains stable through new forms of integration. For example, in place of the kinship ties that provided social cohesion in the past, there are laws, judicial processes, and new values and belief systems.

Functionalists assume that social institutions will not persist unless they continue to contribute to the overall society. This leads functionalists to conclude that deliberately altering institutions will threaten societal equilibrium. Critics note that the functionalist approach virtually disregards the use of coercion by the powerful to maintain the illusion of a stable, well-integrated society (Gouldner 1960). Feminist theorists are among the most outspoken critics of functionalist theory, arguing that it provides a convenient defence of the patriarchal status quo.

Conflict Theory

The functionalist perspective minimizes change. It emphasizes the persistence of social life and sees change as a means of maintaining the equilibrium (or balance) of a society. By contrast, conflict theorists contend that social institutions and practices continue because powerful groups have the ability to maintain the status quo. Change has crucial significance, since it is needed to correct social injustices and inequalities.

Karl Marx accepted the evolutionary argument that societies develop along a particular path. However, unlike Comte and Spencer, he did not view each successive stage as an inevitable improvement over the previous one. History, according to Marx, proceeds through a series of stages, each of which exploits a class of people. Ancient society exploited slaves; the estate system of feudalism exploited serfs; modern capitalist society exploits the working class. Ultimately, through a socialist revolution led by the proletariat, human society will move toward the final stage of development: a classless communist society, or "community of free individuals" as Marx

described it in *Das Kapital* in 1867 (see Bottomore and Rubel 1956:250).

As we have seen, Karl Marx had an important influence on the development of sociology. His thinking offered insights into such institutions as the economy, the family, religion, and government. The Marxist view of social change is appealing because it does not restrict people to a passive role in responding to inevitable cycles or changes in material culture. Rather, Marxist theory offers a tool for those who wish to seize control of the historical process and gain their freedom from injustice. In contrast to functionalists' emphasis on stability, Marx argues that conflict is a normal and desirable aspect of social change. In fact, change must be encouraged as a means of eliminating social inequality (Lauer 1982).

One conflict sociologist, Ralf Dahrendorf (1959), has noted that the contrast between the functionalist perspective's emphasis on stability and the conflict perspective's focus on change reflects the contradictory nature of society. Human societies are stable and long-lasting, yet they also experience serious conflict. Dahrendorf found that the functionalist approach and the conflict approach were ultimately compatible despite their many areas of disagreement. Indeed, Parsons spoke of new functions that result from social change, and Marx recognized the need for change so that societies could function more equitably.

Feminist Theories

Unlike other sociological perspectives discussed above, social change is the hallmark of feminist theories. Feminist sociologists, diverse as they are, share a desire to deepen their understanding of society in order to change the world; it is their desire to make the world more just and humane (Madoo Lengermann and Niebrugge-Brantley 2000). Confronting social injustice in order to promote change for those groups in society who are disadvantaged by their "social location"—their class, race, ethnicity, sexual preference, age, or global location—is a key feature of feminist perspectives. As Patricia Hill Collins explains, change is sought for "people differently placed in specific political, social, and historic contexts characterized by injustice" (1998:xiv).

Increasingly, feminist theories advance the view that acknowledging women's differences must be paramount in guiding the direction of social change. The interests of white, middle-class women, for example, must not be assumed to represent the interests of all women. Social change must be inclusive of the interests of women of diverse backgrounds. Rosemary Hennessy and Chrys Ingraham ask: "What are the consequences of this way of thinking for transforming the inequities in women's lives?" and "How is this way of explaining the world going to improve life for all women?" (cited in Madoo Lengermann and Niebrugge-Brantley 2000:445).

Global Social Change

We are in a truly dramatic period of global social change. Sociologists point to a few of the recent political events: the collapse of communism; the presence of terrorism in various parts of the world, including North America; the dismantling of the welfare system in some developed nations; revolution and famine in Africa and Eastern Europe; the spread of AIDS; the computer revolution; and the cloning of a complex animal, Dolly the sheep.

In this era of massive social, political, and economic change on a global scale, is it possible to predict change? Some technological changes seem obvious, but the collapse of communist governments in the Soviet Union and Eastern Europe took people by surprise in its speed and its unexpectedness. However, prior to the Soviet collapse, sociologist Randall Collins (1986, 1995), a conflict theorist, had observed a crucial sequence of changes that most observers had missed.

In seminars as far back as 1980—and in a book published in 1986—Collins argued that Soviet expansionism in the twentieth century had resulted in an overextension of resources, including disproportionate spending on military forces. Such overextension strains a regime's stability. Moreover, geopolitical theory suggests that nations in the middle of a geographic region (like the Soviet Union) tend to fragment over time into smaller units.

Collins predicted that the coincidence of social crises on several frontiers would precipitate the collapse of the Soviet Union. The success of the Iranian revolution in 1979 led to an upsurge of Islamic fundamentalism in nearby Afghanistan and in Soviet republics with substantial Muslim populations. At the same time, there was growing resistance to communist rule throughout Eastern Europe and within the Soviet Union itself. Collins predicted that the rise of a dissident form of communism within the Soviet Union might facilitate the breakdown of the regime. Beginning in the late 1980s, Soviet leader Mikhail Gorbachev chose not to use military power and other types of repression to crush dissidents in Eastern Europe, offered plans for democratization and social reform of Soviet society, and seemed willing to reshape the Soviet Union into a loose federation of somewhat autonomous states. But, in 1991, six republics on the western periphery declared their independence, and within months the entire Soviet Union had formally disintegrated. (For a different course of events, see Box 21-2, which chronicles the recent, comparatively peaceful revolution in South Africa.)

Sociologist Maureen Hallinan (1997) cautions that we need to move beyond the restrictive models of social change—the linear view of evolutionary theory and the assumptions about equilibrium within functionalist theory. She and other sociologists have looked to "chaos theory" advanced by mathematicians to consider erratic events as a part of change. Hallinan noted that upheavals and major chaotic shifts do occur and that sociologists must learn to predict their occurrence, as Collins did with the Soviet Union. It is not hard to imagine the dramatic nonlinear social change that will result from major innovations in the areas of communication and biotechnology, as we saw in Chapter 20.

Resistance to Social Change

Efforts to promote social change are likely to meet with resistance. In the midst of rapid scientific and technological innovations, many people are frightened by the demands of an ever-changing society. Moreover, certain individuals and groups have a stake in maintaining the existing state of affairs.

Social economist Thorstein Veblen (1857–1929) coined the term **vested interest groups** to refer to those people or groups who will suffer in the event of social change. For example, for many years the Canadian Medical Association (CMA) took a strong stand against the professionalization of midwifery. While the doctors' public objections were based on claims of health risk, there cannot be any doubt that the potential for loss of income and authority over a medical procedure played a major role in determining their resistance. In general, those with a disproportionate share of society's wealth, status, and power, such as members of the Canadian Medical Association, have a vested interest in preserving the status quo (Starr 1982; Veblen 1919).

Economic and Cultural Factors

Economic factors play an important role in resistance to social change. For example, it can increase initial costs for manufacturers to meet high standards for the safety of products and workers. Conflict theorists argue that, in a capitalist economic system, many firms are not willing to pay the price of meeting necessary safety standards. They may resist social change by cutting corners within their plants or by pressuring the government to ease regulations.

Communities, too, protect their vested interests, often in the name of "protecting property values." The abbreviation "NIMBY" stands for "not in my backyard," a cry often heard when people protest landfills such as that intended for Kirkland Lake (Chapter 20), prisons, nuclear power facilities, and even group homes for people with developmental disabilities. The targeted

Sociology in the Global Community

21-2 Social Change in South Africa

p. 277

As recently as 10 years ago, South Africa, a nation of 43 million people, was accurately described as a country where race was the sole determinant of power. Regardless of occupation, education, or family background, white South Africans enjoyed legal rights and privileges that were denied to all people of colour. Ever since 1948, when it received its independence from Great Britain, South Africa had maintained this rigid segregationist policy, known as *apartheid*.

During the 1980s, South Africa felt increasing worldwide economic pressure. At the same time, black South Africans were more and more vocal about their second-class citizenship. They engaged in many forms of nonviolent and violent protest, including economic boycotts, labour strikes, political demonstrations, and occasional acts of sabotage.

In a dramatic turn of events in 1990, South African prime minister F.W. de Klerk legalized 60 banned black organizations and freed Nelson Mandela, the leader of the long-outlawed African National Congress (ANC), after 27 years of imprisonment. The following year, de Klerk and black leaders signed a National Peace Accord, pledging themselves to the establishment of a multiparty democracy.

In 1994, South Africa held its first universal election. Nelson Mandela's ANC received 62 percent of the vote, giving him a five-year term as president. Mandela and his political party were then faced with a difficult challenge: making the transition from a liberation movement fighting for revolution to a governing party that needed to achieve political compromises. Moreover, an end to the racist policy of apartheid—while applauded around the world—was not in itself a solution to all of South Africa's serious problems. At best, one-fifth of the country's blacks could compete in the nation's economy, while the balance formed a huge underclass.

> An end to the racist policy of apartheid—while applauded around the world—was not in itself a solution to all of South Africa's serious problems.

Some of the controversial issues facing the government are very familiar to residents of North America:

- *Employment equity.* Race-based employment goals and other "affirmative action" programs have been proposed, yet critics insist that such efforts constitute reverse apartheid.
- *Illegal immigration.* An estimated 2 to 20 percent of South African residents are illegal immigrants, many of whom wish to escape the poverty and political turmoil of neighbouring African states.
- *Medical care.* South Africa is confronting the inequities of private health care for the affluent (usually white) and government-subsidized care for others (usually people of colour).
- *School integration and upgrading.* Multiracial schools are replacing the segregated school system. As of 1998, 82 percent had no media equipment (televisions or computers), and 57 percent had no electricity.

Perhaps the most difficult issue facing the government is land reform. Between 1960 and 1990, the all-white government forced 3.5 million black South Africans from their land and frequently allowed whites to settle on it. Under legislation adopted in 1994, these displaced citizens can now file for restitution of their land. As of 1998, more than 23 000 such claims had been filed; in many cases, there are sure to be objections from settled whites. Even though government compensation will be offered to current landowners, bitter disputes will be inevitable.

Let's Discuss

1. How would a conflict theorist explain the relatively peaceful revolution in South Africa? What explanation might a functionalist offer?
2. Do you think other nations should use economic pressure to face social change in a country? Why or why not?

Sources: Daley 1996, 1998; Duke 1998; R. Schaefer 2000; Sidiropoulos et al. 1996; South African Institute of Race Relations 1998.

---

community may not challenge the need for the facility but may simply insist that it be located elsewhere. The "not in my backyard" attitude has become so common that it is almost impossible for policymakers to find acceptable locations for such facilities as dump sites for hazardous wastes (J. Jasper 1997).

Like economic factors, cultural factors frequently shape resistance to change. William F. Ogburn (1922) distinguished between material and nonmaterial aspects of culture. *Material culture* includes investigations, artifacts, and technology; *nonmaterial culture* encompasses ideas, norms, communication, pp. 66–67 and social organization. Ogburn pointed out that one cannot devise methods for controlling and utilizing new technology before the introduction of a technique. Thus, nonmaterial culture typically must respond to changes in

"Not in my backyard!" say these demonstrators, objecting to the placement of a new incinerator in their neighbourhood. The phenomenon of NIMBY has become so common that it is almost impossible for policymakers to find acceptable locations for incinerators, landfills, and dump sites for hazardous wastes.

material culture. As discussed in Chapter 20, Ogburn introduced the term *culture lag* to refer to the period of maladjustment during which the nonmaterial culture is still adapting to new material conditions. One example is the Internet. Its rapid uncontrolled growth raises questions about whether to regulate it and, if so, how much.

In certain cases, changes in material culture can add strain to the relationships between social institutions. For example, new techniques of birth control have been developed in recent decades. Large families are no longer economically necessary, nor are they commonly endorsed by social norms. But certain religious faiths, among them Roman Catholicism, continue to extol large families and to disapprove methods of limiting family size such as contraception and abortion. This represents a lag between aspects of material culture (technology) and nonmaterial culture (religious beliefs). Conflicts may emerge between religion and other social institutions, such as government and the educational system, over the dissemination of birth control and family-planning information (M. Riley et al. 1994a, 1994b).

Resistance to Technology

Technological innovations are examples of changes in material culture that have often provoked resistance. The p. 131 *Industrial Revolution,* which began primarily in England during the period 1760 to 1830,

was a scientific revolution focused on the application of nonanimal sources of power to labour tasks. As this revolution proceeded, societies relied on new inventions that facilitated agricultural and industrial production and on new sources of energy such as steam. In some industries, the introduction of power-driven machinery reduced the need for factory workers and made it easier to cut wages.

Strong resistance to the Industrial Revolution emerged in some countries. In England, beginning in 1811, masked craft workers took extreme measures: They conducted nighttime raids on factories and destroyed some of the new machinery. The government hunted these rebels, known as **Luddites**, and ultimately banished some while hanging others. In a similar effort in France, some angry workers threw their wooden shoes (*sabots*) into factory machinery to destroy it, thereby giving rise to the term *sabotage*. While the resistance of the Luddites and the French workers was short-lived and unsuccessful, they have come to symbolize resistance to technology over the last two centuries.

Are we now in the midst of a technological revolution, with a contemporary group of Luddites engaged in resistance? Many sociologists believe that we are now living in a *postindustrial society*. It is p. 131 difficult to pinpoint exactly when this era began. Generally, it is viewed as having begun in the 1950s, when for the first time the majority of workers in industrial societies became involved in services rather than in the actual manufacturing of goods (D. Bell 1973; Fiala 1992). Along the same lines, there are those who argue that we are now living in a period where direction of progress has been shifted away from technological advancement to an emphasis on understanding the world around us from a perspective beyond the realm of science.

Just as the Luddites resisted the Industrial Revolution, people in many countries have resisted postindustrial technological changes. The term **neo-Luddites** refers to those who are wary of technological innovations and who question the incessant expansion of industrialization, the increasing destruction of the natural and agrarian world, and the "throw it away" mentality of contemporary capitalism with its resulting pollution of the environment. Neo-Luddites insist that whatever the presumed benefits of industrial and postindustrial technology, such technology

Today's version of Luddites are protesting techno-logical innovations that they regard as destructive. This Greenpeace demonstrator in Montreal scales a giant corn "monster" in protest of genetically engineered food.

How might some of the theoretical perspectives we examined earlier in the chapter evaluate technology's role in collective behaviour? While Neil Smelser's value-added perspective did not explicitly refer to communication technology, his emphasis on people needing to be mobilized for action takes on new meaning today with fax machines and the Internet. With relatively little effort and expense, we can now reach a large number of people in a short period of time. Looking at the new technology from the assembling perspective, we could consider the Internet's Listservs and chat rooms as examples of non-periodic assemblies. Without face-to-face contact or even simultaneous interaction, people can develop an identity with a large collective of like-minded people via the Internet (Calhoun 1998).

Sociology is only beginning to consider the impact of the latest technology on various forms of collective behaviour. Technology clearly plays a role in disaster research; moreover, a large number of disasters today are technological in origin. A content analysis of the coverage of disasters by *Time* magazine showed that about 40 percent were technological and 60 percent natural during the 1990s (Bernhardt 1997).

We have seen that rumours fly on the Internet. One click of the "Send" button can forward messages to every person in one's address book. Multiply this by the millions of e-mail account holders to get an idea of the reach of the Internet in distributing rumours. We have seen, too, how Internet rumours can stir panics. In the same way, people can be exposed almost instantly to the latest crazes, fads, and fashions. And people are constantly being encouraged to call a telephone number or

has distinctive social costs and may represent a danger to the future of the human species and our planet (Bauerlein 1996; Rifkin 1995b; Sale 1996; Snyder 1996).

Such concerns are worth remembering as we turn to examine technology's contribution to collective behaviour and its possible impact on social change.

Communication Technology and Collective Behaviour

Many of the examples that we have used to illustrate collective behaviour reflect the impact of communication technology—from radio broadcasts proclaiming that Martians have landed, to the Internet as a vehicle for spreading rumours. The World Wide Web is only the latest in a wave of new communication technology that has transformed collective behaviour, and brought about large-scale social change.

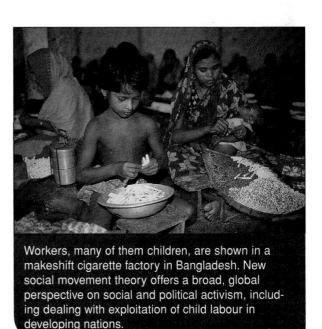

Workers, many of them children, are shown in a makeshift cigarette factory in Bangladesh. New social movement theory offers a broad, global perspective on social and political activism, including dealing with exploitation of child labour in developing nations.

21-3 Virtual Social Movements

We are accustomed to think of social movements in terms of protest marches and door-to-door petition drives. But the World Wide Web allows for alternative ways of trying to organize people and either bring about fundamental change or resist change. The Internet itself has often been referred to as a "virtual community," and as in any community there are people who seek to persuade others to their point of view. Furthermore, the Internet serves to "bring people together"—say, by transforming the cause of the Mexican Zapatista into an international lobbying effort or linking environmentalists on every continent through Greenpeace International or e-mailing information and news from abroad to dissidents in China.

Being like-minded and in face-to-face contact, critical to conventional social movements, is not necessary on the Internet. Moreover, people can engage in their own virtual community with little impact on their everyday lives. On the Internet, for example, one can mount a petition drive to free a political prisoner in another country without taking days and weekends away from one's job and family. Dissidents can communicate with one another using computers in Internet cafes, with little concern for being traced or monitored by the government.

Two new studies by Matthew Zook and research by sociologist Roberta Garner examined how many websites express ideological points of view that are contentious or hostile to existing institutions. Garner looked at 542 websites that could be regarded as "ideological postings"; some reflect the interests of a particular group or organization and some are only the opinions of isolated individuals.

> The Internet itself has often been referred to as a "virtual community," and as in any community there are people who seek to persuade others to their point of view.

Among the sites were postings that reflected extreme patriotic views, white racism, attachment to cults, regional separatism and new forms of nationalism, and expression of militant environmentalism.

While the Garner sample was not random and therefore may not be representative of all ideological postings, the hundreds of sites did show some consistencies, many of them also noted by Zook:

- Like conventional social movements, these sites serve as an alternative source of information, bypassing mainstream sources of opinions found in newspaper editorials.
- These nonmainstream movements enjoy legitimacy because no gatekeeper keeps them off the web. By virtue of being on a website, even an unsophisticated one, the information has the appearance of being just as legitimate as that found on a website for a TSE 300 corporation or CTV news. And because the information appears on *individual* sites, it seems to be more real and even sincere than messages that come from the mass media of television or radio.
- The sites make little reference to time or specific events, except to historic moments. There is not much sense of movement along an agenda.
- The sites rely heavily on written documents, either in the form of

Sources: Calhoun 1998; Castells 1996; Garner 1999; Rosenthal 2000; Van Slambrouck 1999; Zook 1996.

log on to a website to register their public opinion on some policy issue.

Can one be part of a "crowd" via the new communication technology? Television and the Internet, as contrasted with books and newspapers, often convey a false sense of intimacy reinforced by immediacy. We seem to be personally hurt by the death of Princess Diana or moved by the troubles of the Kennedy family. Therefore, the latest technology brings us together in an electronic global village to act and to react. Box 21-3 shows how virtual social movements can develop on the web (Garner 1999).

The new communication technology is also able to create enclaves of similarly minded people. Websites are not just autonomous and independent; they are interconnected through a global electronic network. One website, in turn, lists a variety of other sites that serve as "links." For example, seeking out information on domestic partnerships may lead you to an electronic enclave on the Internet supportive of cohabitation between men and women or alternatively to an enclave that is supportive of gay and lesbian couples. Developments in communication technology have contributed to social change by clearly broadening the way we interact with one another today (Calhoun 1998).

manifestos or established documents such as the Constitution or the Bible. Written testimonials (such as "How I Became a Conservative") also proliferate on these websites.

- The presentations are still fairly unsophisticated. While there are glossy animated websites, most sites look like a printed page.
- Unlike conventional social movements, these virtual sites are generally not geared for action. Despite expressions of concern or foreboding (such as the site "Are You Ready for Catastrophic Natural Disasters?"), there were few calls to do anything. Sites like "Glory to the Cuban Revolution" seek to inform visitors, serve as a resource, and, perhaps, bring people around to their point of view.

Zook as well as Garner and her student researchers found that these sites often seem to define themselves by their choice of links on the web. In other words, with whom do they wish to be associated? This is particularly true of well-established social movements that have expanded to use the Internet. For example, both the leading abortion rights groups and anti-abortion organizations feature links to other groups, but only to those that are like-minded.

The entire process of "links" is very important in the Internet network. How one defines one's ideology determines how a site may be located and who makes links. For example, the website of a female national socialist from Sweden boldly encourages visitors to establish a link from their website to hers as long as they are a part of the "white aryan movement on the Net." Using the term "militia" as opposed to "patriotic" would bring different people to one's site. The terms one uses are important since webpages act as recruiting tools to attract new members to a movement and may, in fact, be the only realistic way that some groups will attract followers.

People in conventional social movements commonly try to infiltrate other groups holding opposing views to learn their strategy or even disrupt their ability to function. There is a parallel to that emerging on the Internet. The term *hactivists* (a merging of "hackers" with "activists") refers to people who invade computer systems electronically, placing embarrassing information on their enemies' webpages or, at the very least, defacing them. During the height of the 1999 NATO attacks on Yugoslavia, movements opposed to the military action bombarded the official NATO website with requests meant to overload it and paralyze its operation.

Research into virtual social movements is still exploratory. Social movement researchers such as Garner and Zook are interested in establishing the relationship between ideological websites and "real" organizations. Do these sites merely reflect a single posting? Or are they the visible manifestation of a broader consensus? And sociologists will be interested in examining a more representative sample of such sites to determine how often they explicitly call for social change.

Let's Discuss

1. What are some of the advantages of having a virtual social movement on the Internet? What might be some disadvantages?

2. If you were to create a webpage designed to attract followers to a social movement, what would it be like?

Lesbian and Gay Rights

The Issue

Despite the large numbers of lesbians and gays in Canada and around the world, homosexuality continues to function in many societies as a master status that carries a stigma. Amnesty International (1994) published a pioneering report documenting that lesbians and gays suffer from governmental persecution in many parts of the world. In response to such discrimination, a social movement for lesbian and gay rights has emerged across Canada and in many diverse nations. This movement is putting pressure on policymakers to pass legislation establishing and protecting gay and lesbian rights.

The Setting

The first social movement to advance the civil rights of lesbians and gays was founded in Germany in 1897 by physician Magnus Hirschfeld and others. The Scientific-Humanitarian Committee fought to abolish legal penalties against homosexual behaviour and to educate people about gay rights and women's rights. The committee was eventually crushed by the Nazis in 1933; subsequently, at least 10 000 to 20 000 people identified as homosexuals died in Nazi concentration camps. As a result, one cherished symbol of contemporary gay activists—worn on buttons and patches—is a pink triangle, the very emblem gay prisoners were forced to wear by the Nazis (Adam 1995; Heger 1980; Lauritsen and Thorstad 1974; Plant 1986).

While the first homosexual organization in North America was founded in Chicago in 1924, early gay rights activism was visible in Canada almost exclusively through the work of one man. From 1949 to 1964, James Egan wrote letters and articles to newspapers and politicians, aimed at correcting stereotypes of homosexuality and arguing for the repeal of laws that criminalized homosexual activity; *The Globe and Mail* published one in 1950 (Bebout 2000). Thirty years later, Egan re-emerged in the forefront of the gay rights fight by bringing one of the first constitutional challenges involving gay rights to the Supreme Court of Canada (CLGA 1996).

The first known gay organization in Canada—Association for Social Knowledge (ASK)—was formed in Vancouver in 1964. The Canadian Council on Religion and the Homosexual emerged shortly after that with a concern for "sympathetic understanding . . . of the problems faced by homosexuals in our society" (CLGA 1982). In 1969, the first gay liberation organization in Canada, the University of Toronto Homophile Association (UTHA), held its initial meetings and by the mid-1970s there were organizations such as these across Canada.

The development of the modern movement coincided with important political events such as the constitutional entrenchment of a bill of rights (Smith 1999) Experiences in early gay rights groups gave activists greater organizing ability—an important component of resource mobilization. In addition, there were spillover effects through involvement in other social movements of the 1960s and 1970s—such as those working for the peace movement (protesting against the U.S. war in Vietnam), for aboriginal rights, and for women's liberation. Many lesbians and gays were led to reflect more directly on their own oppression stemming from their sexual orientation (J. Katz 1992; CLGA 1982).

Building on earlier homosexual activism and on the growth of lesbian and gay subcultures in major cities, the contemporary gay movement publicly began in New York City on June 28, 1969. Police raided the Stonewall Inn,

an after-hours gay bar, and forced patrons onto the street. But, instead of dispersing, the patrons locked police inside the bar and rioted until official reinforcements arrived. For the next three nights, gays and lesbians marched through the streets of New York, protesting police raids and other forms of discrimination. Within months, gay liberation groups had appeared in cities and campuses everywhere. As noted above, UTHA, the first gay liberation organization in Canada was formed four months after Stonewall. Within two years, similar organizations were evident in Great Britain, various Western European countries, and Australia (Adam 1995; Adam et al. 1999, Garner 1996; Gay Archivist 1989). In other words, lesbian and gay rights is an international phenomenon; groups around the world are linked through the development of the International Lesbian and Gay Association (Smith 1999).

It is difficult to speak of one lesbian and gay political movement in Canada. "This movement is not represented in one organization or even in several; rather, it is a pan-Canadian network of activists rooted in the particular geography of local communities, some of whom may belong to gay and lesbian rights organizations, informal networks, or coalitions while they are simultaneously active in or have previously been active in other movements . . ." (Smith 1999:9). While most voluntary associations supporting lesbian and gay rights are primarily local or provincial in their focus, there are national organizations that address gay issues. Among these are EGALE Canada (which advances equality and justice for lesbian, gay, bisexual, and transgendered people and their families across Canada) and Parents, Families, and Friends of Lesbians and Gays (PFLAG), whose chapters in more than 35 cities in Canada and in 11 countries around the world provide support for lesbians, gays, and their families (Brelin 1996).

In response to the AIDS crisis, self-help groups—especially in the gay communities of major cities—have been established to care for the sick, educate the healthy, and lobby for more responsive public policies. The Canadian AIDS Society (CAS) is a national coalition of 115 community-based groups across the country. It advocates, at the federal public policy level, on behalf of people and communities affected by HIV/AIDS, promotes education and awareness, and provides a national framework for community-based participation in Canada's response to AIDS (CAS 2002). The Canadian National Foundation for AIDS Research (CANFAR) is a charitable foundation created in 1987 to generate funds for research into all aspects of HIV and AIDS, but it also provides awareness programs and was one of the co-founders of the Red Ribbon Campaign (CANFAR 2002). The Community AIDS Treatment Information Exchange (CATIE) is a national, nonprofit organization committed to providing free, current, and confidential treatment information for all Canadians living with HIV/AIDS and for their families and care providers (CATIE 2002).

The most outspoken AIDS activist group has been ACT-UP, which has conducted controversial protests and sit-ins in the halls of government and at scientific conferences. In the view of sociologist Barry Adam (1995), while the rise of such self-help and AIDS activist groups has siphoned away many leaders and participants from gay rights organizations, the broad reach of the AIDS crisis has mobilized new constituencies of gays and their friends and relatives into AIDS and gay activism.

Despite its international existence, the gay and lesbian rights movement must deal with the local jurisdictions, including federal and provincial levels of government in Canada. In terms of progress, Canada is quite far ahead of other countries, in particular the U.S.,

After presenting a brief of "demands" calling for changes in the ways public policy discriminated against homosexuals, the first large-scale gay rights demonstration took place on Parliament Hill, on August 28, 1971.

with regard to constitutional rights. In 1967, two years before the Stonewall incident, Pierre Trudeau, then minister of justice, introduced the first version of a sexual offences reform bill with his famous statement about the state not belonging in the bedrooms of the nation. Two years later in May 1969, an omnibus criminal reform bill, C-150, was passed in parliament; it included the legalization of sexual acts between two consenting adults in private if they are aged 21 and over. While homosexuality per se was not "legalized," certain sexual acts considered indecent prior to C-150 were decriminalized in certain circumstances (i.e., in privacy). Another two years later, in the summer of 1971, a brief prepared by Toronto Gay Action and sponsored by Canadian gay groups was presented to the federal government. "We demand" called for law reforms and changes to public policy relating to homosexuals, because the prejudice against them was evident in their daily experiences with police harassment, exploitation, and pressures to conform that denied their sexuality (Waite and DeNovo 1971). The brief was followed a few days later by the first large-scale gay demonstration on Parliament Hill, on August 28, 1971 (Bebout 1997; CLGA 1998).

One of the "demands" was the right of equal employment and promotion at all governmental levels. In 1977, the federal solicitor general Francis Fox declared that homosexuality was not grounds for firing or refusing to hire someone. Several city councils had already passed resolutions banning discrimination in municipal hiring on the basis of sexual orientation, with Toronto being the first to do so in 1973. Throughout the 1970s, calls for inclusion of sexual orientation in human rights codes were made by supporters in provincial and federal legislatures. Late in 1977, the National Assembly amended the *Quebec Charter of Human Rights* to include sexual orientation—the first province to do so, and it took another decade before any other provinces followed suit (i.e., Ontario in 1986, and the Yukon Territory and Manitoba in 1987). In 1996, after a 25-year struggle at the federal level, the *Canadian Human Rights Act* was amended to protect homosexuals from discrimination by the federal government, its agencies, and federally incorporated businesses.

Sociological Insights

While the 1982 *Canadian Charter of Rights* did not include sexual orientation on its list, it did include the words "in particular," which allowed challenges to discrimination on grounds other than those specifically named in the Charter. While the Supreme Court has heard a number of cases related to lesbian and gay issues, probably the most noteworthy was the 1995 Egan & Nesbit old-age pension case. In it, all nine justices of the Supreme Court of Canada confirmed that Section 15 of the *Charter of Rights* must be read to include sexual orientation (CLGA 1998). The Charter, as part of the *Constitution of Canada*, is binding on everyone. Homosexuals in other countries, however, do not enjoy the same legal protection.

Despite the effort of the lesbian and gay rights movement, in 1986 the U.S. Supreme Court ruled, by a narrow 5–4 vote, that the U.S. Constitution does not protect homosexual relations between consenting adults, even in the privacy of their own homes. This decision underscored the fact that heterosexuality remains the socially approved form of sexual relations in the United States; the dominant ideology of our society promotes exclusive heterosexual norms.

Sociologist Steven Seidman (1994:583) notes, "From secondary school books to public images in advertisements, movies, television shows, magazines, and newspapers, heterosexuality is presented as natural and normal." Viewed from a conflict perspective, the dominant ideology encourages antigay prejudice and discrimination by excluding positive images of lesbians and gay men while emphasizing narrow stereotypes.

By the 1990s, lesbian and gay activists had recognized that encouraging people to "come out" could help illustrate the diversity of gay life and assist resource mobilization. Many lesbians and gays had long felt the need to conceal their identities (remain "in the closet") out of fear that they might lose their jobs, be cut off from their families, and fall victim to prejudice and discrimination. However, the gay movement has given many individuals the support and strength to "come out" and assert their identities publicly and proudly—as new social movements frequently do for those who are challenging dominant social norms.

Among the many lesbian, gay, and bisexual organizations in Canada and the United States, there are: gay sports leagues and singing groups; professional associations, such as those of gay doctors and teachers; campus lesbian and gay organizations; and groups of visible minority gays, some of whom have challenged white domination of the lesbian and gay movement (Brelin 1996:34).

Policy Initiatives

Resistance to lesbian and gay rights has also been evident at every step of the way, including the continuing controversy over gays in the military and the battle over possible legalization of same-sex marriage. Antigay discrimination by the Canadian Armed Forces began to be challenged in the mid-1970s, often by service personnel who came out and fought the consequences. Major purges—particularly of lesbians—were reported as early as 1977 when Master Corporal Gloria Cameron and eight other women were dismissed from the Armed Forces because they were lesbians. Cameron launched an appeal and went public with her story, but her appeal was rejected. The Chief of Defence Staff justified it by saying: "Experience has shown that the presence of homosexuals can be most disruptive. . . . There is only one way of insuring our servicemen and women that their rights will be respected: by denying employment to homosexuals" (CLGA 1998:6).

With the *Charter of Rights and Freedoms* in 1985, the federal government pledged to end antigay discrimination in all areas of federal jurisdiction, including the Armed Forces. Though the Forces fought back, seeking exemption, in 1989 they stopped their dismissals but barred gays and lesbians from promotion, training, or security clearances. In 1991 a court ruled that this violated the Charter, and the following year the Forces were required to provide financial settlement to Michelle Douglas, a lesbian who challenged her 1988 dismissal. The Chief of Defence stated that all Canadians, "regardless of their sexual orientation, will now be able to serve their country . . . without restriction" (CLGA 1998:7). Again, in the U.S., military personnel have been less successful. In 1993, President Bill Clinton considered issuing an executive order against antigay discrimination within the military, but was forced to back down because of heated opposition from military leaders and powerful members of Congress. Under a compromise devised in 1994—known as "Don't Ask, Don't Tell"—lesbians and gays can continue to serve in the military as long as they keep their homosexuality a secret, while commanders are prohibited from asking about a person's sexual orientation. But commanders *can* investigate and dismiss military personnel if there is evidence that they have committed homosexual acts. According to a 1998 report the military is discharging 67 percent *more* gay and lesbian troops today than before the new policy was enacted (Weiner 1998).

According to the World Report 2002, from 1994 to 2000, more than 6500 service members were discharged, with a record number of more than 1000 during 2000. Again, as experienced in Canada, women were discharged at a disproportionately higher rate (Weiner 1998; Human Rights Watch 2002).

Same-sex marriage and "spousal" rights have been a battle throughout the 1990s. Not only marriage per se, but income tax, pensions, and other joint benefits such as workplace insurance plan coverage were at issue in attempts to change federal and provincial laws' definitions of "spouse" and "family." Some victories have occurred, such as the granting of benefits to same-sex partners of federal employees. And, for example, in 1997, the British Columbia legislature passed Bill 31, which recognized same-sex domestic partners as spouses, just as in the case of common-law couples. In 2002 Quebec passed the *Civil Union Act*, giving all couples, including gays and lesbians, the choice of registering their union with the province rather than the church.

As noted in Chapter 14, lesbians and gays are forming unions and are even allowed to marry in a number of churches in Canada. The problem comes when attempting to register their union—that is when their rights are denied, effectively ensuring that they are not married by law. Joe Varnell and Kevin Bourassa were married in Toronto in 2002, and challenged the Ontario government to register that marriage (Gessell 2002). As discussed in Chapter 13, the Ontario Superior Court ruled that Canada's definition of marriage was discriminatory and

unconstitutional, opening the door for the federal government to adapt its definitions. Currently, the Justice Minister intends to appeal the Ontario decision, making same-sex marriage an issue for the future.

A common stereotype has been that lesbian and gay organizations are found only in Western industrialized nations. However, the International Lesbian and Gay Association now has about 300 member organizations in 70 countries. In 1995, Japan held its second annual gay pride march; two gay groups were formed in China; and gay groups were founded in Bolivia, Kenya, Pakistan, South Korea, and Sri Lanka. There are more than 50 gay and lesbian groups in South Africa, more than a dozen in Mexico, and at least 7 lesbian organizations in Brazil. The spread of the Internet has assisted the creation of many pioneering lesbian and gay organizations (Adam et al. 1999; Dillon 1997; *The Economist* 1996).

Let's Discuss

1. Viewed from a conflict perspective, how does the dominant ideology of our society encourage antigay prejudice and discrimination?
2. How has the AIDS crisis affected the movement for lesbian and gay rights?
3. In what ways is the social position of lesbians different from that of gay men?

Chapter Resources

Summary

Collective behaviour is the relatively spontaneous and unstructured behaviour of a group that is reacting to a common influence in an ambiguous situation. Sociological theories used to understand collective behaviour and forms of this behaviour are examined, with particular attention to **social movements** and their important role in promoting social change. **Social change** is significant alteration over time in behaviour patterns and culture, including norms and values. This chapter examines sociological theories of social change, resistance to change, and the impact of communication technology on collective behaviour, social movements, and social change.

1. Turner and Killian's **emergent-norm perspective** suggests that new forms of proper behaviour may

emerge from a crowd during an episode of collective behaviour.

2. Smelser's **value-added model** of collective behaviour outlines six important determinants of such behaviour: structural conduciveness, structural strain, generalized belief, precipitating factor, mobilization of participants for action, and operation of social control.

3. The **assembling perspective** introduced by McPhail and Miller sought for the first time to examine how and why people move from different points in space to a common location.

4. In **crowds** people are in relatively close contact and interaction for a period of time and are focused on something of common interest.

5. Researchers are interested in how groups interact in times of disaster.

6. *Fads* are temporary patterns of behaviour involving large numbers of people; *fashions* have more historical continuity.

7. The key distinction between a *panic* and a *craze* is that a panic is a flight *from* something whereas a craze is a mass movement *to* something.

8. A *rumour* is a piece of information used to interpret an ambiguous situation. It serves a social function by providing a group with a shared belief.

9. *Publics* represent the most individualized and least organized form of collective behaviour. *Public opinion* is the expression of attitudes on public policy communicated to decision makers.

10. Social movements are more structured than other forms of collective behaviour and persist over longer periods of time.

11. A group will not mobilize into a social movement unless there is a shared perception that its *relative deprivation* can be ended only through collective action.

12. The success of a social movement will depend in good part on how effectively it mobilizes its resources.

13. Scholars of social movements are realizing how gender affects the way we organize efforts for change, as well as how it reflects the focus of the movement.

14. *New social movements* tend to focus on more than just economic issues and often cross national boundaries.

15. Early advocates of evolutionary theory of social change believed that society was inevitably progressing to a higher state.

16. Comte and Durkheim are examples of the evolutionary theory, which states that all societies pass through the same stages of evolution and reach the same end.

17. Talcott Parsons, a leading advocate of functionalist theory, viewed society as naturally being in a state of equilibrium or balance.

18. Conflict theorists see change as having crucial significance, since it is needed to correct social injustices and inequalities.

19. Feminist theories seek to confront social injustice in order to promote change for those groups in society who are disadvantaged by their class, race, ethnicity, sexual preference, age, and/or global location.

20. In general, those with a disproportionate share of society's wealth, status, and power have a vested interest in preserving the status quo and will resist change.

21. The period of maladjustment when the non-material culture is still adapting to new material conditions is known as *culture lag*.

22. Technological advances are examples of changes in material culture that have often provoked resistance.

23. New communication technology has transformed collective behaviour, and brought about large-scale social change.

24. Advances in communication technology—especially on the Internet—have had a major impact on the various forms of collective behaviour, and advancement of social movements.

25. A growing number of organizations address national and international concerns of lesbians and gays.

Critical Thinking Questions

1. Are the emergent-norm, value-added, and assembling perspectives aligned with or reminiscent of functionalism, conflict theory, feminist theories, or interactionism? What aspects of each of these theories of collective behaviour (if any) seem linked to the broader theoretical perspectives of sociology?

2. Without using any of the examples given in the textbook, list at least two examples of each of the following types of collective behaviour: crowds, disasters, fads, fashions, panics, crazes, rumours, publics, and social movements. Explain why each example belongs in its assigned category. Distinguish between each type of collective behaviour based on the type and degree of social structure and interaction that are present.

3. Select one social movement that is currently working for change in Canada. Analyze that movement, drawing on the concepts of relative deprivation, resource mobilization, and false consciousness.

Key Terms

Apartheid The former policy of the South African government designed to maintain the separation of blacks and other nonwhites from the dominant whites. (597)

Assembling perspective A theory of collective behaviour introduced by McPhail and Miller that seeks to examine how and why people move from different points in space to a common location. (583)

Collective behaviour In the view of sociologist Neil Smelser, the relatively spontaneous and unstructured behaviour of a group of people who are reacting to a common influence in an ambiguous situation. (581)

Craze An exciting mass involvement that lasts for a relatively long period of time. (586)

Crowds Temporary gatherings of people in close proximity who share a common focus or interest. (584)

Disaster A sudden or disruptive event or set of events that overtaxes a community's resources so that outside aid is necessary. (585)

Emergent-norm perspective A theory of collective behaviour proposed by Turner and Killian that holds that a collective definition of appropriate and inappropriate behaviour emerges during episodes of collective behaviour. (582)

Equilibrium model A functionalist view of society as tending toward a state of stability or balance. (594)

Evolutionary theory A theory of social change that holds that society is moving in a definite direction. (594)

Fads Temporary movements toward the acceptance of some particular taste or lifestyle that involve large numbers of people and are independent of preceding trends. (585)

False consciousness A term used by Karl Marx to describe an attitude held by members of a class that does not accurately reflect its objective position. (591)

Fashions Pleasurable mass involvements in some particular taste or lifestyle that have a line of historical continuity. (585)

Luddites Rebellious craft workers in nineteenth-century England who destroyed new factory machinery as part of their resistance to the Industrial Revolution. (598)

Multilinear evolutionary theory A theory of social change that holds that change can occur in several ways and does not inevitably lead in the same direction. (594)

Neo-Luddites Those who are wary of technological innovations and question the incessant expansion of industrialization, the increasing destruction of the natural and agrarian world, and the "throw it away" mentality that results in polluting the environment. (598)

New social movements Organized collective activities that promote autonomy and self-determination as well as improvements in the quality of life. (592)

Nonperiodic assemblies Nonrecurring gatherings of people that often result from word-of-mouth information. (584)

Panic A fearful arousal or collective flight based on a generalized belief that may or may not be accurate. (586)

Periodic assemblies Recurring, relatively routine gatherings of people, such as university classes. (584)

Public A dispersed group of people, not necessarily in contact with one another, who share an interest in an issue. (588)

Public opinion Expressions of attitudes on matters of public policy that are communicated to decision makers. (588)

Relative deprivation The conscious feeling of a negative discrepancy between legitimate expectations and present actualities. (590)

Resource mobilization The ways in which a social movement utilizes such resources as money, political influence, access to the media, and personnel. (590)

Rumour A piece of information gathered informally that is used to interpret an ambiguous situation. (587)

Social change Significant alteration over time in behaviour patterns and culture, including norms and values. (581)

Social movements Organized collective activities to promote or resist change in an existing group or society. (589)

Unilinear evolutionary theory A theory of social change that holds that all societies pass through the same successive stages of evolution and inevitably reach the same end. (594)

Value-added model A theory of collective behaviour proposed by Neil Smelser to explain how broad social conditions are transformed in a definite pattern into some form of collective behaviour. (582)

Vested interest groups Those people or groups who will suffer in the event of social change and who have a stake in maintaining the status quo. (596)

Additional Readings

BOOKS

Adam, Barry D., Jan Willem Duyvendak, and André Krouwel, eds. 1999. *The Global Emergence of Gay and Lesbian Politics: National Imprints of a Worldwide Movement.* Philadelphia: Temple University Press. The editors offer portraits of gay and lesbian organizing in 16 nations, including Australia, Brazil, France, Great Britain, Japan, Romania, and Spain.

Chang, Jen, Bethany Or, Eloginy Tharmendran, Emmie Tsumura, Steve Daniels, and Darryl Leroux (comp.). 2001. *RESIST! A Grassroots Collection of Stories, Poetry, Photos and Analysis from the FTAA Protests in Quebec City and Beyond.* Halifax, N.S.: Fernwood Publishing Company Limited. In this collection of young people's experiences from Quebec City in 2001, we see a reflection of the variety of people who attend protests and hear about how they make the decisions about which to participate in.

Jasper, James. 1997. *The Art of Moral Protest: Culture, Biography, and Creativity in Social Movements.* Chicago: University of Chicago Press. An analysis of how social movements, ranging from nineteenth-century boycotts to contemporary antinuclear, animal rights, and environmental movements, develop and the impact they have on participants and society as a whole.

Miller, David L. 2000. *Introduction to Collective Behavior and Collective Actions.* 2nd ed. Prospect Heights, IL: Waveland. The author, associated with the assembling perspective, covers all the major theoretical approaches of the field. He examines rumours, riots, social movements, immigration, and other forms of collective behaviour.

Ouellette, Grace. 2002. *The "Fourth World": Feminism and Aboriginal Women's Activism.* Halifax, N.S.: Fernwood Publishing Company Limited. Euro-Canadian feminists rarely address the circumstances that are unique to First Nations women; instead, they work with the assumption that all women are a part of a similar struggle. Using interviews with a number of women, the author addresses issues such as Aboriginal women's experiences with oppression, how they view male domination within their societies, and how these women articulate racism and gender oppression.

Riordon, Michael. 2001. *Eating Fire: Family Life, on the Queer Side.* Toronto: Between the Lines. In examining the range in living patterns and relationships among lesbian and gay families across Canada, the author illustrates the rich diversity in how personal and public identities are negotiated.

JOURNALS

Among those journals that focus on collective behaviour, social movements, and social change are *The Futurist* (founded in 1967), *International Journal of Mass Emergencies and Disasters* (1983), the *Journal of Gay, Lesbian, and Bisexual Identity* (1996), the *Journal of Popular Culture* (1967), *Research in Social Movements, Conflicts and Change* (1978), and *Technological Forecasting and Social Change* (1969).

Internet Connection

www.mcgrawhill.ca/college/schaefer

For additional Internet exercises relating to collective behaviour, social movements, and social change, visit the Schaefer Online Learning Centre at **http://www.mcgrawhill.ca/college/schaefer**. *Please note that while the URLs listed were current at the time of printing, these sites often change—check the Online Learning Centre for updates.*

The Network for Creative Change (NCC) was founded in Nova Scotia in 1996, as a means to identify citizenship opportunities for both local and global action. You can learn more about them at **http://www.chebucto.ns.ca/Community Support/NCC**. Go to the web page and find answers to the following questions:

(a) How did the Network come into existence? Why was it established? What is its purpose?

(b) Do you think the NCC would have been possible 20 years ago? Why or why not?

(c) What is meant by "systemic change"? Why is this type of social change important?

(d) How does the organization perceive the role of science in creating change, and/or helping to resolve some of the most critical issues facing contemporary Canadian society?

(e) What is the Multilateral Agreement of Investment? How does it represent a threat to Canadian society?

(f) What is the Genuine Progress Index? Why do its proponents argue that it is a more accurate measure of the improvement of citizens' lives than those measures currently in use by more governments and international organizations?

Killian that holds that a collective definition of appropriate and inappropriate behaviour emerges during episodes of collective behaviour. (582)

Employment equity Plans and programs to identify and eliminate workplace barriers to four designated groups, including women, Aboriginal Peoples, persons with disabilities, and visible minorities. (476)

Endogamy The restriction of mate selection to people within the same group. (363)

Environmental justice A legal strategy based on claims that minorities are subjected disproportionately to environmental hazards. (562)

Equilibrium model A functionalist view of society as tending toward a state of stability or balance. (594)

Established sect A religious group that is the outgrowth of a sect, yet remains isolated from society. (399)

Esteem The reputation that a particular individual has earned within an occupation. (211)

Ethnic group A group that is set apart from others because of its national origin or distinctive cultural patterns. (261)

Ethnocentrism The tendency to assume that one's culture and way of life represent the norm or are superior to all others. (79, 268)

Ethnography The study of an entire social setting through extended systematic observation. (42)

Eurocentrism A world view that assumes European values are the desired standard. (47)

Euthanasia The act of bringing about the death of a hopelessly ill and suffering person in a relatively quick and painless way for reasons of mercy. (343)

Evolutionary theory A theory of social change that holds that society is moving in a definite direction. (594)

Exogamy The requirement that people select mates outside certain groups. (363)

Experiment An artificially created situation that allows the researcher to manipulate variables. (37)

Experimental group Subjects in an experiment who are exposed to an independent variable introduced by a researcher. (40)

Exploitation theory A Marxist theory that views racial subordination in the United States as a manifestation of the class system inherent in capitalism. (274)

Expressiveness A term used by Parsons and Bales to refer to concern for maintenance of harmony and the internal emotional affairs of the family. (301)

Extended family A family in which relatives—such as grandparents, aunts, or uncles—live in the same home as parents and their children. (356)

F

Face-work A term used by Erving Goffman to refer to the efforts of people to maintain the proper image and avoid embarrassment in public. (94)

Fads Temporary movements toward the acceptance of some particular taste or lifestyle that involve large numbers of people and are independent of preceding trends. (585)

False consciousness A term used by Karl Marx to describe an attitude held by members of a class that does not accurately reflect its objective position. (207)

Family A set of people related by blood, marriage (or some other agreed-upon relationship), or adoption, who share the responsibility for reproducing and caring from members of society. (355)

Fashions Pleasurable mass involvements in some particular taste or lifestyle that have a line of historical continuity. (585)

Feminist perspectives Attempts to explain, understand, and eliminate the ways in which gender socially organizes our public and private lives to produce inequality between men and women. (18)

Fertility The amount of reproduction among women of childbearing age. (547)

Folkways Norms governing everyday social behaviour whose violation raises comparatively little concern. (71)

Force The actual or threatened use of coercion to impose one's will on others. (437)

Formal norms Norms that generally have been written down and that specify strict rules for punishment of violators. (70)

Formal organization A special-purpose group designed and structured for maximum efficiency. (148)

Formal social control Social control carried out by authorized agents, such as police officers, judges, school administrators, and employers. (185)

Functionalist perspective A sociological approach that emphasizes the way that parts of a society are structured to maintain its stability. (17)

G

Gemeinschaft A term used by Ferdinand Tönnies to describe close-knit communities, often found in rural areas, in which strong personal bonds unite members. (128)

Gender roles Expectations regarding the proper behaviour, attitudes, and activities of males and females. (101, 297)

Gender socialization The processes through which individuals learn to become feminine and masculine according to the expectations current in their society. (94)

Generalized others A term used by George Herbert Mead to refer to the child's awareness of the attitudes, viewpoints, and expectations of society as a whole that a child takes into account in his or her behaviour. (93)

Genocide The deliberate, systematic killing of an entire people or nation. (275)

Gentrification The resettlement of low-income city neighbourhoods by prosperous families and business firms. (528)

Gerontology The scientific study of the sociological and psychological aspects of aging and the problems of the aged. (329)

Gesellschaft A term used by Ferdinand Tönnies to describe communities, often urban, that are large and impersonal with little commitment to the group or consensus on values. (128)

Glass ceiling An invisible barrier that blocks the promotion of a qualified individual in a work environment because of the individual's gender, race, or ethnicity. (270, 310)

Goal displacement Overzealous conformity to official regulations within a bureaucracy. (152)

Goal multiplication The process through which an organization expands its purpose. (160)

Goal succession The process through which an organization identifies an entirely new objective because its traditional goals have been either realized or denied. (160)

Group Any number of people with similar norms, values, and expectations who regularly and consciously interact. (122, 143)

Growth rate The difference between births and deaths, plus the difference between immigrants and emigrants, per 1000 population. (550)

H

Hawthorne effect The unintended influence that observers or experiments can have on their subjects. (42)

Health As defined by the World Health Organization, a state of complete physical, mental, and social well-being, and not merely the absence of disease and infirmity. (487)

Hidden curriculum Standards of behaviour that are deemed proper by society and are taught subtly in schools. (415)

Holistic medicine A means of health maintenance using therapies in which the health care practitioner considers the person's physical, mental, emotional, and spiritual characteristics. (501)

Homophobia Fear of and prejudice against homosexuality. (134, 298)

Horizontal mobility The movement of an individual from one social position to another of the same rank. (221)

Horticultural societies Preindustrial societies in which people plant seeds and crops rather than subsist merely on available foods. (131)

Human ecology An area of study concerned with the interrelationships between people and their spatial setting and physical environment. (522)

Human relations approach An approach to the study of formal organizations that emphasizes the role of people, communication, and participation within a bureaucracy and tends to focus on the informal structure of the organization. (156)

Human rights Universal moral rights belonging to all people because they are human. (251)

Hunting-and-gathering society A preindustrial society in which people rely on whatever foods and fiber are readily available in order to live. (130)

Hypothesis A speculative statement about the relationship between two or more variables. (35)

I

Ideal type A construct or model that serves as a measuring rod against which specific cases can be evaluated. (13, 150, 204)

Ideological power and authority The ability to change attitudes or agendas by controlling people's perceptions and beliefs. (437)

Impression management A term used by Erving Goffman to refer to the altering of the presentation of the self in order to create distinctive appearances and satisfy particular audiences. (94)

Incest taboo The prohibition of sexual relationships between certain culturally specified relatives. (363)

Incidence The number of new cases of a specific disorder occurring within a given population during a stated period of time. (494)

Income Salaries and wages. (203)

Independent variable The variable in a causal relationship that, when altered, causes or influences a change in a second variable. (35)

Industrial city A city characterized by relatively large size, open competition, an open class system, and elaborate specialization in the manufacturing of goods. (519)

Industrial society A society that depends on mechanization to produce its economic goods and services. (131, 461)

Infant mortality rate The number of deaths of infants under one year of age per 1000 live births in a given year. (549)

Influence The exercise of power through a process of persuasion. (437)

Informal economy Transfers of money, goods, or services that are not reported to the government. (244)

Informal norms Norms that generally are understood but are not precisely recorded. (70)

Informal social control Social control carried out by people casually through such means as laughter, smiles, and ridicule. (185)

In-group Any group or category to which people feel they belong. (144)

Innovation The process of introducing new elements into a culture through either discovery or invention. (65)

Institutional completeness The degree to which an ethnic community provides for its own institutional needs, particularly in the key areas of religion, education, and social welfare. (267)

Institutional discrimination The denial of opportunities and equal rights to individuals and groups that results from the normal operations of a society. (271, 306)

Instrumentality A term used by Parsons and Bales to refer to emphasis on tasks, focus on more distant goals, and a concern for the external relationship between one's family and other social institutions. (301)

Interactionist perspective A sociological approach that generalizes about fundamental or everyday forms of social interaction. (19)

Interest group A voluntary association of citizens who attempt to influence public policy. (448)

Intergenerational mobility Changes in the social position of children relative to their parents. (222)

Interview A face-to-face or telephone questioning of a respondent to obtain desired information. (40)

Intragenerational mobility Changes in a person's social position within his or her adult life. (222)

Invention The combination of existing cultural items into a form that did not previously exist. (65)

Iron law of oligarchy A principle of organizational life developed by Robert Michels under which even democratic organizations will become bureaucracies ruled by a few individuals. (153)

K

Kinship The state of being related to others. (359)

L

Labelling theory An approach to deviance popularized by Howard S. Becker that attempts to explain why certain people are viewed as deviants while others engaging in the same behaviour are not. (179)

Laissez-faire A form of capitalism under which people compete freely, with minimal government intervention in the economy. (461)

Language An abstract system of word meanings and symbols for all aspects of culture. It also includes gestures and other nonverbal communication. (68)

Latent functions Unconscious or unintended functions; hidden purposes. (17)

Law Governmental social control. (70)

Legal–rational authority Power made legitimate by law. (438)

Liberation theology The use of a church in a political effort to eliminate poverty, discrimination, and other forms of conflict and social injustice evident in a secular society. (393)

Life chances Max Weber's term for people's opportunities to provide themselves with material goods, positive living conditions, and favorable life experiences. (219)

Life expectancy The average number of years a person can be expected to live under current mortality conditions. (549)

Looking-glass self A concept used by Charles Horton Cooley that emphasizes the self as the product of our social interactions with others. (92)

Low Income Cut-Off (LICO) Until January 2001, the Canadian equivalent of a poverty line. If the amount a household spends on the basics—food, shelter, and clothing—exceeds a certain proportion of income (the actual figure fluctuates with economic conditions, but generally falls just under 60 percent), then that household is classified as poor. (214)

Luddites Rebellious craft workers in nineteenth-century England who destroyed new factory machinery as part of their resistance to the Industrial Revolution. (598)

M

Macrosociology Sociological investigation that concentrates on large-scale phenomena or entire civilizations. (16)

Majority government A government where one party controls more than half the seats in a legislative house. (442)

Manifest functions Open, stated, and conscious functions. (17)

Market Basket Measure (MBM) A measure that takes into consideration more than subsistence needs, by calculating the amounts needed by various households to live a life comparable to community standards. (214)

Marginalization The process by which an individual, as a result of her or his minority status, is provided only partial access to opportunities. This discrimination is often more intense is the case of women. (270)

Master status A status that dominates others and thereby determines a person's general position within society. (118)

Material culture The physical or technological aspects of our daily lives. (66)

Matriarchy A society in which women dominate in family decision making. (359)

Matrilineal descent A kinship system that favours the relatives of the mother. (359)

McDonaldization The process by which the principles of the fast-food restaurant have come to dominate certain sectors of society, both in the United States and throughout the world. (143)

Mechanical solidarity The social cohesion of simple, preindustrial society, where the division of labour was minimal and people shared very similar lifestyles, performed the same tasks, and had common beliefs. (129)

Megachurches Large congregations that often lack direct ties to a worldwide denomination. (398)

Megalopolis A densely populated area containing two or more cities and their surrounding suburbs. (520)

Mental illness A disorder of the brain that disrupts a person's thinking, feeling, and ability to interact with others. (502)

Meritocracy A system where individuals earn their place in society. (203)

Metis The group of people formed when French male fur traders married First Nations women in the Red River Valley are of Manitoba. (262)

Metropolitan Influence Zones (MIZs) Areas outside of large metropolitan population centres, but still influenced by them. (526)

Microsociology Sociological investigation that stresses study of small groups and often uses laboratory experimental studies. (17)

Midlife crisis A stressful period of self-evaluation that begins at about age 40. (333)

Migration Relatively permanent movement of people with the purpose of changing their place of residence. (554)

Military–industrial complex The close association between the government, the military, and defence industries. (450)

Minority group A subordinate group whose members have significantly less control or power over their own lives than the members of a dominant or majority group have over theirs. (261)

Modernization The far-reaching process by which a society moves from traditional or less developed institutions to those character istic of more developed societies. (239)

Modernization theory A functionalist approach that proposes that modernization and development will gradually improve the lives of people in peripheral nations. (239)

Monogamy A form of marriage in which one woman and one man are married only to each other. (356)

Monopoly Control of a market by a single business firm. (462)

Morbidity rates The incidence of diseases in a given population. (495)

Mores Norms deemed highly necessary to the welfare of a society. (70)

Mortality rate The incidence of death in a given population. (495)

Multiculturalism A policy that promotes cultural and racial diversity and full and equal participation of individuals and communities of all origins as a fundamental characteristic of Canadian identity. (78)

Multilinear evolutionary theory A theory of social change that holds that change can occur in several ways and does not inevitably lead in the same direction. (594)

Multinational corporations Commercial organizations that are headquartered in one country but do business throughout the world. (236)

Multiple-nuclei theory A theory of urban growth developed by Harris and Ullman that views growth as emerging from many centres of development, each of which may reflect a particular urban need or activity. (523)

N

Natural science The study of the physical features of nature and the ways in which they interact and change. (9)

Negotiated order A social structure that derives its existence from the social inter-actions through which people define and redefine its character. (117)

Negotiation The attempt to reach agreement with others concerning some objective. (116)

Neocolonialism Continuing dependence of former colonies on foreign countries. (234)

Neo-Luddites Those who are wary ot techno-logical innovations and question the incessant expansion of industrialization, the increasing destruction of the natural and agrarian world, and the "throw it away" mentality that results in polluting the environment. (598)

Net migration The number of immigrants entering a country minus the number of emigrants leaving the country. (554)

Net worth The amount by which the value of someone's assets exceeds his or her debts. In Canada, it is used interchangeably with wealth. (203)

New religious movement (NRM) or cult A generally small, secretive religious group that represents either a new religion or a major innovation of an existing faith. (401)

New social movements Organized collective activities that promote autonomy and self-determination as well as improvements in the quality of life. (592)

New urban sociology An approach to urban-ization that considers the interplay of local, national, and worldwide forces and their effect on local space, with special emphasis on the impact of global economic activity. (524)

Nonmaterial culture Cultural adjustments to material conditions, such as customs, beliefs, patterns of communication, and ways of using material objects. (67)

Nonperiodic assemblies Nonrecurring gath-erings of people that often result from word-of-mouth information. (584)

Nonverbal communication The sending of messages through the use of posture, facial expressions, and gestures. (21)

Norms Established standards of behaviour maintained by a society. (70)

Nuclear family A married couple and their unmarried children living together. (355)

O

Obedience Compliance with higher authorities in a hierarchical structure. (182)

Objective method A technique for measuring social class that assigns individuals to classes on the basis of criteria such as occupation, education, income, and place of residence. (211)

Observation A research technique in which an investigator collects information through direct participation in and/or observation of a group, tribe, or community. (37)

Oligopoly Control of a market by a small group of companies. (462)

Open system A social system in which the position of each individual is influenced by his or her achieved status. (221)

Operational definition An explanation of an abstract concept that is specific enough to allow a researcher to measure the concept. (35)

Organic solidarity The social cohesion of industrial society, where people are dependent on one another because of the different and specialized tasks each performs. (129)

Organized crime The work of a group that regulates relations between various crimi-nal enterprises involved in the smuggling and sale of drugs, prostitution, gambling, and other activities. (188)

Out-group A group or category to which people feel they do not belong. (144)

P

Panic A fearful arousal or collective flight based on a generalized belief that may or may not be accurate. (586)

Patriarchy A society in which men dominate family decision making. (182, 359)

Patrilineal descent A kinship system that favours the relatives of the father. (359)

Peer group The group of people with whom we associate who are approximately our own age or who have a similar social status. (102)

Periodic assemblies Recurring, relatively routine gatherings of people, such as uni-versity classes. (584)

Personality In everyday speech, a person's typical patterns of attitudes, needs, characteristics, and behaviour. (91)

Peter principle A principle of organizational life, originated by Laurence J. Peter, accord-ing to which each individual within a hier-archy tends to rise to his or her level of incompetence. (152)

Pluralism Mutual respect between the various groups in a society for one another's cultures, which allows minorities to express their own cultures without experiencing prejudice. (278)

Pluralist model A view of society in which many competing groups within the community have access to governmental officials so that no single group is dominant. (450)

Political action committee (PAC) A political committee established by an interest group—say, a national bank, corporation, trade association, or cooperative or membership association—to solicit contributions for candidates or political parties. (448)

Political socialization The process by which individuals acquire political attitudes and develop patterns of political behaviour. (440)

Political system The social institution that relies on a recognized set of procedures for implementing and achieving the goals of a group. (437)

Politics In Harold D. Lasswell's words, "who gets what, when, and how." (437)

Polyandry A form of polygamy in which some women have more than one husband at the same time. (358)

Polygamy A form of marriage in which an individual can have several husbands or wives simultaneously. (358)

Polygyny A form of polygamy in which a husband can have several wives at the same time. (358)

Population pyramid A special type of bar chart that shows the distribution of the population by gender and age. (552)

Postindustrial city A city in which global finance and the electronic flow of information dominate the economy. (519)

Postindustrial society A society whose economic system is primarily engaged in the processing and control of information. (131)

Postmodern society A technologically sophisticated society that is preoccupied with consumer goods and media images. (132)

Power The ability to exercise one's will over others. (208, 437)

Power elite A small group of military, industrial, and government leaders who control the fate of the country. (449)

Preindustrial city A city with only a few thousand people living within its borders and characterized by a relatively closed class system and limited mobility. (518)

Prejudice A negative attitude toward an entire category of people, such as a racial or ethnic minority. (268)

Prestige The respect and admiration that an occupation holds in a society. (211)

Prevalence The total number of cases of a specific disorder that exist at a given time. (494)

Primary group A small group characterized by intimate, face-to-face association and cooperation. (143)

Privilege Access to opportunities provided to people as a direct result of their membership in a particular societal group. (270)

Profane The ordinary and commonplace elements of life, as distinguished from the sacred. (387)

Profession An occupation requiring extensive knowledge that is governed by a code of ethics. (464)

Professional criminal A person who pursues crime as a day-to-day occupation, developing skilled techniques and enjoying a certain degree of status among other criminals. (188)

Proletariat Karl Marx's term for the working class in a capitalist society. (207)

Protestant ethic Max Weber's term for the disciplined work ethic, this-worldly concerns, and rational orientation to life emphasized by John Calvin and his followers. (391)

Public A dispersed group of people, not necessarily in contact with one another, who share an interest in an issue. (588)

Public opinion Expressions of attitudes on matters of public policy that are communicated to decision makers. (588)

Q

Qualitative research Research that relies on what is seen in the field or naturalistic settings more than on statistical data. (33)

Quantitative research Research that collects and reports data primarily in numerical form. (33)

Questionnaire A printed research instrument employed to obtain desired information from a respondent. (40)

R

Racial group A group that is set apart from others because of obvious physical differences. (261)

Racism The belief that one race is supreme and all others are innately inferior. (268)

Random sample A sample for which every member of the entire population has the same chance of being selected. (36)

Reference group Any group that individuals use as a standard in evaluating themselves and their own behaviour. (146)

Relative deprivation The conscious feeling of a negative discrepancy between legitimate expectations and present actualities. (590)

Relative poverty A floating standard of deprivation by which people at the bottom of a society, whatever their lifestyles, are judged to be disadvantaged in comparison with the nation as a whole. (214)

Reliability The extent to which a measure provides consistent results. (39)

Religion A social institution involving a unified system of beliefs and practices relative to sacred things. (387)

Religiosity The intensity of an individual's commitment to a belief system. (394)

Religious beliefs Statements to which members of a particular religion adhere. (394)

Religious experience The feeling or perception of being in direct contact with the ultimate reality, such as a divine being, or of being overcome with religious emotion. (396)

Religious rituals Practices required or expected of members of a faith. (394)

Representative sample A selection from a larger population that is statistically found to be typical of that population. (36)

Resocialization The process of discarding former behaviour patterns and accepting new ones as part of a transition in one's life. (99)

Resource mobilization The ways in which a social movement utilizes such resources as money, political influence, access to the media, and personnel. (590)

Rites of passage Rituals marking the symbolic transition from one social position to another. (98)

Role conflict Difficulties that occur when incompatible expectations arise from two or more social positions held by the same person. (120)

Role exit The process of disengagement from a role that is central to one's self-identity and reestablishment of an identity in a new role. (121)

Role strain Difficulties that result from the differing demands and expectations associated with the same social position. (121)

Role taking The process of mentally assuming the perspective of another, thereby enabling one to respond from that imagined viewpoint. (93)

Routine activities theory The notion that criminal victimization increases when there is a convergence of motivated offenders and suitable targets. (178)

Rumour A piece of information gathered informally that is used to interpret an ambiguous situation. (587)

S

Sacred Elements beyond everyday life that inspire awe, respect, and even fear. (387)

Sanctions Penalties and rewards for conduct concerning a social norm. (72)

Sandwich generation The generation of adults who simultaneously try to meet the competing needs of their parents and their own children. (333)

Sapir–Whorf hypothesis A hypothesis concerning the role of language in shaping cultures. It holds that language is culturally determined and serves to influence our mode of thought. (68)

Science The body of knowledge obtained by methods based upon systematic observation. (8)

Scientific management approach Another name for the classical theory of formal organizations. (155)

Scientific method A systematic, organized series of steps that ensures maximum objectivity and consistency in researching a problem. (33)

Secondary analysis A variety of research techniques that make use of publicly accessible information and data. (43)

Secondary group A formal, impersonal group in which there is little social intimacy or mutual understanding. (144)

Sect A relatively small religious group that has broken away from some other religious organization to renew what it considers to be the original vision of the faith. (398)

Secularization The process through which religion's influence on other social institutions diminishes. (387)

Segregation The act of physically separating two groups; often imposed on a minority group by a dominant group. (277)

Self According to George Herbert Mead, the sum total of people's conscious perceptions of their own identity as distinct from others. (92)

Self-fulfilling prophecy The tendency of people to respond to and act on the basis of stereotypes, leading to validation of false definitions. (264)

Self-segregation The situation that arises when members of a minority deliberately develop residential, economic, and/or social network structures that are separate from those of the majority population. (277)

Senilicide The killing of the old. (343)

Serial monogamy A form of marriage in which a person can have several spouses in his or her lifetime but only one spouse at a time. (356)

Sexism The ideology that one sex is superior to the other. (306)

Sexual harassment Behaviour that occurs when work benefits are made contingent on sexual favors (as a "quid pro quo") or when touching, lewd comments, or appearance of pornographic material creates a "hostile environment" in the workplace. (161)

Sick role Societal expectations about the attitudes and behaviour of a person viewed as being ill. (488)

Significant others A term used by George Herbert Mead to refer to those individuals who are most important in the development of the self, such as parents, friends, and teachers. (94)

Single-parent families Families in which there is only one parent present to care for children. (368)

Slavery A system of enforced servitude in which people are legally owned by others and in which enslaved status is transferred from parents to children. (204)

Small group A group small enough for all members to interact simultaneously, that is, to talk with one another or at least be acquainted. (147)

Social category A group defined by some culturally relevant characteristic; that is, one that has an impact on a person's status within a society. (268)

Social change Significant alteration over time in behaviour patterns and culture, including norms and values. (581)

Social cohesion The degree to which members of a group feel united by shared values and beliefs. (129)

Social constructionist perspective An approach to deviance that emphasizes the role of culture in the creation of the deviant identity. (180)

Social control The techniques and strategies for preventing deviant human behaviour in any society. (182)

Social democracy An economy that is dominated primarily by private businesses operating within a political framework that is responsible for the redistribution of wealth. (462)

Social distance The degree of difference between cultures, which can vary from slight (e.g., the Canadian and American cultures) to great (e.g., the Canadian culture and that of the Mongols of Northern China). (268)

Social epidemiology The study of the distribution of disease, impairment, and general health status across a population. (494)

Social inequality A condition in which members of a society have different amounts of wealth, prestige, or power. (203)

Social institutions Organized patterns of beliefs and behaviour centred on basic social needs. (125, 352)

Social interaction The ways in which people respond to one another. (115)

Socialism An economic system under which the means of production and distribution are collectively owned. (462)

Socialization The process whereby people learn the attitudes, values, and actions appropriate for individuals as members of a particular culture. (89)

Social mobility Movement of individuals or groups from one position of a society's stratification system to another. (221)

Social movements Organized collective activities to bring about or resist fundamental change in an existing group or society. (589)

Social network A series of social relationships that links a person directly to others and therefore indirectly to still more people. (123)

Social role A set of expectations of people who occupy a given social position or status. (120)

Social safety net A system of social programs, such as welfare, employment insurance, Canada Pension Plan, etc., designed to alleviate the harshest conditions associated with being at the bottom of the income chain. (214)

Social structure The way in which a society is organized into predictable relationships. (115)

Societal-reaction approach Another name for labeling theory. (179)

Society A fairly large number of people who live in the same territory, are relatively independent of people outside it, and participate in a common culture. (64)

Sociobiology The systematic study of the biological bases of social behaviour. (92)

Sociocultural evolution The process of change and development in human societies that results from cumulative growth in their stores of cultural information. (130)

Sociology The systematic study of social behaviour and human groups. (7)

Squatter settlements Areas occupied by the very poor on the fringes of cities, in which housing is often constructed by the settlers themselves from discarded material. (522)

Status A term used by sociologists to refer to any of the full range of socially defined positions within a large group or society. (117)

Status consistency The notion that someone with high status in one area—income, for instance—is likely to be similarly ranked in other areas. (208)

Status group A term used by Max Weber to refer to people who have the same prestige or lifestyle, independent of their class positions. (208)

Stereotypes Unreliable generalizations about all members of a group that do not recognize individual differences within the group. (264)

Stigma A label used to devalue members of deviant social groups. (173)

Stratification A structured ranking of entire groups of people that perpetuates unequal economic rewards and power in a society. (203)

Subculture A segment of society that shares a distinctive pattern of mores, folkways, and values that differs from the pattern of the larger society. (78)

Survey A study, generally in the form of interviews or questionnaires, that provides sociologists and other researchers with information concerning how people think and act. (40)

Survey research The gathering of data by directly questioning members of the population being studied. (37)

Symbols The gestures, objects, and language that form the basis of human communication. (93)

T

Teacher-expectancy effect The impact that a teacher's expectations about a student's performance may have on the student's actual achievements. (418)

Technology Information about how to use the material resources of the environment to satisfy human needs and desires. (66, 130, 562)

Telecommuters Employees of business firms or government agencies who work full-time or part-time at home rather than in an outside office and who are linked to their supervisors and colleagues through computer terminals, phone lines, and fax machines. (157, 563)

Terrorism The use or threat of violence against random or symbolic targets in pursuit of political aims. (439)

Theory In sociology, a set of statements that seeks to explain problems, actions, or behaviour. (10)

Total fertility rate (TFR) The average number of children born alive to a woman, assuming that she conforms to current fertility rates. (549)

Total institutions A term coined by Erving Goffman to refer to institutions that regulate all aspects of a person's life under a single authority, such as prisons, the military, mental hospitals, and convents. (98)

Tracking The practice of placing students in specific curriculum groups on the basis of test scores and other criteria. (417)

Trade unions Organizations that seek to improve the material status of their members, all of whom perform a similar job or work for a common employer. (471)

Traditional authority Legitimate power conferred by custom and accepted practice. (438)

Trained incapacity The tendency of workers in a bureaucracy to become so specialized that they develop blind spots and fail to notice obvious problems. (151)

Triad A three-member group. (148)

U

Underclass Long-term poor people who lack training and skills. (216)

Unilinear evolutionary theory A theory of social change that holds that all societies pass through the same successive stages of evolution and inevitably reach the same end. (594)

Urban ecology An area of study that focuses on the interrelationships between people and their environment. (522)

Urbanism A term used by Wirth to describe distinctive patterns of social behaviour evident among city residents. (519)

V

Validity The degree to which a scale or measure truly reflects the phenomenon under study. (39)

Value-added model A theory of collective behaviour proposed by Neil Smelser to explain how broad social conditions are transformed in a definite pattern into some form of collective behaviour. (582)

Value neutrality Max Weber's term for objectivity of sociologists in the interpretation of data. (46)

Values Collective conceptions of what is considered good, desirable, and proper— or bad, undesirable, and improper—in a culture. (73)

Variable A measurable trait or characteristic that is subject to change under different conditions. (35)

Verstehen The German word for "understanding" or "insight"; used by Max Weber to stress the need for sociologists to take into account people's emotions, thoughts, beliefs, and attitudes. (13)

Vertical mobility The movement of a person from one social position to another of a different rank. (221)

Vested interest groups Those people or groups who will suffer in the event of social change and who have a stake in maintaining the status quo. (596)

Victimization surveys Questionnaires or interviews used to determine whether people have been victims of crime. (191)

Victimless crimes A term used by sociologists to describe the willing exchange among adults of widely desired, but illegal, goods and services. (190)

Vital statistics Records of births, deaths, marriages, and divorces gathered through a registration system maintained by governmental units. (549)

Voluntary associations Organizations established on the basis of common interest, whose members volunteer or even pay to participate. (158)

W

Wealth An inclusive term encompassing all of a person's material assets, including land and other types of property. (203)

White-collar crimes Crimes committed by affluent individuals or corporations in the course of their daily business activities. (188)

World systems analysis A view of the global economic system that sees it as divided between certain industrial nations and the developing countries that they control and exploit. (236, 524)

X

Xenocentrism The belief that the products, styles, or ideas of one's society are inferior to those that originate elsewhere. (80)

Z

Zero population growth (ZPG) The state of a population with a growth rate of zero, achieved when the number of births plus immigrants is equal to the number of deaths plus emigrants. (554)

Zoning laws Legal provisions stipulating land use and architectural design of housing and often employed as a means of keeping racial minorities and low-income people out of suburban areas. (532)

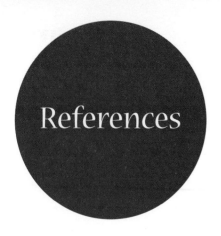

References

A

AARP. 1999. "New AARP Study Finds Boomers Vary in Their Views of the Future and Their Retirement Years." AARP News Release. June 1. Washington, DC.

Abbott, Pamela, and Claire Wallace. 1990. *An Introduction to Sociology: Feminist Perspectives.* New York: Routledge, Chapman and Hall, Inc.

ABC News. 1992. *Primetime Live: True Colors.* Transcript of November 26 episode.

Abegglen, James C., and George Stalk, Jr. 1985. *Kassha: The Japanese Corporation.* New York: Basic Books.

Abelson, Reed. 1997. "When Waaa Turns to Why." *New York Times,* November 1, pp. C1, C6.

Abercrombie, Nicholas, Bryan S. Turner, and Stephen Hill, eds. 1990. *Dominant Ideologies.* Cambridge, MA: Unwin Hyman.

———, Stephen Hill, and Bryan S. Turner. 1980. *The Dominant Ideology Thesis.* London: George Allen and Unwin.

Aberle, David F., A. K. Cohen, A. K. Davis, M. J. Leng, Jr., and F. N. Sutton. 1950. "The Functional Prerequisites of a Society." *Ethics* 60(January):100–111.

Abowitz, Deborah A. 1986. "Data Indicate the Feminization of Poverty in Canada, Too." *Sociology and Social Research* 70(April):209–213.

Abrahams, Ray G. 1968. "Reaching an Agreement over Bridewealth in Labwor, Northern Uganda: A Case Study." Pp. 202–215 in *Councils in Action,* edited by Audrey Richards and Adam Kuer. Cambridge: Cambridge University Press.

Abrahamson, Mark. 1978. *Functionalism.* Englewood Cliffs, NJ: Prentice-Hall.

Abramson, Jeffrey. 1994. *We the Jury: The Jury System and the Ideal of Democracy.* New York: Basic Books.

Abu-Laban, Sharon M., and Susan A. McDaniel. 1995. "Ageing Women and Standards of Beauty." Pp. 97–122 in *Feminist Issues: Race, Class and Sexuality,* edited by Nancy Mandell. Scarborough: Prentice-Hall Canada.

———, Yasmeen, and Daiva Stasiulis. 2000. "Constructing Ethnic Canadians: The Implications for Public Policy and Inclusive Citizenship." *Canadian Public Policy* vol. XXVI (4).

Adachi, Ken. 1976. *The Enemy that Never Was: A History of Japanese Canadians.* Toronto: McClelland and Stewart.

Adam, Barry D. 1992. "Sociology and People Living with AIDS." Pp. 3–18 in *The Social Context of AIDS,* edited by Joan Huber and Beth E. Schneider. Newbury Park, CA: Sage.

———. 1995. *The Rise of a Gay and Lesbian Movement.* Rev. ed. New York: Twayne.

Adam, Barry P., Jan Willem Duyvendak, and André Krouwei, eds. 1999. *The Global Emergence of Gay and Lesbian Politics: National Impact of a Worldwide Movement.* Philadelphia: Temple University Press.

Adam, Kanya. 2000. "Affirmative Action and Popular Perceptions: The Case of South Africa." *Society.* 37(February): 48–55.

Adams, Devon B. 1999. "Summary of State Sex Offender Registry Dissemination Procedures." *Bureau of Justice Statistics Fact Sheet* (August):1–8.

Adamson, Nancy, Linda Briskin, and Margaret McPhail. 1998. *Feminist Organizing for Change: The Contemporary Women's Movement in Canada.* Toronto: Oxford University Press.

Addams, Jane. 1910. *Twenty Years at Hull-House.* New York: Macmillan.

———. 1930. *The Second Twenty Years at Hull-House.* New York: Macmillan.

Adelman, Melvin L. 1993. "Modernization Theory and Its Critics." Pp. 347–358 in *Encyclopedia of American Social History*, edited by Mary Kupiec Coyton, Elliot J. Gorn, and Peter W. Williams. New York: Charles Sculines.

Adler, Patricia A., and John M. Johnson. 1992. "Street Corner Society Revisited." *Journal of Contemporary Ethnography* 21(April):3–10.

———, and Peter Adler. 1998. *Peer Power: Preadolescent Culture and Identity.* New Brunswick, NJ: Rutgers University Press.

———, Steven J. Kless, and Peter Adler. 1992. "Socialization to Gender Roles: Popularity among Elementary School Boys and Girls." *Sociology of Education* 65(July):169–187.

Africa News Service. 1998. "CPJ's 10 Enemies of the Press." Accessed October 8 (www. elibrary.com/ getdoc.cgi?id=113_ rydocid= 435731 @library_F+type=O~&dinst=).

Aguirre, Benigno E. 1984. "The Conventionalization of Collective Behavior in Cuba." *American Journal of Sociology* 90(3):541–566.

———, E. L. Quarantelli, and Jorge L. Mendoza. 1988. "The Collective Behavior of Fads: The Characteristics, Effects, and Career of Streaking." *American Sociological Review* 53(August):569–584.

AIDS Alert. 1999. "AIDS Complacency Leads Back to Risk Behavior." November 14, pp. 127–128.

Akers, Ronald L. 1997. *Criminological Theories: Introduction and Evaluation.* 2d ed. Los Angeles, CA: Roxbury Publishing Co.

Alain, Michel. 1985. "An Empirical Validation of Relative Deprivation." *Human Relations* 38(8):739–749.

Alam, Sultana. 1985. "Women and Poverty in Bangladesh." *Women's Studies International Forum* 8(4):361–371.

Alba, Richard D., and Gwen Moore. 1982. "Ethnicity in the American Elite." *American Sociological Review* 47(June):373–383.

Albarracin, Dolores, Martin Fishbein, and Eva Goldstein de Muchinik. 1997. "Seeking Social Support in Old Age as a Reasoned Action: Structural and Volitional Determinants in a Middle-Aged Sample of Argentinean Women." *Journal of Applied Social Psychology* 27: 463–476.

Albas, Daniel, and Cheryl Albas. 1988. "Aces and Bombers: The Post-Exam Impression Management Strategies of Students." *Symbolic Interaction* 11(Fall):289–302.

Albert, Terry, and Gregory Williams. 1998. *The Economic Burden of AIDS in Canada.* Ottawa: Canadian Policy Research Networks.

Albrecht, Gary L., Katherine D. Seelman, and Michael Bury (Eds.) *2000 Handbook of Disability Studies.* Thousand Oaks, CA: Sage.

Alfino, Mark, John S. Carpeto, and Robin Wyngard. 1998. *McDonaldization Revisited: Critical Essays on Consumer Culture.* Westport, CT: Praeger.

Alinsky, Saul. 1946. *Reveille for Radicals.* Chicago: University of Chicago Press.

Allan, Stuart. 1999. *News Culture.* Buckingham, Great Britain: Open University Press.

Allen, Bem P. 1978. *Social Behavior: Fact and Falsehood.* Chicago: Nelson-Hall.

Allen, John L. 1996. *Student Atlas of World Politics.* 2d ed. Madison, WI: Brown and Benchmark.

Allport, Gordon W. 1979. *The Nature of Prejudice.* 25th anniversary ed. Reading, MA: Addison-Wesley.

Alonzo, Angelo A. 1989. "Health and Illness and the Definition of the Situation: An Interactionist Perspective." Presented at the annual meeting of the Society for the Study of Social Problems, Berkeley, CA.

Alter, Jonathon. 2000. "The Death Penalty on Trial." *Newsweek,* June 12, pp. 24–32, 34.

Altman, Lawrence K. 1998. "Parts of Africa Showing H.I.V. in 1 in 4 Adults." *New York Times,* June 24, pp. A1, A6.

Alvord, Lori Arviso, and Elizabeth Cohen Van Pelt. 1999. *The Scalpel and the Silver Bear.* New York: Bantam.

Alzheimer's Association. 1999. "Statistics/Prevalence." Accessed January 10, 2000 (http://www.alz.org/facts/stats.htm).

Amato, Paul, and Alan Booth. 1997. *A Generation at Risk.* Cambridge, MA: Harvard University Press.

Amazon.com. 2000a. *About Amazon.com.* Accessed September 30, 2000 (http://www.amazon.com/exec).

Ambert, Anne-Marie. 1998. *Divorce : Facts, Figures and Consequences.* Ottawa: The Vanier Institute of the Family, Contemporary Family Trends.

American Association for the Advancement of Science. 2000. *Author abstracts, Conference Proceedings from Arctic Science 2000.* Whitehorse, Yukon: American Association for the Advancement of Science.

American Association of Health Plans. 1998a. "Number of People in HMOs, 1976–96." Accessed August 11, 1998 (http://www.aahp.org/menus/index.cfm?cfid=64953%cftoken=32374).

———. 1998b. "Demographic Characteristics of Health Plan Enrollees." Accessed August 11, 1998 (http://www.aahp.org/menus/index.cfm?cfid=64953%cftoken=32374).

American Association of University Women. 1992. *How Schools Shortchange Girls.* Washington, DC: American Association of University Women.

American Bar Association. 1997. *Section of Individual Rights and Responsibilities. Section of Litigation* (*Capital Punishment*). (February). Chicago: Division for Policy Administration, ABA.

———. 1999. "Commission on Domestic Violence." Accessed July 20, 1999 (http://www.abanet.org/domviol/stats.html).

———. 1999a. "Domestic Partnerships: List of Cities, States and Counties." Accessed September 2, 1999 (http:www.aclu.org/issues/gay/dpstate.html).

———. 1999b. "School Prayer Amendment Returns." Accessed November 8, 1999 (http://www.aclu.org/action/prayer106.html).

———. 2000. "State and Local Laws Protecting Lesbians and Gay Men Against Workplace Discrimination." Accessed January 19 (http://www.aclu.org/issues/gay/gay-laws.html).

American Humane Association. 1999. "Child Abuse and Neglect Data." Accessed July 20, 1999 (http://www.Americanhumane.org/cpfactdata.htm).

American Medical Association Council on Scientific Affairs. 1992. "Assault Weapons as a Public Health Hazard in the United States." *Journal of the American Medical Association* 267:3067–3070.

American Society of Plastic Surgeons. 2002. *National Clearinghouse of Plastic Surgery Statistics.* Accessed February 1, 2002 (http://www.plasticsurgery.org/mediactr/stats_ncs.htm).

American Sociological Association. 1993. *The Sociology Major as Preparation for Careers in Business and Organizations.* Washington, DC: American Sociological Association.

———. 1995a. *Careers in Sociology.* 2d ed. Washington, DC: American Sociological Association.

———. 1995b. *The Sociological Advantage.* Washington, DC: American Sociological Association.

———. 1997a. *Code of Ethics.* Washington, DC: American Sociological Association. Accessible at http://www.asanet.org/members/ecoderev.html.

———. 1997b. *Code of Ethics.* Washington, DC: American Sociological Association.

———. 1997c. *Style Guide.* 2d ed. Washington, DC: American Sociological Association.

———. 1999. *Careers in Sociology.* 5th ed. Washington, DC: American Sociological Association.

———. 2000a. *1999 Guide to Graduate Departments.* Washington, DC: American Sociological Association.

———. 2000b. *2000 Medical School Graduation Questionnaire All Schools Report.* Washington, DC: AAMC.

———. 2000c. *U.S. Medical School Faculty: Annual Data.* Accessed October

1, 2000 (http://www.aamc.org/findinfo/infores/datarsc/facros/frspubs/usmsf.htm).

———. 2001. *Guide to Graduate Departments of Sociology.* Washington, DC: ASA.

Ammerman, Nancy T., Jackson W. Carroll, Carl S. Dudley, and William McKinney, eds. 1998. *Studying Congregations: A New Handbook.* Nashville, TN: Abingdon Press.

Amnesty International and Death Penalty Information Center. 1998. *The Death Penalty: Abolitionist and Retentionist Countries.* Developed by Andrew Redey. December 30. Accessed January 30, 1999 (http:\\worldpolicy.org/americas/dp/maps-dp.html).

Amnesty International USA. 1994. *Breaking the Silence: Human Rights Violations Based on Sexual Orientation.* New York: Amnesty International.

Amnesty International. 1999. "Facts and Figures on the Death Penalty." Accessed August 4 (http://www.amnesty.excite.com/abolish/act500299.html).

———. 2000. "The Death Penalty: List of Abolitionist and Retentionist Countries." April. Accessed August 7, 2000 (http://www.amnesty.org/ailib/aipub/2000/ACT/A5000500.htm).

———. 2001. "Campaigning for Gay and Lesbian Human Rights", AI Online Document 79/002/2001. From September 1999 Focus Vol. 29 No. 5 (www.amnesty.org/aidoc).

Amnesty Now. 2000. "Mexico: Investigation into Mass Graves." 24(Winter):8–9.

Amselle, Jorge, and Amy C. Allison. 2000. "Two Years of Success: An Analysis of California Test Scores After Proposition 227." Washington, DC: READ Institute, Center for Equal Opportunity. Accessed at http://www.ceousa.org/.

Anders, George. 1993. "McDonald's Methods Come to Medicine as Chains Acquire Physician's Practices." *Wall Street Journal,* August 24, pp. B1, B6.

Andersen, Margaret L. 1997. *Thinking About Women: Sociological Perspectives on Sex and Gender.* 4th ed. Boston: Allyn and Bacon.

———. 2000. *Thinking About Women: Sociological Perspectives on Sex and Gender.* 5th edition. Boston: Allyn & Bacon.

Anderson, Elijah, and Molly Moore. 1993. "The Burden of Womanhood." *Washington Post National Weekly Edition* 10(March 22–28):6–7.

———. 1978. *A Place on the Corner.* Chicago: University of Chicago Press.

———. 1990. *Streetwise: Race, Class, and Change in an Urban Community.* Chicago: University of Chicago Press.

———. 1999. *Code of the Streets.* New York: Norton.

———, John Ward, and Molly Moore. 1993. "The Burden of Womanhood." *Washington Post National Weekly Edition* 10(March 22–28):6–7.

———, John Ward. 1994. "Where Birth Control Is a Means of Survival." *Washington Post National Weekly Edition* 11(September):18.

Anderson, Sarah, and John Cavanagh. 2001. "Top 200: The Rise of Corporate Global Power." *The Institute for Policy Studies.* Accessed April 18 (http://www.ips-dc.org/reports/top200text.htm).

Andersson-Brolin, Lillemor. 1988. "Ethnic Residential Segregation: The Case of Sweden." *Scandinavian Journal of Development Alternatives* 7(March):33–45.

Angier, Natalie. 1998. "Drugs, Sports, Body Image and G.I. Joe." *New York Times,* December 22, pp. D1, D3.

Anti-Defamation League. 1998. *Audit of Anti-Semitic Incidents, 1997.* New York: Anti-Defamation League.

Appelbaum, Richard, and Peter Dreier. 1999. "The Campus Anti-Sweatshops Movement." *The American Prospect* (September–October), pp. 71–78.

Appleby, Julie. 1999. "Rethinking Managed Care." *USA Today,* October 7, pp. A1–A2.

Aquilino, William S. 1990. "The Likelihood of Parent–Adult Child Coresidence: Effects of Family Structure and Parental Characteristics." *Journal of Marriage and the Family* 52: 405–419.

Arber, Sara and Jay Ginn. 1991. *Gender and Later Life: A Sociological Analysis of Resources and Constraints.* London: Sage.

Archer, Margaret. 1988. *Culture and Agency: The Place of Culture in Social Theory.* Cambridge: Cambridge University Press.

Armer, J. Michael, and John Katsillis. 1992. "Modernization Theory." Pp. 1299–1304 in *Encyclopedia of Sociology,* vol. 4, edited by Edgar F. Borgatta and Marie L. Borgatta. New York: Macmillan.

Armour, Stephanie. 2000. "Companies Work to Be More Gay-Friendly." *USA Today.* (February 28): B1.

Armstrong, Jane. 2002. "Canada is 30 million, but will that last?" *The Globe and Mail,* March 13, pp. A1, A7.

Armstrong, Pat, and Hugh Armstrong. 1993 *The Double Ghetto, Third Edition.* Toronto: McClelland & Stewart.

———, and Hugh Armstrong. 2000. "Thinking It Through: Women, Work and Caring in the New Millennium." Halifax, Nova Scotia: Healthy Balance Research Program.

Arnold, Wayne. 2000. "Manila's Talk of the Town Isn't Talk at All." *New York Times,* July 5, p. C1.

Aronson, Elliot. 1999. *The Social Animal.* 8th ed. New York: Worth.

Assembly of First Nations (AFN). 2001. *First Nations Children's Health.* Part of series of Fact Sheets.

Associated Press. 1998a. "Environmental Test Case Averted." *Christian Science Monitor,* September 21, p. 18.

———. 1998b. "Doctors Perform Japan's First Lung Transplant from Living Donor." Accessed October 28, 1999 (http://www.ap.org).

———. 2000a. "Opinions on Gay Relationships." *Los Angeles Times,* June 1, p. A31.

———. 2000b. *United States Medical School Faculty: Annual Data.* Washington, DC: AAMC.

Association of American Medical Colleges. 2000a. *2000 Medical School Graduate Report: All Schools Report.* Washington, DC: AAMC.

Association of Universities and Colleges of Canada. 1999. "Trends: The Canadian University in Profile" in *AUCC News: Backgrounder,* June 7, 1999.

———. 2001. "About Canada's Universities." Accessed July 28, 2001 (http://www.aucc.ca/en/acuindex.html).

Astin, Alexander, Kenneth C. Green, and William S. Korn. 1987. *The American Freshman: Twenty-Year Trends.* Los Angeles: Cooperative Institutional Research Program, University of California at Los Angeles.

———, Sarah A. Parrott, William S. Korn, and Linda J. Sax. 1994. *The American Freshman: Thirty Year Trends.* Los Angeles: Higher Education Research Institute.

Astin, John A. 1998. "Why Patients Use Alternative Medicine: Results of a National Study." *Journal of American Medical Association* 279(May 20):1548–1553.

Atchley, Robert C. 1976. *The Sociology of Retirement.* New York: Wiley.

———. 1985. *The Social Forces in Later Life: An Introduction to Social Gerontology.* 4th ed. Belmont, CA: Wadsworth.

Atkinson, Anthony Barnes, and John Micklewright. 1992. *Economic Transformation in Eastern Europe and the Distribution of Income.* Cambridge: Cambridge University Press.

Augustine, Noah. 2000. "Grandfather was a Knowing Christian." *The Toronto Star,* August 9, p. A17.

Austin, Erica Weintraub and Bruce E. Pinkleton. 1995. "Positive and Negative Effects of Political Disaffection on the Less Experienced Voter." *Journal of Broadcasting and Electronic Media* 39(Spring):215–235.

Avni, Noga. 1991. "Battered Wives: The Home as a Total Institution" *Violence and Victims* 6(Summer):137–149.

Axtell, Roger E. 1990. *Do's and Taboos around the World.* 2d ed. New York: John Wiley and Sons.

Azumi, Koya, and Jerald Hage. 1972. *Organizational Systems.* Lexington, MA: Heath.

B

Babchuck, Nicholas, and Alan Booth. 1969. "Voluntary Association Membership: A Longitudinal Analysis." *American Sociological Review* 34(February):31–45.

Bachrach, Christine A. 1986. "Adoption Plans, Adopted Children, and Adoptive Mothers." *Journal of Marriage and the Family* 48(May):243–253.

Bachu, Amara. 1999. "Is Childlessness Among American Women on the Rise?" Working Paper No. 37, Population Division, U.S. Bureau of Census, Washington, DC.

Bailey, Gordon, and Noga Gayle. 1993. *Sociology: An Introduction From the Classics to Contemporary Feminists.* Don Mills, Ontario: Oxford University Press.

Bailey, Sue. 2001. "Aboriginal leaders must set sober example, says chief." (www.canoe.ca/Health0102/28_native-cp.html).

Bailey, Susan McGee, and Patricia B. Campbell. 2000. "The Gender Wars in Education." *Wellesley Centers for Women Research Report* 20(Fall/Winter):20.

Bainbridge, William Sims. 1999. "Cyberspace: Sociology's Natural Domain." *Contemporary Sociology* 28(November):664–667.

Baker, Laurence C. 1995. "Differences in Earnings between Male and Female Physicians." *New England Journal of Medicine* 334(April 11):960–964.

Baker, Linda. 1994. "Day-Care Disgrace." *The Progressive* 58(June):26–27.

Baker, Maureen. 2001a. "Paid and Unpaid Work: How do Families Divide Their Labour?" Pp. 96–115 in *Families: Changing Trends in Canada,* 4th ed., edited by Maureen Baker. Toronto: McGraw-Hill Ryerson.

Baker, Maureen. 2001b. "The Future of Family Life." Pp. 285–302 in *Families: Changing Trends in Canada,* 4th ed., edited by Maureen Baker. Toronto: McGraw-Hill Ryerson.

Baldassare, Mark. 1992. "Suburban Communities." Pp. 475–494 in *Annual*

Review of Sociology, edited by Judith Blake and John Hagan. Palo Alto, CA: Annual Reviews.

Bales, Kevin. 1999. *Disposable People: New Slavery in the Global Economy.* Berkeley, CA: University of California Press.

Ballantine, Jeanne H. 1997. *The Sociology of Education: A Systematic Analysis.* 4th edition. Englewood Cliffs, N.J.: Prentice-Hall. A comprehensive approach to education that includes theoretical frameworks, current educational issues, and the process and structure of education systems.

Banks, Olive. 1981. *Three Faces of Feminism.* New York: St. Martin's Press.

Bannerji, Himani. 1991. "But Who Speaks for Us?" In *Unsettling Relations: the university as a site of feminist struggles.* Toronto: Women's Press.

Barber, Benjamin R. 1995. *Jihad vs. McWorld.* New York: Times Books.

Barkey, Karen. 1991. "The Use of Court Records in the Reconstruction of Village Networks: A Corporative Perspective." *International Journal of Comparative Sociology* 32(January–April):195–216.

Barlett, Donald L., and James B. Steele. 1998. "Corporate Welfare." *Time* 152(November 9):36–39.

Barna Research Group. 1998. "The Cyberchurch Is Coming." April 20, 1998. Accessed November 10, 1999 (http://www.barna.org/cgi-bin/Page-PressRelease.asp?/Press Release ID=9).

Barnard, Robert, Dave Cosgrave, and Jennifer Welsh. 1998. *Chips and Pop: Decoding the Nexus Generation.* Toronto: Malcolm Lester Books.

Barndt, Deborah (ed.). 2000. *Women Working the NAFTA Food Chain: Women, Food and Globalization.* Toronto: Sumach Press.

Barr, Cameron W. 1999. "Get Used to It: Japanese Steel Themselves for Downsizing." *Christian Science Monitor,* November 12, pp. 7–8.

Barrett, Stanley R. 1987. *Is God a Racist? The Right Wing in Canada.* Toronto: U of T Press.

Barrett, David B. 1996. "Worldwide Adherents of All Religions by Six Continental Areas, Mid-1995." P. 298 in *Britannica Book of the Year 1996.* Chicago: Encyclopedia Britannica.

Barron, Milton L. 1953. "Minority Group Characteristics of the Aged in American Society." *Journal of Gerontology* 8:477–482.

Barlett, Donald L., and James B. Steele. 1998. "Corporate Welfare." *Time* 152(November 9):36–39.

Barzansky, Barbara, Harry S. Jonas, and Sylvia I. Etzel. 1995. "Educational Programs in U.S. Medical Schools,

1994–1995." *Journal of the American Medical Association* 274(September 6):716–722.

Basow, Susan A. 1992. *Gender Stereotypes and Roles* (3d ed.). Pacific Grove, CA: Brooks/Cole.

Basso, Keith H. 1972. "Ice and Travel among the Fort Norman Slave: Folk Taxonomies and Cultural Rules." *Language in Society* 1(March):31–49.

Bates, Colleen Dunn. 1999. "Medicine's Gender Gap." *Shape,* October.

Bauerlein, Monika. 1996. "The Luddites Are Back." *Utne Reader* (March–April):24, 26.

Baugher, Eleanor, and Leatha Lamison-White. 1996. "Poverty in the United States: 1995." *Current Population Reports,* ser. P60, no.194. Washington, DC: U.S. Government Printing Office.

Bauman, Kurt J. 1999. "Extended Measures of Well-Being: Meeting Basic Needs." *Current Population Reports,* ser. P-70, no. 67. Washington, DC: U.S. Government Printing Office.

Beaujot, Roderic, and Kevin McQuillan. 1982. *Growth and Dualism: The Demographic Development of Canadian Society.* Toronto: Gage Publishing Limited.

———, Ellen M. Gee, Fernando Rajulton, and Zenaida R. Ravanera. 1995. *Family over the Life Course.* Ottawa: Minister of Industry.

Bebout, Rick. 1997. *The origins of "We Demand."* The Canadian Lesbian and Gay Archives (www.clga.ca/Material/Records/docs/wedemand.htm).

———. 2000. *On the Origin of "The Body Politic": Genealogy* (http://webhome.idirect.com/~rbebout/oldbeep/geneo.htm).

Becerra, Rosina M. 1999. "The Mexican-American Family." Pp. 153–171 in *Ethnic Families in America: Patterns and Variations,* 4th ed., edited by Charles H. Mindel, Robert W. Habenstein, and Roosevelt Wright, Jr. Upper Saddle River, NJ: Prentice-Hall.

Becker, Anne E. 1995. *Body, Self, and Society: The View from Fiji.* Philadelphia: University of Pennsylvania Press.

———, and R. A. Burwell. 1999, *Acculturation and Disordered Eating in Fiji.* Presented at the annual meeting of the American Psychiatric Association.

Becker, Howard S. 1952. "Social Class Variations in the Teacher–Pupil Relationship." *Journal of Educational Sociology* 25(April):451–465.

———. 1963. *The Outsiders: Studies in the Sociology of Deviance.* New York: Free Press.

———. 1973. *The Outsiders: Studies in the Sociology of Deviance.* Rev. ed. New York: Free Press.

———, Blanche Greer, Everett C. Hughes, and Anselm Strauss. 1961. *Boys in White: Student Culture in Medical School.* Chicago: University of Chicago Press.

———, ed. 1964. *The Other Side: Perspectives on Deviance.* New York: Free Press.

Beeghley, Leonard. 1978. *Social Stratification in America: A Critical Analysis of Theory and Research.* Santa Monica, CA: Goodyear Publishing.

Begley, Sharon. 1998. "Why Wilson's Wrong." *Newsweek* 131(June 22):61–62.

———. 1999. "Designer Babies." *Newsweek* 132(November 9):61–62.

Bélanger, Alain, and Jean Dumas. 1998. *Report of the Demographic Situation in Canada 1997.* Ottawa: Ministry of Industry.

Belkin, Lisa. 1999. "Getting the Girl." *New York Times Magazine,* July 25, pp. 26–31, 38, 54–55.

Bell, Daniel. 1953. "Crime as an American Way of Life." *Antioch Review* 13(Summer):131–154.

———. 1999. *The Coming of Post-Industrial Society: A Venture in Social Forecasting.* With new foreword. New York: Basic Books.

Bell, Wendell. 1981a. "Modernization." Pp. 186–187 in *Encyclopedia of Sociology.* Guilford, CT: DPG Publishing.

———. 1981b. "Neocolonialism." P. 193 in *Encyclopedia of Sociology.* Guilford, CT: DPG Publishing.

Bellafante, Ginia. 1998. "Feminism: It's All About Me!" *Time* 151(June 20):54–62.

Belluck, Pam. 1996. "The Symptoms of Internet Addiction." *New York Times,* December 1, p. E5.

———. 1999. "On Assisted Suicide, Kevorkian Is Seen as 'Distraction.'" *New York Times,* March 30, p. A17.

Belsie, Laurent. 1998. "Genetic Research Data Will Double Annually." *Christian Science Monitor,* July 30, p. B4.

———. 2000. "Strange Webfellows." *Christian Science Monitor.* (March 2): 15–16.

Bendavid, Naftali. 1998. "Surge in Executions Just the Beginning." *Chicago Tribune,* January 4, pp. 1, 14.

Bender, William, and Margaret Smith. 1997. "Population, Food, and Nutrition." *Population Bulletin* 51(February).

Bendick, Marc, Jr., Charles W. Jackson, and J. Horacio Romero. 1993. *Employment Discrimination against Older Workers: An Experimental Study of Hiring Practices.* Washington, DC: Fair Employment Council of Greater Washington.

Bendix, B. Reinhard. 1968. "Max Weber." Pp. 493–502 in *International Encyclopedia of the Social Sciences,* edited by David L. Sills. New York: Macmillan.

Benedetto, Richard. 1998. "Turncoats in Key Groups Lead Democratic Rebound." *USA Today,* November 5, p. 4A.

Benford, Robert D. 1992. "Social Movements." Pp. 1880–1887 in *Encyclopedia of Sociology,* vol. 4, edited by Edgar F. Borgatta and Marie L. Borgatta. New York: Macmillan.

Benner, Richard S. and Susan Tyler Hitchcock. 1986. *Life after Liberal Arts.* Charlottesville: Office of Career Planning and Placement, University of Virginia.

Bennet, James. 1996. "The Delegates: Where Image Meets Reality." *New York Times,* August 12, pp. A1, A11.

Bennett, Vanora. 1997. "Russia's Ugly Little Secret: Misogyny." *Los Angeles Times, December 6, pp. A1, A9, A10.*

Bennett, Vivienne. 1995. "Gender, Class, and Water: Women and the Politics of Water Service in Monterrey, Mexico." Latin American Perspectives 22(September):76–79.

Berger, Joan. 1988. "It's Time for Quotas to Go the Way of the Tail Fin." *Business Week* 304(March 7):60.

Berger, Peter, and Thomas Luckmann. 1966. *The Social Construction of Reality.* New York: Doubleday.

Berk, Richard A. 1974. *Collective Behavior.* Dubuque, IA: Brown.

———, and Howard E. Aldrich. 1972. "Patterns of Vandalism during Civil Disorders as an Indicator of Selection of Targets." *American Sociological Review* 37(October):533–547.

Berke, Anne C. 1995. *Body, Self, and Society: The View from Fiji.* Philadelphia: University of Pennsylvania Press.

———, and R. A. Burwell. 1999. "Acculturation and Disordered Eating in Fiji." *New Research Program and Abstracts.* Annual meeting of the American Psychiatric Association, May 3–4.

Berke, Richard L. 1994. "Defections among Men to G.O.P. Helped Insure Rout of Democrats." *New York Times,* November 11, pp. A1, A27.

Berkeley Wellness Letter. 1990. "The Nest Refilled." 6(February):1–2.

Berlin, Brent, and Paul Kay. 1991. *Basic Color Terms: Their Universality and Evolution.* Berkeley, CA: University of California Press.

Bernhardt, Todd. 1997. "Disaster Mythology: A Contest Analysis from 1985 to 1995." Presented at the annual meeting of the Midwest Sociological Society, April, Des Moines, IA.

Bernstein, Anne C. 1988. "Unraveling the Tangles: Children's Understanding of Stepfamily Kinship." Pp. 83–111 in *Relative Strangers: Studies of Step-Family* Press, edited by W. R. Beer, Totowa, NJ: Rowan and Liten Field.

Bernstein, Jared, Elizabeth C. McNichol, Lawrence Mishel, and Robert Zahradnik. 2000. *Pulling Apart: A State-by-State Analysis of Income Trends.* Washington, DC: Center on Budget and Policy Priorities.

Bernstein, Nina. 1997. "On Line, High-Tech Sleuths Find Private Facts." *New York Times,* September 15, pp. A1, A20.

Best, Amy L. 2000. *Prom Night: Youth, Schools and Popular Culture.* New York: Routledge.

Best, Fred, and Ray Eberhard. 1990. "Education for the 'Era of the Adult.'" *The Futurist* 21(May–June): 23–28.

Bettelheim, Bruno, and Morris Janowitz. 1964. *Social Change and Prejudice.* New York: Free Press.

Bharadwaj, Lakshmik. 1992. "Human Ecology." Pp. 848–867 in *Encyclopedia of Sociology,* vol. 2, edited by Edgar F. Borgatta and Marie L. Borgatta. New York: Macmillan.

Bianchi, Suzanne M., and Daphne Spain. 1996. "Women, Work, and Family in America." *Population Bulletin* 51(December).

Bibby, Reginald W. 1990. *Mosaic Madness.* Toronto: Stoddart.

———. 1995. *The Bibby Report: Social Trends Canadian Style.* Toronto: Stoddart.

———. 1996. *Fragmented Gods: The Poverty and Potential of Religion in Canada.* Toronto: Irwin.

———, and Donald C. Posterski. 1992. *Teen Trends.* Toronto: Stoddart.

———. 1995. *The Bibby Report: Social Trends Canadian Style.* Toronto: Stoddart.

———. 1996. "Fragmented Gods: Religion in Canada" In R. Brym (ed.), *Sociology in Question: Sociological Readings for the 21st Century.* Toronto: Harcourt Brace.

Bielby, William T,. and Denise D. Bielby. 1992. "I Will Follow Him: Family Ties, Gender-Role Beliefs, and Reluctance to Relocate for a Better Job." *American Journal of Sociology* 97(March):1241–1267.

Billson, Janet Mancini, and Bettina J. Huber. 1993. *Embarking upon a Career with an Undergraduate Degree in Sociology.* 2d ed. Washington, DC: American Sociological Association.

———. 1994. "What Are Employers Looking for in BA, MA, and PhD Sociology Graduates?" *Student Sociologist* (Spring):1–3.

Bjorkman, Sharon. 1999. "Doing Church: The Active Creation of Worship Style." Presented at the Conference of Sociological Ethnography, February 27.

Black, Donald. 1995. "The Epistemology of Pure Sociology." *Law and Social Inquiry* 20(Summer):829–870.

Black, Jerome H. 2000. "Entering the Political Elite in Canada: The Case of Minority Women as Parliamentary Candidates and MPs." *Canadian Review of Sociology and Anthropology* 37(2).

Black, Naomi. 1993. "The Canadian Women's Movement: The Second Wave." Pp. 151–176 in *Changing Patterns: Women in Canada,* 2d ed., edited by Sandra Burt, Lorraine Code, and Lindsay Dorney. Toronto: McClelland and Stewart.

Blackhall, Leslie J. et al. [5 authors]. 1995. "Ethnicity and Attitudes toward Patient Autonomy." *Journal of the American Medical Association* 274(September 13):820–825.

Blackwell, Tom. 2001. "Michigan Seeks to Stop Delivery of Toronto's Trash." *Ottawa Citizen* March 6, final ed., p. A6.

Blair, Jayson. 1999. "Wrongful Arrest of Actor Is Blamed on Bias." *New York Times,* July 18, p. 30.

Blakely, Earl J., and Mary Gail Snyder. 1997. *Fortress America: Gated Communities in the United States.* Washington, DC: Brookings Institution Press/Lincoln Institute.

Blanc, Ann Klimas. 1984. "Nonmarital Cohabitation and Fertility in the United States and Western Europe." *Population Research and Policy Review* 3:181–193.

Blanchard, Fletcher A., Teri Lilly, and Leigh Ann Vaughan. 1991. "Reducing the Expression of Racial Prejudice." *Psychological Science* 2(March):101–105.

Blanchfield, Mike. 2002. "Troops are promised 'beach, beer.'" In *The Ottawa Citizen.* Wednesday, May 22, 2002, page A3.

Blanco, Robert. 1998. "The Disappearance of Mom and Dad." *USA Today,* December 17, p. D1.

Blank, Rebecca M. 1997. *It Takes a Nation: A New Agenda for Fighting Poverty.* Princeton, NJ: Princeton University Press.

Blau, Peter M. 1964. *Exchange and Power in Social Life.* New York: Wiley.

———. 1972. *Racial Oppression in America.* New York: Harper and Row.

———, and Marshall W. Meyer. 1987. *Bureaucracy in Modern Society.* 3d ed. New York: Random House.

———, and Otis Dudley Duncan. 1967. *The American Occupational Structure.* New York: Wiley.

Blauner, Robert. 1964. *Alienation and Freedom.* Chicago: University of Chicago.

———. 1972. *Racial Oppression in America.* New York: Harper and Row.

Blendon, Robert J. 1986. "The Problem of Cost, Access and Distribution of Medical Care." *Daedalus* 115(Spring):119–135.

Bloom, Stephan G. 1996. "Strangers in a Strange Land." *Chicago Tribune Magazine* (January 28), pp. 10–15.

———. 2000. *Postville: A Clash of Cultures in Heartland America.* San Diego, CA: Harcourt Brace.

Bluestone, Barry, and Bennett Harrison. 1982. *The Deindustrialization of America.* New York: Basic Books.

———, and Bennett Harrison. 1999. *Growing Prosperity: The Battle for Growth with Equity in the 21st Century.* Boston, MA: Harrison Century Foundation/Houghton Mifflin.

Blumer, Herbert. 1969. *Symbolic Interactionism: Perspective and Method.* Englewood Cliffs, NJ: Prentice-Hall.

———. 1995. "Collective Behavior." Pp. 165–198 in *Principles of Sociology,* 2d ed., edited by Alfred McClung Lee. New York: Barnes and Noble.

Boaz, Rachel Floersheim. 1987. "Early Withdrawal from the Labor Force." *Research on Aging* 9(December):530–547.

Bobo, Lawrence. 1991. "Social Responsibility, Individualism, and Redistribution Policies." *Sociological Forum* 6:71–92.

Boeck, Scott, and Marcia Staimer. 1996. "News Wire" *USA Today,* May 28, p. 1.

Bolaria, B. Singh. 1995. *Social Issues and Contradictions in Canadian Society.* 2d ed. Toronto: Harcourt Brace.

Boldt, Menno. 1993. *Surviving as Indians: The Challenge of Self-Government.* Toronto: University of Toronto Press.

Bollag, Burton. 1996. "Bitter Internet Access South for Researchers Around the World." *Chronicle of Higher Education* 42(June 28): A14.

Bonacich, Edna, and Richard Appelbaum. 2000. *Behind the Label: Inequality in the Los Angeles Apparel Industry.* Berkeley, CA: University of California Press.

Bond, James T., Ellen Galinsky, and Jennifer E. Swanberg. 1998. *The 1997 National Study of the Changing Work Force.* New York: Families and Work Institute.

Booth, William. 2000. "Has Our Can-Do Attitude Peaked?" *Washington Post National Weekly Edition* 17(February 7):29.

Boritch, Helen. 1997. *Fallen Woman: Female Crime and Criminal Justice in Canada.* Toronto: ITP Nelson.

Borman, Kathryn M., and Joel H. Spring. 1984. *Schools in Central Cities: Structure and Process.* New York: Longman.

Bornschier, Volker, Christopher Chase-Dunn, and Richard Rubinson. 1978. "Cross-National Evidence of the Effects of Foreign Investment and Aid on Economic Growth and Inequality: A Survey of Findings and a Reanalysis." *American Journal of Sociology* 84(November):651–683.

Boserup, Ester. 1977. "Preface." Pp. xi–xiv in *Women and National Development: The Complexities of Change,* edited by Wellesley Editorial Committee. Chicago: Chicago University Press.

Bosetti, Lynn, Elaine Foulkes, Robert O'Reilly, and Dave Sande. 2000. *Canadian Charter Schools at the Crossroads: The Final Report of Charter schools in Alberta.* SAEE Research Series #5. Kelowna, B.C.: Society for the Advancement of Excellence in Education.

Boston Women's Health Book Collective. 1969. *Our Bodies, Ourselves.* Boston: New England Free Press.

———. 1992. *The New Our Bodies, Ourselves.* New York: Touchstone.

Bottomore, Tom, and Maximilien Rubel, eds. 1956. *Karl Marx: Selected Writings in Sociology and Social Philosophy.* New York: McGraw-Hill.

Bourdages, Jean-Luc, and Christine Labelle. 2000. *Protecting Wild Species at Risk in Canada.* Ottawa: Parliamentary Research Branch. PRB 00-19E.

Bouvier, Leon F. 1980. "America's Baby Boom Generation: The Fateful Bulge." *Population Bulletin* 35(April).

———, and Lindsey Grant. 1994. *How Many Americans? Population, Immigration, and the Environment.* San Francisco: Sierra Club.

Bowen, William G., and Derek Bok. 1998. *The Shape of the River: Long-Term Consequences of Considering Race in College and University Admissions.* Princeton, NJ: Princeton University Press.

Bowles, Samuel, and Herbert Gintis. 1976. *Schooling in Capitalist America: Educational Reforms and the Contradictions of Economic Life.* New York: Basic Books.

Bowles, Scott. 1999. "Fewer Violent Fatalities in Schools." *USA Today,* April 28, p. 4A.

Boyd, Monica, and Doug Norris. 1999. "The Crowded Nest: Young adults at home." In *Canadian Social Trends,* Spring 1999.

———, and Edward Prior. 1990. "Young Adults Living in Their Parents' Home." Pp. 188–191 in *Canadian Social Trends,* edited by C. McKie and K. Thompson. Toronto: Thompson Educational Press.

———. 1998. "Canadian, Eh? Ethnic Origin Shifts in the Canadian Census." *Canadian Ethnic Studies* 31(3):1–19.

Bracey, Gerald W. 1993. "No Magic Bullet." *Phi Delta Kappan* 74(February):495–496.

Bradley, Martin B. et al. [5 authors]. 1992. *Churches and Church Membership in the United States 1990.* Atlanta, GA: Glenmary Research Center.

Bragg, Rick. 1999. "Fearing Isolation in Old Age, Gay Generation Seeks Haven." *New York Times,* October 21, pp. A1, A16.

Brand, Dionne. 1993. "A Working Paper on Black Women In Toronto: Gender, Race, and Class." Pp. 220–241 in *Returning the Gaze: Essays on Racism, Feminism and Politics,* edited by Himani Bannerji. Toronto: Sister Vision Press.

Brandon, Karen. 1995. "Computer Scrutiny Adds to Furor over Immigrants." *Chicago Tribune,* December 5, pp. 1, 16.

Brannigan, Augustine. 1992. "Postmodernism." Pp. 1522–1525 in *Encyclopedia of Sociology,* vol. 3, edited by Edgar F. Borgatta and Marie L. Borgatta. New York: Macmillan.

Brannon, Robert. 1976. "Ideology, Myth, and Reality: Sex Equality in Israel." *Sex Roles* 6:403–419.

Braxton, Greg. 1999. "A Mad Dash for Diversity." *Los Angeles Times,* August 9, pp. F1, F10.

Bray, James H., and John Kelly. 1999. *Stepfamilies: Love, Marriage, and Parenting in the First Decade.* New York: Broadway Books.

Brelin, Christa, ed. 1996. *Strength in Numbers: A Lesbian, Gay, and Bisexual Resource.* Detroit: Visible Ink.

Brewer, Rose M. 1989. "Black Women and Feminist Sociology: The Emerging Perspective." *American Sociologist* 20(Spring):57–70.

Bridges, George S., and Sara Steen. 1998. "Racial Disparities in Official Assessments of Juvenile Offenders: Attributional Stereotypes as Mediating Mechanisms." *American Sociological Review* 63(August):554–570. briefingpapers/nafta01/).

Brimacombe, Glenn G., Pedro Antunes, and Jane McIntyre. 2001. *The Future Cost of Health Care in Canada, 2000 to 2020: Balancing Affordability and Sustainability.* Ottawa, Ontario: The Conference Board of Canada.

Brint, Steven. 1998. *Schools and Societies.* Thousand Oaks, CA: Pine Forge Press.

Brodeur, Paul. 1993. "Legacy." *New Yorker* 69(June 7):114.

Bronson, P. 1999. *The Nudist in the Late Shift and Other True Tales of Silicon Valley.* New York: Random House.

Brower, Brock. 1988. "The Pernicious Power of the Polls." *Money,* March 17, pp. 144–163.

Brown, Amanda, and Jim Stanford. *Flying without a Net: The 'Economic Freedom' of Working Canadians in 2000.* Canadian Centre for Policy Alternatives. Accessed April 18, 2002 (http://www.ccsd.ca/efru2000.pdf).

Brown, Michael, and Amy Goldin. 1972. *Collective Behavior: A Review and Reinterpretation of the Literature.* Pacific Palisades, CA: Goodyear.

Brown, Robert McAfee. 1980. *Gustavo Gutierrez.* Atlanta: John Knox.

Brown, Roger W. 1954. "Mass Phenomena." Pp. 833–873 in *Handbook of Social Psychology,* vol. 2, edited by Gardner Lindzey. Reading, MA: Addison-Wesley.

———. 1965. *Social Psychology.* New York: Free Press.

Brown, William J., and Michael J. Cody. 1991. "Effects of a Prosocial Television Soap Opera in Promoting Women's Status." *Human Communication Research* 18(September):114–142.

Bruce, Judith, Cynthia B. Lloyd, and Ann Leonard, with Patrice L. Engle and Niev Duffy. 1995. *Families in Focus: New Perspectives on Mothers, Fathers, and Children.* New York: Population Council.

Bruni, Frank. 1998. "A Small-But-Growing Sorority Is Giving Birth to Children for Gay Men." *New York Times,* June 25, p. A12.

Bryant, Adam. 1999. "American Pay Rattles Foreign Partners." *New York Times,* January 17, sec. 6, pp. 1, 4.

Bryson, Ken, and Lynne M-Casper. 1999. "Coresident Grandparents and Grandchildren." *Current Population Reports,* ser. P-23, no. 198. Washington, DC: U.S. Government Printing Office.

Buckley, Stephen. 1997. "Left Behind Prosperity's Door." *Washington Post National Weekly Edition,* March 24, pp. 8–9.

Buechler, Steven M. 1995. "New Social Movement Theories." *Sociological Quarterly* 36(3):441–464.

Buffalo News. 1999. "Viewpoints: We Must Continue Fight to Ban Soft Money." November 22, p. 3B.

Bula, Francis. 2000. "This is An International Crisis." *The Vancouver Sun,* November 21, pp. A1, A6.

Bulle, Wolfgang F. 1987. *Crossing Cultures? Southeast Asian Mainland.* Atlanta: Centers for Disease Control.

Bunzel, John H. 1992. *Race Relations on Campus: Stanford Students Speak.* Stanford, CA: Portable Stanford.

Bureau of Labor Statistics. 1998a. "Employer-Sponsored Childcare Benefits." *Issues in Labor Statistics,* August, pp. 1–2.

———. 1998b. "Employment Status of the Civilian Population by Race, Sex, Age, and Hispanic Origin." Accessed on November 18 at ttp://www.bls.gen/news.release/empsit.tp2.htm.

———. 1999a. "Comparative Civilian Labor Force Statistics for Ten Countries 1959–1990." Posted April 13, 1999. Accessed October 9, 1999 (ftp://ftp.bls.gov/pub/special.requests/ForeignLabor/flslforc.txt).

———. 1999b. "What Women Earned in 1998." *Issues in Labor Statistics.* Washington, DC: U.S. Government Printing Office.

———. 2000. "Employment Status of the Civilian Population by Race, Sex, Age, and Hispanic Origin." Accessed at http://www.bls.gen/news.release.

Bureau of Primary Health Care. 1999. Home Page. Accessed January 18, 2000 (http://www.bphc.hrsa.gov/bphcfactsheet.htm).

Bureau of the Census. 1970. *Statistical Abstract of the United States, 1970.* Washington, DC: U.S. Government Printing Office.

———. 1975. *Historical Statistics of the United States, Colonial Times to 1970.* Washington, DC: U.S. Government Printing Office.

———. 1981. *Statistical Abstract of the United States, 1981.* Washington, DC: U.S. Government Printing Office.

———. 1991a. "Marital Status and Living Arrangements: March 1990." *Current Population Reports,* ser. P-20, no. 450. Washington, DC: U.S. Government Printing Office.

———. 1991b. "Half of the Nation's Population Lives in Large Metropolitan Areas." Press release, February 21.

———. 1991c. "Half of the Nation's Population Lives in Large Metropolitan Areas." Press Release, February 21.

———. 1994. *Statistical Abstract of the United States: 1994.* Washington, D.C.: U.S. Government Printing Office.

———. 1995. *Statistical Abstract of the United States, 1995.* Washington, DC: U.S. Government Printing Office.

———. 1996a. *1992 Women-Owned Businesses.* Washington, DC: U.S. Government Printing Office.

———. 1996b. *Statistical Abstract of the United States, 1996.* Washington DC: U.S. Government Printing Office.

———. 1997a. *Statistical Abstract of the United States, 1997.* Washington, DC: U.S. Government Printing Office.

———. 1997b. "Geographical Mobility: March 1995 to March 1996." *Current Population Reports,* P-20, no. 497. Washington, DC: U.S. Government Printing Office.

———. 1998a. "Race of Wife by Race of Husband." Internet Release of June 10.

———. 1998b. *Statistical Abstract of the United States, 1998.* Washington, DC: U.S. Government Printing Office.

———. 1998c,d. Unpub.Tables—Marital Status and Living Arrangements: March 1998 (Update). Accessed July 26, 1999 (http://www.census.gov/prod/99pubs/p20-514u.pdf).

———. 1998e. Voting and Registration: November 1996. Internet release date: October 17, 1997. Accessed July 17, 1998 (http://www.census.gov/population/socdemo/voting/history/vot01.txt).

———. 1998f. "Money Income in the United States: 1997." *Current Population Reports,* ser. P-60, No. 200. Washington, DC: U.S. Government Printing Office.

———. 1999a. *Statistical Abstract of the United States, 1996.* Washington, DC: U.S. Government Printing Office.

———. 1999b. "The Asian and Pacific Islander Population in the United States: March 1998 (Update) (PP1-113). Table 9." *Total Money Income in 1997 of Families.* Accessed August 3, 1999 (http://www.census.gov/population/sucdemo/race/api98/table09.txt).

———. 1999c. "American Indian Heritage Month." News release October 21.

———. 1999d. "Population Estimates for States by Race and Hispanic Origin: July 1, 1998." Accessed September 16, 1999 (http://www.census.gov/population/estimates/state/srh/srhus98.txt).

———. 1999e. "Money Income in the United States." *Current Population Reports,* ser. P-60, no. 206. Washington, DC: U.S. Government Printing Office.

———. 2000a. "Census Bureau Projects Doubling of Nation's Population by 2100. Press release January 13.

———. 2000a. *Statistical Abstract of the United States, 2000.* Washington, DC: U.S. Government Printing Office.

———. 2000b. "Employment Status of the Civilian Population by Race, Sex, Age, and Hispanic Origin." Accessed January 3, 2000 (http://www.bls.gov/news.release/empsit.102.htm).

———. 2000c. "The Hispanic Population in the United States." *Current Population Reports,* ser. P20–527. Washington, DC: U.S. Government Printing Office.

———. 2000d. "National Population Projections." Internet release of January 13. Accessed May 11, 2000 (http://www.census.gov/population/).

———. 2000e. "Money Income in the United States 1999." *Current Population Reports,* ser. P60, no. 209. Washington, DC: U.S. Government Printing Office.

———. 2002f. "Population Pyramid Summary for Canada." *International Data Base.* Accessed April 4, 2002 (http://www.census.gov/cgi-bin/ipc/idbpyrs.

Burek, Deborah, ed. 1992. *Encyclopedia of Associations, 1993.* Detroit: Gale Research.

Burgess, Ernest W. 1925. "The Growth of the City." Pp. 47–62 in *The City,* edited by Robert E. Park, Ernest W. Burgess, and Roderick D. McKenzie. Chicago: University of Chicago Press.

Burkett, Elinor. 2000. *The Baby Boom: How Family Friendly America Cheats the Childless.* New York: Free Press.

Burns, John R. 1998. "Once Widowed in India, Twice Scorned." *New York Times,* March 29, p. A1.

Burstyn, Varda (ed.). 1985. *Women Against Censorship.* Vancouver, B.C.: Douglas & McIntyre.

Burt, Martha R. et al. 1999. *Homeless: Programs and the People They Save.* Washington, DC: Urban Institute.

Burton, Velmer S., Jr. 1990. "The Consequences of Official Labels: A Research Note on Rights Lost by the Mentally Ill, Mentally Incompetent, and Convicted Felons." *Community Mental Health Journal* 26(June):267–276.

Bush, Melanie. 1993. "The Doctor Is Out," *Village Voice* 38, June 22, p. 18.

Butler, Daniel Allen. 1998. *"Unsinkable:" The Full Story.* Mechanicsburg, PA: Stackpole Books.

Butler, Judith. 1990. *Gender Trouble: Feminism and the Subversion of Identity.* London: Routledge.

Butler, Robert N. 1990. "A Disease Called Ageism." *Journal of American Geriatrics Society* 38(February): 178–180.

Butterfield, Fox. 1996. "U.S. Has Plan to Broaden Availability of DNA Testing." *New York Times,* June 14, p. A8.

C

Cable, Sherry, and Michael Benson. 1993. "Acting Locally: Environmental Injustice and the Emergence of Grassroots Environmental Organizations." *Social Problems* 40(November):464–477.

Cahill, Spencer E. 1980. "Directors for an Interactionist Study of Gender Development." *Symbolic Interaction* 3:123–38.

Calhoun, Craig. 1998. "Community Without Propinquity Revisited." *Sociological Inquiry* 68(Summer):373–397.

Calhoun, David B. 2000. "Learning at Home." P. 193 in *Yearbook of the Ency-clopedia Britannica 2000.* Chicago: Encyclopedia Britannica.

Callahan, Tim. 1996. "Trees and Volcanoes Cause Smog!" *Humanist* 56(January–February):29–34.

Calliste, Agnes. 2001. "Black Families in Canada. Exploring the Interconnections of Race, Class and Gender." Pp. 401–419 in *Family Patterns, Gender Relations,* edited by Bonnie J. Fox. Toronto: Oxford University Press.

Came, Barry. 1994. "A Family Tragedy." *Maclean's* 107(November 21):40–43.

Campbell, Anne. 1991. *The Girls in the Gang.* 2d ed. Cambridge, MA: Blackwell.

Campbell, Bruce, Carlos Salas, and Robert Scott. 2000. "NAFTA at Seven." Washington, DC: Economic Policy Institute. Accessed April 18, 2000 (http://www.epinet.org/

Campbell, Jennifer A. 1999. "Health Insurance Coverage," *Current Population Reports Service,* P60 No. 208. Washington D.C.: U.S. Government Printing Office.

Campbell, Paul R. 1996. "Population Projections for States by Age, Sex, Race, and Hispanic Origin: 1995 to 2025." Population Division PPL-47. Washington, DC: U.S. Government Printing Office.

Camus, Albert. 1948. *The Plague.* New York: Random House.

Canada Mortgage and Housing Corporation (CMHC). 2000. *Survey of Canadians' Attitudes Toward Homelessness* (www.cmhc-schl.gc.ca/en/imquaf/ho/ho_014.cfm?).

———. 2002. *No Room of Her Own: A Literature Review on Women and Homelessness.* Accessed April 18, 2002 (http://www.cmhc-schl.

Canadian Broadcasting Corporation. 2000. *Stockwell Day's New Alliance.* Accessed April 5, 2002 (http://www.cbc.ca/insidecbc/newsinreview/Sep2000/stockwell/

Canadian Centre for Justice Statistics (CCJS). 2001a. *Family Violence in Canada: A Statistical Profile 2001.* Ottawa: Minister of Industry and Statistics Canada Catalogue No. 85-224.

———. 2001b. *Religious Groups in Canada: Statistics Profile Series.* Ottawa: Minister of Industry and Statistics Canada Catalogue No. 85F0033MIE.

Canadian Centre for Policy Alternatives. 2001. *New Report Shows NAFTA Has Harmed Workers in All Three Countries.* Accessed August 22, 2001 (http://www.

Canadian Charter Schools Centre (CCSC). 2002. "What are Charter Schools? (www.charterschools.ca/wacs.html).

Canadian Council on Social Development. 2000a. "Unequal Access: A report card on racism." *Perception.* Volume 24, No. 3, December.

———. 2000b. *The Canadian Fact Book on Poverty, 2000.* Ottawa: Canadian Council on Social Development.

———. 2001. *Minimum Wages Rates for Experienced Adult Workers in Canada and the Provinces.* Accessed May 4, 2001 (http://www.

Canadian Education Statistics Council (CESC). 2000. *Education Indicators in Canada: Report of the Pan-Canadian Education Indicators Program 1999.* Toronto: Canadian Education Statistics Council with Statistics Canada and Council of Ministers of Education, Canada.

Canadian Environmental Defence Fund. "Justice at Walkerton." Accessed April 29, 2002 (http://www.edcanada.org/walkerton).

Canadian Human Rights Commission (CHRC). 2002. *Employment Equity Report 2001.* Ottawa: Canadian Human Rights Commission. Catalogue No. HR1-3/2001.

Canadian Institute for Health Information. 1999. *Supply and Distribution of Registered Nurses in Canada.* Ottawa: Canadian Institute for Health Information.

———. 2001. *Health Care in Canada.* Accessed January 27, 2002 (http://www.cihi.ca/HealthReport2001).

Canadian Mental Health Association (CMHA). 2001a. *Submission to the Commission on the Future of Health Care in Canada* (http://www.healthcarecommission.ca).

———. 2001b. *Media Release May 7, 2001 Re: Mental Health Week.* (http://www.cmha.ca/english/info_centre/media_release/compas_2001.htm)

———. 2002. *Mental Health and Mental Illness in Canada: Facts and Figures.* CMHA Mental Health Week—Sharing Our Stories, May 6–12, 2002. (www.cmha.ca/mhw2002/facts_fig.htm).

Canadian National Foundation for AIDS Research (CANFAR). 2002. *CANFAR—About Us—Executive Summary.* www.canfar.com/about/executive.htm)

Canadian Panel on Violence Against Women. 1993. *Changing the Landscape: Ending Violence—Achieving Equality, Final Report.* Ottawa: Minister of Supply and Services. Cat. no. SW45-1/1993E.

Canadian Press Newswire. 2000. "Angus Reid Group changes name to reflect ties with Paris-based Ipsos." Canadian

Business and Current Affairs (CBCA), on-line data base. October 2. Accessed April 8, 2000 (http://delos.lib.sfu.ca: 8366/cgi-bin/slri/z3950.CGI/134.87. 144.15.917141763/?cbca.db)

Canadian Press. 2000. "Garbage-filled Moose Carries Message." *St. John's Telegram*, September 26, final ed., p. 8.

Canadian Race Relations Foundation (CRRF). 2000. *Unequal Access: A Canadian Profile of Racial Differences in Education, Employment and Income.* A report prepared by the Canadian Council on Social Development.

Canadian Society of Environmental Biologists. 2000. "Toronto City's Plans to Ship

Canadian Sociology and Anthropology Association. 2002. *Statement of Professional Ethics.* Accessed April 17, 2002 (http://alcor.concordia.ca/~csaa1/csaa. html).

Canadian Teachers' Federation (CTF). 2002. "Ten Charter School Myths." (www.ctf-fce.ca/E/WHAT/NI/ CHARTER/myths.htm).

Cancel, Cecil Marie. 1997. "The Veil." Accessed October 10, 1999 (http://about.com).

Cancian, Francesca. 1986. "The Feminization of Love." *Signs* 11(Summer):692–708.

Cantril, Hadley. 1940. *The Invasion from Mars: A Study in the Psychology of Panic.* Princeton, NJ: Princeton University Press.

Caplan, Ronald L. 1989. "The Commodification of American Health Care." *Social Science and Medicine* 28(11):1139–1148.

Caplow, Theodore. 1969. *Two against One: Coalitions in Triads.* Englewood Cliffs, NJ: Prentice-Hall.

Cardarelli, Luise. 1996. "The Lost Girls: China May Come to Regret Its Preference for Boys." *Utne Reader,* May–June, pp. 13–14.

Carey, Anne R., and Elys A. McLean. 1997. "Heard It Through the Grapevine?" *USA Today,* September 15, p. B1.

———, and Grant Jerding. 1999. "What Workers Want." *USA Today*, August 17, p. B1.

Carey, Anne R., and Jerry Mosemak. 1999. "Big on Religion." *USA Today,* April 1, p. D1.

Cargan, Leonard, and Matthew Melko. 1991. "Being Single on Noah's Ark." Pp. 161–165 in *Sociological Footprints,* 5th ed., edited by Leonard Cargan and Jeanne H. Ballantine. Belmont, CA: Wadsworth.

Carlen, P., J. Hicks, J. O'Dwyer, P. Christina, and C. Tchaikovsky. 1985. *Criminal Women.* Cambridge: Polity Press.

Carlisle, David M., Barbara D. Leake, and Martin F. Shapiro. 1995. "Racial and Ethnic Differences in the Use of Invasive Cardiac Procedures among Cardiac Patients in Los Angeles County, 1986 through 1988." *American Journal of Public Health* 85(March):352–356.

Carrese, Joseph A., and Lorna A. Rhodes. 1995. "Western Bioethics on the Navaho Reservation: Benefit or Harm?" *Journal of the American Medical Association* 274(September 13):826–829.

Carson, Rachel L. 1962. *Silent Spring.* Boston: Houghton Mifflin.

Carty, Linda. 1991. "Black Women in Academe: A Statement from the Periphery." In Himani Bennerji, Linda Carty, Kari Kehli, Susan Heald, and Kate McKenna. *Unsettling Relations: the university as a site of feminist struggles.* Toronto: Women's Press.

Carty, Win. 1999. "Greater Dependence on Cars Leads to More Pollution in World's Cities." *Population Today* 27(December):1–2.

Casper, Lynne M., and Kenneth R. Bryson. 1998. "Co-resident Grandparents and Their Grandchildren: Grandparent Maintained Families." Population Divison Working Paper no. 26. Washington, DC: Bureau of the Census.

———, and Loretta E. Bass. 1998. "Voting and Registration in the Election of November 1996." *Current Population Reports,* ser. P-20, no. 504. Washington, DC: U.S. Government Printing Office.

Cassidy, Claire Monod. 1982. "Protein-Energy Malnutrition as a Culture-Bound Syndrome." *Culture, Medicine, and Psychiatry* 6:325–345.

Castaneda, Jorge G. 1995. "Ferocious Differences." *Atlantic Monthly* 276(July):68–69, 71–76.

Castelli, Jim. 1996. "How to Handle Personal Information." *American Demographics* 18(March):50–52, 57.

Castells, Manuel. 1983. *The City and the Grass Roots.* Berkeley: University of California Press.

———. 1996. *The Information Age: Economy, Society and Culture.* Vol. 1, *The Rise of the Network Society.* London: Blackwell.

———. 1997. *The Power of Identity.* Vol. 1, *The Information Age: Economy, Society and Culture.* London: Blackwell.

———. 1998. *End of Millennium.* Vol. 3 of *The Information Age: Economy, Society and Culture.* London: Blackwell.

———. 2000. *The Information Age: Economy, Society and Culture* (3 vols.).

2d. ed. Oxford and Malden, MA: Blackwell.

Catalyst. 1998. *The Catalyst Census of Women Board Directors in Canada.* Toronto: Catalyst.

———. 1999. *1999 Catalyst Census of Women Board of Directors of the Fortune 1000.* New York: Catalyst.

Cavanagh, John, and Robin Broad. 1996. "Global Reach: Workers Fight the Multinationals." *The Nation* 262(March 18):21–24.

CBS News. 1979. Transcript of *Sixty Minutes* segment, "I Was Only Following Orders." March 31, pp. 2–8.

———. 1998. "Experimental Prison." *Sixty Minutes.* June 30. ccsd.ca/fs_minw.htm).

Celis, William, III. 1993. "Suburban and Rural Schools Learning That Violence Isn't Confined to the Cities." *New York Times,* April 21, p. B11.

Center for Public Integrity. 1998. *Nothing Sacred: The Politics of Privacy.* Washington, DC: CPI.

Center for the American Woman and Politics. 1999. *Women in Elective Office 1998.* New Brunswick, NJ: CAWP, Rutgers University.

Centers for Disease Control and Prevention. 1995. "Trends in Sexual Risk Behavior among High School Students: United States, 1990, 1991, and 1993." *Morbidity and Mortality Weekly Report* 44(February 24):124–125, 131–132.

———. 2000a. "Abortion Surveillance: Preliminary Analysis—United States, 1997." *Morbidity and Mortality Weekly Reports,* January 7, p. 2.

———. 2000b. "Commentary." *HIV/AIDS Surveillance Supplemental Report 5,* January 18, p. 1.

Cetron, Marvin J., and Owen Davies. 1991. "Trends Shaping the World." *Futurist* 20(September–October): 11–21. cgocable.net/~exworld/cseb/news/ adamsmine.html).

Cha, Ariena Eunjung. 2000. "Painting a Portrait of Dot-Camaraderie." *The Washington Post,* October 26, pp. E1, E10.

Chaddock, Gail Russell. 1998. "The Challenge for Schools: Connecting Adults with Kids." *Christian Science Monitor,* August 4, p. B7.

———, Gail Russell. 1999. "Can This School Make a Difference?" *Christian Science Monitor,* January 2, pp. 13, 18–19.

Chalfant, H. Paul, Robert E. Beckley, and C. Eddie Palmer. 1994. *Religion in Contemporary Society.* 3d ed. Itasca, IL: F. E. Peacock.

Chambliss, William, and Robert B. Seidman. 1971. *Law, Order, and Power.* Reading, MA: Addison-Wesley.

———. 1972. "Introduction." Pp. ix–xi in Harry King, *Box Man.* New York: Harper and Row.

———. 1973. "The Saints and the Roughnecks." *Society* 11(November–December):24–31.

Chan, R.W., B. Rayboy and C.J. Patterson. 1998. "Psychological Adjustment Among Children Conceived via Donor Insemination by Lesbian and Heterosexual Mothers." *Child Development* 69:443–457.

Charmaz, Kathy, and Debora A. Paterniti, eds. 1999. *Health, Illness, and Healing: Society, Social Context, and Self.* Los Angeles, CA: Roxbury.

Charter, David, and Jill Sherman. 1996. "Schools Must Teach New Code of Values." *London Times,* January 15, p. 1.

Chase-Dunn, Christopher, and Peter Grimes. 1995. "World-Systems Analysis." Pp. 387–417 in *Annual Review of Sociology, 1995,* edited by John Hagan. Palo Alto, CA: Annual Reviews.

Chatzky, Jean Sherman. 1999. "The Big Squeeze." *Money* 28(October):129, 131–134, 137–138.

Cheng, Wei-yuan, and Lung-li Liao. 1994. "Women Managers in Taiwan." Pp. 143–159 in *Competitive Frontiers: Women Managers in a Global Economy,* edited by Nancy J. Adler and Dafna N. Izraeli. Cambridge, MA: Blackwell Business.

Cherlin, Andrew J. 1999. *Public and Private Families: An Introduction.* 2d ed. New York: McGraw-Hill.

———, and Frank Furstenberg. 1992. *The New American Grandparent: A Place in the Family, A Life Apart.* Cambridge, MA: Harvard University Press.

———, and Frank Furstenberg. 1994. "Stepfamilies in the United States: A Reconsideration." Pp. 359–381 in *Annual Review of Sociology, 1994,* edited by John Hagan. Palo Alto, CA: Annual Reviews.

Chernin, Kim, 1981. *The Obsession: Reflections on the Tyranny of Slenderness.* New York: Harper and Row.

Chesney-Lind, Meda, and Noelie Rodriguez. 1993. "Women under Lock and Key." *Prison Journal* 63:47–65.

———, and Randall G. Shelden. 1998. *Girls, Delinquency, and Juvenile Justice.* 2d ed. Belmont, CA: Wadsworth.

Chicago Tribune. 1997a. "China Aborting Female Fetuses." October 17, p. 13.

———. 1997b. "In London, Prince Meets a Pauper, an Ex-Classmate." December 5, p. 19.

Child & Family Canada. 1994. *The Distribution of Income in Canada.* Ac-

cessed May 12, 2001 (http://www.cfc-efc.ca/docs/000000327.htm).

Childcare Resource and Research Unit. 2000. *Early Childhood Care and Education in Canada, Provinces and Territories 1998.* Centre for Urban and Community Studies: University of Toronto.

Chilly Collective (Eds.). 1995. *Breaking Anonymity: The Chilly Climate for Women Faculty.* Waterloo: Wilfred Laurier University Press.

Chin, Ko-lin. 1996. *Chinatown Gangs: Extortion, Enterprise, and Ethnicity.* New York: Oxford University Press.

Chow, Esther Ngan-Ling, and S. Michael Zhao. 1995. "The Impact of the One-Child Policy on Parent-Child Relationships in the People's Republic of China." Presented at the annual meeting of the American Sociological Association, August, Washington, DC.

CHRC. 2002b. "Case Summaries" in *Anti-Discrimination Casebook* (www.chrc-ccdp.ca/Legis&Poli/Anti-DiscriminationCasebook_Recueil/DeDecisions/AdcSummaries P1_RDDResumesP1.asp).

Christensen, Kathleen. 1990. "Bridges over Troubled Water: How Older Workers View the Labor Market." Pp. 175–207 in *Bridges to Retirement,* edited by Peter B. Doeringer. Ithaca, NY: IRL Press.

Christiansen, John B. and Sharon N. Barnartt. 1995. *Deaf President Now: The 1988 Revolution at Gallaudet University.* Washington, DC: Gallaudet University Press.

Cimons, Marlene. 1999. "New Data Suggest Limits to AIDS Drugs." *Los Angeles Times,* August 31, pp. A1, 12.

Citizens' Forum on Canada's Future. 1991. *Report to the People and Government of Canada.* Ottawa: Privy Council Office.

Citizenship and Immigration Canada. 2001. *Pursuing Canada's Commitment to Immigration: The Immigration Plan for 2002.* Cat. no. Ci51-105/2001. October. Ottawa: Minister of Works and Government Services.

Civic Ventures. 1999. *The New Face of Retirement: Older Americans, Civic Engagement, and the Longevity Revolution.* Washington, DC: Peter D. Hart Research Associates.

Clark, Brian L. 1999. "Internet Life: Our Town. Online." *Money* 28(September):36.

Clark, Burton, and Martin Trow. 1966. "The Organizational Context." Pp. 17–70 in *The Study of College Peer Groups,* edited by Theodore M. Newcomb and Everett K. Wilson. Chicago: Aldine.

Clark, Candace. 1983. "Sickness and Social Control." Pp. 346–365 in *Social Interaction: Readings in Sociology,* 2d. ed., edited by Howard Robboy and Candace Clark. New York: St. Martin's.

Clark, Charles, and Jason M. Fields. 1999. "First Glance: Preliminary Analysis of Relationship, Marital Status, and Grandparents Items on the Census 2000 Dress Rehearsal." Presented at the annual meeting of the American Sociological Association, August, Chicago.

Clark, S.D. 1979. "The Changing Image of Sociology in English-Speaking Canada." Pp. 393–403 in *Canadian Journal of Sociology,* Volume 4.

Clark, Thomas. 1994. "Culture and Objectivity." *The Humanist* 54(August):38–39.

Clarke, Lee. 1988. "Explaining Choices among Technological Risks." *Social Problems* 35(February):501–504.

———. 1999. *Mission Improbable: Using Fantasy Documents to Tame Disaster.* Chicago: University of Chicago Press.

classif.htm). Geneva, Switzerland: Inter-Parliamentary Union.

Clawson, Dan, and Mary Ann Clawson. 1999. "What Has Happened to the U.S. Labor Movement? Union Decline and Renewal." Pp. 95–119 in *Annual Review of Sociology,* edited by Karen S. Hook and John Hagan. Palo Alto, CA: Annual Reviews.

Cloud, John. 1998. "Sex and the Law." *Time* 151(March 23):48–54.

Cloward, Richard A. 1959. "Illegitimate Means, Anomie, and Deviant Behavior." *American Sociological Review* 24(April):164–176.

———, and Frances Fox Piven. 1993. "The Fraud of Workfare." *The Nation* 246 (May 24):693–696.

Clymer, Adam. 2000. "College Students Not Drawn to Voting or Politics, Poll Shows." *New York Times,* January 2, p. A14.

CNN.com. 2001. "Canadian Falun Gong follower says he was tortured in China." January 19, 2001. (www.cnn.com/2001/ASIANOW/east/01/18/canada.china).

Coatney, Caryn. 1998. "Arrest of Abortion Doctors Puts Australia Laws on Spot." *Christian Science Monitor,* March 25, p. 6.

Cobb, Chris. 2002. "Canadians want diverse society: poll", p. A5 in *The Ottawa Citizen,* Monday, February 18, 2002.

Cockerham, William C. 1998. *Medical Sociology.* 7th ed. Upper Saddle River, NJ: Prentice-Hall.

———. 1999. *Health and Social Change in Russia and Eastern Europe.* New York: Routledge.

Code, Lorraine. 1993. "Feminist Theory." Pp. 19–57 in *Changing Patterns: Women in Canada*, 2d. ed., edited by Sandra Burt, Lorraine Code, and Lindsay Dorney. Toronto: McClelland and Stewart.

Coeyman, Marjorie. 1999. "Schools Question the Benefits of Tracking." *Christian Science Monitor*, September 21, p. 20.

Cohen, David, ed. 1991. *The Circle of Life: Ritual from the Human Family Album*. San Francisco: Harper.

Cohen, Lawrence E., and Marcus Felson. 1979. "Social Change and Crime Rate Trends: A Routine Activities Approach." *American Sociological Review* 44:588–608.

Cohen, Patricia. 1998. "Daddy Dearest: Do You Really Matter?" *New York Times*, July 11, p. B7.

Cole, David. 1999. *No Equal Justice: Race and Class in the American Criminal Justice System*. New York: The New Press.

Cole, Elizabeth S. 1985. "Adoption, History, Policy, and Program." Pp. 638–666 in *A Handbook of Child Welfare*, edited by John Laird and Ann Hartman. New York: Free Press.

Cole, Mike. 1988. *Bowles and Gintis Revisited: Correspondence and Contradiction in Educational Theory*. Philadelphia: Falmer.

Coleman, James William, and Donald R. Cressey. 1980. *Social Problems*. New York: Harper and Row.

Colker, David. 1996. "Putting the Accent on World Wide Access." *Los Angeles Times* (May 21), p. E3.

Collier, Jane, Michelle Rosaldo, and Sylvia Yanagisako. 2001. "Is There A Family? New Anthropological Views." Pp. 11–21 in *Family Patterns, Gender Relations*, 2d ed., edited by Bonnie J. Fox. Toronto: Oxford University Press.

Collins, Gail. 1998. "Why the Women Are Fading Away." *New York Times*, October 25, pp. 54–55.

Collins, Patricia Hill. 1991. *Black Feminist Thought: Knowledge, Consciousness, and the Politics of Empowerment*. New York: Routledge.

———. 1998. *Fighting Words: Black Women and the Search for Justice*. Minneapolis: University of Minnesota.

Collins, Randall. 1975. *Conflict Sociology: Toward an Explanatory Sociology*. New York: Academic.

Collins, Randall. 1979. *The Credential Society: An Historical Sociology of Education and Stratification*. New York: Academic.

———. 1980. "Weber's Last Theory of Capitalism: A Systematization." *American Sociological Review* 45(December):925–942.

———. 1986. *Weberian Sociological Theory*. New York: Cambridge University Press.

———. 1995. "Prediction in Macrosociology: The Case of the Soviet Collapse." *American Journal of Sociology* 100(May):1552–1593.

Comack, Elizabeth. 1996. *Women in Trouble*. Halifax: Fernwood Publishing.

CommerceNet/Nielsen Internet Demographic Survey. 1998. "Who's on Line." Reproduced in *USA Today*, August 25, p. D1.

Commission on Behavioral and Social Sciences Education. 1998. *Protecting Youth at Work*. Washington, DC: National Academy Press.

Commission on Civil Rights. 1976. *A Guide to Federal Laws and Regulations Prohibiting Sex Discrimination*. Washington, DC: U.S. Government Printing Office.

———. 1981. *Affirmative Action in the 1980s: Dismantling the Process of Discrimination*. Washington, DC: U.S. Government Printing Office.

Commoner, Barry. 1971. *The Closing Circle*. New York: Knopf.

———. 1990. *Making Peace with the Planet*. New York: Pantheon.

Communications Canada. 2001. "Facts on Canada." Accessed April 11, 2001 (http://www.infocan.gc.ca/facts/multi_e.html).

CompuSearch/InfoGroup Inc. 1993. *Quantitative Research Study Produced for Lifestyles TV Inc.*, pp. 24–27.

Computer Security Institute. 1999. "1999 CSI/FBI Computer Crime and Security Survey." *Computer Security Issues and Trends* 5(Winter):1–15.

ComQuest Research Group. 1993. *Lifestyles Television Focus Group Report*. Vancouver: Bureau of Broadcast Measurement.

CONGO. 2000. *Beijing Plus Five*. NGO Alternative Global Report to the UN-GASS 5 Years after Beijing, June 5–9 2000. New York: Conference of NGOs (CONGO).

Congressional Quarterly. 1996. "Campaign Finance Reform." *CQ Research Reports*, February 9.

Connidis, Ingrid A. 1989. *Family Ties and Ageing*. Toronto: Butterworths.

Conrad, Peter, and Joseph W. Schneider. 1992. *Deviance and Medicalization: From Badness to Sickness*. Expanded ed. Philadelphia: Temple University Press.

———, ed. 1997. *The Sociology of Health and Illness: Critical Perspectives*. 5th ed. New York: St. Martin's.

Constable, Pamela. 1999. "India's Clock Just Keeps on Ticking." *Washington Post National Weekly Edition* 16(August 30):16.

Contenta, Sandro. 1993. *Rituals of Failure: What Schools Really Teach*. Toronto: Between the Lines.

Cook, P. J., and J. A. Leitzel. 1996. *Perversity, Futility, Jeopardy: An Economic Analysis of the Attack on Gun Control*. Durham, NC: Sanford Institute of Public Policy, Duke University.

Cook, Rhodes. 1991. "The Crosscurrents of the Youth Vote." *Congressional Quarterly Weekly Report* 49(June 29):1802.

Cook, Tom. 2002. "Canadian soldiers easing back to normalcy." In *The Hamilton Spectator*, August 7.

Cooley, Charles H. 1902. *Human Nature and the Social Order*. New York: Scribner.

Coontz, Stephanie. 1997. "Divorcing Realty." *The Nation* 265(November 17):21–24.

Cooper, Glenda. 1997. "Who's Right about Child Care?" *Independent*, February 4, p. 1.

Cooper, Kenneth J. 1994. "Wrong Turns on the Map?" *Washington Post National Weekly Edition* 12 (January 31):14.

Cooper, Richard T. 1998. "Jobs Outside High School Can Be Costly, Report Finds." *Los Angeles Times*, November 6, p. A1.

Corning, Amy. 1993. "The Russian Referendum: An Analysis of Exit Poll Results." *RFE/RL Research Report* 2(May 7):6–9.

Coser, Lewis A. 1956. *The Functions of Social Conflict*. New York: Free Press.

———. 1977. *Masters of Sociological Thought: Ideas in Historical and Social Context*. 2d ed. New York: Harcourt, Brace and Jovanovich.

Coser, Rose Laub. 1984. "American Medicine's Ambiguous Progress." *Contemporary Sociology* 13(January):9–13.

Côté, James E., and Anton L. Allahar. 1994. *Generation on Hold: Coming of Age in the Late Twentieth Century*. Toronto: Stoddart.

Couch, Carl. 1996. *Information Technologies and Social Orders*. Edited with an introduction by David R. Maines and Shing-Ling Chien. New York: Aldine de Gruyter.

Council of Ministers of Education, Canada. 1995. *A Report on Education in Canada, 1995*. Toronto: Council of Ministers of Education, Canada.

Council on Ethical and Judicial Affairs, American Medical Association. 1992. "Decisions Near the End of Life." *Journal of the American Medical Association* 267(April 22–29):2229–2333.

Counts, D. A. 1977. "The Good Death in Kaliai: Preparation for Death in Western New Britain." *Omega* 7:367–372.

Cox, Craig. 1999. "Prime-Time Activism." *Utne Reader* (September–October), pp. 20–22.

Cox, Kevin. 2001. "Nova Scotia Gay Couple Given Legal Recognition." *The Globe and Mail*, June 5, p. A5.

Cox, Oliver C. 1948. *Caste, Class and Race: A Study in Social Dynamics.* Detroit: Wayne State University Press.

Craig, Maxine. 1997. "The Decline and Fall of the Conk; or How to Read a Process." *Fashion Theory* 1(4): 399–420.

Craig, W., and D. Pepler. 1997. "Observations of bullying and victimization in the schoolyard". In *Canadian Journal of School Psychology* 2, 41-60.

Creese, Gillian, Neil Guppy, and Martin Meissner. 1991. *Ups and Downs on the Ladder of Success: Social Mobility in Canada.* Ottawa: Statistics Canada.

Crenshaw, Edward M., Matthew Christenson, and Doyle Ray Oakey. 2000. "Demographic Transition in Ecological Focus." *American Sociological Review* 65(June):371–391.

Cressey, Donald R. 1960. "Epidemiology and Individual Contact: A Case from Criminology." *Pacific Sociological Review* 3(Fall):47–58.

Cresson, Edith. 1995. "Roots and Wings: Remaining European in the Information Age." *New Perspectives Quarterly* 12(Fall):26–28.

Croissant, Jennifer L. 1998. "Developmental Stories for Postmodern Children." Pp. 285–300 in *Cyborg Babies: From Techno-Sex to Techno-Tots,* edited by Robbie Davis-Floyd and Joseph Dumit. New York: Routledge.

Cromwell, Paul F., James N. Olson, and D'Aunn Wester Avarey. 1995. *Breaking and Entering: An Ethnographic Analysis of Burglary.* Newbury Park, CA: Sage.

Crosby, Doug. 1991. *An Apology to Native Peoples.* (www.turtleisland.org/news/oblates.pdf).

Crossette, Barbara. 1996a. "'Oldest Old,' 80 and Over, Increasing Globally." *New York Times,* December 22, p. 7.

———. 1996b. "Snubbing Human Rights," *New York Times,* April 28, p. E3.

———. 1999. "The Internet Changes Dictatorship's Rules." *New York Times,* August 1, sec. 4, p. 1.

Crouse, Kelly. 1999. "Sociology of the Titanic." *Teaching Sociology Listserv.* May 24.

Cuff, E. C., W. W. Sharrock, and D. W. Francis, eds. 1990. *Perspectives in Sociology.* 3d ed. Boston: Unwin Hyman.

Cullen, Francis T., Jr., and John B. Cullen. 1978. *Toward a Paradigm of Labeling Theory,* ser. 58. Lincoln: University of Nebraska Studies.

Cumming, Elaine, and William E. Henry. 1961. *Growing Old: The Process of Disengagement.* New York: Basic Books.

Cunningham, Kitty. 1993. "Caucus Rebuffs Clinton." *Congressional Quarterly Weekly Report* 51(June 12):1452.

Cunningham, Michael. 1992. "If You're Queer and You're Not Angry in 1992, You're Not Paying Attention." *Mother Jones* 17(May–June):60–66, 68.

Currie, Elliot. 1985. *Confronting Crime: An American Challenge.* New York: Pantheon.

———. 1998. *Crime and Punishment in America.* New York: Metropolitan Books.

Curry, Timothy Jon. 1993. "A Little Pain Never Hurt Anyone: Athletic Career Socialization and the Normalization of Sports Injury." *Symbolic Interaction* 26(Fall):273–290.

Curtis, James E., Edward G. Grabbs, and Douglas E. Baer. 1992. "Voluntary Association Membership in Fifteen Countries: A Composite Analysis." *American Sociological Review* 57(April):139–152.

Curtius, Mary. 1999. "Struggling Town Split Over Wal-Mart Plan." *Los Angeles Times,* July 5, pp. A1, A16–18.

Cushman, John H., Jr. 1998a. "Pollution Policy Is Unfair Burden, States Tell E. P. A." *New York Times,* May 10, pp. 1, 20.

———, Jr. 1998b. "Nike Pledges to End Child Labor and Apply U.S. Rules Abroad." *New York Times,* May 13, p. C1.

Cussins, Choris M. 1998. In *Cyborg Babies: From Techno-Sex to Techno-Tots,* edited by Robbie Davis-Floyd and Joseph Dumit. New York: Routledge.

D

D'Emilio, John. 1983. *Sexual Politics, Sexual Communities.* Chicago: University of Chicago Press.

Dahl, Robert A. 1961. *Who Governs?* New Haven, CT: Yale University Press.

Dahrendorf, Ralf. 1958. "Toward a Theory of Social Conflict." *Journal of Conflict Resolution* 2(June):170–183.

———. 1959. Class and Class Conflict in Industrial Sociology. Stanford, CA: Stanford University Press.

Dalaker, Joseph, and Bernadette D. Proctor. 2000. "Poverty in the United States." *Current Population Reports,* ser. P60, no. 210. Washington, DC: U.S. Government Printing Office.

———, and Mary Naifeh. 1998. "Poverty in the United States: 1997." *Current Population Reports,* ser. P-60, no. 201. Washington, DC: U.S. Government Printing Office.

———. 1999. "Poverty in the United States 1998." *Current Population Reports,* ser. P-60, no. 207. Washington, DC: U.S. Government Printing Office.

Daley, Suzanne. 1996. "Apartheid's Dispossessed Seek Restitution." *New York Times,* June 25, p. A3.

———. 1997. "Reversing Roles in a South African Dilemma. " *New York Times,* October 26, sec. WE, p. 5.

Daley, Suzanne. 1998. "A Post-Apartheid Agony: AIDS on the March," *New York Times* (July 23), pp. A1, A10.

———. 1999. "Doctors' Group of Volunteers Awarded Nobel." *New York Times,* October 16, pp. A1, A6.

———. 2000. "French Couples Take Plunge that Falls Short of Marriage." *New York Times,* April 18, pp. A1, A4.

Dalfen, Ariel K. 2000. "Cyberaddicts in Cyberspace? Internet Addiction Disorder." *Wellness Options.* (Winter): 38–39.

Daniels, Arlene Kaplan. 1987. "Invisible Work." *Social Problems* 34(December):403–415.

———. 1988. *Invisible Careers.* Chicago: University of Chicago Press.

Dao, James. 1995. "New York's Highest Court Rules Unmarried Couples Can Adopt." *New York Times,* November 3, pp. A1, B2.

Dart, John. 1997. "Lutheran Women Wait Longer for Pastor Jobs, Survey Finds." *Los Angeles Times,* May 3, pp. B1, B5.

Daskal, Jennifer. 1998. *In Search of Shelter: The Growing Shortage of Affordable Rental Housing.* Washington, DC: Center on Budget and Policy Priorities.

Davidson, Robert C., and Ernest L. Lewis. 1997. "Affirmative Action and Other Special Consideration Admissions at the University of California, Davis, School of Medicine." *Journal of the American Medical Association* 278(October 8):1153–1158.

Davies, Christie. 1989. "Goffman's Concept of the Total Institution: Criticisms and Revisions." *Human Studies* 12(June):77–95.

Davies, Scott, and Margaret Denton. 1996. "The Employment of Masters and PhD Graduates from Eleven Sociology Departments." Accessed January 24, 2002 (http://www.mcmaster.ca/socscidocs/survey.htm).

Davis, Darren W. 1997. "The Direction of Race of Interviewer Effects Among African-Americans: Donning the

Feldman, Linda. 1999. "Control of Congress in Seniors' Hands." *Christian Science Monitor.* (June 21):1–4.

Felson, Marcus. 1998. *Crime and Everyday Life: Insights and Implications for Society.* 2d ed. Thousand Oaks, CA: Pine Forge Press.

Ferman, Louis A., Stuart Henry, and Michael Hoyman, eds. 1987. *The Informal Economy.* Newbury Park, CA: Sage. Published as September 1987 issue of *The Annals of the American Academy of Political and Social Science.*

Fernandez, John R. 1999. *Race, Gender and Rhetoric.* New York: McGraw-Hill.

Fernández, Sandy. 1996. "The Cyber Cops." *Ms.* 6(May–June):22–23.

Fernea, Elizabeth W., and Robert A. Fernea. 1997. "A Look Behind the Veil." *Human Nature.* (January).

Fernea, Elizabeth. 1998. *In Search of Islamic Feminism: One Woman's Global Journey.* New York: Bantam Books.

Ferree, Myra Marx, and David A. Merrill. 2000. "Hot Movements, Cold Cognition: Thinking about Social Movements in Gendered Frames." *Contemporary Society* 29(May):454–462.

Ferrell, Tom. 1979. "More Choose to Live outside Marriage." *New York Times,* July 1, p. E7.

Feuer, Lewis S., ed. 1959. *Karl Marx and Friedrich Engels: Basic Writings on Politics and Philosophy.* Garden City, NY: Doubleday.

Fiala, Robert. 1992. "Postindustrial Society." Pp. 1512–1522 in *Encyclopedia of Sociology,* vol. 3, edited by Edgar F. Borgatta and Marie L. Borgatta. New York: Macmillan.

Fick, Steven. 2001. In "Toronto: A Global Village," by Gwyn Dyer. *Canadian Geographic* (January/February):54.

Fields, Jason M., and Charles L. Clark. 1999. "Unbinding the Ties: Edit Effects of Marital Status on Same Gender Groups." Paper presented at the annual meeting of the American Sociological Assocation, August, Chicago.

Finder, Alan. 1995. "Despite Tough Laws, Sweatshops Flourish." *New York Times,* January 6, pp. A1, B4.

Findlay, Steven. 1998. "85% of American Workers Using HMOs." *USA Today,* January 20, p. 3A.

Fine, Gary Alan. 1984. "Negotiated Orders and Organizational Cultures." Pp. 239–262 in *Annual Review of Sociology, 1984,* edited by Ralph Turner. Palo Alto, CA: Annual Reviews.

Fine, Michelle, and Adrienne Asch. 1988. *Women with Disabilities: Essays in Psychology, Culture, and Politics.* Philadelphia: Temple University Press.

Finkel, Alvin, and Margaret Conrad with Veronica Stong-Boag. 1993. *History of the Canadian Peoples: 1867 to Present.* Toronto: Copp Clark Putnam.

Finkel, Steven E., and James B. Rule. 1987. "Relative Deprivation and Related Psychological Theories of Civil Violence: A Critical Review." *Research in Social Movements* 9:47–69.

Finnie, Ross. 1993. "Women, Men and the Economic Consequences of Divorce: Evidence from Canadian Longitudinal Data." *Canadian Review of Sociology and Anthropology* 30(2):205–241.

Fiore, Faye. 1997. "Full-Time Moms a Minority Now, Census Bureau Finds." *Los Angeles Times,* November 26, pp. A1, A20.

Firestone, David. 1999. "School Prayer Is Revived As an Issue In Alabama." *New York Times,* July 15, p. A14.

Firestone, Shulamith. 1970. *The Dialectic of Sex: The Case for Feminist Revolution.* New York: Bantam.

Firmat, Gustavo Perez. 1994. *Life on Hyphen: The Cuban-American Way.* Austin: University of Texas Press.

Fisher, Carolyn A., and Carol A. Schwartz. 1995. *Encyclopedia of Associations, 1996.* Detroit: Gail Research.

Fisher, Ian. 1999. "Selling Sudan's Slaves into Freedom." *New York Times,* April 25, p. A6.

Fishman, Mark, and Gray Cavender, eds. 1998. *Entertaining Crime: Television Reality Programs.* Hawthorne, NY: Aldine de Gruyter.

Fitzpatrick, Eleanor. 1994. *Violence Prevention: A Working Paper and Proposal for Action.* St. John's: Avalon Consolidated School Board.

Fitzpatrick, Kevin, and Mark LaGray. 2000. *Unhealthy Places: The Ecology of Risk in the Urban Landscape.* New York: Routledge.

Flacks, Richard. 1971. *Youth and Social Change.* Chicago: Markham.

Flanders, John. 2001. "Getting Ready for the 2001 Census." *Canadian Social Trends.* (Spring) Statistics Canada. Catalogue No. 11-008. Ottawa: Minister of Industry.

Flavin, Jeanne. 1998. "Razing the Wall: A Feminist Critique of Sentencing Theory, Research, and Policy." Pp. 145–164 in *Cutting the Edge,* edited by Jeffrey Ross. Westport, CT: Praeger.

Fleras, Augie, and Jean Leonard Elliott. 1992. *The Nations Within. Aboriginal-State Relations in Canada, the United States, and New Zealand.* Toronto: Oxford University Press.

———, and Jean Leonard Elliott. 1999. *Unequal Relations: An Introduction to Race, Ethnic and Aboriginal Dynamics.* Scarborough: Prentice-Hall.

———, and Jean Lock Kunz. 2001. *Media and Minorities: Representing Diversity in Multicultural Canada.* Toronto: Thompson Educational Publishing.

Fletcher, Connie. 1995. "On the Line: Women Cops Speak Out." *Chicago Tribune Magazine,* February 19, pp. 14–19.

Fletcher, Robert S. 1943. *History of Oberlin College to the Civil War.* Oberlin, OH: Oberlin College Press.

Flexner, Eleanor. 1972. *Century of Struggle: The Women's Rights Movement in the United States.* New York: Atheneum.

Floyd, Richard, and Stephen Dooley. 1998. *The Target Inclusion Model: Including Members of the Subject Population on the Research Team.* Paper presented to the Canadian Learneds Society, Lenoxville.

Fong, Petti. 2001. "Brain Diseases 'Loom as Next Big Health Threat.'" *The Vancouver Sun,* March 20, p. A3.

Forcese, Dennis, and Stephen Richer. 1988. "Introduction: Social Issues and Canadian Sociology." Pp. 1–9 in *Social Issues: Sociological Views of Canada.* 2d ed. Scarborough, Ontario: Prentice-Hall Canada Inc.

Fornos, Werner. 1997. *1997 World Population Overview.* Washington, DC: The Population Institute.

Forsythe, David P. 1990. "Human Rights in U.S. Foreign Policy: Retrospect and Prospect," *Political Science Quarterly,* 105(3):435–454.

Fortune. 2000. "The Fortune Global 200." 142(July 24):F1–F24.

Fountain, Monica. 1996. "Not the Retiring Type." *Chicago Tribune,* April 14, sec. 13, p. 6.

Fox, Bonnie. 2001. "As Times Change: A Review of Trends in Personal and Family Life." Pp. 153–175 in *Family Patterns, Gender Relations,* 2d ed., edited by Bonnie J. Fox. Toronto: Oxford University Press.

Francis, David R. 1999. "Part-time Workers Face Full-time Problems." *Christian Science Monitor,* July 1, p. 11.

Franklin, John Hope and Alfred A. Moss, Jr. 1994. *From Slavery to Freedom.* 7th ed. New York: Knopf.

Franklin, John Hope, and Alfred A. Moss. 2000. *From Slavery to Freedom: A History of African Americans.* 8th ed. Upper Saddle River, NJ: Prentice-Hall.

Franklin, Stephen. 2000. "Hard Times at End?" *Chicago Tribune,* January 29, section 2, pp. 1–2.

Frazee, Valerie. 1997. "Establishing Relations in Germany." *Workforce* 76(No. 4):516.

Freeman, Jo. 1973. "The Origins of the Women's Liberation Movement."

American Journal of Sociology 78(January): 792–811.

———. 1975. *The Politics of Women's Liberation.* New York: McKay.

Freeman, Linton C. 1958. "Marriage without Love: Mate Selection in Non-Western Countries." Pp. 20–30 in *Mate Selection,* edited by Robert F. Winch. New York: Harper and Row.

Freeze, Colin. 2001. "Women Outwork Men By Two Weeks Every Year." *The Globe and Mail,* March 13, p. A1.

Freidson, Eliot. 1970. *Profession of Medicine.* New York: Dodd, Mead.

Freire, Paulo. 1970. *Pedagogy of the Oppressed.* New York: Herder and Herder.

French, Howard W. 2000. "Women Win a Battle, But Job Bias Still Rules Japan." *New York Times,* February 26, p. A3.

Freudenheim, Milt. 1990. "Employers Balk at High Cost of High-Tech Medical Care." *New York Times,* April 29, pp. 1, 16.

———. 1998. "Aetna Is Reducing Fertility Benefits." *New York Times,* January 10, pp. A1, A8.

Fridlund, Alan. J., Paul Erkman, and Harriet Oster. 1987. "Facial Expressions of Emotion: Review of Literature 1970–1983." Pp. 143–224 in *Nonverbal Behavior and Communication,* 2d ed., edited by Aron W. Seigman and Stanley Feldstein. Hillsdale, NJ: Lawrence Erlbaum Associates.

Friedan, Betty. 1963. *The Feminine Mystique.* New York: Dell.

Friedland, Jonathon. 2000. "An American in Mexico Champions Midwifery as a Worthy Profession." *Wall Street Monitor,* February 15, pp. A1, A12.

Friedman, Thomas L. 1999. *The Lexus and the Olive Tree: Understanding Globalization.* New York: Farrar, Straus, Giroux.

Friedrichs, David O. 1998. "New Directions in Critical Criminology and White Collar Crime." Pp. 77–91 in *Cutting the Edge,* edited by Jeffrey Ross. Westport, CT: Praeger.

Friends of Clayoquot Sound (FOCS). 2001a. *Who We Are* (www.ancient rainforest.org/home/who_we_are. html).

———. 2001b. *Temperate Rainforest Fact Sheet and Clayoquot Sound Update* (www.ancientrainforest. org/ logging_pdates/fact_sheet. htm).

Fuller, Bruce, and Sharon Lynn Kagan. 2000. *Remember the Children: Mothers Balance Work and Child Care Under Welfare Reform.* Berkeley: Graduate School of Education, University of California.

———, and Xiaoyan Liang. 1993. *The Unfair Search for Child Care.* Cam-

bridge, MA: Preschool and Family Choice Project, Harvard University.

Fullerton, Howard N., Jr. 1997. "Labor Force 2006: Slowing Down and Changing Composition." *Monthly Labor Review* (November):23–38.

———, Jr. 1999. "Labor Force Projections to 2008: Steady Growth and Changing Composition." *Monthly Labor Review* (November):19–32.

Furstenberg, Frank, and Andrew Cherlin. 1991. *Divided Families: What Happens to Children When Parents Part.* Cambridge, MA: Harvard University Press.

———, et al. 1999. *Managing to Make It: Urban Families and Adolescent Success.* Chicago: University of Chicago Press.

———. 1987. "The New Extended Family: The Experience of Parents and Children After Remarriage." Pp. 42–71 in *Remarriage and Stepparenting: Current Research and Theory,* edited by K. Pasley and M. Ihinger-Tallman. New York: Guilford.

G

Gable, Donna. 1993a. "On TV, Lifestyles of the Slim and Entertaining." *USA Today,* July 27, p. 3D.

———. 1993b. "Series Shortchange Working-Class and Minority Americans." *USA Today,* August 30, p. 3D.

Gabor, Andrea. 1995. "Crashing the 'Old Boy' Party." *New York Times,* January 8, sec. 3, pp. 1, 6.

Galant, Debra. 2000. "Finding a Substitute for Office Chitchat." *New York Times,* February 16, sec. Retirement, p. 20.

Gale, Elaine. 1999. "A New Point of View." *Los Angeles Times,* January 11, pp. B1, B3.

Gallup Poll. 1999. "Public Support for the Death Penalty." As reported in *New York Times,* April 3, p. A11.

Galt, Virginia. 1998. "Where the Boys Aren't: At the Top of the Class." *The Globe and Mail,* February 26, p. A6.

Gamson, Josh. 1989. "Silence, Death, and the Invisible Enemy: AIDS Activism and Social Movement 'Newness.'" *Social Problems* 36(October): 351–367.

———. 1998. *Freaks Talk Back: Tabloid Talk Shows and Sexual Nonconformity.* Chicago: University of Chicago Press.

Gans, Herbert J. 1991. *People, Plans, and Policies: Essays on Poverty, Racism, and Other National Urban Problems.* New York: Columbia University Press and Russell Sage Foundation.

Gans, Herbert J. 1995. *The War against the Poor: The Underclass and Antipoverty Policy.* New York: Basic Books.

Ganzeboom, Harry B. G., Donald J. Treiman, and Woult C. Ultee. 1991.

"Comparative Intergenerational Stratification Research." Pp. 277–302 in *Annual Review of Sociology, 1991,* edited by W. Richard Scott. Palo Alto, CA: Annual Reviews.

Ganzeboom, Harry B. G., Ruud Luijkx, and Donald J. Treiman. 1989. "Intergenerational Class Mobility in Comparative Perspective." Pp. 3–84 in *Research in Social Stratification and Mobility,* edited by Arne L. Kalleberg. Greenwich, CT: JAI Press.

Garbage to Adam's Mine." Sept. 13. Accessed February 1, 2002 (http://www.

Gardner, Carol Brooks. 1989. "Analyzing Gender in Public Places: Rethinking Goffman's Vision of Everyday Life." *American Sociologist* 20(Spring):42–56.

Gardner, Carol Brooks. 1990. "Safe Conduct: Women, Crime, and Self in Public Places." *Social Problems* 37(August):311–328.

Gardner, Carol Brooks. 1995. *Passing By: Gender and Public Harassment.* Berkeley: University of California Press.

Gardner, Marilyn. 1998. "Prime-Time TV Fare Rarely Shows a Family Life as It's Really Lived." *Christian Science Monitor,* June 10, p. 13.

Garfinkel, Harold. 1956. "Conditions of Successful Degradation Ceremonies." *American Journal of Sociology* 61(March):420–424.

Garner, Roberta. 1996. *Contemporary Movements and Ideologies.* New York: McGraw-Hill.

Garner, Roberta. 1999. "Virtual Social Movements." Presented at Zaldfest: A conference in honour of Mayer Zald. September 17, Ann Arbor, MI.

Garreau, Joel. 1991. *Edge City: Life on the New Frontier.* New York: Doubleday.

Gartner, Rosemary, Myrna Dawson, and Maria Crawford. 2001. "Confronting Violence in Women's Lives." Pp.473–490 in *Family Patterns, Gender Relations,* edited by Bonnie J. Fox. Toronto: Oxford University Press.

Garza, Melita Marie. 1993. "The Cordi-Marian Annual Cotillion." *Chicago Tribune,* May 7, sec. C, pp. 1, 5.

Gaskell, Jane, Arlene McLaren, and Myra Novogrodsky. 1995. "What Is Worth Knowing?" Pp. 100–118 in *Gender in the 1990s: Images, Realities and Issues,* edited by Edna D. Nelson and Barry W. Robinson. Scarborough: Nelson Canada.

Gates, Henry Louis, Jr. 1991. "Delusions of Grandeur." *Sports Illustrated* 75(August 19):78.

Gates, Henry Louis, Jr. 1999. "One Internet, Two Nations." *New York Times,* October 31, p. A15.

Gauette, Nicole. 1998. "Rules for Raising Japanese Kids." *Christian Science Monitor,* October 14, pp. B1, B6.

Gauette, Nicole. 1999. "Japanese Suburbanites Defy Law." *Christian Science Monitor,* September 28, p. 5.

Gay Men's Health Crisis. 2000. "Facts and Statistics." Accessed February 1, 2000 (http://www.gmhc.org/basics/statmain.html).

Gearty, Robert. 1996. "Beware of Pickpockets." *Chicago Daily News,* November 19, p. 5.

Gecas, Viktor. 1981. "Concepts of Socialization." In Morris Rosenberg and Ralph H. Turner (eds.), *Social Psychology: Sociological Perspectives.* New York: Basic Books, pp. 165–199.

Gecas, Viktor. 1982. "The Self-Concept." Pp. 1–33 in *Annual Review of Sociology,* 1982, edited by Ralph H. Turner and James F. Short, Jr. Palo Alto, CA: Annual Reviews.

Gecas, Viktor. 1992. "Socialization." Pp. 1863–1872 in *Encyclopedia of Sociology,* vol. 4, edited by Edgar F. Borgatta and Marie L. Borgatta. New York: Macmillan.

Geckler, Cheri. 1995. *Practice Perspectives and Medical Decision-Making in Medical Residents: Gender Differences—A Preliminary Report.* Wellesley, MA: Center for Research on Women.

Gee, Ellen M., Barbara A. Mitchell, and Andrew V. Wister. 1995. "Returning to the Parental 'Nest': Exploring a Changing Canadian Life Course." *Canadian Studies in Population* 22 (2):121–144.

Gelles, Richard J., and Claire Pedrick Cornell. 1990. *Intimate Violence in Families.* 2d ed. Newbury Park, CA: Sage.

Gelles, Richard J., and Murray A. Straus. 1998. *Intimate Violence: The Causes and Consequences of Abuse in the American Family.* New York: Simon and Schuster.

General Accounting Office. 2000. *Women's Health: NIH Has Increased Its Efforts to Include Women in Research.* Washington, DC: U.S. Government Printing Office.

Gerber, Linda M. 1990. "Indian, Metis, and Inuit Women and Men: Multiple Jeopardy in a Canadian Context". In *Canadian Ethnic Studies.* Vol. XXII, No. 3:69–84.

Gereffi, Gary, and Miguel Kovzeniewicz, eds. 1994. *Commodity Chains and Global Capitalism.* New York: Praeger.

Gerrows, Henry A. 1988. *Schooling and the Struggle for Public Life: Critical Pedagogy in the Modern Age.* Minneapolis: University of Minnesota Press.

Gerth, H. H., and C. Wright Mills. 1958. *From Max Weber: Essays in Sociology.* New York: Galaxy.

Gesensway, Deborah, and Mindy Roseman. 1987. *Beyond Words: Images from America's Concentration Camps.* Ithaca, NY: Cornell University Press.

Gessell, Paul. 2002. "Young 'marrieds' write a book" in *The Ottawa Citizen.* Wednesday June 12,2002, page C11–12.

Gest, Ted. 1985. "Are White-Collar Crooks Getting Off Too Easy?" *U.S. News & World Report* 99(July 1):43.

Geyh, Paul. 1998. "Feminism Fatale?" *Chicago Tribune,* July 26, sec. 13, pp. 1, 6.

Gibbs, Nancy, 1993. "Rx for Death." *Time,* May 31, pp. 34–39.

Gibson, James William. 1994. *Warrior Dreams: Paramilitary Culture in Post-Vietnam America.* New York: Hill and Wang.

Gidengil, Elisabeth, Andre Blais, Neil Nevitte, and Richard Nadeau. 2000. "Women to the Left, Men to the Right? Gender and Voting in the 1997 Canadian Election." Paper presented at the 2000 Congress of the International Political Science Association, Quebec City, August 2000.

———, Andre Blais, Richard Nadeau, and Neil Nevitte. 2001. "Women to the Left? Gender Differences in Political Beliefs and Policy Differences." Unpublished paper. Accessed April 18, 2002 (http://www.fas.umontreal.ca/POL/Ces-eec/

Gillespie, Mark. 1999. "Poll Releases, April 6, 1999: U.S. Gun Ownership Continues Broad Decline." Accessed July 2, 2000 (http://www.gallup.com/poll/releases/pr990406.asp).

Gilliard, Darrell K., and Allen J. Beck. 1998. *Prison and Jail Inmates at Midyear 1997.* Washington, DC: U.S. Government Printing Office.

Giordano, Peggy C., Stephen A. Cernkovich, and Alfred DeMaris. 1993. "The Family and Peer Relations of Black Adolescents." *Journal of Marriage and Family* 55(May):277–287.

Giroux, Henry A. 1988. *Schooling and the Struggle for Public Life: Critical Pedagogy in the Modern Age.* Minneapolis: University of Minnesota Press.

Given, Lisa. 2000. "The Promise of 'Lifelong Learning' and the Canadian Census: The Marginalization of Mature Students' Information Behaviours." *Canadian Association for the Information Science 2000: Dimensions of A Global Information Science.* Accessed July 23, 2001 (http://slis.ualberta.ca/cais2000/given/htm).

Glascock, Anthony P. 1990. "By Any Other Name, It Is Still Killing: A Comparison of the Treatment of the Elderly in American and Other Societies." Pp. 44–56 in *The Cultural Context of Aging: Worldwide Perspectives,* edited by Jay Sokolovsky. New York: Bergen and Garvey.

Glasser, Susan B., and Juliet Eilperin. 1999. "A New Conduit for 'Soft Money': Critics Decry Big, Largely Untraceable Donations to Lawmakers' Leadership PACS." *Washington Post,* May 16, p. A1.

Glassner, Barry. 1999. *The Culture of Fear: Why Americans Are Afraid of the Wrong Things.* New York: Basic Books.

Glaub, Gerald R. 1990. "Gap between State Funding and School Spending Widens." *Illinois School Board Journal* 58(July–August):24–26.

Glauber, Bill. 1998. "Youth Binge Drinking Varies Around World." *St. Louis Post-Dispatch,* February 9, p. E4.

Gleick, James. 1999. *Faster: The Acceleration of Just About Everything.* New York: Pantheon.

Glick, Paul C., and Sung-Ling Lin. 1986. "More Young Adults are Living with Their Parents: Who are They?" *Journal of Marriage and the Family* 48: 107–112.

Global Reach. 2000. *Global Internet Statistics* (by language). September 30, 2000. Accessed November 7, 2000 (http://www.glreach.com/globstats/index.php3).

Goffman, Erving. 1959. *The Presentation of Self in Everyday Life.* New York: Doubleday.

———. 1961. *Asylums: Essays on the Social Situation of Mental Patients and Other Inmates.* Garden City, NY: Doubleday.

———. 1963a. *Stigma: Notes on Management of Spoiled Identity.* Englewood Cliffs, NJ: Prentice-Hall.

———. 1963b. *Behavior in Public Places.* New York: Free Press.

———. 1971. *Relations in Public.* New York: Basic Books.

———. 1979. *Gender Advertisements.* New York: Harper and Row.

Goldberg, Carey, and Janet Elder. 1998. "Public Still Backs Abortion but Wants Limits, Poll Says." *New York Times,* January 16, pp. A1, A16.

Goldberg, Carey. 1998. "Little Drop in College Binge Drinking." *New York Times,* August 11, p. A14.

Golden, Frederic. 1999. "Who's Afraid of Frankenfood?" *Time,* November 29, pp. 49–50.

Goldman, Benjamin A., and Laura Fitton. 1994. *Toxic Wastes and Race Revisited: An Update of the 1987 Report on the Racial and Social Economic Characteristics of Communities with Hazardous Waste.* Washington, DC:

Center for Policy Alternatives, United Church of Christ Commission for Racial Justice, and NAACP.

Goldman, Robert, and Stephen Papson. 1998. *Nike Culture: The Sign of the Swoosh.* London: Sage Publications.

Goldsby, Richard. 1977. *Race and Races.* 2d ed. New York: Macmillan.

Goldstein, Amy. 1998. "A Transfusion from Patients' Wallets May Be in Order." *Washington Post National Weekly Edition,* September 21, p. 31.

Goldstein, Greg. 1998. "World Health Organization and Housing." Pp. 636–637 in *The Encyclopedia of Housing,* edited by Willem van Vliet. Thousand Oaks, CA: Sage Publications.

Goldstein, Melvyn C., and Cynthia M. Beall. 1981. "Modernization and Aging in the Third and Fourth World: Views from the Rural Hinterland in Nepal." *Human Organization* 40(Spring):48–55.

Gole, Nilofer. 1997. "Lifting the Veil—Reform vs. Tradition in Turkey—An Interview." *Manushi,* May 1.

Goleman, Daniel, 1991. "New Ways to Battle Bias: Fight Acts, Not Feelings." *New York Times,* July 16, pp. C1, C8.

Goliber, Thomas J. 1997. "Population and Reproductive Health in Sub-Saharan Africa." *Population Bulletin* 52(December).

Goode, Erica. 1999. "For Good Health, It Helps to Be Rich and Important." *New York Times,* June 1, pp. 1, 9.

Goode, William J. 1959. "The Theoretical Importance of Love." *American Sociological Review* 24(February):38–47.

Goodgame, Dan. 1993. "Welfare for the Well-Off." *Time* 141(February 22):36–38.

Gottdiener, Mark, and Joe R. Feagin. 1988. "The Paradigm Shift in Urban Sociology." *Urban Affairs Quarterly* 24(December):163–187.

———, and Ray Hutchison. 2000. *The New Urban Sociology.* 2d ed. New York: McGraw-Hill.

Gottfredson, Michael, and Travis Hirschi. 1990. *A General Theory of Crime.* Palo Alto, CA: Stanford University Press.

Gottschalk, Peter, Sara McLanahan, and Gary Sandefur. 1994. "The Dynamics and Intergenerational Transmission of Poverty and Welfare Participation." Pp. 85–108 in *Confronting Poverty: Prescriptions for Change,* edited by Sheldon H. Danziger, Gary D. Sandefur, and Daniel H. Weinburg. Cambridge, MA: Harvard University Press.

Gough, E. Kathleen. 1974. "Nayar: Central Kerala." Pp. 298–384 in *Matrilineal Kinship,* edited by David Schneider and E. Kathleen Gough. Berkeley: University of California Press.

Gouldner, Alvin. 1960. "The Norm of Reciprocity." *American Sociological Review* 25(April):161–177.

———. 1970. *The Coming Crisis of Western Sociology.* New York: Basic Books.

Gove, Walter R. 1987. "Sociobiology Misses the Mark: An Essay on Why Biology but Not Sociobiology Is Very Relevant to Sociology." *American Sociologist* 18(Fall):258–277.

———, ed. 1980. *The Labelling of Deviance.* 2d ed. Beverly Hills, CA: Sage.

Goyder, John. 1997. *Technology and Society: a Canadian perspective.* Peterborough: Broadview Press.

Graham, Hilary, and Anne Oakley. 1981. "Competing ideologies of reproduction: medical and maternal perspectives on pregnancy." In *Women, Health and Reproduction,* edited by Helen Roberts. London: Routledge & Kegan Paul.

———. 1987. "Providers, negotiators and mediators: women as hidden carers." In *Women, Health and Healing: Towards a new perspective,* edited by E. Lewin and V. Olsen. London: Tavistock.

Gram, Karen. 2001. "Hard Times in the Good Ol' Days." *The Vancouver Sun,* May 5, p. A 21.

Gramsci, Antonio. 1929. "Selections from the Prison Notebooks." In Quintin Hoare and Geoffrey Nowell Smith, eds. London: Lawrence and Wishort.

Grant, Judith. 1993. *Fundamental Feminism: Contesting the Core Concepts of Feminist Theory.* New York and London: Routledge.

Graydon, Shari. 2001. "The Portrayal of Women in Media: The Good, the Bad, and the Beautiful." Pp. 179–195 in *Communications in Canadian Society,* 5th ed., edited by Craig McKie and Benjamin D. Singer. Toronto: Thompson Educational Publishing.

Greaves, Lorraine. (1996). *Smoke Screen: Women's Smoking and Social Control.* Halifax: Fernwood Publishing.

Greeley, Andrew M. 1989. "Protestant and Catholic: Is the Analogical Imagination Extinct?" *American Sociological Review* 54(August):485–502.

Green, Dan S., and Edwin D. Driver. 1978. "Introduction." Pp. 1–60 in *W. E. B. DuBois on Sociology and the Black Community,* edited by Dan S. Green and Edwin D. Driver. Chicago: University of Chicago Press.

Greenburg, Jan Crawford. 1999. "Sampling for Census Restricted." *Chicago Tribune,* January 26, pp. 1, 10.

Greene, Jay P. 1998. "A Meta-Analysis of the Effectiveness of Bilingual Education." Sponsored by the Toms River Policy Initiative. Accessed July 1

(http://data.Fas.harvard.edu/pepg/biling.htm).

———, Paul E. Peterson, and Jiangtro Du. 1997a. *Effectiveness of School Choice: The Milwaukee Experiment.* Cambridge, MA: Harvard University's Program on Education Policy and Governance.

———, William G. Howell, and Paul E. Peterson. 1997b. *Lessons from the Cleveland Scholarship Program.* Cambridge, MA: Harvard University's Program on Education Policy and Governance.

Greenhouse, Linda. 1998a. "High Court Ruling Says Harassment Includes Same Sex." *New York Times,* March 5, pp. A1, A17.

———. 1998b. "Overturning of Late-Term Abortion Ban Is Let Stand." *New York Times,* March 24, p. A13.

———. 2000. "Justices Uphold Ceiling of $1,000 on Political Gifts." *New York Times,* January 25, pp. A1, A18.

Greenhouse, Steven. 1994. "State Dept. Finds Widespread Abuse of World's Women," *New York Times* (February 3), pp. A1, A9.

———. 1998. "Equal Work, Less-Equal Perks." *New York Times,* March 30, p. C1.

Greenwood, Ernest. 1957. "Attributes of a Profession." *Social Work* 2(July):45–55.

Greif, Mark. 2000. "Potemkin Villages." *The American Prospect* 11(January 3):54–57.

Grimsley, Kirstin Downey. 1997. "Big Boss May Be Watching—and Listening." *Washington Post National Weekly Edition,* June 2, p. 20.

Grob, Gerald N. 1995. "The Paradox of Deinstitutionalization." *Society* 32(July–August):51–59.

Gross, Jane. 1991. "Surge of Rock Fans, Then Death, Grief, Anger." *New York Times,* January 25, pp. A1, A16.

Grossman, David C. et al. 1997. "Effectiveness of a Violence Prevention Curriculum among Children in Elementary School." *Journal of the American Medical Association* 277(May 28):1605–1617.

Groves, Martha. 1999. "New Adoptions Open Up the Family Circle." *Los Angeles Times,* August 8, p. A3.

Groza, Victor, Daniela F. Ileana, and Ivor Irwin. 1999. *A Peacock or a Crow: Stories, Interviews, and Commentaries on Romanian Adoptions.* Euclid, OH: Williams Custom Publishing.

Guillemin, Jeanne. 1999. *Anthrat: The Investigation of a Deadly Outbreak.* Berkeley: University of California Press.

Guppy, Neil, and Scott Davies. 1998. *Education in Canada: Recent Trends*

———. 1798. *Essays on the Principle of Population.* New York: Augustus Kelly, Bookseller; reprinted in 1965.

Mandell, Nancy, ed. 1998. *Feminist Issues.* 2d ed. Scarborough: Prentice Hall Allyn and Bacon.

Mann, Jim. 2000. "India: Growing Implications for U.S." *Los Angeles Times,* May 17, p. A5.

Manson, Donald A. 1986. *Tracking Offenders: White-Collar Crime.* Bureau of Justice Statistics Special Report. Washington, DC: U.S. Government Printing Office.

Manzo, John. 1996. "Taking Turns and Taking Sides: Opening Scenes from Two Jury Deliberations." In *Social Psychology Quarterly* 59:107–125.

Marcil-Gratton, Nicole. 1999. "Growing up with Mom and Dad? Canadian Children Experience Shifting Family Structures." *Transition* 29 (1), September: 4–7.

Marcuse, Peter. 1991. *Missing Marx: A Personal and Political Journal of a Year in East Germany, 1989–1990.* New York: Monthly Review Press.

Marklein, Mary Beth. 1996. "Telecommuters Gain Momentum." *USA Today,* June 18, p. 6E.

Marks, Alexandra. 1998. "Key Swing Vote in 1998: Women," *Christian Science Monitor,* July 14, p. 3.

Markson, Elizabeth W. 1992. "Moral Dilemmas." *Society* 29(July–August):4–6.

Marmor, Theodore. 1995. P. 1505 in "Medicare Canada's Postwar Miracle, US Management Expert Tells CMA Conference" by J. Rafuse. *CMA Journal* 152 (9).

Maroney, Heather Jon, and Meg Luxton. 1987. *Feminism and Political Economy: Women's Work, Women's Struggles.* Agincourt, Ontario: Methuen Publications.

Marquis, Julie, and Dan Morain. 1999. "A Tortuous Path for the Mentally Ill." *Los Angeles Times,* November 21, pp. A1, A22, A23.

Marsden, Peter V. 1992. "Social Network Theory." Pp. 1887–1894 in *Encyclopedia of Sociology,* vol. 4, edited by Edgar F. Borgatta and Marie L. Borgatta. New York: Macmillan.

Marshall, Kathleen. 1999. *The Gambling Industry: Raising the Stakes.* Statistics Canada. Ottawa: Minister of Industry.

Marshall, Victor W. and Philippa J. Clarke. 1996. *Summary of Facilitating the Transition from Employment to Retirement.* Ottawa: Health Canada, National Forum on Health.

———, and Judith A. Levy. 1990. "Aging and Dying." Pp. 245–260 in *Handbook of Aging and the Social Sciences,* edited

by Robert H. Binstock and Linda K. George. San Diego: Academic Press.

Martelo, Emma Zapata. 1996. "Modernization, Adjustment, and Peasant Production." *Latin American Perspectives* 23(Winter):118–130.

Martin, Joyce A., and Melissa M. Park. 1999. "Trends in Twin and Triplet Births: 1980–97." *National Vital Statistics Reports* 47(September 14).

Martin, Marvin. 1996. "Sociology Adapting to Changes." *Chicago Tribune,* July 21, sec. 18, p. 20.

Martin, Philip, and Elizabeth Midgley. 1999. "Immigrants to the United States." *Population Bulletin* 54(June):1–42.

———, and Jonas Widgren. 1996. "International Migration: A Global Challenge." *Population Bulletin* 51(April).

Martin, Susan E. 1994. "Outsider Within the Station House: The Impact of Race and Gender on Black Women Politics." *Social Problems* 41(August):383–400.

Martineau, Harriet. [1837] 1962. *Society in America.* Edited, abridged, with an introductory essay by Seymour Martin Lipset. Reprint, Garden City, NY: Doubleday.

———. 1896. "Introduction" to the translation of *Positive Philosophy* by Auguste Comte. London: Bell.

Martinez, Elizabeth. 1993. "Going Gentle into That Good Night: Is a Rightful Death a Feminist Issue?" *Ms.* 4(July–August):65–69.

Martinez, Valerie, Kay Thomas, and Frank R. Kenerer. 1994. "Who Chooses and Why: A Look at Five School Choice Plans." *Phi Delta Kappan* 75(May):678–681.

Martyna, Wendy. 1983. "Beyond the He/Man Approach: The Case for Nonsexist Language." Pp. 25–37 in *Language, Gender and Society,* edited by Barrie Thorne, Cheris Kramorae, and Nancy Henley. Rowley, MA: Newly House.

Marx, Karl, and Friedrich Engels. [1847] 1955. *Selected Work in Two Volumes.* Reprint, Moscow: Foreign Languages Publishing House.

Masaki, Hisane. 1998. "Hashimoto Steps Down." *The Japan Times* 38 (July 20):1–5.

Mascia-Lees, Frances E., and Patricia Sharp, eds. 1992. *Tattoo, Torture, Mutilation, and Adornment: The Denaturalization of the Body in Culture and Text.* Albany: State University of New York Press.

Masland, Tom. 1992. "Slavery." *Newsweek* 119(May 4):30–32, 37–39.

Mason, J. W. 1998. "The Buses Don't Stop Here Anymore." *American Prospect* 37(March):56–62.

Mason, Marie K. 1942. "Learning to Speak after Six and One-Half Years of Silence." *Journal of Speech Disorders* 7(December):295–304.

Massey, Douglas S. 1998. "March of Folly: U.S. Immigration Policy After NAFTA." *The American Prospect* (March–April):22–33.

———. 1999. "International Migration at the Dawn of the Twenty-First Century: The Role of the State." *Population and Development Review* 28(June):303–322.

———, and Nancy A. Denton. 1993. *American Apartheid: Segregation and the Making of the Underclass.* Cambridge, MA: Harvard University Press.

Matloff, Norman. 1998. "Now Hiring! If You're Young." *New York Times,* January 26, p. A21.

Matrix Information and Directory Services. 1999. "Current World Map of the Internet." Austin, TX: MIDS. Also accessible online (http://www.mids.org/mapsale/world/index.html).

Matsushita, Yoshiko. 1999. "Japanese Kids Call for a Sympathetic Ear." *Christian Science Monitor,* January 20, p. 15.

Matthews, Jay. 1999. "A Home Run for Home Schooling." *Washington Post National Weekly Edition* 16(March 29):34.

Mauro, Tony, and Jim Drinkard. 1999. "Review Could Jeopardize Campaign-Finance Laws." *USA Today,* October 6, p. A6.

Mauro, Tony. 1999. "Will Every Childish Taunt Turn Into a Federal Case?" *USA Today,* May 25, pp. A1, A2.

Mawhiney, Anne-Marie. 2001. "First Nations in Canada." Pp. 153–166 in *Canadian Social Welfare,* 4th ed., edited by Joanne C. Turner and Francis J. Turner. Toronto: Pearson Education.

Maxwell, Joe. 1992. "African Megachurch Challenged over Teaching." *Christianity Today* 36(October 5):58.

Mayer, Karl Ulrich, and Urs Schoepflin. 1989. "The State and the Life Course." Pp. 187–209 in *Annual Review of Sociology,* 1989, edited by W. Richard Scott and Judith Blake. Palo Alto, CA: Annual Reviews.

Mayor's Task Force on Homelessness. 1997. *Report to Wheaton City Council on the Mayor's Task Force on Homelessness.* Wheaton, IL: Mayor's Task Force on Homelessness.

Maze, Brian, M. Cathey Maze, and Judith Glasser. 1997. "Assessing Alcoholism and Codependency in St. Kitts: Inappropriate Standards and Culture-Bound Syndromes." Presented at the annual meeting of the American Sociological Association, Toronto.

McAdam, D. 1989. "The Biographical Consequences of Activism." *American Sociological Review* 54(October):744–760.

McCaghy, Charles H. 1980. *Crime in American Society.* New York: Macmillan.

McCarthy, John. 2002. *Charter Schools: Hanging in the Balance.* Research paper series of CCSC. (www.charter-schools.ca).

McCarthy, Terry. 1999. "Inside the Falun Gong." *Time* 154(August 9): 48–50.

McChesney, Robert W. 1999. *Rich Media, Poor Democracy: Communication Politics in Dubious Times.* Urbana, IL: University of Illinois Press.

McCloskey, Michael. 1991. "Twenty Years of Change in the Environmental Movement: An Insider's View." *Society and Natural Resources* 4(July–September):273–284.

McClung, H. Juhling, Robert D. Murray, and Leo A. Heitlinger. 1998. "The Internet as a Source for Current Patient Information." *Pediatrics* 10(June 6): electronic edition.

McCormick, John, and Claudia Kalb. 1998. "Dying for a Drink." *Newsweek,* June 15, pp. 30–31, 33–34.

McCreary Centre Society. 2001. *No Place to Call Home.* Burnaby, B.C: McCreary Centre Society.

McCreary, D. 1994. "The Male Role and Avoiding Femininity." *Sex Roles* 31:517–531.

McDaniel, Susan A., and Lorne Tepperman. 2000. *Close Relations: An Introduction to the Sociology of the Family.* Scarborough: Prentice Hall Allyn and Bacon Canada.

McDermott, Kevin. 1999. "Illinois Bill Would Repeal Law Requiring Listing of Campaign Donors on Internet." *St. Louis Post-Dispatch,* November 25, p. A1.

McDonald, Kim A. 1999. "Studies of Women's Health Produce a Wealth of Knowledge on the Biology of Gender Differences." *Chronicle of Higher Education* 45(June 25):A19, A22.

McDonald's. 1999. *The Annual.* Oak Brook, IL: McDonald's.

McDonnell, Patrick J., and Maki Becker. 1996. "7 Plead Guilty in Sweatshop Slavery Case." *Los Angeles Times,* February 10, p. A1.

McDonough, Peggy, and Vivienne Walters. 2000. "Gender, Work and Health: An Analysis of the 1994 National Population Health Survey." *Centres of Excellence for Women's Health Research Bulletin* 1(1):3–4.

McEnroe, Jennifer. 1991. "Split-Shift Parenting." *American Demographics* 13(February):50–52.

McFalls, Joseph A., Jr. 1998. "Population: A Lively Introduction." *Population Bulletin* 53(September).

———, Jr., Brian Jones, and Bernard J. Gallegher III. 1984. "U.S. Population Growth: Prospects and Policy." *USA Today,* January, pp. 30–34.

McFarlane, Bruce A. "Anthropologists and Sociologists, And Their Contributions to Policy in Canada." Pp.281–294 in *Fragile Truths: 25 Years of Sociology and Anthropology in Canada,* edited by William K. Carroll, Linda Christiansen-Ruffman, Raymond F. Currie, and Deborah Harrison. Ottawa, Canada: Carleton University Press.

McGue, Matt, and Thomas J. Bouchard Jr. 1998. "Genetic and Environmental Influence on Human Behavioral Differences." Pp. 1–24 in *Annual Review of Neurosciences.* Palo Alto, CA: Annual Reviews.

McGuire, Meredith B. 1981. *Religion: The Social Context.* Belmont, CA: Wadsworth.

———. 1992. *Religion: The Social Context.* 3d ed. Belmont, CA: Wadsworth.

McIntosh, Peggy. 1988. "White Privilege and Male Privilege: A Personal Account of Coming to See Correspondence Through Work and Women's Studies." Working Paper No. 189, Wellesley College Center for Research on Women, Wellesley, MA.

McKenzie, Cheryl. 2001. *Aboriginal Spirituality: Spirit Beings On A Human Journey.* Five-part series for CBC Radio, CBC Manitoba.

McKenzie, Evan. 1994. *Privatopia: Homeowner Associations and the Rise of Residential Private Government.* New Haven, CT: Yale University Press.

McKinlay, John B., and Sonja M. McKinlay. 1977. "The Questionable Contribution of Medical Measures to the Decline of Mortality in the United States in the Twentieth Century." *Milbank Memorial Fund Quarterly* 55(Summer):405–428.

McKinley, James C., Jr. 1999. "In Cuba's New Dual Economy, Have-Nots Far Exceed Haves." *New York Times,* February 11, pp. A1, A6.

McKinney, Kathleen. 1990. "Sexual Harassment of University Faculty by Colleagues and Students." *Sex Roles* 23(October):421–438.

McKinnon, Jesse and Karen Humes. 2000. "The Black Population in the United States." *Current Population Reports.* Ser. P20 No. 530. Washington, DC: US Government Printing Office.

McLane, Daisann. 1995. "The Cuban-American Princess." *New York Times Magazine,* February 26, pp. 42–43.

McLaughlin, Abraham. 1998. "Tales of Journey from Death Row to Freedom." *Christian Science Monitor,* November 16, p. 2.

McMahon, Colin. 1995. "Mexican Rebels' Struggle in Chiapas Is 'about the Future.'" *Chicago Tribune,* January 1, p. 6.

McNamara, Robert S. 1992. "The Population Explosion." *The Futurist* 26 (November–December):9–13.

McPhail, Clark, and David Miller. 1973. "The Assembling Process: A Theoretical and Empirical Examination." *American Sociological Review* 38(December):721–735.

———. 1991. *The Myth of the Madding Crowd.* New York: De Gruyter.

———. 1994. "The Dark Side of Purpose in Riots: Individual and Collective Violence." *Sociological Quarterly* 35(January):i–xx.

McPherson, J. Miller, and Lynn Smith-Lovin. 1986. "Sex Segregation in Voluntary Associations." *American Sociological Review,* 51(February):61–79.

McQuaig, Linda. 1998. *The Cult of Impotence: Selling the Myth of Powerlessness in the Global Economy.* Toronto: Penguin Canada.

McTeer, Maureen A. 1999. *Tough Choices: Living and Dying in the 21st Century.* Toronto: Irwin Law.

McVey, Wayne W., Jr., and Warren Kalbach. 1995. *Canadian Population.* Scarborough: Nelson Canada.

Mead, George H. 1930. "Cooley's Contribution to American Social Thought." *American Journal of Sociology* 35(March):693–706.

———. 1934. *In Mind, Self and Society,* edited by Charles W. Morris. Chicago: University of Chicago Press.

———. 1964a. *In On Social Psychology,* edited by Anselm Strauss. Chicago: University of Chicago Press.

———. 1964b. "The Genesis of the Self and Social Control." Pp. 267–293 in *Selected Writings: George Herbert Mead,* edited by Andrew J. Reck. Indianapolis: Bobbs-Merrill.

Mead, Margaret. [1935] 1963. *Sex and Temperament in Three Primitive Societies.* Reprint, New York: Morrow.

———. 1973. "Does the World Belong to Men—Or to Women?" *Redbook* 141(October):46–52.

Mechanic, David, and David Rochefort. 1996. "Comparative Medical Systems." Pp. 475–494 in *Annual Review of Sociology,* 1996, edited by John Hagan. Palo Alto, CA: Annual Reviews.

Mehren, Elizabeth and Robert A. Rosenblatt. 1995. "For AARP a Reversal of Fortune." *Los Angeles Times,* August 23, pp. A1, A10–A11.

———. 1999. "Working 9 to 5 at Age 95." *USA Today*, May 5, pp. A1, A21–A22.

Meisel, John. 2001. "Stroking the Airwaves: The Regulation of Broadcasting by the CRTC." Pp. 217–232 in *Communications in Canada*, 5th ed., edited by Craig McKie and Benjamin D. Singer. Toronto: Thompson Educational Publishing.

Melia, Marilyn Kennedy. 2000. "Changing Times." *Chicago Tribune*, January 2, sec. 17, pp. 12–15.

Melson, Robert. 1986. "Provocation or Nationalism: A Critical Inquiry into the Armenian Genocide of 1915." Pp. 61–84 in *The Armenian Genocide in Perspective*, edited by Richard G. Hovannisian. Brunswick, NJ: Transaction.

Men. Washington, NJ: Times Change.

Mendez, Jennifer Brikham. 1998. "Of Mops and Maids: Contradictions and Continuities in Bureaucratized Domestic Work." *Social Problems* 45(February):114–135.

———. 1998. "Of Mops and Maids: Contradictions and Continuities in Bureaucratized Domestic Work." *Social Problems* 45(February):114–135.

Merton, Robert K. 1968. *Social Theory and Social Structure*. New York: Free Press.

———. and Alice S. Kitt. 1950. "Contributions to the Theory of Reference Group Behavior." Pp. 40–105 in *Continuities in Social Research: Studies in the Scope and Method of the American Soldier*, edited by Robert K. Merton and Paul L. Lazarsfeld. New York: Free Press.

———, G. C. Reader, and P. L. Kendall. 1957. *The Student Physician*. Cambridge, MA: Harvard University Press.

Messner, Michael A. 1997. *Politics of Masculinities: Men in Movements*. Thousand Oaks, CA: Sage.

Meyer, David S., and Nancy Whittier. 1994. "Social Movement Spillover." *Social Problems* 41(May):277–298.

Meyers, Thomas J. 1992. "Factors Affecting the Decision to Leave the Old Order Amish." Presented at the annual meeting of the American Sociological Association, Pittsburgh.

Michael, Robert T., John H. Gagnon, Edward O. Laumann, and Gina Kolata. 1994. *Sex in America: A Definitive Survey*. Boston: Little, Brown.

Michels, Robert. 1915. *Political Parties*. Glencoe, IL: Free Press (reprinted 1949).

Mifflin, Lawrie. 1999. "Many Researchers Say Link Is Already Clear on Media and Youth Violence." *New York Times*, May 9, p. 23.

Migration News. 1998a. "Canada: Immigration, Diversity Up." 5(January). Accessed May 22 (http://migration.ucdavis.edu).

———. 1998b. "Immigration in EU, France: New Law, Australia: Immigration Unchanged." 5(May). Accessed May 6 (http://migration.ucdavis.edu).

———. 1999a. "Japan: Korean Illegals." *Migration News* 6(March).

———. 1999b. "Mexico: Demography, Remittances." *Migration News* 6(July).

———. 1999c. "Mexico: NAFYTA" 6(November):16–17.

Milan, Anne. 2000. "One Hundred Years of Families." *Canadian Social Trends*. Statistics Canada, Cat. no. 11-008 (Spring):2–13.

Miles, Angela. 2000. "Local Activism, Global Feminisms and the Struggle Against Globalization" in *Women 2000: Eradicating Poverty and Violence in the 21st Century, Special Issues of Canadian Woman Studies* 20,3(Fall): 6-10.

———. 2001. "Global Feminisms" in *Feminist Issues: Race, Class and Sexuality*, 3d ed. Edited by Nancy Mandel. Toronto: Prentice Hall.

Milgram, Stanley. 1963. "Behavioral Study of Obedience." *Journal of Abnormal and Social Psychology* 67(October):371–378.

———. 1975. *Obedience to Authority: An Experimental View*. New York: Harper and Row.

Miller, D. W. 2000. "Sociology, Not Engineering May Explain Our Vulnerability to Technological Disaster." *Chronicle of Higher Education* (October 15):A19–A20.

Miller, David L. 1973. *George Herbert Mead: Self, Language, and the World*. Chicago: University of Chicago Press.

———. 2000. *Introduction to Collective Behavior and Collective Action*. 2d ed. Prospect Heights, IL Waveland Press.

———, and Richard T. Schaefer. 1993. "Feeding the Hungry: The National Food Bank System as a Non-Insurgent Social Movement." Presented at the annual meeting of the Midwest Sociological Society, Chicago.

———, and ———. 1998. "Promise Keepers and Race: The Stand in the Gap Rally, Washington, DC, 1997." Paper presented at the annual meeting of the Midwest Sociological Society, April, Kansas City, MO.

Miller, G. Tyler, Jr. 1972. *Replenish the Earth: A Primer in Human Ecology*. Belmont, CA: Wadsworth.

Miller, Greg. 1999. "Internet Fueled Global Interest in Disruptions." *Chicago Tribune*, December 2, p. A24.

Miller, Leslie. 1995. "MIT Prof Taps into Culture of Computers." *USA Today*, November 7, pp. D1, D2.

———. 1998. "Finding On-Line Faithful Revives Religious Groups." *USA Today*, March 25, pp. D1, D2.

Miller, Michael. 1998. "Abortion by the Numbers." *The Village Voice* 43, January 27, p. 58.

Miller, Reuben. 1988. "The Literature of Terrorism," *Terrorism*, 11(1):63–87.

Millett, Kate. 1970. *Sexual Politics*. New York: Doubleday.

Mills, C. Wright. 1956. *The Power Elite*. New York: Oxford University Press.

———. 1959. *The Sociological Imagination*. London: Oxford University Press.

Mills, Kim I., and Daryl Henschaft. 1999. *The State of the Workplace for Lesbian, Gay, Bisexual and Transgendered Americans 1999*. Washington, DC: Human Rights Campaign Foundation.

Mills, Robert J. 2000. "Health Insurance Coverage." *Current Population Reports*, ser. P60, no. 211. Washington, DC: U.S. Government Printing Office.

Milton S. Eisenhower Foundation. 1999. *To Establish Justice, To Insure Domestic Tranquility: A Thirty Year Update of the National Commission on the Causes and Prevention of Violence*. Washington, DC: Milton S. Eisenhower Foundation.

Mindel, Charles, Robert W. Habenstein, and Roosevelt Wright, Jr. 1998. *Ethnic Families in America: Patterns and Variations*. 4th ed. Upper Saddle River, NJ: Prentice Hall.

Miner, Barbara. 1997. "Lessons from England: Charters, Choice, and Standards" in *Rethinking Schools: An Urban Educational Journal Online*. Volume 11, No. 3—Spring.

Miner, Horace. 1956. "Body Ritual Among the Nacirema." *American Anthropologist* 58(June):503–507.

Mingle, James R. 1987. *Focus on Minorities*. Denver: Education Commission of the States and the State Higher Education Executive Officers.

Mitchell, Alanna. 1999. "Home Schooling Goes AWOL." *The Globe and Mail*, February 2, p. A1, A6.

Mitchell, Barbara A. 1998. "Too Close for Comfort? Parental Assessments of 'Boomerang Kid' Living Arrangements." *Canadian Journal of Sociology* 23(1).

Mitchell, William J. 1996. *City of Bits*. Cambrige, MA: MIT Press.

Mitchell, William J. 1999. *E-topia*. Cambridge, MA: MIT Press.

Mitofsky, Warren J. 1998. "The Polls-Review. Was 1996 a Worse Year for Polls than 1948?" *Public Opinion Quarterly* 62(Summer):230–249.

Mizrahi, Terry. 1986. *Getting Rid of Patients.* New Brunswick, NJ: Rutgers University Press.

Moffatt, Susan. 1995. "Minorities Found More Likely to Live Near Toxic Sites." *Los Angeles Times,* August 30, pp. B1, B3.

Mogelonsky, Marcia. 1996. "The Rocky Road to Adulthood." *American Demographics* 18(May):26–29, 32–35, 56.

Mollen, Milton. 1992. *"A Failure of Responsibility": Report to Mayor David N. Dinkins on the December 28, 1991, Tragedy at City College of New York.* New York: Office of the Deputy Mayor for Public Safety.

Molot, Maureen Appel, and Fen Osler Hampson, eds. 2000. *Canada among Nations, 2000: Vanishing Borders.* Toronto: Oxford University Press.

Monaghan, Peter. 1993. "Sociologist Jailed Because He 'Wouldn't Snitch' Ponders the Way Research Ought to Be Done." *Chronicle of Higher Education* 40(September 1):A8, A9.

Money. 1987. "A Short History of Shortages." 16(Fall, special issue):42.

Monmaney, Terence. 1995. "Ethnicities' Medical Views Vary, Study Says." *Los Angeles Times,* September 13, pp. B1, B3.

Monteiro, Lois A. 1998. "Ill-Defined Illnesses and Medically Unexplained Symptoms Syndrome." *Footnotes* 26(February):3, 6.

Montgomery, Marilyn J., and Gwendolyn T. Sorrell. 1997. "Differences in Love Attitudes Across Family Life Stages." *Family Relations* 46:55–61.

Moore, David A. 1995. "Public Sense of Urgency about Environment Wanes." *Gallup Poll Monthly* (April), pp. 17–20.

————. 1999. "Americans Oppose General Legalization of Marijuana." Poll Released April 9. Accessible online (http://www.gallup.com/poll/releases/pr990409b.asp).

Moore, Kristin A. 1995. *Report to Congress on Out-of-Wedlock Childbearing.* Washington, DC: Child Trends.

Moore, Thomas S. 1996. *The Disposable Work Force: Worker Displacement and Employment Instability in America.* New York: Aldine de Gruyter.

Moore, Wilbert E. 1967. *Order and Change: Essays in Comparative Sociology.* New York: Wiley.

————. 1968. "Occupational Socialization." Pp. 861–883 in *Handbook of Socialization Theory and Research,* edited by David A. Goslin. Chicago: Rand McNally.

Morehouse Medical Treatment and Effectiveness Center. 1999. *A Synthesis of the Literature: Racial and Ethnic Differences in Acccess to Medical Care.*

Menlo Park, CA: Henry J. Kaiser Family Foundation.

Morehouse Research Institute and Institute for American Values. 1999. *Turning the Corner on Father Absence in Black America.* Atlanta: Morehouse Research Institute and Institute for American Values.

Morello, Carol. 1997. "Opponents Chip Away at Prop. 209." *USA Today,* November 17, pp. A1–A2.

Morin, Richard. 1993. "Think Twice before You Say Another Word." *Washington Post National Weekly Edition* 10, January 3, p. 37.

————. 1997. "An Airwave of Crime." *Washington Post National Weekly Edition,* August 18, p 34.

————. 1999. "Not a Clue." *Washington Post National Weekly Edition* 16(June 14):34.

————. 2000. "Will Traditional Polls Go the Way of the Dinosaur?" *Washington Post National Weekly Edition* 17(May 15):34.

Morland, John, Jr. 1996. "The Individual, the Society, or Both? A Comparison of Black, Latino, and White Beliefs about the Causes of Poverty." *Social Forces* 75(December):403–422.

Morris, Aldon. 2000. "Reflections on Social Movement Theory: Criticisms and Proposals." *Contemporary Sociology* 29(May):445–454.

Morris, Bonnie Rothman. 1999. "You've Got Romance! Seeking Love on Line." *New York Times,* August 26, p. D1.

Morris, Charles. 1996. *The AARP: America's Most Powerful Lobby and the Clash of Generations.* New York: Times Books/ Random House.

Morrison, Denton E. 1971. "Some Notes toward Theory on Relative Deprivation, Social Movements, and Social Change." *American Behavioral Scientist* 14(May–June):675–690.

Morrow, David J. 1999. "A Movable Epidemic." *New York Times,* August 9, p. C1.

Morrow, John K. 1997. "Of Sheep Cloning and Cold Fusion." *Chicago Tribune,* March 7, p. 23.

Morse, Arthur D. 1967. *While Six Million Died: A Chronicle of American Apathy.* New York: Ace.

Morse, Jodie. 1999. "Cracking Down on the Homeless." *Time,* December 2000, pp. 69–70.

Mortimer, Jeylan E., and Roberta G. Simmons. 1978. "Adult Socialization." Pp. 421–454 in *Annual Review of Sociology, 1978,* edited by Ralph H. Turner, James Coleman, and Renee C. Fox. Palo Alto, CA: Annual Reviews.

Moseley, Ray. 2000. "Britons Watch Health Service Fall to Its Knees." *Chicago Tribune,* January 22, pp. 1, 2.

————. 1999. "Dutch Euthanasia Plan Lets Kids Make Choice." *Chicago Tribune,* August 26, p. 1, 22.

Moser, Nancy. 1998. "Wishing for Maybes." Pp. 158–164 in *Generation to Generation: Reflections on Friendships Between Young and Old,* edited by Sandra Martz and Shirley Coe. Watsonville, CA: Papier-Mache Press.

Moskos, Charles C., Jr. 1991. "How Do They Do It?" *New Republic* 205(August 5):20.

Mosley, J., and E. Thomson. 1995. Pp. 148–165 in *Fatherhood: Contemporary Theory, Research and Social Policy,* edited by W. Marsiglo. Thousand Oaks, CA: Sage.

Mossman, M.J. 1994. "Running Hard to Stand Still: The Paradox of Family Law Reform." *Dalhousie Law Journal* 17(5).

MOST. 1999. MOST Quarterly. Internet vol. 1. Accessed July 19, 1999 (http://www.mostonline.org/qtrly/qtrly-index.htm).

Ms. Magazine. 1992. "Family Planning Policies: 1991's Winners and Losers." 2(March–April):10.

Mulcahy, Aogan. 1995. "'Headhunter' or Real Cop? Identity in the World of Internal Affairs Officers." *Journal of Contemporary Ethnography* 24(April):99–130.

Murdock, George P. 1945. "The Common Denominator of Cultures." Pp. 123–142 in *The Science of Man in the World Crisis,* edited by Ralph Linton. New York: Columbia University Press.

————. 1949. *Social Structure.* New York: Macmillan.

Murdock, George P. 1957. "World Ethnographic Sample." *American Anthropologist* 59(August): 664–687.

Murphy, Caryle. 1993. "Putting Aside the Veil." *Washington Post National Weekly Edition* 10 (April 12–18): pp. 10–11.

Murphy, Dean E. 1997. "A Victim of Sweden's Pursuit of Perfection." *Los Angeles Times,* September 2, pp. A1, A8.

Murray, C .J. L., and A. D. Lopez (eds.). 1996. *The Global Burden of Disease: A comprehensive assessment of mortality and disability from diseases, injuries, and risk factors in 1990 and project to 2020.* Cambridge: Harvard University Press.

Mychajlowycz, Maryjka. 1999. *The Friends: 20 Years Young* (www.ancientrainforest.org/history_focs/maryjkas_article.html).

N

Nader, Laura. 1986. "The Subordination of Women in Comparative Perspective." *Urban Anthropology* 15(Fall–Winter):377–397.

Nagel, Joanne. 1996. *American Indian Ethnic Renewal: Red Power and the Resurgence of Identity and Culture.* New York: Oxford University Press.

Naifeh, Mary. 1998. "Trap Door? Revolving Door? Or Both? Dynamics of Economic Well-Being, Poverty 1993–94." *Current Population Reports*, ser. P-70, no. 63. Washington, DC: U.S. Government Printing Office.

Naiman, Joanne. 1997. *How Societies Work: Class, Power and Change in Canadian Society.* Concord: Irwin Publishing.

Nakane, Chie. 1970. *Japanese Society.* Berkeley: University of California Press.

Nakao, Keiko, and Judith Treas. 1990. *Computing 1989 Occupational Prestige Scores.* Chicago: NORC.

———, and Judith Treas. 1994. "Updating Occupational Prestige and Socioeconomic Scores: How the New Measures Measure Up." Pp. 1–72 in *Sociological Methodology, 1994*, edited by Peter V. Marsden. Oxford: Basil Blackwell.

———, Robert W. Hodge, and Judith Treas. 1990. *On Revising Prestige Scores for All Occupations.* Chicago: NORC.

Nakhaie, M. Reza. 2001. "Ethnic and Gender Distribution of Sociologists and Anthropologists, 1971–96: Canada." *Journal of Sociology* 26(2).

Nanda, Serena. 1991. *Cultural Anthropology.* Belmont, CA: Wadsworth Publishing Company.

Nash, Manning. 1962. "Race and the Ideology of Race." *Current Anthropology* 3(June):285–288.

Nason-Clark, Nancy. 1993. "Gender Relations in Contemporary Christian Organizations." Pp. 215–234 in *The Sociology of Religion: A Canadian Focus*, edited by W.E. Hewitt. Toronto: Butterworths.

National Abortion and Reproductive Rights Action League. 1999a. "House Passes HR2436, The So-Called 'Unborn Victims of Violence Act.'" Accessed October 9, 1999 (http://www.naral.org/publications/press/99sep/093099b.htm).

———. 1999b. "NARAL Factsheets: Public Funding for Abortion." Accessed October 9, 1999 (http://www.naral.org/publications/facts/1999/public_funding.html).

National Advisory Commission on Criminal Justice. 1976. *Organized Crime.* Washington, DC: U.S. Government Printing Office.

National Alliance for Caregiving. 1997. *The NAC Comparative Analysis of Caregiver Data for Caregivers to the Elderly, 1987 and 1997.* Bethesda, MD: National Alliance for Caregiving.

National Alliance for the Mentally Ill. 2000. "What Is Mental Illness?" Accessed January 18, 2000 (http://www.nami.org/disorder/whatis.html).

National Anti-poverty Organization. 1998. *Government Expenditure Cuts to Health Care and Post Secondary Education: Impacts on Low Income Canadians.* Ottawa: National Anti-poverty Organization.

National Archives of Canada. 1993. *Nunavut Territory, 1993.* Ref. no. NMC161029. Ottawa: Department of Indian and Northern Affairs.

National Center for Educational Statistics. 1997. "Digest of Education Statistics 1997." Washington, DC: U.S. Government Printing Office. Accessed September 29, 1999 (http://nces.ed.gov/pubs).

———. 1998. *Students' Report of School Crime: 1989 and 1995.* Washington, DC: U.S. Government Printing Office.

———. 1999. *Digest of Education Statistics, 1998.* Washington, DC: U.S. Government Printing Office.

National Center for Health Statistics. 1974. *Summary Report: Final Divorce Statistics, 1974.* Washington, DC: U.S. Government Printing Office.

———. 1990. *Annual Survey of Births, Marriages, Divorces, and Deaths: United States, 1989.* Washington, DC: U.S. Government Printing Office.

———. 1997a. U.S. *Deceased Life Tables for 1989–91.* Washington, DC: U.S. Government Printing Office.

———. 1997b. "Births and Deaths: United States, 1996." *Monthly Vital Statistics Report* 46(September 11).

———. 1998. "Births, Marriages, Divorces, and Deaths: Provisional Data for July 1998." *Monthly Vital Statistics Report* 47(November 27):1–2.

———. 1998. "Expectation of Life at Single Years of Age, by Race and Sex." *National Vital Statistics Report* 47(December 24):10.

———. 1999. "Infant, Neonatal, and Postnatal Mortality Rates by Race and Sex." *National Vital Statistics Report* 47(June 30):86–87.

———. 2000. "Births, Marriages, Divorces, and Deaths: Provisional Data for January 1999." *Monthly Vital Statistics Reports* 48(January 25):1–2.

National Center on Elder Abuse. 1998. *The National Elder Abuse Incidence Study.* Washington, DC: American Public Human Services Association.

National Center on Women and Family Law. 1996. *Status of Marital Rape Exemption Statutes in the United States.* New York: National Center on Women and Family Law.

National Conference of State Legislatures. 2000. *Limits on Contributions to Candidates.* Washington, DC: NCSL.

National Council of Welfare. 1999. *Poverty Profile 1997.* Ottawa: National Council of Welfare.

———. 2000. *Child Poverty Profile 1998.* Ottawa: Minister of Public Works and Government Services Canada, 2000.

———. 2000. *Poverty Profile 1998.* Minister of Public Works and Government Services Canada.

National Gay and Lesbian Task Force. 1999. *Hate Crime Laws in the United States.* Accessed September 7, 2000 (http://www.ngltf.org).

National Homeschool Association. 1999. *Homeschooling Families: Ready for the Next Decade.* Accessed November 19, 2000 (http://www.n-h-a.org/decade.htm).

National Institute of Mental Health. 1999. *The Numbers Count: Mental Illness in America.* Washington, DC: U.S. Government Printing Office.

National Institute on Aging. 1999a. *Early Retirement in the United States.* Washington, DC: U.S. Government Printing Office.

———. 1999b. *The Declining Disability of Older Americans.* Washington, DC: U.S. Government Printing Office.

National Law Center on Homelessness and Poverty. 1996. *Mean Sweeps: A Report on Anti-Homeless Laws, Litigation, and Alternatives in 50 United States Cities.* Washington, DC: National Law Center on Homelessness and Poverty.

National Marriage Project. 2000. *The State of Our Unions.* New Brunswick, NJ: The National Marriage Project.

National Organization for Men Against Sexism (NOMAS). 1999. "Statement of Principles." Accessed October 11, 1999 (http://www.nomas.org/statemt_of_principles.htm).

National Partnership for Women and Families. 1998. *Balancing Acts: Work/Family Issues on Prime-Time TV. Executive Summary.* Washington, DC: The National Partnership for Women and Families.

National Telecommunications and Information Administration. 2000. *Falling Through the Net: Toward Digital Inclusion.* Washington, DC: U.S. Government Printing Office.

———. 1999. *Falling through the Net: Defining the Digital Divide.* Washington, DC: U.S. Government Printing Office.

National Vital Statistics Reports. 2000. "Births, Marriages, Divorces and Deaths: Provisional Data for October 1999." *National Vital Statistics Reports* 48(September 6).

Navarro, Mineya. 1998. "Group Forced Illegal Aliens into Prostitution, U.S. Says." *New York Times,* April 24, p. A10.

Navarro, Vicente. 1984. "Medical History as Justification Rather Than Explanation: A Critique of Starr's The Social Transformation of American Medicine." *International Journal of Health Services* 14(4):511–528.

Neary, Tom. 1997. "Burakumin in Contemporary Japan." Pp. 50–78 in *Japan's Minorities: The Illusion of Homogeneity,* edited by Michael Weiner. London: Routledge.

Neft, Naomi, and Ann D. Levine. 1997. *Where Women Stand: An International Report on the Status of Women in 140 Countries.* New York: Random House.

Negushi, Mayumi. 1998. "A Matter of Life and Death." *Japan Times Weekly* 38(October 26):10–11.

Nelson, Adie, and Augie Fleras. 1998. *Social Problems in Canada: Conditions and Consequences.* 2d ed. Scarborough: Prentice-Hall.

———, and Barrie Robinson. 2002. *Gender in Canada.* Toronto: Pearson Education Canada Inc.

———, and ———. 1999. *Gender in Canada.* Scarborough, Prentice Hall.

Nelson, Jack. 1995. "The Internet, the Virtual Community, and Those with Disabilities." *Disability Studies Quarterly* 15(Spring):15–20.

Nelson, Mariah Burton. 1994. *The Stronger Women Get, the More Men Love Football.* New York: Avon.

NetCoalition.com. 2000. "NetCoalition Joins Friend of the Court Brief in Napster Case." Press release, August 30. Washington, DC: NetCoalition.com.

Neuborne, Ellen. 1996. "Vigilantes Stir Firms' Ire with Cyber-antics." *USA Today,* February 28, pp. A1, A2.

Nevitte, Neil. 1996. *The Decline of Deference: Canadian Value Change in Cross-National Perspective.* Peterborough, ON: Broadview Press.

New York Times. 1992. "Californians Confront Wave of Earthquake Rumors." July 20, p. A8.

———. 1993a. "Child Care in Europe: Admirable but Not Perfect, Experts Say." February 15, p. A13.

———. 1993b. "Dutch May Broaden Euthanasia Guidelines." February 17, p. A3.

———. 1995. "Reverse Discrimination of Whites Is Rare, Labor Study Reports." March 31, p. A23.

———. 1997. "Slave Trade in Africa Highlighted by Arrests." August 10, p. 5.

———. 1998. "2 Gay Men Fight Town Hall for a Family Pool Pass Discount." July 14, p. B2.

———. 1999a. "Woman Strikes Deal to Quit Redwood Home." December 19, p. 33.

———. 1999b. "Cult in Gas Attack Apologizes, But the Japanese Are Skeptical." (December 2), p. A8.

———. 2000. "Technology's Gender Gap." September 5, p. A26.

Newman, Katherine S. 1999. *No Shame in My Game: The Working Poor in the Inner City.* New York: Alfred A. Knopf and Russell Sage Foundation.

Newman, William M. 1973. *American Pluralism: A Study of Minority Groups and Social Theory.* New York: Harper and Row.

Newport, Frank. 2000. "Americans Remain Very Religious, But Not Necessarily in Conventional Ways." *Emerging Trends* 22(January):2–3. news.release. news/stats/caseload.htm).

Newsbytes News Network. 1997a. "Groups Want Intervention in CompuServe/Gernig Case." March 25. Accessed October 8, 1998 (http://www.elibrary.com/ getdoc.cg1?id= 113_ydocid=1183038 @library_ d&dtype=O~o&dinst=).

Newsday. 1997. "Japan Sterilized 16,000 Women." September 18, p. A19.

Neysmith, S.M. 1995. "Feminist Methodologies: A Consideration of Principles and Practice for Research in Gerontology." In *Canadian Journal on Aging* 14(1):100-18.

Ng, Roxana. 1990. "State Funding to a Community Employment Center: Implications for Working with Immigrant Women". In Ng, Roxana, Gillian Walker and Jacob Muller (eds). *Community Organization and the Canadian State.* Toronto: Garamond Press.

Nguyen, S. D. 1982. "The Psycho-social Adjustment and Mental Health Needs of Southeast Asian Refugees." *Psychiatric Journal of the University of Ottawa* 7(1) 6–34.

NHTSA (National Highway Traffic Safety Administration). 1996. *Fatal Accident Reporting System.* Washington, DC: NHTSA.

———. 1997. *Fatal Accident Reporting System.* Washington, DC: NHTSA.

Nibert, David. 2000. *Hitting the Lottery Jackpot: Government and the Taxing of Dreams.* New York: Monthly Review Press.

NICHD. 1999a. "Higher Quality Care Related to Less Problem Behavior." Accessed July 28, 1999 (http://www.nih.gov/nichd/docs/news/DAYCAR99.htm).

———. 1999b. "Child Outcomes When Child Care Center Classes Meet Recommended Standards for

Quality." *American Journal of Public Health* 89(July):1072–1077.

Nie, Norman H. 1999. "Tracking Our Techno-Future." *American Demographics* (July):50–52.

———, and Lutz Erbring. 2000. "Study of the Social Consequences of the Internet." Accessible online (http://www.stanford.edu/group/sigss/). Palo Alto, CA: Stanford Institute for the Quantitative Study of Society.

Nielsen, François. 1994. "Sociobiology and Sociology." Pp. 267–303 in *Annual Review of Sociology, 1994,* edited by John Hagan. Palo Alto, CA: Annual Reviews., pp. 267–303.

Nielsen, Joyce McCarl, Glenda Walden, and Charlotte A. Kunkel. 2000. "Gendered Heteronormativity: Empirical Illustrations in Everyday Life." *Sociological Quarterly* 41(No. 2): 283–296.

NIHCD. 1999a. "Higher Quality Care Related to Less Problem Behavior." Accessed July 28, 1999 (http://www.nih.gov/nichd/docs/news/DAYCAR99.htm).

———. 1999b. "Child Outcomes When Child Care Center Classes Meet Recommended Standards for Quality." *American Journal of Public Health* 89(July):1072–1077.

Nixon, Howard L., II. 1979. *The Small Group.* Englewood Cliffs, NJ: Prentice-Hall.

Noble, Holcomb B. 1998. "Struggling to Bolster Minorities in Medicine." *New York Times,* September 29.

Nock, Steven L., James D. Wright, and Laura Sanchez. 1999. "America's Divorce Problem." Society 36(May/June):43–52.

Nolan, Patrick and Gerhad Lenski. 1999. *Human Societies: An Introduction to Macrosociology.* New York: McGraw-Hill.

Noll, Roger G., and Andrew Zimbalist. 1997. *Sports, Jobs and Taxes: The Economic Impact of Sports Teams and Stadiums.* Washington, DC: The Brookings Institution.

Noonan, Rita K. 1995. "Women against the State: Political Opportunities and Collective Action Frames in Chile's Transition to Democracy." *Sociological Forum* 10:81–111.

NORC (National Opinion Research Center). 1994. *General Social Surveys 1972–1994.* Chicago: National Opinion Research Center.

Norman, Jim. 1996. "At Least 1 Pollster Was Right on Target." *USA Today,* November 7, p. 8A.

Norrie, Kenneth Harold, and Douglas Owram. 1996. *A History of the Canadian Economy.* 2d ed. Toronto: Harcourt Brace.

North Carolina Abecedarian Project. 2000. *Early Learning, Later Success: The Abecedarian Study*. Chapel Hill, NC: Frank Porter Graham Child Development Center.

Novak, Mark and Lori Campbell. 2001. *Aging and Society: A Canadian Perspective*, 4th edition. Scarborough, Ontario: Nelson Thomson Learning.

Novak, Tim, and Jon Schmid. 1999. "Lottery Picks Split by Race, Income." *Chicago Sun-Times*, June 22, pp. 1, 24, 25.

Novick, Peter. 1999. *The Holocaust in American Life*. Boston: Houghton Mifflin.

Nussbaum, Daniel. 1998. "Bad Air Days." *Los Angeles Times Magazine*, July 19, pp. 20–21.

O

O'Donnell, Mike. 1992. *A New Introduction to Sociology*. Walton-on-Thames, United Kingdom: Thomas Nelson and Sons.

O'Donnell, Rosie. 1998. Statement at the National Partnership for Women and Families Annual Luncheon, June 10.

O'Hanlan, Kate. 1995. "Lesbian Health and Homophobia: Perspectives for Treating Obstetrician/Gynecologist." Accessed April 4, 2002 (http://www. ohanlan.com/lhr.htm).

O'Hare, William P., and Brenda Curry-White. 1992. "Is There a Rural Underclass?" *Population Today* 20(March): 6–8.

O'Hearn, Claudine Chiawei, ed. 1998. *Half and Half: Writers on Growing Up Biracial and Bicultural*. New York: Pantheon Books.

O'Rand, Angele M. 1996. "The Precious and the Precocious: Understanding Cumulative Disadvantage and Cumulative Advantage Over the Life Course." *The Gerontologist* 36(No. 2):230–258.

Oakes, Jeannie. 1985. *Keeping Track: How Schools Structure Inequality*. New Haven, CT: Yale University Press.

Obermiller, Tim Andrew. 1994. "Sex by the Numbers." *University of Chicago Magazine* 87(October):34–37.

Oberschall, Anthony. 1973. *Social Conflict and Social Movements*. Englewood Cliffs, NJ: Prentice-Hall.

Observer. 1999. "Another horrific year ends century of blood" in *Guardian Unlimited*. Guardian Newspapers Limited, 2002 (www.guardian.co.uk/ Archive/Article).

OECD. 1995. *Trends in International Migration: Continuing Reporting System on Migration, Annual Report 1994*. Paris: OECD.

———. 1998. "Annual National Accounts: Gross Domestic Product." Accessed April 21, 1998 (http://www. oecd.olrg/std/gdp.htm).

Office of Justice Programs. 1999. "Transnational Organized Crime." *NCJRS Catalog* 49(November/December):21.

Office of the Federal Register. 1997. *United States Government Manual, 1997–1998*. Washington, DC: U.S. Government Printing Office.

Ogburn, William F. 1922. *Social Change with Respect to Culture and Original Nature*. New York: Huebsch (reprinted 1966, New York: Dell).

———, and Clark Tibbits. 1934. "The Family and Its Functions." Pp. 661–708 in *Recent Social Trends in the United States*, edited by Research Committee on Social Trends. New York: McGraw-Hill.

Okano, Kaori, and Motonori Tsuchiya. 1999. *Education in Contemporary Japan: Inequality and Diversity*. Cambridge: Cambridge University Press.

Oliver, Melvin L., and Thomas M. Shapiro. 1995. *Black Wealth/White Wealth: New Perspectives on Racial Inequality*. New York: Routledge.

Omran, Abdel R., and Farzaneh Roudi. 1993. "The Middle East's Population Puzzle." *Population Bulletin* 48 (July).

Ontario Consultants on Religious Tolerance. 2001. "Public Opinion Polls on Same-Sex Marriages: U.S. and Canada" (http://www.religious tolerance.org/hom_marp.htm).

Ontario Human Rights Commission. 2001. Toronto: Queen's Printer for Ontario.

Ontario Ministry of Education. 1994. *Education About Religion in Ontario Public Elementary Schools*. (www.edu. gov.on.ca/eng/document/curricul/ religion/rligioe.html).

Ontario Secondary School Teachers' Federation (OSSTF). 2001. *Private School Tax Credits—A Plan for Inequity: Response to Equity in Education Tax Credit Discussion Paper*. September 2001 (www.osstf.on.ca/www/ issues/charter.html).

Orum, Anthony M. 1989. *Introduction to Political Sociology: The Social Anatomy of the Body Politic*. 3d ed. Englewood Cliffs, NJ: Prentice-Hall.

———. 2001. *Introduction to Political Sociology*. 4th ed. Upper Saddle River, NJ: Prentice-Hall.

Orwell, George. 1949. *1984*. New York: Harcourt Brace Jovanovich.

OSHA (Occupational Safety and Health Administration). 1999. "One Size Doesn't Fit All Approach." National News Release: USDL 99–333. Wash-ington, DC: U.S. Department of Labor.

Ostling, Richard N. 1993. "Religion." *Time International*, July 12, p. 38.

Ouellette, Laurie. 1993. "The Information Lockout." *Utne Reader*, September–October, pp. 25–26.

Owens, Lynn, and L. Kendall Palmer. 2000. *Public Betrayals and Private Portrayals: Activist Intention in Tension on the WWW*. Presented at the annual meeting of the American Sociological Association, Washington, DC.

P

Paddock, Richard C. 1999. "Republic Stirs Debate by Allowing for Multiple Wives." *Los Angeles Times*, August 15, pp. A27–A28.

Pagani, Steve. 1999. "End the 'Culture of Death,' Pope Tells America." Reuters Wire Service, January 23.

Page, Charles H. 1946. "Bureaucracy's Other Face." *Social Forces* 25 (October):89–94.

Palen, J. John. 1995. "The Suburban Revolution: An Introduction." *Sociological Focus* 28(October):347–351.

Palmer Patterson, E. 1972. *The Canadian Indian: A History Since 1500*. New York: Collier-Macmillan of Canada Ltd.

Pamuk, E., D. Makui, K. Heck, C. Rueben, and K. Lochren. 1998. *Health, United States 1998 with Socioeconomic Status and Health Chartbook*. Hyattsville, MD: National Center for Health Statistics.

Pappas, Gregory et al. [4 authors]. 1993. "The Increasing Disparity in Mortality between Socioeconomic Groups in the United States, 1960 and 1986." *New England Journal of Medicine* 329(July 8):103–109.

Park, Robert E. 1916. "The City: Suggestions for the Investigation of Human Behavior in the Urban Environment." *American Journal of Sociology* 20(March):577–612.

———. 1936. "Succession, an Ecological Concept." *American Sociological Review* 1(April):171–179.

Parker, Suzi. 1998. "Wedding Boom: More Rings, Tuxes, Bells, and Brides." *Christian Science Monitor*, July 20, pp. 1, 14.

Parsons, Talcott, and Robert Bales. 1955. *Family, Socialization, and Interaction Process*. Glencoe, IL: Free Press.

———. 1951. *The Social System*. New York: Free Press.

———. 1966. *Societies: Evolutionary and Comparative Perspectives*. Englewood Cliffs, NJ: Prentice-Hall.

———. 1972. "Definitions of Health and Illness in the Light of American Values and Social Structure." Pp. 166–187 in *Patients, Physicians and Illness*, edited by Gartley Jaco. New York: Free Press.

———. 1975. "The Sick Role and the Role of the Physician Reconsidered." *Milbank Medical Fund Quarterly, Health and Society* 53(Summer):257–278.

Pasternak, Judy. 1998. "'Edge City' Is Attempting to Build a Center." *Los Angeles Times*, January 1, p. A5.

Pate, Antony M., and Edwin E. Hamilton. 1992. "Formal and Informal Deterrents to Domestic Violence: The Dade County Spouse Assault Experiment." *American Sociological Reviews* 57(October):691–697.

Patterson, Orlando. 1998. "Affirmative Action." *Brookings Review* 16(Spring):17–23.

Patton, Carl V., ed. 1988. *Spontaneous Shelter: International Perspectives and Prospects*. Philadelphia: Temple University Press.

Paul, Angus. 1987. "Why Does Terrorism Subside? Researchers Offer Preliminary Theories," *Chronicle of Higher Education*, 34 (September 23):A10.

Paulson, Amanda. 2000. "Where the School Is Home." *Christian Science Monitor*, October 10, pp. 18–21.

Pavalko, Ronald M. 1988. *Sociology of Occupations and Professions*. 2d ed. Itasca, IL: F. E. Peacock.

———, ed. 1972. *Sociological Perspectives on Occupations*. Itasca, IL: F. E. Peacock.

Payer, Lynn. 1988. *Medicine and Culture: Varieties of Treatment in the United States, England, West Germany, and France*. New York: Holt.

Pear, Robert. 1983. "$1.5 Billion Urged for U.S. Japanese Held in War." *New York Times*, June 17, pp. A1, D16.

———. 1996. "Clinton Endorses the Most Radical of Welfare Trials." *New York Times*, May 19, pp. 1, 20.

———. 1997a. "New Estimate Doubles Rate of H.I.V. Spread." *New York Times*, November 26, p. A6.

———. 1997b. "Now, the Archenemies Need Each Other." *New York Times*, June 22, sec. 4, pp. 1, 4.

———. 1999. "House Rejects Doctor-Assisted Deaths." *Chicago Tribune*, October 23, p. 4.

Pelton, Tom. 1994. "Hawthorne Works' Glory Now Just So Much Rubble." *Chicago Tribune*, April 18, pp. 1, 6.

Peressini, T., L. McDonald, and D. Hulchanski. 1995. "Estimating Homelessness: Towards A Methodology for Counting The Homeless in Canada." Toronto: Centre for Applied Social Research, University of Toronto. Accessed April 18, 2002 (http://www.

cmhc-schl.gc.ca/en/ imquaf/ho/ ho_005.cfm).

Perkins, Craig, and Patsy Klaus. 1996. *Criminal Victimization 1994*. Washington, DC: U.S. Government Printing Office.

Perlez, Jane. 1996. "Central Europe Learns about Sex Harassment." *New York Times*, October 3, p. A3.

Perrow, Charles. 1986. *Complex Organizations*. 3d ed. New York: Random House.

———. 1999. Normal Accidents: *Living with High Risk Technologies*. Updated edition. New Brunswick, NJ: Rutgers University Press.

Perrucci, Robert. 1974. *Circle of Madness: On Being Sane and Institutionalized in America*. Englewood Cliffs, NJ: Prentice-Hall.

Perry, Suzanne. 1998a. "Human Rights Abuses Get Internet Spotlight." Reuters, February 4.

———. 1998b. "U.S. Data Companies Oppose Primary Laws." Reuters, March 19.

Pescovitz, David. 1999. "Sons and Daughters of HAL Go on Line." *New York Times*, March 18, pp. D1, D8.

Pestello, Frances, Stanley Saxton, Dan E. Miller, and Patrick G. Donnelly. 1996. "Community and the Practice of Sociology." *Teaching Sociology* 24(April):148–156.

Peter, Laurence J., and Raymond Hull. 1969. *The Peter Principle*. New York: Morrow.

Petersen, William. 1979. *Malthus*. Cambridge, MA: Harvard University Press.

Peterson, Deb. 1996. "Kinship Support Differences between African Americans and Whites: Results from an Analysis." Paper presented at the annual meeting of the Midwest Sociological Society, Chicago.

Peterson, Paul E., Jay P. Greene, and William Howell. 1998. *New Findings from the Cleveland Scholarship Program: A Reanalysis of Data from the Indiana University School of Education Evaluation*. Cambridge, MA: Harvard University, Program on Education Policy and Governance.

Petricevic, Mirko. 2002. "Teach about religion, author urges." *The Record.com*. Friday March 1, 2002. (www.therecord.com/cgi-bin/PFP. cgi?doc=news/news_02030191124. html).

Phelan, Michael P., and Scott A. Hunt. 1998. "Prison Gang Members' Tattoos as Identity Work: The Visual Comments of Moral Careers." *Symbolic Interaction* 21(No. 3):277–298.

Philip, Margaret. 2001. "Teens' Dilemma: Cash or Class." *The Globe and Mail*, March 27, p. A7.

Phillips, E. Barbara. 1996. *City Lights: Urban–Suburban Life in the Global Society*. New York: Oxford University Press.

Piaget, Jean. 1954. *The Construction of Reality in the Child*. Translated by Margaret Cook. New York: Basic Books.

Pietila, Hilkka. 2002. *Engendering the Global Agenda: The Story of Women and the United Nations*. UN-NGLS Non-Governmental Liaison Service. New York: United Nations.

Pigler Christensen, Carole. 2001. "Immigrant Minorities in Canada." Pp. 180–209 in *Canadian Social Welfare*, 4th ed., edited by Joanne C. Turner and Francis J. Turner. Toronto: Pearson Education.

Pillemer, Karl, and David Finkelhor. 1988. "The Prevalence of Elder Abuse: A Random Sample Survey." *The Gerontologist* 28(February):51–57.

Piller, Charles. 2000. "Cyber-Crime Loss at Firms Doubles to $10 Billion." *Los Angeles Times*, May 22, pp. C1, C4.

Pinderhughes, Dianne. 1987. *Race and Ethnicity in Chicago Politics: A Reexamination of Pluralist Theory*. Urbana: University of Illinois Press.

———. 1996. "The Impact of Race on Environmental Quality: An Empirical and Theoretical Discussion." *Sociological Perspectives* 39(Summer):231–248.

Pipher, Mary. 1994. *Reviving Ophelia: Saving the Selves of Adolescent Girls*. New York: Ballantine.

Plant, Richard. 1986. *The Pink Triangle: The Nazi War against Homosexuals*. New York: Henry Holt.

Platt, Kevin. 1999. "China vs. Mass Spiritual Thirst." *Los Angeles Times*, August 3, pp. 1, 10.

Platt, Steve. 1993. "Without Walls." *Statesman and Society* 6(April 2):5–7.

Pleck, J. H., and E. Corfman. 1979. "Married Men: Work and Family." *Families Today: A Research Sampler on Families and Children* vol. 1, pp. 387–411.

Plimmer, Martin. 1998. "This Demi-Paradise: Martin Plummer Finds Food in the Fast Lane Is Not to His Taste." *Independent* (London), January 3, p. 46.

Plomin, Robert. 1989. "Determinants of Behavior." *American Psychologist* 44(February):105–111.

Plotnick, Robert D., Eugene Smolensky, Eirik Evenhouse, and Siobhan Reilly. 1998. "Identity and Poverty in the United States: The Twentieth Century Record." *Focus* 19(Summer–Fall):7–14.

Pogrebin, Letty Cottin. 1981. *Growing Up Free: Raising Your Child in the 80's*. New York: McGraw-Hill.

Pogrebin, Robin. 1996. "Hard-Core Threat to Health: Moshing at Rock

Concerts." *New York Times,* May 9, pp. B1, B9.

Pohl, Rudy. 2001. *Homelessness in Canada: Part 1—An Introduction.* Ottawa: Ottawa Innercity Ministries (www.ottawainnercityministries. ca/homepage/homelessnessInCanada _Part1.htm).

policyalternatives.ca/whatsnew/naftaat-sevenpr.html).

Polk, Barbara Bovee. 1974. "Male Power and the Women's Movement." *Journal of Applied Behavioral Sciences* 10(July):415–431.

Pollack, Andrew. 1996. "It's See No Evil, Have No Harassment in Japan." *New York Times,* May 7, pp. D1, D6.

Pollack, William. 1998. *Real Boys: Rescuing Our Sons from the Myths of Boyhood.* New York: Henry Holt.

Pollard, John. 2001. "The Impact of Religious Affiliation and Religious Practices on Attitudes Toward Euthanasia" in *IRS Newsletter.* Institute of Social Research, Vol. 16 No. 1, Fall 2001.

Pollard, Kelvin M. 1994. "Population Stabilization No Longer in Sight for U.S." *Population Today* 22(May):1–2.

———. and William P. O'Hare. 1999. "America's Racial and Ethnic Minorities." *Population Bulletin* 54(September).

polls_061200.html).

Pomfret, John. 2000. "A New Chinese Revolution." *Washington Post National Weekly Edition,* February 21, pp. 17–19.

Ponczek, Ed. 1998. "Are Hiring Practices Sensitive to Persons with Disabilities?" *Footnotes* 26(No. 3):5.

Poole, Teresa. 1998. "Population: China: Draconian Family Planning Has Desired Effect." *The Independent* (London), January 12, p. 11.

Popenoe, David, and Barbara Dafoe Whitehead. 1999. *Should We Live Together? What Young Adults Need to Know About Cohabitation Before Marriage.* Rutgers, NJ: The National Marriage Project.

Population Reference Bureau. 1978. "World Population: Growth on the Decline." *Interchange* 7(May): 1–3.

———. 1996. "Speaking Graphically." *Population Today* 24(June/July):b.

———. 2000a. "More Youths Take Alternative Route to Finish High School." *Population Today* 28(January):7.

———. 2000b. *The World Youth 2000.* Washington, DC: Population Reference Bureau. Accessed April 18, 2002 (http://www.prb.org/Content/NavigationMenu/Other_reports/2000-2002/The_Worlds_Youth_2000 _Data_Sheet.htm).

Porter, John. 1965. *The Vertical Mosaic: An Analysis of Social Class and Power in Canada.* Toronto: University of Toronto Press.

Porter, Rosalie Pedalino. 1997. "The Politics of Bilingual Education." *Society* 34(No. 6):31–40.

Power, Carla. 1998. "The New Islam." *Newsweek* 131(March 16):34–37.

Power, Richard. 1999. "1999 CSI/FBI Computer Curve and Security Survey." *Computer Security Issues and Trends* 5(Winter):1–15.

Powers, Mary G., and Joan J. Holmberg. 1978. "Occupational Status Scores: Changes Introduced by the Inclusion of Women." *Demography* 15(May):183–204.

Prehn, John W. 1991. "Migration." Pp. 190–191 in *Encyclopedia of Sociology,* 4th ed. Guilford, CT: Dushkin.

Preston, Julia. 1998. "Both Carrot and Stick Fail in Chuapas." *New York Times,* May 17, p. 6.

Prince, Raymond. 1985. "The Concept of Culture-Bound Syndromes: Anorexia Nervosa and Brain-Fog." *Social Science and Medicine* 21(2):197–203.

Princeton Religion Research Center. 2000a. "Nearly Half of Americans Describe Themselves as Evangelicals." *Emerging Trends* 22(April):5.

———. 2000b. "Latest Religious Preferences for U.S." *Emerging Trends* 22(March):2.

———. 1998. "U.S. Far Less Protestant Than Half-Century Ago." *Emerging Trends* 20:1.

Pritchard, Peter. 1987. *The Making of McPaper: The Inside Story of USA Today.* Kansas City, MO: Andrews, McMeel and Parker.

Privacy Commissioner of Canada. 2000. *The Personal Information Protection and Electronic Documents Act.* Accessed April 18, 2002 (http://www.privcom.gc.ca/legislation/02_06_01_ e.asp).

Public Interest Research Groups. 1999. *Running for the Money: An Analysis of the 2000 Presidential Wealth Primary.* Boston, MA: PIRG.

Public Legal and Education Service of New Brunswick. 2001. *Sexual Harassment in Schools* (March). Saint John: Public Legal and Education Service of New Brunswick.

Pula, James S. 1995. *Polish Americans: An Ethnic Community.* New York: Twayne.

Purnick, Joyce. 1996. "G.O.P. Quest to Narrow Gender Gap." *New York Times,* November 14, p. B1.

Putnam, Robert D. 2000. *Bowling Alone: The Collapse and Revival of American Community.* New York: Simon and Schuster.

Pyle, Amy. 1998. "Opinions Vary on Studies That Back Bilingual Classes." *Los Angeles Times,* March 2, pp. B1, B3.

Q

Quadagno, Jill. 1999. *Aging and the Life Course: An Introduction to Social Gerontology.* New York: McGraw-Hill.

Quarantelli, Enrico L. 1957. "The Behavior of Panic Participants." *Sociology and Social Research* 41(January):187–194.

———. 1992. "Disaster Research." Pp. 492–498 in *Encyclopedia of Sociology,* vol. 2, edited by Edgar F. Borgatta and Marie L. Borgatta. New York: Macmillan.

———, and James R. Hundley, Jr. 1975. "A Test of Some Propositions about Crowd Formation and Behavior." Pp. 538–554 in *Readings in Collective Behavior,* edited by Robert R. Evans. Chicago: Rand McNally.

———, and Russell R. Dynes. 1970. "Property Norms and Looting: Their Patterns in Community Crises." *Phylon* 31(Summer):168–182.

Quinney, Richard. 1970. *The Social Reality of Crime.* Boston: Little, Brown.

———. 1974. *Criminal Justice in America.* Boston: Little, Brown.

———. 1979. *Criminology.* 2d ed. Boston: Little, Brown.

———. 1980. *Class, State and Crime.* 2d ed. New York: Longman.

R

Radosh, Mary Flannery. 1984. "The Collapse of Midwifery: A Sociological Study of the Decline of a Profession." Southern Illinois University, Carbondale. Unpublished Ph.D. dissertation.

Radosh, Polly F. 1986. "Midwives in the United States: Past and Present." *Population Research and Policy Review* 5:129–145.

Ralston Saul, John. 1993. *Voltaire's Bastards: The Dictatorship of Reason in the West.* Toronto: Penguin Canada.

———. 1997. *Reflections of a Siamese Twin: Canada at the End of the 20th Century.* Toronto: Viking.

Ramet, Sabrina. 1991. *Social Currents in Eastern Europe: The Source and Meaning of the Great Transformation.* Durham, NC: Duke University Press.

Ravitch, Diane. 2000. *Left Back: A Century of Failed School Reforms.* New York: Simon and Schuster.

Raybon, Patricia. 1989. "A Case for 'Severe Bias.'" *Newsweek* 114(October 2):11.

Read, Jen'nan Ghazal, and John P. Bartkowski. 1999. "To Veil or Not to

Veil? A Case Study of Identity Negotiation Among Muslim Women in Austin, Texas." Presented at the annual meeting of the American Sociological Association, August, Chicago.

Reddick, Randy, and Elliot King. 2000. *The Online Student: Making the Grade on the Internet.* Fort Worth: Harcourt Brace.

Rees, Ruth. 1990. *Women and Men in Education: A national survey of gender distribution in school systems.* Toronto: Canadian Education Association.

Reese, William A., II, and Michael A. Katovich. 1989. "Untimely Acts: Extending the Interactionist Conception of Deviance." *Sociological Quarterly* 30(2):159–184.

Reid, Karla Scoon. 2001. "Canadians Debate Education Tax Credits." In *Education Week: American Education's Newspaper of Record.* November 14, 2001.

Reiman, Jeffrey H. 1984. *The Rich Get Richer and the Poor Get Prison.* 2d ed. New York: Wiley.

Reinharz, Shulamit. 1992. *Feminist Methods in Social Research.* New York: Oxford University Press.

Reiss, Ira L. 1995. "Is This the Definitive Sexual Survey?" *Journal of Sex Research* 22(1):77–85.

Reitz, Jeffrey. 1980. *The Survival of Ethnic Groups.* Toronto: McClelland and Stewart.

Religion Today.com. 2000. "Promise Keepers Takes Its Message to Latin America." Accessed February 11, 2000 (http://www.religiontoday.com/Archive/FeatureStory/view.cgi?File=20000113.s1.html).

Religion Watch. 1991. "Current Research: New Findings in Religious Attitudes and Behavior." 6(September):5.

———. 1995. "European Dissenting Movement Grows among Laity Theologians." 10(October):6–7.

Remnick, David. 1998a. "Bad Seeds." *New Yorker* 74(July 20):28–33.

———. 1998b. *King of the World.* New York: Random House.

Rennison, Callie Marie. 1999. "Criminal Victimization 1998. Changes 1997–98 with Trends 1993–98." *Bureau of Justice Statistics National Crime Victimization Survey* (July).

Rensberger, Boyce. 1994. "Damping the World's Population." *Washington Post National Weekly Edition* 12(September 18):10–11.

Renzetti, Claire M., and Daniel J. Curran. 1992. *Women, Men, and Society.* 2nd ed. Toronto: Allyn and Bacon.

Repper, J., R. Perkins, S. Owen, D. Deighton, and J. Robinson. 1996. "Evaluating Services for Women with Serious and Ongoing Mental Health Problems: Developing an Appropriate Research Method." *Journal of Psychiatric and Mental Health Nursing* 3, 39–46.

Reskin, Barbara, and Irene Padavic. 1994. *Women and Men at Work.* Thousand Oaks, CA: Pine Forge Press.

Retsinas, Joan. 1988. "A Theoretical Reassessment of the Applicability of Kübler-Ross's Stages of Dying." *Death Studies* 12:207–216.

Reuters. 1995. "New Chinese Law Prohibits Sex-Screening of Fetuses." *New York Times*, November 15.

Rheingold, Harriet L. 1969. "The Social and Socializing Infant." Pp. 779–790 in *Handbook of Socialization Theory and Research*, edited by David A. Goslin. Chicago: Rand McNally.

Richardson, Diane, and Victoria Robinson. 1993. *Thinking Feminist: Key Concepts in Women's Studies.* New York: The Guildford Press.

Richardson, James T. 1993. "Definitions of the Cult: From Sociological-Technical to Popular-Negative." *Review of Religious Research* 34(June).

———, and Barend van Driel. 1997. "Journalists' Attitudes Toward New Religious Movements." *Review of Religious Research* 39(December):116–136.

Richburg, Keith B. 1985. "Learning What Japan Has to Teach." *Washington Post National Weekly Edition* 3, November 4, p. 9.

———. 2000. "Netherlands Moves to Legalize Assisted Suicide." *Washington Post Foreign Service*, November 29, 2000.

Richey, Warren. 1998. "Counting the People: Court to Settle Dispute." *Christian Science Monitor*, November 30, p. 2.

Richman, Joseph. 1992. "A Rational Approach to Rational Suicide." *Suicide and Life-Threatening Behavior* 22(Spring):130–141.

Richtel, Matt. 2000. "www.layoffs.com." *New York Times*, June 22, pp. C1, C12.

Rideout, Victoria J., Ulla G. Foehr, Donald F. Roberts, and Mollyann Brodie. 1999. *Kids & Media @ the New Millennium.* New York: Kaiser Family Foundation.

Ridgeway, Cecilia L. 1987. "Nonverbal Behavior, Dominance, and the Basis of Status in Task Groups." *American Sociological Review* 52(October):683–694.

Ridgeway, James, and Jeffrey St. Clair. 1995. "Where the Buffalo Roam." *Village Voice* 40, July 11, p. 14.

Riding, Alan. 1993. "Women Seize Focus at Rights Forum," *New York Times* (June 16), p. A3.

———. 1998. "Why 'Titanic' Conquered the World." *New York Times*, April 26, sec. 2, pp. 1, 28, 29.

Ries, Lynn M. 1992. "Social Mobility." Pp. 1872–1880 in *Encyclopedia of Sociology*, vol. 4, edited by Edgar F. Borgatta and Marie L. Borgatta. New York: Macmillan.

Rifkin, Jeremy. 1995a. *The End of Work: The Decline of the Global Labor Force and the Dawn of the Post-Market Era.* New York: Tarcher/Putnam.

———. 1995b. "Afterwork." *Utne Reader* (May–June):52–62.

———. 1996. "Civil Society in the Information Age." *The Nation* 262(February 26):11–12, 14–16.

———. 1998. *The Biotech Century: Harnessing the Gene and Remaking the World.* New York: Tarcher/Putnam.

Riley, John W., Jr. 1992. "Death and Dying." Pp. 413–418 in *Encyclopedia of Sociology*, vol. 1, edited by Edgar F. Borgatta and Marie L. Borgatta. New York: Macmillan.

Riley, Matilda White, and Robert L. Kahn, in association with Karin A. Mock. 1994b. "Introduction: The Mismatch between People and Structures." Pp. 1–36 in *Age and Structural Lag*, edited by Matilda White Riley, Robert L. Kahn, and Ann Foner. New York: Wiley Inter-Science.

———, ———, and Anne Foner. 1994a. *Age and Structural Lag.* New York: Wiley Inter-Science.

Riley, Nancy E. 1996. "China's 'Missing Girls:' Prospects and Policy." *Population Today* (February):pp. 4–5.

Rimer, Sara. 1998. "As Centenarians Thrive, 'Old' Is Redefined." *New York Times*, June 22, pp. A1, A14.

Ringel, Cheryl. 1997. *Criminal Victimization 1996.* Washington, DC: U.S. Government Printing Office.

Ritzer, George. 1977. *Working: Conflict and Change.* 2d ed. Englewood Cliffs, NJ: Prentice-Hall.

———. 1995a. *Modern Sociological Theory.* 4th ed. New York: McGraw-Hill.

———. 1995b. *The McDonaldization of Society.* Rev. ed. Thousand Oaks, CA: Pine Forge Books.

———. 1996. *The McDonaldization of Society.* Rev. ed. Thousand Oaks, CA: Pine Forge Press.

———. 1998. *The McDonaldization Thesis: Explorations of Extensions.* Thousand Oaks, CA: Sage Publications.

———. 2000. *The McDonaldization of Society.* New Century Edition. Thousand Oaks, CA: Pine Forge Press.

Roan, Shari. 1995. "Under Pressure, Isolation: Jury Stress Sparks Concerns." *Los Angeles Times*, September 22, pp. A1, A28.

Contemporary Ethnography 23(July):123–149.

———. 1995. "Scholarly Ethics and Courtroom Antics: Where Researchers Stand in the Eyes of the Law." *American Sociologist* 26(Spring):87–112.

Scarr, Sandra. 1997. "New Research on Day Care Should Spur Scholars to Reconsider Old Ideas." *Chronicle of Higher Education* 43(August 8):A48.

Schaefer, Peter. 1995. "Destroy Your Future." *Daily Northwestern*, November 3, p. 8.

Schaefer, Richard T. 1997. "Placing the Los Angeles Riots in Their Social and Historical Context." *Journal of American Ethnic History,* forthcoming.

———. 1998a. "Differential Racial Mortality and the 1995 Chicago Heat Wave." Presentation at the annual meeting of the American Sociological Association, August, San Francisco.

———. 1998b. *Alumni Survey.* Chicago, IL: Department of Sociology, DePaul University.

———. 2000. *Racial and Ethnic Groups.* 8th ed. Upper Saddle River, NJ: Prentice-Hall.

———. 2002. *Racial and Ethnic Groups.* 9th ed. Upper Saddle River, NJ: Prentice-Hall.

Schaefer, Sandy. 1996. "Peaceful Play." Presentation at the annual meeting of the Chicago Association for the Education of Young Children, Chicago.

Schaller, Lyle E. 1990. "Megachurch!" *Christianity Today* 34(March 5):10, 20–24.

Scheer, Robert. 1998. "The Dark Side of the New World Order." *Los Angeles Times,* January 13, p. B7.

Scheff, Thomas J. 1999. *Being Mentally Ill: A Sociological Theory.* 3d ed. New York: Aldine de Gruyter.

Schellenberg, Kathryn, ed. 1996. *Computers in Society.* 6th ed. Guilford, CT: Dushkin.

Schiraldi, Vincent. 1999. "Juvenile Crime Is Decreasing—It's Media Coverage That's Soaring." *Los Angeles Times,* November 22, p. B7.

Schlenker, Barry R., ed. 1985. *The Self and Social Life.* New York: McGraw-Hill.

Schmetzer, Uli. 1999. "Modern India Remains Shackled to Caste System." *Chicago Tribune,* December 25, p. 23.

Schmid, Carol. 1980. "Sexual Antagonism: Roots of the Sex-Ordered Division of Labor." *Humanity and Society* 4(November):243–261.

Schmidt, William E. 1990. "New Vim and Vigor for the Y.M.C.A." *New York Times,* July 18, pp. C1, C10.

Schmitt, Eric. 1998. "Day-Care Quandary: A Nation at War with Itself." *New York Times,* January 11, sec. 4, pp. 1, 4.

Schnaiberg, Allan. 1994. *Environment and Society: The Enduring Conflict.* New York: St. Martin's.

Schnaiberg, Lynn. 1999a. "Study Finds Home Schoolers Are Top Achievers on Tests." *Education Week* 18(March 31):5.

———. 1999b. "Home Schooling Queries Spike After Shootings." *Education Week* 18(June 9):3.

Schneider, Barbara, and David Stevens. 1999. *The Ambitious Generation: America's Teenagers Motivated but Directionless.* New Haven, CT: Yale University Press.

Schneider, Howard. 1997. "Canada's Culture War Questioned in Battle with U.S., Arsenal of Federal Protections Called Needless." *Washington Post,* February 15, p. A29.

Schneider, Keith. 1995. "As Earth Day Turns 25, Life Gets Complicated." *New York Times,* April 16, p. E6.

Schneider, Linda, and Arnold Silverman. 2000. "Mexico: Nation of Networks." Pp. 61–116 in *Global Sociology: Introducing Five Contemporary Societies,* 2d edition. New York: McGraw-Hill.

Schulman, Kevin A. et al. 1999. "The Effect of Race and Sex on Physicians' Recommendations for Cardiac Catheterization." *New England Journal of Medicine* (February 25):618–626.

Schur, Edwin M. 1965. *Crimes without Victims: Deviant Behavior and Public Policy.* Englewood Cliffs, NJ: Prentice-Hall.

———. 1968. *Law and Society: A Sociological View.* New York: Random House.

———. 1983. *Labelling Women Deviant: Gender, Stigma and Social Control.* Philadelphia: Temple University Press.

———. 1985. "'Crimes without Victims': A 20 Year Reassessment." Paper presented at the annual meeting of the Society for the Study of Social Problems.

Schwab, William A. 1993. "Recent Empirical and Theoretical Developments in Sociological Human Ecology." Pp. 29–57 in *Urban Sociology in Transition,* edited by Ray Hutchison. Greenwich, CT: JAI Press.

Schwartz, Howard D., ed. 1987. *Dominant Issues in Medical Sociology.* 2d ed. New York: Random House.

Schwartz, Joe. 1990. "Earth Day Today." *American Demographics* 12(April):40–41.

———. 1991. "Why Japan's Birthrate Is So Low." *American Demographics* 13(April):20.

Sciolino, Elaine. 1993. "U.S. Rejects Notion That Human Rights Vary with Culture," *New York Times* (June 15), pp. A1, A18.

Scott, Alan. 1990. *Ideology and the New Social Movements.* London: Unwin Hyman.

Scott, Ellen Kaye. 1993. "How to Stop the Rapists? A Question of Strategy in Two Rape Crisis Centers." *Social Problems* 47 (August):343–361.

Scott, Hilda. 1985. *Working Your Way to the Bottom: The Feminization of Poverty.* London: Routledge.

Scott, Katherine, and David Ross. 1996. *The Progress of Children.* Ottawa: Canadian Council on Social Development.

Second Harvest. 1997. *1997 Annual Report.* Chicago, IL: Second Harvest.

Secretan, Thierry. 1995. *Going into Darkness: Fantastic Coffins from Africa.* London, Eng.: Thames and Hudson.

Segall, Alexander. 1976. "The Sick Role Concept: Understanding Illness Behavior." *Journal of Health and Social Behavior* 17(June):163–170.

Segall, Rebecca. 1998. "Sikh and Ye Shall Find." *Village Voice* 43(December 15):46–48, 53.

Segerstråle, Ullica. 2000. *Defense of the Truth: The Battle for Science in the Sociobiology Debate and Beyond.* New York: Oxford University Press.

Seidman, Steven. 1994. "Heterosexism in America: Prejudice against Gay Men and Lesbians." Pp. 578–593 in *Introduction to Social Problems,* edited by Craig Calhoun and George Ritzer. New York: McGraw-Hill.

Selig, Josh. 1998. "Muppets Succeed Where Politicians Haven't." *New York Times,* March 29, p. C45.

Senate of Canada. 1995. "Of Life and Death—Final Report." The Special Senate Committee on Euthanasia and Assisted Suicide, June.

Senior Action in a Gay Environment (SAGE). 1999. *One Family All Ages.* New York: SAGE.

Serrano, Richard A. 1996. "Militias: Ranks Are Swelling." *Los Angeles Times,* April 18, pp. A1, A6.

Sexton, J. Bryan, and Robert L. Helmreich. 2000. "Analyzing Cockpit Communications: The Links Between Language, Performance, Error and Workload." *Human Performance in Extreme Environments* 5(1):63–68.

Shaheen, Jack G. 1999. "Image and Identity: Screen Arabs and Muslims." In *Cultural Diversity: Curriculum, Classrooms, and Climate Issues,* edited by J. Q. Adams and Janice R. Welsch. Macomb, IL: Illinois Staff and Curriculum Development Association.

Shapiro, Isaac, and Robert Greenstein. 1999. *The Widening Income Gulf.*

Washington, DC: Center on Budget and Policy Priorities.

Shapiro, Joseph P. 1993. *No Pity: People with Disabilities Forging a New Civil Rights Movement.* New York: Times Books.

Sharma, Hari M., and Gerard C. Bodeker. 1998. "Alternative Medicine." In *Britannica Book of the Year 1998.* Chicago: Encyclopaedia Britannica, pp. 228–229.

Shaw, Marvin E. 1981. *Group Dynamics: The Psychology of Small Group Behavior.* 3d ed. New York: McGraw-Hill.

Shaw, Susan. 1988. "Gender Differences in the Definition and Perception of Household Labor." *Family Relations* 37(July):333–337.

Shcherbak, Yuri M. 1996. "Ten Years of the Chernobyl Era." *Scientific American* 274(April):44–49.

Sheehy, Gail. 1995. *New Passages: Mapping Your Life across Time.* New York: Random House.

Sheehy, Gail. 1999. *Understanding Men's Passages: Discovering the New Map of Men's Lives.* New York: Ballantine Books.

Shelley, Louise I. 1992. "Review of Crime and Justice in Two Societies." Pacific Grove, CA: Brooks/Cole.

Shenon, Philip. 1995. "New Zealand Seeks Causes of Suicides by Young." *New York Times,* July 15, p. 3.

———. 1998. "Sailor Victorious in Gay Case on Internet Privacy." *New York Times,* June 12, pp. A1, A14.

Sherman, Arnold K., and Aliza Kolker. 1987. *The Social Bases of Politics.* Belmont, CA: Wadsworth.

Sherman, Lawrence W., Patrick R. Gartin, and Michael D. Buerger. 1989. "Hot Spots of Predatory Crime: Routine Activities and the Criminology of Place." *Criminology* 27:27–56.

Sherrill, Robert. 1995. "The Madness of the Market." *The Nation* 260(January 9–16):45–72.

Sherwin, Susan. 1992. *No Longer Patient: Feminist Ethics and Health Care.* Philadelphia: Temple University Press.

Shibutani, Tamotshu. 1966. *Improvised News: A Sociological Study of Rumor.* Indianapolis: Bobbs-Merrill.

Shields, Rob, ed. 1996. *Cultures of Internet: Virtual Spaces, Real Histories, Living Bodies.* London: Sage.

Shilts, Randy. 1987. *And the Band Played On: Politics, People, and the AIDS Epidemic.* New York: St. Martin's.

Shinkai, Hiroguki, and Ugljes̆a Zvekic. 1999. "Punishment." Pp. 89–120 in *Global Report on Crime and Justice,* edited by Graeme Newman. New York: Oxford University Press.

Shioiri, Toshiki, Toshiguki Someya, Daigo Helmeste, and Siu Wa Tang.

1999. "Misinterpretation of Facial Expression: A Cross-Cultural Study." *Journal of Psychiatry and Clinical Neurosciences* 24(March).

Shiver, Jube Jr., 2000. "International Firms Gain Foothold in Washington." *Los Angeles Times,* March 12, pp. A1, A21.

Shogan, Robert. 1998. "Politicians Embrace Status Quo as Nonvoter Numbers Grow." *Los Angeles Times,* May 4, p. A5.

Shogren, Elizabeth. 1994. "Treatment against Their Will." *Los Angeles Times,* August 18, pp. A1, A14–A15.

Short, Kathleen, Thesia Garner, David Johnson, and Patricia Doyle. 1999. "Experimental Poverty Measures: 1990 to 1997." *Current Population Reports,* ser. P-60, no. 205. Washington, DC: U.S. Government Printing Office.

Shorten, Lynda. 1991. *Without Reserves: Stories from Urban Natives.* Edmonton, Can.: NeWest Press.

Shuit, Douglas P. 1995. "Disparity Found in Heart Care for Minorities." *Los Angeles Times,* March 29, pp. A3, A27.

Shupe, Anson D., and David G. Bromley. 1980. "Walking a Tightrope." *Qualitative Sociology* 2:8–21.

Siddiqi, Mohammad A. 1993. "The Portrayal of Muslims and Islam in the U.S. Media." Presented at the conference on The Expression of American Religion in the Popular Media, Indianapolis.

Sidel, Ruth, and Victor Sidel. 1984. "Toward the Twenty-First Century." Pp. 267–284 in *Reforming Medicine,* edited by V. Sidel and R. Sidel. New York: Pantheon.

Sidiropoulos, Elizabeth et al. 1996. *South Africa Survey 1995/96.* Johannesburg: South African Institute of Race Relations.

Sigelman, Lee, Timothy Bledsoe, Susan Welch, and Michael W. Combs. 1996. "Making Contact? Black–White Social Interaction in an Urban Setting." *American Journal of Sociology* 5(March):1306–1332.

Silicon Valley Cultures Project. 1999. The Silicon Valley Cultures Project Website. Accessed July 30, 1990 (www.sjsv.edu/depts/anthropology/ svcp).

Sills, David L. 1957. *The Volunteers: Means and Ends in a National Organization.* Glencoe, IL: Free Press.

———. 1968. "Voluntary Associations: Sociological Aspects." Pp. 362–379 in *International Encyclopedia of the Social Sciences,* vol. 16, edited by D. L. Sills. New York: Macmillan.

Silver, Cynthia, Cara Williams, and Trish McOrmond. 2001. "Learning On Your Own." *Canadian Social Trends.* Statis-

tics Canada. Catalogue No. 11-008. Spring. Ottawa: Minister of Industry.

Silver, Ira. 1996. "Role Transitions, Objects, and Identity." *Symbolic Interaction* 19(1):1–20.

Silverman, Milton, Mia Lydecker, and Philip R. Lee. 1990. "The Drug Swindlers." *International Journal of Health Services* 20:561–572.

Simard, Rene. 2000. *Reaching Out: Canada, International Science and Technology, and the Knowledge-based Economy.* Ottawa: Industry Canada.

Simmel, Georg. 1950. *Sociology of Georg Simmel.* Translated by K. Wolff. Glencoe, IL: Free Press (originally written in 1902–1917).

Simmons, Ann M. 1998. "Where Fat Is a Mark of Beauty." *Los Angeles Times,* September 30, pp. A1, A12.

Simon, Joshua M. 1999. "Presidential Candidates Face Campaign Finance Issue." *Harvard Crimson,* July 2.

Simon, Stephanie. 1999. "In Insular Iowa Town, a Jolt of Worldliness." *Los Angeles Times,* January 25, pp. A1, A8.

Simons, John. 1999. "Are Web Political Polls Reliable? Yes? No? Maybe?" Accessed April 13, 1999 (http://deseretnews.com/dn/view/0,1249,75003 756,00.html).

Simons, Marlise. 1989. "Abortion Fight Has New Front in Western Europe." *New York Times,* June 28, pp. A1, A9.

Simons, Marlise. 1996a. "African Women in France Battling Polygamy." *New York Times,* January 26, pp. A1, A6.

———. 1996b. "U. N. Court, for First Time, Defines Rape as War Crime," *New York Times* (June 28), pp. A1, A10.

———. 1997. "Child Care Sacred as France Cuts Back the Welfare State." *New York Times,* December 31, pp. A1, A6.

Simpson, Ann. 1999. *Public Deliberation Guide. A World in Common: Talking about What Matters in a Borderless World.* Ottawa: Canadian Council for International Cooperation.

Simpson, Sally. 1993. "Corporate Crime." Pp. 236–256 in *Introduction to Social Problems,* edited by Craig Calhoun and George Ritzer. New York: McGraw-Hill.

Sinclair, Pam. 2002. *A Blast From The Past* (www.tla-temagami.com/ tla-temagami/history.html).

Sjoberg, Gideon. 1960. *The Preindustrial City: Past and Present.* Glencoe, IL: Free Press.

Skafte, Peter. 1979. "Smoking Out Secrets of the Mysterious 'Snakers' in India." *Smithsonian* 10(October):120–127.

Skees, Suzanne. 1995. "The Last of the Shakers?" *Ms.* 5(March–April):40–45.

———. 2000k. *Women in Canada: 2000. A Gender-Based Statistical Report.* Catalogue No. 89-503-XPE. Ottawa: Ministry of Industry.

———. 2000l. *Canadian Social Trends.* Catalogue No. 11-008, Spring, p. 16.

———. 2000m. "The Labour Market in the 1990s." *The Daily.* January 20. Accessed May 23, 2002 (http://www.statcan.ca/Daily/English/000120/

———. 2000n. "Part-time by Choice." *The Daily.* November 24. Accessed May 23, 2002 (http://www.statcan.ca/Daily/English/001124/d001124b.htm).

———. 2001a. "Family Income 1999." In *The Daily,* Friday, August 10, 2001.

———. 2001b. "*Average Earnings By Sex and Work Pattern*" in Income Statistics Division. Ottawa: Statistics Canada (www.statcan.ca/english/Pgdb/-People/Labour/labor01b.htm).

———. 2001c. "Census Tables." Catalogue No. 93F0023XDB96003. Ottawa: Statistics Canada (www. statcan.ca/english/census96/nov4. table1.htm).

———. 2001d. "General Social Survey: Internet Use." In *The Daily,* Monday, March 26, 2001 (www.statcan.ca/Daily/English/010326/d010326a.htm).

———. 2001e. "Population Structure and Change in Predominantly Rural Regions." *The Daily.* January 16. No. 21-006XIE.

———. 2001f. *A Report on Adult Education and Training in Canada: Learning a Living.* Ottawa: Ministry of Industry with Statistics Canada and Human Resources Development Canada.

———. 2001g. *The Assets and Debts of Canadians: An Overview of the Results of the Survey of Financial Security.* Ministry of Industry, March 2001, Catalogue no. 13-595-XIE.

———. 2001h. "Census Tables." Catalogue No. 93F0023XDB96003. Ottawa: Statistics Canada (www. statcan.ca/english/census96/ feb17/eolcan.htm).

———. 2001i. "Family Income, 1999." *The Daily.* November 6. Accessed May 5, 2002, (http://www.statcan.ca/Daily/English/011106/d011106b.htm).

———. 2001j. "Household Internet Use Survey." In *The Daily,* Thursday, July 26, 2001 (www.statcan.ca/Daily/English/010726/d010726a.htm)

———. 2001k. "*Labour Force and Participation Rates.*" CANSIM II Tables. Ottawa : Statistics Canada. (www.statcan.ca/english/Pgdb/People/Labour/labor05.htm).

———. 2001l. "University Enrolment" in *The Daily,* Thursday, November 8, 2001. Ottawa: Statistics Canada.

———. 2001m. *The Daily,* August 10, 2001.

———. 2001n. "Survey of Approaches to Education Planning." *The Daily.* April 10. Accessed April 22, 2002 (http://www.statcan.ca/Daily/English/010410/

———. 2001o. "*Visible Minorities in Canada.*" Canadian Centre for Justice Statistics Profile Series. June 2001. Statistics Canada Catalogue No. 85F0033MIE.

———. 2001p. www.statcan.ca/english/Pgdb/People/Labour/Llabor01a.htm. Income Statistics Division.

———. 2001q. "Crime Statistics." *The Daily.* July 19. Accessed August 15, 2001 (http://www.statcan.ca/ Daily/English/010719/d010719b.htm).

———. 2001r. "Social Participation and Inclusion." July. Accessed April 22, 2002 (http://www.statcan.ca/english/freepub/89F0123XIE/32.htm).

———. 2001s. *Family Violence in Canada: A Statistical Profile.* Ministry of Industry. Accessed January 19, 2002 (http://www.statcan.ca/english/85-224-XIE/ 0100085-224-XIE.pdf).

———. 2002a. "A profile of the Canadian population: where we live." From *2001 Census Analysis Series.* Statistics Canada Catalogue: 96F0030XIE010012001.

———. 2002b. "Childcare services industry". *The Daily.* Friday, April 26, 2002.

———. 2002c. "Crime Statistics 2001" in *The Daily.* July 17, 2002.

———. 2002d. *A profile of the Canadian population: where we live.* From 2001 Census Analysis Series. Statistics Canada Catalogue: 96F0030XIE010012001.

———. 2002e. *Profile of the Canadian population by age and sex: Canada ages.* Catalogue no. 96F0030XIE2001002 (www.statcan.ca/english/freepub/96F0030XIE/free.htm)

———. 2002f. "Income of Individuals 2000." *The Daily,* July 10, 2002.

———. 2002g. *Canada at a Glance.* Ottawa: Statistics Canada, Communications Division. Catalogue # 12-581-XPE.

———. 2002h. *Full-time and part-time employment.* (www.statcan.ca/english/Pgdb/People/Labour/labor12.htm).

———. 2002i. "Family Income 2000." *The Daily,* July 28, 2002.

———. 2002j. *Reasons for part-time work.* (www.statcan.ca/english/Pgdb/People/Labour/labor63.htm).

———. 2002k. *Statistical Methods: Definitions of Concepts and Variables - Census Family.* (www.statcan.ca/english/concepts/definitions/cen-family.htm)

———. 2002l. "Family Characteristics: Points for Discussion" in *2001 Census Consultation Guide.* (www.statcan.ca/english/freepub/02-125-GIE/html/fam.htm)

———. 2002m. "Gender Pay Differentials: Impact of the Workplace." *The Daily.* June 19, 2002.

———. 2002n. "Changing Conjugal Life in Canada." In *The Daily.* Thursday, July 11, 2002.

Statistics Sweden. 1999. *Social Report 1997: National Report on Social Conditions in Sweden: February 18, 1999 (Update).* Accessed July 14, 2000 (http://www.sos.se/sos.publ/refereng/9700-72e.htm).

Status of Women Canada. 1995. *Setting the Stage for the Next Century: The Federal Plan for Gender Equality.* Canada: Status of Women Canada. Catalogue no. SW21-15/1995.

———. 2000. *National Day of Remembrance and Action on Violence Against Women.* News Release. December 5. Accessed April 22, 2002 (http://

Stavenhagen, Rodolfo. 1994. "The Indian Resurgence in Mexico." *Cultural Survival Quarterly,* Summer–Fall, pp. 77–80.

Stearn, J. 1993. "What Crisis?" *Statesmen and Society* 6(April 2):7–9.

Stedman, Nancy. 1998. "Learning to Put the Best Shoe Forward." *New York Times,* October 27.

Steffenhagen, Janet. 2001. "City Streets Draw Non-B.C. Youths." *The Vancouver Sun,* March 26, p. A3.

Stein, Leonard. 1967. "The Doctor–Nurse Game." *Archives of General Psychiatry* 16:699–703.

Stein, Peter J. 1975. "Singlehood: An Alternative to Marriage." *Family Coordinator* 24(October):489–503.

———, ed. 1981. *Single Life: Unmarried Adults in Social Context.* New York: St. Martin's.

Steinfeld, Edward S. 1999. "Beyond the Transition: China's Economy at Century's End." *Current History* 98(September):271–275.

Stenning, Derrick J. 1958. "Household Viability among the Pastoral Fulani." Pp. 92–119 in *The Developmental Cycle in Domestic Groups,* edited by John R. Goody. Cambridge, Eng.: Cambridge University Press.

Stephen, Elizabeth Hervey. 1999. "Assisted Reproductive Technologies: Is the Price Too High?" *Population Today* (May):1–2.

Stephenson, Marylee. 2000. "Corporate Profile." Accessed April 4, 2002 (http://www.

Stern, Kenneth S. 1996. *A Force upon the Plain: The American Militia Movement and the Politics of Hate.* New York: Simon and Schuster.

Sternberg, Steve. 1999. "Virus Makes Families Pay Twice." *USA Today,* May 24, p. 6D.

Sterngold, James. 1992. "Japan Ends Fingerprinting of Many Non-Japanese," *New York Times* (May 21), p. A11.

Stevens, Ann Huff. 1994. "The Dynamics of Poverty Spells: Updating Bane and Ellwood." *American Economic Review* 84(May):34–37.

Stevenson, David, and Barbara L. Schneider. 1999. *The Ambitious Generation: America's Teenagers, Motivated but Directionless.* New Haven: Yale University Press.

Stevenson, Robert J. 1998. *The Boiler Room and Other Telephone Sales Scams.* Urbana, IL: University of Illinois Press.

Stoeckel, John, and N. L. Sirisena. 1988. "Gender-Specific Socioeconomic Impacts of Development Programs in Sri Lanka." *Journal of Developing Areas* 23(October):31–42.

Stolberg, Sheryl Gay. 2000. "Alternative Care Gains a Foothold." *New York Times* (January 31): A1, A16.

Stolberg, Sheryl. 1995. "Affirmative Action Gains Often Come at a High Cost." *Los Angeles Times*, March 29, pp. A1, A13–A16.

———. 1997. "U.S. Publishes First Guide to Treatment of Infertility." *New York Times*, December 19, p. A14.

Stoll, Clifford. 1995. *Silicon Snake Oil: Second Thoughts on the Information Superhighway.* New York: Anchor/Doubleday.

Stone, Brad. 1999. "Get a Life?" *Newsweek* 133(June 7):68–69.

Stoughton, Stephanie, and Leslie Walker. 1999. "The Merchants of Cyberspace." *Washington Post National Weekly Edition* 16(February 15):18.

Stout, Madeline Dion. 1996. *Aboriginal Canada: Women and Health: A Canadian Perspective.* Paper prepared for the Canada–USA Forum on Women's Health. Ottawa: Health Canada.

Strassman, W. Paul. 1998. "Third World Housing." Pp. 589–592 in *The Encyclopedia of Housing,* edited by Willem van Vliet. Thousand Oaks, CA: Sage.

Straus, Murray A. 1994. "State-to-State Differences in Social Inequality and Social Bonds in Relation to Assaults on Wives in the United States." *Journal of Comparative Family Studies* 25(Spring):7–24.

———. 1999. *Violence in Intimate Relationships.* Thousand Oaks, CA: Sage.

Strauss, Anselm. 1977. *Negotiations: Varieties, Contexts, Processes, and Social Order.* San Francisco: Jossey Bass.

Strom, Stephanie. 1999. "In Japan, From a Lifetime Job to No Job at All." *New York Times,* February 3, p. A1.

———. 2000a. "In Japan, the Golden Years Have Lost Their Glow." *New York Times* (February 16): 7.

———. 2000b. "Tradition of Equality Fading in New Japan." *New York Times,* January 4, pp. A1, A6.

Struck, Doug. 2000. "A Violent Crime Wave Hits Japan." *Washington Post National Weekly Edition* 17(February 14):12.

Strum, Charles. 1993. "Schools' Tracks and Democracy." *New York Times,* April 1, pp. B1, B7.

Stuckey, Johanna H. 1998. "Women and Religion: Female Spirituality, Feminist Theology, and Feminist Goddess Worship." Pp. 267–287 in *Feminist Issues: Race, Class, and Sexuality.* 2nd ed. Edited by Nancy Mandell. Scarborough: Prentice Hall Allyn and Bacon Canada.

Sugimoto, Yoshio. 1997. *An Introduction to Japanese Society.* Cambridge, Eng.: Cambridge University Press.

Sumner, William G. 1906. *Folkways.* New York: Ginn.

Sunhara, Ann Gomer. 1981. "Deportation: The Final Solution to Canada's 'Japanese Problem.'" Pp. 246–261 in *Ethnicity Power and Politics in Canada,* edited by Jorgen Dahlie and Tissa Fernando. Toronto: Methuen.

Surgeon General. 1999. *Surgeon General's Report on Mental Health.* Washington, DC: U.S. Government Printing Office.

Sutherland, Edwin H. 1937. *The Professional Thief.* Chicago: University of Chicago Press.

———. 1940. "White-Collar Criminality." *American Sociological Review* 5(February):1–11.

———. 1949. *White Collar Crime.* New York: Dryden.

———. 1983. *White Collar Crime: The Uncut Version.* New Haven, CT: Yale University Press.

———, and Donald R. Cressey. 1978. *Principles of Criminology.* 10th ed. Philadelphia: Lippincott.

Suttles, Gerald D. 1972. *The Social Construction of Communities.* Chicago: University of Chicago Press.

Swanson, Stevenson, and Jim Kirk. 1998. "Satellite Outage Felt by Millions." *Chicago Tribune,* May 21, pp. 1, 26.

———. 1999. "Shaker Ranks Down to the Faithful Few." *Chicago Tribune,* April 4, p.6.

Swartz, Leslie. 1985. "Anorexia Nervosa as a Culture-Bound Syndrome." *Social Science and Medicine* 20(7):725–730.

Swiss, Deborah, and Judith Walker. 1993. *Women and the Work/Family Dilemma: How Today's Professional Women Are Finding Solutions.* New York: Wiley.

Synott, Anthony. 1987. "Shame and Glory: A Sociology of Hair." *The British Journal of Sociology* 38: 381–413.

Szasz, Thomas S. 1971. "The Same Slave: An Historical Note on the Use of Medical Diagnosis as Justificatory Rhetoric." *American Journal of Psychotherapy* 25(April):228–239.

———. 1974. *The Myth of Mental Illness* (rev. ed.). New York: Harper and Row.

T

Taeuber, Cynthia M. 1992. "Sixty-Five Plus in America." *Current Population Reports,* ser. P-23, no. 178. Washington, DC: U.S. Government Printing Office.

Tagliabue, John. 1996. "In Europe, a Wave of Layoffs Stuns White-Collar Workers." *New York Times,* June 20, pp. A1, D8.

Takahara, Kanako. 1999. "Preventing an AUM Comeback. Will Bills Save Society from Cult's Menace?" *The Japan Times* (November 18), p. 3.

Takezawa, Yasuko I. 1995. *Breaking the Silence: Redress and Japanese American Ethnicity.* Ithaca, NY: Cornell University Press.

Talbot, Margaret. 1998. "Attachment Theory: The Ultimate Experiment." *New York Times Magazine,* May 24, pp. 4–30, 38, 46, 50, 54.

Tannen, Deborah. 1990. *You Just Don't Understand: Women and Men in Conversation.* New York: Ballantine.

———. 1994a. *Talking from 9 to 5.* New York: William Morris.

———. 1994b. *Gender and Discourse.* New York: Oxford University Press.

Tarnopolsky, Walter Surma. 1991. *Discrimination and the Law in Canada: Race, Ethnic and Cultural Equality.* Vancouver: Western Judicial Centre.

Tashman, Billy. 1992. "Hobson's Choice: Free-Market Education Plan Vouches for Bush's Favorite Class." *Village Voice* 37(January 21): educational supplement, pp. 9, 14.

Taylor, Carl S. 1993. *Girls, Gangs, Women, and Drugs.* East Lansing: Michigan State University Press.

Taylor, Humphrey, and George Terhanian. 1999. "Heady Days Are Here Again: Online Polling Is Rapidly Coming of Age." *Public Perspectives* 10(June/July):20–23.

———. 1999. "No Witchcraft Here." *Public Perspective* 10(August/September):42–43.

Taylor, Verta. 1995. "Watching for Vibes: Bringing Emotions into the Study of Feminist Organizations." Pp. 223–233 in *Feminist Organizations: Harvest of the New Women's Movement,* edited by Myra Marx Ferree and Patricia Yancy Martin. Philadelphia: Temple University Press.

Telecommunications and Information Administration. 2000. Falling Through the Net. Washington, DC: U.S. Government Printing Office.

Telsch, Kathleen. 1991. "New Study of Older Workers Finds They Can Become Good Investments." *New York Times,* May 21, p. A16.

Tenner, Edward. 1996. *Why Things Bite Back: Technology and the Revenge of Unintended Consequences.* New York: Vintage Books.

Terhanian, George. 2000. Correspondence to author, January 7.

Terkel, Studs. 1974. *Working.* New York: Pantheon.

———. 1999. "Looking Toward Cyberspace: Beyond Grounded Sociology."

Contemporary Sociology 28(November):643–654.

Terry, Sara. 2000. "Whose Family? The Revolt of the Child-Free." *Christian Science Monitor*, August 29, pp. 1, 4.

The Canadian AIDS Society (CAS). 2002. *About The Canadian AIDS Society*. (www.cdnaids.ca).

The Canadian Lesbian and Gay Archives (CLGA). 1982. "Victories and defeats: A gay and lesbian chronology, 1964–1982." From *Flaunting It! A decade of gay journalism from "The Body Politic"* (http://www.clga.ca/Material/Records/docs/flitchro/fcint/ htm).

———. 1998. *What we demanded; What we got.* (www.clga.ca/Material/Records/docs/wegot.htm).

The Economist. 1990. "Thick Skins." 314 (February 24):26.

———. 1994. "Parent Power." 331(May 7):83.

———. 1995. "Home Sweet Home." 336(September 9):25–26, 29, 32.

———. 1996. "It's Normal to Be Queer." (January 6), pp. 68–70.

———. 1998. "Cruel and Ever More Unusual." 346(February 14).

The Gay Archivist. 1989. *Our Silver Anniversary: Canadians have been organizing for twenty-five years.* Number 7, June.

Theberge, Nancy. 1997. "'It's Part of the Game'—Physicality and the Production of Gender in Women's Hockey." *Gender and Society* 11(February):69–87.

Third International Mathematics and Science Study. 1998. *Mathematics and Science Achievement in the Final Year of Secondary School.* Boston, MA: TIMSS International Study Center.

Third World Institute. 1997. *Third World Guide 97/98.* Toronto, Ontario: Garamond Press.

Thirlwall, A. P. 1989. *Growth and Development.* 4th ed. London: Macmillan.

Thomas, Gordon, and Max Morgan Witts. 1974. *Voyage of the Damned.* Greenwich, CT: Fawcett Crest.

Thomas, Jim. 1984. "Some Aspects of Negotiating Order: Loose Coupling and Mesostructure in Maximum Security Prisons." *Symbolic Interaction* 7(Fall): 213–231.

Thomas, Pattie and Erica A. Ownes. 2000 "Age Cure!: The Business of Passing." Present at the annual meeting of the American Sociological Association, Washington, DC.

Thomas, Robert McG., Jr. 1995. "Maggie Kuhn, 89, the Founder of the Gray Panthers, Is Dead." *New York Times*, April 23, p. 47.

Thomas, William I. 1923. *The Unadjusted Girl.* Boston: Little, Brown.

Thompson, Linda, and Alexis J. Walker. 1989. "Gender in Families: Women and Men in Marriage, Work, and Parenthood." *Journal of Marriage and the Family* 51(November):845–871.

Thomson, Elizabeth, and Ugo Colella. 1992. "Cohabitation and Marital Stability: Quality or Commitment?" *Journal of Marriage and the Family* 54(May):259–267.

Thornton, Russell. 1987. *American Indians Holocaust and Survival: A Population History Since 1492.* Norman: University of Oklahoma Press.

Tiano, Susan. 1987. "Gender, Work, and World Capitalism: Third World Women's Role in Development." Pp. 216–243 in *Analyzing Gender: A Handbook of Social Science Research,* edited by Beth B. Hess and Myra Marx Ferree. Newbury Park, CA: Sage.

———. 1990. "Maquiladora women: A new category of workers?" Pp. 193–224 in K. Ward (ed.), *Women Workers and Global Restructuring.* Ithaca, NY: Cornell University Press.

Tidmarsh, Lee. 2000. "If I Shouldn't Spank, What Should I Do? Behaviour Techniques for Disciplining Children." *Canadian Family Physician* 46:1119–1123.

Tierney, John. 1990. "Betting the Planet." *New York Times Magazine*, December 2, pp. 52–53, 71, 74, 76, 78, 80–81.

Tierney, Kathleen. 1980. "Emergent Norm Theory as 'Theory': An Analysis and Critique of Turner's Formulation." Pp. 42–53 in *Collective Behavior: A Source Book,* edited by Meredith David Pugh. St. Paul, MN: West.

———. 1994. "Property Damage and Violence: A Collective Behavior Analysis." Pp. 149–173 in *The Los Angeles Riots: Lessons for the Urban Future,* edited by Mark Baldassare. Boulder, CO: Westview.

Tilly, Charles. 1993. *Popular Contention in Great Britain 1758–1834.* Cambridge, MA: Harvard University Press.

Time. 1971. "Suburbia: The New American Plurality." 97(March 15):14–20.

Tobin, Jacqueline, and Raymond Dobard. 1999. *Hidden in Plain View: The Secret Story of Quilts and the Underground Railroad.* New York: Doubleday.

Todd, Douglas. 2001. "Emphasis on Morality." *The Vancouver Sun,* February 26, p. A:15.

Tolbert, Kathryn. 2000. "In Japan, Traveling Alone Begins at Age 6." *Washington Post National Weekly Edition* 17(May 15):17.

Tong, Rosemary. 1989. *Feminist Theory: A Comprehensive Introduction.* Boulder, CO: Westview.

Tonkinson, Robert. 1978. *The Mardudjara Aborigines.* New York: Holt.

Tönnies, Ferdinand. [1887] 1988. *Community and Society.* Rutgers, NJ: Transaction.

Topolnicki, Denise M. 1993. "The World's 5 Best Ideas." *Money* 22(June):74–83, 87, 89, 91.

Touraine, Alain. 1974. *The Academic System in American Society.* New York: McGraw-Hill.

Transport Canada. 1998. *Transportation in Canada: 1997 Annual Report.* Cat. No. T1-10/1997E. Ottawa: Minster of Public Works and Government Services.

———. 2000. *Transportation in Canada 2000 Annual Report.* Ottawa: Transport Canada (www.tc.gc.ca/pol/en/anre2000/tc0003ae.htm).

Treas, Judith. 1995. "Older Americans in the 1990s and Beyond." *Population Bulletin* 50(May).

Trebay, Guy. 1990. "In Your Face." *Village Voice* 35, August 14, pp. 14–39.

Treiman, Donald J. 1977. *Occupational Prestige in Comparative Perspective.* New York: Academic.

Trubisky, Paula. 1995. "Congressional Briefing Highlights Sexual Behavior Survey." *Footnotes* 23(January):1.

Tuchman, Gaye. 1992. "Feminist Theory." Pp. 695–704 in *Encyclopedia of Sociology,* vol. 2, edited by Edgar F. Borgatta and Marie L. Borgatta. New York: Macmillan.

Tuck, Bryan, Jan Rolfe, and Vivienne Adair. 1994. "Adolescents' Attitudes Toward Gender Roles within Work and its Relationship to Gender, Personality Type and Parental Occupations." *Sex Roles* 31, 9–10: 547–558.

Tucker, James. 1993. "Everyday Forms of Employee Resistance." *Sociological Forum* 8(March):25–45.

Tumin, Melvin M. 1953. "Some Principles of Stratification: A Critical Analysis." *American Sociological Review* 18(August): 387–394.

———. 1985. *Social Stratification.* 2d ed. Englewood Cliffs, NJ: Prentice-Hall.

Ture, Kwame, and Charles Hamilton. 1992. *Black Power: The Politics of Liberation.* Rev. ed. New York: Vintage Books.

Turkle, Sherry. 1995. *Life on the Screen: Identity in the Age of the Internet.* New York: Simon and Schuster.

———. 1999. "Looking Toward Cyberspace: Beyond Grounded Sociology." *Contemporary Sociology* 28 (November): 643–654.

Turner, Bryan S., ed. 1990. *Theories of Modernity and Postmodernity.* Newbury Park, CA: Sage.

Turner, Craig. 1998. "U.N. Study Assails U.S. Executions as Biased." *Los Angeles Times*, March 4, p. A1.

Turner, J. H. 1985. *Herbert Spencer: A Renewed Application.* Beverly Hills, CA: Sage.

Turner, Margery Austin, and Felicity Skidmore, eds. 1999. *Mortgage Lending Discrimination: A Review of Existing Evidence.* Washington, DC: Urban Institute.

Turner, Ralph, and Lewis M. Killian. 1987. *Collective Behavior.* 3d ed. Englewood Cliffs, NJ: Prentice-Hall.

Twaddle, Andrew. 1974. "The Concept of Health Status." Social Science and Medicine 8(January):29–38.

Tyler, Charles. 1991. "The World's Manacled Millions." *Geographical Magazine* 63(1):30–35.

Tyler, Patrick E. 1995a. "As Deng Wanes, a Backlash Stalls His Last Big Reform," *New York Times* (June18), pp. 1, 7.

———. 1995b. "For China's Girls, Rural Schools Fail." *New York Times,* December 31, p. 5.

Tyler, William B. 1985. "The Organizational Structure of the School." Pp. 49–73 in *Annual Review of Sociology, 1985,* edited by Ralph H. Turner. Palo Alto, CA: Annual Reviews.

U

U.S. Conference of Mayors. 1999. *A Status Report on Hunger and Homelessness in America's Cities.* Washington: U.S. Conference of Mayors.

U.S. English. 1999. "States with Official English Laws." Accessed July 27, 1999 (http://www.us-english.org/states. htm).

Uchitelle, Louis. 1996. "More Downsized Workers Are Returning as Rentals." *New York Times,* December 8, pp. 1, 34.

———. 1996. "More Downsized Workers Are Returning as Rentals." *New York Times,* December 8, pp. 1, 34.

———. 1998. "Downsizing Comes Back, but the Outcry Is Muted." *New York Times,* December 7, p. A1.

———. 1999. "Divising New Math to Define Poverty." *New York Times,* October 18, pp. A1, A14.

UNAIDS. 2000. *Report on the Global HIV/ AIDS Epidemic, June 2000.* Geneva, Switzerland: Joint United Nations' Programme on HIV/AIDS (UNAIDS).

UNESCO. 1999. "Estimated illiteracy rate and illiterate population aged 15 years and over" in UNESCO Statistical Yearbook 1999: Education and Literacy. (www.uis.unesco.org/en/stats/ statistics/yearbook/tables/Table_II_ S_1_Region.htm).

United Nations Development Programme. 1995. *Human Development Report 1995.* New York: Oxford University Press.

United Nations Development Programme. 1996. *Human Development Report 1996.* New York: Oxford University Press.

———. 1999. *Human Development Report, 1999.* New York: Oxford University Press.

United Nations Human Rights Commission. 1997. "U.N. Human Rights Commission Acts on Texts." M2 Press-Wire. 4/9.

United Nations Population Division. 1998a. "Demographic Input of HIV/ AIDS." Accessed (http://www. undp.org/ popin/wdtrends/demoimp. htm).

———. 1998b. *World Abortion Policies.* New York: Department of Economic and Social Affairs, UNPD.

———. 1998c. *World Population Projections to 2150,* February 1, 1998. Accessed August 10, 1998 (http://www.undp.org/ popin/wdtrends/ execsum.htm).

———. 1999. *The World at Six Billion.* New York: UNPD.

United Nations Population Fund. 2000. *State of World Population 2000: Lives Together, Worlds Apart: Men and Women in a Time of Change.* New York: United Nations Population Fund.

United Nations. 1995. *The World's Women, 1995: Trends and Statistics.* New York: United Nations.

———. 1995. *United Nations and the Advancement of Women 1945–1995.* The United Nations Blue Book Series VI. 1st edition. New York: United Nations.

———. 2000. *Secretary General's Address to the Special Session on Women.* Press Release SG/SM/7430, WOM/1203. New York: United Nations.

University of Calgary Gazette. 2000. "Quid Novi." Gazette, May 29, 30(5). Accessed July 2, 2001 (http://www. ucalgary.ca/unicomm/Gazette/ Archives/index.html).

University of New Hampshire. 2000. "Kentucky Fried Chicken Hoax." Accessed January 20, 2000 (http:// www.unh.edu/BoilerPlate/kfc.html).

USA Today. 1998. "Did Tobacco Company Money Kill the Anti-smoking Bill?" June 22, p. 16A.

Utt, Ronald D. 1998. *Cities in Denial: The False Promises of Subsidized Tourist and Entertainment Complex.* Washington, DC: Heritage Foundation.

Utter, Jack. 1993. *American Indians: Answers to Today's Questions.* Lake Ann, MI: National Woodlands Publishing.

Uttley, Alison. 1993. "Who's Looking at You, Kid?" *Times Higher Education Supplement* 30(April 30):48.

V

Vallas, Steven P. 1999. "Rethinking Post-Fordism: The Meaning of Workplace Flexibility." *Sociological Theory* 17(March):68–101.

van den Berghe, Pierre. 1978. *Race and Racism: A Comparative Perspective.* 2d ed. New York: Wiley.

Van Slambrouck, Paul. 1998. "In California, Taking the Initiative—Online." *Christian Science Monitor,* November 13, pp. 1, 11.

———. 1999a. "Netting a New Sense of Connection." *Christian Science Monitor,* May 4, pp. 1, 4.

———. 1999b. "Newest Tool for Social Protest: The Internet." *Christian Science Monitor,* June 18, p. 3.

van Vucht Tijssen, Lieteke. 1990. "Women between Modernity and Postmodernity." Pp. 147–163 in *Theories of Modernity and Postmodernity,* edited by Bryan S. Turner. London: Sage.

Vancouver Sun. 2000. "Youth Violence in Canada." December 2, p. B4.

Vanderpool, Tim. 1995. "Secession of the Successful." *Utne Reader* (November–December):32, 34.

Vanier Institute of the Family. 1999. "The Cost of Raising a Child." In *Transition Magazine.* Summer 1999, Fol. 29, No. 2.

———. 1999. *Profiling Canadian Families.* Ottawa: Vanier Institute of the Family.

———. 2000a. *Family Facts.* (www.-vifamily.ca/faqs/faq.htm)

———. 2000b. *The Current State of Canadian Family Finances - 2000 Report.* Ottawa: The Vanier Institute of the Family.

Vanneman, Reeve, and Lynn Weber Cannon. 1987. *The American Perception of Class.* Philadelphia: Temple University Press.

Vaughan, Diane. 1996. *The Challenger Launch Decision: Risky Technology, Culture, and Deviance at NASA.* Chicago: University of Chicago Press.

———. 1999. "The Dark Side of Organizations: Mistake, Misconduct, and Disaster." Pp. 271–305 in *Annual Review of Sociology,* edited by Karen J. Cook and John Hagan. Palo Alto: Annual Reviews.

Veblen, Thorstein. 1919. *The Vested Interests and the State of the Industrial Arts.* New York: Huebsch.

Vega, William A. 1995. "The Study of Latino Families: A Point of Departure." Pp. 3–17 in *Understanding Latino Families: Scholarship, Policy, and Practice,* edited by Ruth E. Zambrana. Thousand Oaks, CA: Sage.

Velkoff, Victoria A., and Valerie A. Lawson. 1998. "Gender of Aging." *International Brief,* ser. IB, no. 98–3. Washington, DC: U.S. Government Printing Office.

Venkatesh, Sudhir Alladi. 1997. "The Social Organization of Street Gang Activity in an Urban Ghetto." *American Journal of Sociology* 103(July):82–111.

Ventura, Stephanie J., and Christine A. Bachrach. 2000. "Nonmarital Childbearing in the United States, 1990–91." *National Vital Statistics Reports* 48(October 18).

———, Joyce A. Martin, Sally C. Curtin, T. J. Mathews, and Melissa M. Park. 2000a. "Births: Final Data for 1998." *National Vital Statistics Reports* 48(March 28).

———, ———, and ———. 1998a. *Teenage Births in the United States: National and State Trends, 1990–96.*

Washington, DC: National Vital Statistics System.

Ventura, Stephanie J., T. J. Mathews, and Sally C. Curtin. 1999. "Declines in Teenage Birth Rates, 1991–98: Update of National and State Patterns." *National Vital Statistics Reports* 47(October 25).

Verhovek, Sam Howe. 1997. "Racial Tensions in Suit Slowing Drive for 'Environmental Justice,'" *New York Times*, September 7, pp. 1, 16.

———. 1999. "Oregon Reporting 15 Deaths in Year Under Suicide Law." *New York Times*, February 18, pp. A1, A17.

Vernon, Glenn. 1962. *Sociology and Religion.* New York: McGraw-Hill.

Vernon, Jo Etta A. et al. [4 authors]. 1990. "Media Stereotyping: A Comparison of the Way Elderly Women and Men Are Portrayed on Prime-Time Television." *Journal of Women and Aging* 2(4):55–68.

Vidaver, R. M. et al. 2000. "Women Subjects in NIH-funded Clinical Research Literature: Lack of Progress in Both Representation and Analysis by Sex." *Journal of Women's Health Gender Based Medicine* 9(June):495–504.

Vissandjee, Bilkis. 2001. "The Consequences of Cultural Diversity." *The Canadian Women's Health Network* 4(2): 3–4.

Vladimiroff, Christine. 1998. "Food for Thought." *Second Harvest Update* (Summer):2.

Vobejda, Barbara, and Judith Havenmann. 1997. "Experts Say Side Income Could Hamper Reforms." *Washington Post*, November 3, p. A1.

———. 1993. "U.S. Ends Survey of Its Dwindling Farm Population." *Chicago Sun-Times*, October 9, p. 6.

———, and ———. 1997. "Experts Say Side Income Could Hamper Reforms." *Washington Post* (November 3), p. A1.

W

Wacquant, Loïc J. D. 1993. "When Cities Run Riot." *UNESCO Courier* (February), pp. 8–15.

Wages for Housework Campaign. 1999. *Wages for Housework Campaign.* Circular. Los Angeles.

Wagley, Charles and Marvin Harris. 1958. *Minorities in the New World: Six Case Studies.* New York: Columbia University Press.

Waite, Brian, and Cheri DeNovo. 1971. "Letter accompanying the brief." Letter written for the August 28th Gay Day Committee (www.clga.ca/Material/Records/docs/wedemand.htm).

Waitzkin, Howard, and John D. Stoeckle. 1976. "Information Control and the Micropolitics of Health Care." *Journal of Social Issues* 10(6):263–76.

———. 1986. *The Second Sickness: Contradictions of Capitalist Health Care.* Chicago: University of Chicago Press.

Wake, Bev. 2000. "Home Schooling Gets Top Marks: More Parents are Home Schooling their Children because of Better Internet Access and the Availability of Educational Material." *Ottawa Citizen.* September 7, p. C3.

Waldron, Arthur. 1998. "Why China Could Be Dangerous." *The American Enterprise* 9 (July/August):40–43.

Wallace, Ruth A., and Alison Wolf. 1980. *Contemporary Sociological Theory.* Englewood Cliffs, NJ: Prentice-Hall.

Wallerstein, Immanuel. 1974. *The Modern World System.* New York: Academic Press.

———. 1979. *Capitalist World Economy.* Cambridge, Eng.: Cambridge University Press.

———. 1999. *The End of the World As We Know It: Social Science for the Twenty-first Century.* Minneapolis: University of Minnesota Press.

———. 2000. *The Essential Wallerstein.* New York: The New Press.

Wallerstein, Judith S., Judith M. Lewis, and Sandra Blakeslee. 2000. *The Unexpected Legacy of Deviance.* New York: Hyperion.

Wallis, Claudia. 1987. "Is Mental Illness Inherited?" *Time* 129(March 9):67.

Walzer, Susan. 1996. "Thinking about the Baby: Gender and Divisions of Infant Care." *Social Problems* 43(May):219–234.

Wapner, Paul. 1994. "Environmental Activism and Global Civil Society." *Dissent* 41(Summer):389–393.

Waring, Marilyn. 1988. *If Women Counted: A New Feminist Economics.* San Francisco: Harper and Row.

Warner, Judith. 1996. "France's Anti-abortion Movement Gains Momentum." *Ms.* 7(September–October):20–21.

Washington Post. 2000. "Guidelines of the Dutch Euthanasia Law." November 29, 2000.

Washington Transcript Service. 1999. "Hillary Rodham Clinton Holds News Conference on Her New York Senatorial Bid." November 23.

Watts, Jerry G. 1990. "Pluralism Reconsidered." *Urban Affairs Quarterly* 25(June):697–704.

Weber, Bruce, Greg Duncan, and Leslie Whitener. 2000. "Rural Dimensions of Welfare Reform." *Poverty Research News* 4(September–October):3–4.

Weber, Martha L. 1998. "She Stands Alone: A Review of the Recent Literature on Women and Social Support." *Prairie Women's Health Centre of Excellence.* Winnipeg: Prairie Women's Health Centre of Excellence.

Weber, Max. 1922. *Wirtschaft und Gesellschaft.* Tübingen, Ger.: J. C. B. Mohr.

———. [1904] 1949. *Methodology of the Social Sciences.* Translated by Edward A. Shils and Henry A. Finch. Glencoe, IL: Free Press.

———. [1913–1922] 1947. *The Theory of Social and Economic Organization.* Translated by A. Henderson and T. Parsons. New York: Free Press.

———. [1904] 1958a. *The Protestant Ethic and the Spirit of Capitalism.* Translated by Talcott Parsons. New York: Scribner.

———. [1916] 1958b. *The Religion of India: The Sociology of Hinduism and Buddhism.* New York: Free Press.

Wechsler, Henry et al. 2000a. "College Binge Drinking in the 1990s: A Continuing Program." *Journal of American College Health* 48(March):199–210.

———. 2000b. "What Colleges Are Doing About Student Binge Drinking A Survey of College Administrators." *Journal of American College Public Health* (April). Accessed at www.hsph.harvard.edu/cas/alcohol.surveyrpt2. html.

Wechsler, Henry. 2000c. "Binge Drinking: Should We Attack the Name or the Problem?" *Chronicle of Higher Education* 47(October 20):B12–13.

Weeks, John R. 1988. "The Demography of Islamic Nations." *Population Bulletin* 43(December).

———. 1996. *Population: An Introduction to Concepts and Issues.* 6th ed. Belmont, CA: Wadsworth.

———. 1999. *Population: An Introduction to Concepts and Issues.* 7th ed. Belmont, CA: Wadsworth.

Weigard, Bruce. 1992. *Off the Books: A Theory and Critique of the Underground Economy.* Dix Hills, NY: General Hall.

Weil, Frederick D. 1987. "Cohorts, Regimes, and the Legitimization of Democracy: West Germany since 1945." *American Sociological Review* 52(June):308–324.

Weiner, Tim. 1998. "Military Discharges of Homosexuals Soar." *New York Times*, February 12, p. A21.

Weinfeld, M. 1994. "Ethnic Assimilation and the Retention of Ethnic Cultures." Pp. 238–266 in *Ethnicity and Culture in Canada: The Research Landscape*, edited by J.W. Berry and J.A. Laponce. Toronto: University of Toronto Press.

Weinstein, Deena, and Michael A. Weinstein. 1999. "McDonaldization Enframed." Pp. 57–69 in *Resisting McDonaldization*, edited by Barry Smart. London: Sage.

———. 1999. *Knockin' The Rock: Defining Rock Music as a Social Problem.* New York: McGraw-Hill/Primis.

———. 2000. *Heavy Metal: The Music and Its Culture.* Cambridge, MA: Da Capo.

Weisman, Steven R. 1992. "Landmark Harassment Case in Japan." *New York Times*, April 17, p. A3.

Weiss, Rick. 1998. "Beyond Test-Tube Babies." *Washington Post National Weekly Edition* 15(February 16):6–7.

Weitz, Rose. 1996. *The Sociology of Health, Illness and Health Care: A Critical Approach.* Belmont Cal.: Wadsworth.

Welfare to Work Partnership. 1998. "Survey of Businesses." News Release. April 9. Washington, DC: Welfare to Work Partnership.

———. 1999. "Member Survey: Promotion and Partnership." Accessed September 29, 1999 (http://www. welfaretowork.org).

———. 2000. "Business Partners Find Success but Call for Renewed Community Action." *Trends in Executive Opinions* (2000 Series No. 1), p.1.

Wellman, Barry et al. [6 authors]. 1996. "Computer Networks as Social Networks: Collaborative Work, Telework, and Virtual Community." Pp. 213–238 in *Annual Review of Sociology,* 1996, edited by John Hagan. Palo Alto, CA: Annual Reviews.

Welsh, Sandy. 1999. "Gender and Sexual Harassment." Pp. 169–190 in *Annual Review of Sociology, 1999,* edited by Karen S. Cook and John Hagan. Palo Alto, CA: Annual Reviews.

Wente, Margaret. 2001. "The school with Canada's longest waiting list." In *The Globe and Mail,* May 29, 2001.

West, Candace, and Don H. Zimmerman. 1983. "Small Insults: A Study of Interruptions in Cross Sex Conversations between Unacquainted Persons." Pp. 86–111 in *Language, Gender, and Society,* edited by Barrie Thorne, Cheris Kramarae, and Nancy Henley. Rowley, MA: Newbury House.

———, and ———. 1987. "Doing Gender." *Gender and Society* 1(June):125–151.

———, and ———. 2000. "Doing Gender." Pp. 131–149 in *The Gendered Society Reader,* edited by Michael S. Kimmel. New York: Oxford University Press, Inc.

West, William G. 1993. "Violence in the Schools/Schooling in Violence: Escalating Problem or Moral Panic? A Critical Perspective." *Orbit.* 24 (1), 6–7.

Whyte, William Foote. 1981. *Street Corner Society: Social Structure of an Italian Slum.* 3d ed. Chicago: University of Chicago Press.

———. 1989. "Advancing Scientific Knowledge through Participatory Action Research." *Sociological Forum* 4(September):367–385.

Wickham, DeWayne. 1998. "Affirmative Action not in Real Jeopardy." *USA Today,* April 7, p. 13A.

Wickman, Peter M. 1991. "Deviance." Pp. 85–87 in *Encyclopedic Dictionary of Sociology,* 4th ed., by Dushkin Publishing Group. Guilford, CT: Dushkin.

Wiener, Jon. 1994. "Free Speech on the Internet." *The Nation* 258(June 13):825–828.

Wilford, John Noble. 1997. "New Clues Show Where People Made the Great Leap to Agriculture." *New York Times,* November 18, pp. B9, B12.

Wilhelm, Anthony. 1998. *Buying into the Computer Age: A Look at Hispanic Families.* Claremont, CA: The Thom Rivera Policy Institute.

Wilkinson, Tracy. 1999 "Refugees Forming Bonds on Web." *Los Angeles Times,* July 31, p. A2.

Willet, Jeffrey G., and Mary Jo Deegan. 2000. "Liminality? and Disability: The Symbolic Rite of Passage of Individuals with Disabilities." Presented at the annual meeting of the American Sociological Association, Washington, DC.

Williams, Carol J. 1995. "Taking an Eager Step Back." *Los Angeles Times,* June 3, pp. A1, A14.

Williams, Christine L. 1992. "The Glass Escalator: Hidden Advantages for Men in the 'Female' Professions." *Social Problems* 39(3):253–267.

———. 1995. *Still a Man's World: Men Who Do Women's Work.* Berkeley: University of California Press.

Williams, David R., and Chiquita Collins. 1995. "U.S. Socioeconomic and Racial Differences in Health: Patterns and Explanations." Pp. 349–386 in *Annual Review of Sociology, 1995,* edited by John Hagan. Palo Alto, CA: Annual Reviews.

Williams, J. Allen, Jr., Nicholas Batchuk, and David R. Johnson. 1973. "Voluntary Associations and Minority Status: A Comparative Analysis of Anglo, Black and Mexican Americans." *American Sociological Review* 38(October):637–646.

Williams, Lena. 1995. "Not Just a White Man's Game: Blacks in Business Master the Art of Networking." *New York Times,* November 9, pp. D1, D10.

Williams, Patricia J. 1997. "Of Race and Risk." *The Nation.* Digital Edition. Accessed December 12, 1999 (http://www.thenation.com).

Williams, Robin M., Jr. 1970. *American Society.* 3d ed. New York: Knopf.

———, in collaboration with John P. Dean and Edward A. Suchman. 1964. *Strangers Next Door: Ethnic Relations in American Communities.* Englewood Cliffs, NJ: Prentice-Hall.

Williams, Simon Johnson. 1986. "Appraising Goffman." *British Journal of Sociology* 37(September):348–369.

Williams, Wendy M. 1998. "Do Parents Matter? Scholars Need to Explain What Research Really Shows." *Chronicle of Higher Education* 45(December 11): B6–B7.

Wilmut, Ian et al. [5 authors]. 1997. "Viable Offering Derived from Fetal and Adult Mammalian Cells." *Nature* 385(February 27):810–813.

Wilson, Edward O. 1975. *Sociobiology: The New Synthesis.* Cambridge, MA: Harvard University Press.

———. 1978. *On Human Nature.* Cambridge, MA: Harvard University Press.

Wilson, Jamie. 2002. "The Symbol of Stability"—NAFTA reaches into the lives of farmers in Southern Mexico. The Social Justice Committee papers (http://www.s-j-c.net/NAFTA.htm).

Wilson, John. 1973. *Introduction to Social Movements.* New York: Basic Books.

———. 1978. *Religion in American Society: The Effective Presence.* Englewood Cliffs, NJ: Prentice-Hall.

Wilson, Susannah. 2001. "Intimacy and Commitment in Family Formation." Pp. 144–63 in *Families: Changing Trends in Canada,* 4th ed., edited by Maureen Baker. Toronto: McGraw-Hill Ryerson.

Wilson, Warner, Larry Dennis, and Allen P. Wadsworth, Jr. 1976. "Authoritarianism Left and Right." *Bulletin of the Psychonomic Society* 7(March):271–274.

Wilson, William Julius, ed. 1989. *The Ghetto Underclass: Social Science Perspectives.* Newbury Park, CA: Sage.

———. 1980. *The Declining Significance of Race: Blacks and Changing American Institutions.* 2d ed. Chicago: University of Chicago Press.

———. 1987. *The Truly Disadvantaged: The Inner City, the Underclass and Public Policy.* Chicago: University of Chicago Press.

———. 1988. "The Ghetto Underclass and the Social Transformation of the Inner City." *The Black Scholar* 19(May–June):10–17.

———. 1996. *When Work Disappears: The World of the New Urban Poor.* New York: Knopf.

———. 1999a. "Towards a Just and Livable City: The Issues of Race and Class." Address at the Social Science Centennial Conference, April 23, 1999. Chicago, IL: DePaul University.

———. 1999b. *The Bridge Over the Racial Divide: Rising Inequality and Coalition Politics.* Berkeley: University of California Press.

Winerip, Michael. 1998. "Schools for Sale." *New York Times Magazine,* July 14, pp. 42–48, 80, 86, 88–89.

Winsberg, Morton. 1994. "Specific Hispanics." *American Demographics* 16(February):44–53.

Winter, J. Alan. 1977. *Continuities in the Sociology of Religion.* New York: Harper and Row.

Wirth, Louis. 1928. *The Ghetto.* Chicago: University of Chicago Press.

———. 1931. "Clinical Sociology." *American Journal of Sociology* 37(July):49–66.

———. 1938. "Urbanism as a Way of Life." *American Journal of Sociology* 44(July):1–24.

Wiseman, Paul. 2000. "China's Little Emperors: The Offspring of Policy." *USA Today*, February 23, p. 10D.

Withers, Edward J., and Robert S. Brown. 2001. "The Broadcast Audience: A Sociological Perspective." Pp. 121–150 in *Communications in Canadian Society*, 5th ed., edited by Craig McKie and Benjamin D. Singer. Toronto: Thompson Educational Publishing.

Witt, Matt. 1999. "Missing in Action: Media Images of Real Workers." *Los Angeles Times*, August 30, pp. E1, E3.

Wolf, Naomi. 1990. *The Beauty Myth: How Images of Beauty Are Used Against Women*. New York: Morrow.

———. 1991. *The Beauty Myth*. New York: Anchor Books.

———. 1992. *The Beauty Myth: How Images of Beauty Are Used Against Women*. New York: Anchor.

Wolf, Richard. 1996. "States Can Expect Challenges after Taking over Welfare." *USA Today*, October 1, p. 8A.

———. 1998. "States Slow to Plunge into Covenant Marriage." *USA Today*, June 16, p. 3A.

Wolff, Edward N. 1999. "Recent Trends the Distribution of Household Wealth Ownership." In *Back to Shared Prosperity: The Growing Inequality of Wealth and Income in America*, edited by Ray Marshall. New York: M.E. Sharpe.

Wolinsky, Fredric P. 1980. *The Sociology of Health*. Boston: Little, Brown.

Wolraich et al. 1998. "Guidance for Effective Discipline." *Pediatrics* 101 (April):723–728.

Women's International Network. 1995. "Working Women: 4 Country Comparison." *WIN News* 21(September 9):82.

Wood, Daniel B. 1999. "In Mexico, U.S. Industry Finds Uncertainty." *Christian Science Monitor*, November 1, p. 3.

———. 2000. "Minorities Hope TV Deals Don't Just Lead to 'Tokenism.'" *Christian Science Monitor*, January 19.

Woodard, Colin. 1998. "When Rate Learning Fails against the Test of Global Economy." *Christian Science Monitor*, April 15, p. 7.

Wooden, Wayne. 1995. *Renegade Kids, Suburban Outlaws: From Youth Culture to Delinquency*. Belmont, CA: Wadsworth.

Woolf, Virginia. 1977. *A Room of One's Own*. San Diego, CA: Harvest/HBJ.

World Bank 2001. *World Development Indicators* (www.worldbank.org/data/countrydata).

World Bank. 1990. *World Development Report 1990: Poverty*. New York: Oxford University Press.

———. 1992. *Housing: Enabling Markets to Work: A World Bank Policy Paper*. Washington, DC: World Bank.

———. 1995. *World Development Report 1994: Workers in an Integrating World*. New York: Oxford University Press.

———. 1996. *World Development Report 1996: From Plan to Market*. New York: Oxford University Press.

———. 1997a. *World Development Indicators 1997*. Washington, DC: International Bank for Reconstruction and Development/The World Bank.

———. 1997b. *World Development Report 1997: The State in a Changing World*. New York: Oxford University Press.

———. 1999a. *World Development Report 1998/99: Knowledge for Development*. New York: Oxford University Press.

———. 1999b. *World Development Indicators 1999*. New York: Oxford University Press.

———. 2000a. *World Development Report 1999/2000: Entering the 21st Century*. New York: Oxford University Press.

———. 2000b. *World Development Indicators 2000*. Washington, DC: World Bank.

———. 2000c. *World Development Report 2000/2001*. New York: Oxford University Press.

World Development Forum. 1990. "The Danger of Television." 8(July 15):4.

World Health Organization. 1998. *Unsafe Abortion: Global and Regional Estimates of Incidence of and Mortality Due to Unsafe Abortion*. Geneva, Switzerland: WHO.

———. 2000. *The World Health Report 2000. Health Systems: Improving Performance*. Geneva, Switzerland: WHO.

World Resources Institute. 1998. *1998–99 World Resources: A Guide to the Global Environment*. New York: Oxford University Press.

———. The United Nations Environment Programme, United Nations Development Program, The World Bank. 1996. *World Resources, 1996–1997*. New York: Oxford University Press.

Wresch, William. 1996. *Disconnected: Haves and Have-Nots in the Information Age*. New Brunswick, NJ: Rutgers University Press.

Wright, Eric R., William P. Gronfein, and Timothy J. Owens. 2000. "Deinstitutionalization, Social Rejection, and the Self-Esteem of Former Mental Patients." *Journal of Health and Social Behavior* (March).

Wright, Erik Olin, David Hachen, Cynthia Costello, and Joy Sprague. 1982. "The American Class Structure." *American Sociological Review* 47 (December): 709–726.

Wright, Gerald C., and Dorothy M. Stetson. 1978. "The Impact of No-Fault Divorce Law Reform on Divorce in the American States." *Journal of Marriage and the Family* 40:575–580.

Wright, James D. 1995. "Ten Essential Observations on Guns in America." *Society* 32(March/April):63–68.

Wright, Robin. 1995. "The Moral Animal: Why We Are the Way We Are." *Science of Evolutionary Psychology*. Reprint edition. New York: Vintage Books.

Wu, Zheng. 1990. "Premaritial Cohabitation and the Timing of First Marriage." *Canadian Review of Sociology and Anthropology* 36(1):109–127.

Wurman, Richard Saul. 1989. *Information Anxiety*. New York: Doubleday.

Wuthnow, Robert, and Marsha Witten. 1988. "New Directions in the Study of Culture." Pp. 49–67 in *Annual Review of Sociology*, 1988, edited by W. Richard Scott and Judith Blake. Palo Alto, CA: Annual Reviews.

X

Xinhua News Agency. 1997. "IDB Okays Financing for Child Care in Ecuador." November 19.

Y

Yamagata, Hisashi, Kuang S. Yeh, Shelby Stewman, and Hiroko Dodge. 1997. "Sex Segregation and Glass Ceilings: A Comparative Statistics Model of Women's Career Opportunities in the Federal Government over a Quarter Century." *American Journal of Sociology* 103(November):566–632.

Yap, Kioe Sheng. 1998. "Squatter Settlements." Pp. 554–556 in *The Encyclopedia of Housing*, edited by Willem van Vliet. Thousand Oaks, CA: Sage Publications.

Yaukey, John. 1997. "Blacksburg, VA: A Town That's Really Wired." *Gannett News Service*, April 8, pp. 1–3.

Yax, Laura K. 1999. "National Population Projections." Accessed October 30, 1999 (http://www.census.gov/population/www/projections/natproj.html).

Yglesias, Linda. 1996. "Splitting Hairs." *New York Daily News*, February 18, pp. 50–51.

Yinger, J. Milton. 1970. *The Scientific Study of Religion*. New York: Macmillan.

———. 1974. "Religion, Sociology of." In *Encyclopaedia Britannica*, vol. 15. Chicago: Encyclopaedia Britanica, pp. 604–613.

Young, Gay. 1993. "Gender Inequality and Industrial Development: The Household Connection." *Journal of Comparative Family Studies* 124(Spring):3–20.

Young, Margaret, and Jay Sinha. *Bill D-11: The Immigration and Refugee Protection Act*. Ottawa: Parliamentary Research Branch. LS-397E.

yrendrpt99.html).

Z

Zajac, Andrew. 1999. "Notes from a Wired Community." *Chicago Tribune,* April 5, pp. C3–C4.

Zald, Mayer N. 1970. *Organizational Change: The Political Economy of the YMCA.* Chicago: University of Chicago Press.

Zaslow, M. 1988. "Sex Differences in Children's Response to Parental Divorce: 1. Research Methodology and Postdivorce Family Forms." *American Journal of Orthopsychiatry* 58(July):355–378.

———. 1989. "Sex Differences in Children's Response to Parental Divorce: 2. Samples, Variables, Ages, and Sources." *American Journal of Orthopsychiatry* 59(January):118–141.

Zelizer, Gerald L. 1999. "Internet Offers Only Fuzzy Cyberfaith, Not True Religious Experiences." *USA Today,* August 19, p. 13A.

Zellner, William M. 1978. "Vehicular Suicide: In Search of Incidence." Western Illinois University, Macomb. Unpublished M.A. thesis.

———. 1995. *Counter Cultures: A Sociological Analysis.* New York: St. Martin's Press.

———. 2001. *Extraordinary Groups: An Examination of Unconventional Lifestyles.* 7th ed. New York: Worth.

Zhao, John Z., Fernando Rajulton, and Z. R. Ravanera. 1995. "Leaving the Parental Home: Effects of Family Structure, Gender, and Culture." *Canadian Journal of Sociology* 20(1): 31–50.

Zhou, Xueguang, and Liren Hou. 1999. "Children of the Cultural Revolution: The State and the Life Course in the People's Republic of China." *American Sociological Review* 64(February):32–36.

Zia, Helen. 1990. "Midwives: Talking about a Revolution." *Ms.* 1(November–December):91.

———. 1993. "Women of Color in Leadership." *Social Policy* 23(Summer):51–55.

Zimbardo, Philip G. 1972. "Pathology of Imprisonment." *Society* 9(April):4, 6, 8.

———. 1992. *Psychology and Life.* 13th ed. New York: HarperCollins.

———, Craig Haney, W. Curtis Banks, and David Jaffe. 1974. "The Psychology of Imprisonments: Privation, Power, and Pathology." In *Doing Unto Others: Joining, Molding, Conforming, Helping, and Loving,* edited by Zick Rubin. Englewood Cliffs, NJ: Prentice-Hall.

Zimmer, Lynn. 1988. "Tokenism and Women in the Workplace." *Social Problems* 35(February):64–77.

Zimmerman, Mary K. 1987. "The Women's Health Movement: A Critique of Medical Enterprise, and the Position of Women." Pp. 442–472 in *Analyzing Gender: A Handbook of Social Science Research,* edited by Beth B. Hess and Myra Marx Ferree. Newbury Park, CA: Sage.

Zola, Irving K. 1972. "Medicine as an Institution of Social Control." *Sociological Review* 20(November):487–504.

———. 1983. *Socio-Medical Inquiries.* Philadelphia: Temple University Press.

Zook, Matthew A. 1996. "The Unorganized Militia Network: Conspiracies, Computers, and Community." *Berkeley Planning Journal* 11:1–15.

Zuckerman, M. J. 2000. "Criminals Hot on Money Trail to Cyberspace." *USA Today,* March 21, p. 8A.

Zweigenhaft, Richard L., and G. William Domhoff. 1998. *Diversity in the Power Elite: Have Women and Minorities Reached the Top?* New Haven: Yale University Press.

Census Update References

Human Resources Development Canada. 2003. 2002 *Employment Equity Act Annual Report: Workplace Equity.* Catalogue No. MP31-5/2002.

Statistics Canada. 2003a. *Canada's ethnocultural portrait: The changing mosaic.* 2001 Census: analysis series. Catalogue no. 96F0030XIE2001008. Released January 21, 2003.

———. 2003b. *Aboriginal peoples of Canada: A demographic profile.* 2001 Census: analysis series. Catalogue no. 96F0030XIE2001007. Released January 21, 2003.

———. 2003c. *The changing profile of Canada's labour force.* 2001 Census: analysis series. Catalogue no. 96F0030XIE2001009. Released February 11, 2003.

———. 2003d. *Education in Canada: Raising the standard.* 2001 Census: analysis series. Catalogue no. 96F0030XIE2001012. Released March 11, 2003.

———. 2003e. *Earnings of Canadians: Making a living in the new economy.* 2001 Census: analysis series. Catalogue no. 96F0030XIE2001013. Released March 11, 2003.

———. 2003f. *Income of Canadian families.* 2001 Census: analysis series. Catalogue no. 96F0030XIE2001014. Released May 13, 2003.

———. 2003g. *Religions in Canada.* 2001 Census: analysis series. Catalogue no. 96F0030XIE2001015. Released May 13, 2003.

———. 2003h. *Canada at a Glance 2003.* 2001 Communications Division. Catalogue no. 12-581-XPE.

———. 2003i. *Ethno-Cultural Portrait of Canada, Table 1.* (http://www12.statcan.ca/english/census01/products/highlight/ETO/Table1.)

———. 2003j. *Earnings of Immigrant workers and Canadian-born workers, 1980-2000. The Daily,* Wednesday, October 8.

Acknowledgments

CHAPTER 1

P. 6: Quotation from Katherine Irwin. 1999. "Getting a First Tattoo: Techniques of Legitimization and Social Change," dissertation, University of Colorado. Copyright 1999 by Katherine Irwin. Reprinted by permission.

P. 24: Quotation in Box 1-3 from Carol Brooks Gardner. 1989. "Analyzing Gender in Public Places: Rethinking Goffman's Vision of Everyday Life," *The American Sociologist*, **20** (Spring): 45, 49, 56. © 1989. Reprinted by permission of Transaction Publishers, Rutgers University. All rights reserved.

CHAPTER 2

P. 32: Quotation from *Generation on Hold* copyright ©1995 J.E. Cote and Anton L. Allahar. Reproduced by permission of Stoddart Publishing Co. Limited.

P. 51: Figure 2-3 from the Statistics Canada publication, "Canadian Social Trends," Catalogue 11-008, Spring 2000

P. 53: Figure in Appendix from World Bank. 1999. *Entering the 21st Century: World Development Report 1999/2000*: 226–227. Copyright © 1999 by the International Bank for Reconstruction and Development/The World Bank. Used by permission of Oxford University Press, Inc.

CHAPTER 3

P. 62: Quotation from Horace Miner. 1956. "Body Ritual among the Nacirema," *American Anthropologist*, Vol. 58 No. 3. Reprinted by permission of the American Anthropological Association.

P. 69: Figure 3-2 from Edward B. Espenshade, Jr. 1990. *Rand McNally Goode's World Atlas*, 18/e: 25. Map © by Rand McNally, R. L. #00-S-22.

P. 73: Figure 3-3 "Valued Means of Teenagers and Adults" from *Teen Trends* copyright ©1992 Reginald W. Bibby and Donald C. Posterski. Reproduced with permission of Stoddart Publishing Co, Limited.

P. 76: Figure 3-4 illustration by Jim Willis. 1996. "The Argot of Pickpockets," *New York Daily News* (November 19): 5. © New York Daily News, LP. Reprinted by permission.

P. 79: Figure 3-5 "Applicability of Traits to Canadians and Americans" from *The Bibby Report: Social Trends Canadian Style* copyright ©1995 Reginald W. Bibby. Reproduced with permission of Stoddart Publishing Co., Limited.

CHAPTER 4

P. 88: Quotation from Patricia A. Adler and Peter Adler. 1998. *Peer Power: Preadolescent Culture and Identity*: 2–3. Copyright © 1998 by Patricia Adler and Peter Adler. Reprinted by permission of Rutgers University Press.

P. 91: Quotation from Constance Holden. 1980. "Identical Twins Reared Apart," *Science*, 207: 1323–1328. Copyright 1980 American Association for the Advancement of Science. Reprinted by permission.

P. 99: Quotation from Annette, Cecile, and Yvonne Dionne. 1997. Letter to parents of septuplets, published in *Time* 12/1: 39. © Annette, Cecile, and Yvonne Dionne (represented by Boivin Payette) 1997. Reprinted by permission.

CHAPTER 5

P. 114: Quotations from Philip G. Zimbardo. 1972. "Pathology of Imprisonment," *Society*, **9** (April): 4. Reprinted by permission of Copyright Clearance Center. And from Philip G. Zimbardo, C. Haney, W. C. Banks, & D. Jaffe. 1974. "The Psychology of Imprisonment: Privation, Power, and Pathology." In Z. Rubin (Ed.), *Doing Unto Others: Explorations in Social Behavior*: 61–73. Published by Prentice Hall. Reprinted by permission of the Philip G. Zimbardo, Stanford University.

P. 131: Figure 5-2 from L. K. Altman. 1998. "The Geography of AIDS," *New York Times* (June 24): A1. Copyright © 1998 by The New York Times Co. Reprinted by permission.

P. 135: Figure 5-3 based on data from Roxane Laboratories. Reprinted by permission of Roxane Laboratories, Columbus, OH.

CHAPTER 6

P. 142: Quotation from *Voltaire's Bastards* by John Ralston Saul. Copyright ©1992 by John Ralston Saul. Reprinted by permission of Penguin Books Canada Limited.

P. 159: Table 6-3 adapted from Statistics Canada, "Percentage volunteering and average hours volunteered during the year, Canadians aged 15 and older, 2000." http://www.statcan.ca:8083/english/freepub/71-542-XIE/71-452-XIE00001.pdf

P. 163: Table 6-4 reproduced with permission from Public Legal Education and Information Service of New Brunswick, http://www.legal-info-legale.nb.ca

CHAPTER 7

P. 172: Table 7-1 from William A. Reese II and Michael A. Katovich. 1989. "Untimely Acts: Extending the Interactionist Conception of Deviance," *Sociological Quarterly*, **30** (No. 2, Summer): 159–184. © 1989 by The Midwest Sociological Society. Reprinted by permission of *Sociological Quarterly* and the author.

P. 174: Figure 7-1 Copyright, 1999, Los Angeles Times. Reprinted with permission.

P. 176: Table 7-3 Adapted with the permission of The Free Press; copyright renewed 1985 by Robert K. Merton

P. 191: Figure 7-2 from the Statistics Canada publication, "Crime rates by province and territory," 2001. http://www.statcan.ca/Daily/English/020717/d020717b/htm

CHAPTER 8

P. 202: Quotation from Katherine S. Newman. 1999. *No Shame in My Game: The Working Poor in the Inner City*: 86, 102. Copyright © 1999 by Katherine S. Newman. Reprinted by permission of Alfred A. Knofp, a division of Random House Inc.

P. 206: Figure 8-1 from Adam Bryant. 1999. "American Pay Rattles Foreign Partners," *New York Times* (January 17): D1. Copyright © 1999 by The New York Times Co. Reprinted by permission.

P. 213: Figure 8-2 adapted from Statistics Canada, "The Assets and Debts of Canadians: An Overview of the Results of the Survey of Financial Security" Catalogue 13-595, March 2001.

P. 218: Figure 8-3 "Poverty Rates for Persons by Age Group and Sex, 1998', from *Poverty Profile 1998*. Reproduced with the permission of the Ministry of Public Works and Government Services Canada, 2002.

P. 216: Table 8-3 adapted from the Statistics Canada publication 1999c "Income in Canada," Catalogue No. 75-202.

CHAPTER 9

P. 232: Quotation from *The Ingenuity Gap* by Thomas Homer-Dixon Copyright ©2000 by Resource & Conflict Analysis Inc. Reprinted by permission of Knopf Canada, a division of Random House of Canada Limited.

P. 235: Figure 9-1 adapted from Carl Haub and Diana Cornelius, 2000 World Population Data Sheet. Washington, DC.: Population Reference Bureau, 2000. Reprinted by permission.

P. 237: Table 9-1 adapted in part from Jeremy Kahn. 1999. "Global Five Hundred: The World's Largest Corporations," *Fortune* **140** (August 2): 144–146, f-1–f-24. © 1999 Time Inc. All rights reserved. And adapted in part from World Bank. 2000. *Entering the 21st Century: World Development Report 1999/2000*: 230–231. Copyright 2000. Reprinted by permission of Oxford University Press.

P. 241: Figure 9-2 adapted in part from World Bank. 1997. *World Development Indicators 1997*: 54–56. Copyright 1997. Reprinted by permission of Oxford University Press. And adapted in part from World Bank. 2000. *Entering the 21st Century: World Development Report 1999/2000*: 238–239. Copyright 2000. Reprinted by permission of Oxford University Press.

P. 247: Fig. 9-3 data from the Mexican census as reported in McMahon. 1995. And in World Bank. 1995. *World Development Report 1994: Workers in an Integrating World*. Copyright 1995. Reprinted by permission of Oxford University Press.

CHAPTER 10

P. 260: Quotation from *Web of Hate* by Warren Kinsella, ©1997, HarperCollins Canada, 350–351.

P. 263: Figure 10-1 adapted from the Statistics Canada Web site http://www.statcan.ca/english/census96/nov4/imm1.htm and from the Statistics Canada publication "Canada's Ethnocultural Portrait: The Changing Mosaic, 2001 Census (Analysis series)," Catalogue 96F0030, January 21, 2003, available at: http://www12.statcan.ca/english/census01/products/analytic/companion/etoimm/contents.cfm?

P. 267: Table 10-1 adapted from the Statistics Canada Web site http://www12.statcan.ca/english/census01/products/highlight/ETO/Table1.cfm?Lang=E&T=501&GV=1&GID=0

P. 265: Fig. 10-2 from Richard T. Schaefer. 2000. *Racial and Ethnic Groups*, 8th ed. Copyright 2000. Reprinted by permission of Prentice Hall and the author.

P. 270: Figure 10-3 Source: Canadian Race Relations Foundation, reprinted in Canadian Council on Social Development publication

P. 280: Figure 10-4 adapted from the Statistics Canada publication "Aboriginal Peoples of Canada: A Demographic Profile, 2001 Census (Analysis series)," Catalogue 96F0030, January 21, 2003, available at: http://www12.statcan.ca/english/census01/products/analytic/companion/abor/contents.cfm?

P. 281: Figure 10-5 adapted from the BC Union of Indian Chiefs.

P. 289: Table 10-2 adapted from the Statistics Canada Web site http://www.statcan.ca/english/census96/nov4/table1.htm and from the Statistics Canada publication "Canada's Ethnocultural Portrait: The Changing Mosaic, 2001 Census (Analysis series)," Catalogue 96F0030, January 21, 2003, available at: http://www12.statcan.ca/english/census01/products/analytic/companion/etoimm/contents.cfm?

CHAPTER 11

P. 296: Quotation from Naomi Wolf. 1991. *The Beauty Myth*: 9, 10. Reprinted by permission of Chatto & Windus, a division of Random House U.K., and the author, represented by Abner Stein Literary Agency.

P. 309: Figure 11-2 "Employment of women with children, by family status, 1976–1999," from the Statistics Canada publication "Women in Canada 2000: A gender based statistical report," Catalogue 89–503, September 2000.

P. 310: Table 11-2 adapted from the Statistics Canada publication "Earnings of Men and Women," Catalogue 13–217, 1999.

P. 312: Figure 11-3 from Statistics Canada, "Women in Canada 2000: A gender based statistical report," Catalogue 89–503, September 2000.

P. 312: Figure 11-4 adapted from the Statistics Canada publication "Overview of Time Use of Canadians in 1998," Catalogue 12F0080, page 5.

P. 316: Figure 11-5 adapted from the Statistics Canada website http://www.statcan.ca/english/Pgdb/People/Labour/labor01b.htm and from the Statistics Canada publication "Visible Minorities in Canada," Catalogue 85F00333, Table 1, page 9.

P. 319: Figure 11-6 from Population Division of the Dept. of Economic & Social Affairs of the U.N. Secretariat. 1998. *Global Divide on Abortion*. Reprinted by permission of United Nations Publications Board.

CHAPTER 12

P. 326: Quotation from Nancy Moser. 1998. "Wishing for Maybes." In Sandra Martz and Shirley Coe (Eds.), *Generation to Generation:*

Reflections on Friendships between Young and Old. Papier-Maché Press 1998, pp. 158–160. Reprinted by permission of Nancy Moser.

P. 329: Figure 12-1 "Three Centuries of World Population Aging." From *Long-Range World Population Projections: Based on the 1998 Revision*. The Population Division, Department of Economic and Social Affairs, United Nations Secretariat. Reproduced with permission.

P. 329: Figure 12-2 "Percentage Increase in Age 60 and Over by Region, 2000–2050. Source: "World Population Prospects, The 1998 Revision, Volume II: Sex and Age." The Population Division, Department of Economic and Social Affairs, United Nations Secretariat. Reproduced with permission.

P. 336: Table 12-2 adapted from the Statistics Canada publications "Population Aging and the Elderly", Catalogue 91-533, March 1993 and "Population Projections for Canada, Provinces and Territories", 2000–2026, Catalogue 91-520, March 2001.

P. 337: Figure 12-4 adapted from the Statistics Canada publication "A Portrait of Seniors in Canada, 3ʳᵈ Edition," Catalogue 89–519, 1999 and adapted from the Statistics Canada Web sites http://www.statcan.ca/engligh/PGdb/demo31a.htm and http://www.statcan.ca/english/Pgdb/demo23b.htm.

P. 339: Figure 12-5 adapted from the Statistics Canada Publication "Population Projections for Canada, Provinces, and Territories," 2000–2026, Catalogue 91–520, 2001.

P. 338: Map 12–1 adapted from the Statistics Canada publication "A Portrait of Seniors in Canada, 3ʳᵈ edition, Catalogue 89–519, 1999, page 73.

CHAPTER 13

P. 354: Quotation from Cornel West and Sylvia Ann Hewlett. 1998. *The War against Parents*: 21–22. Copyright © 1998 by Sylvia Ann Hewlett and Cornel West. Reprinted by permission of Houghton Mifflin Company. All rights reserved.

P. 357: Table in Box 13-1 based on Internet version of National Partnership for Women and Families. 1998. "Balancing Acts: Work/Family Issues on Prime-Time TV Executive Summary" Reprinted by permission of National Partnership for Women and Families.

P. 356: Figure 13-1 adapted from the Statistics Canada Publication "Canadian Families: Diversity and Change," Catalogue 12F0061XFE, June 1996.

P. 364: Quotation from Simon Rodberg. 1999. "Woman and Man at Yale," *Culturefront* **8:1** (Spring): 25. Reprinted by permission of the New York Council for the Humanities.

P. 371: Figure 13-4 adapted from the Statistics Canada publication "Family Violence in Canada: A Statistical Profile 2001," Catalogue 85–224, page 27.

P. 371: Figure 13-5 adapted from the Statistics Canada publication "Family Violence in Canada: A Statistical Profile 2001," Catalogue 85–224, page 27.

P. 374: Figure 13-6 adapted from the Statistics Canada publication "Divorces," Catalogue No. 84–213.

P. 377: Quotations from Anthony DePalma. 1998. "Two Gay Men Fight Town Hall for a Family Pool Pass Discount," *New York Times* (July 14): B2. Copyright © 1998 The New York Times Co. Reprinted by permission.

CHAPTER 14

P. 386: Excerpt from "Grandfather was a Knowing Christian" by Noah Augustine. Toronto Star, Aug 9, 2000, page A17. Reprinted with permission of Noah Augustine.

P. 398: Table 14-1 adapted from the Statistics Canada publications "Religions in Canada (data products: nation series: 1991 Census of Population)," 1991, Catalogue 93-319, June 1993; and "Religions in Canada, 2001 Census (Analysis series)," Catalogue 96F0030, May 13, 2003, available at: http://www12. statcan.ca/english/census01/products/ analytic/companion/rel/contents.cfm?

CHAPTER 15

P. 410: Quotation from Contenta, Sandro. 1993. *Rituals of Failure: What Schools Really Teach.* Toronto: Between the Lines, pages 3–6. http://www.btlbooks.com

P. 412: Figure 15-1 adapted from the Statistics Canada publication "Education Indicators in Canada: Report of the Pan-Canadian Education Indicators Program 1999," Catalogue 81–585, page 24.

P. 417: Table 15-1 adapted from the Statistics Canada Web site http://www.statcan.ca/ Daily/english/031008/d031008a.htm

CHAPTER 16

P. 436: Quotation from Robert Bernard, Dave Gosgrave, and Jennifer Welsh. 1998. *Chips and Pop: Decoding the Nexus Generation.* Reprinted with permission of Raincoast Publishers http://www.raincoast.com

P. 447: Figure 16-3 from Inter-Parliamentary Union. 2000. "Women in National Parliaments." Accessed January, 2000, at http://www.pu.org/wmn-e/world.htm. Reprinted by permission of Inter-Parliamentary Union, Geneva.

P. 450: Figure 16-4 from Richard L. Zweigenhaft and G. William Domhoff. 1998. *Diversity in the Power Elite*: 3. Copyright 1998. Reprinted by permission of Yale University Press.

P. 442: Table 16-1 adapted from the Statistics Canada publication "Canadian Social Trends," Catalogue 11–008, Spring 2001.

P. 454: Table 16-2 adapted from the Statistics Canada publication "Canadian Social Trends," Catalogue 11–008, Spring 2001.

CHAPTER 17

P. 460: Quotation from Jeremy Rifkin. 1996. *The End of Work*: 11–13. Copyright © 1995 by Jeremy Rifkin. Reprinted by permission of Putnam Berkley, a division of Penguin Putnam Inc.

P. 468: Figure 17-1 reprinted from "Work Life Balance in the New Millennium: Where are we? Where do we need to go?" by Linda Duxbury and Chris Higgins, 2001. The Work Network. Canadian Policy Research Networks. www.jobquality.ca/indicator_e/dem002.stm

P. 477: Figure 17-2 data based in part from the Statistics Canada publication "The changing profile of Canada's labour force, 2001 Census (Analysis series)," Catalogue 96F0030, February 11, 2003, available at: http://www12. statcan.ca/english/census01/products/ analytic/companion/paid/contents.cfm?

CHAPTER 18

P. 484: Quotation from Peter Gzowski. 2001 "How to Quit Smoking in Fifty Years or Less" in *Addicted: Notes from the Belly of the Beast,* Lorna Crozier and Patrick Lane, eds. Copyright ©2001 Greystone Books (Douglas & McIntyre Publishing Group). Reprinted by permission of the publisher.

P. 490: Figure 18-1 from Carl Haub and Diana Cornelius. 1999. *World Population Data Sheet 1999.* Reprinted by permission of Population Reference Bureau.

P. 499: Figure 18-2 ©2001, CIHI, *National Health Expenditure Trends, 1975–2001,* copied with permission. Published by the Canadian Institute for Health Information., Ottawa, Canada.

P. 508: Figure 18-4 ©2001, CIHI, *National Health Expenditure Trends, 1975–2001,* copied with permission. Published by the Canadian Institute for Health Information., Ottawa, Canada.

CHAPTER 19

P. 516: Quotation from Andrew Ross, PhD. 1999. *The Celebration Chronicles*: 218–220. Copyright © 1999 by Andrew Ross.

Reprinted by permission of Ballantine Books, a Division of Random House Inc.

P. 520: Table 19-1 adapted in part from Gideon Sjoberg. 1960. The *Preindustrial City: Past & Present:* 323–328. Copyright © 1960 by The Free Press. Used by permission of The Free Press, a division of Simon & Schuster. And adapted in part from E. Barbara Phillips. 1996. *City Lights: Urban-Suburban Life in the Global Society:* 132–135. Copyright © 1981 by E. Barbara Phillips & Richard T. LaGates, 1996 by E. Barbara Phillips. Used by permission of Oxford University Press, Inc.

P. 521: Figure 19-1 based on data from Carl Haub and Diana Cornelius. 2000. *World Population Data Sheet 2000.* Reprinted by permission of Population Reference Bureau.

P. 523: Figure 19-2 from Chauncy D. Harris & Edward Ullman. 1945. "The Nature of Cities," *Annals of the American Academy of Political & Social Science,* **242** (Nov): 7–17. Reprinted by permission of the American Academy of Political & Social Science.

CHAPTER 20

P. 546: Quotation from Po Bronson. 1999. *The Nudist on the Late Shift.* 78–79, 80. Copyright © 1999 by Po Bronson. Reprinted by permission of Random House and Curtis Brown Ltd.

P. 551: Figure 20-1 © 1994, The Washington Post. Reprinted by permission of Washington Post Writers Group and Population Reference Bureau.

P. 567: Figure 20-3 from www.glreach.com/ globstats. Reprinted by permission of Euro-Marketing Associates from <www. glreach.com/globstats>.

CHAPTER 21

P. 580: Quotation from Richard Roeper. 1999. *Urban Legends*: 91–94. © 1999 Richard Roeper. Reprinted by permission of Career Press, Franklin Lakes, NJ. All rights reserved.

P. 593: Quotation from Indutai Pantankar. 1986. "If Peasants Build Their Own Dams, What Would the State Have Left to Do?" In Michael Dobkowski and Isidor Walliman (eds.), *Research in Social Movements, Conflicts and Change,* **19**: 209–224. Reprinted by permission of JAI Press.

Photo and Cartoon Credits

ABOUT THE AUTHOR

Michael Bedford Photography, Ottawa,
http://www.mbedford.com

PART OPENERS

Part Opener Photos: © PhotoDisc, Inc., and
Corbis, Inc; CP Picture Archive/Peter Bregg

CHAPTER 1

Chapter Opener: Courtesy of Art Director &
Designer Yoshimaru Takahasi for the Osaka
1st Century Association Bid for the 2008
Oympics
P. 6: Michael Newman/Photo Edit
P. 8: Index Stock (top); Steve Liss/Liaison
(bottom)
P. 10: CP Picture Archive/Tom Hanson
P. 12: Mark Peterson/Saba
P. 15: Corbis-Bettmann
P. 16: Courtesy of the Carleton University
Archives
P. 18: CP Picture Archive/Andre Forget
P. 19: Richard Floyd

CHAPTER 2

Chapter Opener: Stastistics Canada
P. 32: CP Picture Archive/Andre Forget
P. 34: CP Picture Archive/Paul Chiasson
P. 37: Cartoon by Mike Keefe, Denver Post. ©
Mike Keefe, dePIXon Studios, Inc.
P. 43: Betty Press/Woodfin Camp
P. 44: Photofest
P. 45: Mark Reinstein/ImageWorks
P. 47: CP Picture Archive/Dick Loek
P. 48: Bob Daemmrich/Image Works
P. 50: Esbin&Anderson/Image Works

CHAPTER 3

Chapter Opener: Barry Dawson, *Street Graph-
ics India* (New York: Thames & Hudson,
1999), pp.24-25.
P. 62: Robert Bruke/Liaison
P. 63: Chuck O'Rear/Woodfin Camp
P. 65: Fujiphotos/Image Works (top); Wayne
Eastep/Tony Stone (bottom)
P. 67: James Schnepf/Liaison
P. 70: Richard Floyd
P. 71: Courtesy of Marylee Stephenson,
csresors.com and www.sociocomic.com.
P. 72: Richard Floyd
P. 76: Cartoon © 2000 by Sideny Harris
P. 77: Marios Corvetto/Image Works (top);
Cartoon © 2000 by Sideny Harris (bottom)

P. 78: Jerry Alexander/Tony Stone
P. 81: Richard Floyd

CHAPTER 4

Chapter Opener: Setagaya Volunteer
Association, Tokyo, Japan
P. 90: Anthony Susu/Liaison
P. 93: Elizabeth Crews/Image Works
P. 94: Jim Cummins/Taxi/Getty Images
P. 97: Thomas S. England/Photo Researchers
P. 98: Keystone/Sygma
P. 100: Jeff Greenberg/Photo Edit
P. 102: Tom Wagner/Saba
P. 105: 1998 Children's Television Workshop.
Sesame Street Muppets © 1998 Jim
Henson.
P. 106: Mary Kate Denny/Photo Edit
P. 108: Svenne Nordlov/Tio Foto

CHAPTER 5

Chapter Opener: Courtesy of interTREND
Communications, Inc., Torrence,
California
P. 114: © Philip Zimbardo/Stanford University
P. 116: Michael Probst/AP Photo
P. 117: Richard Floyd
P. 120: Richard Floyd
P. 121: Sarah Leen
P. 122: Anna Clopet/Liaison
P. 123: Cartoon TOLES © The Buffalo News.
Reprinted with permission of UNIVERSAL
PRESS SYNDICATE. All rights reserved.
P. 126: Herb Swanson/*Chicago Tribune*
P. 127: Richard Floyd
P. 129: Richard Floyd; Cartoon by Dean
Vietor. Code 1986 0324 040 DVI.HG © The
New Yorker Collection 1986 Dean Vietor
from cartoonbank.com. All rights reserved.

CHAPTER 6

Chapter Opener: Photo by M. Rutledge,
Courtesy of the Canadian Museum of
Flight, Langley, BC. http://www.
canadianflight.org
P. 142: John Berkeley/Artville/Getty Images
P. 144: Cartoon by Robert Weber. Code 1979
10 01 046 RWE.HG © The New Yorker
Collection 1979 Robert Weber from
cartoonbank.com All rights reserved.
P. 146: Courtesy of János John Maté (top);
Photofest (bottom)
P. 147: Theo Westenberger
P. 149: CBS Photo Archive
P. 151: Cartoon © 2000 by Sidney Harris;
Archive Photo

P. 153: CP Picture Archive/Janet Durrans
P. 157: Rob Crandall/Stock Boston
P. 158: ©Ted Dyke Photography
P. 160: Robert C.V. Liebermann/YMCA of
Greater New York
P. 162: Richard Floyd

CHAPTER 7

Chapter Opener: Health Canada
P. 172: Reed Saxon/AP Photo
P. 176: R.F. Hestoft/Saba
P. 177: Stephen Fisch/Stock Boston
P. 179: Richard Floyd
P. 180: Stock Montage
P. 184: © 1965 by Stanley
P. 187: Carolina Kroon/Impact Visuals
P. 188: Cartoon © 2000 by Sidney Harris
P. 189: Stephen Chernin/AP Photo
P. 192: Courtesy of Holly Johnson

CHAPTER 8

Chapter Opener: HotJobs.com, Ltd.
P. 204: Hampton University
P. 209: Richard Floyd
P. 214: Cartoon by Frank Cammuso. The
Herald Co., Syracuse, NY © 1995 *Herald-
Journal*. All rights reserved. Reprinted by
permission.
P. 218: Julius Wilson
P. 219: Peter Gifford/Liasion
P. 220: © 20th Century Fox/AP Photo
P. 223: Richard Floyd
P. 225: Ferry/Liaison

CHAPTER 9

Chapter Opener: Courtesy of Heye &
Partners, Germany
P. 232: Associated Press AP. Photograph by
Vincent Yu
P. 233: Alan Dejecacion/Liaison
P. 238: D. Harse/Image Works
P. 239: CP Picture Archive/Stephan Savoia
P. 242: Charles Gupton/Stock Boston
P. 245: Ann States/Saba
P. 246: Paul Fusco/Magnum
P. 247: Cindy Reiman/Impact Visuals
P. 248: Keith Dannemiller/Saba
P. 249: Mark Richards/Photo Edit
P. 253: Laruent Rebours/AP Photo

CHAPTER 10

Chapter Opener: Courtesy of the Surrey Delta Mulicultural Coordinating Society
P. 260: CP Picture Archive/Tim Fraser
P. 264: Canadian Press TRSTR. Photograph by Rick Eglington
P. 269: Steven Rubin/Image Works
P. 272: Mike Albans/Daily News
P. 275: ©Michael Bedford Photography, Ottawa
P. 276: Art Zemur/Liaison
P. 277: Alon Reininger/Contact Press Images
P. 279: Canadian Press CP. Photograph by Joe Bryska
P. 282: Richard Floyd
P. 283: Canadian Press CP. Photograph by STF Staff.
P. 284: CP Picture Archive/Christine Vanzella
P. 286: Richard Floyd

CHAPTER 11

Chapter Opener: Guerilla Girls
P. 298: © Mike Maloney/San Francisco (top); Picture provided by Harrison G. Pope, Jr., adapted from THE ADONIS COMPLEX by Harrison G. Pope, Jr., Katherine Phillips, Roberto Olivardia. The Free Press, © 2000 (bottom)
P. 301: © Maria Lewpowsky
P. 302: B. Mahoney/Image Works
P. 304: Cartoon © 2000 by Sidney Harris
P. 305: Eric Roxfelt/AP Photo
P. 306: S. Nagendra/Photo Researchers
P. 312: Cartoon by Ed Stein, *Rocky Mountain News*. Reprinted by permission of Ed Stein.
P. 313: Micahel Newman/Photo Edit
P. 314: National Archives of Canada/PA-30212
P. 316: Courtesy of Prudence Hannis
P. 317: Cartoon by Clay Bennett. Bennett © United Feature Syndicate. Reprinted by permission.

CHAPTER 12

Chapter Opener: UN, Programme on Ageing, Division for Social Policy and Development
P. 327: Diane M. Lowe/Stock Boston
P. 331: Patrick Murphy
P. 334: Rich Frishman
P. 335: Thierry Secretain/Cos/Woodfin Camp
P. 340: Lionel Delevigne/Stock Boston
P. 342: Bob Daemmrich/Image Works (top); Richard Lord/Image Works (bottom)
P. 344: *Detroit News*/Liaison

CHAPTER 13

Chapter Opener: Genetica DNA Laboratories, Inc.
P. 356: Saola/Liaison

P. 359: Eastcott/Woodfin Camp
P. 360: Spencer Grant/Liaison
P. 362: Michael Newman/Photo Edit
P. 363: Bill Tuslow/Liaison
P. 365: Cliff Moore
P. 367: Richard Hutchings/Photo Researchers (top); Michael Justice/Liaison (bottom)
P. 369: Blair Seitz/Photo Researchers
P. 370: Courtesy of Karla Jessen Williamson
P. 373: Michael Dean
P. 376: Jon Bradley/Tony Stone
P. 377: CP Picture Archive/Andrew Vaughan
P. 380: © The Andy Warhol Foundation, Inc./Art Resource

CHAPTER 14

Chapter Opener: Thomas Coex/Agence France Press
P. 386: CP Picture Archives/Andrew Vaughan
P. 389: Richard Vogel/Liaison
P. 390: CP Picture Archive/Kevin Frayer
P. 391: Will Yourman/Liaison
P. 393: Lara Jo Regan/Liaison
P. 396: Michael Cogan/Agence
P. 397: Steve McCurry/Magnum
P. 399: Glenn Baglo/*The Vancouver Sun*
P. 400: Glenn Baglo/*The Vancouver Sun*
P. 401: Reuters NewMedia Corbis
P. 403: Cartoon by Kevin Rechin. Copyright 1999, *USA Today*. Reprinted with permission.

CHAPTER 15

Chapter Opener: SchoolNet Magazine, http://www.schoolnet.ca
P. 410: Between the Lines http://www.btlbooks.com
P. 413: ©Michael Bedford Photography, Ottawa
P. 414: Michael Newman/Photo Edit
P. 415: Mary Kate Denny/Photo Edit
P. 416: Joe McNally/Sygma
P. 417: Cartoon © Kirk Anderson kanderson @pioneerpress.org. Reprinted by permission.
P. 418: Marc Riboud/Magnum
P. 421: Richard Floyd
P. 423: Davis Barber/Photo Edit
P. 425: Cartoon by Steve Sack. © Tribune Media Services, Inc. All rights resreved. Reprinted by permission.
P. 426: Bill Bachman/Image Works
P. 427: Reprinted with permission of Graham Harrup
P. 428: Linda Rosier

CHAPTER 16

Chapter Opener: Milton Glaser
P. 436: CP Picture Archive/Fred Thornhill
P. 438: AP Photo
P. 441: CP Picture Archive/Chuck Stoody

P. 443: CP Picture Archive/Jonathan Hayward
P. 445: CP Picture Archive/Roberto Candia
P. 449: Moises Salman/AP Photo
P. 451: Paul Conklin/Photo Edit

CHAPTER 17

Chapter Opener: Carole Conde and Karl Beveridge
P. 463: Reuters/Claro Cortes/Archive Photos
P. 466: Photofest
P. 467: Aaron Haupt/Stock Boston
P. 468: Chiaki Tsukumo/AP Photo
P. 469: Cartoon by Scott Adams. Dilbert by Scott Adams. © United Feature Syndicate. Reprinted by permission.
P. 470: CP Picture Archive/Tannis Toohey
P. 471: Bob Daemmrich/Stock Boston
P. 472: Barry Sweet/AP Photo
P. 473: D. Wells/Image Works
P. 474: Cartoon by Tony Auth © 1999 The Philadelphia Inquirer. Reprinted by permission of Universal Press Syndicate. All rights reserved (top); Stacy Pick/Stock Boston (bottom).
P. 478: Louise Grubb/Image Works

CHAPTER 18

Chapter Opener: © Queen's Printer for Ontario, 2002. Reproduced with permission.
P. 484: CP Picture Archive/Andrew Stawicki
P. 487: Jonathan Nouro/Photo Edit
P. 488: Stephanie Maze/Woodfin Camp (left); David Austen/Stock Bosotn (right)
P. 490: Stephen Agricola/Stock Boston
P. 492: CP Picture Archive/Todd Warshaw Pool
P. 494: Eric Bouvet/Liaison
P. 496: CP Picture Archive/Ryan Remiorz
P. 497: Bill Avon/Photo Edit
P. 501: A. Ramey/Woodfin Camp
P. 504: Betty Press/Woodfin Camp
P. 505: Rhoda Sidney/Stock Boston
P. 509: CP Picture Archive/Fred Chartrand

CHAPTER 19

Chapter Opener: *Chicago/Gary Union of the Homeless* 1990
P. 517: Westenberger/Liaison
P. 518: Image Works
P. 520: Cartoon by Henry Martin. © Tribune Media Services, Inc. All rights reserved. Reprinted with permission.
P. 524: M.J. Griffith/Photo Researchers
P. 525: J. Marshall/Image Works
P. 527: Jean Marc Giboux/Liaison
P. 529: Cartoon © Kirk Anderson kanderson@pioneerpress.com Reprinted by permission.
P. 530: Jim Pickerall/Stock Boston
P. 531: Richard Floyd

Name Index

A

Abbott, P., 182, 493
Abegglen, J.C., 242
Abella, R., 476
Abelson, R., 107
Abercrombie, N., 75, 210
Aberle, R., 125
Abowitz, D.A., 216
Abrahamson, M., 175
Abrahams, R., 116
Abramson, J., 20
Abu-Labau, S.M., 340
Adachi, K., 282
Adair, V., 101, 299
Adam, B.D., 134, 492, 602, 605
Adams, E., 171
Adamson, N., 155, 314
Addams, J., 14–15, 304
Adelman, M., 240
Adler, P.A., 42, 88, 89, 101
Aguirre, B., 441
Aguirre, B.E., 585
Ahlberg, C., 299
Ahmed, K.C., 240
Alain, J.B., 590
Alam, S., 244
Albanese, P., 363
Albarracin, D., 498
Albas, C., 95
Albas, D., 95
Albrecht, G., 119
Alda, Alan, 276
Aldrich, H.E., 584
Alfino, M., 67
Ali, Muhammad, 116
Alinsky, S., 527
Allahar, A.L., 32–33
Allen, B.P., 185
Allport, G.W., 274, 275
Alonzo, A.A., 491
Altman, L., 133
Alvord, L.A., 487, 499
Amato, P., 374
Ambert, A.-M., 372, 375
Ammerman, N.T., 395
Andersen, M., 304
Anderson, E., 181

Anderson, J., 240
Anderson, S., 469
Annan, K., 252
Antunes, P., 498
Appelbaum, R., 233
Aquilino, A.J., 35
Aranami, Y., 486
Arber, S., 339
Armstrong, H., 16, 127
Armstrong, J., 554
Armstrong, P., 16, 127
Arnold, W., 123
Aronson, E., 171
Asahara, S., 401
Ashe, A., 118
Atchley, R.C., 332, 334
Atkinson, A.B, 495
Attaturk, M., 307
Auger, M., 188
Augustine, J.M., 386
Augustine, N., 386, 387
Austin, E.W., 444
Avarey, D.W., 179
Avni, N., 373
Axtell, R.E., 93
Azumi, K., 148

B

Babad, E.Y., 419
Bachrach, C., 368
Baer, D.E., 158
Bailey, S., 487
Bainbridge, W.S., 49, 399, 401
Baker, L.C., 500
Baker, M., 108, 363, 368, 372
Baker, W.E., 239
Baldassare, M., 530
Bales, K., 205
Bales, R., 301–302, 500
Balson, D., 419
Banks, W.C., 114, 115
Bannerji, H., 419
Barkey, K., 44
Barlow, M., 591
Barnard, R., 436, 437
Barndt, D., 239
Barnett, J., 378
Barnevik, P., 460
Barr, C.W., 469
Barrett, S.R., 269
Barron, M.L., 329
Bartkowski, J.P., 307
Barzansky, B., 500

Basow, S.A., 119, 121
Bass, K.R., 444
Basso, K.H., 68
Batchuk, N., 158
Bauerlein, M., 599
Beall, M.B., 327
Beals-Gonzaléz, C.A., 424, 425
Bear, J., 68
Beaujot, R., 276, 285
Bebout, R., 602, 603
Becker, A.E., 63
Becker, H.S., 179, 180, 418, 491
Becker, M., 205
Beckley, R.E., 402, 403
Begley, S., 92, 380
Behrman, J.R., 422
Bell, D., 131
Bell, W., 234, 239
Belsie, L., 560, 563
Bender, W., 550
Benford, R.D., 589
Benner, R.S., 28
Bennett, V., 248
Berger, P., 115
Berk, R.A., 584
Berlin, B., 68
Bernardo, P., 181, 587
Bernstein, A.C., 370
Beshiri, 533
Best, A., 172
Best, F., 425
Bharadwaj, G.T., 561
Bhatia, S., 545
Bhumibol Adulyadej, King, 438
Bianchi, S.M., 372
Bibby, R.W., 73, 79, 398, 403
Bielby, B.B., 361
Bielby, W.T., 361
Bikono, B.E., 422
Billson, J.M., 28, 29
Bjorkman, S., 395
Black, D., 70
Blackhall, L., 493
Black, J.H., 271
Blackwell, T., 560
Blais, A., 442
Blakely, E.J., 528
Blanc, A.K., 376
Blanchard, F.A., 183–184
Blanchfield, M., 504
Blanco, R., 357
Blauner, R., 467
Blau, P.M., 153, 161, 222
Bledsoe, T., 275